D0119164

THE
BEST YEARS
OF
YOUR LIFE

Everything You Need To Know Now
To Plan For The Years Ahead

Bottom Line
Books

www.BottomLineSecrets.com

Contents

1

Preparing to Retire

The Simple Secrets of Planning for Your Retirement

All of us seek levels of comfort in our lives, perhaps more so when we retire. *That includes, along with other things...*

- **Living where we want to live.**
- **Doing what we enjoy doing.**
- **Having work that brings us satisfaction.**

Retiring successfully means staying within our comfort zone while making the transition from working full-time.

We can't rely on others to plan our retirement, because we all have our own unique realm where we want to be. Building retirement comfort zones is something you and your spouse must do on your own. *Key steps...*

- **Prepare for what comes after the honeymoon phase.** That begins with your retirement party. It will end six months to two years later. You've done all the chores and played all the golf you want to play. Many of those who haven't prepared for what happens next become depressed. And they feel unimportant and unappreciated because they aren't doing anything that makes others appreciate them.

Challenge: Don't make vague retirement plans such as, "I'll catch up on jobs around the house," or, "I'll play golf whenever I want to."

Prepare for the end of the honeymoon by making specific, long-range plans to develop a second career, become involved in community service...or go back to school to learn what you didn't have time for when you were working.

Financial trap: The postretirement letdown can come from financial as well as emotional causes—a realization that your finances aren't providing the retirement you had anticipated.

Marion E. Haynes, retirement planning consultant, 3811 Valley View Dr., Springdale, AR 72762. He spent 35 years as a corporate human resources executive, retiring in 1991 as manager of pensioner relations for Shell Oil. He is a past member of the board of the International Society for Retirement Planning and author of the retirement planning book *Comfort Zones.* Crisp.

Be honest in your retirement planning, so you know exactly how far your nest egg will carry you.

Find your comfort zone, matching your retirement plans with your financial resources. Do that by taking inventory of your current financial reserves and by developing a realistic postretirement budget that allows for the impact of future inflation on your reserves.

•Leave excess baggage from your working life behind. One day you are president or general manager or a successful salesperson. The next day, you're retired and sitting at home. Suddenly, you're nothing. Your title, and the perks that went with it, are gone.

Retirement is a move into a new phase of life—just another member of the community. Acknowledge the reality of what you will have to deal with.

Prepare in advance by developing alternative activities that will provide the fulfillment you had been getting from your work life.

My experience: When I retired from Shell Oil, three companies offered me part-time assignments. I did consulting for one company for two years, working about 60 days each year. That proved an excellent transition for me—bridging the period between going to work every day and not going to work at all.

With that transition behind me, I felt comfortable and fulfilled devoting most of my time to community service with organizations in my area.

Be flexible and open to whatever postretirement opportunities come along. You may do consulting in your own field, but you may also find opportunities in areas far removed from what you did during your working life.

Don't assume that when you retire, you have to stop working for good.

Example: Our local newspaper carried an article about a man who had just gone back to work at 73. He said he had already carried out all his plans for retirement. "There's nothing left to do, so I decided to go back to work," he said.

•Include your life partner in all your retirement planning, so that you reinforce each other. Often, it's the husband who makes the retirement plans and the wife—who typically outlives her spouse—who must struggle to make them work.

Some people—including most women—still believe that only men retire. A working wife, however, will have the same problems in retirement as her husband. Less obvious, but still true, is that homemakers often find the transition to be more difficult than someone who has been working outside the home. Women who have been homemakers all their lives must insist on being a full partner when the working spouse retires.

Since retirement involves both husband and wife, all retirement plans must be made jointly. Each partner must agree on when to retire, where to live, the financial resources that will be needed in retirement and how each will deal with the emotional letdown that follows the end of the retirement honeymoon.

Differences: Postretirement living won't be precisely the same for both partners. One may become infirm before the other. One almost certainly will die before the other. That reality isn't easy to think about, but it must be planned for.

I suggest spouses practice some role shifting as they approach retirement. Women need to know how to do routine household repairs, get the car serviced, manage the couple's finances and investments. Men need to know how to prepare their own meals, wash their clothes, keep the house clean.

•Anticipate the phases of retirement— and plan ahead for each. Most people talk about retirement as a single phase—lasting from the day they stop working until they die. Even as we go through retirement, we tend to feel that whatever is happening to us now will last forever.

For most people, retirement will consist of four phases—with different comfort zones required for each. *Those four phases are...*

•Transition. That's the "honeymoon" phase, when you're first getting used to the idea of being retired. The main emphasis in this phase is to build the structure that will sustain you when the honeymoon ends and the posthoneymoon letdown begins.

•Active living. You're healthy, vigorous and over the "posthoneymoon" letdown. Now you can do the extensive traveling you always hoped to do. When my wife and I travel, we fly into a city, rent a car and spend two or three weeks of very busy sightseeing.

•**Slowing down.** You're still basically healthy, but now it's harder to get around. This is a time for catching up on such long-deferred activities as organizing and cataloging the family photographs, and writing your own memoirs so your grandchildren will learn about how you lived as a child. You can still travel, but tours are more your speed—where you sit and are taken from place to place.

•**Assisted living.** No one likes to think he/she will someday have to depend on others for help. In fact, most of us will need some assistance when we become old and truly infirm. Don't spend your retirement years obsessing about it. But think about it well in advance so you will know how to handle it when the time comes.

Much Longer Lives Require Shrewder Retirement Planning

Ruth L. Hayden, a financial educator and consultant based in St. Paul. She is author of *For Richer, Not Poorer: The Money Book for Couples*. Health Communications, Inc.

When the Social Security system was established in 1935, people, on average, lived to the ripe old age of 62.

Today, thanks to advances in medicine, greater awareness of the benefits of good nutrition and an increased awareness of the benefits of physical exercise, we can expect to live as long as 30 years beyond retirement age—into our 80s and 90s.

To avoid financial mishaps during these bonus retirement years requires careful planning. You must keep yourself healthy emotionally, physically, mentally *and* financially. *Take time now to...*

•**Imagine your future.**
•**Plan how you want to live.**
•**Practice making—and sticking to—a financial budget.**

SETTING GOALS

Resolve any fears you may have for your financial future by setting retirement goals. *To start...*

1. *Write down what you want to have* ...to do...to be...and to see during your retirement years. *Ask yourself the following questions...*

•**What is my life going to be like** emotionally, physically, mentally and financially?

•**How will I continue to feel worthwhile** and valuable to society?

•**Will I continue working** part-time or volunteer for a charity?

•**Will I take care of my health** by exercising regularly and eating a healthful diet?

•**Do I have adequate health insurance?**

•**What will my finances be like** in retirement?

This goal-setting stage of planning is the time to fantasize and dream about the future.

Do you want to travel? Move to a different place? Spend more time with your grandchildren? Launch your own business or a new career? Take up a new sport or hobby?

Whatever it is you want to do in retirement, write it all down.

2. *Create a time frame for achieving your goals,* and write that down along the left-hand margin of a piece of paper.

Look at a calendar of years to come and choose actual dates by which each goal will be achieved. For every date, write down the age you'll be at that time.

3. *Fit the hopes and dreams you wrote down in Step One* into the time frame you created in Step Two.

Example: Make a column to the right of your "future dates" that asks, "What do I want?"

Then, add another column next to that one that asks, "What will I need to do by this date to make this goal happen?"

LESS MONEY

The steps you need to take to accomplish your goals may or may not involve the accumulation of money.

No matter what they involve, however, write them down. When you've got a clear picture of what you want to achieve during your retirement years, create a budget that helps you both achieve your goals and get used to the idea of living on a reduced income.

Most of us will find ourselves living on a reduced—if not fixed—income at some time during our three-decade-long retirement. By setting a budget now and sticking to it, you'll know that you can do it. You can trust yourself to plan your finances and, by extension, plan your life.

Software packages can help you create a budget. My favorite is Intuit's *Quicken*. If you need additional help, read a book on budgeting and/or talk to a financial planner.

BUDGETING

Things you'll want to take into account when creating a budget include…

●**Monthly fixed expenses.** Rent/mortgage, phone service, TV, Internet service, electric service, car payments, etc.

●**Nonmonthly fixed expenses.** Quarterly water service, car insurance payments, estimated taxes, etc.

●**Weekly flexible expenses.** Eating out, books, newspapers.

●**Nonmonthly optional expenses.** Gifts, theater tickets, movies, trips, etc.

The budget is your first step to financial security. You'll feel more in control of your finances, now and in the future, when you have your budget in place.

THE FUTURE

To help carry that sense of financial control forward into retirement, adopt the following model for planning and managing your finances.

As circumstances such as health and living arrangements change, adapt the model and your financial plan to address your needs.

●**Between the ages of 60 and 70,** continue accumulating money for retirement. Take a part-time job and use the money you earn for cash-flow needs—buying groceries, paying bills, etc.

If your part-time job offers a 401(k) plan, take advantage of it. Otherwise, invest money in a traditional IRA, a Roth IRA and/or the stock market.

●**Between the ages of 70 and 80,** your health-care costs may go up. You may have quit working altogether. To continue living comfortably, use the income from your investments, but—if at all possible—don't touch the principal. If you do use the principal, your money may not hold out.

●**In life's later years, from the age of 80 on up**, do whatever you need to do financially to maintain autonomy and make your life work.

This is the time to dip into the principal, if necessary, from your investments and enjoy yourself!

How to Be Prepared When Your Spouse Retires

Gloria Bledsoe Goodman, author of *Keys to Living With a Retired Husband*. Barron's Educational Series, Inc.

One of the greatest mistakes a couple can make is to assume that retirement will simply be a continuation of married life as they have known it.

Retirement has its own rhythm, just as the honeymoon years, child-rearing years and empty-nest years had theirs.

Most likely change: You will spend much more time together. *Result:* Trouble spots may arise in the smallest areas of daily life. Many newly retired couples, even those who agree on the major issues of their retirement—where to live, how to handle the finances—are surprised by how infuriating they may suddenly find their comfortable, cherished mate.

Most common trouble spots…

●**Lack of retirement planning.** Many a husband has been shocked to learn that his wife has no desire to move to the fishing village he always pictured as a retirement home. Failure to communicate expectations about retirement, or to do the pre-planning necessary to make your dreams a reality, can cause terrible conflict in retiring couples.

To offset clashes over major issues: Attend a retirement planning workshop at your local

Chamber of Commerce, community college or senior center.

●**Failure to appreciate the psychological impact of retirement.** Couples must realize that retirement can be a traumatic passage, particularly for men. Even men who look forward to retirement may feel fearful and "lost" when they no longer have a routine and the familiar identity of their working selves. Concerns with mortality and self-worth may loom large for the first time.

Best course for women: Respect the grieving period. Don't crowd or smother your husband with suggestions, opinions, questions or demands or push him into a full schedule before he is ready. But do let him know that you are there. This is a good time for extra cuddling, affection and reassurance. Let him percolate a bit, and shift the focus to your own feelings.

Many women feel that they have spent their entire lives deferring to the needs of their husbands and families. They expect retirement to be "their turn," and fear being trapped again by their husbands' needs.

Best course: Have compassion for your husband's feelings, but be very firm regarding your own needs.

Once the transitional period passes, women can help their husbands back into active life. Men are badly needed as community volunteers. Some may just want to "play" a while, others may enjoy part-time work or a second career.

●**Alcoholism/clinical depression.** Alcoholism is under-recognized and badly undertreated in seniors, even though treatment has a high likelihood of success in this age group.

Depression, with or without alcohol, can afflict either sex, but is especially common among those forced to take "early retirement." Depression can also be triggered by many medications. If you suspect either problem in your family, don't hesitate to seek professional help.

Small stuff—but major gripes…

●**Grocery shopping.** It sounds hilarious—but this is a top area of conflict cited by retired couples. Often the wife has been shopping for years, and finds it insulting when her husband suddenly questions every choice and examines every tomato.

I have met many couples who have had bitter arguments over who gets to push the cart!

Solution: Decide that one of you will do all the shopping. Or shop with two lists. He can select the produce, while she does the rest.

●**Territorial strife.** With two people in one house, problems often arise over rooms and routines.

Examples: She wants the spare room as a sewing room, he wants a den. He used to leave for work, so she could drink coffee and watch *Good Morning, America,* before starting her chores. Now he wants to watch CNN and complains when she starts the housework.

Solution: Communication, compassion and compromise. It's your retirement as well as your spouse's. Wives must be willing to cede some domestic territory—it's his kitchen, too. Husbands must face the necessity to "get a life," and not expect their wives to provide one.

●**Comings and goings.** Insecurity often manifests as controlling behavior…Where are you going? When will you be home? Who's on the phone?

Solution: Stay calm and considerate. Reassure your mate, but don't be bullied. *Essential:* Keep your sense of humor.

●**Division of labor.** He expects her to perform the same chores she always has, even if she's still working part-time. She expects that now that he's retired, he'll take on some household chores.

Solutions: It's time to be fair.

Men: You may have retired from work, but not from the partnership of a marriage. Offer to take on the vacuuming. Don't force her to ask.

Women: Acknowledge the work he does do—caring for the yard, garbage, car, etc. Then ask for the help you need from your spouse. But if you ask him to vacuum, let him do it his way. *Helpful:* List chores you each hate, and negotiate for the other to take them on. Hire help for chores you both hate.

●**Sex.** Many men find sex a means of self-proof as well as pleasure. So a pleasant side effect of the anxieties retirement can produce is that many men discover a renewed enthusiasm for sex. Older men often have a stronger sex drive in the morning—so don't be too quick to leap out of bed. You don't have to—you're retired!

Wives: Enjoy it, buy some new lingerie, be willing to try new things.

Caution: Some couples experience the opposite, and shy away from intimacy after retirement. If your sex life is unhealthy, this is a problem that needs to be resolved through frank discussion or counseling.

●**Television.** Get two!

Best Time to Retire Is Early July

A full-time worker will have accumulated the 1,000 hours required during a calendar year for full benefits. Summer retirement lowers stress—major lifestyle changes are easier to handle when days are warm, there is plenty to do outdoors and many people are away from work as well. *Caution:* Retirement in summer can eliminate a year-end bonus, and can have Social Security implications. Consult your financial adviser.

Lee Rosenberg, certified financial planner, Valley Stream, New York.

How to Have a Steady Income for Life

Robert M. Freedman, Esq., Freedman and Fish, 521 Fifth Ave., New York 10175. Mr. Freedman is former chairman of the elder law section of the New York State Bar Association and founder of the National Academy of Elder Law Attorneys.

The peace of mind that comes from knowing you'll have a steady income for life comes at a price—your assets will decline rather than grow. *But if lifetime income is your goal, there are a number of ways to achieve it...*

RETIREMENT PLANS

When you retire, you'll likely have a choice of how to take your money from the company pension plan.

Many financial advisers suggest rolling over a company retirement plan distribution into an IRA to retain maximum flexibility. When the money is in an IRA, you can invest it as you see fit. And you'll have full access to the funds at all times.

But if a steady income for life is your primary goal, you may want to have the pension money paid to you in monthly installments. If your spouse survives you, he/she can continue to receive a monthly income for life.

Caution: Once you've made the election to take pension distributions in the form of a monthly annuity, you can't change your mind.

Alternative: Roll over pension funds to an IRA, and, in effect, create your own fixed flow of income. Simply withdraw the IRA money in regular monthly installments.

Self-defense: Sit down with a financial planner who can work out a withdrawal schedule to provide for a monthly income from the IRA (based on your life expectancy).

While distributions from your IRA must begin by April 1 of the year following the year you turn 70½—you can start taking your annuity payments from the IRA at any younger age you choose. (If you're under age 59½, though, you'll be assessed a 10% early withdrawal penalty, unless payments are made in a series of substantially equal periodic payments.)

BUY A COMMERCIAL ANNUITY

Those who lack the experience of handling large sums of money may want to use insurance proceeds or other lump-sum payments to buy lifetime income from an insurance company in the form of an annuity.

Commercial annuities are investment products offered by insurance companies. They are bought directly from the company or through banks and brokerage firms.

The insurance company paying on the life insurance policy can provide an annuity, but shop around to find the best one for you.

From an investment perspective, commercial annuities may not appeal to you. You must consider the fees the company charges for the annuity in relation to the return.

But if you're prepared to pay the price and the insurance company is sound, then peace of mind can be yours with a commercial annuity.

INCOME OPTION

Annuities pay a fixed monthly amount to you during your lifetime and can be tailored to provide a continued flow of income to your surviving spouse.

TURNING ASSETS INTO INCOME

• **Reverse mortgages.** Older people of moderate means can convert the equity in their home into a monthly retirement income by using a reverse mortgage. Instead of paying principal and interest monthly, you receive a monthly check.

General qualifications...

• Generally you must be age 60 or older.

• There must be little or no other mortgage on the home.

• The home must be single family (or a one-unit condominium that is FHA-approved) and owner-occupied. Owners of mobile homes don't qualify for reverse mortgages.

The monthly income you receive is fixed according to the value of your home, the area in which you live (FHA-insured reverse mortgages set maximum loan caps for various areas) and your current age. There are different payment options to choose from, one being a monthly income for life (or the joint life of the home owners).

Caution: The reverse mortgage becomes due when the owner sells the home, moves or dies.

CHARITABLE REMAINDER TRUSTS

If you have substantial assets, especially appreciated assets such as securities, you can use them to obtain a fixed income for life *and* benefit charity by setting up a charitable remainder trust. *Benefits...*

• **Fixed income.** You receive a fixed monthly income based on the value of the assets in the trust—and the type of charitable remainder trust you use.

You can even obtain inflation protection by using a charitable unitrust. It pays a monthly income based on a percentage of the value of the assets annually. If the assets' value rises, you benefit accordingly.

• **Tax deduction.** You can claim a current income tax deduction for the value of the "remainder interest" of the money that the charity will receive when you die. This deduction is determined by IRS tables, which have recently been changed.

Caution: To achieve tax benefits, the trust must be set up carefully. Consult an attorney for this purpose.

OTHER CHARITABLE OPTIONS

Instead of using a personal charitable trust, consider...

• **Pooled income funds.** Your contribution to the charity goes into a pool with gifts from other donors. The money is invested by professional money managers.

Your income is based on the size of your gift and your age. You also receive an upfront tax deduction for the gift based on the value of what the charity will get upon your death.

• **Charitable gift annuity.** Some of the country's biggest charities will provide you with a monthly income and a tax deduction—in return for a hefty donation. The monthly income payments may not be as large as those from a commercial annuity, but you're providing a benefit to society rather than to an insurance company's shareholders.

Fewer Cars Mean More Retirement Money

Over a 40-year career, someone who buys a new car and keeps it for 10 years—instead of trading it in every three years—could have an extra $385,000 at retirement. *How to do it:* Take the savings in new-car payments and insurance and invest it—aim for an average annual return of 7.5%. Let it compound without withdrawals over the decades.

Jonathan Pond, president, Financial Planning Information, Nine Galen St., Watertown, MA 02472. *www.jonathan pond.com.*

Pension Traps—
Annuity Opportunities

Glenn Daily, a fee-only insurance consultant and author of *The Individual Investor's Guide to Low-Load Insurance Products*. International Publishing Corp.

Before collecting checks from your company pension plan or a single-premium deferred annuity, it pays to investigate your options.

By choosing an immediate annuity, you may wind up with hundreds of dollars more per month in your pocket—at no additional risk.

An immediate annuity is an insurance contract that, in return for a one-time payment, starts paying a fixed sum for your lifetime or for some other period right away.

A single-life annuity, for example, pays the agreed-upon sum every month until the purchaser dies. The payment doesn't have to stop at the first death. It depends on the option you select: Joint and two-thirds survivor, joint and 50% survivor, and joint and 100% survivor. A joint-and-survivor annuity for a married couple, by contrast, pays one larger sum while both spouses are alive, and a lesser amount after the first spouse dies. Payments continue at the lower level during the lifetime of the surviving spouse and end only when that person dies.

IT PAYS TO SHOP

Comparison shopping in the immediate annuity market can pay off quite nicely.

Example: Recently, I checked out rates—which are expressed as monthly income per $10,000 of premium—for a 65-year-old woman. For a $100,000 investment, the monthly income ranged from a high of $915 to a low of $716—a difference of almost $200, or about 28%.

Trap: Don't automatically go for the highest monthly income figure. Given all the turmoil in the insurance industry these days, and the failure of Executive Life, in the example above I decided not even to consider the seven companies paying the top rates because I had reservations about their soundness. Bear in mind that you are purchasing something that you intend to last for the rest of your life.

I wound up recommending my client purchase an annuity that ranked 20th out of 100. It was offered by Northwestern Mutual, the solid, conservative, and well-run Minnesota company. The annuity provided monthly income of $839. The median income figure was $809 a month.

COMPARE CAREFULLY

Two common situations in which investigating what you'd receive with an immediate annuity makes sense...

●**When you're retiring from your company.** Before you automatically accept the monthly pension check your company plan offers, ask if the plan permits a lump-sum distribution instead. Many, but not all, plans do.

See what you can get in monthly income by purchasing an immediate annuity with some of that money. You may be surprised to discover that you'll get a much larger payment with the annuity than with your company pension.

●**When you're ready to start annuitizing, or receiving distributions,** from a single-premium deferred annuity that you purchased years ago. Just because you purchased the annuity from Company A, don't assume that it now offers the best deal in terms of monthly income. You may do better by switching to Company B or C.

Caution: In either case, don't sink all your money into an immediate annuity all at once. You may be purchasing at a trough, and annuity rates may subsequently shoot up. I recommend that people purchase several contracts over time and that they not annuitize more than 50% of their total investable assets.

It's vital that you do your comparative shopping right at the point when you are ready to make your purchase.

Reason: The immediate annuity market is a very fluid one, and rates can fluctuate widely, even within a given company, depending upon the details of your individual situation.

Example: A particular company may post attractive payouts one month, but not the next. Or, it may be competitive at some ages but unattractive at others.

To compare the different rates offered by different companies, you can check with a local broker or contact the following sources...

●**Web Annuities,** 800-872-6684, *www.imme diateannuity.com*. An insurance-brokerage and research firm that specializes in immediate annuities. It also works on a commission basis.

- **TIAA-CREF,** 800-233-1200.

- **AnnuityNet,** *www.annuitynet.com*. Look for the inflation proofer immediate annuity.

Of course, there are some drawbacks to opting for an immediate annuity, rather than for your company pension. Rejecting your pension might be unwise, for example, if your company has a history of increasing its pension payouts from time to time in order to offset inflation. The annuity check you get the first month is the same amount you'll receive 20 years from now—assuming you're still alive to collect.

And—pensions are insured by the Pension Board Guaranty Corporation, while immediate annuities are only as good as the company that issues them.

Before you jump at the highest available rate, you should always very carefully investigate the issuing company's financial health.

Aim: To be reasonably sure it will be able to make those payouts as long as you live.

Caution: Some, but not all, insurers require annuity buyers to pay upfront policy fees or other charges, which can range from $150 to $500. And about 10 states impose premium taxes that amount to 1% to 3% of the amount invested.

Variable Annuity Traps

Beware: A bonus for signing up for a variable annuity is a marketing gimmick. The bonus—up to 5%—rewards new annuity buyers according to how much money they commit to an annuity. But these highly promoted accounts come with little-mentioned fees, such as annual costs that are higher than what competitors offer…steep surrender charges…and surrender charges that last longer than the industry average. The Securities and Exchange Commission is now investigating variable-annuity marketing tactics. *Bottom line:* Do not buy a variable annuity without first consulting an independent financial adviser.

Harold Evensky, CFP, principal, Evensky, Brown & Katz, financial planners, Coral Gables, FL.

Variable annuities are now being aggressively promoted by many insurance companies—but

are appropriate for relatively few investors. Issuers say annuities are good for timid investors because they guarantee that the money will be preserved for heirs despite market fluctuations. But annuities have fees that may be twice those of mutual funds. They carry large penalties for early withdrawals, plus an IRS penalty for withdrawals before age 59½.

J. Michael Martin, president, Financial Advantage Inc., fee-only financial planners, Columbia, MD.

When a Pension Dies With You

A pension can "die" with you—if the payout is limited to lifetime monthly benefits and you aren't married. Pensions provide a joint and survivor payout option *only* to married participants. So unmarried participants can't pass on benefits—and payments cease at death. *Good news:* Plans generally allow participants to take lump-sum distributions in lieu of monthly benefits—although spouses of participants must consent to this and waive survivorship benefits. A lump-sum distribution can be rolled over to an IRA, from which monthly benefits can be taken. Whatever remains in the IRA upon the owner's death can be left to heirs—spouse, child, life partner.

Robert S. Keebler, CPA, Virchow, Krause & Co., Green Bay, WI, and author of *A CPA's Guide to Making the Most of the New IRA*. American Institute of CPAs.

How Safe Is Your Pension?

George E.L. Barbee, executive director of client services, Price Waterhouse, 1251 Avenue of the Americas, New York 10020. He is a contributor to the *Price Waterhouse Retirement Adviser*. Pocket Books.

More and more people are discovering—to their horror—that they can't rely solely on their company defined-benefit pension plan for retirement security. Some companies have even terminated plans. And sometimes plans fail because of a company's financial problems or problems with an insurance company that provided a guaranteed income contract.

What can you do? Not much, if a pension-plan failure catches you unprepared. You could write to the US Department of Labor, but in practice it can't be counted on to do much unless you're with a large company. Nor is the IRS likely to provide much help. The Pension Benefits Guaranty Corporation is supposed to pay when defined-benefit plans fail, but it has payout caps that could be much less than what you were counting on, and some observers claim the organization is overextended. Nearly all lawyers with pension-plan expertise work for plan sponsors, not individual participants.

Avoid bad surprises...

Keep yourself informed about your company's pension plan. *Ask yourself fundamental questions (some of these can be answered by your pension plan's annual report)...*

• **What's the pension plan invested in?**

• **Is the pension portfolio heavily loaded with your company's stocks?**

• **Is the pension plan in sound condition?**

• **If your company offers a guaranteed income contract portfolio,** is it provided by a single insurer? If just one, how solid is it?

• **How sound is your company?** Monitor annual reports, quarterly reports and business news affecting your company.

• **What are the ratings of insurance companies involved with your guaranteed income contract portfolio?** Consider a B- (or lower) rating from A.M. Best, Moody's or Standard & Poor's as a warning flag.

SELF-DEFENSE

• **Consider a pension plan as one part of an overall portfolio.** Don't rely on a company pension plan to provide the bulk of your retirement assets. Put eligible funds into an IRA. Buy an annuity. Build your own portfolio of savings and investments.

Your portfolio should be properly diversified, enabling you to survive in the event that something goes awry. Diversification is especially important for the millions of people who acquired large chunks of their company's stock through employee stock-ownership plans. If you have more than 5% to 10% of your assets in a single stock, look to diversify your portfolio.

• **Think ahead about health care.** Because costs are escalating dramatically, more and more companies are curtailing dollar payouts in many ways. You might not be able to use the doctor or hospital of your choice unless you pay out-of-pocket. Set aside additional savings for adequate health care protection or consider other forms of health insurance appropriate for your circumstances.

Truth About Cash-Balance Pension Plans

Cash-balance plans are a fairly new type of pension plan in which employers pay 4% to 7% of an employee's compensation into the employee's account in the plan. Most accounts have a guaranteed rate of return, often tied to the yield on 30-year Treasury bonds, although some companies give employees investment options.

The money in the account accumulates steadily over time, and when employees retire or change jobs, they generally can take a lump-sum payment from the plan. Or a retiree could elect to receive an annuity based on the amount in the account.

With a traditional defined benefit plan, retirees typically get monthly payments until they die based on how long they were with the firm and their highest level of pay during the five years prior to retirement. Employees have to stay with a company most of their careers for this type of pension to be worth much— one reason why younger workers, who tend to change jobs, prefer the cash-balance plan.

For details, read "Cash Balance Package," free from the Department of Labor, 800-998-7542 or online at *www.dol.gov.*

Nancy Dunnan, financial adviser and author of *Never Short a Stock on Wednesday and 300 More Financial Lessons You Can't Afford Not to Know.* HarperBusiness.

New Strategy to Help You Grow Your 401(k)

William E. Donoghue, chairman of W.E. Donoghue & Co. Inc., registered investment advisers, and publisher of *Donoghue's WealthLetter,* a monthly strategic mutual fund investment newsletter, Box 309, Suite 401, 100 Medway Rd., Milford, MA 01757.

During the past 10 years, three trends have made traditional retirement savings assumptions obsolete…

• **The wave of corporate mergers and acquisitions** has concentrated more assets in fewer large-company stocks.

• **People in these large corporations are investing 30% of their 401(k) money in their own company stocks**…and 30% in large-cap index funds. This drives up demand for large-cap stocks.

• **People are living longer.** The cost of living comfortably into your 90s and beyond has increased dramatically.

Investors should be least conservative with tax-deferred retirement money and instead think long term. These accounts have the greatest compounding power. And with increased longevity, you're going to need a lot of money for a long time.

So—advice such as "diversify your 401(k) portfolio" and "play it safe" adds to your risk of running out of money before you run out of life.

Here are my new rules to boost your chances of saving enough for a long and happy retirement…

• **Focus on large-cap growth stocks.** Spreading your money equally among all your 401(k) plan's funds only dilutes long-term returns.

Better: Concentrate your assets in an S&P 500 index fund and other funds that invest mainly in large-cap growth companies. Large-cap stock funds have been the strongest performers over the past decade. They outperform, on average, small-cap stock funds 9.24% to 13.78%.

Large companies have performed well during this period because, on average, they do business more economically. They also attract the best talent while outperforming or acquiring their smaller competitors.

I haven't seen a scenario in which small-cap stocks will outperform large-cap stocks again. The trend toward investing in large-cap stocks is denying many smaller companies access to the capital markets.

My suggested 401(k) allocation: People in their 30s, 40s, 50s and even nearing retirement can put at least 50% of their 401(k) assets in funds that invest in large-cap domestic stocks.

Once you retire, keep two to three years of cash to cover spending needs in less volatile investments, such as money market funds and income-oriented stock funds. The rest of your assets can remain in large-cap stock funds. Remember, anyone with a 25-year time horizon is a long-term investor. If you are 65 and expect to live to 90, you are a long-term investor.

• **Don't overinvest in overseas stock funds.** International stock funds may offer great short- or intermediate-term investment opportunities. But overall, these funds have not proven to be sound long-term, buy-and-hold investments. Few foreign countries or regions have the long-term economic stamina and vitality to outperform US stocks.

Rule of thumb: If you wish to invest in an international fund, limit your investment to 10% of your portfolio.

Use new 401(k) plan contributions to buy shares of international funds rather than sell off large-cap investments to raise cash. To maximize returns, buy fund shares when bad news abroad sends share prices down and sell shares when good news pushes prices up. Be prepared to move quickly. It is better to keep small profits than to lose big ones.

•Avoid money market and bond funds.
Unless you are retired, there is only a very limited role for a money market fund in a long-term 401(k) portfolio.

With 24-hour phone access to funds and brokers—and no adverse tax consequences of trading in a tax-deferred 401(k) portfolio—it's easy to sell shares to raise cash if you need it.

Parking cash in a 401(k) plan's money market fund while waiting for the right time to invest it is of little value.

Also, limit your investment in bond funds. In a rising interest rate market bond funds lose value.

If you want to buy fund shares, raise cash by selling shares in a fund that you feel has the worst prospects.

•Maximize 401(k) plan contributions.
There are three big reasons for you to contribute the total allowable amount each year, which is $11,000 for 2002, or $12,000 for those age 50 and older.

•You are receiving "free" money if your employer matches some or all of your contributions.

•Plan contributions reduce your current income taxes because contributions are withdrawn from your paycheck before your income is taxed.

•Most 401(k) plans offer low-cost loan programs that come in handy when you need to borrow cash in emergencies.

•Beware of newly started funds. Out of the 3,727 domestic stock funds, only 20 outperformed a low-cost S&P 500 index fund over the past five- and 10-year periods.

New funds are as likely to be in the bottom 100 as they are to fall into the top 100 each year.

Exception: Enhanced index funds, which are designed to beat index returns by investing a portion of funds in a futures-and-options strategy tied to the index and the balance in a money market fund.

Examples: The Rydex Index Trust and Pro-Funds fund families both offer funds that are designed to earn between 1.5 and two times the S&P 500 stock index or the NASDAQ stock index.

Enhanced index funds are likely to make more money in a rising stock market and lose more in a declining market than any managed stock fund.

Ask your employer to consider adding an enhanced index fund to your plan.

•Make the most of a rollover IRA. Most people aren't aware that when they change jobs and move their 401(k) plan assets into a rollover IRA, they have many more investments open to them. If you choose to roll over your IRA to a discount broker, you will have even more investment choices than traditional brokerage firms.

How to Check Up on Your 401(k)'s Performance

Treat your 401(k) as you would other investments—check its performance against comparable investments.

Example: If you have 401(k) money in a growth fund, compare that fund against other growth funds.

If your 401(k) is underperforming, contact the 401(k) administrator. Most companies are responsive to well-researched complaints…it is in their best interest to keep the employees satisfied. Ninety percent of 401(k) plans are at firms that have fewer than 100 employees.

Ted Benna, inventor of the 401(k) and president of The 401(k) Association, 155 Lingwood Ct., Bellefonte, PA 16823.

401(k) Plan Trap

If you borrow funds from your 401(k) retirement account and leave your employer before repaying the loan, the entire outstanding balance will be taxable income to you. If you are under age 59½, it will be subject to an early distribution penalty as well.

Self-defense: If you plan to retire or leave your employer and have 401(k) loans outstanding, repay them before you leave.

Whenever you take out a 401(k) loan, be aware of the tax risk should you leave your employer unexpectedly.

Terry Savage, a syndicated *Chicago Sun-Times* financial columnist and author of *The Savage Truth on Money.* John Wiley & Sons.

Answers to Your Toughest Questions About IRAs

Ed Slott, CPA, E. Slott & Co., 100 Merrick Rd., Rockville Centre, NY 11570. He is editor of *Ed Slott's IRA Advisor*. *www.irahelp.com.*

While the basic rules for IRAs seem straightforward enough, working with the rules is not always easy. Many questions continue to trouble individuals—about putting funds into and taking funds out of IRAs. *Some helpful questions and answers…*

ON CONTRIBUTIONS

Am I permitted to contribute stock to my IRA?

No. Only cash contributions are allowed. Once money is in the IRA, though, you can buy stock with it. And stock that you have in an IRA can be rolled over or transferred directly to another IRA.

Caution 1: The stock you purchase in your IRA must be publicly traded. If you buy stock in a closely held corporation—even a minority interest—you are considered to be "self-dealing." This is prohibited by the law that governs IRAs, and you will be subject to a penalty.

Caution 2: You cannot swap stock into or out of an IRA. For example, if *you* own stock in X Co. and *your IRA* owns stock in Y Co., you cannot exchange one for the other (even though they are of equal value). Doing so would be treated both as a taxable distribution to you and a nonpermissible contribution.

ON DISTRIBUTIONS WHILE YOU'RE ALIVE

I own some great stock in my traditional IRA and must start taking distributions this year because I'm 70½. Must I sell the stock and take a distribution in cash or can the stock be distributed to me?

You can have the stock distributed to you. Since the stock must be publicly traded, it is easy to value it for purposes of taking the required distribution. The stock is valued on the date of the distribution. The dollar amount of the distribution is taxed to you as ordinary income.

I am 72 and took my first required minimum distribution last year. My two children are named as beneficiaries on the account. Since then, I've remarried. What effect does my remarriage have on my future IRA distributions?

None, unless you change the beneficiary, naming your new spouse rather than your children and your new spouse is more than 10 years your junior. Required distributions are smaller when there is a much younger spouse named as the beneficiary. Otherwise, your distributions under the new distribution rules remain the same—whether your children continue as beneficiaries or you name your new spouse (who is not 10 years younger than you are).

ON DISTRIBUTIONS AFTER DEATH

My father died, leaving me as beneficiary of his IRA. What should I do?

First, the title to the account should be changed to read: *(Your parent's name), IRA, deceased (date of death), FBO (for the benefit of) (your name)*. Then take your required distributions.

One way to meet the distribution requirement is to withdraw the entire amount (and pay tax all at once). With this alternative, you must take all by the end of the fifth year following the year of your father's death.

Or, if you wish to keep money in the IRA as long as possible, you can spread distributions out over your life expectancy. Here, distributions must begin by the end of the first year following the year of your father's death.

You can name a new beneficiary (such as your own spouse or child) to inherit the IRA if you should die before exhausting the account. However, your naming a new beneficiary has no impact on your required distributions.

My mother named me and my two siblings as cobeneficiaries of her IRA. She died at age 68. What are our options?

The account can be split into separate shares, one share for each beneficiary. Then each of you can take distributions from the IRA based on your life expectancies.

If the account is not split, then distributions must be based on the age of the oldest sibling.

An itemized income tax deduction can be claimed by a beneficiary who is required to report as income distributions from an inherited IRA. The beneficiary can deduct the portion of federal estate tax allocable to the IRA distribution he/she received. How is this calculated?

There is no clear IRS guidance on this question. It would appear that first you allocate the portion of the federal estate tax to the IRA. This is based on the percentage of the estate that the IRA represents. For example, if the estate is $2 million and the IRA is $800,000, then 40% of the estate tax is applicable to the IRA. Then, of that amount, the portion of the account distributed each year is the same portion of the estate tax deduction used each year.

Example: If one-twentieth of the account is required to be distributed to the beneficiary, then one-twentieth of the 40% allocable portion of the estate tax deduction can be claimed as an itemized deduction in the year of this distribution.

ON ROTH IRAS

I'm 72 and want to convert part of my regular IRA to a Roth IRA. Can I include the required minimum distributions I started taking at 70½ in the conversion amount?

No. Required minimum distributions cannot be converted to a Roth IRA. Amounts in excess of the required distributions can be converted if income for the year is no more than $100,000 (including the required minimum distributions). Starting in 2005, required minimum distributions will not be taken into account in determining eligibility to convert to a Roth IRA.

ON OTHER MATTERS

Can I roll over my IRA into my 401(k)?

If your IRA is a "conduit" IRA, one that consists solely of funds transferred from a qualified retirement plan (and the earnings on those funds), then you can roll over the IRA to a 401(k)—assuming the plan will accept such rollovers.

However, if you also contributed other money to that IRA, then the conduit is considered "tainted" and cannot be rolled into a 401(k) or other qualified plan.

My IRAs are in New York. That state provides protection to IRAs from the claims of creditors. I now live in a state that does not appear to provide such protection. Are my IRAs protected or not?

It would seem that your IRAs are still protected by the laws of New York, since the accounts are still in that state. However, check with a tax attorney in your new state to determine the extent of protection, if any, afforded there.

Valuable Opportunities Playing Roth IRAs by the New Rules

Ed Slott, CPA, E. Slott & Co., 100 Merrick Rd., Rockville Centre, NY 11570. He is editor of *Ed Slott's IRA Advisor*. *www.irahelp.com*.

Roth IRAs are clearly a success for those who have them. Wise use of a Roth IRA helps individuals build tax-free, long-term wealth.

THE BASICS

Traditional IRA: Any individual younger than 70½ with earnings of $3,000 or more can contribute up to $3,000 of *pretax* income for 2002 (plus $500 if the individual is at least 50 years old by the end of the year), although active participants in qualified plans can only make fully deductible contributions for the year 2002 if Adjusted Gross Income (AGI) is below $54,000 on a joint return…or $34,000 on a single return. Earnings grow tax-free until withdrawals begin after retirement—or by age 70½, whichever comes first. Withdrawals are taxed at ordinary income rates.

Roth IRA: You can contribute the same amount to a Roth IRA, but contributions are not tax-deductible. Earnings, however, are completely *tax-free* (not tax-deferred, as with a regular IRA). Withdrawals are never required, as they are with a regular IRA. You can begin to withdraw *earnings* after age 59½ without penalty if the account is owned for at least five years. You can withdraw *contributions* tax- and penalty-free at any time.

WHO QUALIFIES

Roth IRAs are better for lower-bracket taxpayers.

To qualify…

● **You must have earned income equal to the contribution amount.**

● **Allowable contribution starts to phase out at AGI of $95,000** and disappears completely when AGI reaches $110,000 for single individuals…$150,000 and $160,000 for married couples filing jointly.

Distributions are income tax-free to your Roth IRA beneficiaries, who can spread distributions over their life expectancies—possibly another 30 or more years of tax-free growth.

What to do: Your Roth IRA beneficiary should elect the life expectancy term by taking the first required distribution by December 31 of the year after you die. Otherwise, he/she will have to withdraw the proceeds over five years …and will lose a lifetime of tax-free earnings. When you leave a Roth IRA to your spouse, he can roll it over into an existing or new Roth IRA and be exempt from any required distributions.

Caution: A Roth IRA is part of your taxable estate. So when you open one, buy additional life insurance held by a trust or your beneficiaries. The insurance provides liquidity for paying estate taxes without forcing your heirs to make excessive IRA withdrawals to pay the tax.

CHANGES IN IRA CONVERSIONS

● **Converting to a Roth IRA.** When Roth IRAs were first created in 1998, you could pay the income tax owed when you converted a traditional IRA to a Roth IRA over four years.

If you are eligible and convert now, you must pay the tax in the year of the conversion. To simulate the four-year income spread, convert 25% of your traditional IRA to a Roth IRA over four years.

● **Converting from a Roth IRA.** When the market drops, you can save taxes by converting a Roth IRA back to a regular IRA.

Example: You converted a $100,000 regular IRA into a Roth IRA in 2001 that shrank to $30,000 in April 2002, because the market fell. If you recharacterize the Roth account as a regular IRA in April 2002, you'll remove the tax owed on the initial $100,000. You can then convert the $30,000 back to a Roth IRA as a Roth conversion next year—only one conversion is permitted per year. This way, you'll regain the Roth IRA benefits.

Only one "recharacterization" from a Roth IRA to a regular IRA is permitted per year. Filing Form 8606, *Nondeductible IRAs,* removes taxes that were owed when the Roth IRA was opened.

IRA Nightmares

Errors by brokerages, mutual fund companies and other financial institutions are increasing —resulting in costly tax penalties for investors. *Reasons:* The complex tax law and high volume of customer requests. *Self-defense:* Use an IRA-savvy tax adviser to plan retirement investments and payouts. Then send your requests in writing, giving the institution plenty of time to execute them.

Ed Slott, CPA, E. Slott & Co., 100 Merrick Rd., Rockville Centre, NY 11570. He is editor of *Ed Slott's IRA Advisor. www.irahelp.com.*

Don't rely on your IRA trustee to keep records of your beneficiary designations and distribution elections. These may well not be used for decades. In the meantime, the papers can and do get lost, as firms that serve as IRA trustees merge, move, reorganize their offices, etc. *Trap:* If your elections are lost, the trustee will distribute your IRA funds following its "default" options—which may be very different from what you elected. *Safety:* When making beneficiary designations and distribution elections, get acknowledged copies of them from the IRA trustee, and keep them with your will and other estate planning documents.

Seymour Goldberg, Esq., CPA, Goldberg & Goldberg, PC, 666 Old Country Rd., Suite 600, Garden City, NY 11530.

Doublecheck IRA Designations

Check that your IRA beneficiary designations are properly on file.

Trap: IRA trustees can lose the paperwork on elections that were made many years ago.

Horror story: A person named his daughter beneficiary of his $500,000 IRA. But when the bank that managed the IRA merged with another bank, the paperwork didn't carry over. Since there was no named beneficiary, his estate was named beneficiary by default.

Result: When he died, the IRA was liquidated, creating a $200,000 income tax bill and forfeiting an untold amount of tax-deferred growth.

Ed Slott, CPA, E. Slott & Co., 100 Merrick Rd., Rockville Centre, NY 11570. He is editor of *Ed Slott's IRA Advisor.* *www.irahelp.com.*

How to Find Forgotten Assets

One out of every eight Americans has forgotten some financial asset—bank account, utility deposit, etc. These unclaimed assets eventually go to the states. A free Web site, *www. missingmoney.com,* lets you look for assets in 24 states—Arizona, Colorado, Delaware, Florida, Kansas, Kentucky, Maine, Maryland, Massachusetts, Michigan, Minnesota, Missouri, Montana, New Hampshire, New Mexico, North Carolina, Oklahoma, South Carolina, South Dakota, Utah, Vermont, Virginia, West Virginia, Wisconsin, plus the District of Columbia. Check the site as new states are added periodically. (e.g., Nebraska will be added soon).

Joan Caplin, money writer, *Money,* Rockefeller Center, New York 10020.

2

Estate Planning Strategies

Estate Planning For an Increasingly Complex Future

Estate planning today is more complex than ever before, and the need for attention to estate plans will grow and grow. *Three factors have come together to make this so...*

●**Greater longevity.** With lifespans increasing, more people are choosing to combine a program of lifetime gifts, trusts and family limited partnerships with their estate plans. A simple will or even a living trust is no longer sufficient for an estate plan.

●**The unlimited marital deduction,** which gives you the right to transfer any amount of property to your spouse free of gift and estate tax, came into effect in January 1982. It has made estate planning and estate tax deferral easy for many couples. But by now there are many widows and widowers with large taxable estates. Preserving as many assets as possible for their heirs without access to the unlimited marital deduction requires a carefully crafted estate plan.

●**The booming financial markets of the last decade,** combined with a period of economic stability, have given far more people than ever before enough assets to almost guarantee that their estates are potentially taxable.

A TEAM BUSINESS

The best approach to an estate plan is to think of it as a business—one that is focused on people.

To be successful, a business needs a plan and a mission, and it needs a first-rate management team.

Indeed, these business essentials are doubly important for an estate plan.

If you make a mistake in business, you can generally cut your losses and regroup. But, if

---

Owen G. Fiore, Esq., CPA, a nationally recognized estate planning attorney and tax litigator. He is founder of The Fiore Law Group, 101 Park Center Plaza, Suite 1150, San Jose, CA 95113.

your heirs are squabbling after your death, there's obviously nothing you can do.

Your plan and mission: Develop clear ideas about what you're trying to achieve with your estate plan...

- **Keep a family business going.**
- **Provide funds for your grandchildren's educations.**
- **Provide financial security for a surviving spouse or parent.**
- **Set up a really long-term, or "dynasty," trust.**
- **Keep an undisciplined young adult from controlling money too soon.**

Once you've thought out the plan—communicate your goals to your team of advisers so they can set up strategies to implement them.

THE TEAM

You are the CEO of the business of putting together an estate plan. The team members should be able to communicate and work together well with you—and with each other. *The three key team members are...*

- **CPA** is the gatekeeper. He can provide a financial reality check. That goes along with doing the tax returns and supervising the books and records.

- **Attorney** draws up the will, trust documents, and perhaps family limited partnership papers and ought to be able to explain them clearly.

Often, diagrams help—showing what assets go to whom at each step of the plan. A simple outline of the legal documents can also help make a complex plan understandable.

- **Life insurance professional** decides how much coverage is needed and what type is best for an individual or couple to achieve particular goals.

Example: A second-to-die policy that provides cash to pay estate taxes may be useful if a family business is to be passed intact to the next generation.

Depending upon the individual circumstances, other team members may include...

- **Financial planner** or investment adviser, particularly when primary assets are marketable securities.

- **Business valuation expert**—who will be needed if there is a family business or family partnership. The IRS is militant about business valuations, and a detailed, up-to-date appraisal by an outside expert must be included with a gift or estate tax return, if the return is to pass muster.

- **Family counselor or clinical psychologist**—who is sometimes needed when family members do not see eye to eye.

Example: Siblings may vie as to who should be the next CEO of a family business, or even over whether to carry on with the business or sell it. Sort out problems as soon as they are apparent. Do not let them fester.

- **Representative of an institutional trustee,** such as a bank or trust company, who may be needed if there is no individual or family member who alone could serve as executor of an estate. *Caution...*

- Watch out for "trust mills," impersonal "cookie-cutter" packages and the like.

- Interview your attorney, not only about billing, but also about how he plans to achieve your goals and ask him to explain the plan. If the attorney says, "You won't understand it, just trust me," make for the exit.

TAX SAVINGS

Once the team is in place and the estate's goals set, the team can decide on the best way to achieve them while minimizing taxes. It's often possible to save 50% or more of the taxes that might be owed, if assets were simply bequeathed outright. *Frequently used strategies...*

- **Lifetime gifts** are often preferable to leaving assets at death via a will or trust. Of course, each person may give $10,000 a year to each of any number of recipients free of gift and estate tax consequences.

For more sizable gifts, a gift tax return must be filed, but there will be no tax owed until the gift and estate tax-exempt amount ($1 million in 2002) is exceeded.

In any event, if you give securities that are likely to appreciate, the tax will be based on their current value. If you hold onto them and your heirs receive them as bequests in many years, the value, and hence the ultimate estate—and state—tax, could be far higher.

•**Family limited partnership** is frequently an ideal way to make your gifts while retaining control as the general partner.

You can bring the younger generation into the business as limited partners, sharing the income and learning the business.

At the same time, considerable tax savings may be realized due to valuation discounts on the limited partnership units given to family members. Discounts are allowed precisely because the donees do not have control, which makes their shares less valuable than yours.

Example: You put $4 million worth of securities into the partnership. Discounted to 75% of value, only $3 million would be taxable. Because estates of $3 million or more are taxable at 55%, that's quite a tax savings, even after the $15,000 to $20,000 it might cost to set up the partnership. Also, all estate tax is saved on post-gift appreciation in value.

Tax avoidance cannot be the only reason for the partnership, or the IRS will disallow the valuation discounts. But keeping control out of the hands of people who are not yet qualified is a valid reason.

Caution: Proper accounting and representation by counsel will be needed if the IRS challenges a partnership or trust document.

How to Take Advantage Of the Tax Laws

Sanford J. Schlesinger, Esq., partner and head of the wills and estates department of the law firm Kaye, Scholer, Fierman, Hays & Handler, LLP, 425 Park Ave., New York 10022.

Americans will be transferring *trillions* of dollars worth of assets to family members and other beneficiaries and heirs over the next 50 years. Possibly as much as $136 trillion will be given away or bequeathed.

No doubt your wealth, like that of so many others, is rapidly building up. *Impact:* Planning has never been so important.

This is the right time to review plans for gifts and estates, making sure your planning takes full advantage of what the tax laws allow.

Do not fall prey to two widely held misconceptions…

Misconception 1: **Congress has eliminated transfer taxes, so there is no need to act now.**

The new tax law increases the estate tax exemption and cuts estate tax rates over the next decade. However, estate tax is repealed only for those dying in 2010. Thereafter old estate tax rules reapply.

Bottom line: There's a continuing need to plan for estate taxes.

Misconception 2: **My finances are fairly straightforward, so I don't need to worry about a lot of sophisticated planning.**

Even married schoolteachers in their 50s can have more than $1 million in assets today if they bought a home years ago and have contributed regularly to their retirement plans. They need a lesson in estate planning if they want those assets to go to their children without the IRS taking a big cut. *How to get started…*

LIST YOUR ASSETS

First: **Make a list of all your assets.** *Include…*

•**The equity in your home.**

•**Your investment portfolio.**

•**All retirement plans and IRAs.**

•**Investment real estate.**

•**Value of business interests.**

•**Other significant assets** such as artworks and collectibles.

Then: **Update your estate plan.** If total assets exceed $1 million, you should proceed to update your trust and estate plans.

BEST WAYS TO CUT ESTATE TAXES

•**Divide assets with your spouse.** A couple can double the $1 million that is exempt from gift and estate taxes simply by dividing ownership of assets into his and hers, rather than owning them jointly. A his/hers division creates two estates instead of one, fully utilizes each spouse's exempt amount and drastically cuts taxes.

●**Get insurance out of your estate.** Generally, insurance should be owned by an irrevocable life insurance trust or ownership rights should be relinquished. Many people mistakenly think of insurance as tax free.

It is true that beneficiaries do not owe income taxes on life insurance proceeds, but if you—or a business of which you own more than 50%—own the policy, it will be subject to estate taxes, which can far exceed income taxes.

●**Make annual gifts.** Remember, the law allows you to make gifts up to a dollar limit per recipient per year ($11,000 in 2002) to as many recipients as you wish with no gift or estate tax consequences. A gifting program can reduce taxable estates for people whose assets clearly exceed their needs. The best time to make the gifts is early in the year, to get a full year's benefit of unloading the money and its appreciation.

●**Make tuition gifts.** The law allows you to make gift-tax-free gifts—in addition to the annual gift limit—for tuition costs.

Say you want to pay your granddaughter's college expenses. You can pay an unlimited amount of tuition gift tax free as long as you make the payment directly to the university. In limited circumstances, you may even be able to take advantage of this tax break by *prepaying* your granddaughter's tuition.

UPDATE YOUR WILL

If your will was written before the *Taxpayer Relief Act of 1997,* it may use numbers pegged to the former law. That exempted $600,000 from gift and estate taxes and $1 million from the generation-skipping transfer tax. *New amounts...*

●**The estate tax and generation-skipping transfer tax exemption amounts,** $1 million in 2002, will rise to $3.5 million by 2009.

●**The gift tax exemption amount** is $1 million in 2002 (it does not increase thereafter).

As a result of these changes, wills and trusts may need to be revised, using *formulas* rather than absolute numbers.

●**For the charitably inclined,** consider naming a charity as the beneficiary of an IRA, instead of bequeathing it to an individual via your will.

If the IRA goes to your child, say, up to 80% could be gobbled up in income and estate taxes. *Better:* Leave the child assets that are not subject to income taxes and give a charity the asset—the IRA—that would otherwise be subject to income taxes.

FAMILY-OWNED BUSINESSES

The family-owned business deduction, which (combined with the exemption amount) shielded $1.3 million in value of a family business, is repealed starting in 2004. Those owning such business interests need to make new plans to reduce or eliminate the estate tax.

INDIVIDUAL STATE CHANGES

Because many states have passed new laws concerning gift and estate taxes, it is advisable to check with your attorney as to whether your will or trust documents need to be updated because of state law.

●**Gift taxes.** Many states are repealing gift taxes. New York, for example, repealed its gift tax, effective January 1, 2000, and adopted a "soft" estate tax, effective February 1, 2000. A "soft" estate tax is one that is based on the federal return. The switch removes a tax incentive for moving to Florida, as many New York retirees now do. (North Carolina, Connecticut, Tennessee, Georgia and Puerto Rico still levy gift taxes.)

●**Dynasty trusts.** Many states have repealed what is known as "the rule against perpetuities," which prevented assets from being held in trust indefinitely. Now, if you want to put assets, or even a family business, into a long-term trust, you may be able to do so under the laws of your own state instead of setting up an Alaska or South Dakota trust. In practice, many people prefer to set a limit on how long trusts last.

●**Investing trust assets.** States are beginning to look at trusts' overall rate of return, recognizing capital gains as income, not just interest and dividends. Trusts are often set up to pay out income to beneficiaries with what's left over (the "remainder") going to someone else after a set period or upon the deaths of the beneficiaries. This state monitoring of a trust's return has profound implications on how assets are invested. Check with your attorney or trustee concerning the law in your state.

How to Eliminate Family Squabbles

Martin M. Shenkman, CPA, JD, tax attorney in New York and author of numerous books on estate planning, including *The Complete Book of Trusts*. John Wiley & Sons.

Many of the nasty battles that siblings wage over estates arise because their parents failed to consider their feelings when making plans.

While wills and trusts are necessary to protect assets, they very often neglect emotional issues and create long-lasting relationship problems for heirs.

Feelings don't have to be hurt when protecting assets. Changing the wording or softening language in those documents can make a crucial difference in how a parent's wishes are perceived by children.

To anticipate and avoid the biggest problems...

Problem: **Failing to distribute noninvestment assets fairly.** Families have always battled over seemingly worthless items that are left in estates. But the recent jumps in prices for art, antiques and collectibles have raised the stakes.

Even though you have good intentions when you make up your estate plans, problems may arise.

Example: If you leave one child your collection of first-edition books and your other child your favorite desk, the two items may have vastly different values. One child could benefit at the expense of the other.

Fights also erupt when parents completely forget to include such assets in their estate plans or fail to specify which child gets which piece of property.

Solution: Make a list of all of your personal assets. Then let the oldest child choose one item from the list, followed by the next oldest child—all the way down to the youngest child.

Then, in the second selection round, let the youngest child choose first from the list. This list can be circulated by mail or by e-mail, with pictures of the assets if necessary. The children can also submit their selections to you by mail.

When all the children have had a chance to select first, get appraisals of the assets they've chosen. Appraisals can vary in cost, from several hundred dollars to many thousands of dollars.

Balance the value of assets by giving cash in addition to items of lesser value. Values of items in an estate can change over time. So the sooner it is handled and everything is distributed, the better.

If children are unable to agree on who gets what within 60 days, state in your will that everything will be sold at current market value, with each child receiving a share of the proceeds to equalize the value of items distributed.

Problem: **Completely disinheriting a child.** By doing so, you guarantee that the child's only memories of you are bad ones.

Better: Acknowledge in your will that the relationship between the two of you was not the best. Then leave your child something—even if it is not as much as you left other children.

Leaving less-favored heirs something may prevent legal challenges to your will. Naming them makes it legally clear that you intentionally meant to leave to them smaller portions than to their siblings.

Avoid using language that will hurt them, such as, "I leave only $100 to my son Frank, who I hope one day will make something of himself."

Words like these can cause divisions within a family for generations. Use milder language that puts a positive spin on your wishes and urges your family to become closer.

Example: "I leave 10% of my estate to my son Frank. While our relationship was not as close as I had wished, I hope that this bequest will encourage him to remain close with the rest of the family."

Problem: Leaving one child more than the other. If one child is left more than another—despite the fact there may be good reasons for this move—you may ruin their future relationship.

Example: One of my clients was worried about how to divide her estate fairly between her two daughters. One daughter is wealthy...the other is divorced and struggling to bring up her young children without financial support from her ex-husband.

Many parents would leave more to the divorced daughter—but my approach is to treat siblings equally in estate plans to preserve their relationship.

Solution: Because the less fortunate daughter will likely need more support, I suggested that my client leave each daughter 30% of the estate outright. Then the client put the remaining 40% into something I call a *pot trust*.

A pot trust is like a pot of soup—allowing each daughter to ladle out the money that she needs.

It named both daughters as cotrustees, since they were on good terms. If they weren't on good terms, she would have named a bank as trustee.

Each daughter must get the other daughter's permission to withdraw money from the trust.

Once the youngest grandchild, who is the son of the divorced daughter, reaches age 25, the trust will be dissolved. Whatever is left will be equally divided between the two daughters.

Problem: A will that can't adjust to changes in children's circumstances. Your will needs to deal with the differing needs of each child while still making them each feel satisfied.

Sometimes a subtle change in language is all that's necessary.

Example: Recently, I helped a client solve a difficult situation involving his two adult children—one son was a successful businessman and one could never hold a job.

The father wanted to split his estate, giving half to the businessman outright and putting the other half into a trust for the other son, naming his brother as trustee.

I convinced him this was a mistake. Putting the responsible brother in charge of his brother's finances would forever doom their relationship.

Better: We split the estate 50–50, putting each brother's share into a separate trust for life. We also named each son as cotrustee—along with a bank—of his own trust.

Even though the documents looked identical on the surface, there was a crucial difference in the language.

The businessman has the right to independently withdraw some of the principal in the trust without getting prior approval of the bank trustee.

But the other son must first get the consent of the bank before withdrawing funds from the trust, although he is entitled to the income produced by the trust assets.

Grandchild Loopholes

Edward Mendlowitz, CPA, partner, Mendlowitz Weitsen, LLP, CPAs, Two Pennsylvania Plaza, Suite 1500, New York 10121. He is author of several books on taxes, including *IRA Distributions: What You Should Know.* Practical Programs, Inc.

Gifts to grandchildren—or great-grandchildren for that matter—help them and cut the family's overall tax bill. *Here are the best tax-saving gift strategies...*

Loophole: Pay a grandchild's tuition and medical expenses. Generally, you owe gift tax when you give a particular grandchild (or anyone) more than the annual gift tax limit ($11,000 in 2002). In 2002 the tax-free limit is $22,000 per grandchild per year for a married couple who join in making the gift.

In addition to an annual gift-tax-free gift, you can give an unlimited amount to help with education expenses as long as payments are made directly to a school, college or other educational institution.

On top of that, payments you make directly to hospitals or other medical providers to cover a grandchild's *medical* expenses are gift tax free.

Caution: You must make out the gift check directly to the institution (education or medical), not to your grandchildren.

Another form of giving: A married couple can contribute up to $110,000 in 2002 to a qualified state tuition program (QSTP) with the money to be used for a grandchild's education.

The $110,000 can be offset with five years' worth of $22,000 joint annual gift-tax exclusions, making the contribution absolutely gift tax free. The election to apply the five years' worth of $22,000 exclusions is made on IRS Form 709.

Note: Distributions of earnings that are used to pay tuition, fees, books and supplies are now tax free.

Caution: A steep penalty applies to earnings that are distributed but not used to pay for higher education expenses.

Loophole: **Make your grandchildren partners in a family partnership.** The limited partnership interests that you transfer to your grandchildren are valued for gift tax purposes at less than the fair market value of the entire assets. A discount is applied because the partners/grandchildren have no control over the invested assets.

How to do it: Make yourself the general, or controlling, partner and your grandchildren limited partners. You will have complete control over the assets owned by the partnership. Income generated by the partnership assets will be paid to the grandchildren or accumulated for them.

Loophole: **Name your grandchild the beneficiary of your retirement plan.** You must start taking money out of your IRAs and other retirement plans by April 1 of the year after the year in which you turn age 70½. When you withdraw less than the IRS-required minimum amount each year, you owe a penalty.

Strategy: The minimum annual withdrawal is based on the joint life expectancy of you and the beneficiary you've named to your retirement account. You can minimize the annual payout—maximizing the tax-free buildup in the account —by naming a young grandchild as beneficiary of the account.

Reason: Your grandchild has a longer life expectancy than you do, and your combined expectancies would stretch the payout period longer than it would be had you named your spouse or another adult as beneficiary. Also, when you die, the balance in the account would be distributed over the beneficiary's life expectancy.

Loophole: **Set up a custodial account for the grandchild**—a Uniform Transfers (or Gifts) to Minors Act account with a bank or brokerage firm. The account will be owned by the grandchild and generally taxed at his/her lower tax rate. Transfer enough cash or assets to each grandchild so that they have $1,400 of investment income per year.

Reason: Because of the kiddie tax, children under age 14 can earn only $750 of investment income free of tax in 2002. The next $750 of investment income will be taxed at their low 10% rate. Investment earnings above $1,500 will be taxed at the parent's tax rate.

Best assets to give grandchildren under 14...

●**Index funds or growth stocks** that produce little or no current income. The shares can be sold after the children turn age 14, and the gains taxed at their low rate.

●**Series EE or I US savings bonds** that mature after your grandchild's 14th birthday. The taxes are deferred on these bonds until they are cashed in or mature.

●**Zero-coupon municipal bonds,** which don't generate any current income.

Best assets for grandchildren older than 14…

Take advantage of the children's low tax rate by giving them income-producing assets like high-dividend-paying stocks or bonds.

Alternative: Give appreciated assets and have your grandchildren sell them.

Trap: Grandparents who make gifts to custodial accounts should not act as custodians. If they do, any money left in the account when they die will be included in their taxable estates. Avoid this by having one grandparent make a gift to the other grandparent, who then gives the money to the grandchild. That way, the first grandparent can act as custodian without adverse tax consequences.

Loophole: **Put your grandchild to work** as a model or "actor" in advertisements for your business or its products. Children can earn income of up to $4,700 before owing any tax in 2002. Above that, earnings of up to $6,000 are taxed at 10% and earnings above $6,100 but not over $27,950 are taxed at their low 15% rate.

Strategy: Up to $3,000 of earned income a year can be contributed to a Roth IRA and never taxed there.

Caution: The business will owe Social Security and payroll taxes on salaries paid to your grandchildren.

Loophole: **Set up a life insurance trust** to hold policies on your life for the benefit of your grandchildren. When the trust is properly set up, the proceeds paid on your death will not be subject to estate tax.

Trap: Gifts to grandchildren that exceed an exemption amount are subject to the generation-skipping transfer tax. Avoid this tax by transferring $1 million into a life insurance trust. You may owe little or no tax on this gift, depending on your other lifetime gifts. Then direct the trust to buy a single-premium life insurance policy on your life. This should pay a benefit of $2 million to $5 million, depending on your age.

When you die, the policy proceeds will be paid to your grandchildren free of estate tax. *Result:* You have passed on $2 million to $5 million for the price of gift tax on $1 million.

Caution: If the trust is set up incorrectly, the full insurance proceeds could be subject to a generation-skipping transfer tax.

Estate Planning Loopholes

Here are two strategies to consider if you have a disabled family member…

Loophole: **Gift-tax-free gifts to disabled persons.** Expenses paid for medical care or tuition directly to the hospital, provider or school also are exempt from gift tax and the generation-skipping transfer tax.

Caution: You must write a check directly to the institution, not to the individual receiving the care.

Loophole: **"Special needs" trust.** Money can accumulate in a "special needs" trust to provide a disabled person with income without any gift or estate tax or Medicaid consequences.

Caution: You must follow the guidelines outlined in OBRA (Omnibus Budget Reconciliation Act of 1993), Section (d)(4)(c).

Wiser Bequests

Leaving a bequest of cash to charity can be a tax mistake. *Better:* Instead of leaving cash to a charity, have your will fund a charitable bequest with an item that would be subject to income tax if left to heirs.

Examples: Deferred compensation, nonqualified stock options, IRA funds.

Since charities are tax exempt, they can receive these items income tax free. And heirs can receive cash income tax free. So you effectively cut the IRS tax bite.

Contrast: Deferred compensation and IRA funds are subject to income tax at ordinary rates, as are nonqualified stock options when exercised. If you leave the charity cash and bequeath your heirs taxable items, you will be leaving your heirs a tax bill—and making a bequest to the IRS. (See IRS Letter Ruling 200002011.)

Martin M. Shenkman, CPA, JD, tax attorney in New York and author of numerous books on estate planning, including *The Complete Book of Trusts*. John Wiley & Sons.

The "Forever Trust"

David S. Rhine, CPA, regional director of family wealth planning, Sagemark Consulting, a division of Lincoln Financial Advisors Corp., a broker/dealer and registered investment adviser, 395 W. Passaic St., Rochelle Park, NJ 07662.

Stock options, stock market gains, life insurance, family businesses, appreciated real estate…and other new wealth has exposed many more families to the steep estate tax.

NEW LAW

Fortuitously, a new opportunity to escape estate tax now exists. New law in several states makes it possible to place family wealth in a perpetual trust. This trust can protect wealth—and let it accumulate—for the benefit of family members forever.

Moreover, the wealth will pass from generation to generation estate tax free forever into the future—even as it grows.

In the past, it wasn't possible to create a trust that would last forever because of the "rule against perpetuities." That rule generally limits the maximum term of a trust to the lifetime of a living person, plus 21 years.

But now 16 states have repealed the rule—Alaska, Arizona, Delaware, Florida, Idaho, Illinois, Maine, Maryland, Minnesota, Missouri, New Jersey, New York, Ohio, Rhode Island, South Dakota and Wisconsin. Several more states have legislation pending to do so.

OUT OF STATE

The rule does not have to be repealed in your state in order to use a perpetual trust. It's possible to fund a trust during your lifetime in a state other than where you live.

Competition between states for this trust business is a large part of what's driving the spreading repeal of the rule against perpetuities.

Over time, the power of compound interest can produce staggering gains.

Examples: If a trust grows 7% per year—the average long-run return from the stock market over inflation—$1 million will grow to $867 million in 100 years. Yes, $867 million!

And if a trust grows just 1% faster, at 8%, $1 million will become $2.2 billion in 100 years.

Growth much less than this would probably be enough to secure your family's financial welfare—and their gratitude to you—for generations to come.

ESTATE TAX RULES

The initial transfers that fund a perpetual trust are subject to gift and estate tax under normal rules—but there are ways to minimize or eliminate the tax.

The tax advantage of a perpetual trust is that future "layers" of estate tax between generations are eliminated.

Estate tax applies at rates up to 50% in 2002 (45% by 2007). So, on transfers through two generations (to grandchildren), almost 80% of an estate can be consumed by estate tax—and through three generations (to great-grandchildren), the figure is 90%.

It is these future layers of estate tax that are eliminated by a perpetual trust.

Two kinds of taxes must be planned for when establishing a perpetual trust…

● **Gift or estate tax.**

● **Generation-skipping tax.**

Every individual has a personal gift- and estate-tax-exempt amount of $1 million in 2002. The estate tax exemption rises to $3.5 million by 2009, which can be used to fund the trust. A couple can make use of two exempt amounts with proper planning.

To make your exemption more valuable…

● **Life insurance can be used to fund the trust** and with proper planning, the insurance proceeds can escape being part of your taxable estate. The premium going into the trust may be subject to transfer tax, but that's just a fraction of the proceeds, particularly if you use second-to-die insurance. Or use split-dollar life insurance to get the transfer costs even lower.

● **Make your gift before it appreciates.** Appreciating assets can be placed in the trust before you die, so future appreciation escapes estate tax.

● **Minority interests in private businesses** often can be valued at discounts of 30% or 40%. You may be able to cover $1.4 million or more of underlying value with your $1 million tax-exempt amount.

GST

The generation-skipping tax (GST) is a special consideration whenever a transfer is made across more than one generation—such as to grandchildren as happens with the perpetual trust.

In order to prevent persons from avoiding layers of estate tax with transfers across more than one generation, Congress created the GST.

It applies to such transfers in addition to any gift or estate tax. But the GST can be minimized as well. *Planning opportunities...*

●**Every individual has an exemption amount from GST** (it's the same as the estate tax exemption).

●**GST applies only once to funds left in a properly drafted trust,** even if the trust eventually benefits many generations.

Example: In 2002, you can fund a trust with up to $1 million with no GST. If you fund the trust with more, GST will apply to the excess—but after it is paid, trust funds will pass from generation to generation in the future with no estate tax or GST, so future layers of estate tax will still be eliminated.

TRUST RULES

A perpetual trust is irrevocable. Once created, it cannot be changed or modified by the creator.

You can give beneficiaries limited power over disposition of the assets for succeeding generations.

A trustee selected by the trust's creator becomes responsible for managing the assets. Distributions may be discretionary, or set as a percentage of trust assets or trust income. You should also give a roadmap for the appointment of successor trustees by the beneficiaries. Do the trustees appoint their own successors? Or some hybrid? Typically, a corporate trustee will also play a role.

Flexibility: You can even give each beneficiary the right to demand a distribution of up to 5% of principal annually. *Advantage:* If you split up the trust by family, and a beneficiary doesn't need the money, it will remain in the trust and pass tax free to his/her family.

A perpetual trust does owe income tax on its income, so trust investments typically will be geared toward appreciation—which fits well with holding an interest in a growing family business or growth stock portfolio.

In some states, a perpetual trust can also function as a charitable lead trust—combining tax and charitable benefits. To minimize transfer taxes, each year for a set number of years after the trust starts, funds are paid to charity. The value of this charitable income stream reduces the taxable gift.

FAMILY PLANNING

Setting up a perpetual trust requires far-reaching vision...faith on your part in the trustee, who will require a great deal of flexibility...and procedures for selecting a succession of trustees in the future.

The trust will last far beyond what you can foresee, so you must make provisions for the unexpected.

Example: The trust's investments may grow much more quickly or slowly than expected—and your family may grow more quickly or slowly than expected as well.

Thus, careful thought will have to go into designing distribution standards that will keep the trust from...

●**Being prematurely depleted** due to excess distributions during a time of slow growth.

●**Retaining funds and "growing for growth's sake"** when it could be helping family beneficiaries while investments are booming.

Important: Specific legal rules for perpetual trusts vary in each state. And these trusts have many legal, tax and estate planning considerations that must be carefully considered with experts.

But if you have accumulated wealth and wish to make it really last for your family, a perpetual trust is a new option to consider.

Congress Killed the Estate Tax...or Did It?

Gideon Rothschild, Esq., CPA, partner in the law firm Moses & Singer LLP, 1301 Avenue of the Americas, New York 10019.

S tarting in 2002 and continuing through 2010, the rules for passing on property change dramatically. But in 2011, all the new rules expire, with estate tax reverting to its 2001 status.

During this nine-year period, some individuals will no longer have their estates depleted by taxes. Others are not out of the woods entirely and still need to plan to minimize estate and gift taxes.

TAX RATES AND EXEMPTIONS

Starting in 2002, estate taxes drop in the following manner...

● **The top tax rate declines from 55% to 50%.** It continues to fall by one percentage point each year until it reaches 45% in 2007. It stays at that rate until 2010, when the federal estate tax is repealed entirely.

Caution: In 2011, the repeal *expires*. It remains to be seen whether Congress will act before the expiration date to make the repeal permanent.

● **The amount exempt from estate tax—** $1 million in 2002 and 2003—increases to $1.5 million in 2004, $2 million in 2006 and $3.5 million in 2009.

In 2010, there is no exemption amount because there is no estate tax that year. When the old rules take effect again in 2011, the exemption amount reverts to $1 million.

Impact of these changes: Wills and trusts must be reviewed. Revisions may be necessary.

Requiring special scrutiny: Wills that contain credit shelter trusts, trusts designed to fully utilize the exemption amount in the estate of the first spouse to die.

Why: Because of the escalating exemption amount, it may no longer be desirable in an estate of less than $5 million to funnel the maximum exemption amount to the credit shelter trust.

Example: A couple has a combined estate of $2 million ($1 million each) and wills requiring credit shelter trusts to be funded with the "maximum federal estate tax exemption amount." If one spouse dies in 2006, when the exemption amount is $2 million, his/her entire estate would be placed in the trust. In essence, the other spouse would be disinherited.

Gift taxes: The gift tax exemption amount for lifetime transfers is $1 million in 2002 and, unlike the estate tax exemption, increases no further.

The gift tax is *not* repealed in 2010. Instead, it becomes a flat tax at the highest individual income tax rate—35%.

Wealthy individuals who have already used up the $675,000 lifetime exemption amount should make additional tax-free gifts in view of the current $1 million exemption.

Gift tax exclusion: In 2002, the annual gift tax exclusion of $11,000 per recipient (or $22,000 if married), and the exclusion for direct payments of tuition or medical expenses were not changed by the new law. Thus, in addition to the lifetime exemption amount, wealthy taxpayers can continue to make these tax-free gifts year-in and year-out to reduce the size of their taxable estates.

FAMILY BUSINESSES

The special additional deduction for family-owned business interests currently available— up to $675,000—is repealed for individuals dying after 2003. Business owners whose estates fall below the increasing exemption amount are not adversely impacted by this repeal. Those with substantial holdings need to consider other transfer-planning strategies to minimize taxes.

Review succession plans with tax advisers. If you don't have a succession plan, make one now.

CARRYOVER BASIS

While the new law reduces or eliminates the estate tax burden, it potentially *increases* the income tax burden on heirs and can result in an overall tax increase.

Property inherited after 2009 no longer receives a stepped-up basis to its value at death. Instead, carryover basis rules are set to apply. Heirs take over the same basis that the decedent had. This may be substantially lower than the property's current value.

When heirs sell their inherited property, they'll have to pay tax on the resulting gain— the difference between what they've realized on the sale (current value) and the decedent's original basis.

Exceptions: Two exceptions allow stepped-up basis rules to be used...

•**Up to $1.3 million of basis increase** can be allocated to appreciated assets passing to any heir. This dollar limit is increased by unused capital losses, net operating losses and unused built-in losses.

•**Up to $3 million of additional basis** for appreciated assets passing to a surviving spouse.

Example: A married individual dies in 2010, leaving an estate of $5 million, $4 million of which is bequeathed to the surviving spouse. The assets have a basis of $1 million for the spouse's bequest and $500,000 for the remaining assets. The executor can allocate $3 million of basis to the assets passing to the spouse and $500,000 of basis passing to other heirs. *Note:* The stepped-up basis allocation cannot exceed the fair market value of the assets.

In the absence of contrary instructions in a will, it's up to the executor to decide which property can enjoy the stepped-up basis. It may be helpful to revise wills to include guidance to an executor on allocating the stepped-up basis amount.

PLANNING STRATEGIES

Individuals whose estates do not become tax free despite the exemption increase should continue transfer planning to ease the tax burden for their heirs.

•**The generation-skipping transfer tax (GST) is modified by the new law.** Now the exemption amount is the same as that for estate tax purposes. The same estate tax rate applies to generation-skipping transfers until repeal of estate tax. Thereafter, the same 35% rate used for gift tax applies to lifetime generation-skipping transfers. Thus, GST is still a planning issue to address.

•**Flexibility will have to be written into estate-planning documents.** Wills and trusts should consider using "but if" clauses so provisions can be tied to tax changes. *Remember:* An existing formula clause may leave too much to the credit shelter trust and nothing to the spouse.

Example: A will might say that *if* the exemption amount is $1 million (and the individual dies in 2002), property passes in a certain way, *but if* the exemption amount is $2 million (and the individual dies in 2006), property is distributed in another way.

•**Trusts** continue to play an important part in estate tax planning. Dynasty trusts allowing assets to pass from one generation to another and another have not lost their appeal. Similarly, asset protection trusts should not be overlooked for the protection they can offer from creditors' claims.

•**Don't assume** that life insurance to provide estate tax liquidity is no longer needed. Don't be quick to cancel—wait and see what ultimately happens to the estate tax.

•**Valuation discounts** (such as those associated with family limited partnerships) remain an important tool for reducing estate taxes when used in conjunction with lifetime gifts.

Minimize Estate Taxes

Family Limited Partnerships (FLPs) are becoming increasingly popular for minimizing estate taxes. *Caution:* If most of the assets you transfer are appreciated stocks and bonds, you may inadvertently trigger all unrealized capital gains. To avoid this huge cost, have your accountant run through the "investment company rule" calculations. If they are violated, either change the transaction or don't do it at all.

Martin M. Shenkman, CPA, JD, tax attorney in New York and author of numerous books on estate planning, including *The Complete Book of Trusts.* John Wiley & Sons.

Taking a Chance On an FLP

Setting up a family limited partnership (FLP) is the latest game of Russian roulette rich people play with the IRS. If your estate tax return does not get audited, your beneficiaries win with a family limited partnership. But—if there is an audit, your beneficiaries could lose. They'll probably end up in a lengthy court battle, facing steep legal bills and possibly IRS penalties and interest charges.

How the game is played: Cash and marketable securities are transferred to a limited partnership. Each year interests in the partnership are given to family members. The value attributed to the assets owned by the FLP is always less than the market value of the cash and securities that were transferred to it, since those assets are subject to restrictions that would not exist if the assets were owned outright.

Why You Must Review Your Will

Common mistake with wills: Most people update their will when something happens to their family—such as a birth, death or divorce. But they neglect to do so when the law that applies to them changes.

Examples: Numerous recent changes in the federal estate tax affect basic issues such as the amount that a person can leave tax free. And when you move your residence from one state to another, an entirely new set of state laws will govern your will. Key parts of your old will may simply become invalid.

Important: Review your will with your attorney and estate tax adviser periodically even if your personal situation does not change.

Sidney Kess, attorney and CPA, 10 Rockefeller Plaza, Suite 909, New York 10020. Mr. Kess is coauthor of *1040 Preparation, 2001 Edition.* CCH Inc.

Durable Power of Attorney

A durable power of attorney gives a trusted adviser the power to handle your financial affairs during any period in which you are incapacitated.

Important: The power of attorney should include specific authority for that person to deal with the Internal Revenue Service on your behalf. This is often overlooked but may prove vital if your adviser must take responsibility for your tax affairs.

Martin M. Shenkman, CPA, JD, tax attorney in New York and author of numerous books on estate planning, including *The Complete Book of Trusts.* John Wiley & Sons.

How to Avoid the Naming of an Administrator

Encyclopedia of Estate Planning by Robert S. Holzman and John J. Tuozzolo. Bottom Line Books.

To ensure that an executor of your selection will serve, this is what you should do:

●**Sound out your designated executor** to see whether he will actually serve if named in your will. Do this periodically. Is his health still satisfactory? Has he taken on full-time responsibilities elsewhere? Is he still interested in you and your beneficiaries? If not, replace him.

●**Seek to ensure your designated executor's agreement** to serve by recommending to him knowledgeable and able attorneys, accountants, and (where appropriate) appraisers and brokers who can help him to carry out his responsibilities without excessive detail work with which he isn't familiar.

●**Name one or more successor or contingent executors,** so that if the person of your choice doesn't serve, at least it will be your second or third choice, rather than an administrator that you would never have engaged.

●**Name a trust company as coexecutor.** This virtually assures the permanence and continuity of an executor you have seen fit to name.

●**Make certain that your will is valid so that the executor chosen by you will qualify.** Have an attorney familiar with state law check such requirements as the minimum number of witnesses required. State laws vary as to the technicalities to be met.

●**Be sure that your will can be found when the time comes to have it probated.** A perfectly executed and technically correct will is useless if nobody knows where it is. Have your will in your attorney's office, or with your federal income tax workpapers.

Wiser IRA Management

Consider setting up a separate IRA for each heir to maximize the accounts' value to your family. If you have one IRA with multiple beneficiaries, required payouts are determined by the age of the oldest person. That means more must be paid out each year, with less left to keep growing tax-free. But if you set up separate accounts—each with only one beneficiary—younger beneficiaries, such as grandchildren, can stretch out withdrawals much longer.

Caution: Calculations can be complex—be sure to consult a financial adviser.

Edward Slott, CPA, E. Slott & Co., 100 Merrick Rd., Rockville Centre, NY 11570. He is editor of *Ed Slott's IRA Advisor. www.irahelp.com.*

3

Investment Opportunities

New Income-Boosting Essentials

Yesterday's conventional wisdom held that as people neared or reached retirement age, they had to reduce risk by moving most of their savings into conservative investments, such as bonds.

Today's reality: You can't afford not to be invested in equities to some degree, even after you've retired. Stocks or stock mutual fund investments keep your income ahead of inflation. *Fact:* Stocks have outpaced inflation better than any other investment over time.

Best allocation: Keep at least 20% to 50% of your investments in stocks and stock mutual funds. The rest of your portfolio can be in less risky investments, such as bank CDs and government bonds.

For more conservative investments: Consider US Treasuries. Depending on how competitive bank rates are in your area, Treasury bills, notes and bonds will earn 1% to 4% more than bank savings products—particularly passbook accounts. And while earnings on Treasuries are subject to federal income tax like CDs, they are not subject to state and local income taxes. *Three kinds of Treasuries...*

● **Treasury bonds are sold in $1,000 increments with maturities up to 10 years.** These and other Treasury instruments are available from banks and brokerage firms for about a $50 transaction fee. Or you can purchase them directly from the Federal Reserve without a fee through a program called Treasury Direct. *For information:* 800-722-2678 or *www.treasurydirect.gov.*

● **Treasury bills are sold in one-, three- and six-month maturities** and cost a minimum of $1,000 from Treasury Direct, with additional increments of $1,000.

● **Treasury notes are sold in two- to 10-year maturities in $1,000 increments through Treasury Direct.**

Barbara O'Neill, PhD, CFP, a professor of family and consumer sciences at Rutgers University. She is author of *Saving on a Shoestring* and *Investing on a Shoestring.* Dearborn Financial Publishing.

Strategy: "Ladder" maturities when buying CDs and Treasuries.

Instead of buying a single $10,000 CD, say, buy 10 $1,000 CDs and stagger their maturities so that one comes due in year one, a second comes due in year two, a third in year three and so on.

Benefits: You won't tie up all your money in a single CD or bond—you will receive a regular check as each one matures—and you can more easily take advantage of changing interest rates.

How: If rates increase, you can move some of your money into a higher rate CD as soon as one matures, instead of having to wait until a longer-term CD matures.

INVESTMENT APPROACHES

• **Never put your money in an investment product you don't completely understand.** Too many people, while chasing high yields, put money into investments only because they've been told they'll get a high return.

• **Follow the "four-year-old-kid rule."** Don't invest in anything you can't quickly and easily explain in a way that a four-year-old would understand.

• **Don't avoid an investment simply because it has a duration longer than your life expectancy.** Just because someone is age 70 doesn't mean he/she shouldn't buy a 30-year Treasury bond. These long-term investments generally produce higher returns than ones with shorter terms. Remaining principal will become part of your estate and will be passed on to your heirs.

• **Continue to set financial goals.** Reaching retirement doesn't mean you've reached your financial goals. You may need more money in retirement than you had planned. *Retirement expenses may include...*

   • Travel, which can be expensive.

   • Unanticipated health-care needs plus long-term-care insurance.

   • Building up your estate to leave more to your heirs.

   • Helping grandchildren pay for college.

   • One or more new cars.

Expenses such as these may require you to shift assets to higher producing, riskier investments.

Required: A sound financial strategy to increase the odds that these new goals will be met.

CONTINUE TO WORK

There's a growing sentiment in this country that retirement is a dead end. More and more people say they don't want to retire—ever. They want to continue to work, at least part-time, as long as their health holds out, well past age 65. *If this is your intention...*

• **Check with former employers about returning to work.**

• **Get a part-time job.**

• **Split a full-time job with somebody in a time-sharing arrangement.**

• **Turn a hobby into a business.**

CUT EXPENSES

One of the easiest ways to increase your retirement income is simply to spend less by cutting expenses. This will enable you to save more. *Some painless strategies for reducing costs include...*

• **Review your insurance policies** to make sure you're not paying for coverage you no longer need.

• **Play the "age card,"** and get a Senior ID through your local Office of the Aging. This card entitles you to a wide array of discounts.

• **Shift to a low-interest credit card.**

• **Join a co-op** to buy food in bulk.

• **Choose basic clothing styles** that can be dressed up or down. And build your wardrobe around a few colors that complement you.

• **Revive the lost art of letter-writing,** or better still, send e-mail, instead of making expensive long-distance telephone calls.

• **Call the local utility company** for an energy audit and take advantage of its cost-saving advice.

• **Consider low-cost entertainment options,** such as early bird dinners, college theater presentations and inexpensive adult education classes.

• **Swap services,** such as pet-feeding and house-sitting, with neighbors and friends.

Before Hiring a Financial Adviser...

Edward Mendlowitz, CPA, partner, Mendlowitz Weitsen, LLP, CPAs, Two Pennsylvania Plaza, Suite 1500, New York 10121. He is author of several books on taxes, including *IRA Distributions: What You Should Know.* Practical Programs, Inc.

When choosing a financial adviser, look for someone whose style meshes with your needs.

The best way to find an adviser is through referrals from friends or your accountant. Get at least three referrals.

All referrals should have a recognized credential, such as CFP (Certified Financial Planner) or PFS (Personal Financial Specialist). That tells you he/she has completed educational requirements...and follows a strict code of ethics.

Contact the Certified Financial Planner Board of Standards (888-237-6275, *www.cfp-board.org*) or The American Institute of CPAs, PFS Division (888-777-7077, *www.cpapfs.org*) for information about complaints that may have been filed against a potential adviser.

Questions to ask each referral...

•**How do you charge for your services?** "Fee-only" advisers charge by the hour. Others charge a percentage of your total assets...or earn commissions on financial products they sell to you. The best advice generally comes from those who make the same money, no matter what the investment.

•**What is your investment philosophy?** Ask for samples of investment policy statements he helped clients prepare. If you are 35 and have no dependents, you likely want to be more aggressive than someone who is 35 and has children.

•**Beyond providing financial advice, how do you earn money?** If an adviser also sells life insurance, he may be more interested in selling products than in creating a sound financial plan for you.

•**How do you keep up to date in the financial field?** Any adviser you hire should read trade journals and financial publications ...and attend conferences and seminars.

•**How do you keep your clients informed about important financial issues?** An adviser's style must suit you—and he must be able to explain matters to you clearly.

Who Needs a Full-Service Broker?

Full-service brokers still have value for investors who are uncomfortable making their own investment decisions but who do not want to pay recurring fees to an investment manager.

Also: People who are easily influenced by cocktail party conversation about stocks might be better off with a wise full-service broker.

Caution: Choose a broker only after calling several references. Avoid anyone who strongly encourages buying into high-commission investments—particularly load mutual funds and annuities.

William G. Brennan, CPA, certified financial planner at Columbia Financial Advisors, LLP, Washington, DC.

Switching Brokers

It takes two to three weeks to switch brokers after completing an account-transfer form. But delays can occur. *Reasons:* Incorrect information on transfer forms...use of an incorrect form...transfer includes a margin or retirement account...transfer between two different *types* of accounts...change in the account owner. *Self-defense:* Fill out transfer forms carefully...monitor the transfer process.

John Gannon, acting director, Office of Investor Education and Assistance, Securities and Exchange Commission, Washington, DC.

Social Security Savvy

When planning an investment portfolio for retirement, count Social Security benefits as an asset. *Example:* You retire with $500,000 in savings, and plan to invest half in US bonds for safety and half in stocks for growth. You also receive a $1,000 monthly Social Security benefit. *Key:* Social Security benefits are as secure as the interest paid on US bonds. If you expect to receive $12,000 annually for 20 years, that's the equivalent of $150,000 in bonds. So, if you invest half your savings ($250,000) in bonds, that's too much. Your best safety/growth mix is $375,000 in stocks, $125,000 in bonds—with the consideration that your Social Security is the equivalent of $150,000 in bonds.

John Markese, American Association of Individual Investors, 625 N. Michigan Ave., Suite 1900, Chicago 60611.

Safer than Banks

Investors suffering from high anxiety are turning more and more to the safest investment there is: US Treasury securities.

Treasury bills (maturing within six months), notes (maturing in two to 10 years) and bonds (maturing after 10 years) are actually safer than government-insured bank accounts. *Trap:* There's only pennies in government insurance for every dollar of insured bank accounts. *Even worse:* Some of the insurance funds aren't in cash, but in illiquid receivables accepted from troubled banks.

By contrast, every penny of a T-bill is guaranteed by the full faith and credit of the federal government. And the government has never failed to pay its obligations.

Bonus: Liquidity, especially if they're purchased through a mutual fund that offers check-writing privileges. *Special tax status:* T-bills, notes and bonds bought by individuals aren't subject to state income taxes. When these securities are purchased through a mutual fund, 25 of the 40 income-tax states levy a tax.

James M. Benham, chairman, Benham Capital Management Group, 755 Page Mill Rd., Palo Alto, CA 94304.

Dividends Can Mean a Lot

Investors who need income should take dividends seriously. As more and more companies plow money into research and development instead of paying out earnings to shareholders, dividends may no longer be a market fixture. But they do provide investors with an important income stream. Dividends and interest should cover at least 60% of the income needs of anyone who lives on money from investments, with the balance coming from growth of assets, such as a program of systematic withdrawal from an equity mutual fund. That way, if the market drops, the income stream continues with less of a draw on assets.

Madeline Noveck, CFP, president, Novos Planning Associates, Inc., 120 E. 56 St., New York 10022.

Where to Park Your Money for the Short Term

Here are some suggestions for money you will need soon...

●**Money market accounts** pay more than bank accounts and are safe.

●**Ultrashort bond funds** yield slightly more at some increased risk. They invest in issues averaging six-month terms. Best for people who don't want to risk principal.

●**Short-term municipal bond funds** invest in issues with terms up to three-and-a-half years. They go up more than ultrashort funds when interest rates drop but fall more when rates increase.

●**Prime-rate funds** invest in floating-rate bank loans taken by corporations. Yields can be good. Withdrawals are usually allowed only once per quarter. Best for people who need withdrawals at predictable times.

Peter DiTeresa, senior editorial analyst, Morningstar. com, 225 W. Wacker Dr., Chicago 60606.

Warren Buffett's Focused Investment Strategy Made Easy

Robert Hagstrom, manager of Legg Mason Focus Trust, which is modeled on Warren Buffett's investment strategy. He is author of several books on Warren Buffett's investment strategy, including *The Warren Buffett Portfolio: Mastering the Power of the Focus Investment Strategy.* John Wiley & Sons.

I've known Warren Buffett for 15 years, and I have closely studied his investment strategies. One of the secrets of his success is that he owns a small number of stocks—and only those with brand names that are extremely strong and will attract consumer demand over the long term.

You don't need to be a financial wizard to succeed at focused investing. *Here are my rules, based on what I have learned from Warren Buffett...*

●**Limit your portfolio to between 10 and 20 companies.** The majority of Berkshire Hathaway's portfolio is invested in about seven stocks...and Buffett believes a portfolio of 10 stocks is plenty for most people. The focused fund I manage owns only 16 companies.

I realize this type of focused approach may seem counter to conventional wisdom, which preaches the virtues of diversification. But Buffett believes that owning too many stocks hampers, rather than improves, performance.

●**Understand each company's business.** The key stocks Berkshire Hathaway owns—American Express, Coca-Cola, Gillette, Freddie Mac, Walt Disney, The Washington Post and Wells Fargo—are all household names. They operate in industries they dominate.

Buffett says he doesn't understand technology so he doesn't own technology or Internet stocks...but people who can understand technology should consider investing in great technology companies. He also doesn't own startups with new products that haven't been tested in the marketplace.

●**Look for a long history of superior performance.** We pick companies whose five-year trends of earnings growth and returns on equity exceed those of the S&P 500. Right now,

the earnings growth rate of the average stock in the S&P 500 is between 13% and 16%, while its return on equity is between 15% and 20%.

I'm less concerned with how much a company's growth rate exceeds the S&P 500 average than with its *consistency*. I would rather own a company that I'm confident will continue to post 20% annual earnings growth than one with highly erratic annual earnings over the past 10 years that average out to 30%.

●**Use the annual report to assess management and cash allocation.** One way that anyone can gauge the quality of management is to read the chairman's letter in the company's annual report. Even the best companies face some market difficulties. I look for those whose annual reports contain frank discussions of what went right and—equally important—what went wrong over the past year. If there's no mention of problems and challenges facing the company—that's a red flag.

I also like companies that disclose in their annual reports exactly how they are allocating their capital. You can find this information by reading the narrative section usually titled "Management Discussion of Cash Flow Statement."

Example: We sold an alcoholic beverage company because it persistently took cash that is generated by its high-margin distilling operations and allocated the money to its low-margin china business. That just didn't make sense to us.

●**Reinvest in your most promising holdings.** Most people purchase new stocks when they invest rather than buying more shares of what they already own. In most cases, this strategy reduces returns.

If you believe the companies whose stocks you own have bright futures, continue to invest in them.

Important: Each time you invest new cash, concentrate most of your money in the one or two stocks you think have the most promising prospects at that time.

●**Don't trade often.** When you buy a company's stock, plan to hold it for at least five years. Buffett says you should pretend that you have only 20 investment choices available to you during your entire lifetime.

This will force you to be choosy about where you invest and also is an incentive to leave your investments alone once you've made them.

●**Sell a stock if it becomes overpriced compared with the rest of the market.** We don't hang on to expensive stocks if we think their estimated future returns will be less than that of the overall market. We sell when the stock's price rises to a level that makes its future rate of return equal to or below what the future rate of return of the market will be.

Example: Earlier this year, we purchased shares of America Online. We had been early buyers of the stock, but once its price shot past $160 a share, we sold our position. At that price level, its future rate of return was equal to what we believed would be the stock market's future rate of return. After the price slid back down below $100 a share, we bought more.

Investment Lessons

George Stasen, a venture capital expert and chief operating officer of Supra Medical Corp., and Robert Metz, a financial journalist. They are coauthors of *It's a Sure Thing: A Wry Look at Investing, Investors, and the World of Wall Street.* McGraw-Hill.

There's no shortage of financial advice on Wall Street. The problem is that much of this financial advice is conflicting and leaves individuals confused or stuck in bad investments. So what's an investor to do?

Decisions, decisions…

●**"Buy low and sell high" is sound financial advice—but there are actually four decisions to make.** Stock market experts like to say that timing is everything, and most investors strive to sell at the top of a market and buy at the bottom.

This strategy is also known as the "contrary opinion"—doing the opposite of what most other investors are doing at a given time.

But moving successfully against the crowd is very difficult.

Trap: Market cycles contain many small, deceptive movements—so the buy-sell phases aren't always clear. *Here are four decisions a contrarian investor must make…*

●**When the market is approaching the bottom of a cycle,** sellers no longer have the stomach to buy. This creates an opportunity for bargain hunters. To determine when the market has reached this point, you can evaluate stocks using historically low valuations of revenues, earnings and dividends. Or you can wait for an uptrend before buying.

●**After you buy,** don't sell immediately after the bull trend becomes obvious to everyone. Let the crowd join you as the movement upward progresses.

●**When serious overvaluation is reached,** go against the majority and sell. Determine this moment by setting a price objective beforehand. Or base your timing on the heat of the market. Wait for the first sign of market weakness.

●**As the downward cycle advances,** resist the temptation to buy back your stock at a lower price. Wait until the market approaches the bottom again before buying.

●**Don't confuse portfolio activity with progress toward investment goals.** A common mistake made by many investors is rapid portfolio activity. They regard time as the enemy and believe that if they wait too long, that is an invitation for something to go wrong.

It's unrealistic, however, to expect that instant profits are easy to grab. When too much attention is focused on achieving short-term goals, the real opportunity—which is long-term—is forgotten. Think of time as an ally, not as an enemy.

●**Beware of the company that offers creative excuses for underachievement.** Some companies have a talent for making excuses for problems. Be especially wary of companies that wrap bad news in good news. *Danger signs:*

●When shortfalls and disappointments come with good-news announcements, such as the introduction of a new product or overhead-reduction programs.

●When you find your mailbox jammed with "We love you, shareholder" letters from the company.

●When bad news is accompanied by an announcement of a management shake-up. Did the company also say what took so long for them to clean up the problem? If not, incompetents may still be in charge.

Once credibility has been destroyed, it takes a long time for a company to win it back. When management repeatedly says, "Things will be better next year," it's time to sell.

●**Focus on essentials...skip the merely interesting.** Experienced investors are humble. They've learned that they can't possibly know everything. Less seasoned investors, on the other hand, may feel that if they had only a few more hours to do research, their investment returns would be considerably better. Usually this is hogwash.

Save time by not seeking out the opinions of yet another expert. Formulating intelligent questions that you then go out and seek answers to is much more valuable than collecting opinions.

Focus on an industry's prospects, the strength and track record of a company, and the long-term implications of a new development.

●**Good corporate news can lead to a dangerous sense of euphoria.** When there's good news, companies can't wait to circulate it. Many ladle it out in advance, tipping off key stock-market analysts. The result is that these stocks often rise before the news hits the media and afterward rise only slightly—or even fall.

Reasons: Many pros "sell on the news"—or take profits as the news becomes widely known and the price rises—and companies often use good news as an opportunity to seek more equity financing.

Similarly, beware of remarkably upbeat presentations at investment conferences. Instead, wait a few weeks or a month, and you'll almost always be able to buy the stock cheaper.

Opportunity: Look at the volume in the weeks before an "announcement." If it's high, this tells you that you may be late in getting the word.

●**Study the composition of a company's board of directors.** The role of a company's board of directors is to represent the interests of all stockholders. One way to determine whether the directors are representing your interests is to look at the people who make up the board. *How to tell a good board from a bad one...*

●**Determine how many directors come from the company and how many are from the outside.** If most are from the inside, the board may not be independent enough to resist undue pressure from top management.

●**Examine the credentials of the outsiders. If they are not particularly distinguished,** they may have been chosen as "good buddies."

●**If the board is small—fewer than five members—it's likely that outside directors were chosen for their cooperative attitude toward management preferences.** On the other hand, a large board—more than 10—is probably too unwieldy to support much independence on the part of outside directors.

●**The company's proxy statement will reveal the extent of each director's stock ownership and options and interest in the future of the company.** Token holdings are danger signs.

●**Learn to distinguish the truly underappreciated stock from the real losers.** *Key question:* Is the stock misunderstood by Wall Street or is it more likely that management misunderstands what's happened to its market?

Don't be fooled by a company's aura or unduly impressed by its past glories. "What have you done for me lately?" is a legitimate question to ask. "What do you plan to do tomorrow?" is an even better one.

Don't jettison a stock simply because it's the biggest loser in your portfolio. That's a short-term balm that usually turns into a long-term mistake.

How to Find Hot Stocks At Bargain-Basement Prices

Wallace Weitz, manager of Weitz Partners Value Fund and one of the country's shrewdest value investors, Wallace Weitz & Co., 1125 S. 103 St., Omaha 68124.

Value stocks are attracting more and more investors. *Wallace Weitz, a leading value investor, offers his investment secrets...*

Much of my approach to value investing I learned from Benjamin Graham, the master of finding stocks selling for less than their true business values. This approach made him a millionaire at age 35.

Graham was more concerned with a company's true value as a business, not the price the market put on its stock. Once you know the business's value, you know whether it is selling at a discount in the market.

Most people think that value investing means using their computers to screen for some stocks that sell at low price-to-earnings ratios (P/Es) or low price-to-book ratios.

But while seeking a low P/E and price-to-book ratio may eliminate some expensive stocks, ratios do not measure business value.

HOW I MEASURE VALUE

Business value is a function of how much discretionary cash a company will generate for its owners over the next 10 to 20 years.

Discretionary cash flow is the cash the business has left over at the end of the year—after paying taxes and interest and after spending on maintenance. It is also the amount of cash the company can take out of the business—to pay to shareholders or invest in the future—without wrecking the company's ability to function.

The more discretionary cash flow a company holds, the more valuable its business is to you, "the owner."

If you can buy that cash flow at a discount to the market price, you have a true value investment.

SIZING UP CASH FLOW

Start by adding the company's reported earnings per share and its depreciation and amortization. You can find these figures in the company's published income and cash-flow statements. However, distinguishing between maintenance, which is required, and expansion or acquisition, which is optional, can be difficult. The cash-flow statement sometimes gives clues.

Rule of thumb: Companies with lots of plants and equipment require lots of maintenance and replacement.

MANAGEMENT MATTERS, TOO

Not all value shows up on the balance sheet. Management quality adds or subtracts value. I want managers whose goals for the company are consistent with the long-term goals of shareholders. I won't buy a company whose management aims for quick but unsustainable profits just to please financial analysts.

Helpful: Look for senior management that demonstrates its commitment to the business by owning substantial amounts of company stock. This information can be found in annual reports.

Price Earnings Ratios

Price earnings (P/E) ratios have little to do with whether a stock is a good or bad buy. Many analysts recommend stocks with low P/Es as "cheap" and warn that stocks with high P/Es are "expensive." But history shows otherwise.

Study: During the 33 years from 1953 to 1985, the stock market had an average P/E of 15. But the top-performing stocks of this period started their market run-ups with an average P/E of 20 and ended with an average P/E of 45.

Reality: Firms with low P/Es often have them simply because they are poor stocks, while firms with high P/Es usually have demonstrated superior prospects. The simple truth is that most firms have P/Es that fairly reflect their value.

How to Make Money in Stocks: A Winning System in Good Times or Bad by William J. O'Neil, publisher, *Investor's Business Daily.* McGraw Hill.

Adding International Stocks to Your Portfolio Reduces Risk

Every monitored investment newsletter that recommends a blend of US and international investment has increased its return and lowered its risk by doing so.

Why: International stock markets do not move in lockstep with US markets, so when US markets are down, foreign ones are likely to be up and vice versa. Thus, buying international stocks reduces the risk that your whole portfolio will decline in value at one time. And international markets have equaled or surpassed the performance of the US market in recent years. Investments in international stocks are easily made through high-quality mutual funds.

Mark Hulbert, editor, *Hulbert Financial Digest,* 316 Commerce St., Alexandria, VA 22314.

Shift Investments From Stocks to Bonds

Shift investments from stocks to bonds at a gradual rate as you grow older.

Rule of thumb: The percentage of your portfolio invested in stocks should equal 100 minus your age. So if you are 55, you should be 45% invested in stocks and 55% invested in bonds or cash.

Rationale: Stocks are risky in the short run, but over the long run they consistently outperform bonds. You'll need this extra income for retirement. The money you keep in bonds will meet your short- and medium-term cash needs, letting you maintain your stock investments long enough for them to recover from any short-term market drop and protecting you from ever having to cash in your stocks while the market is low.

It's Never Too Late to Get Rich by James Jorgensen, editor, *It's Your Money* newsletter. Dearborn Financial Publishing.

Bonds vs. Stocks

Bonds are riskier than stocks much of the time—contrary to the belief of conservative investors. For much of this century, bonds have been poor investments because of losses in purchasing power, drops in value and low returns compared with other assets. *Important:* Look at a bond's total return—the change in its value plus its coupon amount—to compare it

fairly with other investments. The results may surprise bond buyers.

Kenneth Fisher, founder and CEO, Fisher Investments, a money management firm, Woodside, CA.

Bond Investment Trap

Before investing in bonds check to see if they are subject to a call provision that lets the issuer pay them off before maturity.

Key: Bonds go up in value when interest rates go down. But if bonds are subject to a call provision when interest rates decline, you can expect the issuer to redeem them and refinance at a lower rate. Thus, the call provision limits the potential for gain from a bond while leaving you with the full downside risk of loss if interest rates go up.

Point: While a call provision is onerous on bonds, it is especially so on high-yield "junk" bonds because of the greater risk involved in owning them.

Ben Weberman, financial columnist, *Forbes*, 60 Fifth Ave., New York 10011.

About Munis

Tax-free municipal bonds usually have better after-tax returns than US Treasury bonds for those in the 27% tax bracket—or higher. And there is minimal risk on AA or better municipals. Munis can be a great place to put profits from the stock market when you rebalance your portfolio. *Muni funds:* Look for low expense ratios and administrative costs. And check which munis they invest in—higher yield comes with higher risk.

James Lynch, editor, *Lynch Municipal Bond Advisory*, Box 20476, New York 10025.

Redeem E Bonds or Lose Interest

Barbara Weltman, an attorney with offices in Millwood, NY, and author of *J.K. Lasser's New Rules for Small Business Taxes* (John Wiley & Sons) and *The Complete Idiot's Guide to Making Money After You Retire* (Macmillan).

You may have been given US Series E or EE Savings Bonds as an anniversary gift or when you were married. Or maybe you even bought them through a payroll savings plan at work many years ago.

You probably stashed the bonds in the back of a drawer and then forgot about them, as so many people do.

Problem: E and EE bonds stop paying interest when they reach their final maturity date. The Federal Reserve says there are now billions of dollars worth of unredeemed savings bonds that are no longer paying interest.

What to do: Dig out your savings bonds and turn them in if they've matured. Put the money in something that pays interest.

E bonds issued before December 1965 have a 40-year final maturity, so a bond issued in March 1962 stopped paying interest in March 2002.

E bonds issued from December 1965 through June 1980 and EE bonds issued from January 1980 onward have a final maturity of 30 years, so a bond issued in March 1972 stopped paying interest in March 2002.

Deferring taxes: When you redeem the bonds, instead of paying tax on all the interest that has accrued, you can roll them over into US Government Series HH bonds.

HH bonds pay interest semiannually, but you will put off paying tax on your EE bonds until the HH bonds mature. HH bonds reach their final maturity after 20 years.

All About Cash

William E. Donoghue, chairman of W.E. Donoghue & Co. Inc., registered investment advisers, and publisher of *Donoghue's WealthLetter,* a monthly strategic mutual fund investment newsletter, Box 309, 100 Medway Rd., Suite 401, Milford, MA 01757.

When financial experts talk about allocating a portion of your assets in cash, they usually mean cash equivalents, such as brokerage money market accounts, bank money market deposit accounts and taxable and tax-free money market mutual funds.

These cash equivalents can be liquidated quickly, can earn a competitive money market rate of return (interest or daily dividends) and offer a high degree of safety from loss of principal.

There are several sound reasons for using these safe and convenient accounts...

●**To park money when you are between stock or bond investments.**

●**To maintain a reserve for short-term cash needs.**

●**To reduce the risk of your portfolio by allocating a portion to nearly risk-free investments during periods of heightened market risk.**

That is fine if you need the money in the short term, but these cash equivalent accounts should not be considered for long-term investments of a year or more, unless you intend to use them for checking accounts. There are more profitable places to park your money.

●**Always the best choice is to pay down your high outstanding credit card balances.** Some credit cards still charge as much as 19% interest annually. For many, eliminating this high nondeductible interest cost is the equivalent of finding a risk-free investment yielding as much as 30% before taxes. That's one of the best investments you will ever discover.

●**A well-managed, high-yield bond fund account is often an excellent choice for investors.** Principal losses can occur during periods of rising interest rates or market instability. Some advisers can demonstrate track records of up to 15% total return with conservative trading discipline. You could do this yourself if you wish.

Avoid load (sales commission) bond funds. There are plenty of no-load bond funds available to investors. Paying a 3% or 4% commission to buy a bond fund often defeats the purpose of investing, which is to earn 3% or 4% more than a money fund.

Be especially wary of insured municipal bonds, which are only as good as the insurance companies that back them. A study of these insurance companies indicates that they are grossly overrated. If the insurance companies are overrated, the bonds that rely on their ratings for credibility are overpriced. A realistic evaluation by the marketplace could cause these investments to lose market value, an uninsured loss.

Bottom line: There are several strategies for managing cash balances that can provide you with extra returns and lowered risks.

What to Look For In a Fund

Check a fund's cash position before deciding whether or not to invest. A fund that has more than 10% in cash may have more money than the portfolio manager can handle—unless the fund's prospectus specifically calls for it to maintain a large cash position. And it may signal trouble if a fund you already hold has a growing cash position—so watch its performance carefully. *Best:* Check the fund's cash position quarterly. A fund that can't put its cash to work over a 12-month period is out of step with today's market. Also watch out if a fund grows too quickly—the manager may be unable to invest new money without compromising the investing style that led you to buy into the fund in the first place.

Don Phillips, president, Morningstar, Inc., Chicago.

When It's Year-End Portfolio Review Time

Madeline Noveck, CFP, president, Novos Planning Associate Inc., 120 E. 56 St., New York 10022, and past president for the Institute of Certified Financial Planners.

It's important to review your portfolio well before the end of the year. Mutual fund distributions are taxable even if they are reinvested. You may consider realizing capital losses to offset these taxable gains by selling stocks or funds that have proved disappointing. But don't let the end-of-year urge to save taxes govern your investment decisions. Instead, identify those funds or stocks that have proved disappointing and evaluate them on their merits.

SELL? HOLD? BUY MORE?

If your shares in a mutual fund have been declining, it's time to reevaluate the holding, but not necessarily to sell. *Before unloading a fund that has been declining in value, consider the following...*

• **How has the fund performed relative to its peers?** It could be that the whole asset class is suffering—as has happened with Real Estate Investment Trusts, even though fundamental real estate values have been improving. Make your decision based on the fund's relative performance and the fundamentals of the asset class.

• **Have other investors been pulling out?** This isn't easy to learn, but you can often get leads from the financial press or the mutual fund tracking services. Or call the fund and inquire about monthly money flows. Are they positive or negative?

• **What is the impact of other shareholders withdrawing from the fund?** It is not easy for a fund manager to maintain his/her strategy when the crowd is pulling money out of the fund. In addition, if stocks need to be dumped to meet redemptions, this will create capital gains and add to your tax bill.

• **What has the fund returned on your investment?** A lower net asset value is a clue, but factor in dividends and capital gains distributions to determine total return. Compare your initial investment with the current value of your holding.

●**Has the manager stuck to the fund's investment goals?** If the prospectus promised small undervalued companies but the manager bought midsized growth companies, that's called "style drift." It's not bad if the stated strategy of the fund is to seek opportunities among small and midsized companies. But, if you don't want more mid-cap exposure, you might prefer another purely small-cap fund.

Caution: Before switching to a new fund, be sure you know its expected capital gains distributions and when they will come. These days, most funds are better prepared to give this information and many are being run more tax efficiently.

●**Are there any surrender charges?** If you bought B shares of a load fund and are selling within the first five years, you probably have surrender charges. These increase your loss. However, you can avoid them by switching within the same fund family if there is an appropriate fund. *Note:* You can still report your losses for tax purposes.

REBALANCING

Year-end is also a good time to rebalance your portfolio, which may have strayed from your original asset allocation due to the market's ups and downs.

Example: If large-cap growth stocks, which have done very well in recent years, have grown to, say, 44% of your portfolio instead of the allotted 30%, sell 14% and reinvest the money in an asset class that is now short of its allocation due to poor performance.

Benefit: This strategy leads to buying low and selling high. When an asset class is out of favor and with lower prices, underweighted in your portfolio, it may be a fine time to buy more.

Similarly, when an asset class becomes over-weighted because prices are high, it may be appropriate to take some profits. Prices may go higher (or lower), but over the long run you'll be well served by using this discipline—it helps remove emotion from investing.

Understand that markets tend to go too far up or down in response to temporary factors (sometimes irrational). Then they're apt to reverse in the future.

Wash sale trap: You lose the tax benefits if you buy back the same holding you sold within 30 days, but you can buy a similar fund immediately to maintain your allocation. Just be sure to keep transaction costs to a minimum.

Do not let year-end tax-saving motives dictate your investment decisions. Change your asset allocation strategy only when your investment outlook changes, not to save a few dollars in taxes.

If you conclude that an investment is a loser, get rid of it. If a winner has become too prominent in the portfolio or you think it may be topping out, don't let taxes stop you from doing what is smart from an investment standpoint.

Example: Investors who were overweighted in IBM as it reached $139 earlier this year and didn't lighten up because of the tax bite, have ended up with a stock that went down as low as $90 shortly after.

There are nontaxable ways to get out of an investment. You can donate it to charity or give it to a family member in a lower tax bracket.

Trap: Watch out for gift taxes when you give assets to family members. The limit on gift-tax-free gifts is $11,000 per recipient in 2002—$22,000 if your spouse joins you in making the gift.

Netting gains and losses: Add up all of your losses for the year, short-term and long-term. Then match them up against your gains. For tax purposes, net capital losses can be used to offset otherwise taxable capital gains dollar for dollar—there's no limit to the amount. Up to $3,000 of excess capital losses can then be applied against salary and other ordinary income. Additional losses are carried forward to future tax years to offset capital gains and other income.

How to Get Money Out of A Mutual Fund...Quickly

Sheldon Jacobs, editor and publisher of *The No-Load Fund Investor,* 410 Saw Mill River Rd., Suite 2060, Ardsley, New York 10502.

Most mutual fund investors don't think about getting their money out of a fund when they put it in. Too often, when financial markets dip and they want to redeem their shares, they find that getting their money back is time-consuming, frustrating and sometimes costly. *Reasons:*

● **The phones are tied up.** Mutual fund offices can be so inundated with orders to buy and sell shares that their switchboards may be busy at critical times. When you call requesting information about how to redeem shares, you may have to let the telephone ring for a few minutes before someone answers.

● **The procedures for redeeming shares are bureaucratic.** With most funds you must not only write a redemption letter requesting a check for the value of your investment, but you must also have your signature guaranteed by a commercial bank or by your broker. That can be time consuming, especially if you bought your shares directly from the fund instead of through a broker, and you don't happen to have an account with a commercial bank. Notarized signatures aren't acceptable and most funds will refuse to accept guarantees from savings-and-loan institutions. If your personal bank is an S&L, you'll have to go to a commercial bank that your bank has established a relationship with to have your signature guaranteed.

To avoid these obstacles:

● **Make a copy of the section of the fund prospectus that refers to redemption procedures—and keep it handy.** That way you won't have to make a phone call to get information on redemption procedures.

● **Prepare a redemption letter in advance. Have your signature guaranteed by your broker or commercial bank so you can simply date the letter whenever you decide to pull out of the fund.** Follow prospectus instructions for writing a redemption letter (usually, all you need to do is request that a check be sent to your home address, and give the number of shares owned and your account number).

● **Consider buying shares only in stock or bond funds managed by firms that also have money market funds to which you can switch part or all of your account by telephone.** That way you have access to the money via money market account checks, usually

within two days. *Caution:* It's always a good idea to call in a switch as early in the day as possible, because after 3 pm on heavy-volume days, many fund offices can be especially busy.

● **When you fill out the forms to purchase fund shares,** complete the section for authorizing wire transfers of redemptions to your bank. That service allows you to have shares redeemed and the proceeds deposited directly in your checking or savings account, usually on the same day you make the request. If you need the money fast and you have trouble getting through by phone, you can request a bank transfer in a redemption letter sent by overnight mail.

Five Rock-Bottom Investment Truths

Sheldon Jacobs, editor and publisher of *The No-Load Fund Investor,* 410 Saw Mill River Rd., Suite 2060, Ardsley, New York 10502.

In 2000, mutual funds had their first down year since 1994 and registered their worst performance since 1974. No wonder so many investors are questioning their basic strategy.

I've been reexamining my own beliefs, trying to isolate a few market basics that are always true, no matter what is happening in our economy or the world. *I've come up with five rock-bottom truths...*

1. It's hard to predict which way the market will go. Over the past 120 years, the stock market has done well in years ending in five. Does that mean that you should predict a good year in 2005? I don't believe so, because it seems to be coincidence.

On the other hand, the first year of a presidential cycle is traditionally a bad year for the stock market.

All those TV prognosticators can't predict the future any more than you can.

The goal is to invest sensibly even though you can't know which way the market is headed.

2. The stock market is reasonably efficient. There used to be any number of theories about how investors could make millions by finding undiscovered bargains. That's a lot harder to do today, with so many sophisticated computer programs sorting through the data.

For most of us, the best way to profit from market efficiency is to invest in total market index funds.

3. Diversification is critical. The wisdom of this old saw was driven home to many investors who went too heavily into tech and Internet stocks.

Throughout the 1990s, big-cap growth stocks were the clear winners. Now, value stocks are getting more attention. Small-cap value is doing particularly well. Investors who neglected fixed income lived to regret it, as bonds handily outperformed stocks.

Lesson: Don't overinvest in any one sector of the market.

4. It's vital to keep transaction costs low. There's no need for investors to pay sales loads when buying mutual funds. Also—it's important to pay close attention to funds' annual fees.

Studies have shown dramatic differences in long-term returns between high- and low-cost funds. This is a strong argument for low-cost index funds. These are tax efficient, too, because they have relatively low turnover—so you don't get big unexpected capital gains.

5. Take full advantage of compounding. Time is essential here—the longer you hold an investment, the more your money grows. To get the full benefit of compounding, you must also reinvest dividends.

4

Tax Savvy

Best States to Retire to In Terms of Taxes

Gone are the days when retirement meant whiling away the hours sitting in a rocking chair. Americans are retiring younger, living longer and planning full, active lives. Many are moving to locales where sunny weather, old friends, family or amenity-filled planned communities beckon.

KEY TAX BREAKS

Now, thanks to laws in recent years, even more Americans may be moving to another state to pursue their retirement dreams.

●**Source taxing forbidden.** What was known as "source taxing" has been generally banned.

Example: New York (or California) would tax payouts from a pension earned there, even though the taxpayer had moved to another state.

●**Tax-free home sales.** An exclusion in the tax law makes it unlikely that you'll owe capital gains tax on the sale of your home.

●Gains of up to $500,000 for a couple or $250,000 for a single person on the sale of a principal residence are tax free.

●Even those who have already taken the former one-time exclusion of $125,000 can take the new $500,000/$250,000 exclusion.

This change will free many people who have been staying in too large a home because they did not want to incur capital gains taxes. It could also make it possible for retirees—people who are widowed, for example—to move again without worrying about the tax consequences of selling their homes.

Stanley Hagendorf, JD, LLM, and Wayne Hagendorf, JD, CPA, who have spoken to the American Institute of Certified Public Accountants on the tax issues involved when retiring to another state. Stanley Hagendorf is a lawyer in private practice. Wayne Hagendorf is senior partner in the law firm of Hagendorf & Abernethy, Los Angeles.

OTHER TAX ISSUES

In addition to these issues, people should consider a number of other tax matters when moving to another state. *Consider these also...*

- Income tax
- Sales tax
- Domicile
- Estate tax
- Property tax

INCOME TAX

Income tax is generally the biggest worry retirees have. Most people rank Nevada and Florida as the best states to retire to—two states with no income tax.

Contrast: Residents of New York City, for example, pay state and local income taxes that often are equal to one-third of their federal income taxes.

Florida does have an intangibles tax. This is a tax on the value of stocks, bonds, mutual funds and certain other items an individual brings into the state. But the intangibles tax is small in comparison with income taxes. It is only two-tenths of a cent per dollar.

Very few people—if any—pay a higher tax in Florida than in New York or in the Midwest.

Other states without income taxes: Alaska, South Dakota, Texas, Washington and Wyoming.

New Hampshire and Tennessee do not tax earned income (salary, etc.), but they do tax interest and dividends—an important source of money for many retirees.

DOMICILE

It is not unusual for people who retire to a new state to keep some ties to their former state—a business or investment property, for example, or even a house or an apartment, just in case they want to go back and visit. They think they have moved, but legally they may now be residents of two states, and liable for taxes in both.

High-tax states like New York, California and Massachusetts are aggressive in trying to collect taxes from such people, and the burden of proof is on the taxpayer to prove that he/she has abandoned the old state.

Remedy: When you move, really move...

- **Sever all ties to the former state.**
- **Sell off all your real estate there.**

- **Move your physical assets.**
- **File federal and state tax returns with your new address.**
- **Join social, civic or religious organizations** in your new state and resign membership in such groups in the former state.
- **File an affidavit of domicile in the new state.**
- **Change your driver's license, bank and brokerage accounts** to the new state.
- **Register to vote in the new state as soon as you can.**
- **Buy a new cemetery plot.**

To establish your new domicile, do as many of these things as possible.

ESTATE TAX

Estate tax is generally due at the federal level on estates that exceed $1 million in 2002. The exemption amount will rise over the next decade.

To calculate what your estate is worth, add up the value of your home, retirement accounts, securities portfolio, real estate or business interests that you own, and any other valuables.

Some states model their estate tax laws on the federal rules, but others levy taxes on much smaller estates.

So, if you want your assets to go to your heirs after your death instead of being gobbled up by taxes, it is important to check on the rules and rates of the state to which you are moving.

A will or trust documents written in one state may be valid in another. Even so, it could prove costly for your executor to have to track down witnesses who live in another state.

The prudent thing to do when you move is consult a local attorney who specializes in trusts and estates to find out if any legal changes are needed.

If you own property in two or more states, each may try to levy estate taxes on the whole estate. This gets back to the issue of domicile, and each state is free to set its own rules. However, the Supreme Court has ruled that total state estate taxes cannot exceed 100% of the value of an estate—but they can go that high.

Avoidance: The simple way to avoid handing your heirs this problem is to sell all property in one state when moving to another. That is not always possible, however. A property may be listed with a broker but take a while to sell. The sale of a business can be very complex.

Bottom line: If you move and still own property in another state, be sure to consult a local attorney who specializes in trusts and estates.

If you own property in two states, it may be wise to set up a trust in your lifetime, so a trustee can transfer property in the event of death.

SALES TAX

Sales taxes are often levied by both states and localities. *Important:* Check into the sales tax rates of a particular community before moving to it. Sales tax is of particular importance for people who spend a high portion of their income.

PROPERTY TAX

Property tax is nearly always a local issue, so again, check the property tax rates in a particular municipality before buying a new house or condominium there.

The Big, Bad Retirement Tax Traps

Stephen Pennacchio, partner, KPMG, LLP, 345 Park Ave., New York 10154.

People who are charting retirement finances better watch out for the minefield of tricky IRS rules. Here are the ones that are apt to trip you up and strategies to help you negotiate around them…

Trap: Mandatory withholding on retirement plan distributions. Plan sponsors must withhold 20% of any money that is not directly rolled over into a traditional IRA or another company's plan. *Double trouble:* The IRS views the withheld amounts as premature withdrawals if you're under 59½, so you owe a 10% penalty plus income tax on those amounts.

Example: You take $10,000 from your company plan when you leave the firm, but the plan sponsor only gives you $8,000 in cash. You owe a $200 penalty plus tax on $2,000.

Avoidance: If you replace the $2,000 with your own money and roll this amount over within 60 days of receipt into an IRA or other qualified plan, you can sidestep the penalty and tax. That money is returned to you by the IRS at tax time in the form of a tax refund. But there can be a significant delay. If you withdraw money from the plan in February, you won't receive the refund until April of the following year, or 14 months later.

Better: Ask the plan sponsor to roll the money directly into another qualified plan or into an IRA. That way, no money will be withheld and no penalties will apply.

Strategy: If you're not sure which investment is best for your plan money, or you haven't found another job yet, have the plan sponsor roll the money into an IRA money market fund.

Strategy: If you need to use part of the money, have your company directly roll the entire sum into an IRA first. That way, you avoid withholding on the entire amount and just owe the early withdrawal penalties of 10% plus tax on the money that you take out. If you replace the money in 60 days, you won't owe anything at all.

Trap: Failing to take the required minimum distributions from IRAs. You must begin withdrawing money from traditional IRAs by April 1 following the year in which you turn 70½. The penalty for people who fail to do so is steep—50% of the amount that should have been distributed, but wasn't. When these amounts are ultimately distributed they are subject to income tax. Some banks and mutual funds alert their investors when distributions must begin, but the final responsibility rests with you.

The minimum required to be withdrawn is now based on a joint life expectancy of you and a beneficiary who is automatically treated as 10 years younger than you (whether or not you've named a beneficiary and whether that beneficiary is older or younger than you). *Exception:* You can reduce required distributions if your spouse is more than 10 years your junior—here distributions are figured over your actual joint life expectancy.

You do not need to begin required minimum distributions from company retirement plans until April 1 following the year in which you turn 70½ or when you retire, whichever is later. (This alternative does not apply if you own more than 5% of the business.)

Trap: Not making the most of tax-free compounding. When you retire, use your investments and other money held outside retirement plans first. That way, you defer taxes on the money inside the plans longer.

Example: You have a large sum inside an IRA and smaller amount in other investments. If you had used the after-tax money to cover living expenses for two years, your IRA would have grown at the rate of return you invested it, with the additional benefit of tax-free compounding.

Trap: Paying too much tax on retirement plan distributions. If you were born before 1936, you can elect more favorable tax treatment called 10-year forward averaging when you take a lump sum from a retirement plan. This method treats the money as if it had been taken in 10 equal installments rather than all at once, thus taxing more of the money in the lowest tax brackets.

Caution: Remember to factor in the impact of state taxes when you do the calculations.

Caution: Generally, as the lump-sum distribution is larger, rolling the money into an IRA and delaying distributions is more beneficial than averaging.

Simple Tax Mistakes That Can Be Very, Very Costly

Edward Mendlowitz, CPA, partner, Mendlowitz Weitsen, LLP, CPAs, Two Pennsylvania Plaza, Suite 1500, New York 10121. He is author of several books on taxes, including *IRA Distributions: What You Should Know.* Practical Programs, Inc.

The mistakes you make with tax filings, paperwork and elections can cost you big tax dollars.

RETIREMENT SAVINGS ERRORS

Many families have *most* of their wealth saved in retirement accounts.

● **Self-employed qualified retirement plan mistake.** Not filing a form in the 5500 series. The exact form depends on the number of participants and assets in the plan. These information returns must be filed for all plans that provide benefits to employees and for one-person plans that had more than $100,000 of assets in any year after 1993. The late-filing penalty is up to *$1,000 per day.*

Trap: With a booming stock market over the last decade, owners of one-person plans may not realize their accounts are now worth more than $100,000.

Self-defense: If you are behind on filing the 5500 form, consult a retirement plan expert *immediately.* File the form, and have your adviser ask that penalties be waived. You have a *much* better chance of reducing potentially huge penalties if you correct the delinquency before the government catches it.

● **401(k) plan mistake.** Taking a distribution of employer stock from a 401(k) and rolling it over into an IRA.

Snag: When you finally cash in the stock and withdraw the proceeds from the IRA, they will be taxable as ordinary income. You will lose favorable capital gains treatment for the shares.

Better: If you intend to hold the shares, take a distribution so you own them. You'll owe a current tax on their appreciation since your 401(k) account acquired them. All further long-term gain will be taxed at a rate of up to 20%.

● **IRA mistake #1.** Not naming beneficiaries—either your estate will become your beneficiary or default provisions established by your IRA's trustee will go into effect. *Either case is bad...*

● If your estate becomes your beneficiary, you forfeit your ability to have your heirs stretch out the distribution.

● If default provisions go into effect, your IRA probably won't be distributed as you wished.

● **IRA mistake #2.** Changing the name on the IRA to that of the beneficiary when the owner of an IRA dies. This accelerates IRA distributions.

Better: Keep the IRA in the name of the deceased owner to extend the IRA distribution period.

FILING ERRORS

● **The worst mistake anyone can make is not filing.**

● If you are owed a refund, the statute of limitations expires after three years. After that, you lose the ability to collect your refund.

● If you owe tax, the statute of limitations *never* expires. You will accumulate nonfiling penalties, plus late-payment penalties and interest. Even if you can't afford to pay the tax, file a return to avoid nonfiling penalties. Use the IRS's new installment payment option by filing IRS Form 9465, *Request for Installment Agreement.*

• **Filing a joint return when one spouse owes a bill for the past year and the other is due a refund.** The IRS may take the refund to pay back taxes.

Better: File separate returns to protect the refund. While this may increase the overall tax rate for the couple, if the back tax bill is paid within three years, you can file an *amended* return claiming joint filing status for that year. This lowers the tax rate, and you can file for a refund.

• **Not completing the tax return and filing all required supporting documents.** Such mistakes cost you deductions…or increase your risk of being audited. *Examples…*

• For charitable gifts of property valued at more than $500, you must file Form 8283, *Non-cash Charitable Contributions.* You will need qualified appraisals for donated property worth more than $5,000.

• When claiming a home-office deduction, you must file Form 8829, *Expenses for Business Use of Your Home.*

• On Schedule B of Form 1040, check a "yes" or "no" box for the question asking if you have a foreign bank account.

• **Not filing the IRS's Form 8822, *Change of Address,* when you move.** If you don't, IRS notices sent to your old address may be deemed effective even if you never receive them…and you may lose a tax case by default.

FAMILY ERRORS

Errors in family finances that can boost the tax bill…

• **A grandparent puts money in a child's name** in a Uniform Gifts to Minors Act (UGMA) or Uniform Transfers to Minors Act (UTMA) account…then acts as custodian of the account.

Trap: Because the grandparent retains control over the funds, they remain taxable to the grandparent's estate in spite of the gift.

Better: Name someone else as custodian of the UGMA/UTMA account.

• **A couple separates,** and one spouse voluntarily pays support to the other until they work out a formal separation or divorce agreement.

Trap: The payments are not deductible as alimony because they are not made under a written agreement.

Better: Have a written agreement covering such payments from the start.

• **A will doesn't specify the account from which estate taxes are to be paid.**

Trap: A conflict over who pays the tax may arise. The *entire* cost of estate tax may fall on beneficiaries paid from the "residual estate"—the amount left after bequests of specific items and amounts—with other beneficiaries paying *nothing.*

Better: Have your will explicitly state how estate tax will be paid.

Avoiding The Biggest Mistakes Investors Make

Ted Tesser, CPA, Waterside Financial Services, 30 Waterside Plaza, #9G, New York 10010, which assists clients with tax, investment and retirement plan strategies. He is author of *The Serious Investor's Tax Survival Guide.* Traders' Library.

Mistake: **Not considering taxes until you begin preparing tax returns.** By then it's often too late to adopt strategies that could have cut the tax bill. Monitor the tax implications of your investments throughout the year, and periodically consult with your accountant.

Mistake: **Failing to take responsibility for tax and investment strategies.** Some investors rely completely on accountants, brokers, lawyers or other advisers. Of course, you should seek advice from tax and investment professionals, and use their expertise when implementing the strategies you decide upon. But it's important to remember that you are the person who will have to live with the results, so take responsibility and begin planning ahead now to make the most of your investments.

Mistake: **Not quantifying tax consequences when comparing investment options.** This means looking at the dollar numbers earned after taxes from investments that receive different tax treatment.

Example: Consider the after-tax returns paid out over 10 years by a 10% taxable investment and an 8% tax-free or tax-deferred one. *Let's assume the investments were made by a person paying both a combined federal/state tax rate of 46%.*

| | Before taxes | | After taxes | |
	10%	8%	10%	8%
Starting value	$10,000	$10,000	$10,000	$10,000
After 10 yrs.	$25,937	$21,589	$17,690	$21,589
Net return	$15,937	$11,589	$7,690	$11,589

Without working through the numbers, you are likely to be surprised that taxes cut the return from the higher-yielding investment by more than half (from $15,937 to $7,690)—and that the "lower" yielding investment in fact pays over 50% more after taxes ($11,589 vs. $7,690).

This example is simpler than most real cases. Some investments are partially taxable—for example, US Treasury issues are exempt from state tax but not from federal tax. Also, your own tax bracket will vary according to local law, income level, and the deductions and credits available to you. Although this calculation appears to be complicated, it is made simple with the worksheets I provide in my book.

In some cases, it may pay to increase tax exposure.

Example: If you live in a low- or no-tax state, it may pay to move funds from Treasury bonds to a portfolio of AAA-grade corporate bonds, to receive more income after taxes with almost the same safety, even though more total tax will be due.

The way to know which investment plan is best for you is to work through the numbers illustrating different options.

Mistake: **Not making full use of retirement plans.** Tax-favored retirement programs let you obtain the higher returns offered by taxable investments in a tax-deferred environment. Today, personal retirement accounts such as IRAs, Simplified Employee Plans (SEPs), SIMPLEs and other qualified retirement plans can invest in almost anything except collectibles, mortgaged rental properties or a business in which you own an interest of 5% or more.

Many employer-provided 401(k) savings plans also offer self-directed investment options.

Common error: Thinking the main tax benefit from a retirement-plan contribution is the deduction for it, and making contributions at the last minute each year. In fact, over the long run, the tax-deferral obtained for compound retirement-plan earnings can be more valuable than the contribution deduction.

Example: A $3,000 IRA contribution saves $1,200 for a person in a 40% combined federal and state tax bracket. But a contribution made early in the year will also earn tax-deferred income within the account during the year. If the IRA earns 10%, $3,000 contributed a year before the deadline for just one year will earn $300, and over 30 years this $300 will compound to over $5,000—all of which is forfeited if you make your contribution at the last minute instead. If this contribution is made early each year, the increase in total retirement funds available is significant.

Make plan contributions as early in the year as possible. Also consider making contributions to a Roth IRA to obtain tax-free returns. While there's no deduction for contributions, the potential tax-free returns make this a great investment strategy.

ESTATE-PLANNING MISTAKE

Not averting estate taxes is a big mistake. Many people put off estate planning simply because thinking about death is not pleasant. Others underestimate the cost of estate taxes because they believe the applicable exemption amount ($1 million in 2002, rising gradually to $3.5 million by 2009) will protect them, or because they know they can pass assets tax-free to a spouse. *Traps:*

● **Your estate may be pushed far over the applicable exemption amount ($1 million in 2002)** by assets that you don't think of—such as life-insurance proceeds, the value of retirement accounts or appreciation in the value of your home.

● **Passing all your assets to your spouse can be a costly mistake,** because he/she will be able to pass no more than the applicable exemption amount to the next generation tax-free—while the two of you could plan together to pass double that amount.

Self-defense: Have the insurance on your life owned by your spouse, a child or a trust benefiting family members. You can provide the money needed to pay the premiums through annual tax-free gifts. When you die, the insurance proceeds will not be part of your taxable estate.

Self-defense: If your assets exceed the applicable exemption amount, pass up to that amount of your assets to children directly. *Alternative:* Use a trust that pays income to your spouse for life and then distributes its assets to your children, while leaving the remainder of your assets to your spouse. The applicable exemption amount will be available both for your disposition of property, and for your spouse's disposition of property inherited from you.

Self-defense: Use gifts to cut your estate. You can make gifts of up to $11,000 each to as many separate recipients as you wish in 2002, free of gift tax. The limit is $22,000 if the gift is made jointly with your spouse. You can also make larger tax-free gifts by using part of your applicable exemption amount. Although this will reduce the amount that will be available to your estate, it can pay off if you expect the gift assets to appreciate in value before you die.

Gifts of income-producing assets to family members in lower income-tax brackets, such as children over age 14, can cut family income taxes as well. And gifts of appreciated assets to low-bracket family members can be cashed in by these family members with less gains tax resulting.

Strategy: When older family members have less than the applicable exemption amount in assets, a reverse gift can save big taxes. You can make gifts to them of assets that have appreciated in value. When they die, the assets will pass back to you or to other family members with stepped-up basis—revalued for tax purposes at market value—so potential gains tax on their appreciation is eliminated.

MORE TAX-CUTTING IDEAS

● **Earmark stock and mutual fund shares to maximize the tax advantage when shares are sold.**

Example: Say you bought shares in a stock or mutual fund at different times at different prices, and now wish to sell some. If you have price records for specific shares, you can sell the particular shares that produce the optimal gain or loss—perhaps to minimize taxable gain, or to maximize a capital loss that will protect other gains

from tax. If you do not have price records, the IRS will treat the first shares bought as the first sold.

● **Get the IRS to absorb part of the sales load on a mutual fund.** Do this by buying shares in a money fund offered by a family of funds. After three months or more, transfer out of the money fund and into one of the other fund options (stocks, bonds, etc.). The sales load will produce a loss on the sale of the money fund shares, which you can deduct or use to shelter other gains from tax.

● **Look for losses in your portfolio that can be used to offset gains or generate deductions.**

Tactic: Use tax swaps to produce paper losses that can shelter gains from tax. *How:* Sell a security to produce a loss, then immediately buy back a similar security.

Example: You can sell a bond and then buy back a bond from a different issuer that pays the same interest and has the same maturity date and credit rating. You get a loss deduction while maintaining your investment position. You cannot buy back the same security within 30 days to produce a tax loss.

The 30-day time limit does not apply if you sell a security to produce a gain. So if you already have a loss, you can sell a security at a gain, shelter the gain with the loss, then immediately buy back the same security, avoiding future tax that would otherwise have been due on its appreciation.

● **Consider "trader" status.** If you actively manage your portfolio to profit from market swings—instead of profiting from appreciation, and dividend and interest payments—you may qualify as a professional stock trader and become eligible to deduct investment costs on Schedule C as business expenses. This enables you to fully deduct items that provide only limited deductions to investors, such as interest and investment expenses.

Although you cannot make deductible contributions to SEP, SIMPLE or other qualified retirement plans from trading gains, trading gains are not subject to self-employment taxes either. Consult your tax adviser about how the rules may apply to your situation.

Leaving-the-Nest Loopholes

Edward Mendlowitz, CPA, partner, Mendlowitz Weitsen, LLP, CPAs, Two Pennsylvania Plaza, Suite 1500, New York 10121. He is author of several books on taxes, including *IRA Distributions: What You Should Know.* Practical Programs, Inc.

When your children have all moved out and you're huddled in an empty nest, give some thought to the tax breaks that await you...

Loophole: **Use the home sale exclusion to downsize your living space on a tax-free basis.** If you don't need the size home you now have, consider selling it and buying or renting a smaller place.

Break: You don't pay any tax on the profit you make when you sell your home unless the profit exceeds $500,000 on a joint return or $250,000 if you're single.

Requirement: You must have owned and used the home as your principal residence for at least two out of five years preceding the date you sell it. If you're married, it does not matter that the title is in one name as long as both spouses lived in the home for the requisite two years.

Use the proceeds from the sale of the house to buy a smaller home or to create income used to pay rent on a smaller home. Invest the balance for retirement income.

Loophole: **Modify your investment strategies.** You no longer are saving for your child's college education but instead for your own retirement. With this long-term focus, you can concentrate on tax-deferred investment vehicles, such as growth stocks and bonds and CDs maturing in five or more years.

Caution: In making personal investments, coordinate your holdings with assets in company 401(k) plans and your IRAs. Remember that distributions from these retirement plans are taxed as ordinary income at rates as high as 39.6%, regardless of the underlying investment producing that income.

Thus, concentrate bond holdings and dividend-paying stock inside these plans, while holding growth stock and stock mutual funds in personal investments. This will allow sales of these personal investments to yield capital gains taxed to you at no more than 20% (top IRS rate).

Loophole: **Rethink life insurance needs.** You may have been carrying life insurance as a vehicle to replace income if you died while your child was still in school. You may no longer need the same amount of coverage. *Consider the following...*

● **Reduce the level of coverage** and save on future premium costs.

● **Convert an existing policy** to a paid up policy and stop paying premiums altogether.

● **Donate the policy to charity** (for example, to set up a scholarship at your alma mater) and obtain a tax deduction. Without making a formal agreement to do so, continue donating cash each year to the school to cover the premiums and claim a deduction for your cash donations.

Caution: Before canceling a policy, consider whether it's needed for liquidity for your estate. If you die, make sure your estate has sufficient liquid assets—cash and securities—to pay administrative costs and estate taxes (due nine months after death).

Loophole: **Review your will.** Update your will to delete references to guardians you had named to care for your child in the event both you and your spouse died while he was a minor. Now that your child is grown, you may also want to consider eliminating trusts used for bequests to him and/or name him as your executor or coexecutor.

Loophole: **Review beneficiary designations.** When your child was young, you may have named custodians or trustees of trusts for his benefit as beneficiary of various assets. Now that he's mature, change your beneficiary designation to his name alone. *Review the following for designations you may have made...*

● **Company retirement plans.**

● **IRAs.**

● **Life insurance** (including company-provided coverage).

● **Annuities.**

Loophole: **Buy a long-term-care insurance policy.** If you're in your mid-50s or older, have assets you want to protect (especially if you need to protect a spouse), but don't have millions of dollars, then you should consider a long-term-care policy. The policy will pay for care in your home or in a nursing home if you have a condition or disease requiring custodial care (the type of care not covered by Medicare).

Without such coverage, you'll be forced to deplete the assets you built up over your lifetime before you'll qualify for Medicaid (a needs-based federal–state benefit program).

While odds are you won't need this care until you're much older, the younger you are when you take out the policy, the lower your premiums for life. Expect to pay about $2,000 annually, depending on the extent of the coverage you take.

Tax benefit: You can reduce your out-of-pocket cost for coverage by taking a deduction for premiums. Long-term-care premiums are deductible as itemized medical expenses (subject to the 7.5% floor) according to your age.

Deduction Limits for Long-Term Coverage Premiums for 2002

Age before year-end	Deduction limit
40 or younger	$240
41 through 50	450
51 through 60	900
61 through 70	2,390
71 and older	2,990

Caution: In buying a long-term-care policy, make sure it has a cost-of-living adjustment (inflation rider) to keep pace with increased medical costs over the years.

Loophole: **Do old age and estate planning for your parents.** Every suggestion for your estate planning review applies with equal force to your parents. *Make sure your parents have…*

•**Reviewed their wills and had them updated,** if necessary.

•**Reviewed the beneficiary designations they've made for IRAs,** insurance policies, etc.

•**Prepared and signed health-care proxies and living wills.** A health-care proxy will let you make medical decisions if your parent can't speak for himself. A living will sets out the kind of care your parent would want should he become seriously ill.

•**Purchased long-term-care insurance** to cover the cost of nursing-home care.

If your parents fail to get matters in order, you'll have additional problems when they become ill or die.

Retirement Plan Loopholes

Edward Mendlowitz, CPA, partner, Mendlowitz Weitsen, LLP, CPAs, Two Pennsylvania Plaza, Suite 1500, New York 10121. He is author of several books on taxes, including *IRA Distributions: What You Should Know.* Practical Programs, Inc.

Those who take full advantage of tax-deferred retirement plans have a real chance of living out their golden years in financial comfort. *Consider these tax-wise strategies…*

Loophole: **Shelter part-time business income with tax-deferred retirement plans.** People with sideline businesses can build big retirement nest eggs. They can set up a qualified retirement plan and effectively contribute up to 20% of "self-employed earned income." There's a limit—contributions to a defined contribution plan can't exceed $40,000 in 2002.

Alternative: A Simplified Employee Pension (SEP) plan is easier to administer than a qualified plan, requires no government filings and, in 2002, has the same limit as above.

Deadlines: Contributions to SEPs and qualified plans can be made as late as the return's extended due date—and still be deductible. *Catch:* A qualified plan must have been set up by December 31 for you to make deductible contributions to the plan next year.

New alternative: Companies that are making large amounts of money might want to consider a combination of defined benefit and defined contribution plans. The plan is complex, so consult your tax adviser.

Loophole: **Consider a SIMPLE retirement plan if your business earns $40,000 or less.** When your net income from a part-time or start-up business is less than $40,000, you may be better off with a Savings Incentive Match Plan for Employees (SIMPLE).

Reason: Assuming you're under age 50, you can put away the lesser of earned income or $7,000 and make a matching contribution of as much as $7,000, depending on your income. With net income of $40,000, the match would be limited to $1,200. (The match is 3% of net income.)

You must set up a SIMPLE by October 1 to take deductions. After the plan is in place, you can make contributions up until the time you file your tax return.

Your Health And Your Taxes

Medical deductions have been allowed for the following items…

●**Apartment rent when the apartment was rented for an ailing dependent, because it was cheaper than hospitalization.**

Sidney J. Ungar, TC Memo 1963-159.

●**Elastic stockings recommended by a doctor for a person with varicose veins.**

Bessie Cohen, TC Memo 1/21/51.

●**Fluoridation device installed at home on the recommendation of a dentist.**

Revenue Ruling 64-267.

●**Stop smoking programs and prescription drugs to alleviate nicotine withdrawal.**

Revenue Ruling 99-28.

●**Hair removal through electrolysis performed by a licensed technician.**

Revenue Ruling 82-111.

●**Mattresses and boards bought solely to alleviate an arthritic condition.**

Revenue Ruling 55-261.

●**Mobile phone installed in a car to enable a person who has heart disease to immediately call a doctor in an emergency.**

George M. Womack, TC Memo 1975-232.

●**Telephone calls made long-distance to a therapist for psychological counseling.**

Letter Ruling 8034087.

●**Reclining chair bought on a doctor's advice to alleviate a heart condition.**

Revenue Ruling 58-155.

●**Transportation to AA meetings.**

Revenue Ruling 63-273.

John J. Tuozzolo, associated with the law firm Collins, Hannafin, Garamella, Jaber and Tuozzolo, PC, 148 Deer Hill Ave., Danbury, CT 06810.

Medical Deductions for Nursing Home Expenses

William G. Brennan, partner, Ernst & Young, CPAs, 1225 Connecticut Ave. NW, Washington, DC 20036. He is the editor of the *Ernst & Young Financial Planning Reporter*.

Deductions for nursing home care fall into various areas of the tax law. There are different types of expenses that can be taken as medical deductions.

GUIDELINES

●**Long-term care services.** Costs of care in a nursing home for someone who is chronically ill that are not otherwise covered by insurance are treated as medical expenses deductible to the extent they exceed 7.5% of Adjusted Gross Income.

●**Long-term care insurance.** Premiums are treated as deductible medical expenses (the dollar amount depends on the insured's age for the year and is adjusted annually for inflation).

●**Lump-sum payments.** In some cases, a lump-sum fee is paid for lifetime care in a nursing home. The home should be able to provide you with a statement detailing the portion of the fee that will be required for the patient's future medical care, based on the nursing home's past experience. This amount is generally deductible in the year it is paid—even though it is for future medical care.

●**Dependents' medical expenses.** You may deduct medical expenses that you pay for your spouse or a qualifying dependent. Your parents or other relatives generally qualify as your dependents if you could claim a personal exemption for them on your tax return.

Note: The gross income test, which says that a dependent must earn less than $3,000 for 2002, does not apply when claiming a dependent's medical expenses. The person must be your dependent either at the time care was received or when the expenses were paid.

●**Nature of services.** Whether or not an expense is deductible is determined by the nature of the services provided, not by the qualifications or experience of the provider.

Example: Assume you broke your hip and hired domestic help. If that person also helped with your in-home physical therapy, you could claim as a medical expense the charges for the time spent on your exercises. It wouldn't matter if the provider were not a qualified medical professional, as long as the physical therapy program was for legitimate medical reasons and was prescribed by a doctor. However, the cost of having the same person do housework would not be deductible. The fact that your injury made you unable to do the housework yourself is irrelevant.

Reminder: Medical expenses are only deductible to the extent that they have not been reimbursed by insurance and exceed 7.5% of your Adjusted Gross Income.

What the IRS Won't Tell You About Audits

Frederick W. Daily, Esq., tax attorney, 302 Warren Dr., San Francisco 94131. He is author of *Stand Up to the IRS* and *Tax Savvy for Small Business*. Both from Nolo Press.

Most taxpayers who face an IRS auditor fear how much the IRS knows about them. Auditors use this fear to intimidate taxpayers into making concessions and revealing more.

With the right tactics, you can keep the IRS auditor from learning any more...and help move the audit to its best possible conclusion.

WHAT THE IRS KNOWS

When you appear for an IRS audit, the auditor will have a file on your case that typically contains only three sources of information about you...

●**Tax return being audited.**

●**Your tax-filing history for the past six years.** This tells whether you filed tax returns ...were audited...or had a tax bill adjusted for those years. It does *not* include copies of prior years' tax returns.

●**List of third-party payments made to you** that were reported to the IRS on W-2 and 1099 forms or other information returns.

In 90% of cases, that's all the information the auditor will have about you before the audit begins.

If information that could cause you audit problems is not contained among these three items, the overwhelming odds are that the auditor doesn't have it.

Then the only way the auditor can get it is from you or by issuing a summons on the record keeper.

The auditor will not have: Copies of bank statements, motor vehicle records, property deeds or police records.

Nor will the auditor have copies of 1099s or other information returns sent to the IRS under a Social Security or taxpayer ID number other than yours.

Key: Don't volunteer any information to the IRS auditor that you aren't legally obligated to give—even if he/she asks for it.

THE BIGGEST MISTAKE

By far the most common audit mistake is providing copies of your other years' tax returns just because the audit notice asks you to do so.

Doing so greatly expands audit risk by giving the auditor many things to look at that he otherwise would not see.

Patterns of income and deduction amounts reported over multiple years may raise questions that would not arise when looking at just a single year's return.

The fact that an auditor doesn't have information doesn't mean he won't ask for it. So it's important to know what you are legally required to provide to an auditor...and what you aren't.

Rule: You are required to provide an IRS auditor only the information relating to the specific tax year listed in the audit notice. You are not required to provide information relating to any

55

other tax year, except as it might relate to the year under audit—as carryover items might.

SAYING NO

Most people never imagine saying no to an IRS auditor for fear the auditor might retaliate by expanding the audit.

This fear is greatly exaggerated—retaliation is unlikely. IRS auditors have no incentive to expand an audit. They are evaluated by how quickly they close cases and work through their caseloads. And those caseloads are very heavy.

Inside secret: An auditor who feels there is good reason to examine another year's tax return can obtain it from the IRS's own files, but it may take weeks or months for the IRS to retrieve that old return. One who doesn't take the trouble to do so probably is "just fishing" for the taxpayer to reveal something.

The way to say *no* safely to such an auditor is to respond politely, "I don't believe that this relates to the year or issues being examined." Almost always, that will end the matter.

THE RIGHT REPRESENTATION

If there is information you want to protect from the IRS, consider being represented at your audit by a tax professional—instead of attending the audit personally. They are experienced at dealing with auditors.

A professional representative will not have the answers to some of the auditor's questions —including any information that you might reveal unintentionally.

Your representative will ask the auditor to put the request in writing. Then, in responding to a written request, your representative can discuss things with you and draft as narrow an answer as possible.

The whole process will slow the audit, which the auditor doesn't want. So attempts by the auditor to "go fishing" will be frustrated.

The IRS cannot conduct a "lifestyle or economic reality audit," asking questions that are unrelated to the preparation of the return being examined, unless it already has a reasonable indication that income has been understated.

A professional representative will also prevent your emotions or personal factors from complicating an audit. No matter how difficult the audit may be, your representative should be able to deal with the auditor in a calm and professional manner.

The fee you pay may be a bargain for both the taxes it saves and the anxiety you avoid by not dealing with the auditor personally.

And, last but not least, fees paid to a tax professional for defending an audit are deductible.

5

Your Insurance Edge

Early Retirement & Social Security Benefits

The age at which you can begin to collect full Social Security retirement benefits is going up. It will rise gradually, in two-month increments, from age 65 for persons born in 1938 and later, to age 67 in the year 2027.

Ultimate impact: Persons born in 1960 and later won't be able to collect full benefits until they reach age 67. (Refer to the chart below).

Retirement Age Increases

The normal retirement age will increase in stages to 66 through 2009, and then, starting in 2022, gradually to 67 by 2027.

Year of Birth	Age for Full Benefits
1937 and earlier	65
1938	65 & 2 months
1939	65 & 4 months
1940	65 & 6 months
1941	65 & 8 months
1942	65 & 10 months
1943 through 1954	66
1955	66 & 2 months
1956	66 & 4 months
1957	66 & 6 months
1958	66 & 8 months
1959	66 & 10 months
1960 and later	67

The *early retirement age,* however, will *not* change. You'll still be able to begin collecting *reduced* Social Security benefits at age 62.

REDUCED BENEFITS

Quandary: When you opt for early retirement, your monthly benefits are reduced from what you'd get if you waited until the normal retirement age to start collecting Social Security.

The benefit reduction for taking early retirement at 62 is 20% of what you'd get if you waited until age 65. Those who retire early

Peter J. Strauss, Esq., a partner in the law firm Epstein Becker & Green, PC, 250 Park Ave., New York 10177. He is a fellow of the National Academy of Elder Law Attorneys and coauthor of *The Elder Law Handbook—A Legal and Financial Survival Guide for Caregivers and Seniors.* Facts on File.

must take a percentage reduction for each month that they retire before their "normal" retirement age. A percentage of the full benefit is lopped off.

The percentage of full benefits lost is five-ninths of 1% for the first 36 months of retirement before normal retirement age and five-twelfths of 1% for each additional month. (The chart below spells out the reductions for various ages.)

Reduction in Retirement Benefits
Depending On Early and Normal Retirement Age

EARLY RETIREMENT AGE	PERCENTAGE BENEFIT REDUCTION...		
	for those with normal retirement age of 65	for those with normal retirement age of 66	for those with normal retirement age of 67
62	20%	25%	30%
63	13⅓%	20%	25%
64	6⅔%	13⅓%	20%
65	—	6⅔%	13⅓%
66	—	—	6⅔%

Example 1: A person who opts for early retirement at age 62 would have his/her monthly Social Security benefit check permanently reduced by 20% of the full retirement benefit. So, if benefits at 65 would be $1,000 a month, taking retirement at 62 will reduce benefits to $800 a month.

Example 2: Someone born after 1959 who takes early retirement at age 62 (when the normal retirement age has gone up to 67) will have benefits reduced by 30%. If full benefits are $1,000 a month, early retirement benefits will be $700 a month.

If you're thinking about early retirement, you need to get an estimate of your benefits. This is sent to you automatically about three months before your birthday if you are 25 years old or older. If you don't receive it, request it from the Social Security Administration at 800-772-1213 or from its Web site at *www.ssa.gov.*

SHOULD I TAKE EARLY RETIREMENT?

Opting for early retirement means that benefits commence early, before age 65, even though at a reduced rate.

Advantage: This gives you additional years of collecting benefits.

Bottom line: Suppose your normal retirement age is 65, but you take early retirement at 62 with reduced benefits. In terms of total benefits, you'll be ahead of what you would have received had you waited until age 65 to start collecting, until you reach a "crossover point" at age 77. Beyond that point your total benefits would be greater if you retired at age 65.

As the normal retirement age increases to age 67 (and the reduction in early retirement benefits also increases), it will take about 14 years (until the same age of 77) before the later retiree can catch up with the early retiree in total benefits received.

WORKING WHILE COLLECTING

•**Under current law, retirement benefits are reduced** for those *under age 65* if their earnings from employment exceed a set amount ($11,280 in 2002). Then, Social Security benefits are reduced by $1 for each $2 of excess earnings.

•**Those age 65 and older** and still working are not subject to an earnings penalty and can earn any amount without a reduction in benefits.

Note: The earnings limit does not change even though the normal retirement age has been increased.

If you plan to work full time or otherwise earn more than the modest earnings limit for those under age 65, it may not make sense to commence benefits before retirement.

MEDICARE

Benefits under Medicare do not start before age 65. This is so even if you opt for early retirement at age 62.

However, the Medicare starting age does not change. This is the case even though the Social Security normal retirement age will increase. The Medicare eligibility age remains 65.

DECISIONS, DECISIONS

Whether or not to start receiving Social Security benefits at the early retirement age depends on your personal situation. *Questions to ask yourself...*

•**Life expectancy.** What is your personal health history (and family health history)? If you do not anticipate a long life, then opting for early commencement of benefits may prove more financially rewarding than waiting until your normal retirement age.

•**Capacity for work.** If you are planning to continue at a job or to work at your own business, then waiting until you cease working—or, depending on your earnings, at least attain age 65—may make much more sense for you than starting benefits early.

Social Security Tax-Saving Strategy

Barbara Weltman, an attorney with offices in Millwood, NY, and author of J.K. Lasser's New Rules for Small Business Taxes *(John Wiley & Sons) and* The Complete Idiot's Guide to Making Money After You Retire *(Macmillan).*

Social Security recipients lose a significant portion of benefits to taxes if their income exceeds certain limits. More specifically, when Modified Adjusted Gross Income (MAGI) —which is Adjusted Gross Income increased by tax-free interest on municipal bonds, certain exclusions and a portion of Social Security benefits—exceeds...

●**$32,000 on a joint return or $25,000 on a single return,** up to 50% of Social Security benefits are included in taxable income.

●**$44,000 on a joint return, $34,000 on a single return or zero if married filing separately,** up to 85% of Social Security benefits are included in taxable income.

TAX-SAVING STRATEGY

Reduce tax on your Social Security benefits by reducing your MAGI. *How...*

●**Defer income.** Invest for growth rather than income. Postpone realizing gains on investments and taking discretionary distributions from IRAs and other retirement plans.

●**Make tax-free investments.** Roth IRA payouts of earnings are tax free if certain conditions are met, so fund a Roth IRA rather than a regular IRA.

Interest from tax-free municipal bonds is included in MAGI for purposes of determining tax on Social Security benefits—but municipals pay a lower interest rate than taxable bonds.

●**Shift income.** Make estate-tax-reducing gifts of property to younger family members by shifting income-producing property.

●**Deduct losses.** At year-end, take "paper" investment losses to offset income from gains and up to $3,000 of ordinary income. You can repurchase the loss investment after 31 days, or a similar, but not identical one, immediately.

Social Security Rip-off

There are now four million illegal users of fake Social Security numbers. *Result:* Someone else may be receiving your benefits.

Self-defense: Call the Social Security Administration (800-772-1213) to request your summary statement of earnings. Compare it with your past W-2 statements. Lower annual figures may mean benefits are being misdirected. Higher figures could mean your number has been stolen and could attract the IRS, which scans this data to uncover hidden income.

Statute of limitations for an appeal: Three years, three months, and three days from the contested year.

How You Can Make the Most of Medicare Coverage

David S. Landay, Esq., president of NVR, Inc., a New York City company that provides financial counseling to people who have serious health conditions. He is author of Be Prepared: The Complete Financial, Legal and Practical Guide to Living with Cancer, HIV and Other Life-Challenging Conditions. *St. Martin's Press.*

As you may already know, Medicare has two key advantages over private health insurance. It costs little (or nothing) and is available to every US citizen or legal resident age 65 or older—even those with preexisting conditions that would make them ineligible for private insurance.

Eligible people can receive an enrollment form in the mail a few months before turning 65. Once they fill it out and send it back, they're in the program.

But like most federal programs, Medicare is enormously complex. To help you take full advantage of it, we spoke with David S. Landay, a lawyer specializing in counseling people with serious illness…

•I know that Medicare has two parts. Could you please explain them? Part A covers in-patient hospital care and—under some circumstances—home health care, treatment in a nursing facility and hospice care.

This part of the program is free to any Medicare enrollee who has accumulated—or whose spouse has accumulated—about 40 credits. That generally means 10 years of full-time work.

Part B covers doctors' fees, outpatient medical and surgical services, diagnostic tests and more. This part is optional. It costs $54 per month in 2002.

You'll automatically be enrolled in Part A if you complete the Medicare application. When you enroll in Part A, you're automatically enrolled in Part B, unless you check a box on the enrollment form.

•Is Part B worth the expense? For most people, the answer is yes. Otherwise, unless you're covered by private insurance, you'll be responsible for paying doctors' fees as well as the costs of diagnostic tests. Compared with other insurance plans, the monthly premium is very reasonable.

Some people decline Part B because they're covered by a group insurance plan at work and feel they don't need additional coverage.

This may be unwise, particularly for people who have a medical problem or who come from a family with a history of medical problems, since Part B picks up many of the co-payments and deductibles.

•Where does Medigap coverage fit in? Since Medicare doesn't cover everything, many people get additional coverage through a so-called Medigap policy.

Medigap policies are sold by private insurance companies, but the benefits they offer are standardized. This makes it easy to compare prices and coverage levels among companies.

There are 10 Medigap policies, designated by the letters A through J. Plan A provides the most basic coverage, Plan J the most comprehensive. Each policy covers some or all of Medicare's coinsurance payments. A few pay the deductibles as well.

Which plan makes sense for you depends upon your health, the cost of any prescription medications you take and, of course, what you can afford to pay in monthly premiums.

Medigap policies can be confusing, and there's a great deal of overlap among them. For free help in picking one, call your state health insurance assistance program. Look in your phone book in the state government section under "Insurance" or "Department of Insurance."

•Can I switch Medigap policies if my health starts to decline? Yes, but try to do so within six months of the time you first enroll in the program. Otherwise, you'll have to pay a higher premium because of your preexisting condition.

By law, every Medigap policy comes with a money-back guarantee. If you're dissatisfied with the coverage, ask for a refund and switch to another insurer.

•What's the best policy for covering prescription drugs? The most comprehensive Medigap policy, Plan J, pays 50% of the cost of prescription drugs up to an annual maximum of $3,000. Plans H and I also pay 50% of the cost, but the annual cap will be lower.

Except for medications you receive in the hospital and some cancer drugs, Medicare does not pay the cost of medications.

•What is Medicare managed care? It's an arrangement whereby an HMO or another managed-care program provides Medicare coverage.

Signing your benefits over to an HMO typically extends your coverage to things not traditionally covered by Medicare—dental care, hearing aids, prescription medications, etc. And the fees with a Medicare HMO are more predictable than those in fee-for-service coverage.

The disadvantages with this arrangement are the same as those you would face in any managed-care organization. You'll have to choose a primary-care physician from the plan's roster, and you'll have to get all of your care within the plan. The plan—and not you—will be managing your care.

If you sign up for managed care and decide you're unhappy with your treatment, you can switch back to standard Medicare at any time.

•**How do I protect myself in case I need long-term care?** Neither Medicare nor the various Medigap policies pay for indefinite nursing home care. Review your policies carefully to determine exactly what's covered, and then decide whether you need extra insurance. Consult a lawyer, social worker or your insurance broker if you need assistance.

A companion program to Medicare, Medicaid does provide long-term nursing care.

Ordinarily, only low-income people and those who meet certain financial criteria are eligible for Medicaid. But home owners and others with substantial financial assets who anticipate that they may need extended long-term care should consult a lawyer. In many cases, it's possible to take advantage of the Medicaid safety net without liquidating all of your assets.

To Find a Good Archer Medical Savings Account (MSA)...

Shop around. Fees and interest rates for Archer MSAs vary widely. Carefully review the details of the savings account part of the MSA. Think of it as a money market account. Compare interest rates...enrollment fees...monthly membership fees...withdrawal process. *Also:* Check with Independent Insurance Agents of America, 800-221-7917 or *www.iiaa.org,* for a free comparison of offerings. Check separately with insurers that sell exclusively through their own networks of agents.

Edward Slott, CPA, E. Slott & Co., 100 Merrick Rd., Rockville Centre, NY 11570. He is editor of Ed Slott's IRA Advisor. www.irahelp.com.

How to Choose the Best Health Insurance

Bruce Pyenson and Jim O'Connor, principals with Milliman & Robertson, a consulting firm that works with insurance companies and health-care providers, Two Pennsylvania Plaza, New York 10121. Mr. Pyenson is author of several books, including *J.K. Lasser's Employee Benefits for Small Business.* Prentice-Hall.

Most health insurance is provided through group policies in the workplace. But there are millions of people who are self-employed or between jobs who have to find individual coverage on their own. Medicare also offers different coverage options.

While there are plenty of good policies out there, finding one that fits your needs takes some digging.

SIZE UP YOUR NEEDS

The health-care needs of families with young children are different from those of singles starting new jobs...couples without children...and empty nesters. Families with infants want a full range of care that covers everything from routine vaccinations to ear infections. Healthy singles may only need bare-bones coverage for unexpected catastrophes.

In these days of managed care, there are four basic types of coverage...

HEALTH MAINTENANCE ORGANIZATIONS (HMOs)

A very prevalent type of group coverage, HMOs provide comprehensive medical care through networks of physicians. Typically, you pay $5 or $10 per in-network doctor visit and don't have to fill out forms after each appointment or worry about meeting a deductible requirement.

If you have a special health problem, you typically must first consult your primary care physician—also known as the *gatekeeper.* This physician may treat you or may refer you to a specialist. If you decide to use an out-of-network specialist or hospital, coverage—if any—is limited.

With limited choice about which doctors and hospitals to use and limited access to specialists, these plans are usually the most economical. Your out-of-pocket costs are fairly low for the wide range of coverage you get.

Best for: People with children who are new to a community—they have no relationships with physicians or hospitals. Also good for people with children whose current physician and hospital are part of the HMO network.

PREFERRED PROVIDER ORGANIZATIONS (PPOs)

These types of policies—which are more expensive than comparable HMOs—give you the ability to go outside the plan network for your medical care. Most PPO plans don't have a gatekeeper system, so you usually don't need approval to see specialists.

If you see a physician within the network, you get one level of benefits (usually 80% of a claim is covered). If you see a physician outside the network, you get another, lower level of benefits (only 60% to 70% of the claim might be covered).

Best for: People who want more choice about health-care providers...and whose doctors are part of the PPO network.

INDEMNITY POLICIES

These plans pay benefits for most services no matter what doctor or hospital you go to. Such traditional policies appeal to people who have lived in the same community for a long time and have established ties to physicians and hospitals. While they guarantee you the most latitude in terms of choosing your health-care providers, indemnity plans are also the most expensive. Sometimes people who want the flexibility of an indemnity policy opt for high deductibles of as much as $10,000 to reduce monthly premiums.

"ANY DOCTOR" POLICIES

These hybrid plans use a PPO approach for hospitals but allow you to see any licensed physicians you wish. They are cheaper than indemnity policies but more expensive than full-fledged PPOs.

Best for: People who feel comfortable with the hospitals in the PPO network but want the flexibility of using any doctor they choose.

FINDING THE BEST PLAN

●**Research what is available in your state.** Because each state regulates insurance, choices will be limited. Not all insurance companies offer policies in all states. And a company's policies may be different in different states.

If your car and homeowner's insurance is with a company that sells through a network of agents, start by calling your agent.

If you belong to a professional or trade group or a college alumni association, find out if these organizations offer special health policies for members. Such policies often cost less than individual policies but more than group policies. If you have chronic health problems, these policies can be a good deal since you may not be able to get an affordable policy on your own.

●**Determine what different types of policies will cost you.** Call two major companies that write health insurance nationwide.

For HMOs: Aetna (800-872-3862)...United Health Group (877-311-7848).

For PPOs, "Any Doctor" and indemnity: Fortis Health (800-211-1193)...Mutual of Omaha (800-775-6000).

Simplify your search by using the Internet. Two sites that provide up to 20 different premium quotes are *www.quotesmith.com* and *www.insweb.com*.

Be sure to get the answers to some crucial questions...

●**Does the plan cover maternity, mental health and substance abuse?**

●**What are the rules concerning preexisting conditions** (health problems you had before taking out the policy)?

●**Ask the insurer about rate increases.** You want to know how often and by how much insurers boost their premiums each year. Ask what the increases have been for the past several years. Some companies charge very low initial rates but then raise premiums by a large amount. Rate increases are currently running 10% to 15% a year. If your insurer is boosting rates by 30% or more annually, it's time to shop around.

●**Find out if customers are satisfied.** Get the names of current HMO members. Ask if they've experienced delays in obtaining membership cards, problems communicating with physicians, difficulty getting pharmacies to accept their coverage, trouble getting doctor's appointments quickly or trouble getting prompt referrals to specialists.

You can also call your state insurance or health department (they usually are listed in the state government pages of your telephone directory). Some states develop statistics that indicate complaint ratios of HMOs.

If you have an established doctor, you might also call him/her for feedback on the plan you are considering, particularly for HMOs.

How to Outsmart Your Managed-Care Organization

Bruce A. Barron, MD, PhD, associate professor of clinical obstetrics and gynecology at Columbia–Presbyterian Medical Center and a former senior medical director at Empire Blue Cross/Blue Shield, both in New York City. He is author of *Outsmarting Managed Care: A Doctor Shares His Insider's Secrets to Getting the Health Care You Want.* Times Books.

Before the era of managed care, people who sought medical care were known as patients.

Nowadays many of us are customers of a health-maintenance organization, preferred-provider organization or another managed-care organization (MCO).

Customers of MCOs don't always get what they pay for...

•**Some MCOs deny patients key diagnostic tests.**

•**Some MCOs refuse to pay for costly medications.**

•**Some MCOs push customers into surgery with a surgeon who has substandard training**—in a second-rate hospital.

There's really no need to be a victim of managed care. *Here's how to fight back...*

PLAIN FACTS ABOUT MCOs

Managed care is big business. Your doctor may focus on easing symptoms and healing disease, but MCOs inevitably focus on the *bottom line.* This may be especially true of for-profit MCOs, which now constitute the majority of plans. Whatever their fancy brochure says, their allegiance is to their shareholders—not to you.

Like all businesses, MCOs try to maximize revenues while minimizing expenditures. Raising premiums is one way MCOs improve their bottom lines. They also reduce the *medical loss ratio.* In plain English, that means delivering as little health care as possible.

CHOOSING A DOCTOR

In most MCOs, customers must choose a primary-care physician from a roster of participating doctors. These doctors are listed by medical specialty.

Trap: Just because a doctor is listed as an internist, cardiologist, etc., does not mean he/she has had the extra training and has passed the rigorous tests required for board certification.

It's common for MCOs to hire doctors who are not board-certified, even though board certification has long been considered a mark of medical expertise.

What to do: Call your MCO or the doctor's office to find out about board certification.

For a list of board-certified physicians in the US, consult the *Directory of Medical Specialists.* This book—available at most public libraries—also details doctors' training, experience, etc.

The American Medical Association offers similar information on its Web site, *www.ama-assn. org.* Or you can contact the American Board of Medical Specialties at 866-ASK-ABMS. *www. abms.org.*

Important: If a doctor you are considering practices as part of a group, check the credentials of his partners, too.

The doctor you select must be your ally. Will he help you fight for proper medical care? Will he help you get critical tests, treatments and referrals even if the MCO doesn't want to provide them?

Although it is hard to know how a doctor will behave until a problem arises, it is important to find out his general feelings on the subject.

GETTING FIRST-RATE CARE

Some doctors like to joke that managed care is fine—as long as you don't get sick. Unfortunately, the joke contains a kernel of truth. And the more serious your illness, the harder it can be to get state-of-the-art medical care.

Example: An endoscopic examination of the stomach is often the best way to check for a peptic ulcer. But an MCO may refuse to cover endoscopy, arguing that this $1,200 procedure falls outside its "practice guidelines."

Each time you discuss treatment options with your doctor, ask whether his recommendations are constrained by rules set down by the MCO.

If so, ask what he *would* do—which tests, procedures, medications, etc., he would recommend—if there were no such constraints.

If this recommendation differs from his original one, ask that he explain his position *in writing*. That way, you'll have a record if you need to appeal an MCO decision.

If you need a specialist, do the ones affiliated with the MCO have the best qualifications? Or are there better specialists outside of the MCO's network?

If you need surgery, how do the surgical track records of hospitals affiliated with the MCO compare with the track records of hospitals unaffiliated with the MCO?

Death rates tend to be much lower in hospitals that do a high volume of a given procedure.

If you believe the MCO's rules will adversely affect your health, the MCO is required *by law* in some states to review your case. But you'll have a battle on your hands.

TAKING IT TO THE TOP

When you telephone the MCO to appeal a decision, you'll probably talk first to a "case manager." In many cases, this person is a nurse who simply explains the MCO's treatment guidelines.

If the case manager rejects your appeal, insist on speaking to a "medical director"—a doctor who works for the MCO.

Do *not* let yourself be intimidated. Nonphysicians tend to be deferential around medical doctors. That's inappropriate here. You're dealing not with Marcus Welby, but with a representative of a giant corporation.

Find out the medical director's specialty. If he's a dermatologist and you have cancer, he may know less about your condition than you do. In such a case, ask to speak to a medical director who has training in oncology.

If this medical director rules against you, ask to speak with the MCO's "medical director for policy." This company official has greater power to help you.

Crucial: Each time you speak with a representative of the MCO, ask for a report of the conversation or ruling *in writing*. It's essential that you create a paper trail. That way, you'll have all the documentation needed if you choose to get an external review, in which an expert outside the MCO evaluates your case.

At some point as you make your way up the hierarchy, the MCO will probably give in to your demands.

If the MCO does not give in, file a complaint with the agency that regulates insurance companies. In some states, it's the department of consumer affairs.

Another option: Contact the media. When TV or newspaper reporters cover cases in which an MCO customer has been denied care, the MCO almost always capitulates.

Long-Term-Care Insurance And Your Taxes

Thomas Orr, CPA, partner with the accounting firm Bregante & Co., 180 Howard St., San Francisco 94105. The head of his firm's insurance tax practice, he has published opinions on the taxability of long-term-care insurance.

The *Health Insurance Portability and Accountability Act* (HIPAA) of 1996 divided the world of long-term-care insurance (LTC) into two types of policies—tax-qualified and non-tax-qualified.

Tax-qualified policies' major benefits…

•**Premiums may be tax deductible.** The deductions for long-term-care insurance range up to set limits, depending on your age each year, according to the following schedule for 2002…

Age	Maximum Deduction
40 or under	$240
41–50	450
51–60	900
61–70	2,390
71+	2,990

● **Benefits you receive won't be taxable.** This exclusion applies to amounts received up to $210 per day in 2002, indexed for inflation, on long-term-care contracts that pay a per diem benefit.

Bonus benefit: Amounts over $210 per day also will be excluded if the money reimburses the policyholder for LTC expenses.

TESTS FOR TAX BENEFITS

In order to qualify for these tax benefits, LTC policies must meet certain key standards...

● **The insured individual must be unable to perform** at least two of the following "activities of daily living" (ADLs)—eating, bathing, dressing, getting out of bed, toileting and continence.

● **A licensed health-care professional** must certify that these conditions will last for at least 90 days.

BARRIERS TO BENEFITS

Even with tax-qualified policies the tax benefits aren't certain.

Example: Premiums are deductible only if you itemize.

Trap: Premiums on a tax-qualified policy are added to other medical expenses and only those expenses that exceed 7.5% of your AGI are deductible.

Example: Frank Fisher is a 61-year-old single taxpayer with $70,000 in AGI. Assume he's in the 27% tax bracket. Only those medical expenses over $5,250 per year are deductible and then, only if he itemizes deductions.

Suppose Mr. Fisher has $4,588 in total medical expenses this year, not counting long-term-care premiums. If he pays a $2,200 premium for a tax-qualified LTC policy, he'd raise his total medical expenses to $6,788. His federal tax savings from his deductible LTC policy would be less than $415.

If Mr. Fisher had $100,000 in AGI, the LTC deduction would have no value, because his total medical expenses would be well under 7.5% of his AGI.

The age limits given in the chart on page 64 further restrict deductions for LTC insurance premiums.

As a result, many taxpayers won't be able to deduct all or part of their LTC premiums, even if they have a tax-qualified policy.

Tax professionals generally believe that the premiums on a tax-qualified policy will be deductible, as long as all the conditions are met. Premiums on a nonqualified policy won't be deductible.

CONTROVERSY

However, the taxability of policy benefits is a controversial issue.

Example: Mary Adams, an elderly widow, goes into a nursing home and collects benefits of $100 per day under her LTC policy. That's $36,500 a year. Will those benefits be considered taxable income? *Some answers...*

● **They won't be taxable income if Mary owns a tax-qualified policy.**

● **They won't be taxable income if Mary has an LTC policy** bought before 1997, because such policies were grandfathered by HIPAA.

Strategy: If you have such a policy, don't exchange it or modify it without careful consideration.

If Mary owns a post-1996, nonqualified policy, though, her $36,500 is not specifically excluded from income—it is not included in income either.

TRACKING THE TAX CODE

It is likely that such benefits are not meant to be included in income. Prior to the passage of HIPPA, benefits received under an LTC policy were treated as nontaxable and the premiums paid for such coverage were not deductible.

Accordingly, benefits received now under a nonqualified LTC contract probably should not be included in income. This is especially true for those benefits that reimburse the policyholder for the expenses of qualified long-term-care services.

IRS position: Informally, an IRS spokesman has declared that benefits from a nonqualified LTC policy likely will be considered income if the money was spent to help an elderly individual go shopping—but benefits used for custodial care won't be taxed.

Paper trail: Insurance companies must report LTC benefit payments to the IRS, noting whether or not the policy is tax qualified. This will make it easier for the IRS to pinpoint such benefits.

However, the federal tax return doesn't have a line specifically for the inclusion of LTC benefits and the instructions for the "other income" line of Form 1040 are unclear, to say the least, when it comes to benefits from a nonqualified LTC policy.

Key: In most cases, the after-tax cost of paying tax on LTC benefits would wind up being modest, in relation to the benefits received.

WEIGHING THE ALTERNATIVES

As indicated, not all long-term-care policies meet these standards. *However, some nonqualified policies may provide more benefits than tax-qualified policies...*

•**Nonqualified policies may pay if policyholders can't meet the two-activities-of-daily-living test** but are unable to perform other functions, such as walking around or getting to a doctor's appointment.

•**Nonqualified policies generally don't include a 90-day test,** so they may pay off in cases of shorter term disabilities.

•**Some require only that a doctor state a patient can't care for himself/herself** any more and that care is "medically necessary."

Thus, buying a nonqualified LTC insurance policy means you won't be able to deduct your premiums—which you might not be able to deduct anyway. In a worst case scenario, you might owe some tax on any benefits received.

Trade-off: In return for such tax disadvantages, you might be getting a policy that provides better coverage.

Faced with a choice between safer tax benefits and more comprehensive coverage, how should you or your elderly parents decide?

One option is to buy a nonqualified policy that includes an option to convert to a tax-qualified policy if the tax situation becomes clearer—and such a conversion seems desirable. That may prove to be a prudent hedge against another round of "tax simplification."

If you do buy a policy with a conversion feature, make sure...

•**You won't have to pay a higher premium** because of your age at the time of conversion.

•**You won't incur tax consequences** due to a policy exchange.

Long-Term Care ...New Option

A problem with obtaining long-term-care insurance is that most people won't need long-term care, in which case the expensive premiums are wasted.

But new combined life insurance/long-term-care policies address this problem. The policies pay a standard life insurance benefit, but should you need long-term care, you can tap the policy benefit tax free. The life insurance benefit may be reduced by amounts spent on care needs. Whether you eventually need care or not, your premiums will earn a return. Ask your insurance adviser for details.

Lee Slavutin, MD, CPC, CLU, principal of Stern Slavutin-2 Inc., insurance and estate planners, 530 Fifth Ave., New York 10036.

Give Your Life Insurance Policy a Checkup

Glenn Daily, a fee-only insurance consultant and author of *Life Insurance Sense and Nonsense,* available from the author.

After a life insurance policy is purchased, most people put the papers in a file and just pay the premium when the bill arrives.

Problem: A family's life insurance needs may change every few years.

Depending upon the type of policy you own, performing a life insurance checkup might take as little as an hour or so and save you big, big money.

Before you begin...

•**Understand the policy you already own.** Many people don't know what type of insurance coverage they have. *Questions to ask yourself...*

•Do you have a term...whole life...universal...or variable universal policy? If you're uncertain, review your policies—or ask your life insurance agent for in-depth explanations.

In short, term insurance provides coverage for a set period of time—such as 10 years. The other three types are cash-value policies, meaning that in addition to a death benefit, part of your premium is placed in a savings vehicle and can be withdrawn or borrowed. Each type has different fees and investment returns. The checkup process is different for each one.

• How much insurance coverage do you have currently? Chances are you've forgotten the amount, so verify it with the company or agent. Coverage levels that seemed appropriate even four or five years ago may look out-of-date when compared with your family's current financial realities.

Important: If you also receive life insurance coverage from your employer, add that to any personal policies you own to obtain your total coverage level.

• **Gather all relevant policy documentation.** If you own a cash-value policy—whole life, universal or variable life—pull your most recent annual statement and ask your agent for an up-to-date, in-force illustration that estimates your future premium and policy values based on current assumptions. For term policies, the illustration will show you estimated premiums.

• **Compare existing total coverage with your family's actual insurance needs.** A family's insurance needs keep changing. Many financial planning books have worksheets to estimate insurance needs.

Key events that signal more coverage is probably needed: Birth of a child…purchase of a home…new job with a higher salary.

Key events that signal less coverage is probably needed: Child's college graduation…divorce…retirement.

• **Start thinking about adjusting your coverage levels to suit your family's current needs.** If you don't need as much coverage as you did in the past, cutting your annual premiums can be as simple as calling your agent and asking to reduce your coverage.

Opportunity: If your insurer permits you to reduce the face amount of an existing policy, you'll be able to skip new application fees and a medical exam. Find out if there are any changes or tax consequences before you act.

If your insurance needs have increased, it may be possible to reduce your costs. *Here's how to tell, depending on the type of insurance you own…*

• **Term insurance.** This is the quickest, easiest checkup to perform. *Goal:* To determine if your premiums are attractive compared with those offered by your insurer's competitors.

Strategy: Call Quotesmith (800-556-9393) for free comparisons. If competitors' prices are lower, it may be time to switch to another insurer. *It may be time to switch if…*

• Your family's insurance needs change.

• Your insurer raises your premiums unexpectedly.

• You own a level-premium term policy—which means you are charged the same premium for a set number of years—and the term is about to expire.

• **Cash-value insurance.** With cash-value policies—which provide coverage plus a savings account or investment—the checkup process is more complicated but not impossible. *Whether you own a whole life, universal or variable universal policy, start with these two steps:*

• Order a rate-of-return analysis from the Consumer Federation of America (CFA) (202-387-6121). CFA takes the values from your in-force illustration and computes a rate of return you can compare with other policies and investments.

Mistake: Automatically canceling a cash-value policy because you learn that it is underperforming the market. You have paid a lot in commissions, and there is going to be a charge to forfeit the policy.

Better: Consult with your agent about other options if you're unhappy with your policy. Such options may include repaying a loan, using dividends to buy paid-up additions or shrinking the face value of your policy.

• Evaluate your current insurer's financial stability. Ask your agent to send you current, full-scale reports on your insurer from rating agencies—A.M. Best, Standard & Poor's, Moody's and Duff & Phelps. If the ratings look shaky, consult your agent about your options.

•**Whole life insurance.** If you determine that your insurer is stable and your policy's investment returns are competitive, look for ways to get better value from your policy.

Helpful: Pay premiums annually rather than paying them semiannually...quarterly...or monthly. *Savings:* 8% to 12% in interest charges.

Use dividends to buy paid-up additions. This is one of the best bargains offered by insurers—equivalent to making a single-premium, no-commission addition to your coverage.

Scrutinize policy riders. If you can eliminate extra cost benefits that you no longer need, you'll lower premiums.

•**Universal life insurance allows policyholders to pay more or less than the suggested premium.** If they pay less, the policy will last for fewer years than established at the outset because less money is going to maintain the policy.

Key: Determine whether the amount you plan to pay in premiums is sufficient to keep your policy going as long as you'll need it.

Ask your agent when the policy will expire under various assumptions about premium payments and interest rates.

Important: You're particularly vulnerable if you bought your policy during the 1980s, when interest rates were higher than today. If your insurer anticipated a much higher rate of return than your policy has actually earned, your coverage may expire sooner than you expect or desire unless you take steps now to increase the premium or reduce coverage.

•**Check competitors.** If you need to increase coverage, make certain that what your insurer is offering still seems competitive. In addition to the Consumer Federation of America, call the Wholesale Insurance Network to get comparisons with new low-load policies. They charge lower commissions so more of your premium goes toward insurance.

Life Insurance If You Can't Pass a Physical

Can't pass the life insurance physical? Don't give up—there may be a way.

Find an agent who knows his way with insurance companies. Their standards vary on overweight, blood pressure, smoking, and other medical conditions. *Example:* Six-foot middle-aged man weighing 270 pounds—many companies would add a big surcharge premium for his weight. But one company will insure him with no surcharge at all.

The agent's job is to find the exceptional company and know how to present the application in the most favorable light. Few agents do this well. You've got to insist the agent shop for you.

If an individual policy isn't available (or only at very high cost), group policies can be found in clubs, fraternal orders, religious orders, volunteer firemen. It may pay to join a club just for the group insurance. The saving on the premium is usually more than the dues.

Frank J. Crisona, attorney and principal of the Crisona Agency, Box 130, Carle Place, NY 11514.

You Can Fight Insurance Companies...and Win

William M. Shernoff, a consumer-rights lawyer who practices in Claremont, CA. He is author of *How to Make Insurance Companies Pay Your Claims and What to Do If They Don't.* Hastings House.

I hear horror stories every day from families whose insurance companies refused to make timely payments on legitimate claims. Individuals are inhumanely hounded by collection agencies because their insurance companies haven't paid the bills they are legally obligated to pay. The disabled are forced to go on welfare. Some people have even been driven to attempt suicide.

Very few people—fewer than 1% of those with insurance claims—question claim denials. By not questioning a denied claim, there's a good chance you're letting the insurance company cheat you out of money that rightfully belongs to you.

Good news: Most of those who do challenge insurers either win their cases or significantly improve their positions.

WHAT IT TAKES TO WIN

●**Positive attitude.** Don't assume "they" must be right and take the first no for a final answer. Insurance companies count on the fact that most people simply accept their decisions.

●**Persistence.** The adage, "a squeaky wheel gets the grease," is true when it comes to dealing with a claim denial.

●**Knowledge.** Educate yourself on specific issues and the tools available to help you fight a large insurance company.

YOU BE THE JUDGE

On any claim refusal, exercise your rights as a consumer…

●**Insist on a written explanation.** Most state laws require an insurance company to give you one.

●**Compare the explanation you get from the company with the language of the policy.** Insurers notoriously write policies that are difficult to understand and then interpret them to their own advantage. But in court, where language is unclear, the meaning is construed against the insurance company. Some courts have even held that the reasonable expectation of the policyholder governs the meaning of policy language.

●**Rely on your own common sense. Judge for yourself "what is fair" and "what you expected."** If what the insurance company offers doesn't seem fair, there is a good chance that it isn't.

●**Don't be put off if your claim is denied for technical reasons.** An insurer cannot deny benefits because you filed late or filled out a form improperly unless the company can show it has been harmed by your failure. That's very, very rarely the case.

●**Use intermediaries to press your claim.** The agent who sold you the policy, or if you have a group policy, the administrator who handles claims for your company, can often give a decisive nudge to the insurer.

●**Always put your claim in writing.** Arm yourself with supporting evidence. One of the most common reasons insurers give for rejections is that a bill exceeds regular and customary charges. But some companies use outdated fee schedules or averages that don't apply to your case. Get written estimates from other doctors for the same treatment to prove your point.

Example: One woman who received much less than she expected for a Cesarean delivery called 27 doctors in her area and asked what they charged for a C-section. Only three charged less than her gynecologist, 10 charged more. Faced with these figures, the insurer paid up.

●**Pursue your claim up the company's chain of command.** Keep written notes of every conversation—who you talked to, his/her telephone extension, what was said.

GO THE EXTRA MILE

If the insurer continues to stonewall, seek outside help. *Sources:*

●**States' department of insurance.** Most try to identify and prevent unfair claims practices. Strong ones—like California, New York and Illinois—will even act as a referee between you and your insurance company.

●**Small claims court.** Sue the insurer yourself if the claim does not exceed the maximum recovery amount for small-claims court, usually between $1,000 and $2,500. Rather than spending their time and money to defend themselves against you, the company may well settle.

●**Lawyer.** It isn't hard to find one who will work on a contingency basis if you have a really strong case. You may end up collecting not just the claim amount, but additional sums for economic loss, emotional distress and—if the company has been really unscrupulous—punitive damages for wrongful conduct.*

Example: A client of mine had a $48 gripe against his insurance company, which refused to pay for medicine. After we proved the company had fraudulently changed its basic policy coverage, the jury awarded him $70,000 in compensatory damages—and $4.5 million in punitive damages.

*Group policyholders governed by Employee Retirement and Income Security Act (ERISA) regulations can recover only policy benefits from successful lawsuits.

Whichever routes you take, the important thing is to keep pushing to get the benefits you rightfully deserve. Don't be a victim.

Mistakes When Filing Insurance Claims

● **Failure to accurately calculate losses.** It's hard to believe, but many people can't accurately determine their losses—whether by damage or theft.

Reason: They fail to maintain effective accounting and record-retention procedures to document the losses. It's not uncommon to hear of a situation in which a theft loss amounted to $250,000 but the claimant could substantiate only $100,000 of the loss. It's important to plan ahead with your accountant to determine the best procedures for demonstrating what you own in case you have to make a claim.

● **Overstating the loss.** This is a subtle problem. If a claimant purposely overstates the loss to the point where the insurance company could question his integrity, the latter will take a hard line. Generally, if the claimant takes a fair position, the insurer will still bargain over the loss claim but will be more reasonable.

● **Underestimating the loss.** This sounds like a contradiction of the above, but it's not. Immediately after losses are claimed, the adjuster will ask the claimant for an estimate of the damage, not an accurate, justified number. The insurer requires such a rough estimate, but be wary of providing a number before taking the time to get a reliable estimate. If the adjuster reports a number that's too low and then must go back later to the insurer and restate it much higher, both his credibility and yours are hurt. He looks foolish. Those hurt feelings can make future loss negotiations tricky. So tell the adjuster about any problems you have in coming up with a number.

6

Smart Banking

Your Bank Is Still Ripping You Off

The average American family is paying far more than it should in bank fees, including ATM charges and mortgage interest. *Some of the latest bank rip-offs and how you can avoid them...*

LOAN RIP-OFFS

•**Interest rates.** Two customers walk into a bank and ask for loans. One has a great credit rating and a 20% down payment. The other has an okay credit rating and a 10% down payment. Which customer gets the better deal from the bank? *Neither!* Both get the same quote.

Banks will not offer below-standard rates without some prompting. But they generally will when good customers push.

The best customers have clean credit ratings, ongoing relationships with the lender and adequate collateral. These customers should ask for the loan rate to be lowered by one-half to one percentage point.

On a typical 30-year, $100,000 mortgage, that's a saving of up to $25,000 over the life of the loan.

•**Loan type.** When you're ready to accept the rate offered, tell the loan officer you want to borrow on a *simple-interest, single-payment note* that allows for monthly payments or an *installment note calculated by simple interest*. Do not take the standard front-end loaded installment note that is usually offered.

With a standard installment note, the borrower pays interest on the entire loan amount through the life of the loan—despite the fact that an increasing portion of the loan is paid off over time. With a simple-interest, single-payment note, you pay interest on only the amount of the loan outstanding.

Edward F. Mrkvicka, Jr., former chairman of a national bank and current president of Reliance Enterprises, Inc., a national financial consulting firm, 22115 O'Connell Rd., Marengo, IL 60152. He is author of *Your Bank Is Ripping You Off*. St. Martin's Griffin.

Example: For a $10,000, four-year loan at 10.25% Annual Percentage Rate (APR), you'll save $140 by requesting a simple-interest note.

Also tell the loan officer that you don't want *Credit Life and Disability Insurance* on your loan. This coverage protects the bank's interests—not yours. While not required, such insurance is often slipped into the loan—increasing its cost—without the customer knowing or understanding that he/she could have refused coverage. The premium is then subject to hidden finance charges.

You can get better coverage at less cost from your insurance agent.

FEE RIP-OFFS

•Overdraft checking. With this type of account, if you write a check that exceeds your balance, the bank automatically lends you the money to cover it. But it's not as good as it sounds. The bank lends this money at a high interest rate, and these accounts often carry additional charges, such as transaction fees—even if you pay off the overdraft right away.

Better: Ask to have your checking account *red flagged*. Many banks—particularly small ones—allow such no-cost arrangements, under which customers are called if they overdraw. If the customer can cover the checks that day, the bank waives the overdraft fees.

•Unadvertised account options. Don't assume the checking and savings policies in a bank's literature are the only ones available.

Example: Free low-balance checking accounts often are available for senior citizens, students and the disabled—but only if you ask.

•Bank consolidation. The number of banks continues to fall, from a peak of nearly 15,000 in 1983 to roughly half that today. Less competition is never good for consumers. Large banks generally charge more and provide less than small banks. Whenever two banks merge, they inevitably adopt the fee structure and charges of the more expensive bank.

Better: If you're currently shopping for a new bank, consider a credit union. These institutions typically offer better rates than banks and are less likely to be taken over. Contact the Credit Union National Association (CUNA) to find credit unions in your area that you are eligible to join. 800-358-5710…or *www.cuna.org*.

CREDIT CARD RIP-OFFS

•Disappearing grace periods. Not long ago, credit card users could be relatively confident that if they paid off their bills within 30 days, they wouldn't pay interest. But more credit card companies are doing away with "grace periods" and charging interest from the *moment* of purchase.

Today, the top priority for those not carrying balances should be a grace period, not interest rates or special features.

•Debit card downsides. *Two problems to be aware of…*

•Debit cards withdraw funds from your account immediately.

•Married couples are more likely to incur overdraft fees when using debit cards. Before debit cards were introduced, if both partners wrote big checks on the same day, one could run to the bank with a deposit to cover the shortfall. But today the immediacy of debit cards means that overdrawn is overdrawn.

How to Protect Yourself from Your Banker

Edward F. Mrkvicka, Jr., former chairman of a national bank and current president of Reliance Enterprises, Inc., a national financial consulting firm, 22115 O'Connell Rd., Marengo, IL 60152. He is author of *Your Bank Is Ripping You Off*. St. Martin's Griffin.

Reality: While there are certainly some smart and some honest bankers in the United States, as an industry, bankers have not run their business at all well. *In the past 10 years…*

…on average, more than 100 banks a year have failed. Taxpayers may have to bail out savings and loans to the tune of up to $500 billion or more before it's over. And many individuals have lost all of their life's savings.

…bank insurance reserves dwindled from $18 billion to a deficit of $7 billion before being rebuilt.

Self-defense: Ask questions and look out for your own interests in any dealings with your bank.

COMPARISON SHOP

No matter how convenient your bank may be or how long you've done business there, it's important today to at least call around and see what's available from other banks in the area.

Example: All banks today are trying to increase their earnings through added fees. Just the fees for an average checking account can cost you several hundred dollars annually, net of any interest you may earn on that account. So, it pays to shop around for the bank with the lowest fees.

Bargains: If you qualify as a senior citizen by whatever standards a given bank uses, it will often give you free checking. But most banks don't advertise this. You must ask for it. If your bank doesn't offer free checking, it may pay to switch to another bank.

Ask around, too, to see whether other banks have senior citizen clubs that offer discounts on local restaurant meals, transportation, travel, etc.

WHAT'S REALLY INSURED?

Of course it's comforting to know that your deposits are insured for up to $100,000, but don't make the mistake of thinking that just because there's an FDIC symbol on the door, all transactions with your bank are protected. They're not...and often bank employees don't know (or don't tell you) that.

Safe-deposit box contents, for example, aren't considered deposits and may or may not be insured by the bank.

Any mutual funds that you may have with a bank's broker don't fall under FDIC insurance either.

At best, they're covered by the Securities Investor Protection Corporation (SIPC), which protects brokerage accounts against fraud, but not market declines.

Rule: If a bank tries to sell you anything other than a Certificate of Deposit, which is covered under FDIC protection, find out whether it is insured. What happened in the notorious Charles Keating (Lincoln Savings & Loan) bank failure was that investors had been switched out of CDs and into bank bonds that were not insured.

Don't simply take the word of bank employees. They may have been told that bank products are insured in order to sell them.

Better: Verify the information with the FDIC in your region, the state banking authority or—for banks with "National" in their names—the US Comptroller of the Currency. If investments are not insured and the bank gets into trouble, it could take years to get your money back, if you ever do.

FORM A RELATIONSHIP

It's important for everyone—especially seniors—to get to know their banker by name. When your banker knows you, he/she can be helpful if an emergency arises.

Many banks are now charging $15 to $25 per bounced check, for example, and it can cost even more for overdraft protection. Once you're known, instead of buying expensive overdraft protection, ask to speak to the bookkeeper and request that he/she red flag your account and call you immediately if there's an overdraft. Then, at no cost, you have until the end of the business day to add funds. Again, if your bank won't do this, find one that will.

Don't trust trust departments: If you must deal with a bank trust department, pick a big bank. I have real reservations about using bank trust departments, especially when you don't have enough money to command adequate attention from senior officers. Banks are known more for their mismanagement of trust moneys than for astute investment advice. You can probably do better with a smart trust accountant, trust attorney or trust company.

WHAT TO AVOID

●**ATMs.** Young people may swear by them, but most seniors are not comfortable with automatic teller machines (ATMs). That's fine because it's becoming more and more costly to use the machines and, since they can be a magnet for criminals, elderly people could easily become victimized.

●**Bank-sponsored mutual funds.** Many banks are now pushing to sell mutual funds to depositors. But you should be aware that almost all of what they sell are load funds that carry a sales commission of up to 8%. And most banks offer a very limited universe of funds with only one or two selections in each category. By doing a little research at your library and reading financial publications, you can easily find many well-managed funds with good histories and invest in them directly without paying a sales load.

●**Reverse mortgages.** With so much current emphasis on getting the equity out of your home, more banks can be expected to offer some form of reverse mortgage financing—an annuity-like upside-down mortgage—to seniors. I don't recommend it because essentially you're giving away your home—at least a big share of the equity you've built up over the years—to the bank in order to stay there. Diluting your (and your heirs') hard-earned equity in your home should be a last resort.

For younger seniors with a longer life expectancy, the monthly income from a reverse mortgage probably won't be enough to make much difference and, because the interest compounds over a long period, it becomes a very expensive way to borrow.

Better: Sell your home to your children and let them pay you $300 to $400 a month. Or sell to an outsider under an arrangement that allows you to live there as long as you wish.

Check with your state information office. There are many programs to help with real estate taxes, repairs and maintenance, and assistance for health reasons. These programs may be enough to ensure you don't have to move.

Bank-Failure Loophole

If your bank fails and your deposits exceed $100,000 (the maximum amount insured by the FDIC), you may be able to use the uninsured portion to pay off any outstanding debt to the bank you may have.

Self-defense: Request a "voluntary offset" from the bank's claims agent.

Example: Someone with $120,000 in deposits and a $50,000 bank loan can ask that the $20,000 not covered by the FDIC be used to pay down the loan.

Rationale: You probably won't see the $20,000 for some time, and when you do, you aren't likely to receive the full amount. Meanwhile,

your debt would be reduced by the amount offset, dollar for dollar.

Cody Buck, former senior executive of the FDIC's division of liquidation. He is author of The ABCs of FDIC: How to Save Your Assets from Liquidation. *CoStarr Publications.*

Bank Safe-Deposit Box Trap

In effect, many banks don't insure safe-deposit boxes for theft. If there is insurance, it is very difficult to collect because you can't prove the box's contents. You could have a bank officer sign a safekeeping receipt each time you visit to confirm the contents…but this sacrifices your confidentiality and doesn't guarantee coverage.

Best: A home safe. Models that exceed the fire safety of a bank vault cost less than $250 and losses are covered by your homeowner's insurance. List each item in a policy rider.

Edward F. Mrkvicka, Jr., former chairman of a national bank and current president of Reliance Enterprises, Inc., a national financial consulting firm, 22115 O'Connell Rd., Marengo, IL 60152. He is author of Your Bank Is Ripping You Off. *St. Martin's Griffin.*

Beware of Bank IRAs

Edward F. Mrkvicka, Jr., former chairman of a national bank and current president of Reliance Enterprises, Inc., a national financial consulting firm, 22115 O'Connell Rd., Marengo, IL 60152. He is author of Your Bank Is Ripping You Off. *St. Martin's Griffin.*

Retirement planning: One cannot overstate the importance of it. And…in investigating all of your Individual Retirement Account (IRA) options, I believe you'll find that a bank IRA is one of the least acceptable alternatives.

In fact, a bank IRA could be the most unrewarding investment you ever make.

Some banks advertise how you can "easily" accumulate a million dollars in your IRA.

Unfortunately, a Government Accounting Office study revealed that if inflation continues at its historical pace, your million dollars may be worth, in buying power, only $50,000. In other words, you'll be lucky to get back exactly what you put in.

There are other investments that could return much more for your retirement—even if you have to pay taxes on them.

Problem: Banks like IRAs for one reason and one reason only—they are cheap money for the banks. Bank IRA interest rates are historically one to three percentage points below those of other market IRA vehicles available from brokers and mutual fund families. In later years, when your IRA balance is substantial, that could mean tens of thousands of dollars in interest lost every year.

Bigger problem: The banks' below-market IRA interest rates can be even more unfavorable. Under some plans, the bank also maintains the right to change the basis on which it pays interest, at its own discretion.

The insurance trap: Too many older investors say to me, "Never mind that I may be sacrificing some interest—at least I know that my retirement funds are insured by the full faith and credit of the US government."

For many years investors could have confidence in government insurance, at least up to the maximum insured limit—currently $100,000 (IRA balances in excess of $100,000 are not insured). But in the past 10 years, everything has changed.

We should have learned from the savings-and-loan disaster about the questionable value of government-backed deposit insurance.

Sooner or later there will be failures of major money-center banks—banks that have been getting away with privatizing their profits—and socializing their losses by claiming they're "too big to fail."

As with the savings-and-loan bailout, this means that US taxpayers—you and I—will pay for those bank losses caused by illegal behavior, greed, incompetent regulatory agencies and a Congress that looks the other way.

Don't invest in a bank IRA because of bank insurance that is coming right out of your pocket.

Checkbook Checklist

Your check register is a good record of deposits and spending if you record all transactions in it. Be sure to include date, check number, name and invoice number or date of invoice. *More ideas...*

● **Keep a spare check or two in your wallet.**

● **Paper clip the checkbook on the page you are working.**

● **Write check numbers in the register ahead of time.**

● **Color code in the register. Use red for tax-deductible items.**

● **Round up check amounts to the nearest dollar.**

● **Cut addresses off extra deposit slips for address labels.**

● **Keep a small, thin calculator in your register.**

● **Use black or blue ink. Light colored ink doesn't copy as well.**

● **Keep track of monthly expenses at the back of the book.**

Heloise, whose syndicated column *Hints from Heloise* appears in more than 500 newspapers internationally. She is author of a number of books, including *Heloise: Household Hints for Singles*. Perigee Books.

Beware of Playing The *Float* on Checks

The time between writing a check and having it clear keeps shrinking. Most checks now clear in three business days or less...and mortgage and car payments may go through immediately. *Trap:* If several of your checks reach the bank at the same time, the largest one may be sent through first—hitting you with multiple "insufficient funds" fees if the first check wipes out your balance. *Self-defense:* If your bank offers overdraft protection free or at low cost, sign up. Checks that would otherwise bounce are advanced by the bank or charged to your credit card. Just be sure to pay off your balance immediately. *Also helpful:* Accounts that allow you to transfer money by phone.

Edward F. Mrkvicka, Jr., former chairman of a national bank and current president of Reliance Enterprises, Inc., a national financial consulting firm, 22115 O'Connell Rd., Marengo, IL 60152. He is author of *Your Bank Is Ripping You Off*. St. Martin's Griffin.

More from Ed Mrkvicka...

ATM Self-Defense

Discarding your ATM receipt at the bank may help thieves loot your account. High-tech bandits are using video cameras to observe/record customers punching in ID numbers at teller machines. Then they match it to the account numbers on receipts left behind.

Self-defense: Guard your PIN number... retain receipts to match up against monthly bank statements. If there's a withdrawal discrepancy, report it immediately to the bank.

Save ATM Fees

To avoid ATM surcharges, open an account at a bank that gives rebates when you use the machines. *Example:* USAA Federal Savings, 800-531-2265, will refund up to 10 ATM charges per month. *Alternatives:* Switch to a bank that has many ATMs in your area, and use only that bank's machines...pay with ATM cards at supermarkets—many markets let you take out extra cash with no fee.

Jean Sherman Chatzky, financial writer, *Money*, Rockefeller Center, New York 10020.

Do-Gooder Credit Cards Do Little

So-called affinity cards claim to give a portion of what you charge to a cause in which you believe. Cards are available with tie-ins to environmental and family-oriented organizations. But charities get very little money from your use of the cards. *Example:* If you charged $800 a month for a year—a total of $9,600—on one major bank's do-good card, its tie-in fund would get only $48. *Also:* Affinity cards often carry high interest rates.

Robert McKinley, president and publisher, CardWeb. com, Inc., which closely follows the credit card industry, Frederick, MD.

Cosigner's Trap

To obtain credit for their children, parents often cosign credit cards or other loans for them. But parents should be aware that creditors in some states are not required to notify cosigners when a borrower exceeds a credit limit or falls behind on loan payments. So a cosigning parent can become liable for overdue payments and penalties without ever knowing there is a problem. The parent's credit rating may be harmed as well.

Defense: If you cosign a child's borrowings, monitor payments and monthly statements closely.

Better: Consider having the child cosign your credit card. That way, the child will have access to the credit line and build a credit history while monthly statements come directly to you.

Gerri Detweiler, education adviser of Myvesta.org, a nonprofit personal finance organization.

Dangers of Cosigning A Loan

You will be listed with credit bureaus as responsible for the loan—and your credit could be damaged if payments are missed. Since the amount of the loan appears as your debt, you may find it harder to qualify for a loan of your own. If payment trouble develops, you may not find out until the borrower has defaulted and your credit has been damaged. *Extra danger:* Cosigning on credit cards. Since credit lines may be increased periodically, you may end up being responsible for much more than you planned.

Gerri Detweiler, education adviser of Myvesta.org, a nonprofit personal finance organization.

Credit Card Traps

Credit card balance-transfer traps can make some low-rate offers almost worthless. *Examples:* The low-rate introductory period may start when you open an account, not when the transfer is made—and may end shortly after the transfer is done. Card issuers may charge high fees—up to 4%—for balance transfers that then have a low interest rate. Missing a single payment date on any card—not necessarily the low-rate one—can cause the low-rate card company to increase your rate significantly. Low rates may apply only to transfers—new purchases may still incur high rates.

Also, when you cancel a credit card, be sure it's listed as closed on your credit report. If the report still lists the account as open, your ability to borrow may be reduced. After canceling a card, ask for written verification that it has been canceled. A month later, ask for a copy of your credit report. If the report still shows the account as open, inform the credit bureau and send it a copy of the verification letter showing the account to be closed. By law, credit bureaus must verify disputed information with the source within 30 days.

Gerri Detweiler, education adviser of Myvesta.org, a nonprofit personal finance organization.

Don't Pay Too Much

Nearly three out of four mortgage holders pay too much into escrow accounts—set up by lenders with a borrower's money to pay real estate taxes and home-insurance costs.

Self-defense: Check monthly payments carefully against copies of all tax and insurance bills. If what's due in taxes is less than the funds in escrow—seek a refund immediately.

Bottom line: While you pay monthly, the lender might pay only quarterly—or even annually. Any funds held in escrow until those payments come due are the equivalent of giving the lender a no- or low-interest loan.

Edward F. Mrkvicka, Jr., former chairman of a national bank and current president of Reliance Enterprises, Inc., a national financial consulting firm, 22115 O'Connell Rd., Marengo, IL 60152. He is author of *Your Bank Is Ripping You Off*. St. Martin's Griffin.

Smarter Home Loans

You'll find that when applying for a home-equity loan, home appraisals are almost always lower than the *market-value* appraisal of a home. The bank does this for protection in case of a default on the loan. If you want a larger loan than the original appraisal would allow, there is recourse. Have your home independently appraised—this can usually be done through a real estate agent. Ask for a *Comparative Market Analysis,* which reports on your home in relation to others in your area, and for an estimate of your home's fair market value. Then call the bank with the new information and ask it to reconsider. If the bank is still uncooperative, go to a new bank with your appraisal. The second bank will likely be more flexible than the first because its appraiser won't feel comfortable deviating greatly from the information you provided prior to his appraisal.

Edward F. Mrkvicka, Jr., former chairman of a national bank and current president of Reliance Enterprises, Inc., a national financial consulting firm, 22115 O'Connell Rd., Marengo, IL 60152. He is author of *Your Bank Is Ripping You Off*. St. Martin's Griffin.

Auto Financing

Those who have to take out a five-year car loan in order to afford the payments probably can't afford the car.

Better: A less expensive model that can be paid off in three or four years.

David L. Scott, PhD, professor of accounting and finance, Valdosta State University, GA. He is author of *The Guide to Managing Credit: How to Stretch Your Dollars Through Wise Credit Management*. The Globe Pequot Press.

Internet Banking... Consider This

Internet banks operate without retail outlets and big staffs, so they often offer higher interest rates and lower fees than traditional banks. *But consumers may pay a high price in other ways...*

•**Poor service.** Internet banks are often bad at dealing with problems.

Example: If an improperly recorded deposit causes checks to bounce, it is nearly impossible to set things straight, according to customers with whom I've spoken.

Resolving problems is a hassle at any bank—but when you have a location, you can meet with a real person.

•**Lack of insurance.** Not all Internet "banks" have FDIC insurance, yet some claim they do.

Alternative: Consider a brick-and-mortar bank that also has an Internet presence.

There are several Web sites you can use to research a bank. Both *www.bankrate.com* and *www.gomez.com* focus on E-banks.

Edward F. Mrkvicka, Jr., former chairman of a national bank and current president of Reliance Enterprises, Inc., a national financial consulting firm, 22115 O'Connell Rd., Marengo, IL 60152. He is author of *Your Bank Is Ripping You Off*. St. Martin's Griffin.

7

Stretching Your Dollars

Be Sure You Collect All the Benefits to Which You're Entitled

Don't let ignorance or false pride prevent you from getting all you're entitled to in the way of aid. Some of the benefits may surprise you.

Some benefits are provided on the basis of age alone...others depend on financial need.

AGE-BASED BENEFITS

These benefits are yours simply because you've reached a certain birthday. *Included...*

● **Social Security benefits.** As a general rule, provided you've worked for a certain number of years over your lifetime, you qualify for Social Security benefits starting at age 62... though the benefits are reduced at that age.

Full benefit checks don't begin until your normal retirement age—currently age 65, but it will increase to 67 over the next several years.

Spouses, former spouses and widow(er)s may be entitled to benefits based on the other spouse's (or former spouse's) earnings and may start as early as age 60.

● **Medicare.** Unless you receive Social Security disability benefits for 24 months, your Medicare coverage doesn't start until age 65, even if you elected to begin receiving Social Security benefits at age 62.

Once you turn 65 you're covered under Part A of Medicare (hospital, skilled nursing facility, home health and hospice coverage) if you worked a certain length of time.

To receive Part B of Medicare (doctors' coverage, some home health and other outpatient services), you must pay a monthly premium.

LOCAL BENEFITS

Check local papers for seniors' activities and the minimum age for participation. Also look for discounts and other help. *What you'll find...*

Judith A. Stein, an attorney and executive director of the Center for Medicare Advocacy, Inc. She is president of the National Academy of Elder Law Attorneys.

79

●**Clubs, trips and programs for seniors.** Local governments generally help seniors' groups that meet for social and recreational purposes.

Examples: Daily recreational facilities…bus trips to a wide variety of places…field programs.

●**Senior discounts.** Retailers may offer discounts to seniors of a certain age. Many places provide senior ID cards to those as young as age 50 (for example, members of American Association of Retired Persons) that can be used to cash in on discounts in the area.

●**Help with local transportation.** Cities and counties, in many places, run bus services for seniors.

BENEFITS BASED ON NEED

A number of benefits for seniors can only be obtained if there is a financial need. The eligibility requirements may change from year to year. *Included…*

●**Supplemental Security Income (SSI)** provides income to seniors.

●**Food stamps.** Monthly allotments are available for the purchase of food items. The amount depends on household size and income. *Note:* The right to food stamps is not dependent on age.

●**Meal programs.** Homebound seniors may be entitled to receive daily meal deliveries.

●**Medicare beneficiary programs** provide assistance with premiums, deductibles and copayments.

These Medicare programs are entitled QMB, SLMB, QI-1 and QI-2—depending on the benefits provided. They are limited to those age 65 or older with financial need.

●**Medicaid** pays for medical costs for those age 65 or older who have income and assets below a certain level (which varies by state). It also provides coverage for the blind and disabled, regardless of age.

●**Prescription aid.** In some states, low-income prescription drug programs help those age 65 or older who do not have Medicaid or other insurance to cover drug costs.

●**Property tax relief** lets senior home owners reduce their property tax bill. Rules differ in each locality, but may provide relief of up to 50% of the bill for those age 65 or older with income below a certain amount.

●**Rent subsidies.** As with property tax relief, some localities provide rent assistance for those in need.

●**Home energy assistance** for both renters and home owners gives cash (or makes payments to energy suppliers) in some localities if monthly income is below a threshold amount.

No minimum age: There may not be any minimum age for eligibility for the following…

●**Emergency assistance cash** for food, rent, moving, etc., for those with income below SSI limits.

TO FIND OUT ABOUT BENEFITS

There's an elder network operating in every state that can provide information and assistance. You can tap into this network by contacting your local agency on aging or state department on aging.

Note: If you're investigating benefits for someone else, you can obtain general information without authorization. But if you need to discuss confidential information with a particular governmental agency, you may need authorization from the person you're helping.

●**Departments on Aging.** Every state has some administrative agency or subdivision for the elderly. It may go by a different name in your location—Office of Aging, Commission on Aging, Division of Senior Services, etc. Some state departments have regional offices. This is your first contact point. *This state office can provide…*

●Information about benefits and eligibility requirements.

●Referral services to agencies providing specific types of assistance.

●**Federal resources.** The Social Security Administration can provide information and help on Social Security benefits, Medicare and more. 800-772-1213 or *www.ssa.gov.*

●**The Health Care Financing Administration (HCFA)** also provides information and help with Medicare. 800-633-4227 or *www.medicare.gov.*

●**Access America for Seniors Web site** makes it easier to connect with various federal agencies. *www.seniors.gov.*

- **Administration on Aging** provides information for older Americans about opportunities and services. *www.aoa.dhhs.gov.*

- **Department of Veterans Affairs** provides information about VA programs for veterans and their families. 800-827-1000 or *www.va.gov.*

- **Private seniors organizations.** They can give you information on assistance programs. *These organizations include…*

  - American Association of Retired Persons (AARP) at 800-424-3410 or *www.aarp.org.*

  - Gray Panthers at 800-280-5362.

  - Older Women's League (OWL) at 800-825-3695 or *www.owl-national.org.*

- **The Center for Medicare Advocacy** provides assistance regarding Medicare and health-care rights. 860-456-7790 or *www.medicare advocacy.org.*

- **Other organizations.** The National Academy of Elder Law Attorneys (NAELA) distributes brochures to explain various benefit programs for the elderly. 520-881-4005 or *www.naela.org.*

Frugality Secrets from An Expert

Amy Dacyczyn, author of *The Complete Tightwad Gazette: Promoting Thrift as a Viable Alternative Lifestyle.* Random House. She lives in Leeds, ME, with her husband and their six children.

Frugality is nothing to be ashamed of. Frugal people are just making choices—the trade-offs necessary to reach their financial goals.

Wealth is not how much you earn…it is how much you accumulate. Wealthy people tend to be those who work hard, save and thoughtfully invest money.

Golden rule of penny-pinching: Use materials you have before you spend money on new items. *Here are the best ways to do that, along with my favorite money-saving strategies…*

BEST BARGAINS EVER

- **Toothpaste and dental floss.** Next time you're at the dentist, think about how much toothpaste and floss you could buy for the cost of that filling.

- **Paper and crayons**—they are still the best gifts for any child.

- **Noncable television.** People like to bash TV, but there are plenty of worthwhile programs.

- **Postage stamps.** The sheer volume of material that can be included in a one-ounce letter is amazing—and the post office will carry it thousands of miles for only 34 cents.

And e-mail, of course, is a great bargain for computer owners.

- **Potatoes.** Pound for pound, potatoes offer more nutrients for lower cost than any other food.

My favorite cheap-and-easy meal: Baked potato (cooking in the microwave costs less than the oven) topped with chopped, steamed broccoli and cheese sauce. Sprinkle with bacon bits. I feed my entire family for about $1 because I buy economy-size bags of potatoes and make my own sauce.

Other tasty-but-tightwad topping combinations: Chili and cheese…sour cream and chives…cheese and mushrooms…meat sauce.

FREEBIES

- **Free attractions.** Look in your local paper for museums, gardens, historical buildings, etc. They are often listed in the calendar section. Check the library for *Guide to Free Attractions, USA* and *Guide to Free Campgrounds.*

- **Free information.** The federal government publishes hundreds of free consumer guides, from *College Handbook* to *Understanding Social Security.* For a free catalog of publications, call 888-878-3256…or go to *www.pueblo.gsa.gov.*

- **Free posters.** The US Postal Service sends promotional posters for new stamps to every post office in the country. If you see one you like, ask the postmaster if you can have it when the office is done with it.

Also ask at your video store for outdated movie posters.

- **"Free" health club membership.** See if you can work part-time in exchange for free membership. Many clubs have child-care rooms and are looking for moms to staff them.

●**Freebies from your congressperson.** Elected officials occasionally offer free calendars and other items. If you're planning a trip to Washington, DC, ask your congressional representative for free passes to restricted Senate and House galleries.

IN YOUR CAR

●**Car repairs.** Inquire at a local vocational school—students may need cars to fix. Most schools charge only for paint and parts.

●**Obey the speed limit.** This saves on gasoline, of course, but it also reduces wear on tires, brakes and other car components. And it reduces your risk of costly (and dangerous) accidents and speeding tickets—and the increased insurance premiums that go along with them.

IN THE KITCHEN

●**Save energy when cooking.** When preparing rice or pasta, bring water to a boil…add noodles or rice…bring back to a boil…and turn off the burner. Leave covered for 10 to 20 minutes, stirring occasionally to prevent sticking.

Many other foods can be prepared using residual heat, rather than keeping the burner on the entire time.

●**Watch what you drink.** Tap water is the cheapest thirst quencher. Homemade iced tea costs five cents per eight-ounce glass…Kool-Aid, 13 cents…apple juice, 25 cents.

If you must have a soft drink, a serving from a one-liter bottle costs about 20 cents, versus 30 cents for the same amount from a can.

AROUND THE HOUSE

●**Carpeting.** When replacing wall-to-wall carpeting, cut out sections from under the beds and sofas where the carpet is not worn. Take them to your carpet dealer for binding and use them as area rugs.

Opportunity: Ask your carpet store for old samples, which are often thrown out. Use them in the car, bathroom, doorways or basement.

●**"Free" paint.** Don't throw out old, half-empty cans of paint. Instead mix them together, and use to repaint the basement, garage or tool-shed—someplace where you're not picky about the color.

Caution: Don't use paint from before 1980—it may contain lead. And never mix oil-based paint with latex paint. But you can mix interior paint with exterior…and flat with semigloss.

20 Easy Ways to Save Hard Dollars… Year In…Year Out

Amy Dacyczyn, author of *The Complete Tightwad Gazette: Promoting Thrift as a Viable Alternative Lifestyle.* Random House. She lives in Leeds, ME, with her husband and their six children.

Small changes in your lifestyle can add up to significant savings over the course of a year. *If you adopt just half of these suggestions, you'll save over $1,000 a year…*

●**Switch from a bank to a credit union.** The average checking account now costs $185 a year in service charges to maintain. Credit unions are nonprofit organizations that return surplus funds to members in the form of low-cost services. Larger credit unions offer free checking, low or no annual fees on credit cards and excellent rates on car loans.

Disadvantages: Fewer branch offices, and the branches may not have automatic teller machines. But, remember, not very long ago, we all survived without ATMs.

●**Buy your home heating oil in the summer.** In my area, prices drop 20¢ a gallon during the off-season, so filling a 275-gallon tank in the summer saves $55. If you are a do-it-yourselfer with extra space, you can buy a used second tank, so you'll have two tanks that can be filled in the off-season. Check local laws about installation and inspection of the second tank. You will have to monitor prices for some weeks to get the best deal in your area, but the bottom should hit some time between July and early September.

Caution: Don't wait until November, when prices go back up, to get your first fill-up.

●**Change the oil in your car yourself.**

●**Review your insurance policies.** Take higher deductibles where you can afford them, and eliminate coverage you don't need for your lifestyle.

Examples: Many people past childbearing age are still paying for maternity benefits. Most car insurance policies cover car rental reimbursement when the car is in the shop—but will you use this? Maybe you have a second car or friends who will help out. Are there extra drivers listed on your insurance who no longer live with you? Many homeowners' policies cover furs, jewelry, computers or other items you may not own.

Also, check with your agent to make sure you are getting any discounts you qualify for.

Examples: Nonsmoking on health insurance, alarm systems or safe driving records on car insurance, owning multiple policies with one company.

•**Make your own popcorn.** A family that pops two batches of traditional generic popcorn a week instead of an equivalent amount of microwave popcorn will save $100 in a year. And it can take less time to make popcorn in a hot-air popper than in a microwave.

•**Reduce your smoking by three cigarettes a day.** (Or give up smoking altogether and save even more.)

•**Rent videos instead of going to the movies.** Even better, check them out of the library.

•**Make pizza from scratch instead of having it delivered.**

•**Give personal services rather than store-bought presents.** Offer to garden, clean bathrooms or baby-sit for your friend in the hospital. Bring your hostess potted herbs from your kitchen or a homemade casserole. Give the new graduate "free résumé service" or 100 pages of thesis typing. Fill out change-of-address forms for your friend who just moved. Refinish a chest of drawers for newlyweds. And don't forget to make your own greeting cards.

•**Share a newspaper subscription with your neighbor.** Are you finished with the paper before you leave for work in the morning? Does your neighbor read the paper before supper? Share magazine subscriptions, too. Many public libraries microfilm, then discard magazines every six months. Request the outdated issues be held for you. Raid recycling bins.

•**Hang four loads of laundry a week instead of running the dryer.**

•**Drink four fewer cans of soda per week—saves at least $100 a year.**

•**Tape 10 pieces of music from the radio rather than buying commercially recorded audiotapes.**

•**Cut your family's hair yourself.** A child's haircut costs as much as $8 to $10 every six weeks. An adult haircut at $25 every six weeks adds up to $217 a year. If you learn to trim it yourself you will only need to have a professional job at the hairdresser half the time. This will save you $100.

•**Bake one batch of bread (two loaves) once a week.**

•**Write one good letter a month instead of making an $8 long-distance telephone call.**

•**Use half your usual amount of cleaning and personal care products.** Find the minimum effective level of shampoo, conditioner, laundry detergent, bleach, dishwasher detergent, toothpaste, shaving cream, lotion, perfume, etc. You may find you can make do with less than half your usual amount.

•**Buy articles of clothing from thrift shops and yard sales rather than paying store prices.** This is also a fun way to shop.

•**Barter for one regular service.** Handy with graphics? Arrange to make fliers and do an advertising layout for your massage therapist in return for monthly sessions. Want help cleaning? Offer to take your cleaning person's kids for a weekly activity in return for two hours of housecleaning. Are you an accountant? Trade tax preparation for lawn care or TV repair.

Consider three-party trades to get what you need.

Example: You want ten $10 computer lessons, the computer instructor needs a $100 repair on her car, so you prepare the mechanic's tax return in exchange for fixing the car, in exchange for your lessons.

Be creative!

•**Use dry milk.** A gallon of whole milk costs up to $2.59 per gallon. Dry milk, purchased in the 20-quart store-brand box, costs $1.60 per gallon. Dry milk is 100% fat-free, while whole milk contains 4% fat. By mixing the two kinds of milk, half dry milk and half whole milk, you can make your own 2% milk. If you use a gallon of milk every three days, you will easily save $100 in a year by substituting dry milk in cooking, homemade cocoa mix and in using the half-and-half mixture for drinking.

Secrets of Big-Time Food Bill Savings

Linda Bowman, professional bargain hunter and author of *The More for Your Money* series of guides, including *Free Food...& More* and *Freebies (& More) for Folks Over 50.* Probus Publishing Co.

Most of us have had the thought, "I can't believe I'm paying this much for one bag of stuff," as the supermarket cashier finishes ringing up the "few things" we ran to the store for.

"Did I really buy that much?" we wonder. Usually, we haven't bought that much—just paid too much. Here are some ways to save big on the family food bill...

SUPERMARKET SAVINGS

• **Shop with a list...or you'll spend more than you save.**

• **Clip coupons—and keep them organized.** Don't throw money away with the garbage. Coupons can easily save you $1,000 a year.

Be willing to give up brand loyalty in favor of a meaningful discount. One brand of tomato paste or dish detergent is much like another.

File coupons in envelopes by category—canned goods, cereals, pet foods, paper products, etc. Put coupons you plan to use right away and those with short expiration dates in the front. Take them with you to the store, along with an empty envelope to put coupons in for the items you select, so you don't have to sort them at the checkout counter.

Shop at a supermarket that honors double the value on the face of coupons. You can also increase your savings by combining in-store sales with coupons. Be sure to calculate the per-unit price of products when using coupons.

Example: A six-ounce jar of instant coffee may cost $3.29, or 55¢ an ounce, and a 10-ounce jar $4.99, or 50¢ an ounce. Normally, the larger size is the better buy. But with a 75¢ coupon, at a double-coupon store, the six-ounce jar costs $1.79, or 30¢ an ounce, while the 10-ounce jar is $3.49, or 35¢ an ounce.

• **Companion product offers.** Companies and supermarkets often issue coupons for a free item, with the purchase of a companion item.

Examples: A free gallon of milk with the purchase of a breakfast cereal...a free box of pasta with the purchase of spaghetti sauce.

• **Refund and rebate offers.** You may need to clip UPC symbols or save register receipts as "proof of purchase" to send for these offers. They are worth the trouble—and can be very lucrative, whether you get a cash rebate, additional coupons or free products.

• **Senior discounts.** Many large chain stores and some independent markets issue senior discount cards that allow cashiers to subtract as much as 5% to 10% off the final bill.

• **Generic brands.** Not only are they here to stay, they are growing and growing. Generics can provide substantial savings, especially on grooming products, cereals and canned goods.

• **Track savings.** Most supermarkets total the amount saved with coupons at the bottom of the register receipt. You can deposit monthly savings from coupons, refunds, etc., in an account earmarked toward a goal.

SUPERMARKET ALTERNATIVES

• **Join a wholesale or warehouse shopping club.** These huge operations are in metropolitan and suburban areas nationwide. Shopping is a no-frills enterprise, and products must often be purchased in bulk or large sizes. Brand selection may be limited and may change at any given time. But savings can be excellent. *Key:* Know your prices. Some warehouse club prices are not significantly better than prices at the discounters.

• **Shop at farmers' markets,** where vegetables and fruits are fresher, tastier and cheaper. Buy in bulk in-season, then can or preserve.

• **Shop at bakery outlets and "thrift stores."** Thrift stores are one-brand outlets for companies such as Entenmann's, Pepperidge Farm, Arnold's Bakery, Sunbeam Bread and

Wonder Bread/Hostess. Prices run 30% to 50% off retail for day-old goods.

●**Food co-ops and buying clubs.** Consumer cooperatives are run by members and usually buy food in bulk and then repackage it for buyers. Members can save 15% to 50% on most items, because brokers, middlemen and costly packaging are eliminated from the exchange.

●**Do it yourself.** Grow a vegetable garden, make your own frozen dinners from leftovers.

RESTAURANT SAVINGS

●**Happy hour buffets.** Between 4 pm and 6 pm, for the price of a drink—not necessarily alcoholic—many restaurants provide free buffets. If you don't mind eating early, many people find these feasts to be filling, fun dinners and a change in daily routine.

●**Early bird specials.** Many restaurants offer much lower prices for those who order dinner between 4 pm and 6 pm. You get the same food as on the dinner menu, often with dessert and beverage included, for less than you'd pay for the entrée alone during peak hours. To find specials, check local newspapers or call the restaurants that you are interested in.

●**Senior menus.** Some restaurants, particularly large chains, have senior menus, which offer smaller portions at lower prices. Carry your identification.

●**Two-for-one or free item coupons.** Check newspapers and circulars for coupons from area restaurants for "buy one entrée, get the second of equal or lesser value free" or "free wine or dessert with entrée" offers.

●**Restaurant discount books.**

Examples: Entertainment Publications publishes regional guides, with about 200 coupons for 2-for-1 meals and discounts at restaurants, fast-food chains and specialty shops. 2125 Butterfield Dr., Troy, MI 48084, 248-637-8400. The Dinner on Us Club qualifies you for 2-for-1 or other discounts at member restaurants nationwide. 300 W. Schrock Rd., Westerville, OH 43081. 800-346-3241.

INVEST IN SAVINGS

Other companies publish local or regional discount books as well. These can be a wise investment if you like to dine out a lot—but shop around. Prices and services vary substantially.

Key: Make sure the book contains enough discounts you will really use to pay for itself.

Saving Money With Coupons

Linda Bowman, professional bargain hunter and author of *The More for Your Money* series of guides, including *Free Food…& More* and *Freebies (& More) for Folks Over 50*. Probus Publishing Co.

Most of us pay more than we should for groceries, household products and other goods and services. The biggest mistake we make is failing to take full advantage of cents-off coupons, refund offers, two-for-one deals and other money-saving offers. Compared with the billions of coupons issued every year, not that many are actually redeemed.

Reasons: Many shoppers are too embarrassed to present coupons to checkout clerks. Others are not aware or interested in the available deals, or they feel that clipping coupons is too time-consuming.

Today, however, more consumers are looking to cut weekly costs and stay on a budget. There are several ways to clip coupons and save up to 25% on your supermarket bill. *How I do it…*

●**Set up a system.** Spend a few minutes each week looking over newspaper inserts and other likely sources of coupons. Clip the ones you think you might use and toss them into a shoe box, then separate them by category. Mark each grouping of coupons with its own labeled note card. Be as general or as specific as you like with your categories.

Just prior to each trip to the grocery store, review your shopping list. Transfer the coupons you plan to use from the storage box to an envelope labeled "unused." Take this envelope and a second, empty one (labeled "used") along to the store. As you toss each item on your list into your shopping cart, transfer its coupon from the first envelope to the second.

●**Be choosy.** Coupons should be used to buy only two types of products—those you use regularly and those you'd like to try. Don't let coupons entice you to buy products you neither need nor truly want. Don't be trapped by brand loyalty. Buy whatever brand you have coupons for.

●**Accumulate as many coupons as possible.** Today coupons are available from a wide variety of sources, including product labels and cartons, supermarket ads, inserts in your Sunday newspaper and displays placed along supermarket shelves. Coupons may also be distributed directly through the mail, on airline flights and at movie theaters.

●**Save unused coupons.** Take them along to the supermarket. *Reason:* Some markets maintain informal coupon-exchange bins where customers can exchange coupons they don't want for those they do.

●**Join a coupon-exchange club.** There are several large clubs to choose from, all offering the same basic service.

How they work: Upon joining, members fill out a form specifying which products they use. Periodically, members mail in coupons they don't need…and the club mails back coupons they do.

●**Shop at "coupon-friendly" supermarkets.** Some markets accept coupons only grudgingly. Others not only accept them, but will give you twice their face value.

●**Use coupons in conjunction with other savings offers.** When reading through your local newspaper's supermarket ads, watch for "double plays"—items discounted by both coupons and special sale prices.

Even better: Triple plays. These occur when prices are reduced not only by coupons and specials, but also by a mail-in refund offer.

To keep track of the thousands of refunds being offered at any given time, there are refunding newsletters. They not only list all the offers, but also detail the often Byzantine regulations governing how to obtain the refunds.

My favorite: Refundle Bundle, Box 140, Centuck Station, Yonkers, NY 10710.

●**Bank your savings.** Because coupons net you only a few dollars each time you shop, it's easy to squander the money saved by using them. *Solution:* Open a savings account specifically for your coupon savings. Decide on a particular item to save for. Don't dip into the account until you've accumulated enough to make the purchase.

Wintertime Money Savers

Andy Dappen, author of *Cheap Tricks: 100s of Ways You Can Save 1000s of Dollars*. Brier Books.

Winter is the season of higher electricity and gas bills, car maintenance and repair bills, bills for cold and flu medications and so on. But there are several ways that you can cut down on expenses without sacrificing great comfort.

AVOID COSTLY CAR REPAIRS

●**Keep your gas free of water.** The most frequent problems mechanics see in winter are caused by water in the gas. To prevent problems, add a drier (such as Prestone Gas-Drier or Heet) to your gas every few fill-ups.

●**Check your radiator fluid and the condition of the radiator hoses.** If the fluid is low, add a 50/50 mixture of antifreeze and water. In the coldest parts of the country or when an extreme cold snap strikes, you may want to alter this by using more antifreeze. *Best:* Use a mixture of 70% antifreeze and 30% water. Muddy-looking fluid should be changed. Make sure that the rubber hoses leading from the radiator to the engine are not cracked, brittle, bulging or mushy when they are squeezed.

●**Keep your battery terminals clean to avoid starting problems (and costly towing bills).** Clean the battery terminals occasionally with baking soda and then reduce the corrosion problem by smearing them with a thin coating of petroleum jelly.

●**Promptly repair any nicks in your windshield.** Stop those smaller than a quarter from spawning spider legs and ruining the windshield by covering them on both sides with transparent tape (duct tape works too). Then get the car to a windshield-repair specialist. Cost for a nick ranges from $30 to $50, compared with the $300 to over $600 it can cost to replace the whole windshield.

●**Check tire inflation every few weeks with an accurate gauge.** Changes in temperature alter tire pressure, and under-inflation increases tire wear and gas consumption by as much as 5%. *Important:* Check the pressure while tires are cold. Know how many pounds of pressure they require. Then check them again at the gas station (after they've warmed from being driven on) and add the pounds of pressure that were needed when they were cold.

SAVE ON HEATING

●**Put on an extra sweater and modify your heating habits.** Keep the daytime thermostat at 65 degrees Fahrenheit (rather than 70) and the nighttime temperature at 55 degrees Fahrenheit (rather than 60 or 65). This can reduce your heating bill 15% or more. And turn down the heat when you leave to run errands.

●**Keep fireplace dampers closed when not in use.** Install glass fireplace doors. Then heat won't escape through the chimney.

●**Have your home's insulation checked by your utility company.** Many utilities perform this inspection service free or for a nominal fee. Make sure your home's insulation meets the US Department of Energy's recommendations.

●**Wrap fiberglass insulation around heating ducts and hot water pipes in basement,** attic and crawl space. Putting 2½ inches of insulation around these ducts and pipes will pay for itself in one season.

SAVE ON LIGHTING

●**Replace incandescent lights with fluorescent lights in areas that need light for hours each day.** Today's fluorescent tubes produce warmer hues that won't make your home feel like a factory, and they're three to four times more efficient. If you don't want to install the tubes, use compact fluorescent bulbs. They screw into standard sockets.

●**Use outdoor light fixtures that turn on and off by means of built-in heat/motion detectors and timers.** They're far more economical than those that burn nonstop.

●**Don't turn lights on and off frequently.** Turning the lights out every time you leave the room for a few minutes may seem like it's doing good, but it shortens the life of the bulbs. So don't turn out the light unless leaving for more than a few minutes.

GRANDMA'S REMEDIES

●**Get an annual flu shot if you're 65 or older or suffer from cardiac or respiratory problems.** It's cheap insurance against the major problems a flu can precipitate.

●**Have prescriptions filled at a discount drugstore.** It is much cheaper than using your hospital's pharmacy.

MISCELLANEOUS MONEY SAVERS

●**Freeze your credit.** This is a good idea any time of year, but works especially well around the holiday season. Put your credit cards in a bowl of water and place them in the freezer. It sounds crazy, but by the time the ice melts enough to retrieve the cards, the urge to buy may have passed. And writing checks or paying cash for items forces you to do a "reality check" on how much you really have to spend.

●**Put rubber half-soles on the bottom of your shoes.** In damp or wet weather, the leather soles of your shoes are constantly absorbing water, which slowly damages the leather and reshapes the shoe. Half-soles cost $12 to $15 and add years of life to your shoes. *Also:* Alternate the shoes you wear each day. Having a day to dry and air between uses greatly extends shoe life.

Big, Big Money to Be Saved by Making the Most of Rebates

Tim Duffy, private legal investigator in Covina, CA, who works on product liability and advertising practices cases. His Web site, *www.timduffy.com*, features 50 rebate links as well as consumer stories and alerts. He is a former consultant to the US Department of Agriculture's Division of Weights and Measurement Standards on matters of consumer fraud.

Only 8% of the people who buy products that offer cash rebates ever take advantage of them. That leaves stores and manufacturers sitting on millions of dollars they were prepared to hand out. Here's how to make the most of rebate offers…

●**Keep an eye on the deadlines.** Before you buy a product for its rebate, search the small print on the packaging, in the rebate certificate and in ads for the rebate's expiration date.

Helpful: Check one of the many Internet resources available that list manufacturer rebates and deadlines, including…

●*www.rebateplace.com* for computer-related manufacturer rebates.

●*www.freakyfreddies.com/rebate.htm* and *www.mycoupons.com,* which offer details on coupon and rebate offers.

If you're considering a specific product rebate, also check for details on that company's Web page.

Another good source is *Refunding Makes Cents,* Box 969, Bountiful, UT 84011 *(www. refundcents.com).* It lists hundreds of major manufacturer rebates, contact addresses, qualifications and deadlines.

●**Shop on Sundays.** Many stores offer rebates on products only while supplies last. Some stores even purposefully keep low supplies of products that have the best rebate offers. But nearly all stores first announce their rebate offers in local Sunday newspaper ads. Once you've circled the items you want, shop early that day.

Trap: Stores that offer rain checks on their rebates often won't offer extensions on products with manufacturer rebates.

●**Shop at stores that brag about their low prices.** Many of these stores have underutilized policies that guarantee instant rebates if you find their products sold for less elsewhere.

Examples: Three large office-supply chains —Office Depot, Office Max and Staples—back their low-price guarantees. If you find a lower price advertised locally on their merchandise, they will match that price. Office Depot and Office Max may also offer a rebate of up to $55. (The exact amount varies with the difference between the prices.) Check with individual stores for their requirements.

Once you confirm a store offers such a guarantee—and you've decided on what you want —call a few other local retailers or drop in to compare prices. If their price is even $1 less

than the store with the rebate guarantee, pick up a store ad or flyer that shows the lower price. Or ask the store to write down the price on its stationery or fax a written quote to you as proof of the lower price.

●**Hold the store accountable if a manufacturer fails to pay up.** If a rebate check has not arrived within the time stated in the rebate—usually six to eight weeks—and you followed the rebate's rules, politely ask the store manager for the cash amount. Or call the store's customer service line.

A recent court case in Palm Springs, California, decided that a major retail chain that had advertised a manufacturer's rebate was responsible for the rebate amount—plus damages— when the consumer complained because he had not received it more than two months after the promised date.

Important: You may be asked to provide copies of the original materials you mailed in to claim the cash offer.

Avoid firms that sell rebate offers. Most of these offers are scams. They are for products that too few want…the offers have expired or involve hidden charges, such as excessive shipping costs…or they duplicate information in coupons mailed for free by the millions.

Guerrilla Shopper's Guide To Outlet Malls

Elysa Lazar, author of *Outlet Shopper's Guide.* Lazar Media. Her Web site, *www.lazarshopping.com,* includes a database of factory outlets nationwide and mail-order companies.

Hundreds of factory-outlet stores have popped up around the country—all claiming to offer great bargains.

Careful…many of those bargains can be buried under loads of inferior merchandise.

Here's how to avoid the big traps and how to find the best deals…

●**Order coupons to maximize savings.** *With very little effort, you can cut your bill at outlet stores by an extra 25%...*

•Visit *www.outletbound.com* before you shop, and request a free VIP Voucher. It is redeemable for coupons or special offers worth hundreds of dollars at more than 200 participating outlet centers nationwide. The site also lets you search outlets by location, store, brand or product category.

•Request a coupon book from the store manager. These books are presented to members of bus tours, not to individuals. But the store will usually let you have a coupon book as a gesture of goodwill. Another place to find these books is at an outlet center's information desk or management office.

●Ask for "early markdowns." Most stores will give you the sale prices on any items you're buying that will go on sale within the next two weeks. Ask the store what its policy is.

●Sign up for the store's mailing list. You will receive advance notices of special sales, as well as vouchers for 5% to 15% off.

My favorite outlet-store mailing lists: Donna Karan...Joan & David.

●Ask for a "volume discount" from store managers if you're buying a large amount of merchandise at once.

●**Beware of items that were never sold in retail stores.** Many popular stores create lower-priced lines, with the same brand name and style, and sell them through their outlet stores.

Examples: I've seen outlet coats and sweaters with plastic buttons instead of the leather ones on the retail versions. Other garments lack quality work, such as reinforced stitching around the sleeves.

How to spot the difference: Most inferior made-for-outlet merchandise has "factory store" stamped on its label or tag. Items from the designer's retail stores will have labels that are sliced in half or are marked with ink. When in doubt, ask a salesperson.

●**Give clothing the quality test before buying.** I perform a wrinkle test on every garment I buy. I grab a fistful of the fabric, squeeze it, then release. Except for linen, the item should retain its shape and wrinkle very little.

Many outlet stores post charts that decode the flaws in the merchandise. *But you can do your own quick check...*

Bath towels: Are the hems even? Are the stitches near the borders tight?

Belts: Does it say "full-grain" leather? Full-grain is almost twice as thick as "split-grain" leather, which is brittle and wears out quickly.

Dress shirts: Turn the shirts inside out to see if the lining at the collar and armholes is sewn well. Pay more for 100% two-ply cotton. It stands up much better to repeated washings than polyester blends.

T-shirts: Is there strong, close stitching around the neck, shoulder seams and armholes? If not, the shirt will lose its shape quickly.

●**Consider items that fail to meet manufacturers' standards.** These are marked off by up to 70%. The items that are worth buying are labeled "irregular." They have minute flaws, such as crooked waistband seams or missing buttons.

Usually not worthwhile: Clothes that are labeled "seconds." They typically have serious flaws, such as stains or seams that pull. Clothes made of 100% silk rarely hold their color or shape more than one season.

●**Ask about the store's refund and exchange policy.** They vary greatly, especially during the holidays.

Before you buy, find out if you can return outlet items through the mail...or to full-price retail stores. *Examples...*

●Ann Taylor outlets let you return items to their full-price branches.

●Levi's outlets will take back an irregular garment—even after you've washed it.

Self-defense: Save the tags. If you purchase an "all-sales-are-final" item and then discover you want to return it, look for a defect. If the garment wasn't specifically marked imperfect, you can bargain to get a refund.

Or find a substitute garment in the store that costs a bit more. Ask the manager if you can use your "final sale" purchase as partial payment for the new one you chose.

●**Don't assume outlet stores have the lowest prices.** Many stores mix in full-price items with discount merchandise. So—an item on sale at the company's retail store can be priced less than in the outlet. Research prices at retail stores. Then look to pay at least 25% less for the same item at the outlet store.

Also, ignore the "suggested retail price" listed on the merchandise tag at outlets. It is usually inflated to make the saving look big.

Focus on quality rather than the discount. If you don't love a garment, you won't wear it, no matter how much you've saved.

Formula: Before I buy, I ask myself a simple question—*If the item was full price at the retail store, would I still buy it?* If I hesitate when answering, I put it back.

•**Shop from home or online before making the trip to the outlet.** Some stores allow you to make purchases over the phone with a credit card if you describe what you're looking for. Others offer a catalog of their outlet merchandise.

Resource: OutletsOnline has a complete listing of names, locations and phone numbers of outlet centers and their stores in the US by state. It indicates which ones will let you shop online. *www.outletsonline.com.*

Bargaining Secrets at Flea Markets, Tag Sales And Antique Shows

Susan Dresner, president, Ways & Means, wardrobe-management and retail consulting firm, New York. She has been dubbed "The Blackbelt Shopper" by *Money* magazine.

B ringing home bargains from flea markets, antique shows and yard sales is very satisfying, but negotiating prices can be intimidating for many people.

Vendors, on the other hand, expect haggling. It is a time-honored tradition in markets throughout the world. Prices are padded for haggling. I find bargaining a lot of fun—a dance of wills and knowledge.

Using these strategies will help you feel more in control during the trading process.

BARGAINING BASICS

•**Make a quick circuit of the area to see if anything is of interest,** no matter the price. If nothing "tugs at your heart," leave. There will always be another opportunity with a better payoff for your time and money.

•**Calculate your price.** If you spot a *must-have,* mentally calculate the most that you would be willing to pay to acquire it. Consider the item's value in the real world...what you think the vendor will want for it...and its value to you.

Scenarios: You spot a battered World War II medal. In better shape, it might go for $50, but the way it has been just tossed in a pile of costume jewelry, the seller might accept $10. You decide you would love it for your collection even if you had to spend $15.

If you do not know an object's worth: Compare prices around the market for similar pieces...or bid at another time, after you have done some research.

•**Engage the vendor.** First, hang around the vendor's stall to watch how the vendor operates. Does he/she set firm prices? How far does he budge from his asking price? Is he pleasant? Knowledgeable? Or scattered and careless?

Once you have sized up the situation, eye the object you want. Pick it up. Examine it carefully for defects. Look for a manufacturer's mark, which makes it more desirable, etc. The vendor will notice your interest, and the courtship game begins.

THE DIALOGUE OF TRADE

For those embarrassed or intimidated by the thought of bargaining, here's how a typical bargaining session progresses. *Use it as a basic script to guide you through the process...*

You make eye contact with the vendor and eye the object to acknowledge you are interested in a deal.

How much? you ask casually. He responds firmly with a dollar amount. You examine the object again, taking your time.

If you decide to continue, make a counteroffer—usually one-half to one-third lower than the initial price. Say hesitantly, *I don't know. I don't really need it. How about $____?*

The vendor might communicate *nothing doing* by shaking his head or muttering something like, *It's worth more to me to just cart it away.*

If the vendor appears unwilling to play (he walks off or doesn't respond), move on.

If, on the other hand, he studies you and/or the item and maybe relates a tale about it, you might then ask, *What's your best price?*

For good measure, suggest that you may sell it to someone else. Doing so drives home the point that you need a competitive price. At this juncture, you rejoin with, *My absolute ceiling figure is $____!* Choose a number that is just a bit lower than your real limit...or wait for the vendor's final offer.

CLOSURE

While the bargaining process might seem confrontational, closure should be a win-win situation.

Once you agree on a price, handshakes, a joke or two and smiles all around are in order. As the vendor wraps your prize, tell him how much you love the object and what a treasure trove his stall is. Along with your cash, this cements the deal and opens the door for future trading.

BARGAINING SAVVY

Not all outdoor markets are the same. Modify your tactics for where you are and what is being sold.

●**Roadside flea market.** A regularly held market where anybody can sell anything— soap, household gadgets, handmade items, baked goods, old books, etc.

Prices are marked, but bargaining is expected. If you buy two or more things from a dealer, always get a special deal.

Make sure you want what you buy and are not just swept up in the "high" of trading. This year's prize can land in your garage sale next season.

●**Outdoor antique show.** For serious collectors of old postcards, quilts, antique furniture, etc. Trade publications, which can often be found in antique stores, and Web sites, such as *www.openair.org* or *www.collectors.org*, post details about these fairs.

Arrive before the show opens (admission fees may be higher at that time) when antique dealers are searching for finds.

●**Estate sales.** The contents of an upscale property must be disbanded. The sales are often professionally run. Find out about them from local newspapers or roadside signs.

Offerings can range from antiques and rugs to linens and kitchen items. My best deals have come from these.

Example: A green-painted armchair, for which I paid $25, turned out to be a 19th-century mahogany piece worth $800 once the finish had been restored and the seat re-covered.

Prices are marked, but negotiations are always in order. At the end of the tag sale or flea market, things fly out at unbelievable bargains.

●**Garage sales/yard sales.** Basically offer other people's "junk." Chances to mine diamonds in the rough improve when you confine yourself to nicer neighborhoods.

Heirlooms picked up for a song can be sought-after antiques...and throwaway doodads can be transformed into treasures for your home with some imagination.

Much Shrewder Car Buying

No matter what car price you have negotiated, a salesperson typically will make at least three more attempts to raise the price.

He/she will tell you that the manager won't approve the deal—but in reality he won't talk with the manager until he has tried to bump up the price several times. *Self-defense...*

●**Before shopping,** use the Internet to find the "true" best price for the car you are considering at Web sites such as *www.carsdirect.com* and *www.kbb.com.*

●**Use prices from one dealer** (or the Internet) to work against the others. This improves your chances of getting the best deal.

●**Not happy?** Leave your number and walk out. Many salespeople will call within 24 hours to match the price quoted by the competition.

David Solomon, president, Nutz & Boltz, automotive information membership organization, Box 123, Butler, MD 21023. *www.motorminute.com.*

How to Cut the Cost Of Car Insurance

Jack Gillis, director of public affairs at the Consumer Federation of America, 1424 16 St. NW, Washington, DC 20036. He is author of *The Car Book*. HarperCollins.

Despite declining auto insurance rates, 75% of car owners haven't changed their insurance policies—or even inquired about doing so—within the last five years.

How can you pay less for your insurance coverage...

• **Compare policy rates on the Web.** This process takes about a half hour. First look at the sample rates charged by all insurers that do business in your state.

• *www.insure.com* provides a link to every state insurance department. At the home page, enter your state in the box labeled "insurance in your state."

Once you have a benchmark rate, visit a site that can locate policies with the lowest rates.

• Insweb *(www.insweb.com)* and Quicken Insurance *(www.insuremarket.com)*. You type in the information about your driving history. Then these Web sites sift through the insurance companies in their databases to find the ones that have the lowest prices. These services are free.

• **Shop aggressively every two years.** Different insurers target certain types of drivers at different times and then offer lower rates based on how closely you fit their preferred "top tier" profiles.

You're a candidate for a lower rate whenever...

• Points are removed from your license.

• One of your cars is removed from your policy.

• Your kids no longer drive your car.

• Your car is no longer used for commuting.

• **Maximize your policy's discounts.** Discounts can cut your premium in half. Most insurers offer as many as 20 different discounts. Most don't tell you about all of them unless you specifically ask. *Helpful...*

• Air bags

• Antilock brakes

• Antitheft devices

• Car-pool drivers

• Graduates of driver-training courses

• Low mileage

• Multiple policies

• No accident in three years

• Nonsmokers

• Older drivers who don't drive at night

• **Ask groups if they offer low-rate policies.** More insurers now offer organizations group policies that have discounted rates for members.

Examples: Retirement organizations, alumni associations, credit unions...and some credit card issuers, too.

• **Eliminate unnecessary coverage.** Increasing your monthly deductible from $200 to $500 could reduce your collision and comprehensive premiums by as much as 30%.

Consider eliminating collision and comprehensive coverage if your car is paid off...more than four years old...or worth less than $4,000.

To research car values: National Automobile Dealers Association *(www.NADA.com)*...or Kelley Blue Book *(www.kbb.com)*.

• **Buy a less desirable—or safer—car.** Buying a model that is a favorite with thieves or statistically in frequent accidents can send your premiums sky-high.

For cars with low theft rates: The National Insurance Crime Bureau *(www.NICB.com)*.

For cars with the highest safety ratings: Insurance Institute for Highway Safety *(www. highwaysafety.org)*.

Car Buying Trap

Used fleet and rental cars are rarely good bargains for personal transportation. While these cars are maintained by the fleet or rental-service garage, only the *normal* service maintenance schedule is followed—even though the cars experience severe usage and should receive extra maintenance. *Result:* They are more likely to develop mechanical problems than used cars purchased from individuals. *Self-defense:* Ask to see documents of previous ownership before buying a used car. Have your mechanic check for neglect, abuse, odometer rollback or flood damage.

David Solomon, president, Nutz & Boltz, automotive information membership organization, Box 123, Butler, MD 21023. *www.motorminute.com.*

Slash New-Car Costs

Car buyers can save hundreds of dollars by *factory-ordering* a car. *Reasons:* You pay only for options you want…and can negotiate with multiple dealers for *precisely* the same car. *Downside:* Delivery may take six weeks or longer…and if a major incentive is due to expire before you take delivery, the deal may not be extended. *To get the best deal:* Determine the precise model, options, etc. that you want …research prices at such free Web sites as Kelley Blue Book *(www.kbb.com)* and Edmunds *(www.edmunds.com)*…then check the average transaction price at *www.AutoAdvisor.com.* Use the lowest Internet price as leverage with local dealers.

Ashly Knapp, CEO of AutoAdvisor.com, nationwide vehicle buying and consulting service.

Free or Almost Free Health Care

Matthew Lesko, a syndicated columnist based in Kensington, MD, who specializes in advice on receiving free services. He is author of *Free Health Care!* Information USA. His Web site is *www.lesko.com.*

There are many ways to get free or low-cost checkups…vaccinations…drugs… even surgery and dental care.

To receive this care, it's not necessary to be unemployed, elderly or in a low-income bracket. Nor is it essential to have some rare disease. In many cases, all that's required is the willingness to do a little detective work on the phone or on the Internet…

●**Visit a government health clinic.** Free checkups, vaccinations and other kinds of care are offered at clinics operated by state and municipal governments. Some clinics provide free prenatal and well-child care, too.

More information: Call your state public health department. The number should be listed in your phone book's "blue pages." Or call your state medical association.

Hint: Bring along a book or magazine. Government health clinics are busy—and noisy—places and they don't make appointments. Expect to spend more time than usual in the waiting room.

●**Get free medications.** Most pharmaceutical manufacturers have programs that provide medicine for free. These are often called "indigent programs." In fact, however, the income requirements are often quite lenient. People with an annual household income of up to $45,000 are sometimes eligible.

The request for the medication must come from the patient's doctor.

More information: Visit the Web site of the Pharmaceutical Research and Manufacturers of America at *www.phrma.org/patients.* The site lists companies that provide free medication, types of medication available and information about applying.

●**Get care at a dental school.** There are 53 dental schools in the US. All operate clinics that provide basic services at great savings. That includes checkups, cleaning, X rays and fillings.

More advanced services such as fitting bridges, dentures and implants may also be available.

Student dentists do the work but are closely supervised by their professors.

Bonus: Care may be free for conditions the professors are studying.

More information: To locate a nearby dental school, visit the American Dental Association Web site at *www.ada.org.* Click on "Education" and follow the links. Or call local universities and ask if they have dental schools.

●**Join a clinical study.** The National Institutes of Health (NIH) spends billions of dollars annually to study cutting-edge treatments for every imaginable ailment. Physicians conducting these studies always need patients to participate.

The NIH conducts some studies at its Clinical Center in Bethesda, Maryland. But most are conducted at academic medical centers across the country.

Important: Some NIH studies compare the effectiveness of new treatments with placebos and/or standard treatment. Participants are assigned randomly to study groups and they cannot choose the treatment they will receive.

More information: Visit the NIH Web site at *www.clinicaltrials.gov*. It lists studies by condition, explains requirements for joining and identifies researchers to contact.

If you lack access to the Internet, call the NIH Clinical Center at 800-411-1222.

• **Get a free "second opinion."** The proliferation of Web sites devoted to health and medicine makes it easy to learn about virtually any condition. *Some reliable sites...*

• MayoClinic.com, the site of the Mayo Clinic *(www.mayohealth.org)*.

• CBS Health Watch, the consumer health Web site maintained by Medscape, a comprehensive site for physicians *(www.cbshealthwatch.com)*.

• Intelihealth, featuring Harvard Medical School's consumer health information *(www.inteli health.com)*.

Another option: For nearly every condition, there's an organization and/or government agency that provides printed material for no more than the cost of a stamped, self-addressed envelope.

More information: Contact the National Health Information Center in Washington, DC. *www.nhic.org*. 800-336-4797. It will direct you to the appropriate organization for your condition.

8

Secrets of Living Longer and Better

It's Important to Take Charge of Old Age Now

It's no longer news that more Americans are living longer—the 75-plus and 85-plus age groups are the fastest growing segments of the US population. But for the first time, we can benefit from studies that tell us not only who is living longer, but why—and what we can do to enrich and lengthen our lives.

Research consistently shows that there is more to healthful aging than just staying physically fit. Maintaining strong social ties plays an essential role. And a third factor, less frequently discussed, is also important…a sense of personal purpose. *Bottom line:* People who lead purposeful lives live longer than those who do not.

PHYSICAL HEALTH: BASIC LIFE-EXTENDERS

•**Eliminate tobacco,** regardless of your present age and health status.

•**Drink alcohol in moderation,** if at all. If you are one of the nation's 10 million alcoholics, get help. There are very, very few elderly alcoholics.

•**Lower the amount of fat in your diet.** Most Americans get up to 40% of their calories from fat. *Better:* 10% to 20%.

•**Mediate the effects of stress with exercise and other techniques.**

•**Exercise for a half-hour daily, five days a week.** Choose a solid cardiopulmonary program. Fast walking is inexpensive and effective.

Caution: Golf is not recommended. It is not an aerobic exercise, and can be stressful if combined with business.

MENTAL HEALTH AND ABILITIES

Contrary to popular belief (and barring disease), intelligence does not decline with age.

Robert N. Butler, MD, chairman of the department of geriatrics at Mount Sinai School of Medicine, Mount Sinai Hospital, New York. He is coauthor of *Aging and Mental Health.* Macmillan.

While reaction speed does slow, some abilities such as judgment, accuracy and general knowledge may actually increase as learning continues. *Important:* Ongoing stimulation.

In terms of human development, one of the essential tasks of old age is to find ways to understand and use the lessons of one's lifetime. This entails learning to apportion one's strengths and resources, and to adapt to changes and losses as they occur.

Key: People must continue to adapt to stay healthy, both mentally and physically. Failure to adapt to changing circumstances can result in physical or mental illness at any age.

A comprehensive Seattle study found wide variation in intellectual changes among individuals as they aged. A large number showed little decline, even in their 80s. *What they had in common:* These people had no cardiovascular disease, were not poor, were actively involved in life...and their attitudes and behavior were already flexible in midlife, and remained so.

Expect some emotional changes with aging. *Most common:* Family authority roles begin to reverse, usually in the mid-50s. Women tend to grow more active and assertive, while men tend to become more nurturing. This pattern occurs in many cultures, and should be supported, as each sex explores potentials that may have been neglected in earlier life.

Recommended: Encourage men to share and network, women to be more self-determining and active in the world beyond their families.

Helpful to men: Beginning to recognize and develop your nurturing side now, whatever your age, can help prevent or alleviate the common syndrome of stress, coronary disease and shortened life expectancy associated with overidentification with work and subsequent "retirement shock."

OTHER CHANGES TO EXPECT—AND SUPPORT

•**Desire to leave a legacy.** *This can take many forms:* Artwork, fortune, grandchildren, possessions, family recipes, memories in the minds of others. Many older people find the role of "elder" (counselor, mentor, teacher) to be particularly enriching.

•**Altered sense of time.** Older people tend to lose both "time panic" and boredom, in favor of a sense of time based on the appreciation of the truly important things in life... human relationships, nature, etc. *Result:* An ability to live in the moment that can make old age a richly enjoyable time, filled with emotional and sensory awareness. Older people also experience a personal sense of the cycle of life and one's place in the cycle...for many, a deepening of spiritual beliefs.

•**Creativity and curiosity.** Most older people stay productive and active their entire lives, barring ill health or social problems, such as poverty. *Less well known:* Many older people become creative for the first time in their lives. *Keys:* An attitude of curiosity and the ability to be surprised throughout one's lifetime.

•**Feelings of serenity, wisdom, fulfillment.** As older people come to accept the inevitability of death, feelings of satisfaction with one's life, of having done one's best, of having survived life's challenges, are more common than generally believed—though not as common as possible. The process of reminiscence that characterizes old age is essential to the emotional well-being of older people, as they work to resolve past conflicts and find significance in their life history.

Recommended: Make examining personal conflicts and reviewing your life a habit. Listen and support the process in the elderly. It can be hurtful, even devastating, for an older person to be told his/her life story is boring or unimportant.

SOCIAL HEALTH

People who have healthy social networks have less disease and live longer than those who do not. A study of men and women over age 65 conducted at Duke University Medical Center found the risk of mortality to be four times greater in people who had little social support, even when other factors, such as gender, health, smoking, economic status, depression, etc., were considered.

A Swedish study found that social isolation is one of the best predictors of mortality from all causes. Other studies have found that individuals who are "self-starters," able to initiate new social contacts and activities, have the least disease and the longest survival rates.

Researchers are just starting to appreciate the importance of friendship at all phases of life. In addition to immediate family, friends are seen as "family" by many older persons, and they lend important support in times of need.

Studies are beginning to show that one reason women may outlive men is their greater skill in seeking and maintaining friendships. Mortality following the loss of a spouse is also lower in women, due in part to their better social networks.

Recommended: Use the telephone, write letters and cards, attend reunions. Nurture friendships with people of all ages throughout your lifetime. While many consider retirement communities to be artificially segregated environments, studies show older people who live among other older people make more friends than those who live among the young.

Caution: American cultural beliefs about independence and "doing for oneself" can foster a sense of isolation in people who resist help when it is needed. By contrast, people in group-oriented societies (Israeli kibbutzim, for example) can accept the support of others with no loss of self-esteem or feelings of dependence.

Recommended: Make use of support groups in the times of grief, stress or loss that are an inevitable part of life: Illness, widowhood, family crisis. *Also very useful:* Humor, a healing mechanism and coping skill that is underused in the elderly.

A SENSE OF PURPOSE

One's goal or purpose in later life (or any other time) need not be lofty. A sense of purpose can be derived from volunteer work, one's role as a grandparent or an attachment to the New York Yankees. Retirees who organize their daily lives to accommodate their goals live longer than those who do not.

Example: A University of Michigan study found that men who did volunteer work at least once a week were two-and-a-half times less likely to die than those who did none.

Caution: The highest suicide rate in America is among white men in their 80s. *Reason:* This group suffers the greatest loss of power, influence and status, and can therefore experience the greatest sense of helplessness and impotence.

Essential: Maintaining the deep sense of self-esteem that is derived from inner purpose.

Recommended: Begin now to make good use of your time...tutor, fund-raise, work for a cause you admire. *Key:* Choose a regularized activity that is outside yourself.

Make Your "Real Age" Younger

This is the age that reflects your health and life expectancy, rather than chronological age. An analysis of hundreds of factors in numerous health studies identifies how they affect your "Real Age"—some very surprisingly.

Example: Flossing regularly reduces "Real Age" by 6.4 years because bacteria that attack gums can trigger an immune reaction that harms arteries and leads to stroke, heart disease and memory loss.

Over two million people have taken the comprehensive "Real Age test" on the Internet at *www.realage.com,* a site which also has many other useful health resources.

Michael Roizen, MD, dean of the College of Medicine and vice president for biomedical sciences, State University of New York, Upstate Medical University, Syracuse.

Living Life to the Fullest... In the Later Years

Phillip Berman and Connie Goldman, authors of *The Ageless Spirit: Reflections on Living Life to the Fullest in Our Later Years.* Ballantine Books.

Aging is so often thought of in our society as an entirely negative experience. So—we spoke with 40 people over the age of 60 about their experiences in aging.

We asked each person: "What can you say in praise of age?" *Their answers were inspiring...*

Maturity turns out to give us a chance to do many new things and to develop ourselves in new ways. *Suggestions from the people we interviewed...*

• **Develop a new avocation.** It's important to develop a vital, challenging interest that you can take up when you retire. This is especially important for people who, after years of work, have grown tired of their jobs. They look forward to retirement and then find themselves bored, with too much time on their hands, and they become depressed or even ill.

If you develop an avocational interest that's an alternative to your work well in advance of retirement, you will be able to make the transition with much less stress and sense of loss.

Example: Radio and television broadcaster Art Linkletter has used his "retirement years" to start a new career as a writer, using his personal experiences of aging as the basis for his work. His book, *Old Age is Not for Sissies,* which focuses on the joys and pains of late life, became a national best-seller.

• **Retirement is a full-time job.** A regular job consumes 35 or 40 hours a week—more if you factor in commuting. But if you're retired, you're retired 24 hours a day, seven days a week. And you alone have the responsibility for how your day turns out. Structuring your own time is a skill that has to be learned. That's particularly so if you've spent your life in a corporation, where a lot of structure was provided. Some retired people can't find enough activities they enjoy to fill their time, while others, like former Time Warner executive Dick Munroe, find retirement to be busier than full-time work. "I love what I'm doing. I love not doing what I used to do," explains Munroe, "I'm just doing too many things and I should fix that!"

So find things you love to do and learn to say no to anything else.

• **Value your own experience.** Americans undervalue experience. We're so hooked on youth that we haven't yet recognized that inexperience isn't always a virtue, and knowing what you're doing isn't a handicap.

For people who stay open to change and growth throughout their lives, the mature years can prove to be unexpectedly rewarding.

The late writer May Sarton told us she was glad to be old. She had solved a lot of problems that are very anguishing for young people, and she had come to terms with her own life in ways that made life much easier.

The late Norman Cousins spoke very specifically about being in the harvest years. He told us that he was using everything he had ever learned, everything he had ever done or known, and using it better than he ever had before. He could accomplish things with greater economy of effort than when he was younger.

The more you learn, the more you will ultimately be able to do. In a long life, you will have time to develop skills you don't have now but would like to. And when you have assembled them you will be able to use and truly enjoy them.

• **Become wise.** You don't necessarily grow wise as you grow old. Wisdom isn't part of the biological process of aging. But you can work to develop it. Wisdom comes from wrestling with our experiences, making sense out of them...enjoying life's pleasures, letting go of its sorrows and mistakes, and moving forward.

Many of the people that we interviewed found great security in the knowledge gained through aging of what their moral values were and what's valuable in life. Dancer and choreographer Bella Lewitsky told us, "As I've aged I've grown more confident in my own values and at the same time more tolerant of differences."

• **Take time to enjoy the simple things in life.** We have the idea as we come into the later years that if we do nothing, or very simple things, we're not using our time very well.

The late writer Eve Merriam talked about how she relished the change of seasons, particularly the coming of spring, finding what she called daily joy in the colors and fragrances of the trees and flowers.

●**Explore your inner life.** Young adulthood and middle age don't leave us much time to explore the heart and spirit deeply. As the outer life shrinks, there's room for a great deal of inner growth for most people. Although we continue to need the nourishment of other human beings of all ages in our lives, we also need quiet and solitude to explore the inner self.

Through this self-exploration, many of the people we interviewed developed a strong spiritual sense as they grew older—and found that to be one of the richest aspects of aging. This spirituality was often connected with a reverence for nature.

Clarinetist Rosario Mazzeo finds his spiritual connection in nature and takes long walks in the woods every day.

●**The challenge of physical changes.** There's general agreement that the worst thing about aging is the physical erosion that often accompanies the later years—the slowing up of the body.

The attitude that you take toward your physical aging is extremely important. Actor Hume Cronyn spoke about the lines on his face, "Let them get deeper—particularly the laugh lines!"

Important: Deal with physical limitations and needs to care for yourself. Then move past them and focus on the many satisfactions that are possible out there.

While the body is subject to deterioration, the person inside has a continued capacity for growth, whatever the body's age.

●**Understand the value of life.** The best way to get the most out of life is to come to terms with mortality. The late actor Jason Robards once told us that to him, life is like a hotel—everybody checks in and everybody checks out. Once he fully grasped this, he was able to truly savor each day.

It is in fact the sense of the preciousness of time that we acquire as we get older which should fill our later years with a new richness and intensity.

The late songwriter and singer Burl Ives found that contemplating death gave him a renewed sense of joy in life.

●**Forget the myths.** If we want a richer later life, we have to take responsibility for achieving it. We can't accept the myths that "old is over," and that only youth matters. We must learn to appreciate and give thanks for the many gifts that aging brings us.

How We Can Slow Our Aging Processes

Deepak Chopra, MD, executive director for the Institute for Mind/Body Medicine, San Diego, CA. He is author of *Ageless Body, Timeless Mind: The Quantum Alternative to Growing Old*. Harmony Books.

Today, people are living longer, but enjoying it less. Many of us fear old age as a period of declining powers and failing health. But if we learn to replace that fear by a positive attitude, an enhanced physical and spiritual awareness of our bodies and a sensible pattern of activity, we can expect to enjoy the blessings of a vigorous and healthy old age.

A century ago, less than one person in 10 reached the age of 65. Most of those who did live that long had been worn out by a lifetime of inadequate nutrition…widespread disease …backbreaking physical labor. Their remaining years were difficult not because they were old, but because their bodies were in a state of breakdown.

Today, relieved of those harsh external pressures, most of us will live well into our 60s and 70s…and the physical disease and mental breakdown we fear in old age is largely a result of internal stress we can learn to avoid.

PEOPLE AGE DIFFERENTLY

Your well-being depends far less on your chronological age—how old you are according to the calendar—than on two other indicators…

●**Biological age tells how old your body is** in terms of critical life signs and cellular processes.

Every individual is affected differently by time…in fact, every cell and organ in your body ages on its own timetable.

Example: A middle-aged marathon runner may have leg muscles, heart and lungs of someone half his age, highly stressed knees and kidneys that are aging rapidly and eyesight and hearing declining on their own individual paths.

Most 20-year-olds look alike to a physiologist...but at 70, no two people have bodies that are remotely alike.

●**Psychological age indicates how old you feel.** Depending on what is happening in your life and your attitude to it, your psychological age can change dramatically within a very short period.

Examples: An old woman recalling her first love can suddenly look and sound as if she has just turned 18...a middle-aged man who loses his beloved wife can become a lonely old man within a few weeks.

AGING IS REVERSIBLE

It is not news that psychological age can decrease. *We all know the old proverb:* You are as old as you feel. And—now scientists have learned that biological aging can be reversed.

Example: Muscle mass is a key factor in the body's overall vitality...and it was believed until recently that it inevitably declined with increasing age. But Tufts University researchers discovered that isn't so. They put 12 men, aged 60 to 72, on a weight-training program. After three months, the men could lift heavier boxes than the 25-year-old workers in the lab...and milder weight-training programs proved equally successful for people over 95!

That's not all the good news for aging bodies. *The Tufts team found that regular physical exercise also reverses nine other typical effects of biological age...*

●**Reduced strength**
●**Lower metabolic rate**
●**Excess body fat**
●**Reduced aerobic capacity**
●**Higher blood pressure**
●**Lower blood-sugar tolerance**
●**Higher cholesterol/HDL ratio**
●**Reduced bone density**
●**Poorer body temperature regulation.**

To get optimum benefits from exercise, the type and amount have to be expertly tailored to your individual constitution. You don't have to

be a fitness freak to gain from exercise...just 20 minutes of walking three times a week improves the cholesterol/HDL ratio. No expert advice is needed to benefit from another important route to longevity...a balanced lifestyle.

A study of 7,000 Southern Californians found that the longest-lived followed seven simple rules:

●**Sleep seven to eight hours a night.**
●**Eat breakfast.**
●**Don't eat between meals.**
●**Don't be significantly over- or underweight.**
●**Engage in regular physical activity**...sports...gardening...long walks.
●**Drink moderately**...not more than two alcoholic drinks a day.
●**Don't smoke.**

The study found that a 45-year-old man who followed these rules could expect to live another 33 years...but if he followed only three of them or less, he would probably die within 22 years.

ROLE OF STRESS

The human body reacts to stress by pumping adrenaline and other powerful hormones into the bloodstream. This "fight or flight" response provides energy for taking rapid action and is vital when you are actually faced with pressing external danger.

But it makes your metabolism work in the direction of breaking your body down instead of building it up.

If it occurs too often or continues too long it produces lasting harmful effects including muscle wasting...diabetes...fatigue...osteoporosis...hypertension...effects typical of aging.

That is why a major contribution to the aging process in modern life comes from situations that do not present real physical dangers but produce dangerous levels of stress.

Example: Our cities are full of unavoidable noise, a serious source of stress. Studies have shown increased levels of mental disorder in people who live under the flight paths near airports... elevated blood pressure in children who live near the Los Angeles airport...more violent behavior in noisy work environments.

Fortunately, we have discovered a number of measures that can reduce the aging effects of stress and other hazards of modern life.

To reduce stress and slow the aging process...

●**Experience silence.** Research has shown that people who meditate have higher levels of DHEA, a hormone that protects against stress and decreases with age. Spending 20 minutes twice a day in calm silence pays great benefits in detaching you from the mad bustle of the world and finding your true self.

●**Avoid toxins**...not only foods and drinks that stress your system, but relationships that produce anger and tension.

●**Shed the need for approval by others** ...it's a sign of fear, another stress factor that promotes aging.

●**Use relationships with others to learn your own self.** People we love provide something we need...those we hate have something we need to get rid of.

●**Change your inner dialogue.** Change from *What's in it for me?* to *How can I help others?* Selfishness is bad for you. Psychologist Larry Scherwitz found that people who used the words *I, me, mine* most often in their conversations had the highest risk of heart disease.

●**Be aware of your body's needs.** You will be healthier if you learn to respond to its signals.

Example: Don't eat by the clock...eat when you're hungry...stop when you're full.

●**Live in the moment.** Much stress comes from living in the past or the future instead of the present.

Example: If you're angry at something that already happened...or fearful of something that may happen...your stress can't produce any useful result now. When those feelings occur, bring yourself back to the present.

●**Become less judgmental.** Don't get stressed by other people's decisions...your viewpoint may not be right for them.

●**Stay in contact with nature.** It will make you feel you want to stay around to enjoy it longer...and your body will respond.

How to Change Your Biological Age

William J. Evans, PhD, chief of the human physiology lab at the Human Nutrition Research Center on Aging, a Boston-based facility operated jointly by the US Department of Agriculture and Tufts University. He is coauthor of *Biomarkers: The 10 Keys for Prolonging Vitality.* Fireside Books.

Gray hair, wrinkled skin, growing flabbiness, loss of vitality and reduced resistance to injury and disease...

To most Americans, these are harbingers of old age, unwelcome but inevitable milestones along a path that leads inexorably to the grave.

In fact, research suggests something quite different—that the body's gradual decline stems not from the passing of years but from the combined effects of inactivity and poor nutrition. So no matter what your present health status or your chronological age, regular exercise and improved eating habits will lower your biological age.

Benefits: Reduced body fat...increased muscle mass...strength increases of 200% to 300%...increases in aerobic capacity by 20% or more...and reduced risk of heart disease, diabetes, osteoporosis and other age-related ailments.

To lose fat and gain muscle: Be sure to combine a low-fat diet with regular exercise.

●**Aerobic capacity.** To gauge fitness, doctors often measure the body's ability to process oxygen during exercise. The greater this aerobic capacity, the faster oxygen is pumped through the body—and the fitter the individual. Like other biomarkers, aerobic capacity often declines with age. Typically, by age 65 it is 30% to 40% below its level in young adulthood.

●**Blood-sugar tolerance.** For most Americans, aging brings about a gradual decline in the body's ability to metabolize blood sugar (glucose). So common is this problem that by age 70, 20% of men and 30% of women are at an increased risk of diabetes, a potential killer.

At special risk for problems: The overweight, the sedentary and those who eat a fatty diet.

Good news: A low-fat, high-fiber diet, combined with regular exercise, will cut your diabetes risk. Be sure to include both strength-building and aerobic exercise in your routine.

• **Cholesterol ratio.** As most of us already know, a high cholesterol level boosts your risk of heart disease. But total cholesterol isn't the only thing that counts.

Very important: The ratio of total cholesterol to HDL (good cholesterol). For older people, the ideal ratio is 4.5 or lower. A person whose total cholesterol is 200 and whose HDL is 50, for example, has a ratio of 200/50, or 4.0.

To lower your ratio: Stop smoking, lose weight, reduce your intake of fatty, cholesterol-rich foods (especially animal products) and exercise regularly.

• **Blood pressure.** In many countries, advancing age brings little, if any, change in blood pressure. In the US, however, where older people tend to be overweight and sedentary, blood pressure does rise with age.

To keep pressure in check: Stay slim, don't smoke, get regular exercise and limit your consumption of fat, salt and alcohol. If these steps fail to regulate pressure, pressure-lowering drugs may be necessary.

• **Bone density.** As we age, our skeletons slowly become weaker and more brittle. While some mineral loss is inevitable, the severe and potentially deadly condition known as osteoporosis is not.

Prevention: Although consuming adequate amounts of calcium a day will retard the loss of bone, that alone rarely does the trick. *Also needed:* Weight-bearing exercise, such as walking, running or cycling.

Not helpful: Swimming and other forms of exercise that do not subject the long bones to the stress of gravity do not build bone strength.

• **Body temperature regulation.** Compared with young people, old people sweat less, get less thirsty and excrete more water in their urine. These seemingly minor changes, which are a part of aging—plus the loss of muscle tissue needed for efficient shivering—hinder the body's ability to regulate its internal temperature, which raises the risk of dehydration in summer and hypothermia in winter.

Important: Force yourself to drink during exercise and in hot weather, even if you're not thirsty.

Sleep Deprivation Danger

While chronic sleep deprivation doesn't make you age *faster,* it appears to increase risk for age-related chronic disorders—such as hypertension and diabetes—earlier in life. *Bottom line:* Adequate and restful sleep is as important for your health as proper nutrition and exercise.

Karine Spiegel, PhD, a research assistant at Free University of Brussels in Belgium. Her study of young men and the impact of sleep debt on metabolic and endocrine function was published in *The Lancet,* 84 Theobald's Rd., London WC1X 8RR.

When researchers deprived 11 young men of four hours' sleep a night for six nights, they found deteriorations in the men's carbohydrate metabolism and endocrine function. These are effects that normally occur with aging, suggesting that sleep deprivation may increase the severity of disorders related to age. *To get a better night's sleep:* Don't eat large meals or drink a lot or exercise close to bedtime...don't smoke...avoid caffeine and alcohol before bed...establish a regular bedtime schedule.

Eve Van Cauter, PhD, research professor, department of medicine, University of Chicago.

Optimists Live Longer

Healthy elderly people living in the community who rated their health as "poor" were two to six times more likely to die within the next four years than those who said their health was "excellent."

Study of individuals 65 and older, and a review of earlier studies by Ellen L. Idler, PhD, associate professor, Institute for Health, Health Care Policy and Aging Research, Rutgers University, New Brunswick, NJ.

Your Ever-Growing Brain

Biologists at Princeton University have found that brains continue to grow new cells throughout life. The study, done on monkeys, whose brains are very similar to humans, showed that no matter how old the brain, new cells are added daily to the cerebral cortex—the part of the brain that controls advanced functions such as learning and memory. It seems likely that this is also true for humans. If so, it reverses previous thinking that the cerebral cortex of adults cannot produce new cells.

Margery Hutter Silver, EdD, associate director, New England Centenarian Study, Harvard Medical School Division on Aging/Beth Israel Deaconness Medical Center.

The Seniors Win!

Older people score higher than younger people on some mental tests. In a recent study, two groups of people, one aged 18 to 39 and the other aged 65 to 85, were asked to press a button when they saw a particular sequence of two letters on a computer screen. The reaction time of both groups was comparable, but the older group made fewer errors, particularly when more distracting letters were added to the test. Researchers theorize that the older people made fewer errors because the age-related decline in memory function makes them less likely to be led astray by misleading contextual information.

Todd Braver, PhD, assistant professor of psychology, Washington University, St. Louis.

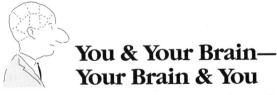

You & Your Brain— Your Brain & You

Vernon H. Mark, MD, FACS. He is coauthor, with Jeffrey P. Mark, MS, of Brain Power. *Houghton Mifflin.*

We've all been taught to take care of our bodies so we can live longer, healthier lives. But mere physical survival does not guarantee quality of life. A meaningful life requires the use of a healthy brain.

Although today's Americans live longer than ever, we fill nursing homes at a record rate. *Reason:* It's not loss of physical function that forces most people into a nursing home...it's the loss of mental faculties.

Good news: Barring severe injury or progressive disease—Alzheimer's, Parkinson's, etc.—much loss of brain function is preventable.

AGING AND THE BRAIN

Failing brain function is not normal. It is a sign of disease, injury or neglect.

Although we may lose brain cells as we age, maturing brains compensate for cell loss in ways that increase brain function.

How: The sheath around the nerve fibers grows thicker, improving the transmission of electrical signals in the brain. And the nerve fibers, or dendrites, grow new branches. *Result:* More interconnections for richer, deeper thinking.

Certain kinds of intelligence, however, do decline as we age.

Example: People slowly lose their ability to work out complex problems in theoretical mathematics...although their ability to do simple calculations isn't impaired.

Applied skills—law, medicine, engineering, architecture, etc.—do not deteriorate with age. And areas that depend on interpretation—art, music, drama, etc.—are actually enhanced as wisdom and judgment deepen. The ability to speak and write also improves from age 50 to 70. And philosophers don't hit their stride until they reach 70 or 80.

PREVENTABLE BRAIN DRAINS

For every patient I see with Alzheimer's or another serious brain disorder, I see 20 who are impaired by something that is preventable or treatable. *Common culprits:*

•**Depression.** The number-one reversible cause of memory loss in the elderly.

People who are depressed enough to warrant professional attention suffer from reduced attention span and poor concentration. *Result:* Impaired performance and a loss of the ability to form new memories.

In severe cases, depressed brain function lessens a person's ability to retrieve old memories. In the elderly, depression can mimic Alzheimer's disease.

●**Medication.** Many of the medicines that a lot of older people take—for high blood pressure, sleep disorders, anxiety, emotional problems, etc.—have side effects, some of which can impair the brain.

Older people are often overmedicated, a result of seeking relief from pain and other problems. Most do not tolerate drugs in the same doses they once did. And certain medications—that are perfectly safe on their own—can cause trouble when combined with others.

●**Alcohol.** The number-one brain poison in our society, it's abused by six million Americans. Alcohol breaks down the blood-brain barrier—a built-in defense that normally protects our brain cells from poisons that enter the bloodstream. A person who is alcohol-poisoned can suffer as much disability as a person with a stroke, tumor or brain injury. The difference is in duration, not degree.

Alcohol abusers run a 30% greater risk of suicide than the general population. *Other risks:* Memory loss, vitamin B1 deficiency, seizures, Korsakoff's psychosis (a brain disorder with severe memory loss).

●**Cocaine and other illicit drugs.** Opiates, stimulants, depressants and hallucinogens all penetrate the blood-brain barrier and alter brain function. Cocaine can cause convulsions, stroke and outbursts of violence.

●**Lack of stimulation.** This alone can seriously depress brain function.

Example: A partially blind stroke victim spent two years in a bed positioned so her sighted side faced a blank wall. It appeared her mental faculties were failing, until she was turned to face the world. *Result:* Remarkable improvement.

An interesting, challenging environment promotes increased brain function. Lacking stimulation, brain function and development are interrupted.

Other potential brain drains are physical illness, including stroke, pain, stress, head injury and poor nutrition.

BUILD A BETTER BRAIN

Our brains improve with stimulation. We can enrich our thinking, sharpen our response time and improve our memory with simple techniques of diet and exercise.

●**Diet.** For optimum brain efficiency, avoid excessive salt, saturated fats and sugar. Breakfast should be the big meal of the day. Eat a full breakfast high in protein such as fish, chicken, turkey or soy products. The last meal of the day should be light, and several hours before bed.

Although many doctors do not think that vitamin/mineral supplements are necessary, I do recommend them. *Reason:* Most recommendations are based on what our body needs to avoid vitamin-deficiency-induced diseases, such as scurvy, rickets and pellagra. That's not enough to keep the brain healthy. Various studies correlate increased vitamin intake with improved verbal and nonverbal intelligence, behavior, memory and visual acuity. *Note:* Check with your doctor before you take any supplements.

●**Exercise.** The brain benefits from mental exercise the same way the body does from physical activity. *Suggested:*

●Balance your checkbook without using a calculator. The mathematical centers atrophy with disuse. Math exercises maintain skills and improve concentration and attention.

●Practice printing with your nondominant hand. Start by making large letters. Don't worry if they're not perfect. *Goal:* To develop speech abilities in the nondominant side of your brain. This will facilitate quicker recovery in the event of a stroke.

●Draw geometric figures and designs. You can do this while you're on the phone. Then copy the drawings with your nondominant hand. *Goal:* Improved perception of complex spatial relations and integration of both brain hemispheres.

●Put information you want to remember in a verse or song. Melody and versification are generated in the nondominant hemisphere. Combining melody with lyrics employs the whole brain and improves retrieval.

●Read challenging material. Good choices include histories, technical information, biographies, quality novels by writers with a good grasp of language (Proust, Austen, Stout, etc.). Read aloud. Listen to books on tape.

• Punctuate brain activity with brain rest. Brain rest is not the same as napping or watching TV. Brain rest requires temporarily shutting down some brain function.

Example: Sit quietly, close your eyes and progressively relax the parts of your body that use the brain most—the lips, tongue, thumbs, index fingers and big toes. Learn this exercise when you are not stressed.

• Stay active. Doing is more rewarding and enriching than watching. Sensory stimulation in its active rather than passive forms is terrific brain food. *Suggested:* Don't just look at art—paint...don't just listen to music—play an instrument...don't just read—write.

How to Sharpen Your Memory as You Grow Older... Nine Simple Strategies

Cynthia R. Green, PhD, director of the memory enhancement program at Mount Sinai School of Medicine in New York. She is author of *Total Memory Workout: 8 Easy Steps to Maximum Memory Fitness.* Bantam.

Research suggests that the popular herb *ginkgo biloba* is moderately beneficial in cases of Alzheimer's disease or other forms of dementia.

But there is little indication that ginkgo—or any other herbal or nutritional supplement—boosts mental function in individuals who are healthy.

Memory expert Dr. Cynthia Green shares her strategies for boosting memory and mental function as you grow older...

• **Make a conscious effort to remember.** The brain sorts information by routing it to short-term memory and then either discarding it or storing it in long-term memory.

Memories held in short-term storage are fleeting. Unless you make a conscious effort to remember new events, names, etc., they won't make the transition to long-term storage.

Suppose you're meeting someone for the first time. You may be a bit anxious about making a good impression. If so, you're probably *not* paying close attention to the person ...and you're likely to forget his/her name the instant you hear it.

• **Better approach:** Run the name through your mind several times as soon as you hear it. Repeat it aloud to the person. Also—once it's convenient to do so, you might even jot the name down on a piece of paper.

This process of focusing will help shift the information from short-term storage to long-term storage.

• **Give meaning to information you'd like to remember.** It's easier to recall new information if you embed it with meaning. *There are several ways to do this...*

• Chunking. This involves grouping different bits of information into manageable—and meaningful—groupings.

Consider telephone numbers. They're easy to remember because they're written in chunks. There are three digits for the area code, three for the exchange and four final digits. Remembering an "unchunked" 10-digit number is much more difficult.

Chunking can be used for any number. You can also chunk information in lists. For instance, you might try mentally categorizing the items on a shopping list—produce, cleaning supplies, grain products, etc. That should make it easy to remember them.

• Mental images. Information is easier to remember if you create a mental image to go along with it.

Suppose you meet someone named Chris. You might envision a Christmas tree as a way of giving the name meaning. If you meet a Laura, you might think of a laurel leaf.

• Connections. Grammar school pupils are taught to spell "principal" by mentally connecting it with the word "pal." You can form analogous links for almost any new bit of information.

Say you've been assigned to locker #84 at a health club. To remember your place, consciously take the time to connect it with something already stored in your long-term memory—Orwell's classic novel *1984,* for instance.

• **Commit information to writing.** Date books, calendars and electronic organizers are invaluable memory tools. If you use one, make it a point to consult it at the same time each morning and evening—to make sure things aren't overlooked.

Often, the mere act of writing something down makes it easier to recall—even if you never refer back to what you've written. Of course, if you do forget, you'll have a written record.

• **Create "forget-me-not" spots.** To keep track of car keys, wallets, sunglasses and other easy-to-misplace items, choose a special place in your home where you'll always put them.

Examples: Bowl on a tabletop...kitchen drawer...drawer near the door.

Forget-me-not spots can also be used to hold your to-do lists, letters to be mailed, videotapes to be returned and receipts.

• **Talk to your doctor about your medications.** Memory can be disrupted by certain common medications, including the heartburn drug *cimetidine* (Tagamet) and the antianxiety drug *diazepam* (Valium).

In many cases, memory trouble can be minimized simply by changing to a different drug or lowering the dosage. If you are taking numerous drugs (polypharmacy) ask your doctor whether this could be affecting your memory.

• **Get regular exercise.** In addition to boosting cardiovascular fitness, taking a brisk walk or doing some other form of aerobic exercise every day enhances blood flow to the cerebral cortex. That's the part of the brain most involved in memory and other cognitive skills.

Exercise also reduces the risk for cardiovascular disease, high blood pressure and diabetes. These conditions are risk factors for *vascular dementia,* a memory-robbing condition caused by multiple tiny strokes.

• **Limit caffeine and alcohol intake.** A little caffeine can help you stay alert, but too much can cause anxiety and make it difficult to concentrate. Alcohol can affect the ability to focus.

• **Boost your consumption of fruits and vegetables.** Individuals with high levels of vitamin C and beta-carotene in their blood score better on tests of memory than do similar people with low levels of antioxidants.

Researchers theorize that antioxidants—which are abundant in fruits and veggies—guard against memory loss by helping to deactivate cell-damaging substances known as *free radicals.*

Good sources of antioxidants: Broccoli, kale, oranges, red peppers and strawberries.

• **Take a daily multivitamin.** Over time, there's a gradual decline in the small intestine's ability to absorb nutrients—vitamin B-12 in particular. Along with thiamine and other B vitamins, B-12 plays a key role in memory and mental function.

To counter this problem, take a daily multivitamin containing 100% of the RDA for vitamins B-6, B-12 and folic acid, in addition to the minerals zinc and boron.

Myths About Memory... And the Realities

Myth: **You can improve your memory by taking dietary supplements**—ginkgo biloba, choline, DHEA, phosphatidylserine, L-carnitine, vinpocetine, etc.

Reality: For most of us, our memory is neither sick nor broken, so it doesn't need to be "cured." You don't need to take a magic potion to have a good memory.

Myth: **Memory lapses are a sign of growing old age.**

Reality: More often than not, they're simply a sign of the times we live in—the Age of Information Overload.

Myth: **Some people just don't have a good memory.**

Reality: There's no such thing as having a "bad" memory. Like other functions, most people have strengths and weaknesses. Some people have good visual memory while others have good aural memory.

Myth: **Memory is a purely intellectual skill.**

Reality: Our memory is an integral part of ourselves, affected by many aspects of our daily lives.

Myth: **Serious memory loss is an inevitable consequence of aging.**

Reality: Only about 15% of adults age 65 and older develop a degenerative memory disorder such as Alzheimer's disease.

Cynthia R. Green, PhD, director of the memory enhancement program at Mount Sinai School of Medicine in New York. She is author of *Total Memory Workout: 8 Easy Steps to Maximum Memory Fitness.* Bantam.

Predicting Longevity

Childhood personality predicts longevity. Children described as being conscientious and dependable were 35% more likely to live to age 70 than those described as being optimistic and having a sense of humor. The reason for this difference in longevity is unknown.

Howard Friedman, PhD, professor of psychology, University of California, Riverside. His review of data from a study of 1,178 children begun in the early 1920s was published in the *Journal of Personality and Social Psychology,* 750 First St. NE, Washington, DC 20002.

Most Causes of Death Are Preventable

Officially, the top 10 causes of death in the US, in order, are heart disease, cancer, stroke, accidental injury, lung disease, pneumonia/influenza, diabetes, suicide, liver disease and AIDS.

But these categories camouflage the true, underlying causes of death—most of which are preventable.

In a single year...

...tobacco kills 400,000 people. Causes cancer, heart disease and stroke.

...diet/inactivity kills 300,000 people. Causes high blood pressure, diabetes and cancer of the colon, breast and prostate.

...alcohol kills 100,000. Causes cirrhosis of the liver, cancer and unintentional injury from car wrecks and other mishaps.

...infections kill 90,000. Includes meningitis, encephalitis and other parasitic diseases.

...toxic agents kill 60,000. Includes contaminated food and water, chemical additives, asbestos, lead and radon.

...motor vehicles kill 47,000. Using seat belts, air bags, child car seats and motorcycle helmets would halve this number.

...firearms kill 36,000.

...sexually transmitted diseases kill 30,000. Includes AIDS, hepatitis and cervical cancer.

...illegal drugs kill 20,000. Drugs account for a large portion of the deaths officially attributed to suicide, homicide, car accidents, AIDS and more.

J. Michael McGinnis, MD, deputy assistant secretary for health (disease prevention and health promotion), US Department of Health and Human Services, Washington, DC. His research on the actual causes of death was published in the *Journal of the American Medical Association,* 515 N. State St., Chicago 60610.

Grains for Longevity

In a recent 10-year study, the death rate among people who ate at least one serving of *whole* grains a day was 15% to 20% below the death rate among those who ate only white bread, white rice and other refined grains.

Whole grain foods include whole-wheat, pumpernickel and oatmeal breads...whole-wheat pasta...bulgur...and oatmeal.

David Jacobs, PhD, professor of epidemiology, University of Minnesota School of Public Health, Minneapolis. His study of 38,000 women was published in the *American Journal of Public Health,* 800 I St. NW, Washington, DC 20001.

 # Learning Not To Smoke

The American Way of Life Need Not Be Hazardous to Your Health by John Farquhar, MD. W.W. Norton & Co.

Kicking the cigarette habit has less to do with willpower than with acquiring the skills to stop smoking. One widely successful treatment uses a gradual, self-directed learning program.

First, plan to stop smoking during a relatively stable period in your work and social life. Understand your smoking habits by keeping a simple diary that records how many cigarettes you smoke daily and how badly you want each one. Score the craving on a scale of one (automatic, boredom) to four (powerful desire). Firm up your commitment by enlisting a nonsmoking buddy to call up and encourage you several times a week.

Phase out the cigarettes in three stages:

1. Taper. Heavy smokers should reduce to 12 to 15 cigarettes daily. If that's your present level, then reduce to eight or nine a day. Use a smoke suppression drill, a mental learning process, each time you have an urge to smoke. Begin by focusing on the craving; then immediately associate it with a negative effect of smoking, such as filthy lung passages, clogged, fatty arteries or skin wrinkled and aged by carbon monoxide and nicotine. *Next:* Relax and imagine a peaceful scene. Follow up with a pleasant image associated with nonsmoking (smooth skin or greater vitality).

2. How to withdraw. One week before your scheduled quitting date, smoke only four cigarettes a day. Smoke two cigarettes in a 15-minute period. Wait at least an hour, and then smoke the other two. While gulping down the cigarettes, concentrate on the negative sensations: Scratchy throat and lungs, foul breath. Keep up negative thoughts for at least five minutes after finishing the last cigarette.

3. Quit. When a smoking urge arises, conjure up the negative image, relax and follow it with a pleasing fantasy. Also, call your nonsmoking buddy for moral support.

Note: Never label yourself a failure. If you have a relapse, return to the tapering phase, and try the procedure again.

9

Family and Friends

How to Enjoy the Birth Of a New Grandchild

 To fully experience the special event, plan to be there for the delivery. If that's not possible, make a trip to see the infant—and the *parents,* of course—as soon as you can.

Why is it so important? Because a grandchild's birth brings the family together. With you on the scene to welcome the baby, the occasion becomes a family celebration. *Special reasons for doing special things…*

• **You can be the family reporter,** recording the birth and accompanying celebration with a camera or a videocamera.

• **Your presence can be a great help to the parents.** Chances are the new parents will have their hands very, very full.

• **The new baby's siblings** will need the kind of attention and support that loving grandparents can provide so well.

A new birth in the family is an important enough event for you or your spouse to take time off work to attend. When you look back on it, a few days of missed work will seem inconsequential by comparison.

PLAN AHEAD

• **Discuss the visit with the parents-to-be** so you'll be able to comply with their wishes.

• **If travel will be necessary,** schedule your vacation for the time of the expected birth—but keep a bag packed, in case your grandchild makes an early arrival.

• **Coordinate your plans with those of the other grandparents** to avoid any conflicts.

• **Find out the hospital rules** from the doctor who'll be performing the delivery. Sometimes grandparents (even grandfathers) are allowed in the delivery room, perhaps in the background to respect the mother's modesty.

Arthur Kornhaber, MD, psychiatrist and president, Foundation for Grandparenting, 108 Farnham Rd., Ojai, CA 93023. He is author of *Grandparent Power: How to Strengthen the Vital Connection Among Grandparents, Parents, and Children.* Crown.

CLOSE ENCOUNTERS

You don't have to be looking over the doctor's shoulder when the baby comes. Indeed, hospital policy or the new parents' wishes may prohibit such an intimate presence. *Exception:* Grandmothers may be allowed in the delivery room, especially if it's their own daughter who's giving birth.

One grandmother who was fortunate enough to help her daughter in the delivery room put it this way: "Helping my daughter give birth was truly an incredible experience. She had a beautiful, unmedicated birth...love and her family surrounded her."

The moment of truth: My own experience delivering babies has shown me that the emotion flowing between new mother and new grandmother at the moment of birth is especially powerful, a time both will cherish forever.

If you can't witness the birth, you can be in the waiting room. Then you can hold the newborn, and present your new grandchild with his/her first teddy bear.

Key: Not only should you be there to welcome the new baby, you should thank the new parents for the incredible gift of a grandchild.

Sometimes, the new parents won't want anyone—even grandparents—in the hospital at all. The thought of relatives sitting impatiently in the waiting room may add to the expectant mother's stress. If that's the case, let the parents-to-be decide how to keep you posted.

SAFE AT HOME

Today, hospitals don't encourage long maternity stays. In most cases, Mom and Baby will be home within a day or two. That's when Grandma and Grandpa are *really needed.*

The new parents may not have provided anything to eat for their return home. If that's the case, why not bring in something special for the happy couple, so they'll have meals for several days?

Grandparents can help in countless ways, from basic housekeeping to making sure that older grandchildren get to and from school and playdates, etc. If there's no live-in housekeeper, one grandparent may actually move in for a while to ease the burden.

Just keeping your eyes open may provide some insights as to how you can help. "I noticed how gingerly my daughter-in-law eased herself into the maple rocker she sat in to nurse my grandson," one grandmother wrote. "I brought her a doughnut pillow and she said it was the best present she received, aside from the baby himself."

Most important: Be sensitive to the wishes and comfort level of the new parents, yet make it clear that you want to provide meaningful support.

In particular, first-time parents may not know what they will need until that need actually arises. Exercise resourcefulness, creativity and good judgment in suggestions you offer.

If you do so, your presence can add immeasurably to this memorable event. The happiness, fulfillment and spiritual joy that every baby brings reach far beyond the new parents to resonate within the hearts of all family members—and that goes double for grandparents!

How to Be a Better Grandparent

Eda LeShan, educator and family counselor. She is author of *Grandparenting in a Changing World.* Newmarket Press.

Those of us who are grandparents grew up in a world far different from today's world.

It was a world of stable families...strict rules of behavior...conventional ideas about the roles of men and women...little concern about crime and environmental destruction. As children, we led a slower paced and far less-stressed life than our grandchildren.

With a more complex world full of more choices, only one thing has not changed...the unconditional love and support grandparents can give their grandchildren.

PARENTS AND GRANDPARENTS

To be good grandparents, we need to accept that our experience bringing up our own children does not entitle us to second-guess them in their current adult role as parents. They have the right to decide how to run their household and bring up their children.

When your children raise their children differently from the way you raised them, it is because they think their ways are better.

If you are uneasy about their choices, make sure you make any suggestions in a diplomatic fashion…and if they still think their way is right, accept it.

Example: Edna insisted her daughter Gloria follow formal rules of behavior from a very early age. Gloria did not want to be so strict with her own child, Antoinette. Edna feels that Gloria has gone too far in the other direction.

She should not say, "Antoinette is never going to learn how to behave herself unless you teach her some manners!"

A better approach: "Do you feel she's too young to learn to say 'please' and 'thank you'? I know there's a difference of opinion whether to teach children by example or by reminding them."

When you "take out" your grandchildren, don't be afraid to spoil them a little bit. Most parents fondly remember similar experiences with their own grandparents and regard it as part of the grandparents' role.

Exception: Be very strict about following health and safety rules set by your children. Grandchildren have to learn that their parents set the rules to protect them and that unconditional love does not mean dangerous permissiveness.

HOW MUCH HELP?

A basic fact of life is that grandparents are older than their children. It is often hard to cope with the demands of lively grandchildren, but it is well worth making an effort to find creative ways to help.

Example: When Eric's wife had to go to the hospital, he called his mother to ask her if he could bring his three young children to stay in her house. Grandma agreed on the spot…and immediately called a nanny agency and hired a full-time baby-sitter.

Later, she told me, "I love the children, they're very cute. I played with them 10 minutes here, 10 minutes there—and it worked out just fine!"

A DEVELOPING RELATIONSHIP

If you live close to your children, they may expect you always to be ready to drop everything and baby-sit at a moment's notice. Don't feel guilty about saying no if it's too much for you.

The most exciting part of being a grandparent is watching a new generation grow up, without all the worries and responsibility you had with your own children.

WHAT TO EXPECT AT DIFFERENT STAGES

●**Infancy.** Small babies need lots of attention…and the new parents need relief. Grandparents can give some by baby-sitting or providing financial aid and moral support.

●**Preschool.** The years from two to five are critical to children's development. Grandparents can help them learn to cope with the complexities of language, feelings and relationships. *Key message to communicate:* Accept feelings, but learn to control behavior.

Example: If your three-year-old grandson calls you a dope, don't just tell him, "It's naughty and rude to say that!" *Better:* "If you're angry at me, you can tell me, but calling me 'dope' hurts my feelings."

●**School age.** Children become more interested in their peers than their grandparents …but they still enjoy educational adventures. You can read to them…take them to museums and zoos…go on special trips. Show interest in their everyday activities…celebrate their birthdays…express joy at their successes but not disappointment at their failures.

●**Teenagers.** At 12 or 13 they are likely to feel they have outgrown you and may refuse to come along with the family to visit you. Don't despair…they will come back later. You can provide sympathetic reactions to their problems and gently give advice they will accept more easily than their parents'.

●**At all ages.** Tell your grandchildren tales about how you grew up. They will be fascinated to learn what the world was like in a different era…and develop a sense of where they came from.

GRANDCHILDREN WITH DIVORCED PARENTS

With divorce more prevalent than ever before, grandparents can provide the emotional support that their grandchildren need to cope with the emotional damage.

Your grandchildren love both their parents. Avoid taking sides in front of the children, regardless of your opinion of who is at fault.

Try to do your best to maintain a good relationship with your child's ex-spouse, particularly if he/she has custody of your grandchildren.

When divorce is followed by remarriage, you may find yourself with a new set of step-grandchildren. You will help keep the new family stronger if you don't demonstrate favoritism to your own grandchildren.

The most important thing you can teach your grandchildren…

According to a Puerto Rican saying: "If someone has to boast about himself, other people say, 'I guess he has no grandmother.'"

By providing unconditional love to our grandchildren just because they were born, we give them a sense of high self-esteem, the key to a worthwhile life.

Very Tax-Wise Ways to Help Your Grandchildren

Edward Mendlowitz, CPA, partner, Mendlowitz Weitsen, LLP, CPAs, Two Pennsylvania Plaza, Suite 1500, New York 10121. He is author of several books on taxes, including *IRA Distributions: What You Should Know*. Practical Programs, Inc.

Grandparents who are in a financial position to help out their grandchildren may be rewarded for doing so with special tax breaks. *Ways to be of help…*

●**Pay for college.**

Options…

●Fund a Qualified State Tuition Plan (QSTP). Most states now offer some form of qualified tuition plan that allows you to contribute on behalf of your grandchild. If you're married—and your spouse consents to the gift—gifts up to $100,000 can be fully tax free. *Here's how…*

For example, you can elect on a gift tax return to treat the $100,000 as having been made over five years. You won't pay gift tax because $100,000 spread equally over five years is $20,000 a year, and that's the maximum amount you and your spouse can jointly give a grandchild annually without owing gift tax.

Impact: The estate tax savings potential to you is enormous if you have several grandchildren and can afford to make this gift to each.

Bonus for some: You may be entitled to a state income tax deduction for a portion of your contribution.

●Contribute to a Coverdell education savings account. Depending on your Adjusted Gross Income, you may be able to put up to $2,000 per grandchild into a Coverdell education savings account (ESA). Your grandchild isn't taxed on contributions you make to the ESA, nor on the earnings on the contributions. And—withdrawals for qualified education costs are tax free.

●Pay tuition directly to the school. You can pay tuition for grandchildren or other relatives of any age, in any amount, directly to the school at no gift tax cost to you. This gift tax benefit is in addition to the annual gift tax exclusion (in 2002, $11,000, or $22,000 for a married couple who join in making the gift).

●**Pay medical expenses.** Like direct payments of tuition to schools, direct payments of medical expenses on behalf of a grandchild are exempt from gift tax.

●**Make interest-free loans.** As a general rule, if a lender fails to charge interest of at least the applicable federal rate (AFR)—an interest rate set by the IRS and published monthly on *www.irs.gov*—then the lender must report "imputed interest income." This is the interest that would have been earned using the AFR rate.

Exceptions: There's no imputed interest income on loans of up to $10,000. And loans up to $100,000 are free of imputed income if the grandchild's net investment income (investment income minus investment expenses) is $1,000 or less.

If net investment income is more, then imputed interest charged to *you* is limited to the extent of your grandchild's net investment income.

●**Make grandchildren beneficiaries of your IRAs and pensions.** When you die, amounts remaining in your plans will belong automatically to your grandchildren.

Naming a grandchild as beneficiary will allow you to reduce your required post-70½ minimum distributions from the plan.

When you name your grandchild as beneficiary, you can figure your minimum annual distributions based on the longer joint life expectancy of you and your beneficiary/grandchild, minimizing payouts.

●**Transfer assets to grandchildren.** By giving assets to them you may be able to turn income that would be taxable to you at your high tax rate into tax-free income to the grandchildren. Income earned by your grandchildren on the assets may be shielded by their income tax exemption or taxed at their low rates.

●If your grandchild is under age 14, then he/she can receive investment income up to $750 tax free in 2002.

The next $750 of investment income of a child under age 14 is taxed at 10%. Investment income over $1,500 is taxed to the grandchild at his parents' top income tax rate.

●If he is 14 or older, he can have investment income up to $750 tax free. Investment income over this amount is taxed at the grandchild's tax rates.

●If he is taxed at the 10% or 15% rate on regular income, the rate he pays on capital gains is only 10%.

Opportunity: Capital gains are subject to only an 8% tax for those in the 10% or 15% bracket—on assets held more than five years.

Assets acquired by gift include the donor's holding period, so if you give appreciated stock you've owned for more than five years and your grandchild sold it in 2002, the top tax on the gain is only 8%.

●**Set up custodial accounts.** Even if your grandchild is just a baby, you can start him off with savings through the use of gifts to custodial accounts. You can set up these accounts with banks, brokerage firms or mutual funds under the *Uniform Transfers (or Gifts) to Minors Act.* Use these accounts to put money aside for your grandchild.

Since the grandchild's Social Security number is on the account, the income is taxed to him under the rules discussed above—the under 14 years of age, over 13 rules.

Caution I: Don't act as the account's custodian yourself. Doing so can result in the money being included in your estate when you die, even though the funds are owned by your grandchild.

Caution II: Before you give money to your grandchild, consider the impact it might have on college financial aid he may be entitled to later on. Funds in a grandchild's name count heavily against grants of aid.

●**Set up a trust fund.** If you want to give substantial assets to your grandchild, it's generally wise to use a trust. This will provide greater control over assets. As long as the trust meets certain requirements, gifts to the trust will qualify for the annual gift tax exclusion even though the grandchild can't touch the money immediately.

Caution: Consult a tax expert to ensure that the trust is a Section 2503(b) or Section 2503(c) trust. These are special trusts endorsed by the Tax Code that allow money put into the trust to qualify for the annual gift tax exclusion.

●**Use life insurance.** Give your grandchild substantial amounts through life insurance. If your child doesn't need the money (he's already got an estate of his own), consider naming a grandchild as beneficiary of your life insurance policy.

If the policy is owned by a trust that's properly set up, your estate will escape tax on the proceeds.

Caution: Consider the impact of the generation-skipping transfer tax.

●**Bring your grandchildren into the business.** You can provide income to your grandchildren while reducing your estate on favorable tax terms. *Here's one way…*

Set up a Family Limited Partnership (FLP). Transfer stocks, real estate or other appreciated assets into the company. Give interests in the FLP to your grandchildren at a discount to the value of the underlying assets of about 30%.

●**Put business assets in a trust for your grandchildren.** If your business is about to buy an asset, consider setting up a trust to buy the asset. Make your grandchild the trust beneficiary and have the business lend the trust the funds to buy the asset.

Charge the trust the AFR to avoid gift tax issues. *Result:* The grandchild will obtain the benefit of the asset's future appreciation—which will be kept out of your estate.

Variation: Instead of using a trust, the same objectives can be accomplished through an FLP.

How to Organize A Family Reunion

Harry McKinzie, author of *Family Reunions: How to Plan Yours*. McKinzie Publishing Co.

You want to reunite with relatives you haven't seen in years, and meet some you've never even heard about.

You want to have a chance to reestablish relationships—even mend some bridges—and make new friendships. That's what a family reunion is all about...and it's worth the effort to organize one.

KEEP IT SIMPLE

Since putting together a reunion takes lots of time and you must pay attention to detail, it is important that you start off right at the beginning with the motto: *Keep it simple.* In order to keep it simple, you need a plan and must be organized. *Here's how to begin...*

GOAL: A BIG TURNOUT

One of the easiest ways to generate enthusiasm for a family reunion is to plan it around a 50th wedding anniversary or the 75th (or 100th) birthday of an older, much-loved family member. Knowing that a great-grandmother or grandfather or the family's oldest living great-aunt will be holding court at the reunion adds excitement to the event and attracts the mature—and the younger—family members to be part of what will be a historic family event.

PULLING YOUR TEAM TOGETHER

Once you have selected the family relative whom you will fete and a date for the reunion, you'll need to plan three initial mailings:

First mailing: Write to every family member and announce the date and occasion for the reunion...and ask for nominations for chairperson, secretary and treasurer for a Family Reunion Executive Committee.

Enclose a form for each position that includes full name, address, date of birth, phone number and qualifications of nominees.

Request that the form be returned within two weeks so a decision can be made quickly. Don't be surprised if you, as the driving force behind the reunion, wind up as chairperson.

Second mailing: Send everyone the names of the nominees, and include a ballot due back in two weeks. This democratic process will imbue the newly elected with legitimate authority.

Third mailing: Announce the names of the Executive Committee, and begin to get the entire family involved by calling for volunteers for the following committees:

- **Communications Committee.** Develops the mailing list. Keeps track of all the correspondence and forms that will be sent to and received from a growing list of family members, including the introductory letter, mailing list, family address and telephone numbers, birthday list and reservation forms.

- **Host Committee.** Chooses the ideal location for the reunion, such as an inn, dude ranch, spa, resort or family home.

- **Travel Committee.** Works with a travel agent to coordinate travel and accommodations...and gets the best price.

- **Welcoming Committee.** Greets and directs family members upon arrival in the host town.

- **Events Committee.** Plans raffles, scholarship awards, family member achievement awards.

- **Meals Committee.** Organizes the food for formal and informal indoor and outdoor events such as picnics, lunches and dances.

How to Help Yourself Heal from Your Spouse's Serious Illness

Rachael Freed, MSW, founder of Minneapolis-based Heartmates, Inc., which provides resources for heart patients and their families.

After a heart attack, life changes forever. We mourn our old innocent ways and our lost certainties. And—we face changes in lifestyle, financial security, retirement and our spouses' physical capabilities.

Learning to live with uncertainty is one of the greatest challenges for the partner of a person with heart disease.

Over the years, you have developed an idea of security. Now the rules have changed.

Important: Give yourself permission to break with family protocol and do whatever it takes to get all of you through. The task of a cardiac couple is to develop a "new normal" that incorporates heart disease.

The upside: A brush with mortality can reorder a couple's priorities for the better.

You don't have the power to eradicate your spouse's heart disease or to eliminate its effects on your life. Your goal is to be prepared to support his/her recovery—*and yours.*

Years after a cardiac event, people expect the heartmate to be a constant cheerleader.

My experience: During the crisis period, friends asked only about the patient. When the emergency was over, they were too uncomfortable to rally around. But I needed help—a lot of help.

GRIEF AND LOSS

After my husband's heart attack, I was coping, but I felt overwhelmed by strong feelings that took months to define. It was the grief that accompanies loss.

Since my husband was alive, how could I be feeling grief and loss? Because our life together had changed forever.

During an early presentation I made to spouses of heart attack survivors, I said, *"You are feeling grief."* Their tears and thanks convinced me that I was on the right track.

YOU'RE A TOP PRIORITY, TOO

The most important person in a heart patient's recovery is not the doctor, but the spouse. To maintain your role as a positive caretaker, you must pay attention to your own recovery.

Example: Airplane travelers are instructed to put their own oxygen masks on before helping someone else.

Taking care of yourself helps you come to terms with a life-changing crisis. *Steps to take...*

● **Make a list.** It should contain actions that would nourish your body, feelings, mind and spirit. Write one on your calendar every day—and do it.

Examples: Listen to music...sit in a chapel...take a walk.

● **Gather information.** Learn how diet, exercise and stress affect heart patients.

● **Confide in someone.** To reduce your sense of isolation, share your concerns with a nonjudgmental sibling, close friend or neighbor.

Many people find great relief by communicating with others in similar situations. *Good resource:* The Heartmates Web site at *www.heartmates.com.*

TAKE YOUR TIME

The nagging fear of another attack always churns below the surface. The fear never disappears entirely, but you'll begin to believe that your mate won't collapse every time he coughs.

Healing is a process, not an event. It takes at least a year, often two, to recover from a spouse's heart attack or cardiac event. No one but you can know the limits of your grieving period.

EMBRACE YOUR HEALING ROLE

Take these steps to reinforce family bonds and your vitality as a couple...

● **Involve the whole family.** The patient and family members may experience different realities. Learn what your family is feeling. At weekly problem-solving meetings, ask each person to describe his greatest concerns. Then discuss them.

Example: If your children are grown and living elsewhere, performing this exercise even once during a visit can break the tension and be extremely helpful.

●**Fight your guilt and fear of stressing the patient.** Use caution in all things, but be aware that the patient won't die if you accidentally sprinkle a little salt on his food...use a noisy vacuum cleaner...take some time for yourself...or cry.

●**Repair the heartmate connection.** Fear of communicating is common after the hospital stay has threatened the marriage bond.

The trauma pulls some cardiac couples apart, intensifying existing conflicts. For others, the crisis provides an opportunity for enriching the relationship.

Honest confrontation of the changes in your relationship is a step toward deepening the marriage connection. *Avoid these traps...*

●Concealing your concerns from the patient.

●Thinking you can reduce stress by withholding your anger and other negative feelings.

●Assuming you must always agree with the patient.

●Disregarding your own emotional needs.

●Letting TV preempt precious time to communicate with each other.

SEX: THE UNASKED QUESTION

At my group presentations, people almost never ask about sex. Privately, they are distraught by the silence, isolation and lack of information about impotence.

These misconceptions contribute to spouses' fear and apprehension...

Myth: Sexual activity is hazardous for heart patients.

Reality: For most, not so. The amount of energy expended during sex is roughly equivalent to climbing two flights of stairs. A patient who can do the latter can probably do the former safely.

Myth: Heart disease decreases sexual drive and impairs sexual functioning.

Reality: Fatigue, depression and medications for angina, high blood pressure or palpitations can cause impotence. Fatigue and depression can be treated. If medications are the problem, the doctor may be able to prescribe a different one.

Myth: Heart disease signifies the end of normal sexual activity.

Reality: After a few weeks of recuperation, the overwhelming majority of cardiac couples can resume their sexual relationship...and mend their bond through affection and physical intimacy.

How to Choose Support Groups

Audrey Gartner, director of the National Self-Help Clearinghouse in New York.

Whether you're coping with chronic illness, the loss of a loved one or any of a hundred other problems, chances are there's a support group to help you.

Getting support from people facing the same problems is reassuring...and therapeutic. Studies suggest that participation in a support group lowers psychological stress ...reduces depression...and raises self-esteem. It can also improve the prognosis for a range of ailments, from cancer to heart disease to infertility.

Recent finding: Women with metastatic breast cancer who belonged to a weekly support group survived 18 months longer than similar patients without peer support.

Support groups also provide their members with useful information about diseases and treatment options. That makes these groups more popular than ever in today's managed-health-care-environment, where time with doctors is limited.

INSIDE SUPPORT GROUPS

Groups generally range in size from a few members to about 25. Meetings are held anywhere from once a day to once a month. They usually last an hour or two.

Groups are led by trained lay members or by medical or mental health professionals. Some groups pass the hat or ask for nominal dues.

At meetings, members share feelings and coping strategies. Some groups also enlist experts to talk about relevant topics.

Examples: A diabetes support group asks a doctor to discuss blood sugar management...a phobia group brings in a psychologist to talk about desensitization techniques.

FINDING A GROUP

The nonprofit National Self-Help Clearinghouse (NSHC)* refers callers to one of about 50 regional self-help clearinghouses. Each of these keeps a directory of local support groups.

If there's no regional clearinghouse in an area, the NSHC refers callers to an appropriate national organization, such as the American Cancer Society or the American Heart Association.

Caution: Clearinghouses cannot vouch for every organization in their directories. A referral is not necessarily an endorsement. The responsibility is on the individual to determine if a group is appropriate and likely to be a productive source of help.

ONLINE SUPPORT

Self-help through the Internet can be a godsend for people who are housebound... geographically isolated...lack transportation... or have a condition so rare that their community doesn't have enough potential group members.

It's also appealing to people who want anonymity when discussing embarrassing topics. Internet support groups are great equalizers, too. Members know nothing of each other's age, ethnicity or economic status.

Online support group members may "meet" in chat rooms, post messages to public newsgroups or forums or e-mail other members.

Caution: In the largely unregulated realm of cyberspace, people are free to post inaccurate advice—with none of the accountability inherent in face-to-face group encounters.

As with all information you find on the Web, consider the source. Groups affiliated with well-known national organizations are safe bets, although these account for relatively few of the thousands of online self-help options.

*The NSHC can be reached at 212-817-1822. Or mail a request for information, along with a self-addressed, stamped, business-sized envelope, to the NSHC at 365 Fifth Ave., Suite 3300, New York 10016-4309.

For the remainder, it's a good idea to visit a new group several times to get a feel for its content and members before joining.

Whenever possible, send an e-mail to the group's administrator, whose address may be posted on the Web site. He/she can give you basic information about the group (group size, focus, etc.) before you decide to sign on.

FINDING ONLINE HELP

Three Web sites can be especially helpful in locating an online group that is right for you...

●**drkoop.com** *(www.drkoop.com).* Headed by former Surgeon General C. Everett Koop, MD, this site hosts message boards on a range of physical and mental ailments.

●**Mental Health Net** *(http://community.mentalhelp.net/forum/newforums.html).* This site provides links to dozens of groups focusing on topics from anxiety to depression to eating disorders.

●**Psych Central** *(www.psychcentral.com).* This site has links to hundreds of live chats and newsgroups on psychology and general mental health topics.

QUALITY CHECKS

As you assess an online or face-to-face group to decide if it's right for you, watch for these signs of potential trouble...

●**One or two people monopolize the conversation.** Every participant should feel free to contribute—or not. Groups should not become sounding boards for a few members' troubles.

●**The advice seems inappropriate.** Group members may insist, for instance, that other members take a particular action or use a certain medication or therapy. If you feel bullied, leave the group.

●**Members are urged to substitute self-help for professional diagnosis and treatment.** Self-help is a valuable adjunct to proper medical care—never a replacement for it.

Funeral Planning Trap

Prepaying for a funeral is a bad investment. *Problems:* It locks in arrangements that do not take into account that the person's wishes may change—such as after a divorce or remarriage. Also, the funeral industry is undergoing significant restructuring as more low-cost funeral operations are opening. The cost of a funeral may be significantly less in the future than it is today. *Better:* Fund funeral expenses within your estate assets unless you are applying for Medicaid. *Average funeral cost today:* $500 to $1,500 for a basic cremation…and $5,000 to $10,000 for an elaborate funeral.

Lisa Carlson, executive director, Funeral Consumers Alliance, a nonprofit group that monitors the funeral industry, Hinesburg, VT, and author of *Caring for the Dead*. Upper Access Publishers.

Lessons from Widowhood

Dr. Joyce Brothers, noted psychologist and author of *Widowed*. Ballantine Books.

My husband, Dr. Milton Brothers, died several years ago. As a psychologist, I knew that bereaved people pass through a predictable series of stages in the normal course of grieving, but this knowledge did not make my personal emotional turmoil any less.

EMOTIONAL RECOVERY

For months after losing Milton, after almost 40 years of an intensely happy marriage, I was in a state of despair…even though I was financially secure and my career kept me constantly busy. All my lecturing, writing and traveling seemed meaningless without my husband to share it. I was overcome by agonizing loneliness.

Today, the loneliness is still there, but it is much less intense. Life has recovered its meaning. Once again, I am able to look forward to new experiences and when I think of my husband, most of the time it brings not tears but smiles because of the legacy of happy memories he left me.

STAGES OF GRIEF

British psychiatrist Dr. Colin Parkes discovered the predictable stages of grief following the loss of a spouse or other close relative.

First stage: Immediately following the death is shock…followed by numbness.

Even though Milt had been struggling for 18 months with terminal cancer, his death still came as a dramatic shock to me.

In the immediate aftermath, I was kept so busy notifying relatives and friends and arranging the details of the funeral that I was essentially operating on autopilot, feeling nothing.

To this day, I still cannot remember the details of those days immediately following Milt's death…not even what I wore to the funeral.

Second stage: Suffering. When the numbness wears off, the pain begins.

Every person's pain is different…a different blend of emotions…a different period of time needed to recover.

The pain seems to be least for those who have suffered a lot in life and learned to accept the vicissitudes it brings.

I was not one of those people, because my life had been full of love, happiness and achievement…all shared with Milt.

Now I recognize that my major emotional problem was self-pity. *I cried…*

- **When someone asked how I was.**
- **When I reached out for Milton**—and once again—I remembered him in his absence.
- **Whenever I passed our favorite restaurant.**
- **When I saw Milt's car.**
- **When I recognized Milton's signature.**

Value of tears: When someone cries, it makes others uncomfortable and they usually try to make the person crying feel better. But research has shown that crying fulfills a valuable physiological function.

Tears of sadness or anger contain leucine enkephalin, a natural pain reliever, and prolactin, a hormone that encourages the secretion of tears. These chemicals are produced in the brain at times of stress. This has led biochemists to suggest that crying is an emotionally helpful process that relieves stress by washing out the chemicals that stress builds up.

So I believe that tears are really a widow's friend, helping her deal with the frustrations and difficulties of life without her helpmate.

As I began to emerge from the stage of intense suffering, the nature of my tears began to change. One day, on the farm where my husband and I had spent so many of our favorite hours together, I noticed the coffee pot. I touched it, remembering how much pride Milt always took in the coffee he made, and I cried.

But this time, I realized that I was not shedding tears for myself and my constant loneliness...they were for Milt, dead at only 62, missing out on decades of vibrant life he should have continued to enjoy. I was emerging from the depths.

OTHER REACTIONS

•**Anger.** Along with sadness, I was full of anger, like many widows. I was angry at Milt for leaving me alone to deal with many unfamiliar aspects of life. I was angry at him for continuing to smoke even though he, a physician, certainly knew the association between smoking and disease, including the cancer that killed him. And I was angry whenever I saw couples together, enjoying what I had lost.

It is natural for widows to be angry. The loss of emotional security accompanied by loneliness produces tremendous stress. Stress, say experts like Dr. John Larson of the Institute of Stress Medicine at Norwalk Hospital, deprives brain cells of essential nutrients and leaves the victim irritable and angry.

•**Insecurity.** Widowhood lowers a woman's social status and leaves her feeling insecure in many different ways.

Even though I am something of a celebrity, professionally successful and financially comfortable, I was not immune from insecurity.

One afternoon, a major talk show failed to call me back to confirm the date I was tentatively scheduled for. Normally, I would not have been concerned. But, just six months after Milt's death, I felt they didn't want me on their show...and nobody else would, ever again.

I was only reassured when the scheduler called me again the next morning, explaining that she hadn't been able to speak to the producer earlier.

COPING WITH LOSS

My experience has taught me that nothing can prepare you for the devastating experience of the loss of a loved one. I was not able to manage my grief better than anyone else. *But I have learned firsthand a number of ways a widow can help herself...*

•**Stay in control of your life.** It is very helpful if a child or other close relative offers to take care of all your bills, taxes and financial matters...but don't let the person do it for more than a month or two.

It shouldn't take long to learn how to take care of basic bill paying and check balancing yourself. For tax expertise, you may want to hire an accountant or other professional...but you make the decisions.

•**Avoid hasty decisions.** If possible, a widow should not make any major decisions for at least a year after her husband's death. If you cannot avoid it, get the best advice you can from a variety of sources.

I regret that a few weeks after Milt died I sold his big farm tractor to a neighbor, thinking I would never need it. Now I regret that I didn't keep it and learn to operate it, so that every time I used it, Milt's memory would have ridden along with me.

•**Maintain your regular routine.** Losing a husband is such a shock that it seems hard to do anything. If you succumb to that, you may end up in a long-term state of depression. Pushing yourself to continue your regular activities serves as an early therapy for grief. Later, when the grief has eased, you will find it easier to make changes.

•**Plan anniversaries and holidays**—they are more painful because of the memories they evoke.

Helpful: Surround yourself with people. The first Thanksgiving after Milt's death, I invited 18 people to the farm for Thanksgiving weekend. I was far too busy to feel miserable. If you can't do it with your own family, invite people you know who will be alone otherwise. You will do good for them as well as yourself...always a rewarding experience. Weekends are also times of potential loneliness, so be sure to plan ahead so you have something worthwhile to do…religious services…sports or hobbies.

●**Be good to yourself.** Widows need coddling…so coddle yourself. Get your hair done …have a facial or massage…and be sure to exercise.

●**Check your progress.** Every three months, see how you have progressed. Do you feel better? Are you less depressed? The answer will not always be yes. But as the months pass, you will notice signs of improvement. There is no timetable, but if you see no progress after a year, it may be a good idea to consult your doctor or therapist for advice and reassurance. You will always feel your loss, but with time you should be able to smile once again. I know that I do, especially when the many happy hours I spend with our grandchildren remind me what a joyous legacy Milton left behind.

How to Make New Friends

To create opportunities to strike up new friendships:

●**Carry an interesting book or pamphlet with you.**

●**Wear an unusual T-shirt.**

●**Walk a dog.**

●**Go window shopping.**

●**Have a party and invite each guest to bring a friend, too.**

Take active steps to meet new people…and to become closer to people you already know.

Suggestion: Get more involved with people who share some of your interests.

●**Always attend large family gatherings.** You will find that your relatives are more interesting than you thought when you were a kid.

●**Find out more about the people at work.** Take every opportunity to attend trade shows and conventions where you will have the chance to meet new people.

●**Join service, sports or volunteer organizations.** The other people there all share at least one of your interests. When you get to know them better, you will find some who have even more in common with you.

●**Join specialty clubs such as chess and card clubs.**

●**Enroll in continuing education classes** in subjects you want to learn more about.

●**Visit libraries and bookstores,** especially for author readings and literary discussion groups.

Getting started…

Make a list of specific things you might do to make a friend. If you have trouble thinking of any, begin with some of the suggestions above. Then choose one from your list—*and do it.*

Two weeks later, go back to your list and choose another reaching-out activity.

Perry Treadwell, PhD, a consultant on relationships. He is author of Making Friends, Leaving Loneliness Behind. Health Communications.

An Openhearted Hug

When you hug someone you love, take hold of the person and in the first breath, in and out, be totally present with him/her—no place else in the world.

Then hold the person for three breaths.

Nothing more.

Nothing less.

Thich Nhat Hanh, Nobel Peace Prize nominee from Plum Village, France, and author of more than 75 books, including The Miracle of Mindfulness. Beacon Press.

The Astounding Healing Power of Pets

Gail Vines, PhD, a science journalist based in Cambridge, England, and author of Raging Hormones. University of California Press.

Animals, like babies, can do wonders for the image, which is why politicians try to be photographed with both as often as possible. Every American president in living memory has exploited his pet's electoral appeal.

Millie Bush, the former president's Spaniel, wrote a best-seller and Socks Clinton, former First Cat of the White House, had his own newsletter. But are companion animals as good for your health as they are for the profile?

Public health experts have long been skeptical. After all, dogs bite and pass on parasites, pigeons and parrots cause lung disease, cats can provoke asthma and tortoises can transmit salmonela. Yet animal lovers should take heart from several findings.

In 1991, researchers at the University of Cambridge discovered that just months after acquiring a cat or a dog, some Britons suffered less from perennial health problems such as headache, backache and flu. And Australians who keep pets were found to have less cholesterol in their blood than non-pet owners with comparable lifestyles, making them less likely to develop heart disease.

These findings may be little more than puzzling correlations. Why should owning a pet make you less likely to suffer from backache? Why should it reduce your cholesterol level? But many researchers suspect that the answers are in the subtle links between mental and physical well-being.

PETS AND LONGEVITY

The first hint that pets could help some people to live longer came from a discovery made by Erica Friedmann, at the time a graduate student at the University of Maryland and later at the City University of New York. She investigated whether a person's social life and degree of social isolation might influence his/her ability to survive a heart attack.

Friedmann interviewed 92 convalescing male patients and quizzed them in detail about their lifestyle, a few questions touching upon pets. A year later 14 of the 92 men had died. Friedmann went back to her data to look for differences between those who had and those who had not survived. She found that socially isolated people were more likely to succumb, and that those who had pets were more likely to recover.

So unexpected was this finding that Friedmann began to look for other explanations. Perhaps the benefits came from the extra exercise dog owners took walking their pets. Yet she found that people with other sorts of pets that needed no exercise were also more likely to survive. She then investigated the possibility that pet owners were healthier to start with and so had less severe heart attacks. This theory also proved to be false.

Nor did pet owners appear to have different psychological make-ups from those without pets, at least judging from their responses to a wide range of standard psychological tests. Friedmann concluded that owning a pet really did help people to recover after a heart attack.

The benefit she found was small: A 3% decline in the probability of death. But given that more than a million people in the US die of heart disease every year, that means that pets could help 30,000 Americans to survive in any given year.

In another study by Warwick Anderson at the Baker Medical Research Institute in Prahran, Australia, 5,741 people attending a heart disease risk clinic were questioned about their lifestyle and whether they had any pets. Researchers found that the average cholesterol level of the 784 patients who owned pets was 2% lower than those who did not own pets. Epidemiologists estimate that this might lower the risk of heart attack by 4%. Pet owners also had lower levels of triglyceride fats in their blood and lower blood pressure, which indicated that owning a pet was as efficient at reducing blood pressure as eating a low-salt diet or cutting down on alcohol.

FISHY EXPERIENCE

No one has yet suggested a mechanism by which pets could lower levels of cholesterol or triglyceride fats. But Friedmann and her team have at least established that people sometimes produce physiological responses to animals. They measured the blood pressure of volunteers who were either resting, talking, reading out loud or greeting their dogs. As expected, blood pressure levels rose as the volunteers performed the slightly stressful tasks of talking or reading to the experimenters. But when the volunteers talked to their dogs, their blood pressure fell to resting levels or below.

121

What's more, it seems that such responses do not necessarily depend on stroking or talking to a pet. In various tests involving psychological questionnaires and standard observational checks of anxiety levels, adults and children proved to be more relaxed simply in the presence of a friendly dog. Aaron Katcher, a psychiatrist at the University of Pennsylvania, showed that people who watch an aquarium full of tropical fish experience a fall in blood pressure greater than those who merely stare at a blank wall.

Yet such studies do not prove there is anything special about our reactions to animals. It has long been known that anything that distracts our attention from our preoccupations has a calming effect on the body. In another experiment by Katcher, watching a videotape of tropical fish proved more absorbing and relaxing than watching a tankful of real fish, judging from measurements of blood pressure. Could pets improve human health simply by distracting and absorbing us?

Many researchers think this is unlikely. According to advocates of "pet therapy," animals can also make us feel better indirectly, by making strange settings or people seem less threatening. It is hard to design experiments to test this theory rigorously, but anecdotal evidence abounds. In the late 1960s, for example, Boris Levinson, an American psychiatrist, noticed that severely withdrawn children who were afraid to communicate with people made rapid contact with his dog Jingles. By carefully insinuating himself into the child-dog relationship, Levinson found he was able to reach his child patients.

Animals can even promote social contact between strangers. Peter Messent, a British zoologist, spent days hanging around public parks watching people strolling through. Those with dogs were much more likely to experience positive encounters with other people, including prolonged conversations with people who were alone or with children.

Pets may thus be "confirming cultural symbols of harmless respectability," says James Serpell, formerly director of the Companion Animal Research Group at the University of Cambridge and later at the University of Pennsylvania. But his research shows that they are far more than this. According to questionnaire responses, pet owners value their pets "as distinctive personalities with whom they have affectionate relationships." And it is here, in friendship, argues Serpell, that we find the real explanation for pets' beneficial effects on our health.

Study after study has shown that people who feel isolated and depressed are more likely to succumb to illness than people who claim to be content. And Serpell and his colleagues were the first to show that pets could improve an ordinary person's general health. They recruited three groups of people. At the start, there was no significant difference between their scores on a questionnaire monitoring minor health problems. Then one group of people were given dogs, another cats.

A month later, they filled in the questionnaire again. Those who owned new pets reported a marked improvement in their general health, which lasted throughout the 10-month study. In contrast to Friedmann's earlier study, dog owners fared slightly better than cat owners, perhaps partly because they also increased the amount of exercise they took. Serpell then repeated the study over 18 months, with three times as many people, all of whom had the same socioeconomic status. He also had access to doctors' assessments of their patients' health. The results supported the conclusions of the earlier study.

GOOD LISTENERS

Part of the explanation, argues Serpell, is that pets can provide owners "with a special kind of emotional support which is lacking, or at least uncommon, in relationships between people." He claims that an animal's muteness is a boon, not a burden. The problem with language is that although we use it to communicate our deepest thoughts and emotions, we also use it to deceive, misinform, criticize and insult others. The fact that pets listen and seem to understand but do not question or evaluate may be one of their most endearing assets as companions, says Serpell. It resembles the relationships some psychotherapists try to build.

Dogs and cats are the most cherished animal companions, largely because they are adept at feeding us with nonverbal signs of affection, argues Serpell. They make us feel respected, admired and wanted. The typical feline expression of slightly detached contentment is enormously appealing to humans, while the way dogs' facial muscles are arranged enables them to express a wide range of human-looking emotions.

"Our confidence, self-esteem, ability to cope with the stresses of life and, ultimately, our physical health depend on this sense of belonging," says Serpell. The sense of responsibility involved in caring for an animal is especially significant. Such nurturing gives meaning to our lives, a sense of being needed that can deeply sustain an ability to set personal goals. "Far from being perverted, extravagant or the victims of misplaced parental instincts, most owners are normal rational people who make use of animals to augment their existing social relationships," says Serpell.

CHILDHOOD EXPERIENCES

Why, then, doesn't everyone keep pets? Serpell has found that childhood experiences with pets are the key. Children brought up with pets are much more likely to have them as adults. Those who went without pets as children seem to remain indifferent to companion animals throughout their lives.

Childhood experience also seems to direct preferences for animals in specific ways. People brought up with dogs remain dog lovers, those with cats, cat lovers. Only those who had both as children remain fond of both. No one has yet found consistent personality differences between cat and dog lovers, nor between pet owners and nonpet owners.

Yet people who have, or have had, pets do tend to have something distinctive about them. In a survey of undergraduates, Serpell's colleague Elizabeth Paul found that people who have had experience with pets tend to have a more positive and humane attitude to animals and the environment, and a tendency to have greater "emotional empathy" for people, too.

Pet ownership has its disadvantages, however, not least of which is the risk of catching something from your companion animal. Britain's canine population deposits about 4.5 million liters of urine and one million kilograms of feces every day, some of it in public places where it can be a health hazard.

Dogs can transmit *toxocariasis* (visceral larva migrans)—infection by a roundworm parasite—which can cause blindness in children. But the condition remains rare—about 10 cases of toxocariasis are reported each year in England and Wales—and can be prevented by giving puppies and nursing bitches antiworm drugs.

More common is *toxoplasmosis*, with symptoms like glandular fever, caused by a parasitic protozoan. About 700 cases are reported each year in Britain, and most people catch it by eating undercooked meat from sheep, goats and pigs, or by coming in contact with cat feces. The parasite can be avoided by wearing gloves when gardening or handling cat litter, and washing hands after handling raw meat. Bird-fanciers need to be on guard for *psittacosis*, caused by a viruslike organism inhaled in the dust from the droppings or feathers of infected birds. The flulike symptoms can be treated with antibiotics.

Pet animals also cause significant injury to people: In Britain alone, more than a quarter of a million dog bites are registered each year. Yet many of these problems could be minimized by public education and restrictions on dogs in recreation areas, according to the report of a working party on companion animals in society, set up by the Council for Science and Society in London.

There are more grounds for concern, perhaps, from the pets' point of view—not all pet owners are good for their animal's health.

Every summer, animal shelters run by charities fill up with pets abandoned as their owners go on holiday. New forms of exploitation may emerge if the health benefits of keeping pets becomes widely accepted. According to Nicholas Tucker, a psychologist at the University of Sussex, "pet burnout" (tiredness and irritability) has been recorded among some of the dogs and cats acting as four-footed therapists among the mentally ill or socially deprived. In the US, castrated, de-toothed monkeys have been trained to act as domestic servants to paraplegic patients. "Being de-clawed or un-voiced may be fairer on the furniture or the neighbors,"

Tucker says, "but what might it be doing to the pets?"

Canine Tips

To cure dogs of pulling without jerking or tugging them, simply stop in your tracks whenever you feel tension on the lead from the dog pulling. Do not move until the dog turns around or backs up to get slack in the leash. Then praise the dog and continue walking. Most dogs will quickly learn that they get to keep moving forward only when the leash is slack, not when they pull on it and make it tight.

Dennis Fetko, PhD, dog trainer and applied animal behaviorist, San Diego, quoted in *Your Dog,* Box 2626, Greenwich, CT 06836.

Feline Tips

Danger to cats: Dog flea products. Cats are very sensitive to high concentrations (45% to 65%) of the chemical *permethrin,* which is found in some dog "spot-on" flea products. Severe illness or death can result when cats are exposed to this ingredient. *Self-defense:* Protect cats from fleas only with products made specifically for cats. Don't use even small amounts of products made for dogs. Follow all usage instructions carefully. Contact your veterinarian at any sign of a problem. *Caution:* Products with identical brand names may contain different ingredients, depending on whether they are designed for dogs or cats. Be sure to buy the right formula.

E. Kathryn Meyer, VMD, coordinator, US Pharmacopeia Veterinary Practitioners' Reporting Program, Rockville, MD.

10

Home Smarts

Safety for Seniors

Each year many older Americans are injured in and around their homes. The kitchen and bathroom are two of the areas in which accidents are most likely to occur. Here's some advice that can keep you from paying a visit to a hospital emergency room…

IN THE KITCHEN

Keep anything that might catch fire away from the range—that includes flammable and combustible items, towels and curtains.

Don't wear garments with loose long sleeves when cooking; besides the likelihood of catching fire, they are apt to catch on pot handles, overturning pots and pans and causing scalds.

Avoid shocks or even electrocution by keeping electrical appliances and power cords away from the sink and hot surfaces. *Precaution:* Move appliances closer to wall outlets or to different outlets so you won't need extension cords.

Low lighting and glare can be contributors to burns or cuts. *Remedy:* Improve lighting by opening curtains and blinds (unless this causes too much glare); use maximum wattage bulbs allowed in each fixture; reduce glare by using frosted bulbs, indirect lighting, shades or globes or partially closing blinds; install under-cabinet or countertop lighting.

Guard against falls. Don't stand on chairs or boxes to reach high shelves. Buy a step stool (preferably one with a handrail). Before climbing on a step stool, make sure it's opened and stable. Tighten screws and braces on step stools. Discard any step stool with broken parts.

IN THE BATHROOM

Equip bathtubs and showers with nonskid mats, abrasive strips or surfaces that are not slippery.

Grab bars can help you get into and out of your bath or shower, and can help prevent falls. *Warning:* Test existing bars for strength

Consumer Product Safety Commission, Washington, DC 20207.

125

and stability. Attach grab bars, through the tile, to structural supports in the wall, or install bars specifically designed to attach to the sides of the bathtub.

Keep your hot water heater set to "low" or 120 degrees. Water temperature above 120 degrees can cause tap water scalds.

Always check water temperature by hand before entering bath or shower.

Tip: Taking baths, rather than showers, reduces the risk of a scald from suddenly changing water temperatures.

Financing a Retirement Home

Maureen Tsu, CFP, San Juan Capistrano, CA, quoted in *Where to Retire,* 1502 Augusta Dr., Suite 415, Houston 77057.

When buying a retirement home, a key decision is whether to purchase it with cash or finance it with a mortgage.

Many people prefer the security of buying with cash and not owing any debt on their home.

Drawback: Using so much cash may leave you cash poor and limit the lifestyle you can afford in retirement.

Contrast: Buying a home with a mortgage can leave you with more spendable cash. The debt on the home can be paid off or refinanced upon your death.

Issues if you decide to finance with a mortgage...

●**Can you obtain tax benefits** from deducting mortgage interest? Do you have enough total deductions to itemize deductions? Are you in a high enough tax bracket to make it worthwhile?

●**Can you invest the cash saved** by buying with a mortgage to earn a higher after-tax rate of return than you will pay on the mortgage?

●**Are you willing to have your estate deal** with the debt on your home by selling it, or by having heirs refinance it at your death?

Issues if you buy with cash...

●**Will you have a way of tapping your equity in the home** to raise cash in an emergency?

●**After spending cash on the home,** will you have enough money to enjoy a comfortable retirement lifestyle?

●**Will your estate eventually sell the home for cash**—so that you might as well take the cash while you are alive by financing the home?

Best: Consider these issues before you retire, while you are still working. You will have more options and a stronger credit standing to make any arrangement you finally choose.

Simple System to Help You Find the Right Retirement Community

Deborah Freundlich, copublisher of *Briefing,* a restaurant marketing newsletter from American Express, and author of *Retirement Living Communities.* Macmillan.

While you are strong and healthy, energetic and living comfortably in a community where you have good support services, friends and family, you probably give little thought to the prospect of moving to a full-service retirement community.

But—this is precisely the time to investigate possible future living arrangements. You don't want to delay the search until you are sick, injured or have lost a helpful spouse.

Look for a retirement living community (RLC) leisurely and carefully. The search can be very enjoyable.

●**Start with a paper search.** Think of it as gathering information for a vacation spot. Ask friends...and the children of people you know who have moved to such communities...and senior citizen groups in your community what places they know of *both good and bad.* Send for literature on RLCs located in areas you might find attractive.

Try to be open about location. Don't think only about how convenient a place is to your children or other family members. You will be there 100% of the time and that's what counts most.

● **Review your finances.** This will be your first opportunity to analyze the financial implications of a move to an RLC. You will have to make a substantial advance payment—in many cases more than $100,000—to qualify for most RLCs.

Be realistic about what you can afford. Above all, ask lots of questions and compare the costs of your prospective RLC with your current expenses.

CHECK THEM OUT

Visit as many RLCs as you can. Arrange short excursions or vacation travel so that you can spend some time at a prospective RLC. Call ahead in plenty of time to arrange a stay—at least one night but preferably longer—in a guest house or guest room in the community. *Check out...*

● **The food and ambience of the communal dining facilities.** Meals tend to be a focal point of your life at any such facility.

Opportunity: The dining room is the best place to meet and talk with the residents to get an idea of whether they are people you would like to spend time with.

● **Nursing and custodial services and facilities.** *Preferable:* A special wing for residents with Alzheimer's or other forms of dementia. Such people need special care and may disrupt other residents who require health care.

Extras: Be sure to get a clear—preferably written—explanation of what extra costs might be involved if one spouse needs special nursing care while the other is well enough to live independently in the RLC with minimal care.

● **Transportation.** Even if the RLC has its own golf course, swimming pool and other sports and community facilities, you will probably want the ability to travel easily to nearby shopping malls, theaters, concert halls and houses of worship. Make sure there is regular, convenient and economical van or bus service. Use it during your visit even if you have your own car.

WHAT IT COSTS

Once you narrow down your prospects, talk seriously about finances with staff members of the RLC.

Don't be pushed into a premature discussion of a contract and finances by overeager staffers during your visit. The most desirable RLCs have waiting lists. In fact, beware of those with an occupancy rate under 85%—*and* hard-sell tactics. *Ask about...*

● **Advance payments.** What is refundable, partially refundable or nonrefundable.

● **Monthly charges.** And what they cover—specifically. Ask what the guarantee is that the charges will not increase—or how such increases will be determined.

● **Added charges.** Charges that might be added if you need more intensive nursing or medical services...or if you have to be moved to an affiliated hospital, rehabilitation facility or medical center.

● **All special fees.**

● **Special benevolent funds.** Should you or your spouse live well beyond any reasonable life expectancy, you could run out of money and you may need to rely on these special funds.

Once a particular RLC begins to seem like an attractive possibility, ask for a complete package of its financial statements. The RLC must make them available to you.

Be sure the statements are recent and audited by a reputable professional. Even if you feel comfortable making sense of balance sheets and profit-and-loss statements, have a CPA evaluate them. You don't want to make a substantial advance payment and then find yourself in a community that begins to skimp on services because of financial problems.

If you decide to sign a contract and get on the waiting list, you can be confident that you've done all that you can to assure yourself the best of care for the last years of your life.

The Very Best Mortgage

Avoid a 30-year mortgage if you do not expect to be in the house for anything close to 30 years. The shorter the time period for which you borrow, the lower the interest rate. So if you plan to stay in a house for only five or so years, you are overspending by taking out a 30-year mortgage. *Alternatives:* Balloon mortgages, which have a fixed rate for five or seven years and then jump to a higher rate...or adjustable-rate mortgages if you plan to stay just a few years.

Robert Van Order, chief economist, Freddie Mac, McLean, VA.

Moving Does Not Have to Be Traumatic

Cathy Goodwin, PhD, author of *Making the Big Move: How to Transform Relocation into a Creative Life Transition.* New Harbinger Publications. She has moved more than 12 times in her life and is currently professor of marketing at Nova Southeastern University in Fort Lauderdale, FL.

Whether you are moving to a smaller space in the same city...to a retirement community in another state ...or to an apartment across the country, there are steps you can take to minimize the disruption that relocation invariably causes.

First, make sure moving is something you want to do. People who feel forced to move often experience anger and resentment on top of all the normal relocation-induced feelings of loneliness, anxiety, excitement and expectation.

PSYCHOLOGICAL ISSUES

If moving is something you've decided is right for you, make it easier on yourself by working through some of the psychological issues ahead of time.

●**List the activities you most enjoy doing.** Think of the roles you play in life that define you. Ask yourself what it is about your home environment that energizes you.

It's often the seemingly trivial routines and comforts—like a morning cup of cappuccino at the local coffee shop—that we miss most in a new location. If you make careful note of these comforts, you'll be able to duplicate them in your new home.

●**Prepare for moving by deciding who you are.** Decide what you need around you in order to fully express your identity.

Exercise 1: Who are you? As quickly as you can, complete the sentence, "I am a ____" 10 times.

Examples: I am a mother, I am an artist, I am a gardener, etc.

Review what you've written and think about what it reveals about you. What, if anything, will change if you move to a new location?

Exercise 2: Which routines are important to you? You will gain an understanding of the importance of your daily routines by writing them down. *As thoroughly as possible, write down...*

1. What you do on weekday mornings.

Example: Wake up without an alarm clock ...walk the dogs...drive to the local newsstand for the paper...stop at the corner coffee shop.

2. What you do to relax in the evening.

3. How you spend Saturday mornings.

When you've completed this exercise, ask yourself how you'd feel about interrupting these routines.

Though the details you record may seem trivial, it's often these little changes and losses that increase the psychological trauma of moving.

PRESERVING COMFORTS AND ROUTINES

By understanding which routines and comforts are important to you, you'll more easily develop replacements in your new community. *Do some homework before the move...*

●**Learn all you can about your prospective community.** Use the Internet to research the community and learn about its character/ culture.

By typing in the city and state you're considering, you can learn about museums and theater programs...local businesses and restaurants ...opportunities for continuing education... medical services...transportation, etc.

Use the library to research the archives of the local newspaper.

Better: Make a premove visit to the area you're considering and talk to people of all ages about what it's like to live in the area.

• **Visualize how you'll spend a day in the new location.** Begin by visualizing your new home for 15 to 20 minutes. Relax, close your eyes and get comfortable.

Ask yourself: What is my ideal home? Where does the sun rise and set? Are there skylight windows? Lamps? Overhead lighting? What is the shape of each room, and what kind of furniture do I see in each? Who or what do I see in the home with me (spouse, dog, cat)?

After you've pictured your new home in your mind, visualize a day in your new community. See yourself waking up. What will you do next? What familiar roles might be useful in your new location? What new roles or activities might you engage in? What problems might you encounter (e.g., no coffee shop!) and how will you deal with these problems?

When you've completed this exercise, write down any insights you've gained, then compare your notes with your real life in the new location after you've moved.

FOR RENTERS

If you choose to rent, place a "Rental Wanted" classified ad in the local paper. I've done this twice. As a result, I've learned about really fine properties that are typically only rented by word-of-mouth.

And, contrary to what many people think, I didn't get any crank phone calls.

Sample ad: *Model tenant with steady income seeks single-level, three-bedroom apartment. References provided.*

PLANNING A NO-TEARS MOVE

• **Use checklists provided by moving companies as well as lists found in books, such as...**

• *Moving: A Complete Checklist and Guide for Relocation* by Karen G. Adams (Silvercat Publications).

• *Steiner's Complete How to Move Handbook* by Clyde Steiner (Dell).

• **Put together an emotional first-aid kit.** Your kit can include coping statements such as, "I will just let go and relax"..."I can deal with this"...or "I've survived this before...I can do it again."

Add to the kit meditation and visualization books and tapes. Also include the phone numbers of old friends—at least one to laugh with, one to listen to you and one who moved recently and can give good advice. Pick up a journal in which you can record your thoughts, concerns and feelings.

Moving to a New State

Get expert advice from a local real estate broker and a local real estate attorney before looking at any houses. *Reason:* Real estate laws and prevailing practices can be different among states and mistakes can be costly. *Questions to ask...*

• **What is the customary spread between list and sale prices?**

• **How much inventory is on the market?** And what is the average time a house stays on the market?

• **Do I need a lawyer to close?**

• **How much are transfer taxes?** When real estate is bought and sold, a tax is paid to transfer the property. This may be paid by the buyer or the seller...or split between them.

• **How long am I committed to a broker with which I sign?**

• **How have property taxes increased over time?** How are they evaluated? Sometimes, the property tax increases upon the completion of a purchase.

• **How much money do I have to give when the offer is made?** How much when the contract is written?

• **What if I want to back out after signing an agreement** and paying a deposit?

Useful resources: Relocation Directors Council (312-726-7410 or *www.rdcrelo.org*) ...Employee Relocation Council (202-857-0857 or *www.erc.org*).

Marge Fisher, management and relocation consultant in Riverside, CT.

Pitfalls When Buying a New Condominium

Dorothy Tyrnon, author, *The Condominium: A Guide for the Alert Buyer.* Golden-Lee Books.

Buying a condominium is more complicated than buying a house. *Reason:* The purchase is really for two separate pieces of property—your unit and the property held in common. *Before signing any contract for a new condominium, which is harder to check out than an established condominium, buyers should study the prospectus for any of these pitfalls:*

• **The prospectus includes a plan of the unit you are buying,** showing rooms of specific dimensions. But the plan omits closet space. *Result:* The living space you are buying is probably smaller than you think.

• **The prospectus includes this clause:** "The interior design shall be substantially similar." *Result:* The developer can alter both the size and design of your unit.

• **The common charges set forth in the prospectus are unrealistically low.** Buyers should never rely on a developer's estimate of common charges. *Instead:* They should find out the charges at similarly functioning condominiums.

Common charges include: Electricity for hallways and outside areas, water, cleaning, garbage disposal, insurance for common areas, pool maintenance, groundskeeping, legal and accounting fees, reserves for future repairs.

• **Variation on the common-charge trap.** The developer is paying common charges on unsold units. But these charges are unrealistically low. *Reason:* The developer has either underinsured or underestimated the taxes due, omitted security expenses or failed to set up a reserve fund.

• **The prospectus includes this clause:** "The seller will not be obligated to pay monthly charges for unsold units." *Result:* The owners of a partially occupied condominium have to pay for all operating expenses.

• **The prospectus warns about the seller's limited liability.** But an unsuspecting buyer may still purchase a condominium unit on which back monthly charges are due, or even on which there's a lien for failure to pay back carrying charges.

• **The prospectus makes no mention of parking spaces.** *Result:* You must lease from the developer.

• **The prospectus is imprecise about the total number of units to be built.** *Result:* Facilities are inadequate for the number of residents.

• **The prospectus includes this clause:** "**Transfer of ownership (of the common property from the developer to the home-owners' association) will take place 60 days after the last unit is sold.**" *Trap:* The developer deliberately does not sell one unit, keeps on managing the condominium and awards sweetheart maintenance and operating contracts to his subcontractors.

• **The prospectus specifies that the developer will become the property manager of the functioning condominium.** But the language spelling out monthly common charges and management fees is imprecise. *Result:* The owners cannot control monthly charges and fees.

Is Your Property's Assessed Value Too High?

The effective real estate tax is the tax rate multiplied by the assessed value. There's not much an individual can do about the tax rate, but assessment can often be challenged successfully. *Requirements:* Proof that either the property is overvalued or the assessment is higher than on comparable property in the same area. *When to ask for a reduction:*

• **Just before making necessary repairs of damages that have lowered the value.**

• **Local tax records err in description by overstating size or income.**

• **Net income drops due to factors beyond owner's control.**

• **When the price paid for the building in an arm's length transaction is lower than the assessed value.**

What to do:

●**Determine the ratio of the assessed value to the present market value.** Compare with average ratios of similar properties recently sold in the same area. *Sources:* Ratios are available to the public in tax districts. Real estate brokers or professional assessors can also be consulted.

●**Check tax records for a description of the property.**

●**Consult a lawyer on the strength of the case,** whether it can be handled by an informal talk with the assessor, and how much it will cost if a formal proceeding and appeal are necessary.

When the New House Is a Lemon

A home buyer may be able to get out of the entire purchase contract if the seller has misrepresented a house with many serious defects.

Normally, when defects show up after the buyers move in, they can sue for damages. Some state courts have ruled that two reasons for suing may void the entire sale: (1) Misrepresentation of an important aspect of the house. (2) The presence of many serious defects.

One case: The builder had assured the buyer that there would be no water problem. But the house was flooded soon after the closing. The court said the related damage would be impossible to repair.

Chastain v. Billings, 570 SW2d 866.

When to Watch Your Broker Closely

A company or individual listing property for sale with a real estate agent may find it's no longer listed after an offer is turned down.

Reason: The agent is trying to make the commission by temporarily taking the property off the active list in the hope the owner will give up and accept the offer. The agent may keep other agents from sending around prospects by removing the file or spreading the word that the property has been sold.

How to Sell Your Own Home Fast

William Supple, Jr., publisher of *Picket Fence Preview,* for-sale-by-owner real estate magazines serving Vermont, New York and New Hampshire. He is also co-founder of the National For Sale By Owner Association, a nonprofit group that helps home owners sell their own property. Mr. Supple is author of *How to Sell Your Own Home.* Picket Fence Publishing.

When my wife and I wanted to sell our home several years ago, we found that real estate agents weren't for us.

Agents typically charge a commission of around 6%. That means they'll take $9,000 of your equity from the sale of a $150,000 home.

In fact, the biggest myth in real estate is that you need an agent to sell your home.

Selling your house yourself often means selling it faster, and saving thousands of dollars in the process. Since you don't have to inflate your price by the amount of the commission, you'll sell sooner than a comparable agent-listed property.

Almost 60% of all real estate agent listings don't sell during the listing period. Many of these home owners then take matters into their own hands and sell by themselves. *Here's how to sell your own home...*

●**Set the right price.** Few home sellers know the market value of their property. Get a professional appraisal ($200 to $300). This will tell you the highest possible price to expect for your home in the current market.

Price your home using the appraisal and the market's supply and demand. *Example:* If you're in a tough buyer's market (with many similar homes on the market), price your home at or below appraised value. Our experience shows us that buyers are more likely to make a reasonable offer on a fairly priced home, and no offers on an overpriced one.

●**Fix and clean everything.** A potential buyer expects a home to be in move-in condition. Buyers will tolerate a little wear and tear, but you're more likely to get a full price offer when the buyer falls in love with your immaculate home.

Pay particular attention to your home's exterior. If the exterior is not in good condition, potential buyers will drive right by without stopping to go inside.

●**Use a multipronged approach to advertise your house.** A classified ad in the local paper is the traditional route, and sometimes these ads are effective.

But if you want to sell your home fast, yard signs and for-sale-by-owner publications are the way to go.

According to a survey of home buyers by *USA Today,* an astounding 49% of them found their future residence simply by noticing a sign in the front yard.

The most effective way to find buyers is by advertising in magazines that exclusively feature homes for sale by owner. Many regions of the nation now have these widely distributed publications. Also consider making a fact sheet about your house with a photo.

Internet sites are another relatively new—and inexpensive—way to reach potential buyers. *Our favorite: www.nfsboa.com,* a national network of for-sale-by-owner Web sites.

Fast Home Fix-Ups Attract the Right Buyers

Patricia MacDonald, owner of Innovative Interior Design, a consultation firm in Orange County, CA, that specializes in helping homeowners prepare their property for sale.

First impressions are critical when it comes to winning over undecided home buyers. *Before putting your house on the market...*

●**Give the front of your home a "haircut."** Look at your home from the street. Trim hedges and overgrown landscaping. Add a coat of semigloss paint to the front door. Buy a new doormat.

●**Make the entryway look big.** When I enter a house, the first thing I like to see is a table with a mirror above it. That makes the entryway feel spacious. Setting a lamp on the table—perhaps with a vase of flowers—also helps.

Remove coat stands, keys and mail from the entryway.

●**Open up first-floor traffic patterns.** Rearrange furniture to create more spacious walkways. *Examples...*

●If you have a sofa dividing your living room from the dining area, move it against a wall.

●Take a piece of furniture out of the room if you have to make more space. Store the furniture in the garage or attic, where clutter won't come as a surprise.

●Remove the leaves from your dining room table.

●**Shine up the kitchen.** Put away large countertop appliances. Take down the magnets and kids' drawings from the refrigerator.

Place a big wooden bowl on the counter, and fill it with lemons or oranges.

No plants should be hanging from the ceiling. They clutter kitchens and block window views. The windows should be clean and offer a clear view. Get rid of any leftover hooks on the walls or ceiling.

●**Clean up the patio.** If your furniture is missing some parts, either repair the items or throw them out.

Put bikes and toys in the garage, and move your grill against the exterior wall of your home.

Garage Sale Before Home Sale

Get rid of as much clutter as possible before putting your house on the market. An uncluttered house looks larger and is more attractive to buyers. Clear out everything you no longer use or do not expect to need when you move. The cleaning-out process may reveal things you should fix or clean before selling your home. After the garage sale and a sprucing-up, list your home for sale.

Robert Irwin, real estate investor and broker in Los Angeles, and author of the *Tips & Traps* home book series. McGraw-Hill.

Simple Secrets Of a Chemical-Free Lawn

Warren Schultz, author of *The Chemical-Free Lawn*. Rodale.

There is no doubt that Americans love their lawns—all of our five million acres of lawns. And so we spend $6 billion a year on lawn care and cultivation.

Problem: The excessive—and largely unnecessary—use of pesticides, herbicides and fertilizers could be avoided. They are damaging our soil, contaminating our water systems and exposing our families to hazardous chemicals.

A healthy lawn has no need for chemicals. It can keep out weeds, disease and insects by itself. Think of your lawn as a garden of grass, and simply follow the principles of good gardening. Consider climate, soil and available light. And—select plant varieties with care—and learn to feed, mow and water correctly.

GRASS GARDENING MADE EASY

If you are planting a new lawn: Consult a reputable garden center for recommendations on grass varieties and advice on sowing or sodding. Many new grasses are resistant to insects and disease.

Grasses are bred to thrive in specific climates and conditions. You may want to have a soil sample analyzed by your state's agricultural college or cooperative extension service. When choosing a grass, consider how you use your lawn. Color is important for perfect vistas, whereas toughness (the ability to bounce back from wear) is crucial in heavy traffic areas such as children's play areas.

To convert to and maintain a chemical-free lawn:

●**Fertilizers.** Use a slowly soluble organic fertilizer, with no more than two pounds of nitrogen per 1,000 feet per year.

Fertilize only once a year, in the fall. Then you won't be fertilizing your weeds...they are not programmed to germinate and grow strongly in the fall. But grass leaves and roots both grow vigorously well into the fall. Fertilizing before winter sets in allows the roots to build up carbon reserves that carry over to spring.

●**Weeds.** Weeds are crowded out by healthy turf. They appear only when a lawn is suffering. *Usual culprit:* Wrong type of grass in the wrong place. *Best approach:* To avoid damage to the surrounding turf, weed by hand. Many of the new, long-handled weeding tools are excellent. Then go back to the bare spots and reseed.

Note: Just because it doesn't look like a blade of grass doesn't mean it's a weed. Enjoy the many plants, such as violets and speedwell that were brought to this country as ornamentals. They add color and attract beneficial insects.

●**Mowing.** Most people mow too often—and too low. *Problem:* When grass is cut too short the roots stop growing. Longer grass shades out weeds—and has deeper roots. *Best:* Raise mower blades to maintain grass at three to four inches high. Never cut more than 40% of the height of grass at one time. Keep mower blades sharp to avoid shredding the grass. Mow higher and less often in hot, dry weather. Let grass grow one inch higher in the shade for increased photosynthesis. To cut back on mowing, plant ground cover around trees, on banks, etc.

●**Watering.** Most people water too often—and too lightly. Sprinkling induces roots to stay near the surface. *Best:* Allow water to soak six to 10 inches deep into the soil. Hold off watering again until the grass begins to wilt. This forces roots to grow deeper, for a healthier lawn. Too much water on the surface can encourage disease. So water in the morning after dew has dried, or in the afternoon—not at night.

•**Insects.** Insects are rarely troublesome when turf and soil are healthy. *Best:* Add shrubs and trees to encourage grub-eating birds. Plant wildflowers and herbs to encourage beneficial insects. If your lawn is actually being damaged by a specific pest, consider reseeding with a resistant strain of grass. *Last resort:* Apply an organic pesticide at the risk of also killing useful bugs.

•**Diseases.** Diseases are usually a symptom of grass that has been overwatered and overfertilized. Most are caused by fungi. *Solutions:* Improve drainage, overseed with resistant strains of grass, stop using chemicals.

Lawn care companies...

Negotiate with your lawn service to do less. Ask them to set mower blades higher. Look for an organic fertilizer program. Discontinue routine weed-spraying, pest treatments, etc. Then, tell your neighbors how you got your lawn to thrive.

Is That House Environmentally Safe?

Gary T. Deane, EdD, executive director of the National Society of Environmental Consultants, a fee-based group that trains realtors, bankers and appraisers to detect environmental hazards of commercial and residential properties, 303 W. Cypress St., San Antonio 78212.

Does the neighborhood in which the property is located appear on any government hazards lists? This is not something that the owner of the property is likely to know. The information is available by calling your regional Environmental Protection Agency (EPA) Superfund office. It will tell you whether the EPA has targeted the area for cleanup.

In some cases, you must rely on the Freedom of Information Act,* a process that often takes six weeks or more. If the EPA is unable to help you, there are several fee-based information groups. *They include:*

•**Fidelity National Information Solutions.** This fee-based firm in Santa Barbara has

*Contact your local EPA office for more information.

developed residential reports that are available by mail and overnight delivery. *Information:* 888-934-3354.

•**How has the property been used during the past 40 or 50 years?** Not all hazardous sites are listed in state or federal records. Check with the city's or town's zoning records. Speak with people who have lived there for a long time.

Harmful: Was the property ever used as an auto-repair facility...a pottery, art or photo studio ...a dry cleaner...a printer...a farm...or a junkyard? The chemicals used by these businesses may have leached into the ground, raising the chances of health hazards from contaminated soil.

•Is the property—or adjoining properties—built on a former landfill? Landfill dirt can contain asbestos and other outlawed substances. Over time, these substances can create harmful gases or contaminate the surrounding land or ground water. Check with your state's Solid Waste Management Office or Landfill Office.

•Is there, or was there ever, a gas station, chemical plant or factory within one-quarter mile of the property? The underground storage tanks for facilities built in the 1950s and 1960s are prone to leakage. There have been cases in which leaks went undetected for years and gasoline or chemicals permeated the soil of entire neighborhoods.

The locations of such facilities will appear on a Fire Insurance Map—available at most public and university libraries, at your fire department, in the databases of ERIIS and Vista, in city or county site records or on the federal government's Leaking Underground Storage Tanks list.

•**Has a radon screen been performed on the property?** Many states require the seller to do a radon test on behalf of the buyer. Your state or regional radon office will tell you if radon is a problem in your area. Home test kits, available in hardware stores, are adequate. *Cost for a kit:* $10 to $50. Or hire an EPA-certified radon inspector. The EPA will send you a free list of all certified radon inspectors in your state. *Cost for an inspection:* $100 to $300.

Dangerous Chemicals Are in Our Homes

Ruth Winter, author of *A Consumer's Dictionary of Household, Yard, and Office Chemicals.* Crown Publishers.

According to the Environmental Protection Agency's estimates, the average household contains between three and 10 gallons of hazardous chemicals—and many of them are organic compounds that vaporize at room temperature.

In the effort to save money by sealing our homes to reduce heating and air-conditioning bills, and by becoming do-it-yourselfers for many tasks once left to professionals, we expose ourselves and our families to high levels of these toxic substances.

READ THE LABEL

"We are all guilty of not thoroughly reading labels," according to Charles Jacobson, compliance officer at the US Consumer Products Safety Commission.

If vapors may be harmful, it doesn't do much good to read the label after you have used the product and inhaled the vapors.

Important: Read the labels before buying a product to select the safest in a category. If you find any of the 11 ingredients listed below on a container, avoid buying it. If you must buy it, use extreme caution when working with…

1. Methylene chloride. A widely used solvent, it is in pesticide aerosols, refrigeration and air-conditioning equipment, cleansing creams, and in paint and varnish removers. Some paint strippers are 80% methylene chloride. Its toxic effects include damage to liver, kidneys and central nervous system. It increases the carbon monoxide level in the blood, and people with angina (chest pains) are extremely sensitive to the chemical. Methylene chloride has been linked to heart attacks and cancer.

2. Dichlorvos (DDVP). Used to control insects. It has a wide range of uses in the home, agriculture and commercial establishments. Currently, dichlorvos is undergoing a special review by the EPA on the grounds that exposure to this compound may pose an unreasonable risk of cancer as well as present other dangers. People may be exposed to dichlorvos by consuming foods with residues of the chemical.

3. 2,4-D. A weed killer related to Agent Orange—which allegedly caused health problems in exposed Vietnam veterans—2,4-D is widely used by home gardeners and farmers. It does not cause acute toxicity, but its long-term effects are scary—much higher incidence of non-Hodgkin's lymphoma and other cancers have been associated with its use among farmers. The National Cancer Institute also reports that dogs whose owners use 2,4-D on their lawns have an increased rate of a type of cancer closely related to human non-Hodgkin's lymphoma.

4. Perchlorethylene. The main solvent employed in the dry-cleaning process, metal degreasing, and in some adhesives, aerosols, paints and coatings, it can be absorbed through your lungs or your skin. The most common effects of overexposure are irritation of the eyes, nose, throat or skin. Effects on the nervous system include dizziness, headache, nausea, fatigue, confusion and loss of balance. At very high exposure it can cause death. California has banned the use of perchlorethylene.

5. Formaldehyde. An inexpensive and effective preservative used in more than 3,000 household products. They include disinfectants, cosmetics, fungicides, preservatives and adhesives. It is also used in pressed-wood products—wall paneling, fiberboard and furniture, and in some papers. There are serious questions about its safety. It is estimated that 4% to 8% of the population is sensitive to it. Vapors are intensely irritating to mucous membranes and can cause nasal, lung and eye problems.

6. Benzene. Among the top five organic chemicals produced in the United States, this petroleum derivative's use in consumer products has, in recent years, been greatly reduced. However, it is still employed as a solvent for waxes, resins and oils and is in varnish and lacquer. It is also an "antiknock" additive in gasoline—thus, make sure your house is well ventilated and insulated from vapors that arise from an attached garage.

Benzene is highly flammable, poisonous when ingested and irritating to mucous membranes. Amounts that are harmful may be absorbed through the skin. *Possible results:* Blood, brain and nerve damage as well as cancer.

7. Cyanide. One of the most rapid poisons known, it is used to kill fungus, insects and rats. It is in metal polishes (especially silver), art materials and photographic solutions.

8. Naphthalene. Derived from coal, it is used in solvents, fungicides, toilet bowl deodorizers and as a moth repellent. It can be absorbed through the skin and eyes as well as through the lungs. It may damage the eyes, liver, kidneys, skin, red blood cells and the central nervous system. It has reportedly caused anemia in infants exposed to clothing and blankets stored in naphthalene mothballs. This chemical can cause allergic skin rashes in adults and children.

9. Paradichlorobenzene (PDB). Made from chlorine and benzene, it is in metal polishes, moth repellents, general insecticides, germicides, spray deodorants and fumigants. PDB is also commonly found in room deodorizers. Vapors may cause irritation to the skin, throat and eyes. Prolonged exposure to high concentrations may cause weakness, dizziness, loss of weight and liver damage. A well-known animal cancer-causing agent, the chemical can linger in the home for months or even years.

10. Trichloroethylene (TCE). A solvent used in waxes, paint thinners, fumigants, metal polishes, shoe polish and rug cleaners. Tests conducted by the National Cancer Institute showed TCE caused cancer of the liver. A combination of alcohol ingestion with exposure to trichloroethylene can cause flushing of the skin, nausea and vomiting.

11. Hydroxides/lye products. These include automatic dishwasher detergents, toilet-bowl cleaners, fire proofing, paint remover and drain cleaners. Ingestion causes vomiting, prostration and collapse. Inhalation causes lung damage. Prolonged contact with dilute solutions can have a destructive effect upon tissue, leading to skin irritations and eruptions.

Smoke Detector Alert

The most popular type—an *ion detector*—will detect fast-developing fires, such as wastepaper basket or kitchen grease fires. It won't detect the more common smoldering fires, such as those started by cigarettes in mattresses. Every home needs two types—ion and photoelectric.

B. Don Russell, PhD, associate vice chancellor of engineering and deputy director, Texas Engineering Experiment Station, Texas A&M University, College Station. He has researched smoke detectors for more than a decade.

Bug Zapper Alert

Bug zappers do more than kill mosquitoes and other flying bugs. They shower the area with allergy-causing insect parts...and with disease-causing viruses and bacteria carried by the bugs. *Best bet:* Get rid of zappers in and around the house and keep bugs away with a repellent containing DEET. *Next best:* Position zappers away from areas where food is served and people congregate.

Alberto B. Broce, PhD, professor of entomology, Kansas State University, Manhattan. His study was presented at a meeting of the American Society for Microbiology.

Very Carefully Researched Ways To Clean Your Home

Cheryl Mendelson, Esq., a graduate of Harvard Law School and author of *Home Comforts: The Art & Science of Keeping House*. Scribner.

Eight years ago, when my home was undergoing major renovations, I found myself with some knotty cleaning questions. I couldn't find effective information for removing many stains or getting all the different surfaces of my home as clean as I wanted.

For answers, I consulted manufacturers, private businesses and craftsmen around the country. *Here is what I learned...*

KITCHENS

●**Sweeping.** Use a broom with even nylon or synthetic bristles. It collects dirt better than corn brooms.

Start sweeping at the walls, and move dirt toward the center so you push it the shortest distance. Don't lift the broom high off the floor after a stroke—this flings dirt into the air.

Store brooms with the bristles up. Otherwise bristles break or bend.

●**Coffee or tea stains on china, plastic and glassware.** Mix one-eighth cup of regular chlorine bleach with one cup of water. Pour into the bottom of your dishwasher before starting the wash cycle.

Important: Make sure nothing aluminum or silver is in the machine—it can become discolored.

BATHROOMS

●**Hardened soap scum on tiles.** Coat the entire surface with undiluted liquid detergent, and allow it to dry overnight. Wet the surface and scrub with a stiff brush and scouring powder. Rinse and buff with a bath towel.

●**Nonslip treads on bathtub floor.** Try Naval Jelly or KRC-7, a porcelain and tile cleaner (both available at plumbing supply stores). These cleaners may remove mineral stains without eating away at the treads.

●**Rust around faucets and fixtures.** Use a powder containing oxalic acid, such as Barkeeper's Friend or Zud (both available at hardware stores).

Important: Never mix these rust removers with chlorine bleach. The fumes are toxic.

●**Concentrate on the spots where fingerprints accumulate**—if you want to disinfect your bathroom in addition to just cleaning it.

Examples: Toilet handles, light switches and knobs on the shower door, medicine cabinet and door.

FURNITURE

●**Water rings on hardwood surfaces.** Try mildly abrasive substances, such as mayonnaise mixed with a bit of ashes or toothpaste. The secret is to rub gently for a long time—as long as 45 minutes—so you remove the stain without scratching the finish.

Afterward, wax the whole surface to even the finish. Use paste wax (sold at home centers and hardware stores). It is more protective than oils or liquid waxes.

●**Minor scratches on wood.** I use Old English Scratch Guard (sold at hardware stores). If in doubt about which color to use, start with a lighter color. Apply the product to your wiping cloth, not directly on the furniture.

●**Use the right dust rag.** Soft white flannel or cheesecloth is best because dust adheres to it so well. Dampen the cloth very slightly with water. For heirlooms and valuable antique woods, use distilled water to dampen rags. For carved furniture, china, ceramics, chandeliers and vases, use a small artist's paintbrush made from natural- or hog's-hair bristles.

UPHOLSTERY

●**Stains from eggs, milk, chocolate.** Rub with a solution of one tablespoon household ammonia and one-half cup of water.

●**Coffee, cola and beer stains.** Rub with a solution of one-third cup of white vinegar mixed with two-thirds cup of water. Avoid soap, which can set the stain permanently.

●**Ink stains.** Sponge with rubbing alcohol.

WALLS

●**Nonwashable wallpaper.** For grease stains, place an absorbent towel over the stain and cover it with an iron set at low for several seconds. For ink or pencil marks, try rubbing with cleaning putty such as Absorene (available at home centers) or a wadded-up piece of fresh, soft, white bread.

● **Washable vinyl wallpaper.** For stubborn stains, such as crayon, tar or adhesives, use WD-40 (available in hardware stores).

● **Painted walls.** Mix a thick paste of baking soda and water. Dip your cloth in it, and rub marks very gently to remove fingerprints, crayon, etc.

CARPETS

● **Spills.** Use as little water as possible. Blot as much of the spill as possible with paper towels. Then, in a bowl, whip up a sudsy foam using water and mild detergent. For delicate carpets, I use Orvus WA paste from Procter & Gamble (available at antique stores, or call 800-332-7787).

Dip your brush into the *foam,* not the water. Brush stain lightly, then wipe off excess foam with a clean cloth. Rinse with a 50/50 solution of white vinegar and water. Then rinse with plain warm water. Blot thoroughly.

● **Use a vacuum with low dust emissions.** If you have asthma or other allergies, consider investing in a vacuum with a HEPA filter—I use the Miele White Pearl (800-694-4868).

WOOD FLOORS

● **Scuffs and heel marks on hard-finish or urethane-type floors.** Dampen a cloth with a small amount of mineral spirits (available at hardware stores). Rub gently in the direction of the grain.

● **Oil or grease stains on natural-finish floors.** Saturate a cotton ball with hydrogen peroxide, and place over the stain for several minutes. Saturate a second cotton ball with ammonia, and place over the stain for several minutes. Repeat until the stain is removed. Let the area dry, then buff with a soft cloth.

COMPUTERS

● **Keyboards.** Try rubbing alcohol or de-greaser sprays (available at electronics stores) to clean off the grime.

● **Computer screens.** Make sure screen is off. Use a slightly damp cloth. Avoid those spe-cial-purpose towelettes sold in office-supply stores. They leave a soapy residue.

Best Home Water Filters

Richard P. Maas, PhD, professor of environmental stud-ies at the University of North Carolina, Asheville. He is codirector of the university's Environmental Quality Insti-tute, a leading center for research on tap-water purity.

With regular news reports about water contamination—even in the best communities—more and more peo-ple are turning to home water filters to protect their families' health…

DETERMINE YOUR NEEDS

To choose the best filter for you, have your tap water tested.

Larger water utilities are now required to send an annual report to customers with the results of tests for about 80 different contaminants. If you haven't received one, call your local utility.

If you have well water—or if you want to do more extensive testing—look in the *Yellow Pages* under "Water Testing" or "Laboratories–Testing." Test price depends on what contaminants you look for. The range is wide—between $17 and $800. The most likely contaminant is lead (20% of US households), which can be picked up by the household plumbing system.

Clean Water Lead Testing (828-251-6800) pro-vides a two-sample, mail-in test (first drawn and after running water for one minute) for $17. *Warning:* Home testing kits may be unreliable.

CARAFE FILTERS

Water flows by gravity, and there's plenty of the filtering medium with which it interacts to remove lead, reduce chlorine byproducts and improve taste and smell. Inexpensive (less than $30).

Drawbacks: Slow…holds only two to three quarts…filters must be changed often, gen-erally every 50 to 100 gallons, depending on the level of contaminants in the water.

Top carafe filter: **Pur Pitcher CR-500.** Half-gallon pitcher uses carbon and an active agent to improve water taste while reducing levels of lead, chlorine, copper and zinc. Safety gauge indicates when filter needs replacing. $20. *Replacement filters:* $8 each. 800-787-5463.

FAUCET-MOUNTED

Inexpensive (less than $50)…easy to install and change filters.

Drawbacks: Units are small, and water pressure forces water through the filter too quickly to thoroughly remove all impurities.

Top faucet filter: Pur Plus FM-3000. Removes microorganisms, such as giardia and cryptosporidium, as well as contaminants, including lead, chlorine and mercury. Automatic shut-off stops water flow when filter needs replacing. Filters last for 100 gallons. $30. *Replacement filters:* $15 each. 800-787-5463.

UNDER-SINK FILTER

Contains a reservoir so water has more time to pass through the filtering mechanism...long-lasting filters.

Drawbacks: Costs $100 or more...may require a plumber for installation.

Top under-sink filter: Waterpik IF-100A. Dual-filter unit removes lead, chlorine and some pesticides—such as lindane—while improving water odor and taste. Installs easily and comes with extra-long tubing and a movable base for quick filter changing. Filters last for approximately 1,200 gallons. $159. *Replacement filters:* Lead filter/$38.59...chlorine/pesticide/taste and odor filter/$12.49. 800-525-2774.

WHOLE-HOUSE FILTER

For homes on well water and not connected to a municipal water system.

Contains sophisticated filtering material tailored to meet the home's specific needs...removes hardness...neutralizes water...removes bacteria. Filtered water is supplied to the whole house, including taps, showers and washing machine.

Drawbacks: Expensive ($1,000 to $3,000 installed plus filtering materials)...requires monthly maintenance...changing filters and/or adding filtering materials.

There is no *best* whole-house system—it depends on your water-treatment goals. Leading manufacturers include Culligan, Flek and Hauge. The company that services your well can provide guidance following a comprehensive water test. Or look in the *Yellow Pages* under "Water Purification & Filtration Equipment."

Stress-Free System to Unclutter Your Home

Donna Smallin, Troy, New York-based author of *Unclutter Your Home: 7 Simple Steps, 700 Tips and Ideas.* Storey Books. She writes for several major manufacturers and retailers and has contributed articles to *Bridal Guide* and *Running Times* magazines.

Too much stuff in your house? Many of us are troubled by the clutter...and overwhelmed by the imposing task of doing something about it. Here is a no-stress system to unclutter your home. *Key questions...*

If I had 20 minutes to evacuate my home, what would I take? That's when you realize that most things aren't very important.

How much is enough? On a scale of zero to 10—with 10 being everything you now own and zero being nothing—what amount of stuff would you prefer to own? Nine? Eight? Five? If five seems about right, your goal should be to eliminate half of your belongings.

If that seems like a lot, remember—you'll be getting rid of things you don't want, use or need.

TOSS OBVIOUS JUNK

Walk around your house with a plastic garbage bag. Toss out expired coupons or packages of food no one will eat...single or worn socks...old, rusted tools and utensils. Do this the night before garbage pickup so you aren't tempted to retrieve anything.

SORT YOUR THINGS

Now comes the hard part—deciding what to keep. Bring a laundry basket or large box into a room, and gather everything that doesn't belong there. Carry these items into the rooms where they belong, and put them away properly.

When you're done with the last item, look around the room you're in. Repeat the process, gathering all the things that don't belong and taking them where they do belong. Keep going until all your rooms are clutter-free.

For items that belong in a room, you need to make some decisions.

If you haven't used an item for a year or you don't like it anymore—get rid of it. If you really want it—put it back.

If it's hard for you to toss things, organize a cleaning party. Find a few people willing to help—in exchange for you helping them another time.

Touching an item increases your attachment. So ask a friend to hold each item while you decide whether to keep it.

Place items you're unsure of in a box. Seal the box and date it. After six months, if you haven't gone back to retrieve anything from the box, get rid of it or have a tag sale. Bring items to a church sale or donate them to the Salvation Army or another charity.

STAYING AHEAD OF CLUTTER

Organizing is a process, not a one-time event. If you spend 15 minutes a day on the task—while watching TV or waiting for dinner to cook—you'll stay ahead of the clutter. *Other strategies...*

•**Watch what you bring home.** When you buy something, get rid of something else. If you get two new sweaters for your birthday, get rid of two old sweaters.

•**Stay current.** Open, sort and file your mail every day. After you read a newspaper or a magazine, get rid of it. If you want to save an article, tear it out and file it. Clean up the kitchen every night. Hang up your clothes or put them in the hamper when you take them off.

11

Looking Good

Cosmetic Surgery Dos and Don'ts

These days with so many people undergoing some kind of cosmetic surgery—whether it's a face-lift, a nose job or a tummy tuck—it's important to remember that plastic surgery is, after all, surgery. It is not to be taken lightly. *Here are my dos and don'ts for people now considering a cosmetic-surgery procedure...*

•**Choose a doctor you trust.** First, you want a surgeon who's competent—he/she should be board-certified or at least board-eligible. If you're not sure, ask the surgeon directly—or check with your local medical society. But equally important is the way you feel about this doctor.

•**Ask the surgeon for references**—former patients who can testify to his competence. Choose a doctor you feel comfortable with. If you know former patients, talk to them. If you are uncomfortable with your doctor, it may affect your willingness to approach him with questions.

•**Ask questions.** Informed patients make good patients. You're paying good money to talk with an expert, so get your money's worth by asking everything you want to know about the procedure—the anticipated outcome, recovery time, costs...

If you don't understand something, ask to have it explained again. Write down the responses. During an initial consultation there's usually so much technical information discussed that the average patient retains only about 50% of it. Having written answers in hand will be a tremendous plus after you leave the office.

•**Keep an open mind.** People often come in to see the surgeon already loaded down with information—so many statistics and anecdotes from friends, relatives and magazine articles that they don't tune in to what the doctor is saying.

It's okay to challenge the surgeon's remarks with something you may have read or heard,

Stephen Cotlar, MD, a Houston-based plastic surgeon certified by the American Board of Plastic Surgery.

but remember that everyone responds to procedures differently—your neighbor's experiences may not be the same as yours. Put aside your own beliefs and preconceptions long enough to really focus on what the doctor is telling you.

●**Don't ignore the risks.** Too many people assume that a nose job, say, or liposuction is so common that it's risk free. All surgery carries risk.

Examples: It's very rare, but it's possible for a facial nerve to be damaged during a face-lift and result in partial paralysis of the face. And TV talk-show host Jenny Jones went public with the serious problems she experienced with her breast implants, which she subsequently had removed.

The doctor should explain what your risks are—and if he doesn't, you should ask.

●**Be wary of doctors who recommend procedures you didn't ask for.** It's quite possible that a surgeon will give you a good suggestion you never considered. For instance, you might come in for a nose job, and the doctor might suggest that you also have a chin implant, to better balance your entire face.

But be alert to someone who suddenly tries to encourage you to have, say, breast implants when you're there for a face-lift.

●**Answer all questions honestly.** During the initial consultation, the surgeon will—and should—ask you a lot of questions involving your health, your habits and even your personal life that may seem irrelevant or nosy...but they're not. They will help him assess whether you're a good candidate for surgery, as well as how well the procedure will turn out.

These questions may include:

●Do you smoke?

●Do you take any medications?

●Do you have a heart condition?

For whatever reason, you may not want to answer the questions, but it's critical that you do so.

Examples: You might not want to admit that you smoke or when you had your last cigarette. But smoking can compromise the circulation to the skin, and smokers who have face-lifts have a higher incidence of complications, so I generally tell patients to stop smoking six to eight weeks prior to surgery.

Or, a doctor may tell you to stop taking aspirin for a week before surgery, because aspirin has a blood-thinning effect—and you want your blood to clot properly during the operation. If the surgeon doesn't ask, volunteer any information you think might be important.

●**Don't assume you know the best solution to your particular problem.** The surgeon should, of course, consider any procedure you request, but he might recommend an alternative that may work better for you.

Example: You want surgery done on your eyelids to help correct a tired look, but what you might actually need is a forehead lift to raise your eyebrows.

Or you believe that liposuction will "cure" your obesity, but liposuction is not a weight-reduction operation—it's a procedure designed to improve certain parts of the body that can't be trimmed any other way, such as "saddlebags" on an otherwise slim person.

The professional doctor will steer you in the right direction.

●**Don't assume you can't have plastic surgery because you're "too old."** The age of the patients coming to the operating table these days is getting older and older. Although the optimum age for a first face-lift is from about 48 to 60 years old, people in their 80s are having them now.

The state of your health is more important to a plastic surgeon than your age, and if you're in generally good health, you may be a fine candidate for surgery.

●**Examine your reasons for having surgery.** During the initial consultation the doctor will probably ask, "Why are you having this surgery done?" If you're having a face-lift because you think it'll enhance your chances to get a job, or simply because you want to like what you see in the mirror better, those are valid reasons.

But if you're doing it to win back a wife who left you for a younger man or because your new girlfriend wishes you would, those are poor reasons.

Plastic surgery should never be done to solve an emotional crisis or because you expect it to make you a different person. If you're doing it for someone else, rather than for yourself…reconsider.

Plastic Surgery Problems

Linton A. Whitaker, MD, chief of the division of plastic surgery, the Hospital of the University of Pennsylvania, and professor of surgery, University of Pennsylvania School of Medicine. Dr. Whitaker specializes in facial surgery.

Whether it's an ordinary nose job or the removal of a rib to achieve a smaller waistline, cosmetic surgery performed by a qualified surgeon is usually safe and effective.

As with any medical procedure, however, cosmetic surgery occasionally results in complications—in a small portion of all procedures. And when complications occur, the results can be devastating.

COSMETIC SURGERY RISKS

•**Persistent infection.** The most common complication—and usually the easiest to correct. Antibiotics are effective in most cases, although implants sometimes have to be removed.

Exception: Cartilage infections, especially those following a nose job (rhinoplasty), rarely may persist for a year or longer even with aggressive antibiotic treatment…and they can destroy the nose's shape.

Self-defense: Choose a qualified surgeon—one who has performed the same procedure dozens of times.

•**Bad nose job.** Nose jobs involving excessive cartilage removal can cause big trouble later in life. As the patient ages, the skin thins, and the nose appears to shrink—sometimes to little more than a tiny nubbin.

In extreme cases, a nubbin nose causes not only acute embarrassment, but also breathing difficulties. The only way to correct the problem is to transplant cartilage taken from elsewhere in the body.

Self-defense: The less tissue removed during any cosmetic surgery, the safer.

•**Lumpy skin.** Surgeons performing liposuction must wield the cannula (fat-sucking instrument) very deftly, since uneven removal of fat results in lumpy or rippled skin. These defects are difficult or impossible to fix, even with additional liposuction or fat transplantation.

In very rare cases, fat cells liberated during liposuction cut off the supply of blood to the heart or brain. Although rare, some fat embolisms are fatal.

Also in rare cases, liposuction can result in inadvertent damage to the spleen or other internal organs. A ruptured spleen usually necessitates emergency surgery to control bleeding.

Self-defense: Use an experienced surgeon. Check out the doctor's reputation, enlist word-of-mouth recommendations and directly ask the doctor questions about his/her background.

•**Barbie Doll hair.** Hair transplantation is safe and effective, but the process takes months or even years to complete. Impatient patients who fail to see it through to the end often wind up with obvious plugs of hair arrayed in regular rows across the scalp.

Self-defense: Start hair transplants only if you intend to see them through.

•**Distorted eyes.** Surgeons performing eye tucks (blepharoplasties) must be careful to remove just the right amount of tissue around the eyes. Otherwise, the patient may be left with eyes that seem to turn downward or outward, or with an exposed mucous membrane around the eyes.

Sometimes the eyelids are stretched so tight by surgery that the eyes cannot fully close. Botched eye jobs can also result in acute glaucoma…even blindness.

Self-defense: Choose a highly experienced surgeon.

•**Lopsided face.** In rare instances, face-lifts damage the facial nerve. *Result:* Diminished muscle tone or even partial paralysis. The patient may develop a crooked smile, sagging cheeks or may have difficulty blinking.

Similarly, implants in the chin, cheeks and other parts of the face must be firmly attached to bone, or over time they may be mobile. More than an annoyance, mobile facial implants can result in a lopsided appearance.

Self-defense: Make sure the surgeon plans the implants so they are placed on bone.

• **Rashes and redness.** Collagen used to fill in acne scars and other skin defects can cause severe rashes and persistent redness. Theoretically, collagen injected directly into a blood vessel rather than just under the skin could interrupt the flow of blood to an eye—resulting in blindness.

Self-defense: The doctor should make sure the patient is not allergic to collagen before large quantities are injected. This can be done by test injections, introducing a small amount of collagen into the body in an inconspicuous place.

• **Too-tight face-lift.** This usually occurs on repeat face-lifts and strictly skin lifts. Newer face-lifts include both deeper layers and skin and give a more natural look.

Self-defense: Ask what technique the surgeon uses and how much experience he/she has with the procedure. Ask to see other patients …or their photographs.

Fat Removal Technique And Its Pitfalls

Liposuction—surgery performed to remove excess fat from various parts of the body—is now the most popular cosmetic operation in the United States. The doctor inserts a thin tube called a cannula through a small incision in the skin and moves it back and forth to break up a fatty deposit. The dislodged fat is then evacuated through this tubing by strong suction.

In cases where a person has good skin elasticity—up into their early 40s for most people—a double chin can be fixed without undergoing a face-lift. Liposuction can remove fat from a full neck, giving the patient a clean jawline and only a tiny scar.

Dr. Henry Zackin, a plastic and reconstructive surgeon in private practice in New York City.

Liposuction is safest when performed as an outpatient procedure under local anesthesia—in a doctor's office, not in a hospital. The doctor should be a board-certified dermatologic surgeon. Avoid doctors who plan to extract large amounts of fat at one time…and those who perform multiple procedures at the same time. Liposuction is usually safe, but serious complications do occur in rare cases—usually when general anesthesia is used. *These include:* Shock, blood clots, infection, bowel perforation in abdominal procedures.

William Coleman III, MD, clinical professor of dermatology, Tulane University, New Orleans, and leader of a study of 257 liposuction-related insurance claims, published in *Dermatalogic Surgery*.

Simple Exercises for a Nonsurgical Face-Lift

Judith Olivia, national spokesperson for Advanced Dermatology Care, an organization that lectures to medical professionals on advancements in the field, and creator of the videos *Face Aerobics* and *Advanced Face Aerobics* (available through her company, Judith Olivia Inc., Box 181706, Casselberry, FL 32718).

Face-lifts make the skin tighter, but the benefits are often temporary because the underlying muscles continue to sag. Then a second—or even a third—face-lift is often necessary.

Free and painless alternative: Strengthen and firm the facial muscles. Facial exercises pull the muscles upward so that the skin looks firm and youthful.

These exercises hit the main trouble spots. Do each exercise once a day for two weeks. After that, weekly workouts are fine. Facial muscles are small, so you'll see improvements quickly.

UNDER-EYE BAGS

Using both hands, gently place one forefinger under each eye, just below the lower lid. Use the muscles of the lower lids to try to lift the weight of your fingers. Do this exercise 20 times, twice a day.

SAGGING JOWLS

Lift your bottom lip so it covers the top lip. Tilt your head up slightly, and smile toward the tops of the ears. Hold for a count of 10, then relax. Repeat five times.

You'll know you're doing it right when you feel a tingle in the muscles of the jaw and throat.

Male advantage: Men move their faces around almost every day when they are shaving, so this exercise is less important for men than it is for women.

DOUBLE CHIN

Lie on your back, with your knees slightly bent and feet flat on the floor. Slowly raise your head and tuck your chin against your chest. Hold this position for a second, then slowly lower your head. Try to repeat it 10 times at first...and gradually work up to 50 repetitions.

DROOPY EYELIDS

Using both hands, put a forefinger on each eyebrow, exerting enough pressure so the eyebrows won't move easily. Try to close your eyes, working against the resistance of your fingers. Don't scrunch your forehead—just try to push the upper lashes into the lower ones as hard as you can. Repeat between five and 20 times, holding for a count of five each time.

FOREHEAD LINES

Cover your forehead with the palm of one hand, holding it firmly. Try to push the forehead muscle toward the top of the head, pushing against the resistance of your hand. Hold for a second, then relax. Repeat 10 times.

Bonus: This exercise not only tightens skin on the forehead—it also helps smooth frown and worry lines. It trains the forehead muscles to work together, instead of rippling.

LOOSE THROAT

Flex throat muscles—as a weight lifter's neck would look straining to lift weights. Hold for a minute, then relax.

Wrinkle Magic

Egg whites smooth facial wrinkles by temporarily tightening the skin.

Directions: Beat an egg white until frothy, then apply it to wrinkles. Let it dry for five minutes, then rinse—first with warm water and then with cool water.

Important: Use fresh egg whites.

Seth L. Matarasso, MD, associate clinical professor of dermatology, University of California, San Francisco, School of Medicine.

Secrets of Youthful-Looking Skin

Nicholas V. Perricone, MD, assistant clinical professor of dermatology at Yale University School of Medicine in New Haven, CT. He is author of *The Wrinkle Cure: Unlock the Power of Cosmeceuticals for Supple, Youthful Skin.* Rodale. For more on skin care, see Perricone's Web site at *www.nvperriconemd.com.*

In their quest to keep a youthful appearance, growing numbers of men and women are using costly—but ineffective—wrinkle creams and undergoing painful procedures like face-lifts and dermabrasion.

There is an effective alternative. It's not a quick fix, but a science-based change in the way you eat and live.

OXIDATION AND INFLAMMATION

What we call "aging" of the skin—wrinkles, age spots, etc.—is *not* the fault of time. It's the result of inflammation. In fact, you might say that aging *is* inflammation...and that if you want to attack the first, you must defend against the second.

Inflammation is usually thought of as something obvious—the redness of sunburn, for instance, or painful swelling associated with infection. Actually, inflammation goes on invisibly—and constantly—at the cellular level.

Oxidation is a cause of underlying inflammation. You may have heard that this cell-damaging process is caused by highly reactive molecular fragments known as free radicals.

Ultraviolet radiation from sunlight creates free radicals in the skin. So does air pollution. And so do the natural metabolic processes that the body uses to convert food into energy.

Free radicals are especially damaging to the membrane that encases every cell. As each cell membrane oxidizes, inflammation-promoting compounds known as *prostaglandins* and *leukotrienes* are created. With its membrane damaged, the cell can't bring in essential nutrients...or expel wastes.

The key to stopping or reversing "aging" is to minimize oxidation—and inflammation.

ANTI-INFLAMMATORY DIET

• **Cut back on sugar.** It's responsible for 50% of skin aging. Sugar molecules react with *collagen,* the protein that gives texture to the skin. That makes skin saggy instead of resilient. And each time sugar reacts with collagen, it releases a burst of free radicals.

In addition to cake, candy and other sweets, it's best to avoid pasta, potatoes, white rice, fruit juices, grapes and cooked carrots. These foods have a high glycemic index—meaning that they are converted into blood sugar very rapidly.

Most fresh fruits and vegetables like broccoli, eggplant, tomatoes and greens are okay because they are absorbed slowly.

•**Eat more protein.** The skin needs a constant supply of amino acids to repair cellular damage. But not all of us get enough of the proteins that supply these amino acids.

Daily protein intake should be 35 g to 60 g for women, 70 g to 80 g for men. Men tend to get enough protein, but the average woman gets just 20 g of protein a day.

Protein comes from dairy products, beans and peas, poultry, etc. But from the perspective of skin health, the best protein sources are cold-water fish like sardines, anchovies and especially salmon.

Cold-water fish are rich sources of omega-3 fatty acids, which exert a potent anti-inflammatory effect. These fish are also rich in a little-known compound called *dimethylaminoethanol* (DMAE). DMAE is the raw material used by the body to synthesize acetylcholine, the chemical that carries messages from nerve endings to muscles. By boosting acetylcholine synthesis, DMAE keeps the muscles that support the skin well-toned.

If you don't like fish, fish oil supplements are an alternative. But they contain only omega-3s, not protein or DMAE.

•**Take supplements.** Vitamins C and E, the mineral selenium and other antioxidants work in concert to inhibit free radical activity.

Because it's difficult to get enough antioxidant protection from foods alone, ask your doctor about taking the following daily supplements...

•Vitamin C...1,000 mg to 2,000 mg.

•Vitamin E...400 international units (IU) of *natural* vitamin E.

•Coenzyme Q10...30 mg for people under age 40...60 mg for people in their 40s...100 mg for people age 50 or older.

•DMAE...50 mg to 100 mg.

•Lipoic acid...50 mg.

•Selenium...200 micrograms.

SUNLIGHT AND THE SKIN

To get a sense of just how significant sun exposure really is, compare your facial skin with skin on a part of your body that's always covered.

To minimize damage: Use sunscreen every day. SPF 15 is okay for day-to-day sun exposure. Use SPF 30 and a hat and other protective clothing if you plan to be out for an extended period.

THE ROLE OF EXERCISE

Exercise dilates blood vessels, bringing nutrients to the skin. And sweating expels toxins from the skin. Exercise also promotes synthesis of growth hormone. High levels of growth hormone are linked to youthful-looking skin.

Running, brisk walking, cycling or using a stair-climber for 30 minutes, five times weekly should suffice. If possible, fit in two or three days per week of strength training. Concentrate on shoulders, back, arms, legs and abdominals. Each session should last about 30 minutes.

AVOIDING IRRITANTS

Avoid contact with cosmetics, soaps, etc., that cause redness or irritation. Prescription retinoic acid preparations like *tretinoin* (Renova) are generally okay, though they may cause temporary pinkness. If severe pinkness lasts for more than four weeks, consult a physician.

Retin-A Repairs Damaged Skin

Retin-A doesn't just smooth wrinkles—it repairs damaged skin. In a study, 29 people with sun-damaged skin applied either 0.1% tretinoin (Retin-A) or a placebo cream once a day. After one year, those using tretinoin showed an 80% increase in formation of collagen, the protein that gives skin its elasticity.

Those receiving the placebo cream had a 14% decrease in collagen synthesis.

Albert M. Kligman, MD, PhD, professor of dermatology, University of Pennsylvania, Philadelphia. His study was published in *The New England Journal of Medicine,* 10 Shattuck St., Boston 02115.

Help for Irritated Skin

Soothe irritated skin by adding one to two cups of milk and one-half to one cup of oatmeal to your bath water. You can also use equal parts of milk and water as a face wash or cold compress…or make an oatmeal face mask for skin inflamed by sunlight or an allergic reaction. *Caution:* Those with food allergies should test a small amount on the skin and wait 48 hours for a reaction.

Diane Berson, MD, assistant clinical professor of dermatology, New York University School of Medicine, New York.

Hair Dye/Cancer Connections

Black hair dye may boost the risk of some cancers. In a study, women who used black dye for 20 years or longer faced an increased risk of death from non-Hodgkin's lymphoma and multiple myeloma. Other colors were found to be safe—even with long-term use.

Good news: Less than 1% of hair-dye users have used black dye for more than 20 years.

Michael J. Thun, MD, MS, director of analytic epidemiology, American Cancer Society, 1599 Clifton Rd. NE, Atlanta. His study of hair dye use among 570,000 American women was published in the *Journal of the National Cancer Institute,* 9030 Old Georgetown Rd., Building 82, Room 209, Bethesda, MD 20814.

Blow-Dryer Alert

Daily blow-drying *can* damage hair, especially dyed or permed hair.

Problems: The heat may cause strands to break or may lead to the development of little pimples (called *folliculitis*) on the scalp. It can also worsen facial acne.

In rare cases, if hair is often pulled tightly to straighten it during drying, hair may fall out, leaving bald spots. Frequent tight braiding/cornrows and constant twirling of hair can also lead to baldness.

Self-defense: If you must use a blow-dryer, dry hair on a medium setting, not hot…keep the dryer at least eight inches from your head and face…don't pull hair tight while drying…use a cream rinse or detangler after shampooing and prior to drying.

Deborah S. Sarnoff, MD, assistant clinical professor of dermatology, New York University School of Medicine, New York. She is author of *Beauty and the Beam: Your Complete Guide to Cosmetic Laser Surgery.* St. Martin's Griffin.

For Men Only

New hair-transplant procedures—*mini-* and *micro*-grafts—give a more natural look than older techniques. Risk is minimal as long as antibacterial ointments are used to prevent infection. *Cost:* About $2,000 to $8,000. *Also very popular for men:* Liposuction—surgical fat removal—to eliminate double chins, "love handles" and other bulges. *Cost:* $1,500—and up. Using local instead of general anesthesia greatly reduces both the risks and postsurgical "downtime" of liposuction. More men are turning to cosmetic surgery to stay competitive in the youth-oriented workplace.

Bruce Katz, MD, dermatologist and director, Juva Skin and Laser Center, New York.

What Causes Teeth to Become Yellowed

Yellowed teeth are usually caused by coffee, tobacco or *gastroesophageal reflux disease* (GERD). In this condition, corrosive stomach acids back up into the esophagus and mouth …eroding teeth and eventually causing them to break off. GERD can often be controlled with *omeprazole* (Prilosec) or other prescription or over-the-counter medications.

Pat Schroeder, MD, gastroenterology fellow, University of Alabama School of Medicine, Birmingham.

Secrets of Exercise Stick-to-it-iveness

Seventy-five percent of people who start an exercise program quit within a year. *To be an exercise veteran…*

•**Choose a program that is fun for you.** *Best:* Lifetime sports—hiking, swimming, walking, dancing, gardening, volleyball, tennis, golf (no golf carts please). Add appropriate conditioning exercises once you are comfortable with the regime.

•**Pick a motivating role model**—someone you've seen on the tennis court or in your aerobics class.

•**Join—or create—a team** to add fun, competition and socializing.

•**Treat exercise times like "appointments."** Those who miss three consecutive exercise sessions are more likely to abandon the program altogether.

Robert Hopper, PhD, gives seminars on health and fitness nationwide. He is based in Santa Barbara, CA.

Walking Boosts Brainpower

In a recent study, sedentary adults 60 to 75 years of age started walking briskly three times a week, gradually increasing the length of the walks from 15 to 45 minutes. After six months, their mental function had improved by 15%. Similar adults who did stretching and toning exercises for one hour three days a week showed no improvement. *Theory:* By increasing oxygen flow to the brain, walking averts the earliest mental changes that occur with aging.

Arthur Kramer, PhD, professor of psychology, University of Illinois, Urbana-Champaign.

Exercises to Do in the Car

Double chin: Lift chin slightly and open and close mouth as though chewing. *Flabby neck:* Move head toward right shoulder while looking straight ahead at the road. Return head to center, then toward left shoulder. *Pot belly:* Sit straight with spine against back seat. Pull stomach in and hold breath for count of five. Relax, then repeat. The exercise also relieves tension and helps fight sleepiness.

Exercise and Your Immune System

Brisk walks strengthen your immune system—but too-strenuous workouts can lower immunity to colds and flu. Exercising near your maximum capacity for just 45 minutes—or more—produces a six-hour "window" of vulnerability afterward. *Better:* Exercise at a moderate level—the equivalent of a brisk walk —if not training for competition.

David Nieman, DrPH, professor of health, department of health and exercise science, Appalachian State University, Boone, NC.

Tai Chi Helpful for Older People

Tai chi improves balance and may help reduce the risk of falls in elderly people. The ancient Chinese exercise—which involves gentle turning and pivoting—teaches participants to focus on how their weight is distributed. Older women who did tai chi three times a week for six months, along with leg presses and brisk walking, experienced a 17% improvement in their ability to balance on one leg. Those who only stretched and practiced tai chi once a week had no significant improvement.

James Judge, MD, assistant professor of medicine, University of Connecticut School of Medicine, Farmington. His study of 21 women was reported in *Physical Therapy,* American Physical Therapy Association, 1111 N. Fairfax St., Alexandria, VA 22314.

Treadmill Traps

Setting the speed too fast or the incline too steep...keeping your ankles too stiff, which can lead to shinsplints...flailing your arms, which can twist your torso and stress the back...locking your arms in one position, which prevents your body from making subtle adjustments to better absorb impact.

Helpful: Keep your gait smooth, upper body loose and arms close to your torso, moving them back and forth in a relatively straight line.

Mike Motta, president, Plus One Fitness, New York, quoted in *American Health,* 28 W. 23 St., New York 10010.

Real Cause of Flabby Muscles

Lack of exercise—not aging. Muscle mass does decline between ages 30 and 70. But isotonic—strength-building—exercises can reverse the decline. Half an hour of isotonics two or three times a week can increase strength within two weeks and double it in 12 weeks—by changing the ratio of muscle to fat. *Bonus:* Increased bone density—helping prevent fractures caused by osteoporosis.

William J. Evans, PhD, director of Noll Laboratories of Human Performance Research, Pennsylvania State University, University Park, and coauthor of *Biomarkers: The 10 Determinants of Aging You Can Control.* Simon & Schuster, Inc.

Exercise and Lactic Acid

Lactic acid builds up during exercise and may contribute to the uncomfortable burning sensation that many exercisers feel.

To remove lactic acid faster: Have an active recovery period after a workout, like walking after running...instead of a passive one, like lying down.

Karen Segal, PhD, associate professor of physiology in pediatrics, director of exercise physiology lab, Cornell University Medical College and New York Hospital, New York.

Elderly and Weight-Lifting

Weight-lifting exercise boosts muscle strength and size as well as mobility in the elderly. Nutritional supplements, on the other hand, have no benefit on these outcomes—either alone or in conjunction with exercise.

Maria A. Fiatarone, MD, chief of the human physiology laboratory, Human Nutrition Research Center on Aging, Tufts University, Boston. Her 10-week study of 100 frail nursing home residents was published in *The New England Journal of Medicine,* 10 Shattuck St., Boston 02115.

Smarter Running

Many seniors cannot run because of joint or other problems. For those who can, running may be a good choice. You can do it anywhere, cost is low and health benefits are significant. *Smart runners…*

•**Run every other day to give your body a day to recover.**

•**Invest in good running shoes,** the one essential item of equipment a runner needs. Running places great stress on feet, knees, hips and lower back. So consult a physical therapist who specializes in sports medicine.

•**Replace shoes when they lose shape,** even if the soles aren't worn.

•**Take care of your feet.** Check them daily for blisters and calluses, and remedy other small problems before they become big ones.

Arthur Safalow, PT, CPed, director of Nassau Rehabilitation and Sports Therapy, Mineola, NY.

Exercising for Weight Loss

John Jakicic, PhD, assistant research professor of psychiatry and human behavior at Brown University School of Medicine, Providence, RI. His study of the role of exercise in weight loss was published in The Journal of the American Medical Association, 515 N. State St., Chicago 60610.

If you're exercising primarily as a way to lose weight, you may have read that 30 minutes three to five times a week is all that's needed.

Not true. A study recently published in *The Journal of the American Medical Association* suggests that a total of at least 40 minutes —and preferably 60—is needed *each* day of the week to lose weight and keep it off.

An hour a day probably sounds pretty daunting. But that's mainly because few of us exercise as effectively—or as creatively—as we could. *Here are some helpful suggestions…*

•**Find a form of exercise that you truly enjoy.** That way, you're more likely to stick with your exercise routine. If you like bicycling, for example, don't try to become a runner. If you like swimming, don't commit yourself to long sessions on a stair-climbing machine.

Structured exercise isn't the only way to lose weight. You can burn calories just by increasing the intensity of everyday activities.

Shoveling snow burns about 400 calories an hour. That's four times as many calories as you would burn off with an hour of walking. An hour of raking leaves burns about 270 calories.

You probably wouldn't shovel snow or rake for a solid hour. But that's not the point. The idea is that any kind of movement done at moderate intensity can help with weight loss.

•**Put exercise on your calendar.** Individuals who pencil their workouts into their calendar are much more likely to follow through.

Give exercise the same priority as you would a business meeting or lunch with a friend.

•**Exercise early in the day.** Morning workouts burn no more calories than workouts late in the day. But they do give you more options if your schedule changes.

If an unforeseen circumstance forces you to cancel a workout that you've scheduled for the morning, you'll still have the rest of the day to break a sweat.

If you're forced to cancel an evening workout, you've lost your chance for the entire day.

•**Break up your workouts.** If you cannot fit a 60-minute workout into your daily schedule, do several shorter workouts throughout the day. You might go for a 30-minute walk in the morning, then take three 10-minute walks later on in the day.

Helpful: If there's any concern that weather or darkness might keep you from working out, invest in a treadmill. Recent research suggests that it's the most effective exercise machine for weight loss.

Whatever exercise you do, it should keep your heart rate elevated to at least 60% of its theoretical maximum capacity for at least 10 minutes at a time, for a total of 40 minutes a day.

To calculate your theoretical maximum heart rate, the old formula still holds true: Subtract your age in years from 220. A 60-year-old, for instance, has a theoretical maximum heart rate of 160 (220 minus 60).

•**Use a heart monitor.** This electronic device—typically consisting of an electrode-studded strap that's worn around the chest and a wristwatch-like digital display—gives a continuous readout of your heart rate.

With a heart monitor, there's no need to stop exercising to take your pulse. That's something you must do if you take your pulse using a finger held against your wrist.

Bonus: Heart monitors give you a clear target heart rate to shoot for, so they can be a tremendous source of motivation.

Heart monitors sell for $50 and up. They're available at sporting goods stores and via mail order.

One good mail-order source of heart monitors is Road Runner Sports, 800-636-3560, *www.roadrunnersports.com.*

•**Exercise to music.** When people listen to fast-tempo music, research shows, they tend to exercise more vigorously than they otherwise would. They also tend to keep at it longer.

Caution: Listening to headphones when running or walking outside can be dangerous.

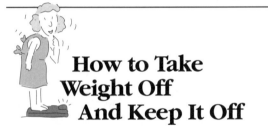

How to Take Weight Off And Keep It Off

Kathleen Thompson, coauthor of *Feeding on Dreams: Why America's Diet Industry Doesn't Work & What Will Work for You.* Macmillan.

Each year, Americans spend billions on commercial diet programs—and much of that is essentially wasted.

Reason: The premise on which these programs are based—cut calories, and you'll lose weight—is out of date. In study after study, it's been thoroughly discredited.

Weight loss just isn't that simple. As we all know, the hard part isn't losing weight, but *keeping* it off. Unless you're willing to eat frozen dinners and drink low-cal shakes for the rest of your life, keeping the weight off is almost impossible on most of the commercial weight-loss programs.

Not surprising, then, that many dieters shuffle unsuccessfully from one diet plan to the next—losing weight on one program, putting it back on and then moving on to another plan.

In fact, counselors working for the leading commercial diet plans freely admit that perhaps nine of 10 people who try one commercial diet program wind up trying two or three or more.

WEIGHT-LOSS PRINCIPLES

How do you take weight off and keep it off —once and for all? *There are three fundamental principles for effective and lasting weight loss...*

Principle #1: **Take control of your life and your weight.** Turning responsibility for what you eat and what you do over to anyone else is deadly. You need to design a program for yourself. You also need to open up your life to self-inspection.

Often, eating is a survival skill. It's a way of coping with frustrations and disappointments. Life can be very difficult. Eating can get you through it.

Overeating becomes a way to maintain emotional health—although, of course, physical health is jeopardized as a result.

To overcome this self-destructive approach to food, you must learn to separate food itself from its emotional symbolism. You may need the help of a psychologist specializing in weight problems.

For referrals to a psychologist in your area, contact the National Association of Anorexia Nervosa and Associated Disorders, P.O. Box 7, Highland Park, IL 60035. 847-831-3438.

Principle #2: **Accept your body.** Focus not upon how your body looks, but on what it enables you to do. And don't compare yourself with the ideal body put forth in sexy movies or magazine ads. After all, body shape is determined largely by heredity. We tend to look like our mothers and fathers—and that persists even if we're successful at losing weight.

Principle #3: **Make food a pleasure.** Avoid thinking of food as a moral issue. "Good" foods are those you think you should be eating— fruits, vegetables, beans, pasta, etc. "Bad" foods taste good but are fattening—cakes, candy, sugary soft drinks, etc.

Substituting good foods for bad sounds like a good idea, but odds are it's just setting you up for failure. *Problem:* Even if you could steer clear of "bad" foods for several months, you'd give in to temptation—possibly by going on an eating binge.

Better way: If you like cheesecake, allow yourself the freedom to eat it on occasion. By removing this cheesecake "taboo," you reduce your obsession with it.

DIETING VS. YOUR SET-POINT

The only way to ensure lasting weight loss is to lower your set-point. That's the weight your body "thinks" it should be.

When people overeat, they generally gain weight only temporarily, returning to their usual weight, or "set-point" when they resume their previous eating habits.

Similarly, when you go on a low-calorie diet, your body wants to keep you from starving. As a result, your metabolism slows to maintain your set-point. *Result:* Weight loss occurs very slowly. When you resume your normal eating patterns, your weight quickly rises to its former level.

To lower your set-point, you must reduce your intake of dietary fat *and* increase your lean muscle mass. In other words, lighten up your eating habits and get enough exercise to build muscle.

CUTTING OUT DIETARY FAT

●**Start small.** You're not going on a diet—you're changing the way you eat for the rest of your life. So there's no need to cut out dietary fat all at once.

You might start by switching to milk instead of cream in your coffee, then switching to low-fat mayonnaise on your sandwiches, etc.

●**Eat what you like. If you already enjoy certain low-fat foods,** make them staples of your diet. Make a list of your favorite high-fat foods, and find a way to substitute low-fat versions for some of them.

●**Keep track of your fat intake.** Buy a nutritional guide that lists the fat content of each food. Use it to calculate how many grams of fat you consume each day.

The maximum number of grams of fat you can eat each day and still lose weight is determined by your age, sex (men burn fat faster than women) and medical condition, among other things.

A woman over 30 should probably consume no more than 20% of her calories in the form of fat. A man over 30 can probably get away with up to 25%. (One gram of fat equals about nine calories.)

●**Make sure the whole family adopts healthful eating habits.** If your spouse has an ice cream sundae for dessert, you probably won't feel satisfied with a pear. But if everyone in the family starts eating healthfully, there's less temptation.

THE IMPORTANCE OF EXERCISE

The more you exercise, the more muscle you build. And because muscle cells burn dietary fat more efficiently than fat cells do, gaining muscle mass speeds your metabolism. *Payoff:* A thin person can eat much more fat than a fat person without gaining weight.

If you've been inactive for a long time, begin by exercising just five or 10 minutes a day. Gradually build until you're exercising at least 20 minutes a day, three to four days a week.

The point is to do what you like. Otherwise, you'll quickly give up exercising. If you used to thrive on volleyball or softball, for example, try to work these activities back into your schedule. If you're joining a gym, look for one where you feel comfortable. One reason people stop going to the gym is that they feel they don't measure up. If you feel intimidated by a chic club, try the local "Y" instead.

Consider hiring a personal trainer (for $15 to $50 per session). If you can't afford one, pool your money with a few friends and hire a trainer to come to one of your homes. Invest in headphones and a few good exercise tapes.

Dieting Magic

Barbara Rolls, PhD, professor of nutrition and head of Laboratory for the Study of Human Ingestive Behavior, Pennsylvania State University, University Park. She is coauthor of *Volumetrics: Feel Full on Fewer Calories.* HarperCollins.

Diets that work don't require you to follow drastic eating regimens or feel guilty if you sneak a brownie.

The real secrets: Portion control…moderation…and variety. Use these secrets to trim calories. General strategies…

● **Make small changes over time.** Eating habits are the hardest ones to change. But small, gradual changes are fairly easy.

Examples: If you drink 2% milk (121 calories/eight ounces), switch to 1% (102 calories) and then to skim (86 calories) over several months. Use reduced-fat sour cream and cottage cheese.

● **Substitute lower-calorie ingredients** in your favorite recipes and still enjoy the taste. You can make healthful, low-calorie foods tastier by adding spices.

● **Don't avoid treats completely.** Quite simply, sugar tastes good. And it doesn't make you fat unless you eat a great deal of it. So— use sugar to your advantage.

Examples: Add one teaspoon of sugar to a bowl of oatmeal if that's the only way you'll eat it. If you want chocolate, eat it at the end of a meal, when you are less likely to overindulge.

NEW WAY TO LOOK AT FOOD

One way to reduce your calorie intake is to eat the same volume as usual—but choose foods that are lower in calories than your regular high-calorie favorites.

● **Eat "high-water" foods.** Fruits, vegetables, nonfat milk and broth-based soups contain a lot of water—so you get a lot of volume and few calories.

Other high-water foods: Hot cereal… boiled eggs…pasta.

Eat less of "low-water" foods, which have a lot of calories by volume.

Examples: Most meats, cheeses and bread …most snack foods (including dried fruit)…oil… crackers…nuts…cookies…candy.

Myth…you'll eat less if you drink a glass of water before a meal. *Reality:* Water alone doesn't satisfy hunger. But thick water-rich drinks, such as tomato juice or milk, will.

● **Choose proteins carefully.** A 2.9-ounce serving of lean sirloin steak is comparable in calories to a 4.8-ounce serving of perch or 3.9 ounces of turkey breast. The larger portions of fish and turkey are more satisfying. Beans, low-fat milk and yogurt are also low-calorie, high-volume ways to eat protein.

HEALTHFUL WAYS TO FILL UP

● **Adjust the balance of foods.** Change the fat and calorie content of sandwiches by using low-fat meat, more garnish—dark lettuce, tomato and sprouts—with reduced-fat mayonnaise and spicy peppers or mustard for punch.

Increase the amount of vegetables in stir-fries, soups and stews. Use lean ground turkey breast in chili instead of ground beef.

Add extra vegetables, such as spinach, mushrooms and eggplant, to lasagna—and use less cheese. Take larger helpings of healthful "side" dishes and smaller portions of meat.

Healthful alternative to sugary soft drinks: Fill a glass with one-quarter juice and three-quarters club soda.

● **Add air to pump up food volume.** Food filled with air tricks your senses into thinking you're eating more than you are.

The longer you blend a fruit smoothie, the frothier it becomes. A large glass filled to the brim has more appeal than the same ingredients that fill only two-thirds of the glass.

For a low-fat frozen dessert, blend low-fat whipped topping with fruit, flavored yogurt or fruit-flavored extract…then freeze.

● **Choose snacks carefully.** Try a high-volume bunch of grapes rather than a comparable handful of raisins. Eat reduced-fat versions of your favorite snack foods—but watch the portions.

PORTION CONTROL

● **Make servings look more plentiful.** At home, eat on small plates rather than on dinner plates. At restaurants, order half servings—or ask that half be wrapped before the meal is served and take it home.

● **Freeze foods in single-serving portions,** so you can easily control how much you eat when you reheat.

● **Serve yourself**—rather than letting others serve you.

● **Buy the smallest packages available of snacks such as cookies or chips**…or buy the more economical size and repackage right away into single servings. Big packages encourage you to eat more.

● **Keep a daily food diary.** Most people underestimate how much they eat. By keeping a log, you'll discover ways to change mindless snacking habits.

Certain Aromas Promote Weight Loss

Certain aromas, including banana, peppermint and green apple, "fool" the brain into thinking the stomach is full. *Result:* Diminished appetite and significant weight loss. *To promote weight loss:* Sniff food before eating...chew food thoroughly...and if your tablemates can tolerate it, blow air through your carefully chewed food before swallowing. Hot food produces more odor—and therefore is more filling—than the same food eaten cold.

Alan R. Hirsch, MD, neurologic director, Smell & Taste Treatment and Research Foundation, 845 N. Michigan Ave., Chicago 60611.

Spotting Fraudulent Weight-Loss Programs

Dieters would be wise to avoid weight-loss programs that:

• **Promise rapid weight loss** (substantially more than 1% of total body weight per week).

• **Try to make clients dependent on special products** rather than teaching how to make good choices from conventional foods.

• **Do not encourage permanent, realistic lifestyle changes.**

• **Misrepresent salespeople as "counselors"** supposedly qualified to give guidance in nutrition and/or general health.

• **Require a large sum of money at the start,** or require clients to sign a contract for an expensive, long-term program.

• **Fail to inform clients** about the various health risks associated with weight loss.

• **Promote unproven or spurious weight-loss aids.**

• **Claim that "cellulite" exists in the body.**

• **Claim that the use of an appetite suppressant or bulking agent** enables a person to lose fat without restricting caloric intake.

• **Claim that a weight-control product** contains a unique ingredient or component, unless that component really is not available in other weight-loss products.

William T. Jarvis, PhD, president of the National Council Against Health Fraud, quoted in *Nutrition Forum*, George F. Stickley Co., Philadelphia 19106.

Good News for Dieters

Yo-yo dieting does not increase overall body fat or permanently slow the body's metabolism...so it doesn't make future weight loss more difficult. Previous studies had suggested just the opposite.

Lesson: If you are overweight, it's a good idea to lose weight—even if there's a chance you'll gain it back. Of course, it's better to maintain a healthy weight via regular exercise and a balanced diet.

Susan Yanofsky, executive secretary, National Task Force on the Prevention and Treatment of Obesity, Bethesda, MD. For more information, write to Weight Control Information Network, One WIN Way, Bethesda, MD 20892.

A Fish a Day...

Eating fish is a valuable part of a weight-loss program. A study of more than 60 overweight, hypertensive patients found that those who ate a meal with fish each day as part of a weight-loss program not only lost weight, but showed decreases in triglycerides and "bad" low-density cholesterol—and an increase in "good" high-density cholesterol—when compared with those who did not eat fish daily.

Lawrence J. Beilin, MD, FRCP, FRACP, professor of medicine, University of Western Australia, Perth.

12

Eating Right ...and Wrong

The Foods and Nutrients That Protect the Heart

There's now compelling evidence that certain foods contain special nutrients that guard against heart disease. The most important of these so-called "nutraceuticals" is *carnitine,* an amino acid found in red meat and in smaller amounts in chicken, fish, dairy products and certain fruits and vegetables.

Carnitine's primary function in the body is to ferry fatty acids from the foods we eat into the mitochondria. These microscopic "furnaces"—found inside every cell—convert fatty acids into the chemical energy that is put to use throughout the body.

CARNITINE SUPPLEMENTS

Biologists have been studying carnitine since the 1940s. Recent studies suggest that high levels of carnitine improve cardiac function in people suffering from coronary artery disease.

Other studies have shown that carnitine given immediately before or after a heart attack helps stabilize the heart rhythm. That improves the heart's pumping efficiency.

Carnitine has also been shown to minimize damage to the heart in the aftermath of a heart attack.

No one can predict when a heart attack will strike. For this reason it's often a good idea for people age 35 or older to take a daily carnitine supplement—to ensure that carnitine levels in the body are sufficient to protect the heart. Consult your doctor.

Carnitine supplementation is especially important for individuals with one or more risk factors for heart attack—obesity, family history of heart disease, elevated cholesterol level, high blood pressure and diabetes.

Stephen L. DeFelice, MD, chairman of the Foundation for Innovation in Medicine, *www.fimdefelice.org*, in Cranford, NJ, and former chief of clinical pharmacology at Walter Reed Army Institute of Research in Washington, DC. DeFelice coined the term "nutraceutical" and was among the first researchers to study carnitine's effects on the heart. He is author of *The Carnitine Defense*. Rodale.

Carnitine supplements are sold over the counter in drugstores and health food stores. Check labels carefully. Animal studies suggest that carnitine *fumarate* is more cardioprotective than other forms of carnitine.

Typical daily dosage: 1,500 mg to 3,000 mg. Taking carnitine twice daily—in divided doses 12 hours apart—helps keep blood levels consistent.

At this dosage, carnitine is extremely safe. Any excess is simply excreted in the urine.

BEYOND CARNITINE

Carnitine isn't the only heart-healthy nutraceutical. Vitamin E, magnesium, folic acid and other B vitamins, chromium and alcohol *in moderation* are proven to reduce heart attack risk.

Since these compounds are present in food only in small quantities, it's sometimes hard to get enough of them from food alone. For this reason, supplementation is often a good idea.

VITAMIN E

Vitamin E helps neutralize free radicals, helping keep these highly reactive molecular fragments from triggering the buildup of fatty deposits in coronary arteries.

Typical daily dosage: 400 international units (IU). To get that much vitamin E from food alone, you'd have to eat 48 cups of wheat germ or 100 cups of spinach.

One recent study of patients at high risk for heart disease seemed to suggest that vitamin E supplementation did not protect the heart against a lack of oxygen. This study contradicts numerous other studies showing that the supplements are heart-protective.

It may turn out that vitamin E is more effective at *preventing* high cholesterol and high blood pressure than at reducing heart attack risk in individuals who already have these risk factors.

Decades of clinical experience suggest that vitamin E supplementation is safe.

Caution: Check with a doctor if you've had a stroke or are on daily aspirin therapy and/or are taking *warfarin* (Coumadin) or another prescription anticoagulant. In such cases, vitamin E supplementation can thin the blood to the point that hemorrhage is likely.

MAGNESIUM

Magnesium prevents platelets from clumping together and clogging coronary arteries. It also stabilizes heart rhythm, reducing the risk of damage to the heart muscle during a heart attack.

Typical daily dosage: 400 mg to 500 mg. Divide into two doses and take twice a day to keep blood levels up all day.

Dietary sources of magnesium include artichokes, beans, shellfish, nuts and whole grains.

B VITAMINS

The B vitamin folic acid cuts blood levels of *homocysteine,* a blood protein that's been linked to heart disease. Folic acid's homocysteine-busting effect is especially pronounced when it's taken in combination with vitamins B-6 and B-12.

Typical daily dosages: 400 micrograms (mcg) folic acid...400 mg vitamin B-6...500 mcg to 1,000 mcg vitamin B-12.

ALCOHOL

Moderate drinking fights heart disease three ways. It boosts levels of HDL (good) cholesterol...helps rid the body of LDL (bad) cholesterol...and helps prevent platelet clumping.

Typical daily "dosage": The equivalent of one drink for women...one or two drinks for men. One drink equals 12 ounces of beer, four ounces of wine or 1.5 ounces of distilled spirits.

If you have a family or personal history of alcohol abuse: Consult a doctor before using alcohol. Pregnant women should not drink alcohol.

CHROMIUM

Chromium has been shown to reduce insulin resistance, in which cells' increasing resistance to insulin causes glucose levels to rise. This is a significant problem for people with diabetes.

Typical daily dosage: 500 mcg to 1,000 mcg.

Dietary sources of chromium include brewer's yeast, liver, egg yolks, wheat germ and whole-grain cereal.

MAKING IT WORK

If it's too hard to keep track of which supplements to take once a day and which twice a day, divide all the doses in half and take all your supplements twice a day.

Caution: Consult a doctor before taking any nutritional supplement. Like prescription medications, supplements can interact with other drugs you take.

Your doctor should carefully monitor the effects of the supplements…and, if necessary, adjust dosages.

New Guidelines for Eating Right

Suzanne Havala, RD, MS, FADA, registered dietitian based in Chapel Hill, NC. She is author of several books, including *The Complete Idiot's Guide to Being Vegetarian* (Macmillan) and *Good Foods, Bad Foods: What's Left to Eat?* (John Wiley & Sons).

The *new* word is out. A government-appointed panel of scientists has issued the fifth edition of *Dietary Guidelines* for Americans, the federal government's official word on the best nutritional practices. *Here is what they say…*

1. Aim for a healthful weight. There are a variety of ways to assess your weight. Check with your doctor to determine if you have excess abdominal fat. This puts you at a higher risk for a variety of diseases.

2. Be physically active every day. Greater emphasis is placed on the importance of regular physical activity and its role in weight control.

3. Let the Food Pyramid guide your food choices. The old guidelines said simply to "eat a variety of foods." Now people are encouraged to refer to the US Department of Agriculture's Food Pyramid for specific advice about what to eat. *www.nal.usda.gov/fnic/,* click on "Food Guide Pyramid."

4. Eat a variety of grains daily—especially whole grains. Previous recommendations lumped grains together with fruits and vegetables. The new guidelines emphasize grains as the foundation of a healthful diet.

5. Eat a variety of fruits and vegetables daily. Along with grains, fruits and vegetables are considered the pillars of a healthful diet. They are linked to lower rates of all types of disease, including diabetes, heart disease, some types of cancer, high blood pressure, etc.

6. Keep food safe to eat. For the first time, the guidelines address safe handling of foods to prevent food-borne illnesses.

Examples: Cooking and reheating food thoroughly…keeping preparation surfaces clean …keeping raw and prepared foods separate.

7. Eat a diet that is low in saturated fat and cholesterol…and moderate in total fat. No more than 30% of daily calories should come from fat.

8. Limit your intake of foods with added sugars. Foods and beverages that contain added sugar displace nutrient-dense foods from your diet. Cut down on sweets and junk foods.

9. Choose and prepare foods with less salt. Americans continue to be advised to limit their sodium intake. *Heaviest sources:* Processed foods…salt added in cooking.

10. If you drink alcoholic beverages, do so in moderation—no more than one drink per day for women…two per day for men. The new guidelines acknowledge a heart-health benefit to moderate amounts of alcohol —particularly in women over age 55 and men over age 45. Alcohol consumption in younger women is associated with an increased risk of breast cancer.

The full text of Dietary Guidelines for Americans can be viewed online at *www.ars.usda. gov/dgac.*

Elderly People May Need More Protein

Elderly people may need more protein— 25% to 50% more—than the familiar recommended daily allowance (RDA).

Current guidelines call for 0.36 gram of protein per pound of body weight per day (equaling 61 grams for a 170-pound person and 51 grams for a 143-pound person). But in a study, healthy subjects 56 to 80 years of age who ate a diet containing the RDA for protein excreted more protein than they ate. Inadequate protein intake may result in muscle mass loss, which can lead to frailty.

Self-defense: Elderly men of average build should consume at least 93 grams of protein a day, elderly women at least 78 grams.

Food	Grams of protein
One cup of 1% fat milk	8
One cup of lowfat yogurt	10
Three ounces of tuna	24
One cup of cooked lentils	39

Wayne Campbell, PhD, research associate, Noll Physiological Research Center, Pennsylvania State University, University Park.

Poor Nutrition in The Elderly

Eating alone is the leading factor behind poor nutrition among old people. Women who eat alone tend to eat too few calories…while men who eat alone tend to eat too much fat.

Other contributors to poor nutrition: Low education level…belonging to a racial minority…living in a low-income neighborhood…smoking…wearing dentures…taking multiple medications.

Katherine Tucker, PhD, assistant professor, Tufts School of Nutrition, Boston. Her study of 700 people ages 60 to 89 was published in *Food & Nutrition Research Briefs,* US Department of Agriculture, 6303 Ivy Lane, Fourth Floor, Greenbelt, MD 20770.

Caffeine and Your Health

Timothy McCall, MD, a Boston internist and author of *Examining Your Doctor: A Patient's Guide to Avoiding Harmful Medical Care.* Citadel Press.

Over the years, conflicting information has been written about the risks of caffeine. Studies have shown that drinking coffee has been tied to pancreatic cancer…high cholesterol…heart attacks…and birth defects.

Reality: The results of these studies have been called into question by health experts. That's because people who drink a lot of coffee tend to have other bad habits as well, such as smoking or not exercising—which may be the culprits.

CAFFEINE AND OSTEOPOROSIS

While caffeine in coffee, tea, cola, chocolate and some medications can cause jitteriness, trembling, irritability and insomnia, studies have not substantiated most of the claims about caffeine's negative *long-term effects.*

Exception: There appears to be a connection between consuming high levels of caffeine and osteoporosis—the thinning of bones that can lead to hip fractures, especially in older women. Risk factors for osteoporosis include being female, thin, white—particularly of Northern European or Asian ancestry—not exercising, smoking and having a family history of the disease.

Self-defense: If you are at high risk for developing osteoporosis, you should significantly reduce your caffeine intake and be sure to include enough calcium in your diet. In one study, women who drank at least one glass of milk per day were protected from the bone-thinning consequences of caffeine.

If you can't drink milk, take a calcium supplement. Calcium carbonate, sold in supermarkets, drugstores and health food stores, is an inexpensive and effective source.

Premenopausal women should take 1,200 mg/day…postmenopausal women, 1,500 mg/day. For best absorption, take no more than 500 mg at one time.

CAFFEINE WITHDRAWAL

People who are accustomed to drinking several cups of coffee a day may develop headaches, have difficulty concentrating, and experience fatigue and depression if they eliminate caffeine from their diets.

If you decide you want to cut down on caffeine, it's best to do so slowly. Cut back by about 20% a week over a month—or more.

Slowly reducing the amount of caffeine in your system prevents withdrawal reactions. If headaches or other symptoms develop, increase your consumption slightly, then continue to slowly lower it over time.

Skim Milk Alert

Drinking skim milk deprives you of a powerful cancer fighting substance. Recent studies have found that conjugated linoleic acid, a compound present in milk fat, is one of the most potent of all natural substances in fighting colon and breast cancers in animals. While human studies have not yet been performed, the research suggests that milk drinkers seeking to reduce fat consumption without losing milk's many nutritional benefits might try 1%-fat milk rather than fat-free milk.

Dale E. Bauman, PhD, Liberty Hyde Bailey professor of animal science, Cornell University, Ithaca, NY.

Chili Pepper Danger

Eating too many hot peppers may boost your risk of stomach cancer. Those who identified themselves as "heavy" consumers of chili peppers were 17 times more likely to develop stomach cancer than those who did not consume chilies. *Possible culprit:* Capsaicin, the hot-tasting component in chili peppers.

Robert Dubrow, MD, PhD, associate professor of epidemiology and public health, Yale University School of Medicine, New Haven, CT. His study of 220 stomach cancer patients and 752 healthy individuals was published in the *American Journal of Epidemiology,* 2007 E. Monument St., Baltimore 21205.

Green Tea Fights Disease

Green tea fights heart disease, cancer, flu—even tooth decay. It's rich in a class of natural antioxidant compounds called *polyphenols*. Green tea is derived from the same plant as the more common black tea, but it's processed differently. Black tea is fermented before drying—green tea is not. The fermentation process reduces the levels of polyphenols.

Hasan Muktar, PhD, professor and director of research, Case Western Reserve University School of Medicine, Cleveland.

Green tea eases arthritis—at least in rodents. In a recent study, mice drank water containing *polyphenols*—antioxidant compounds derived from green tea—or plain water.

After 10 days, the mice were injected with a compound that ordinarily triggers a rheumatoid arthritis-like disorder.

Result: Less than half of the mice that drank water with the polyphenols developed the disorder. In contrast, 94% of the mice that drank plain water developed the disorder.

Human trials are being planned. In the meantime, there's no downside to drinking green tea. Black tea contains lower levels of polyphenols, and so may not provide the same benefit.

Tariq M. Haqqi, PhD, associate professor of medicine and rheumatology, Case Western Reserve University School of Medicine, Cleveland. His study of green tea and arthritis in mice was published in the *Proceedings of the National Academy of Sciences,* 2101 Constitution Ave. NW, Washington, DC 20418.

One More Reason to Eat Green Leafy Vegetables

They seem to help prevent *age-related macular degeneration,* the leading cause of blindness among elderly people. In one study, people who ate the most of certain types of carotenoids—found in spinach and other dark, leafy greens—had a 43% lower risk of developing the eye disorder than those who ate the least.

Johanna M. Seddon, MD, associate professor of ophthalmology, Harvard Medical School and Harvard School of Public Health, and director of the epidemiology unit, Massachusetts Eye and Ear Infirmary, all in Boston. Her study of 356 men and women, age 55 to 80, with age-related macular degeneration and 520 healthy people with normal vision was published in the *Journal of the American Medical Association,* 515 N. State St., Chicago 60610.

Garlic Danger

Fresh garlic mixes can cause botulism if stored at room temperature. The preservatives found in *commercial* garlic preparations retard spoilage only when refrigerated. Because they lack preservatives, *homemade* garlic mixes may spoil even if stored in the refrigerator. After two weeks, throw them out.

Joseph M. Madden, PhD, strategic manager for microbiology, Center for Food Safety and Applied Nutrition, Food and Drug Administration, Washington, DC.

All About Genetically Engineered Foods

Sheldon Krimsky, PhD, professor of urban and environmental policy at Tufts University, Medford, MA. He is author of *Hormonal Chaos: The Scientific and Social Origins of the Environmental Endocrine Hypothesis* (Johns Hopkins University Press) and *Agricultural Biotechnology and the Environment* (University of Illinois Press).

Some nutrition experts and geneticists have expressed concern that genetically engineered foods will have unintended, and dangerous, side effects.

●**What exactly is genetic engineering?** It's a technique for snipping individual genes from one organism—plant, animal or microbe —and slipping them into another. This is done to introduce new traits or to enhance existing traits in crops.

One common goal of genetic engineering is to render crops resistant to attack by insects and the herbicides applied to control weeds.

Another goal is to lengthen the timespan that fruits and vegetables stay fresh. The *Flavr Savr* tomato, which made headlines when it was introduced in 1993, contained a gene that suppresses *polygalacturonase,* an enzyme that causes ripening.

●**Are genetically engineered foods safe to eat?** There's no evidence to suggest that genetically altered foods are harmful—or that they're less nutritious than their unaltered counterparts.

However, there is no compelling evidence that they're safe either. That's because food producers are not required to conduct safety tests on genetically engineered foods that they deem to be equivalent to the natural foods from which they are derived.

Perhaps of greatest concern is the use of genetically engineered *bovine growth hormone* (BGH), which is widely used in the dairy industry to increase cows' milk production.

Cows given BGH are more likely than other cows to develop mastitis, an infection of the udders.

Preliminary research involving animals suggests that drinking milk from cows treated with BGH causes high levels of *insulin-like growth factor* (IGF-1), which are linked to higher cancer risk.

Also, since infections are more common among cows that have been given genetically engineered BGH, they receive more antibiotics.

If dairy farmers could ensure that these powerful drugs didn't get into the human food supply, this might not matter. But antibiotics do slip through.

Widespread use of antibiotics—by doctors as well as food producers—has contributed to the surge in antibiotic-resistant streptococcal infections and other bacterial infections.

●**What can I do to protect myself?** Given what we now know, it's prudent to buy dairy products from producers who don't use BGH.

This information is sometimes included on carton labels. I look for it when I buy milk.

• **Which other foods are likely to have been genetically modified?** Today, more than 60% of soybeans sold in the US have been genetically modified using gene-splicing techniques.

Other crops whose DNA has been altered include apples, broccoli, cranberries and peanuts. These are not yet on the market, but may be soon.

Except for soybeans, corn and some varieties of tomatoes and potatoes, few "whole" foods on the market have been genetically modified.

It's difficult to avoid genetically modified soybeans because they're an ingredient in so many different products. I don't even bother looking for it on the label.

I do try to avoid genetically engineered foods when doing so is feasible. I buy organic produce because I know that federal regulations prohibit labeling genetically altered foods as organic. And I buy free-range chicken because I know that it hasn't been treated with hormones.

If you don't have access to organic foods—or prefer not to pay the premium price—consider buying produce at a local farmers' market.

Small farms are less likely than large growers to use genetically modified seeds.

• **Isn't gene-swapping a problem for those with food allergies?** It can be. The FDA now requires food producers to alert consumers when a genetically engineered food contains a known allergen.

In one highly publicized case, a company was considering transferring a gene from a Brazil nut into a soybean. Then a study showed that individuals allergic to Brazil nuts also became allergic to the genetically modified soybeans. Ultimately, the company did not market the soybean.

Currently, there is no required testing for new allergens created by genetically modified foods. Consequently, as genetic engineering becomes more common, people may find themselves experiencing allergies to foods that never gave them problems before.

• **Do genetically engineered foods taste different?** Food producers say there's no difference, but I'm not so sure.

Once I asked my students to do a blindfolded taste-test on two tomatoes, one of which had been genetically modified. The genetically engineered tomato looked fantastic, but it wasn't nearly as tasty. Some students said it tasted like cardboard.

With other foods, you may never notice the difference.

Salt Substitute Danger

Salt substitutes containing a mixture of sodium chloride and potassium chloride can be dangerous for those on sodium-restricted diets.

Danger: Used liberally by such individuals, these products can result in a potassium buildup, leading to irregular heartbeat or even a fatal heart rhythm disturbance.

Better way: Instead of salt substitutes, add flavor to food with garlic, onion, lemon juice or herbs. Salt substitutes are generally safe for healthy individuals.

Randall Zusman, MD, associate professor of medicine, Harvard Medical School, and director, division of hypertension and vascular medicine, Massachusetts General Hospital, both in Boston.

Margarine Problem

Semisolid, hydrogenated fats are less healthful than the oils they're made from. A group of people with high cholesterol went on a cholesterol-lowering diet that contained corn oil...and their LDL (bad) cholesterol fell an average of 17%. But LDL fell only 10% when researchers replaced the corn oil with corn oil margarine in stick form.

Alice Lichtenstein, DSc, assistant professor of nutrition, lipid metabolism group, Human Nutrition Research Center on Aging, Tufts University, Boston. Her study of 14 men and women ranging in age from 44 to 78 was published in *Arteriosclerosis and Thrombosis,* 7272 Greenville Ave., Dallas 75231.

All About Antioxidants

Kenneth H. Cooper, MD, founder of the Cooper Aerobics Center, 12200 Preston Rd., Dallas 75230. He is author of *Dr. Kenneth H. Cooper's Antioxidant Revolution*. Thomas Nelson, Inc.

Antioxidants may be a popular health catchword, but many people are confused about what antioxidants are and what the conflicting data imply about their usefulness.

To clear up the confusion, we spoke to Dr. Kenneth H. Cooper, whose book *Aerobics* revolutionized America's attitude toward fitness more than 25 years ago. He continues to direct research into exercise, diet, health and fitness at The Cooper Aerobics Center in Dallas.

● **What are antioxidants, and why are they important?**

To understand antioxidants, you must first understand the concept of free radicals.

A free radical is an unstable type of oxygen molecule. It lacks one of its electrons, and must therefore "steal" an electron from another molecule. When that unstable oxygen molecule seeks to replace its missing electron, it causes a chain reaction that can damage cell membranes and DNA.

Free radicals are unavoidable: They're a by-product of normal metabolism, as well as a response to environmental factors like air pollution, cigarette smoke, radiation, pesticide residues and other food contaminants, physical injury, excessive exercise and possibly emotional stress.

Another source of free radicals is ischemia, the cutoff of oxygen to cells, such as during surgery, followed by *reperfusion,* when blood rushes back into the deprived organ.

Free radicals aren't all bad: They're thought to help the immune system and are necessary for the proper function of organs and blood vessels. *But when these renegade molecules get out of control, they can be very destructive...*

● Free radicals promote cancer.

● Free radicals change LDL (bad) cholesterol into the harmful form that clogs arteries.

● Free radicals promote signs of aging, such as deterioration of the skin and other organs.

● Free radicals have also been linked to a variety of medical problems, from cataracts to stroke to rheumatoid arthritis and Parkinson's disease.

Fortunately, the body has weapons to keep free radicals under control—the antioxidants. These molecules prevent and repair free radical damage by sacrificing their own electrons ...and by "mopping up" unstable molecules before they do damage.

Some antioxidants are endogenous, meaning they are produced within the body. The most important of these are superoxide dismutase, catalase and GSH. Others are exogenous, or taken from outside in the form of nutrients.

The primary exogenous antioxidants are vitamin C, vitamin E and beta-carotene.

● **Can you get enough of these exogenous antioxidants from food?**

Researchers are still trying to answer this question. A diet high in vitamin-rich fruits and vegetables—especially greens and cruciferous vegetables like cabbage and broccoli—is associated with a lower incidence of cancer and many other diseases. This may well be due to the foods' antioxidant properties, although the connection has yet to be proven.

Theoretically, it's possible to get all the vitamin C and beta-carotene you need from your diet—if you consume seven to nine servings of fruits and vegetables a day, prepared with minimal cutting, peeling, trimming and cooking so as to minimize vitamin loss.

But most Americans simply don't eat that many fruits and vegetables every day.

As for vitamin E, it's found primarily in fatty foods like nuts and seeds—making it virtually impossible to get enough of this vitamin through diet alone and still keep calories and fat under control.

Vitamin supplements are not a substitute for a healthful diet, regular exercise or controlled weight. But they probably enhance what we're getting from other sources—and at very little financial cost or physical risk.

Think of them as a kind of insurance policy in our stress- and pollution-filled world.

•Didn't a Finnish study find that taking vitamins increases health risk?

This study did find that subjects who took beta-carotene supplements were more likely to develop lung cancer—a result trumpeted in the media around the world.

Since then, however, a number of experts have pointed out flaws in the research. The subjects had all smoked heavily for many years. The cases of lung cancer and heart disease that occurred might well have already been present—undiagnosed—before the study began. (Antioxidants are thought to have a protective, not a curative, effect.) The effects of supplements on nonsmokers weren't studied at all.

To say that beta-carotene is dangerous based on that one study is irresponsible. Far more research suggests that beta-carotene supplements protect against lung and other types of cancer.

Example: A study in China found a 13% reduction in all cancers, and a 9% reduction in overall mortality, among subjects who took supplements of beta-carotene, selenium and vitamin E.

The Finnish study did find that even minimal doses of vitamin E—50 international units (IU) per day—were linked to a 34% reduction in death from prostate cancer, a 16% reduction in death from colon cancer and a 5% reduction in death from heart attack. Yet the press ignored these encouraging findings.

•What doses of vitamin supplements do you recommend?

Based on the existing research, *I believe that most adults should take a daily antioxidant "cocktail" containing...*

•1,000 milligrams (mg) vitamin C. That's 500 mg taken twice a day. Costly sustained-release capsules seem to be no more effective than regular tablets.

•400 IU vitamin E. The natural form—d-alpha tocopherol—is preferable to synthetic dl-alpha tocopherol.

•25,000 IU beta-carotene. Beta-carotene is a precursor of vitamin A, which can be toxic in large doses.

•What role does exercise play in the free radical/antioxidant equation?

Moderate exercise appears to enhance the activity of the body's own antioxidants. However, excessive exercise—such as training for a marathon—seems to increase free radical production.

While I wouldn't presume to tell a marathon runner to stop training, I do think it makes sense to take higher levels of antioxidant supplements.

•3,000 mg vitamin C.

•1,200 IU vitamin E.

•50,000 IU beta-carotene.

•Can these vitamins have toxic side effects?

Not at the above doses, in most cases. *Exceptions...*

•Don't take beta-carotene within four hours of drinking an alcoholic beverage. The interaction of alcohol and beta-carotene can cause liver damage. Heavy drinkers probably shouldn't take beta-carotene at all.

•People on anticoagulant therapy should avoid vitamin E, since it can cause excessive bleeding.

•People with kidney stones should avoid large doses of vitamin C.

•Pregnant women should check with their doctors before taking vitamin supplements or any other type of medication.

Even if you are not in any of the above categories—but especially if you are—check with your doctor before beginning a vitamin regimen. And whenever you're asked about the kinds of medications you're taking, remember to include the supplements on your list.

•Do you recommend any other antioxidant supplements?

The compound Coenzyme Q10 and the mineral selenium help neutralize free radicals. However, Coenzyme Q10 hasn't yet been studied extensively. And excess selenium can cause hair loss, fatigue and other toxic effects. I need more data before I can recommend either of these as supplements.

•What else can I do to head off free radical damage?

Avoid sources of environmental stress. If you exercise outdoors, do so early in the morning or after sundown, when pollution levels are low. Stay away from major highways.

Limit your exposure to sunlight. Give some thought to the other environmental hazards you're likely to encounter—then think of ways to minimize them.

Don't try to change your whole life all at once, however. Pick one factor, address it—and once you've got it under control, start on another.

•What about aspirin?

Aspirin is not an antioxidant, but it has been recommended as protection against heart attacks. Yet most of the research indicates that aspirin is most beneficial to individuals who already have cardiovascular disease...and it may sightly increase the risk of hemorrhagic stroke.

Consequently, for healthy people with no known history of heart disease, I do not recommend taking aspirin regularly.

Prostate Cancer Risk

In a study of 48,000 men, those who ate the most red meat, butter and chicken with skin were two-and-a-half times more likely to develop late-stage prostate cancer than men who ate the least of these foods. By age 80, two-thirds of men have prostate cancer. But whether the cancer lies dormant for years or quickly becomes life-threatening may depend upon the amount of animal fat in the diet.

Edward Giovannucci, MD, ScD, instructor of medicine, Harvard Medical School, Boston.

Save on Vitamins

Nearly all vitamin supplement makers buy their raw vitamins from the same suppliers.

Just three major manufacturers—Roche, BASF and Rhone-Poulenc—produce 90% of the world's vitamins. So, no matter which brand you buy or how much you pay, and regardless of the appearance of the vitamin pill, you are getting the same basic vitamin product. You can save a lot of money if you buy the drugstore's house brand.

Caution: How the raw vitamin is formulated for use—tablets, gel caps, capsules, etc.—can affect how well it dissolves in your body. Look for "USP" on the label to be sure the product meets US Pharmacopeia standards for dissolvability.

V. Srini Srinivasan, PhD, director, dietary supplements division, US Pharmacopeia, 12601 Twinbrook Pkwy., Rockville, MD 20852.

Myths About Minerals

Mia Parsonnet, MD, a member of the clinical faculty of the New Jersey College of Medicine and Dentistry. She is author of *What's Really in Our Food? Fact and Fiction about Fat and Fiber, Vitamins and Minerals, Nutrients and Contaminants.* Shapolsky Publishers, Inc.

Thanks to everything we've read and heard lately about fat, fiber and food additives, we've all become much smarter about what we're eating—and that's great.

However—a surprising number of myths remain concerning the minerals we take in, both in our daily diets and in the form of supplements. And that misinformation can be dangerous...even deadly.

What we do know for certain is that minerals are essential for life. To a large extent, the body is composed of minerals. For example, our blood carries significant amounts of sodium, potassium and chloride. And our bones and teeth are rich in calcium, phosphorous and magnesium.

The news about minerals is generally good: If you eat a healthy, varied diet—including adequate amounts of milk, fruits and vegetables—your body should get all the minerals it requires. Special needs do arise, however.

Example: As people age, calcium is less well utilized, and extra amounts are recommended, especially for women. Prolonged gastrointestinal illness, and certain drugs, may also change requirements.

Minerals are an often-misunderstood category of nutrients, and you may do well to let go of some of the myths:

Myth: A salty taste is a reliable indicator of salt content.

Truth: Food-content labels must be read very carefully—some items that you would never suspect to be high in sodium are. For example, ounce for ounce, certain dry cereals contain more salt than potato chips.

As most of us now know, too much salt in the diet can promote high blood pressure—and possibly strokes in susceptible individuals. We require only a tiny amount of salt to maintain good health—just 500 milligrams daily, or the equivalent of a quarter-teaspoon. Chances are you're getting more than that amount naturally from the foods you eat each day—you need never go near a salt shaker. In fact, the average American consumes closer to 4,000 to 5,000 milligrams per day—10 times what's needed.

If you're a salt-lover, you'd be wise to wean yourself off it. Our taste for salt (or any other flavor) is acquired and thus can be unlearned at any age.

To keep your kids from getting hooked on salt, don't serve them salty food or snacks.

Myth: Calcium deficiency is really only of concern to women approaching menopause.

Truth: Women are never too young to step up their calcium intake to help ward off future osteoporosis. Even teenage girls should start taking calcium supplements to build bone strength, especially if they don't drink milk. Bones that are strong at an early age are less likely to leach out calcium, a process that leads to fractures and other problems later on.

Between the ages of 19 and 24, women (and men) should be sure to get 1,200 milligrams of calcium per day—the amount provided by approximately a quart of milk. If you know you're not taking in sufficient quantities of calcium from your food—and most people's diets are imperfect—by all means take a calcium supplement.

Myth: "Health" foods are better sources of minerals than ordinary foods.

Truth: Some so-called "health" or "natural" foods can in fact be harmful.

Example: Health food fans will often buy "natural" calcium supplements. These supplements are generally produced from limestone and are rich in calcium and magnesium, but they can also contain dangerous impurities, including lead.

In general, it's unwise to buy foods that haven't been carefully inspected and analyzed by government agencies. *Problem:* Many products found in health food stores have not undergone rigorous inspection. If you choose a food or a supplement that hasn't been government-approved, you run the risk of ingesting impurities. While some of them are harmless, others are not.

Myth: Minerals lost through sweat during strenuous exercise should be replaced via a mineral-rich drink such as Gatorade or by taking salt tablets.

Truth: Gatorade, a dilute solution of some of the minerals found in the body, is a perfectly fine product, but you rarely need it. Your body will restore its lost minerals on its own.

It's far more important to replenish the water your body has lost in sweat.

As for salt tablets, athletes used to rely on them, but nowadays we know that these tablets can do more harm than good. Again, it's best to stick to plain water after your workout, unless the salt loss was truly excessive.

Exception: Pedialyte is a solution that pediatricians may give to children who've become dehydrated from excessive vomiting or diarrhea. That's because youngsters have a much more delicate constitution than adults, and so their water and mineral levels must be restored quickly and completely.

MINIMUM DAILY REQUIREMENTS

•**Sodium.** 500 mg. (¼ teaspoon of table salt). *Sodium-rich foods:* Those that have been pickled, canned, smoked or cured...soy sauce...luncheon meats...salted snack foods.

•**Potassium.** 2,000 mg. *Some potassium-rich foods include:* Bananas (four)...orange juice (four 8-ounce glasses)...carrots (six).

•**Chloride.** 750 mg. (or ¼ teaspoon of table salt). *Chloride-rich foods:* Most processed foods.

•**Calcium.** 1,200 mg. (ages 19 to 24)...800 mg. (age 25 and over). *Some calcium-rich foods:* Milk (three 8-ounce glasses)...plain yogurt (three 8-ounce cups)...cheddar cheese (6 ounces).

●**Phosphorus.** 1,200 mg. (ages 19 to 24)... 800 mg. (age 25 and over). *Phosphorus-rich foods:* Same as those rich in calcium.

●**Magnesium.** 350 mg. (men), 280 mg. (women). *Some magnesium-rich foods:* Green beans (five cups)...Brazil nuts (12).

●**Sulfur.** A daily requirement has not been established. *Sulfur-rich foods:* Cheese, eggs, milk, meat, nuts, vegetables.

Some essential trace elements—needed by the body in miniscule amounts...

●**Iron.** *Daily requirement:* 10 mg. (men)... 15 mg. (women ages 19 to 50)...10 mg. (women 51 and over). *Some iron-rich foods:* Liver (4 ounces)...breakfast cereal, such as Cheerios or Raisin Bran (2 ounces).

●**Selenium.** *Daily requirement:* 70 micrograms (men)...55 micrograms (women). *Some selenium-rich foods:* Canned tuna (2½ ounces) ...molasses (2 ounces).

●**Iodine.** *Daily requirement:* 150 micrograms. *Some iodine-rich foods:* Iodized salt...haddock (4 ounces)...milk (8 ounces)... plain yogurt (two 8-ounce cups).

How Herbs Can Keep You Healthy

Sandra McLanahan, MD, director of the stress management training program at Dr. Dean Ornish's Preventive Medicine Research Institute in Sausalito, CA, and executive medical director of the Integral Health Center and Spa, Buckingham, VA. For more information on herbs or for information on starting an herb garden, Dr. McLanahan recommends *The Healing Herbs,* by Michael Castleman. St. Martin's Press.

I never stop being amazed by the remarkable healing power of herbs. As a practicing physician, I've been recommending them to my patients for more than 25 years. Unfortunately, few physicians have taken the initiative to learn enough about herbs.

Herbs have several advantages over conventional drugs. They're inexpensive, potent and—if you take care not to overdose—far less likely to cause allergic reactions or other side effects. (Some potentially dangerous herbs, including sassafras and chaparral, have been taken off the market.) Herbs are readily available without a prescription at health food stores—although it's best to check with your doctor before using herbs.

HERE ARE HERBAL REMEDIES I FIND MOST USEFUL

●**Aloe vera is wonderful for soothing minor burns and preventing subsequent infection.** Although it's available in gel form, research suggests that fresh aloe vera leaves are more potent in their anesthetic and antibacterial properties. I urge my friends, family and patients to keep an aloe vera plant in the kitchen and use its leaves to dab on minor burns.

●**Chamomile tea contains oils that have antispasmodic and anti-inflammatory effects.** It's good for indigestion, anxiety, insomnia and exhaustion. Babies given chamomile tea in their bottle fall asleep faster.

●**Comfrey contains allantoin,** a compound that speeds healing by promoting growth of muscle and connective tissue. It helps prevent bruising and swelling associated with muscle sprains and strains. Applied to the skin as a paste...not to be taken by mouth.

●**Echinacea**—sometimes blended with the natural antibiotic goldenseal—stimulates the body's production of the virus-fighting compound interferon and boosts the number and activity of white cells. That makes it a perfect all-around remedy for colds or flu. It's also good for urinary tract infections. Often taken as drops mixed in a glass of water.

●**Garlic lowers cholesterol,** boosts the immune system and kills disease-causing germs. People who eat lots of garlic get fewer colds. *Important:* Deodorized garlic preparations—used by individuals worried about bad breath—are somewhat less potent than fresh garlic. Parsley helps eliminate bad breath.

●**Ginger tea relieves nausea caused by motion sickness,** morning sickness, influenza or radiation therapy. In tincture form, ginger is also effective against flatulence and indigestion. It may also be useful for lowering serum cholesterol, although at this point the data is preliminary.

●**Milk thistle is widely used in Japan to treat liver problems, including hepatitis A,**

B and C. It contains compounds that promote the flow of bile and stimulate production of new liver cells. Taken in capsule form.

●**Nettle contains the compounds choline, acetylcholine and histamine.** Together, they reduce inflammation, helping to relieve runny nose, watery eyes and other allergy symptoms. It also stimulates the immune system. Studies at the National College of Naturopathic Medicine in Portland, Oregon, demonstrated that two nettle capsules a day reduced symptoms of hay fever. Taken as capsules or brewed as a tea.

●**Saw palmetto contains liposterol,** a compound that inhibits action of the male hormone *dihydrotestosterone.* It's an extremely potent remedy for prostate problems, including frequent urination, prostatitis (prostate inflammation) and benign prostatic hypertrophy (prostate enlargement).

●**St. John's Wort contains an antibacterial oil.** It's good for treating stubborn colds or coughs—and possibly flu and other viral infections. A study found it to be an effective treatment for mild to moderate depression. Taken as capsules or drops.

What to Eat to Prevent Cancer...and What Not to Eat

Leonard A. Cohen, PhD, head of the section of nutritional endocrinology, the American Health Foundation, One Dana Rd., Valhalla, NY 10595. Dr. Cohen's specialty is in the area of nutritional carcinogenesis.

Although scientists continue to debate the role specific foods play in the development of cancer, there's now a consensus that Americans could dramatically lower their cancer risk by altering their eating habits—specifically, by eating less fat and more fiber.

THE FAT CONNECTION

Most Americans consume 38% to 40% of their total calories in the form of fat—well above the 25% to 30% fat consumption considered desirable.

This appears to make us more susceptible to cancer of the colon, breast, pancreas and prostate.

No one knows exactly why eating too much fat promotes the development of cancer, but the evidence—drawn from studies on both animals and humans—is compelling.

Different foods contain different types and quantities of fat...

●**Saturated fats are found in beef and other meats, fried foods and poultry skin.**

●**Monounsaturated fats are found in peanuts, olives and a few other foods.**

●**Polyunsaturated fats are found in corn, safflower and other cooking oils.**

●**Omega-3 fatty acids are found in cold-water fish,** such as herring and salmon.

It's important to keep track of what kinds of fats you eat because nutritionists now recommend that these fats be eaten in equal amounts. In other words, each day we should eat equal portions of polyunsaturated, monounsaturated and saturated fats. For most of us, this means cutting down on saturated fats while increasing intake of monounsaturated and polyunsaturated fats.

To reduce your consumption of saturated fats, eat fewer fried foods, trim the fat off beef and other meats, and remove the skin from poultry. These small sacrifices have big health payoffs.

About fish: Although fish contains oils that are highly unsaturated, it's still unclear what, if any, role this oil plays in preventing cancer. There is some evidence, however, that eating large amounts of fish reduces cancer risk and lowers serum triglycerides—lipids that may be associated with heart disease.

THE FIBER CONNECTION

While we're eating too much fat, we're also eating too little fiber. On the average, Americans consume only 10 to 12 grams of fiber a day. Instead, we should be eating 25 to 30 grams of fiber every day.

Big problem: Our diet consists of highly refined, easy-to-chew foods instead of high-fiber fruits, vegetables and grains.

There are two basic kinds of fiber...

●**Insoluble fiber, found primarily in wheat bran,** is fiber that is not broken down by bacteria in the intestine. By helping waste pass quickly through the colon, it helps prevent colon cancer, diverticulitis and appendicitis.

• **Soluble fiber,** found in oat bran and in most fruits and vegetables, is fiber that is broken down by bacteria. It helps to prevent heart disease (by lowering cholesterol) and diabetes (by lowering the blood sugar).

Nutritionists now recommend that Americans should double their intake of dietary fiber...fruits and vegetables as well as grains. Pears, for instance, at 4.6 grams of fiber each, contain more fiber than any other fruit. *Other good fiber sources:* Red kidney beans (7 grams), lentils (4 grams), apples (3.3 grams), bananas (2.7 grams) and grapefruit (1.5 grams per half).

Caution: Don't consume more than 40 grams of fiber a day. Too much can be almost as bad as too little. In animals, excessive consumption has been found to cause bulky stools that can result in a form of constipation.

There also is some early evidence that alfalfa and certain other grains may actually increase the risk of developing colon cancer. *Self-defense:* Until the final verdict is in, don't rely just on grains for your fiber...eat a wide variety of fiber-rich foods.

BEYOND FAT AND FIBER

Other than increasing fiber and reducing fats, evidence linking dietary choices to cancer is less reliable.

Still, there are things to do that probably will help prevent cancer...and which won't hurt in any case.

• **Eat a wide variety of foods.** This limits your exposure to any carcinogens that might be found in a particular food...and eliminates the need for vitamin and mineral supplements.

• **Increase your consumption of vitamin A.** A powerful antioxidant, it keeps our cells from being attacked by oxygen, and thus prevents cancer. Vitamin A seems particularly effective in helping prevent lung cancer in smokers. To a lesser extent, it also seems to help stave off colon cancer, breast cancer and lung cancer. *Best vitamin A sources:* Carrots, squash and other orange and leafy vegetables.

• **Increase your intake of selenium.** Selenium is a trace element found in most vegeta-

bles. To get more into your diet, eat more vegetables. *Alternative:* Selenium supplements.

• **Limit your consumption of smoked and pickled foods.** They have been tied to stomach cancer. An occasional dill pickle won't hurt you, and neither will an occasional barbecued meal. But a daily regimen of pickled vegetables and smoked meats is imprudent.

Evidence: At the turn of the century, stomach cancer was common in the US. Now that refrigeration is almost universal—and we rely less on pickling and smoking to preserve our foods—it is a rarity. In Japan, however, where pickled and smoked foods remain common, stomach cancer rates are among the highest in the world.

• **Avoid obesity.** Obesity is clearly linked to cancer of both the endometrium (the lining of the uterus) and the breast. Also, obese women with breast cancer are far more likely to succumb to the disease than are normal-weight women diagnosed with similar breast cancer.

Keeping track of your diet is one step toward controlling your weight. *Also extremely helpful:* Exercise.

Watching TV, working in an office and other aspects of a sedentary lifestyle all are associated with cancer.

Although it's not yet clear exactly how exercise helps prevent cancer, the incidence of colon cancer is much higher in men with sedentary occupations than men who are active. Women athletes have lower rates of reproductive-tract cancer than sedentary, out-of-shape women. And animal studies have demonstrated that moderate exercise cuts the risk of breast, pancreas, liver and colon cancer.

Caution: Too much exercise may actually be almost as bad as too little. Several studies have indicated that extreme exertion (like that necessary to complete a marathon) temporarily weakens the immune system, opening the way for infectious bacteria and viruses—and possibly the development of cancer.

• **Limit your consumption of simple carbohydrates (sugars).** Evolving man ate very little sugar. As a result of this, our bodies are not set up to properly digest it.

Problem: Simple carbohydrates cause the pancreas to produce a large amount of insulin very rapidly, and there is now some evidence suggesting that this can have a harmful effect on the pancreas. *Better:* Complex carbohydrates—found in pastas and breads.

•**Limit your caffeine consumption.** Caffeine has been tied to a variety of cancers, including those of the pancreas and bladder. More recent data suggests caffeine does not cause cancer. Nonetheless, caffeine is very clearly a potent drug, and it makes sense to consume it in moderation.

•**Limit your alcohol consumption.** Drinking to excess (more than a couple of drinks a day) has been linked to cancer of the mouth and throat. People who drink and smoke are at high risk. Most patients with head or neck cancer are alcoholics or near-alcoholics with poor nutritional habits who smoke regularly.

Vegetarianism vs. Calcium

Strict vegetarianism can lead to a calcium deficiency. A so-called "vegan" diet—which excludes dairy products as well as meat and eggs—is unlikely to provide enough calcium for the average adult. That's true even for vegans who avoid salt, protein, caffeine and other substances that trigger calcium loss…and for those who eat plenty of calcium-rich vegetables, such as broccoli and kale. Vegans should bolster their calcium intake with calcium-fortified foods and calcium supplements, after checking with a doctor about their specific calcium needs.

Connie Weaver, PhD, head, department of foods and nutrition, Purdue University, West Lafayette, IN.

Seafood Savvy

Lisa Y. Lefferts, an environmental-health consultant in Hyattsville, MD, who specializes in food safety, environmental policy and risk assessment.

Seafood and fish are excellent sources of protein and are low in saturated fat, light on calories, and high in vitamins, minerals, and the omega-3 fatty acids that help reduce the risk of heart disease.

But there are risks. More than 80% of the seafood eaten in the US has not been inspected for chemical or microbial contaminants. *Fortunately, there are things that you can do to enjoy maximum health and minimum risk…*

•**Avoid chemical contaminants.** When you buy fish, choose younger, smaller ones, since they've accumulated fewer contaminants. Low-fat, offshore species like cod, haddock and pollack are especially good choices. Always trim the skin, belly flap and dark meat along the top or center, especially when it comes to fatty fish such as bluefish. Don't use the fatty parts to make sauce. Don't eat the green "tomalley" in lobsters or the "mustard" in crabs.

•**Avoid natural toxins.** When traveling in tropical climates, avoid reef fish such as amberjack, grouper, goatfish or barracuda, which are more likely to be contaminated. Buy only seafood that has been kept continuously chilled, especially mahimahi, tuna and bluefish, which produce an odorless toxin when they spoil.

•**Avoid disease-causing microbes.** Bite for bite, raw or undercooked shellfish is the riskiest food you can eat.

Self-defense: Don't eat shellfish whose shells remain closed after cooking. Do not eat raw fish or shellfish if you are over 60, HIV-positive, pregnant, have cancer or liver disease or are vulnerable to infection. Cook all fish and shellfish thoroughly. Raw clams, oysters and mussels should be steamed for six minutes.

•**Don't buy fresh fish that has dull,** sunken eyes, or fish that smells "fishy." Do not buy ready-to-eat seafood that is displayed too close to raw seafood.

Fish-Dish Danger

Ciguatera fish poisoning is a hard-to-diagnose illness caused by consumption of fish that carry a hard-to-detect toxin. *Symptoms:* Nausea…vomiting…diarrhea…cramps…

numbness or tingling of the lips, tongue and throat...reversal of hot and cold sensations...blurred vision...low blood pressure...labored breathing...depression.

Danger: There is no diagnostic test for the toxin, and symptoms are easily confused with those of other ailments. The only known remedy—large doses of the sugar mannitol—must be administered within 48 hours.

Self-defense: When traveling in tropical areas, avoid grouper, red snapper or any dish containing unspecified fish...never eat barracuda...avoid fish liver, where the toxin is most concentrated. *Usually safe:* Yellowtail snapper and mahimahi.

Donna Blythe, MD, a ciguatera expert from Coral Gables, FL.

Food Additives Appear Safe for Most People... But Not All

Richard W. Weber, MD, staff allergist, Allergy Respiratory Institute of Colorado, 5800 E. Evans Ave., Denver 80222. Dr. Weber has also served as director of allergy training programs for the US Army and the University of Michigan.

Although food additives are safer than many people imagine them to be, certain additives can cause allergic reactions, including hives, childhood hyperactivity—and worse.

MOST COMMON CULPRITS

•**Antimicrobials,** including benzoates like sodium benzoate and benzoic acid, are used to fight growth of yeasts and bacteria in many canned or pickled foods and some cereals.

Problem I: Benzoates can cause asthma and hives.

Problem II: They may cause hypersensitivity in some children. Other problems, including joint pain and diarrhea, have also been reported.

•**Antioxidants,** such as BHA and BHT, are used to retard spoilage of cereal, margarine, potato chips, pastries and other packaged foods.

Problem I: Some people have developed contact dermatitis after handling products treated with antioxidants. In rare cases, people sensitized through skin contact with antioxidants later become sensitive to these additives in foods.

Problem II: Like benzoates, antioxidants may cause hives.

•**Azo dyes are colorfast dyes used in pills,** foods and clothing. One azo dye—tartrazine (FD&C yellow #5)—was dubbed the *yellow peril* 20 years ago when it was suspected of causing asthmatic reactions, hives and hyperactivity.

In fact, tartrazine and other azo dyes, such as sunset yellow (FD&C yellow #6), *do* cause hives in susceptible people—but not asthma as previously thought.

Azo dyes, including tartrazine, can cause hyperactivity but not as commonly as once suspected.

Most vulnerable: Children of preschool age—especially boys.

•**Monosodium glutamate** (MSG) is used as a flavor enhancer in Chinese and Japanese cooking, soup bases and convenience foods. It has been linked to *Chinese restaurant syndrome.*

This ailment—marked by flushing, headache, nausea and a feeling of warmth across the shoulders—typically occurs an hour or so after eating food that contains MSG. Chinese restaurant syndrome is not thought to be dangerous.

MSG also has been blamed for fullblown asthma attacks, which have occurred up to 12 hours after eating food that contains this flavor enhancer. We don't yet know what percentage of the asthmatic population is affected by this susceptibility...but it is thought to be quite small.

•**Sulfites are used to prevent food discoloration**—and to retard growth of mold and bacteria.

Sulfites are often found in dried fruits, wines, some beers and shrimp. At one time they were sprayed on the produce in salad bars. In most localities, legislation now restricts this use.

At highest risk: Asthmatics. For them, ingesting sulfites can cause shortness of breath—and in very sensitive people, a potentially fatal asthma attack.

Inhaling sulfites—which might occur when sulfur dioxide gas is released upon opening a bag of dried fruit—can temporarily irritate the mouth and nose of asthmatics and nonasthmatics.

DO RESTRICTED DIETS HELP?

Asthmatics should avoid sulfites and possibly MSG. For others, however, there is no good evidence that dietary restrictions are necessary or helpful.

Some people susceptible to hives have shown improvement after several months on a diet free of dyes and preservatives as well as natural salicylates (the active ingredient in aspirin, which also occurs naturally in apples and lingonberries).

Important: Because drastically restricted diets may be deficient in key nutrients, check with a doctor or nutritionist before attempting to eliminate additives from your diet.

How You Cook Has a Lot to Do With Fiber Content

How much fiber a food gives you depends considerably on the method of preparation. Leaving the skins on vegetables and fruits enhances their fiber content. Browning bread increases its fiber (which is why crusts have more fiber than the interior of a loaf). Stir-frying or sautéing vegetables adds fiber more than boiling because less soluble fiber is removed. Deep-frying increases fiber, too, but at great cost in fat and calories. On the other hand, puréeing food decreases fiber, and reducing foods to juice almost completely destroys fiber content.

Cookware Alert

Stainless steel cookware boosts the iron content of some foods an average of 14%.

Recent study: Iron leached into scrambled eggs, hamburgers, stir-fried chicken breast and pancakes...but not into rice, green beans or medium-thick white sauce. Six percent of Americans are believed to have too little iron in their bodies, while 1% are believed to have too much. Either condition can be dangerous. If you're unsure of your iron status, ask a doctor about getting tested.

Helen C. Brittin, PhD, professor of food and nutrition, Texas Tech University, Lubbock. Her study of 10 foods cooked in stainless steel and glass pots was published in the *Journal of the American Dietetic Association*, 216 W. Jackson Blvd., Chicago 60606.

Happier and Healthier Restauranting

Theresa Henkelmann, co-owner of the Thomas Henkelmann restaurant at The Homestead Inn, Greenwich, CT.

Dining out shouldn't mean deprivation if you're trying to eat healthfully. *What* you eat is not as important as *how much* you eat. *To control portion size...*

●**Request a half portion or one to share.** Restaurants will often do this for appetizers or desserts—but rarely for entrées other than pasta.

●**Ask for a doggie bag.** Never feel embarrassed to do this, even at gourmet restaurants. Whatever you pay for is yours to take home and savor a second time.

●**Make special requests.** *Best:* Call the restaurant in advance to find out whether the chef can customize a dish—or a meal.

Second best: When you arrive, inform the captain or maître d' of your preferences—avoiding fats, salt, cream sauces, etc.

Upscale restaurants can do the most customizing because most dishes are prepared to order. Most other places will grill fish on request.

Chicken dishes are less flexible—they are often prepared in advance.

Surprising: Sauces may be more healthful than you suspect. Many chefs make them through reduction—slow cooking to develop the richness that used to come from butter or cream.

Excellent choices when dining out: Veal, sautéed lightly in a trace of oil (the meat is very lean)...steamed vegetables...salad with vinaigrette dressing or lemon juice and oil on the side—most people don't feel satisfied if their dressing contains absolutely no oil.

Special-Order Food

You can special-order food at practically any fine restaurant. Dining out can be troublesome for people on special diets—to cut fat or salt...if you are a vegetarian...if you have a food allergy, etc. Most chefs will modify dishes at your request. If your needs are very specific or you want to be sure of getting what you need, call the chef. *Note:* If you're calling,

remember that chefs are busiest from 12 pm to 2 pm and 6 pm to 9 pm. Call the restaurant during off hours prior to your reservation.

Tim Zagat, president of Zagat Survey, which publishes the best-selling guides to restaurants in major US cities, Four Columbus Circle, New York 10019.

Best Time to Eat in a Restaurant

Late-afternoon restaurant meals can be great bargains—with much better service than at lunch or dinner. Some expensive, hard-to-get-into restaurants in major cities are now serving during mid-to-late afternoon, from about 2:30 pm to 5 pm. Portions tend to be smaller and lower-priced than at regular mealtimes, and service is very attentive since few people dine during these hours. Call in advance—not all restaurants offer late-afternoon service.

New York Magazine, 755 Second Ave., New York 10017.

13

The Mind/Body Connection

Healing and the Mind/Body Connection

Over the past century, physicians have learned much about the workings of the various organs in the human body...and have also found effective treatments for many diseases.

This focus on the machine-like aspects of the human body has led many doctors to ignore the many natural ways people can heal themselves when they are aware of the connection between the mind and the body.

THE MIND/BODY CONNECTION

The human body is a complex mechanism that regulates itself using naturally occurring chemical substances. When something is wrong in one organ, messenger molecules of various kinds flow through the body and cause the release of other chemicals that help correct the situation.

Example: When you cut your finger, your body reacts by releasing chemical clotting factors, which thicken the blood in the vicinity of the cut, preventing you from bleeding to death from a cut.

Blood clotting occurs unconsciously, but every process that happens in our bodies, including thought, involves chemical reactions.

Scientists have learned about important chemicals such as peptides—chains of amino acids that transmit chemical messages. And they've learned about endorphins—proteins that are powerful natural painkillers.

Peptides are found throughout the body, not just in the brain. It has become evident that there is no clear distinction between mind and body.

Since antiquity, we have known that chemicals like drugs and alcohol affect both the mind and the body. Changes in the balance of the chemicals in our bodies also affect the way we feel.

Example: When we have a problem in just one part of the body...like a toothache...our whole self tends to feel down.

Bernie S. Siegel, MD, a surgeon and writer. He is author of *How to Live Between Office Visits: A Guide to Life, Love and Health*. HarperCollins.

173

More surprisingly, the mind/body connection also works the other way. We are finding more evidence every day that the way we feel about life does not simply reflect the state of our health—it also affects it.

Doctors long ago observed that about 30% of patients respond positively even when given a placebo—an inert pill with no curative properties.

The placebo effect occurs because those patients believe that they are being given a useful medicine…and their bodies follow that belief by fighting their sickness better than they would have otherwise.

Unfortunately, many doctors themselves encourage a reverse placebo effect. By emphasizing that a certain treatment has only a small statistical chance of success, they encourage patients to expect failure…and their bodies are likely to get the message.

Better way: Doctors should discuss procedures more positively, encouraging patients to adopt a hopeful attitude, so their bodies will be more likely to react favorably. Patients should not let themselves be convinced by statistics… because every person is a unique human being, not a statistic.

THE BODY'S NATURAL WISDOM

Today, a growing number of physicians recognize that their patients have an ally in the body's natural wisdom. Sensitivity to signals sent by our bodies helps us detect emerging health problems before standard medical tests reveal them.

Example: Journalist Mark Barasch had a terrifying dream that he was being tortured by hot coals beneath his chin and thought he had cancer in his throat. Months later, he felt symptoms and went to a doctor, but his blood tests were normal. However, during a later and more complete examination, a thyroid tumor was found.

And, conversely, by sending hopeful signals back to the body, we encourage our bodies to respond with their surprising self-healing capabilities.

Example: In December, Mary was told she had only a few weeks to live. Her daughter, Jane, tried to cheer her up by buying her a new winter nightgown. Mary, who had always been very frugal, said she didn't want the gown, but would like a new summer purse.

This reaction surprised Jane until she interpreted it as a signal that her mother thought she could survive another six months. Jane demonstrated that she shared that belief. Mary recovered enough not only to enjoy her new purse but was active enough to wear it out…and a half dozen more.

One of the most striking examples of the mind/body connection is susceptibility to disease. Many years ago, researchers at the University of Rochester found that people who adopted an attitude of helplessness and hopelessness were those most likely to contract a variety of diseases.

Other studies have found that people who repress their emotions because of unhappy childhood relationships with their parents are prone to suffer heart disease, hypertension, mental illness and cancer.

Mental attitudes also affect the ability to overcome disease.

Patients who take an active part in treatment ask doctors and nurses many questions, insist on finding out what lies behind every request before complying and want to be given a choice between a variety of treatment options. They want to be told what the choices and the priorities are for each. A Yale study showed that these most "difficult" patients were those with the most active immune systems. They survived longer than "good" patients who were quiet and submissive.

HOW TO SURVIVE

You are most likely to survive serious illness if you can answer "yes" to the following questions:

- **Does your life have meaning?**
- **Do you express your anger appropriately—in defense of yourself?**
- **Are you willing to say "no"?**
- **Do you make your own choices?**
- **Are you able to ask for help?**
- **Do you have enough play in your life?**

People who answer "yes" are survivors because their minds give their bodies a good reason to fight for survival. Everyone is eventually going to die. I see life as a labor pain. But like a mother willing to suffer labor pains to give birth to a child, survivors accept the pain of fighting back against disease as part of giving birth to their own renewed life.

Your Imagination And Your Health

Martin L. Rossman, MD, clinical associate professor of medicine, University of California, San Francisco, and codirector of the Academy for Guided Imagery, Mill Valley, CA. He is author of *Healing Yourself: A Step-by-Step Program to Better Health by Imagery*. Pocket Books.

One key to better health lies not with proper nutrition or regular doctor's visits...but with your imagination.

More than a tool for daydreaming or creativity, your imagination can affect your body as well as your mind.

See for yourself: Imagine quartering a lemon. See the bright yellow. Smell the citrus. Now imagine biting into a piece and swallowing the juice.

By now, you're probably starting to salivate. Your jaw may ache. Clearly, what you think affects your body as well as your mind—and this demonstration gives only the tiniest inkling of the vast potential of the mind/body link.

IMAGINATION IS POWERFUL

With practice, you'll be conjuring up images that help you ease psychological stress and alleviate the symptoms of many disorders. Imagery may even be able to heal these disorders.

Mental imagery can also help you change destructive habits or behavior patterns.

Imagery is how we represent things to ourselves—mentally. It's the natural way our nervous system processes information. Memories, dreams, daydreams, planning and creativity are most readily available to us through images—essentially thoughts that you can see, taste, smell and/or feel.

IMAGERY FOR RELAXATION

The most basic use of imagery is for relaxation...

The imagery used in relaxation and stress reduction is really a directed daydream. In fact, it's the reverse of creating tension by worrying and imaging all the things that frighten you—and make you anxious.

What to do: Close your eyes. Breathe deeply and focus on each body part from head to toe. Invite each one to relax. Then imagine a place that's beautiful and serene—a stress-free "hideaway."

Some people imagine a windswept mountaintop. Others see a field full of wildflowers... or a warm, sunny beach.

Whatever you imagine, immerse yourself in the sights, sounds, aromas and feelings of being in this hideaway. After doing this for five to 15 minutes, you'll probably feel very peaceful and relaxed. Practiced regularly, this technique can be used to help alleviate a variety of medical problems—pain, allergies, high blood pressure, etc.

Caution: Imagery can change your body's need for—and tolerance of—certain medications. So if you're taking medications, make sure you're closely monitored by your doctor.

HELP HELPS

Most people can master simple visualization techniques on their own. Others do best when they use a guided-imagery audio- or videotape.

For especially complex problems, it may be necessary to seek the guidance of a professional "guide"—a psychotherapist experienced in the use of guided imagery.*

Such a guide can quickly lead you into a "quiet place" where it's possible to create an identity for the particular problem that's troubling you...and to confront this identity.

HOW IMAGERY HELPED BEAT STOMACH PAIN

One of my patients asked me to help her overcome the chronic pain in her chest and abdomen.

This woman—who had already received treatment for an ulcer—had been imagining her pain as a fire burning inside her stomach. She had visualized dousing this fire with water. That worked for a while, but the pain always came back.

*While many hypnotists, psychotherapists and social workers may be able to help you apply visualization techniques, few professionals are trained in guided imagery. For more information, and to locate guides in your area, call the Academy for Guided Imagery, 800-726-2070.

I suggested that she let another image come to mind, and she saw a little hand pinching her stomach. She asked the hand why it was doing that. It angrily shook a fist at her.

She didn't understand what this meant. So I told her to ask. When she did, the fist opened up and a finger pointed directly at her heart.

Then she got an image of her heart encased in a burlap sack filled with sharp objects. These objects were piercing her heart. The hand, she concluded, wanted to protect her heart.

With my help, she went on to visualize opening the sack and releasing each object. One of the first images to emerge was of her stepfather, who had been very violent. We eventually discovered that her current pain flared up in situations where she was treated abusively by her employer and where she felt powerless.

Creating awareness of this relationship between her emotions and her pain helped her develop assertiveness and ultimately relieved her pain.

So working with receptive imagery as above can be a form of education or psychotherapy that can help teach us about ourselves, expand our problem-solving abilities and train our minds to promote healthy bodies.

Like any other skill, guided imagery can be mastered only after considerable practice. Also, some people are more gifted at it than others. But almost anyone who pursues imagery derives deep relaxation and comfort. Most people also gain spiritual and possibly physical healing.

How to Use Your Mind To Heal Body Pains

John Sarno, MD, professor of clinical rehabilitation medicine at New York University School of Medicine, and attending physician at Howard A. Rusk Institute of Rehabilitation Medicine, New York University Medical Center. He is author of *The Mindbody Prescription—Healing the Body, Healing the Pain.* Warner Books.

My early work in the treatment of back, neck and shoulder pain was unpleasant and frustrating. I found that the conventional diagnoses and therapy methods yielded inconsistent and disappointing results.

THE SPINE

Usually, the pain was attributed to a variety of abnormalities of the structure of the spine such as a herniated or narrow disk and other aging or congenital defects.

These normal deviations were easy to spot on X rays—which show the bones and, indirectly, the general disk structure, but reveal nothing about soft-tissue changes in muscles, nerves or tendons.

In the early 1970s, I began to doubt the validity of these conventional diagnoses, and the spinal "treatments" that went with them—manipulation, acupuncture, stretching, other physical therapy and the most drastic of all, surgery.

Studies of people without back pain have shown that such spinal abnormalities have no connection with back pain itself. The abnormalities are blamed for this pain simply because they are in the same general location.

THE REAL PROBLEM: TMS

My growing experience, along with my study of the medical literature, suggested to me that the primary sites of the pain were the muscles running from the back of the head to the buttocks. Usually pain occurred in one part of the neck or back, often associated with pain in an arm or leg due to nerve involvement as well.

I call this malady *Tension Myositis Syndrome,* or TMS. Myositis refers to a physiologic alteration of muscle tissue.

TMS is a painful but harmless change in the muscles brought on by emotional factors, which set off a reaction in certain tissues of the body, resulting in pain and other neurological symptoms.

HOW IT WORKS

The circulation of the blood is controlled by a part of the central nervous system known as the autonomic nervous system.

When confronted with threatening unconscious feelings, the autonomic nervous system reacts in milliseconds, reducing blood flow to the involved muscle tissue to create a state of mild oxygen deprivation.

CURING TMS

I frequently see patients who have been suffering chronic pain for years—and yet their symptoms often disappear in a matter of days, after just a 45-minute consultation followed by two lectures on TMS.

Understanding the nature of TMS is key to thwarting the brain's avoidance strategy.

Caution: First, make sure you have nothing serious like cancer or a tumor. Consult with your regular doctor.

My therapeutic program involves three key steps...

● **Repudiating the structural diagnosis.** The first thing I tell each patient is that the structural abnormalities identified by doctors are not the cause of his/her symptoms. Instead, the pain, stiffness, burning, pressure, numbness, tingling or weakness he feels is caused by mild oxygen deprivation in the muscles, nerves and tendons.

By themselves, these symptoms are harmless. Even though they may cause severe pain, this pain leaves no residual damage once it vanishes —meaning there's no need for you to "baby" your back or take any special precautions.

● **Acknowledging the psychological basis of the pain.** When back pain or other symptoms occur, instead of concentrating on where the pain is and how bad it feels, I encourage patients to begin thinking about any repressed rage. Even though you may consciously prefer to be angry than to feel pain, your unconscious mind is terrified by rage, and reacts accordingly. *Sources of rage...*

● Rage from trauma in infancy or childhood that has never dissipated.

● Internal rage resulting from self-imposed pressure to be "good" or "perfect" or "successful."

● Rage as a reaction to the very real pressures of everyday life.

It's important to realize that this internal rage is a universal part of the human condition—we all put pressure on ourselves to accomplish tasks and be a "good person," and we all have negative feelings from childhood that reside in our unconscious minds.

When a lifetime of stored anger reaches a critical level and threatens to erupt into consciousness, the brain creates back pain or some other physical symptom as a distraction. This prevents a violent emotional explosion.

In other words, the symptoms of TMS are a strategy for avoiding painful emotions, by diverting attention to your physical body.

● **Accepting the psychological basis for pain and dealing with it.** To counter this built-in tendency, you need to use your conscious mind to "talk to" your unconscious...

● First, tell yourself, *It's all right to be enraged, unconsciously and illogically, like a child having a tantrum. That's part of being human.*

● Next, whenever you feel pain, try to think consciously about repressed rage and its possible reasons. Remember, you are contradicting what your brain is trying to do. But it's essential to focus on threatening thoughts to deny your pain its purpose, which is to divert attention from these feelings.

When your pain is severe it's hard to concentrate on emotions, but think of this process as a contest—pitting your conscious will against the unconscious reactions of your brain.

Example: When you feel a twinge of pain, talk or shout at yourself—tell your mind that you know what it's doing, that you know the physical pain is harmless and a distraction from repressed rage and that you no longer intend to be diverted and intimidated. You might even tell your brain to increase the blood flow to the affected areas.

By becoming aware of what's going on in your body physically and psychologically, you can learn to frustrate your brain's strategy and lead a full, pain-free life.

Once you change your focus of attention from your body to your psyche, you will render your pain useless—taking away its purpose, and revealing what it was trying to hide.

The Taoist Principles Of Preventive Medicine

Kenneth S. Cohen, MA in psychology, a master scholar of Chinese healing arts. A former faculty member of Boulder Graduate School psychology department, he is currently director of the Taoist Mountain Retreat in Nederland, CO.

Many Chinese follow a way of life called Taoism. Its goals are to promote balance and harmony…in both the immediate environment and the universe. Taoists believe that anyone can reach a state of enlightenment called *hsing ming shuang hsiu*, the balance of mind and body. *Required:* Great self-discipline and personal effort, including the cultivation of health and longevity.

Interesting: The Taoist emphasis on preventive medicine is so strong that in old China people paid their physician only when they were well. If they got sick, the treatment was free.

THE BREATH OF LIFE

Taoists believe in an internal energy called *Qi*, the breath of life. Qi corresponds closely to Western concepts of bioelectricity, the body's electrical program. By changing this inner program, people can influence their metabolism in a way that actually strengthens the immune system.

Taoists believe that Qi flows through a system of subtle veins, called meridians. If the Qi is blocked anywhere in the body, you'll have too much Qi—too much energy—on one side of the blockage, and too little on the other.

To open the blocked areas along the meridians so the Qi can flow freely, the Chinese use a series of exercises that involve breathing, gentle movement and visualization.

Called *Qi kung,* these exercises are based on five animals—the crane, bear, monkey, deer and tiger. Each exercise affects a specific internal organ and bodily system. Qi kung exercises, which resemble tai chi exercises, are easy to learn.

THE THREE TREASURES

In addition to the meridian system, Taoists believe that the human body contains three basic forms of energy that create health when they are in balance with each other.

●**Qi is breath energy.** It resides in the chest and lungs.

The three sources of Qi are the air we breathe, the food we eat, and the energy and strength of the immune system that we inherit from our parents. The more Qi you accumulate, the greater your vitality and better your health.

Exercise: Stand with your feet about shoulder-width apart, legs slightly bent, back straight but not stiff, chest relaxed, abdomen loose, with your palms at waist height, facing downward. Inhale and allow the lower abdomen and back to expand as though you were filling a balloon. When you exhale, the lower abdomen and back should contract. Continue to do this exercise as long as you can comfortably. If there's pain there's no gain.

This exercises the diaphragm, gently massaging the internal organs. And because the lower lobes of the lungs are stretched downward, the body can take in more air…and more Qi.

●**Jing is sexual energy,** which is believed to be stored in the lower abdomen and cultivated through balanced sexual relationships.

Exercise: To enhance Jing, stimulate the endocrine system, and improve sexual health, men should contract the muscles of the perineum (the soft band of muscles located between the scrotum and anus) when they inhale and release when they exhale. Women should contract and release the anal and vaginal muscles while continuing to breathe naturally. These exercises, known in the West as Kegel exercises, also help solve sexual problems, including prostate enlargement in men and irregular menstruation in women.

●**Shen is spiritual or intuitive energy.** Shen, which means clarity of mind, requires the ability to temporarily shut off the interference of constant thinking. Most people's minds are like a TV that they can't turn off. Without the clarity and fullness of Shen, which is developed through meditation, none of the other techniques are possible.

Exercise: Sit upright in a chair and breathe at a natural pace. At the same time, observe any thoughts that pass by, as if you were watching passing clouds. Make no judgments and don't try to control or manipulate your thoughts. I call this being an open window of awareness. And although it may sound quite easy, it is very difficult for most Westerners, who always have to be doing something.

BASIC TAOIST PRINCIPLES

There are two underlying principles of Taoist philosophy that tell us how to live in a manner that promotes health and well-being.

●**Tzu jan** involves things that grow from the inside out rather than being created outside. *Translation:* Spontaneity, which shouldn't be confused with impulsiveness. Spontaneity means sensing what is coming from inside you and allowing it to express itself.

●**Wu wei,** or effortlessness, involves going with the flow, lacking artifice, using only those muscles needed for the task at hand.

Taoists think that these two principles should be applied consistently on every level—lifestyle, relationships, exercise, movement, etc.

Example: Unless sexual partners surrender completely to the experience, there can be no exchange of energy. *Result:* None of the elaborate Taoist sex techniques will work until both partners are willing to go with the flow of the experience and express whatever they feel.

Everyday Soul-Soothing

Soul-soothing objects you place where you will see them regularly can boost your spirits when stress starts to get you down.

When creating your own personal "shrine," consider just how much of your inner self you want to reveal. It may be seen by coworkers or visitors to your home, too.

Display the meaningful object(s)—such as an intriguing stone, a shell or a baby's shoe—in a way that evokes inspiration, memory or reverence. Pick objects that remind you of people and places that lift your spirit. You can change shrines frequently or leave them untouched for years.

Jean McMann, PhD, architectural historian and professional photographer, and author of Altars and Icons: Sacred Spaces in Everyday Life. *Chronicle Books.*

Stress/Cancer Connection

Long-term psychological stress can cause cancer of the colon and rectum. Patients who had serious job problems in the previous 10 or more years were 5.5 times more likely to develop colorectal cancer than adults without such problems.

Theory: Stress-induced hormonal changes boost production of tissue-damaging substances called *free radicals.* The higher the concentration of free radicals, the greater the cancer risk. *Also:* Stress weakens the immune system. This limits the body's ability to kill cancer cells, allowing them to grow into tumors. Further, stressful life events may lead to poorer diets and reduced levels of physical activity, also raising risk.

Joseph G. Courtney, PhD, research epidemiologist, University of California, Los Angeles, School of Public Health.

Stress Reliever

Proper breathing reduces stress and helps you relax. It slows your heart rate and lowers blood pressure. *Technique:* Rapidly blow out all the air in your lungs...slowly breathe in through your nose. *Helpful:* Think of it as caressing your lungs with air...relax your stomach muscles...when lungs are full and without stopping to hold your breath, breathe out slowly and completely...repeat six times.

Sexual Pleasure: Reaching New Heights of Sexual Arousal and Intimacy by Barbara Keesling, PhD, sex therapist and teacher at Pepperdine University, Malibu, CA. Hunter House, Inc.

Depression Fighter

To fight depression, exercise can be just as effective as drugs. In a recent study, volunteers diagnosed with major depressive disorder were divided into three groups. One group participated in 30-minute exercise sessions three times a week…another took the antidepressant *sertraline* (Zoloft)…and the third did both. Patients in the medication-only group improved fastest—but after 16 weeks, all three groups showed similar significant improvement.

James Blumenthal, PhD, professor of medical psychology, Duke University Medical Center, Durham, NC. His study of 156 men and women was published in *Archives of Internal Medicine,* 515 N. State St., Chicago, 60610.

Sleeplessness and Depression

Sleeplessness—a common problem among people with depression—can be controlled with supplements of the hormone melatonin. *Recent finding:* Depressed people who took a slow-release formulation of melatonin for four weeks reported marked improvements in sleep quality, compared with similar individuals who took a placebo. If you suffer from depression, check with your doctor to see if melatonin is right for you.

Ornah T. Dolberg, MD, director, division of psychiatry, Sheba Medical Center, Ramat Gan, Israel. Her four-week study of 24 people with major depression was published in *The American Journal of Psychiatry,* 1400 K St. NW, Washington, DC 20005.

Dealing with "Blue" Moods

Richard O'Connor, PhD, a psychotherapist with practices in Canaan, CT, and New York City. He is author of *Undoing Depression: What Therapy Doesn't Teach You and Medication Can't Give You.* Berkley Books.

Sadness is as much a part of life as happiness—there are times to cry as well as smile. But in the course of their lives, one American in five suffers dark moods that deepen and linger. This includes six million older folks.

In the past, depression was often accepted as a "natural" part of aging. After all, sickness often strikes in later life, careers may come to

an end, those we love pass away. No wonder older people get depressed, it was thought.

But we now know that even in the face of such losses, most people mourn, recover and move on. When a blue mood settles in and remains severe, it needn't be endured.

Modern treatments with medication and psychotherapy can help the vast majority of depressed people. But these treatments only go so far. If you feel so persistently "down" that it's hard to enjoy life, *you must take an active role in your recovery.*

THE HABIT OF DEPRESSION

Depression may be caused by a shift in the chemicals that carry messages between brain cells (which is why antidepressant drugs are effective)—or it can be triggered by a major loss. Once it takes hold, it can establish a self-defeating pattern that's hard to escape.

Most depressed people develop a cluster of habits that make it hard to maintain a healthful, positive mood. Even after successful treatment, they may remain somewhat down and are prone to another severe episode of depression a few months or years down the road.

These habits include ways of thinking, feeling and behaving that protect people from their own painful emotions. Instead of being open to experiences that may leave them emotionally vulnerable, they live closed off from other people, and ultimately become emotionally paralyzed—unable to participate in their own lives.

Overcoming these habits means following a program of recovery. This demands effort, self-discipline and courage. *Among the most important steps…*

UNDERSTAND YOUR MOODS

When blue moods strike, they often seem to come out of nowhere…feeling you're at their mercy creates a sense of helplessness and hopelessness.

But in fact, a bad mood is almost always triggered by events or thoughts that you can identify.

Helpful: Keep a *mood journal* to track your ups and downs. Note the circumstances (where you were, with whom, what you were doing) that surround each drop in spirits.

Try to catch and record the internal events that preceded them—thoughts, memories, fantasies. Then imagine how a nondepressed person might feel in these circumstances—remembering the difference between a feeling (it passes quickly) and a mood (it lasts).

FEEL YOUR FEELINGS

Emotions that we refuse to feel don't just go away. When we avoid experiencing the anger that we may have been taught is bad, or insulate ourselves against the acute pain of grief, these emotions turn into less intense, but more lasting, negative moods.

Getting in touch with your feelings is a skill you can develop. As a first step, try to be alert to the slightest glimmer of emotion—a surge of rage, spasm of fear, pang of sadness. Instead of avoiding it, amplify it...allow yourself to feel it more fully.

Also helpful: Talk about your feelings with people you trust, with a therapist or in a support group. Or write them out...many people find that when they sit down for 15 to 20 minutes and write quickly and spontaneously about events of the day, memories or whatever comes to mind, feelings begin to emerge, and become stronger as the words flow to describe them.

CHALLENGE DISTORTED THOUGHTS

People who are prone to depression tend to think in ways that make their moods worse. They dismiss positive events as "flukes" or only temporary...when they feel bad, they're sure it will last forever. They tend to blame themselves and overgeneralize ("I never do anything right") and to believe they are powerless to make things better.

Not only are such thoughts depressing, they're unrealistic. A person who thinks, "I never do anything right" is forgetting the vast majority of things he/she has done that turned out well. To believe that you'll always be alone or unhappy implies fortune-telling powers that you don't have.

With practice, you can catch yourself thinking negative, self-defeating thoughts that darken your mood. When you do, challenge them.

Example: A friend fails to return your phone call and you think, "She doesn't like me. No one cares." Ask yourself: "What other explanation could there be?" Your friend could be busy...forgetful...out of town. And is it really true that you have no other friends?

TAKE CARE OF YOURSELF

When you're depressed, it's hard to get involved in pleasurable activities. Your energy is low and you can't believe that anything will bring you enjoyment. It's a self-fulfilling prophecy—doing nothing is virtually guaranteed to keep you from feeling better.

Instead: Plan activities that are likely to improve your mood, and do them whether you want to or not. Schedule times when you'll visit friends...listen to music...go to the movies... take a long walk in the park.

Almost always, once you've overcome lethargy and put yourself in action, you'll enjoy yourself more than you expected.

Exercise is especially beneficial. It produces natural chemicals—endorphins—that actually elevate your mood, in addition to giving you energy.

BE OPEN-HEARTED

Giving your time, energy and concern to others keeps you from ruminating on your own problems. It boosts your self-esteem to know that you've done something to make someone else feel better.

Generosity can begin close to home. Open your heart to friends and their troubles. Beyond that, time spent in volunteer work—serving the homeless in a soup kitchen, tutoring, reading to children in a hospital—is such a potent mood lifter that researchers have called it "the helper's high."

KNOW WHEN TO SEEK HELP

Depression severe enough to interfere with your life (you sleep poorly, lose your appetite, can't enjoy activities that used to give you pleasure) for more than a few weeks may need more than self-help alone.

Ask your doctor for a referral to a therapist and/or psychiatrist. Particularly if you've been treated for depression in the past, taking prompt action can save you a lot of unnecessary suffering.

Anxiety Disorder

Anxiety disorder is our nation's most prevalent psychiatric problem. At some point in their lives, nearly 15% of the population will suffer from panic attacks, obsessive-compulsive disorder or some other anxiety disorder.

Steve Dager, MD, associate professor of psychiatry and bioengineering, University of Washington, Seattle.

Healing with Life Force

Julie Motz, an energy healer who works in major hospitals across the country and teaches energy healing to inner-city teenagers. She is author of *Hands of Life.* Bantam Books.

Every living thing exudes energy—and this energy can be manipulated to improve your health and to heal both your body and your mind.

A system to explain the body's energy and utilize it in healing exists in every major culture.

•**The Chinese believe that the body's vital life force,** or *qi* (pronounced *chee*), is an energy —think microwaves—that flows unseen and connects all organs and systems.

When qi is disrupted and out of balance, illness results. Qi can be toned, through meditation and exercise. And it can be adjusted, if necessary, by acupuncture.

•**From India comes the concept at the heart of Ayurvedic medicine that there are seven chakras,** or centers of energy located along the spine, that govern a person's emotional and physical well-being.

•**In Western medicine an electrocardiogram (EKG),** for example, measures electrical signals from the heart to tell a doctor a variety of information about heart function.

THE CAUSES OF PAIN

The body's energy correlates with four of the most powerful emotions a human can feel— fear...anger...pain...love. These forces manifest themselves on a physical level, because emotions are a kind of energy.

Anger is the most important because it's the emotion that is so often suppressed. One powerful way to control someone else is to suppress that person's anger.

Parents control their children by not honoring their anger or by not allowing it to be expressed. Most children learn early to hide their feelings of anger. Instead, they're trained by their parents to cry, which is more acceptable.

But the feeling behind the tears is rage. Even when a child does have a temper tantrum, some parents are unlikely to intervene. Instead, they ignore this outburst, so the emotion behind it goes unheard.

THE HEALER'S JOB

As an energy healer, I can "receive" these emotional messages from specific parts of the body, even parts of a cell, which are related to whatever ailment the patient is suffering.

How it works: I scan the body, lightly touching it with my hands, to find where the energy is strong, where it is weak and where it is "blocked." I don't physically "manipulate" the energy—instead I send it a silent "message" to move where it's needed and relieve the blockage. Once it begins flowing smoothly, healing can begin.

This sometimes involves enlisting the patient's help.

A large part of my job as an energy healer is to convince the patient to let go of all of this stored emotion.

While I long ago found myself endowed with the power to feel what others are feeling, it is something that can be learned.

HOW TO HELP YOURSELF

•**Follow your instincts.** When you hurt yourself, say, by catching your thumb in a closing door, your instinct is to grab it and hold it. You should continue holding or touching that body part until you feel some kind of change come over it. This can be the disappearance of the pain, a change in temperature, a tingling that stops or a return of what I call "lost energy." *Helpful:* You have to really concentrate on the thumb to understand what I mean.

Also: Convey to the body part, either verbally or silently, that it is loved and appreciated. This may sound strange at first, but too often people reject and isolate a part of the body that becomes injured or afflicted with a disease. *Better:* Take time to concentrate on the part, to embrace it with the rest of your body and bring it "home."

●**If the problem is internal, place your hand over the area to attract ambient energy to where it's needed.** I often ask patients to visualize themselves entering the organ to tell me what it looks and feels like. Then I ask them how old they are in that place. This often reveals the root cause of their disease.

●**Enlist the help of others.** Others can help us heal. It's a mistake to think we have to be strong when we're ill.

Let yourself be taken care of. When friends and family offer themselves, allow them to do so.

Ask them to send their thoughts, prayers and good feelings to you. People are pleased to help and this positive energy will help you overcome the illness.

●**Additional education.** To learn more about energy healing, attend a class in any of the healing arts, including Reiki…polarity… healing touch.

Good health food stores usually have information about local classes. You'll also find ads in the back of alternative medicine magazines such as *New Age Journal* and *Natural Health.*

You'll find that, once you're with others who understand these techniques, energy healing is relatively easy to learn—and can help you live a healthier, happier, more productive life.

Music & Healing

Postoperative pain can be minimized by listening to soft, soothing music.

Surgical patients who listened to music for as little as 15 minutes a day while recovering reported significantly less pain than did those who relied only on painkillers.

Also helpful: Relaxation techniques such as slow, rhythmic breathing. Music and relaxation

should be considered adjuncts to painkilling medication—not replacements for it.

Marion Good, PhD, RN, associate professor of nursing, Case Western Reserve University School of Nursing, Cleveland. Her study of 500 surgical patients was published in *Pain*, 666 W. Baltimore St., Room 5E-08, Baltimore 21201.

The Healing Power Of Plants

Diane Relf, PhD, assistant professor of horticulture, Virginia Polytechnic Institute and State University, Blacksburg. She is the former president of the American Horticultural Therapy Association, 362A Christopher Ave., Gaithersburg, MD 20879.

You've probably heard that keeping a pet is good for your health. Close contact with animals has been shown to lower blood pressure, ease feelings of depression, boost feelings of self-esteem—and more.

Now we know that you can get many of the same health benefits by tending a garden. Studies have demonstrated that plants…

●**Reduce stress.** A study of college students worried after taking an exam found that the simple act of viewing plants increased positive feelings and reduced fear and anger. Other studies showed that viewing plants lowers blood pressure and reduces muscle tension.

●**Boost self-esteem.** As plants grow, so do their owners' feelings of self-worth. That's why plants are often used in psychiatric rehabilitation. Plants are also used in physical therapy. Caring for them requires balance, flexibility and coordination.

●**Raise job performance.** Studies have shown that workers whose offices afforded a view of trees and flowers experienced less job stress, enjoyed greater job satisfaction and experienced fewer ailments and headaches than those who could see only man-made elements from their windows.

●**Speed recovery.** In another study, gallbladder surgery patients whose rooms looked out on greenery had shorter postoperative hospital stays than patients without a view. Those with the view also used less painkilling medication, suggesting they were in less pain.

If you're intrigued by the idea of using plants for therapy, I recommend filling your home with plants. Just be sure not to buy more than you can comfortably care for. Neglected, sick plants are depressing.

Beware: Plants sold at discount stores tend to have more problems than those bought at a reputable nursery.

To derive maximum health benefits from your plants, I recommend caring for them yourself. If you don't have the time, consider hiring someone else to care for them for you. Simply being around plants is better than not being around them—even if you're not the gardener.

If you're a novice gardener, choose easy-to-raise plants, such as pothos, philodendron, cactus or dracaena marginate.

Rosemary, basil and thyme also do well inside, but they need more light.

Despite their popularity, ficus trees, schefflleras and corn plants are often tricky to care for.

If you'd like to derive physical as well as psychic nourishment from your plants, plant tomatoes, lettuce, etc., in pots on your patio—where you can enjoy watching them grow.

Prayer Heals

Four-hundred and sixty-six heart patients who were the object of other people's prayers during their hospital stay had 11% fewer complications than did 524 patients who were not prayed for. Patients did not know prayers were said for them. Those who did the praying knew only the patients' first names…and prayed only for "a speedy recovery with no complications." The researchers note that, statistically, such a difference between the groups would occur by chance only one in 25 times.

William S. Harris, PhD, heart researcher, Lipids and Diabetes Research Center, Saint Luke's Hospital, Kansas City, MO. His study of 990 coronary care unit patients was published in the *Archives of Internal Medicine,* 515 N. State St., Chicago 60610.

Secrets of Self-Hypnosis To Overcome Bad Habits

C. Roy Hunter, a certified hypnotherapy instructor in Tacoma, WA. He is author of *Master the Power of Self-Hypnosis* (Sterling) and *The Art of Hypnosis* (Kendall/Hunt).

Finding it hard to quit overeating? Smoking? Drinking? You're not alone. As we all know, the vast majority of people who try to break a bad habit fail at first. Many fail repeatedly.

You can remind yourself a hundred times a day that your habit is bad for you. Unfortunately, it's the *unconscious* mind that fuels bad habits. It doesn't care about logic. All it wants is the physical and emotional satisfactions your habit supplies.

Hypnosis helps you let go of the negative unconscious desires…and replace them with positive, habit-breaking emotions.

Hypnosis isn't magic. You will still have to work hard at breaking your bad habit. But hypnosis can give you the edge you need to succeed.

MYTH vs. REALITY

Hollywood has given hypnosis an unrealistic image. The hypnotic trance is not a mystical state in which you lose all self-control. You cannot be forced to quack like a duck or do other humiliating things when you're under hypnosis. In fact, you won't do anything you don't want to do.

The hypnotic trance is nothing more than a state of very deep relaxation.

This state is similar to the one that exists just before you fall asleep, when the beta brain waves that predominate during consciousness are replaced by alpha waves.

You're still fully conscious, but your rational mind is less active than usual…and your imagination is more active. This shift is critical because imagination is the language of the unconscious.

With practice, the emotions you generate during each hypnosis session become permanently embedded in your unconscious. That gives your willpower a much-needed boost.

DO IT YOURSELF

Many psychologists practice hypnosis, but it's also effective when done on your own. *Here's how to do it...*

●**Carefully consider the emotional benefits associated with breaking your habit.** Odds are you've already given a great deal of thought to the physiological benefits—reduced risk for heart attack, stroke, cancer, etc.

But you must also consider all the *emotional* reasons you have for changing. These might include feeling more in control...pleasing your family...having more energy...looking better.

●**Put yourself in a trance.** Find a comfortable and quiet place to lie down or sit. Unplug the phone and turn off the lights.

Take several deep breaths as you imagine your cares slipping away. Then imagine a beach at sunset, a mountain meadow or some other relaxing scene.

Tell yourself, "My toes are relaxed...my breathing is relaxed...I'm getting more and more relaxed."

You've entered a trance when you feel totally relaxed and your mind starts to wander. For most people, this takes about five minutes.

●**Imagine the pleasure you will feel upon successfully breaking your habit.** Once you've entered the trance, imagine that you have already reached your goal. Savor the emotions that thought triggers.

You might think, "My family is so proud of me"..."I look great"..."I feel so much better."

Over time, these feelings will become part of your unconscious...and will stay with you even when you're fully awake and going about your business.

●**Replace old "triggers" with new ones.** Still in the trance, imagine new ways of behaving.

Perhaps you tend to have a cigarette each time you relax with a cup of coffee. During the trance, imagine that having the coffee triggers a *different* response from you.

You might say, "I don't *really* want a cigarette with my coffee. I'd rather focus on reading that novel I just started."

Repeat this scenario again and again.

●**Come out of your trance.** Count slowly from one to five. When you reach five, say, "Fully awake."

Most people notice a diminution in their cravings after just a few sessions of self-hypnosis.

For the first three weeks, it's best to do self-hypnosis for about 20 minutes each day. After that, you can cut back to 20 minutes once or twice a month.

Of course, you can always intensify your self-hypnosis schedule if you find your resolve weakening.

Simple Secrets Of Better and Sounder Sleep

William C. Dement, MD, PhD, director of the Sleep Disorders Center at Stanford University School of Medicine, Palo Alto, CA. He is author of three books, including *The Promise of Sleep*. Delacorte Press. For more information about sleep disorders, contact the National Sleep Foundation at 888-673-7533...or at *www.sleepfoundation.org*.

Lying awake at night. Waking up too early. Feeling drowsy during the day. As we grow older, these and other sleep problems can become more than major annoyances. They can jeopardize our health.

Sleep deprivation can cause diminished performance, apathy and drowsiness. Falling asleep at the wheel is now known to contribute to an estimated 4% of all fatal automobile accidents.

What can be done to curb sleep problems? You may have heard that it's important to cultivate good sleep habits. But few people realize just how important proper "sleep hygiene" really is. *The basics...*

●**Go to bed at the same time each night.** Wake up at the same time each morning.

●**Take a hot bath or perform some other relaxing ritual 30 to 60 minutes before bedtime.**

●**Make sure that your pillow, blanket and mattress are comfortable**...and that your bedroom is dark and quiet. Most people sleep best when the room temperature is around 65°F.

●**Banish computers and other reminders of work from your bedroom.**

•**Avoid caffeinated beverages for six hours before bedtime.** Have no more than three alcoholic drinks in the evening.

•**Avoid exercise for three hours before bedtime.** Working out early in the day is relaxing, but working out before bed boosts alertness.

If revamping your sleep hygiene fails to improve your sleep, try these strategies...

•**Take steps to alleviate worry.** Worry has a way of descending at bedtime. To keep this from happening, spend a few minutes after supper jotting down your concerns—and composing your "to do" list for the next day. Then relax until you go to bed.

•**Go to bed *only* when you feel sleepy.** Your biological clock sends out wake-up messages twice a day—one in the morning, another in the late afternoon. Trying to sleep before the second message has worn off—a process that can take an hour or more—can result in insomnia.

If you tend to fall asleep early and wake up before dawn, your biological clock may be running fast. To overcome this problem, try taking melatonin in the morning or exposing yourself to bright light late in the day.

•**Spend less time in bed.** If you typically spend eight hours in bed—but spend two of those worrying about being awake—try staying in bed for six hours instead. Odds are you'll get the same amount of sleep—but will feel less frustrated.

That's significant, since insomnia-related frustration often sets the stage for even greater sleeplessness.

•**Watch out for too much sleep.** If you pay off your entire "sleep debt" each night, your sleep drive is weakened and you may sleep poorly the next night.

Getting slightly less than a full night's sleep means that you carry some sleep debt into the next day—and sleep more soundly that night. Ten to 20 minutes of sleep debt should keep you sleeping well. More than that leaves you drowsy the next day.

•**Consider physiological causes of sleep trouble.** Thirty million Americans suffer from obstructive sleep apnea, a condition marked by repeated pauses in breathing during sleep. These pauses—up to 200 a night—make it impossible to get deep, restorative sleep.

Most cases of sleep apnea are caused by excessive tissue in the back of the throat. At night, this tissue collapses onto the trachea, shutting off the flow of air until the sleeper gasps and then resumes breathing normally again.

Apnea sufferers tend to snore heavily—and to snort periodically as they sleep. If you suspect that you have sleep apnea, consult a doctor.

In many cases, apnea can be controlled with *continuous positive airway pressure* (CPAP), in which an air mask worn at bedtime continuously pumps air and regulates pressure. For those unable to tolerate the mask, surgery may be necessary.

•**Take steps to control restless legs.** Restless legs syndrome (RLS) causes a creeping, pulling sensation in the legs, particularly at night. The urge to move the legs makes it almost impossible to fall asleep. If you think you might have RLS, ask a doctor about *carbidopalevodopa* (Sinemet) and *gabapentin* (Neurontin). These prescription medications are highly effective at curbing RLS.

•**Consider the possibility that you're depressed.** Early morning awakening is a hallmark of depression and, to a lesser extent, of anxiety. See your doctor if symptoms of these disorders, including hopelessness and worthlessness, persist.

•**Watch out for drug-induced insomnia.** Many different medications, including some antidepressants and heart drugs, can cause insomnia.

If you take any medication regularly, ask your doctor if it might be interfering with your sleep. If so, he/she may be able to alter the dosage or switch you to another medication.

•**Consider sleeping pills.** Short-term use of a sleeping aid is often helpful—especially during periods of stress. The prescription drug *zolpidem* (Ambien) is highly effective and is far less likely to cause addiction than other prescription sleeping pills.

Over-the-counter sleeping aids seem to be effective but have not been carefully studied.

14

Take Charge of Your Medical Needs

Wisest Ways to Treat Home Medical Emergencies

It is difficult to stay calm when you are confronted with a health emergency, such as a bad cut…a serious allergic reaction…or sudden and debilitating back pain.

Don't panic. Even if you are waiting for an ambulance or driving to the emergency department, taking the appropriate action right away—and avoiding common mistakes—will improve the chances of a complete and fast recovery.

The most common home emergencies—and what you should do for them immediately…

ALLERGIC REACTIONS

Some people suffer a life-threatening allergic reaction called anaphylaxis. It can follow insect bites or stings…eating certain foods…or taking a medication to which you are sensitive.

Prime symptoms: Difficulty breathing, dizziness, nausea or a sudden and severe rash.

Do: Take Benadryl (*diphenhydramine*) right away. Follow dosage recommendations on the label. If you have a known allergy and carry an epinephrine self-injector, use it right away. Then get to an emergency department.

Don't: Wait for a serious allergic reaction to go away on its own. It can escalate very, very quickly.

HEAD INJURIES

Head trauma is responsible for more than two million emergency department visits a year. If you or someone you're with loses consciousness—even briefly—following a head injury, get emergency treatment. There could be a concussion or other type of brain damage.

Do: Be alert for symptoms like lethargy or sleepiness…nausea…weakness…changes in vision, etc. These are signs of brain injury that require immediate attention.

Don't: Assume the worst. Most people recover quickly from head injuries. As long as

Ted Christopher, MD, chief of the division of emergency medicine at Thomas Jefferson University Hospital in Philadelphia.

187

you're not feeling dazed, weak or disoriented, you can treat the discomfort at home with an ice pack and by taking acetaminophen. Do not take aspirin or ibuprofen, which may increase bleeding.

HEART ATTACK

Chest pain, often accompanied by sweating, shortness of breath or nausea, is the most common symptom of a heart attack. Call an ambulance if the discomfort doesn't go away promptly or if you have a history of heart problems.

Do: Take an aspirin at the first sign of symptoms. It can help prevent heart damage.

Don't: Wait to get medical attention, even if the discomfort improves. Intravenous medications that are used to dissolve blood clots are most effective when given within just a few hours of symptom onset.

DEEP CUTS

Get help right away for any cut that is longer than one inch or in which you can see underlying tissue.

Do: Use a lot of water pressure when cleaning deep cuts. It spreads the tissues apart and provides more thorough cleaning. Use cool or tepid water, and flood the cut for two to three minutes. Wash with soap (regular bath soap is fine) to prevent infection. Apply pressure with gauze or a clean cloth to stop the bleeding.

Don't: Wash cuts with hot water. It dilates blood vessels and may increase bleeding. And don't use hydrogen peroxide to disinfect cuts—it can damage the tissue.

Warning: If the area surrounding the wound is numb or turns blue, a nerve or major blood vessel may have been damaged. Get to an emergency department right away.

PUNCTURE WOUNDS

Cuts from animal bites or stepping on a nail and other puncture wounds are always serious. The wounds are narrow and deep—they are difficult to wash and there is little bleeding—so bacteria can get trapped inside.

Do: Get to an emergency department quickly. Puncture wounds have a high infection rate. You'll probably need prescription antibiotics and a tetanus shot.

Don't: Remove nails, pencils, etc. that have penetrated deeply into the body. Pulling them out may increase the damage.

Better: Fasten the object in place with a clean bandage and tape...and get to an emergency department.

SUDDEN BACK PAIN

Most cases of back pain are caused by muscle strains. Acting quickly can mean the difference between a fast recovery and spending days—or even weeks—in bed.

Do: Take aspirin or ibuprofen right away. These medications block the action of prostaglandins—chemicals in the body that cause inflammation after an injury. Or try acetaminophen, a good pain reliever. However, seek medical attention immediately for back pain associated with fever or loss of control of your bladder or bowels. Do not self-medicate.

Do: Apply a cold pack or ice cubes wrapped in a cloth to the area for at least 20 minutes, every few hours. The cold will constrict blood vessels and help prevent swelling.

Don't: Apply heat right after a back injury—it may increase swelling. After 24 hours, however, applying heat may help relax muscle spasms.

Warning: Back pain is rare in children. In the absence of an obvious injury, it may be a symptom of a more serious illness. Get it checked out right away.

Also, persistent back pain in the elderly should be checked by a physician. It could be a symptom of a serious medical problem.

HEAT BURNS

Even small burns can be slow to heal, and infections are common.

Do: Flood the area with cool water for five minutes. It lowers the temperature in the skin and helps prevent damage from residual heat. Cool water also acts as an anesthetic to reduce the pain.

Pat the area dry, and apply a triple antibiotic ointment. Then loosely cover with a gauze pad.

To reduce swelling and pain, take aspirin or ibuprofen.

Don't: Apply ice or very cold water to burns—extreme cold damages the skin. Also, don't "protect" the burn with petroleum jelly or butter.

The oils trap heat and restrict air circulation. Do not pop burn blisters intentionally. Intact blisters help prevent infection.

POISONING

If you or someone you're with has ingested a toxic substance (including a large amount of over-the-counter or prescription medicine), get to an emergency department right away.

Do: Call an emergency department or your local poison control center for advice while you're waiting for help. If possible, have the product container in front of you so you can describe exactly what was taken.

Don't: Induce vomiting without medical advice. Many substances will cause additional damage on the way back up. There's also the risk that the vomit will be aspirated into the lungs.

FIRST-AID KIT/ESSENTIALS

- **Several sizes of gauge pads**
- **Rolls of bandage tape**
- **Aspirin, acetaminophen and ibuprofen**
- **Benadryl** (diphenhydramine)
- **Triple antibiotic ointment**
- **Elastic bandage**
- **Chemical ice pack**
- **Epinephrine self-injector** for serious allergy sufferers (requires a prescription)

Do Your Own Medical Research

Gary Schine, president of the medical research agency Schine On-Line, Providence, RI. He is author of *If the President Had Cancer...*. Sandra Publications.

A doctor's advice is usually accepted at face value. Yet when it comes to treating a serious illness, that advice should be given close scrutiny.

Reason: Even the most caring, compassionate physician is ultimately performing a job. He/she has less at stake than the person who's

sick—and whose life may be on the line. In a world where medical breakthroughs occur on an almost daily basis, no doctor can be expected to be up-to-date on every new treatment for every illness.

If you assume that your doctor has all the pertinent information, and accept his suggestions about the "best" course of action without providing any input of your own, you're behaving dangerously.

When your well-being is at stake, you must be your own best advocate. To do that, you must educate yourself about your condition—the various treatment options...and what the latest research reveals about new and possibly experimental treatments. You must then work with your caregivers to assure optimal care.

HOW I SAVED MY LIFE

Four years ago my doctor told me I had a rare and incurable form of leukemia. What he did not know—and what my own research revealed—was that a new anti-leukemia drug had become available three months before my grim diagnosis.

This new drug was especially effective against the rare form of leukemia I was suffering from—80% of those treated achieved a complete and lasting remission. Because of that new treatment I am alive and cancer-free today. *Here is how you or a loved one can learn what you need to know about a serious illness...*

SECOND OPINIONS

If you heed no other advice in this article, be sure to get a second opinion. It can literally spell the difference between life and death.

Example: Six years ago, a friend of mine was diagnosed with advanced liver cancer. My friend's doctor offered him no treatment and gave him only months to live. But on the advice of his brother-in-law, a hospital administrator, Frank sought a second opinion from a major cancer research center. The doctors there recommended a new type of surgery. Frank got the surgery—and he is now healthy and cancer-free.

Moral of this story: Medicine is an inexact and rapidly evolving science. Doctors vary widely in their knowledge. Some are diligent about keeping up with advances in their field. Others aren't. By seeking out a second or perhaps even a third or fourth opinion, you boost your odds of finding a practitioner knowledge-able about every form of therapy that might prove beneficial to you.

Caution: The choices garnered from multiple opinions aren't always clearly black or white, right or wrong. One doctor might recommend a treatment that has an 80% cure rate—but a 20% risk of serious long-term adverse effects. Another might recommend a treatment with a 50% cure rate—but with only a 5% chance of serious side effects. Which is the better option? It's up to the patient to decide.

USING A MEDICAL LIBRARY

Medical information—including information on the latest developments in treatment for virtually every illness, is readily available. The key is knowing how—and where—to find it.

Libraries affiliated with medical schools or major hospitals tend to have the most complete information.

If you're already hospitalized, federal law requires that you be given access to the hospital library—and that the hospital librarian respond to your requests for help in doing research.

If you're not hospitalized, call the library and find out if it's open to the public. If not, ask which local medical libraries are. If none are, ask about exceptions to the restricted access policies. In most states, at least one health library is open to the public.

In addition, at least two medical libraries in the US are geared specifically to lay people…

• **Center for Medical Consumers,** 237 Thompson St., New York 10012.

• **Planetree Health Resource Center,** 2040 Webster St., San Francisco 94115.

PINPOINTING INFORMATION

Pinpointing information in a medical library can be a daunting task to the uninitiated.

To start, ask the librarian to help look up relevant studies in the *Index Medicus,* the master index of medical information. Copy down the names of relevant articles in respected medical journals—such as *The New England Journal of Medicine,* the *Journal of the American Medical Association* and *The Lancet,* a British periodical.

What are you looking for? A general overview of your illness, plus details of the latest research. In particular, you'll want to know dif-ferent methods of treatment—including their success rates and their possible complications—and whether there's been any recent development that your primary physician may not yet know about.

You also want to know about clinical trials—experiments that test new treatments at the cutting edge of medicine. Participating in these experiments carries some risk, but it also offers hope where previously none existed. Despite the risks, far more people have been helped than hurt by clinical trials in this country.

If you find an article that details a promising new treatment, call the author of the article—or ask your doctor to call for you. Some researchers prefer talking to other medical professionals rather than to patients.

ONLINE MEDICAL DATABASES

Thanks to powerful computers and high-speed modems, medical information is now readily available via the Internet.

Benefit: Research that might take days of labor in a library can now be compiled in a matter of minutes.

Useful resources: Medline, a vast compilation of medical articles and Physician's Data Query (PDQ), a database that provides detailed information about new drugs and other treatments for all types of cancer.

If you are not familiar with the Internet or are having difficulty searching for the information you need, consider hiring a medical research firm to do the research for you. *Three excellent services:*

• **The Health Resource,** 564 Locust St., Conway, AR 72032. 501-329-5272.

• **Planetree,** 2040 Webster St., San Francisco, CA 94115. 415-923-3681.

• **Schine On-Line,** 39 Brenton Ave., Providence, RI 02906. 800-346-3287 or 401-751-0120.

The Homeopathic Medicine Chest

Asa Hershoff, ND, DC, a naturopathic doctor and chiropractor who practices homeopathy in Santa Monica, CA. He is author of *Homeopathic Remedies: A Quick and Easy Guide to Common Disorders and Their Homeopathic Treatments.* Avery.

Many Americans are returning to *homeopathy.* This 200-year-old system makes use of more than 2,000 preparations that are designed to support the body's innate healing powers.

These remedies are derived from herbs… animal products, such as snake venom and cuttlefish ink…and mercury, sulfur and other minerals.

LIKE CURES LIKE

The basic idea behind homeopathy is that the symptoms of an illness represent the body's attempt to repair itself or rid itself of disease.

By extension, homeopaths argue, any substance that would cause similar symptoms when taken by a healthy person would bolster the body's healing powers in someone who is sick.

This philosophy is often summed up as: Let like be cured by like.

Example: Raw onion can irritate the eyes and cause a runny nose. The homeopathic remedy for hay fever—which causes similar symptoms—is an extract of onion called *allium cepa.*

Why don't homeopathic preparations exacerbate symptoms? Because the active ingredient is present in an extremely dilute form.

In fact, the concentration is typically so low that not a single molecule of the active ingredient is present.

What's left, homeopaths say, is the *information* contained within the original substance. This "blueprint" instructs the body how to cure itself, much as software tells a computer what to do.

Mainstream physicians contend that this explanation violates laws of chemistry. But centuries of experience suggests that homeopathic remedies really do work.

And recent studies demonstrate that the effectiveness of homeopathy cannot be explained by the placebo effect.

In 1997, the British medical journal *The Lancet* published a study that analyzed more than 100 controlled trials on homeopathy. The study's authors concluded that homeopathic remedies—applied for a range of ills including dysentery and hay fever—were significantly more effective than placebos.

NO SIDE EFFECTS

One clear advantage of homeopathy over conventional drug therapy is the absence of side effects.

What's more, homeopathic remedies do not interact with prescription or over-the-counter drugs…and they are compatible with herbs, surgery and even chemotherapy.

In its purest form, homeopathy involves close collaboration between the homeopath and the patient. The doctor takes a thorough medical history, zeroing in on the exact nature of the symptom, when it occurs, what causes it, etc. He/she also assembles a detailed psychological and physiological profile of the patient.

HOMEOPATHIC SELF-CARE

Homeopathic remedies can also be self-administered. The preparations are readily available in health-food stores and drugstores. Reliable manufacturers include B&T, Boiron, Dolisos and Standard.

Preparations come in liquid or pellet form, at various concentrations. For do-it-yourself use, use 6c, 12c and 30c concentrations. The higher the number, the more dilute the preparation—and the greater its potency. Follow dosage directions carefully.

Useful homeopathic remedies to keep on hand include…

● **Allium cepa.** The onion extract is good not only for hay fever, but also for the early stages of a cold.

● **Arnica.** An extract of the mountain daisy, this anti-inflammatory preparation speeds relief from aches and bruises. Taken just before exercise, it increases stamina and helps prevent muscle soreness. It can also speed healing if taken before surgery or dental work.

● **Arsenicum.** Derived from arsenic—but containing none of it in the final preparation—

191

arsenicum is an effective remedy for stomach flu…mild food poisoning…diarrhea…and hypochondria and other forms of anxiety.

- **Belladonna.** Derived from a nightshade plant, belladonna is a powerful remedy for inflammation of all sorts. It's good for bursitis, sore throat and arthritis as well as styes and skin inflammation. It's also effective for pounding headaches and for fever.

- **Bryonia.** This anti-inflammatory agent— derived from the cucumber plant—is effective for migraine, joint pain and other conditions made worse by movement. It can also be used to treat early symptoms of flulike illness.

- **Carbo veg.** This charcoal preparation is a classic remedy for belching, bloating and flatulence. It's also an effective adjunct to conventional medical treatment for serious respiratory disorders such as asthma and emphysema.

- **Nux vomica.** This remedy, derived from an east Indian plant known as Quaker's buttons, is a natural sedative. In addition to relieving anxiety and irritability, it helps alleviate back pain and muscle tightness.

Nux vomica is also an antidote for the edginess caused by overindulgence in coffee and tobacco. It can ease a hangover in minutes. Taken at bedtime, it can help prevent a hangover the following day.

Homeopathic preparations should be used only for acute or minor conditions. Contact a homeopath and your doctor to see if a homeopathic approach is right for you.

To locate a homeopath in your area, contact the National Center for Homeopathy at 703-548-7790 or *www.homeopathic.org.*

Steering Clear of Incompetent Doctors

Martin L. Gross, an investigative journalist and social critic. He is author of The Medical Racket: How Doctors, HMOs and Hospitals Are Failing the American Patient. Avon.

Too many health-care workers are either incompetent or dangerously sloppy. Here are the threats consumers face— and what we can do to protect ourselves…

- **What sorts of incompetence are you talking about?** American doctors are generally well-trained, but a surprisingly large number are woefully inept in one way or another.

Consider these disturbing findings…

- **Poor stethoscope skills.** In a study involving 453 medical residents, only one in five heart abnormalities that should have been easily diagnosed with the stethoscope was correctly diagnosed.

- **Bad care for diabetes.** The most important diagnostic tool for the treatment of adult-onset diabetes is the *glycosylated hemoglobin* test. Yet in a Medicare study of 97,000 diabetics, 84% of doctors failed to administer the test.

- **Misread mammograms.** Radiologists fail to spot malignant breast tumors that are present on mammograms 46% of the time, a Yale study found.

- **Bad care for people with pneumonia.** Doctors often fail to follow crucial guidelines when treating older pneumonia patients.

In a study of more than 14,000 pneumonia patients, many doctors failed to take blood cultures and to give antibiotics correctly and on a timely basis.

- **How can I tell if a particular doctor is competent?** There's no easy way for a lay person to tell. The best you can do is look for evidence that other *medical experts* have judged the doctor competent.

In addition to a medical school diploma and admitting privileges at an accredited hospital, your doctor should be board-certified in his/her specialty.

To learn if he is board-certified, consult the *Directory of Physicians in the US* and the *Directory of Board Certified American Medical Specialists*. These references are available at most municipal libraries.

Another helpful resource is the American Medical Association. Visit its Web site—*www.ama-assn.org*—and go to "Doctor Finder."

For most people, the best bet is to find a private practitioner who has a faculty appointment at a medical school. Such doctors tend to be more up to date than other doctors.

If you have a particular medical problem, call the nearest medical school. Speak with the chair of the appropriate department or one of his colleagues. Many take private patients.

●**Is there any way to find out if a doctor has been disciplined?** Citizens must write to the agency that oversees the licensing of physicians—this varies from state to state—and ask for information on a particular physician.

The Washington, DC-based consumer advocacy group Public Citizen publishes *21,125 Questionable Doctors*. This book lists physicians who have run afoul of their licensing boards or who have been hit with disciplinary actions by state medical boards or by the federal government.

Some doctors whose names appear on the list may be perfectly competent. But inclusion on the list should lead you to question your doctor closely about why he has this dubious distinction.

If you can't find a copy of the book at your library, you can call Public Citizen at 202-588-7780 to order a report covering your home state.

Friends or relatives who are doctors may have privileged access to information about doctors in your area. Ask what they know.

●**What should I look for in a hospital?** The best hospitals are those that have been accredited "with commendation" by the Joint Commission on Accreditation of Healthcare Organizations (JCAHO). "Regular" accreditation is virtually meaningless.

On request, this not-for-profit agency will send a free report on any hospital. It can be reached at One Renaissance Blvd., Oakbrook Terrace, IL 60181, 630-792-5800. *www.jcaho.org.*

If no nearby hospital has the top JCAHO ranking, opt for the nearest university (teaching) hospital. For serious medical problems at least, teaching hospitals tend to offer better care than community hospitals.

●**What threats do hospitalized patients face?** There are two primary threats—medication errors and infections.

To avoid being given the wrong drug and/or the wrong dosage, take pills only if they are offered to you by a registered nurse (RN), licensed practical nurse (LPN) or physician.

Your doctor should tell you the generic and trade names of any drug he prescribes, the size and color of the pills, how many pills you should take and how often—and any possible side effects, too.

For intravenous (IV) drugs, you should know the drug's name and how often the bag should be changed.

Medication errors and side effects kill an estimated 50,000 Americans each year.

---

6 Ways Doctors Let Older Patients Down

Robert N. Butler, MD, professor of geriatrics at Mount Sinai School of Medicine and president of the International Longevity Center-USA, both in New York City. He is the former director of the National Institute on Aging in Bethesda, MD. In 1976, Dr. Butler won a Pulitzer Prize for his book *Why Survive? Being Old in America.* HarperCollins.

As we grow older, we're more likely to have health problems that require first-rate medical care.

Unfortunately, as many seniors have learned, it can be hard to find a doctor suited to care for *their* special needs.

How can older people be sure to get good medical care? Dr. Robert Butler, a well-known crusader for elder rights, explains how important it is to watch out for mistakes doctors sometimes make when treating elderly patients…

Mistake: **Failing to appreciate the physical changes that come with age.** A disease that causes one set of symptoms in a young person may manifest itself quite differently in an older person. Not all doctors realize that. And an unwary doctor can easily miss the diagnosis.

Example I: If a 30-year-old man suffers a heart attack, he is likely to experience severe chest pain. But chest pain affects fewer than 20% of older heart attack victims. Instead, older victims may simply seem weak or confused.

Example II: An older person suffering from an overactive thyroid may exhibit apathy instead of hyperactivity, the classic symptom.

Mistake: **Urging older people to "take it easy."** Even if you've been disabled by a stroke or another medical problem, leading an active lifestyle helps keep you healthy—and happy.

Even people in their 80s and 90s can develop big, powerful muscles with a program of weight lifting. Such a program can literally put a bedridden patient back on his/her feet.

Mistake: **Being too quick to blame health problems on old age.** Doctors often assume that health problems are inevitable in older people, exhibiting a defeatist "what-can-you-expect-at-your-age?" attitude.

They order fewer diagnostic tests and generally treat disease less aggressively in old people than in young people.

Example: An elderly woman seems confused and disoriented. Assuming that she has Alzheimer's disease, her doctor neglects to order tests that might show the real culprit to be an easily correctable drug reaction.

Mistake: **Not giving the patient enough time.** A good physician takes the time to ask about your work status and lifestyle as well as your medical problems...and, in general, makes you *feel* taken care of.

At each office visit, the doctor should ask about symptoms you have reported in the past. He should also review your response to medications... and ask about new problems.

Your first visit to a new doctor should be devoted to giving a thorough medical history and undergoing a physical exam and lab tests. This can take more than an hour. Once this comprehensive exam is completed, you probably won't need another exam for a year—unless there's a health crisis.

Mistake: **Failing to advocate preventive measures.** Some doctors seem to think, "Why bother trying to lower an elderly patient's cholesterol level. He's just going to decline anyway."

We now know that heart patients of *any* age can benefit from a program of dietary modification, lifestyle change and—if necessary—medication or surgery.

Mistake: **Giving inappropriate prescriptions.** Doctors are too quick to order tranquilizers and antidepressants for their older patients, thinking—incorrectly—that psychotherapy is of

no use. And they often fail to realize that older bodies respond differently to drugs.

Example: It can take an older person twice as long to "clear" *diazepam* (Valium) from his body as a young person. A dose that would be appropriate for a young person could make an older person drowsy.

If you're not sure that your doctor knows about all the drugs you're taking, put all of your medications (including nonprescription drugs and herbal remedies) in a paper bag and bring them with you to your next office visit.

For referral to a certified geriatrician in your area, call the American Geriatrics Society at 800-247-4779.

Your Doctor's Doctor

Fewer than one-third of US doctors have a personal physician. These doctors are less likely to go for regular checkups or undergo routine screenings for cancer and other diseases. They're also less likely to discuss such preventive health measures with their patients.

Gary Gross, MD, associate professor of medicine, Yale University School of Medicine, New Haven, CT.

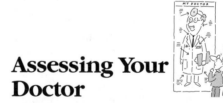

Assessing Your Doctor

Ask yourself these questions to gauge the level of care you're getting...

●**Do I have the chance to express comfortably all that I feel?**

●**Does the doctor really listen to me?**

●**After communicating with my doctor, do I feel relieved or frustrated?**

●**Do I share with my doctor the responsibility for my own well-being?**

●**Am I given the freedom of choice among different treatment plans?**

• **When in doubt, do I feel comfortable in voicing my need for a second opinion?**

• **Does the doctor share his/her knowledge without intimidation?**

• **Do I follow my doctor's instructions, or do I use my own judgment?**

• **Do I perceive that my doctor is doing everything possible to help me?**

• **Does the relationship with my doctor fulfill my expectations and needs?**

Holistic Medicine, 4101 Lake Boone Trail, Raleigh, NC 27607.

How to Be a Better Patient

David Biro, MD, PhD, assistant clinical professor of dermatology at State University of New York Downstate Medical Center and a dermatologist in private practice, both in Brooklyn. Biro has recovered fully since his bone marrow transplant in February 1996. He is author of *One Hundred Days: My Unexpected Journey from Doctor to Patient*. Pantheon.

At age 31, having earned an MD from Columbia University and a PhD from Oxford University in England, my life seemed too good to be true.

I was finishing my first novel and working in my father's dermatology practice. And I was happily married.

But the "good life" was about to go bad. I was about to become…a desperately ill patient.

SHOCKING TEST RESULTS

After noticing a strange flashing sensation in my right eye, an ophthalmologist found a clot in the retinal vein. Blood tests showed that I was anemic and suffering from leukopenia—a condition in which there are dangerously low levels of infection-fighting white blood cells. I also had thrombocytopenia—low levels of platelets.

Four doctors and numerous diagnostic tests later, I was finally diagnosed with *paroxysmal nocturnal hemoglobinuria* (PNH), a rare and often fatal bone marrow disease.

MY DIFFICULT DECISION

I was told that medication might keep my PNH under control. But the only *cure* for the disease was a bone marrow transplant. Only about 70% of patients survive this procedure, in which the marrow—which generates blood cells—is destroyed with drugs and radiation and then replaced with marrow from a donor. Faced with a lifetime of coping with a deadly disease, I opted for the transplant.

Five years later, life is good again—I'm writing another novel, practicing dermatology and still happily married. But having seen medicine as a seriously ill patient as well as a doctor, I have a new perspective on all things medical.

Here's what I learned…

• **Don't expect an immediate diagnosis.** Most patients seem to think that doctors know everything. I certainly felt that way before I got sick.

In fact, doctors often have a hard time making an accurate diagnosis. You'll cope better with the inevitable uncertainty if you anticipate it—if you realize that doctors don't always have all the answers.

• **Learn all you can about your illness.** When I learned that I had PNH, I read all I could about the disease.

Do the same for any condition you might have. Go to a medical library at a local hospital or university…buy a book about the problem…and search the Internet. Knowledge of your condition gives you a sense of control over it. And as an informed patient, you can ask your doctor better questions about your care.

Caution: Information is not expertise. You're educating yourself so that you can ask better questions, not answer them.

• **Get additional opinions.** One doctor was unable to diagnose me. He said we should test my blood regularly and "wait and see" what developed.

Another doctor made an accurate diagnosis —and recommended drug therapy.

It wasn't until I talked with a third doctor that I understood all my options and could make a rational decision.

Tell your doctor you want additional opinions—and ask for referrals. If a second opinion doesn't settle things, go for a third. Don't stop asking until you're satisfied.

●**Decide how much you want to know about side effects and complications.** Yes, I read about PNH. But I did not want to know about *all* the possible side effects of the drugs I'd be taking and *all* the possible complications of the medical tests and procedures I'd undergo.

As a doctor, I'd always felt that reciting a list of possible side effects and complications — most of which happen to only a tiny percentage of patients—was more frightening than useful. So, when I became a patient, I didn't press my doctors to tell me about every risk I faced. I didn't want to worry needlessly.

Best: Ask your doctor about the *likely* problems associated with your medical care. That way, you'll be informed about the important risks without being scared to death.

●**When making a decision, trust your "gut."** I had three main treatment options, and my doctors couldn't agree on what was right for me.

I could have had infusions of *antithymocyte globulin* (ATG), a drug that corrects some of the problems associated with marrow failure. But ATG requires transfusions—which might have increased the risk for complications had I gone on to have a marrow transplant.

I could have taken cyclosporine. But having prescribed it for my patients suffering from psoriasis, I knew it could cause serious side effects, including kidney damage.

My third option was the marrow transplant. But there were two types to consider—and doctors disagreed about which one was right for me.

In the end, I realized that no doctor can make a decision for his/her patients. Yes, there are some conditions for which every doctor makes the same recommendation. But in many cases, there is a "conservative" option and a "radical" option—and you have to choose.

The best way to make a tough medical decision is to evaluate all the facts, become as informed as possible and then choose the option that feels right—the one that best fits with your personality and lifestyle.

●**Fight pessimism.** *Believing* that your treatment will prove effective helps lift your spirits —and that kind of attitude gives you the best chance of recovery.

To stay "up," I used a support network that included my wife, Daniella…my family—one of my three sisters wound up being the marrow donor…and friends.

I exercised every day—even with an armful of intravenous needles. I covered the walls of my hospital room with photos of loved ones and favorite places.

Whatever it takes to make you feel that everything will turn out all right—that's the most important thing to do to see you through a medical ordeal.

Complexities Of At-Home Nursing Care

Peter J. Strauss, Esq., a partner in the law firm Epstein Becker & Green, PC, 250 Park Ave., New York 10177. He is a fellow of the National Academy of Elder Law Attorneys and coauthor of *The Elder Law Handbook—A Legal and Financial Survival Guide for Caregivers and Seniors.* Facts on File.

Only the very rich can afford not to be concerned about the likelihood that some day they will need home care or nursing home care.

But the rest of us do have to worry about becoming incapacitated. And most of us would prefer to be cared for at home. *Questions we all have…*

●**How much does home care cost?**

●**Will Medicare pay for some of it?**

●**What quality of care can one expect from the government?**

●**Do I need a Medigap policy?**

●**What about a long-term-care insurance policy?**

MEDICARE

Medicare generally covers a very limited portion of the cost of care provided in the home. Although home care typically follows a hospital stay, Medicare does not make hospitalization a prerequisite for coverage.

As long as the care is necessary for treatment of an illness or injury, Medicare coverage applies. This coverage, however, includes only the items defined as "home health care benefits." *These include...*

- **Medical social services.**
- **Nursing care** (part-time or intermittent).
- **Medical supplies/equipment.**
- **Physical therapy.**
- **Occupational therapy.**
- **Speech therapy.**
- **Home health aides** (part-time or intermittent), but only if a skilled service—such as therapy—is provided also.

The benefits *must* be prescribed by a doctor and provided by a home-care agency that has been certified by Medicare.

Your share: You pay an annual $100 deductible and copayments for benefits under Medicare Part B. You must also make a 20% copayment for medical supplies—hospital beds, walkers, wheelchairs, etc.

Exception: People under a managed care type of Medicare do not have to make a copayment for benefits received under Medicare Part B.

- **Medicare does not cover everything.** For instance, Medicare limits coverage for part-time or *intermittent* home care—fewer than five days a week on an infrequent basis—to 35 hours per week. If continuing care is needed—care for a period of up to 21 days—then coverage can be for up to seven days a week, but only for up to 56 hours a week.

If a home health aide and nursing services are needed, the amount billed must be kept under 35 hours a week to be considered intermittent.

- **Medicare does not cover the cost of long-term care or personal assistance care.** These are considered custodial-type care rather than medical care. This kind of care applies to those with chronic conditions, such as Alzheimer's disease, Parkinson's disease, etc., who need assistance with daily living activities (eating, bathing, getting in and out of bed, going to the bathroom, etc.).

- **Medicare does not cover the cost of housekeeping.** This is often needed by a person with a chronic condition.

MEDIGAP COVERAGE

Supplemental Medicare insurance—Medigap insurance—picks up only the amounts of Medicare *covered expenses* that Medicare does not pay for, such as copayments and deductibles.

Medigap *does not* cover the cost of long-term care, since Medicare doesn't provide this coverage.

MEDICAID

The cost of custodial care provided in the home may be covered by Medicaid in a few states.

Medicaid is designed to pay only for those who are "poor." So, to be eligible for Medicaid, a person's income and assets must be below limits set by law. Only a few states have a broad home-care program.

Loophole: In most states, people who transfer assets so that Medicaid will pay for *in-home care* are *not* subject to the federal government's 36-month look-back rule. That rule disqualifies people who unload assets within that time period from getting Medicaid to pay for their stay in a nursing home.

Beware: Individual states may impose look-back rules that bar people who transfer assets from getting government assistance for in-home care.

LONG-TERM-CARE INSURANCE

A growing number of older people are buying private insurance policies—long-term-care insurance—to cover the cost of nursing care. The policy should cover both care in a nursing home *and* care in their own home.

You can also buy policies that cover only in-home care or only nursing home care, but this is usually not wise.

Caution: Make sure a policy labeled a "nursing home policy" also covers at-home care.

These policies are expensive: They get more expensive the older you are when you buy them. *Best:* Buy them by the time you are in your 60s. Make sure you take an inflation rider!

CONSIDERATIONS

- **What is the extent of insurance coverage?** Some policies pay for home care only a fraction of what they pay for nursing home care.

●**What is the "triggering event" for payment** of expenses under the policy? Some policies pay much more quickly than others. Find out what the lag time is in policies you're considering.

Bottom line: Make sure that the level of coverage and the event that triggers payment are clearly spelled out in the policy.

TAX INCENTIVES

The tax law now provides breaks that defray some custodial care costs. A person needing home care can take an itemized deduction for "qualified medical expenses" to the extent that total expenses exceed 7.5% of Adjusted Gross Income (AGI). *Deductible medical expenses include...*

●**Out-of-pocket medical costs,** including out-of-pocket payments to home health aides.

●**Medicare copayments and deductibles.**

●**Long-term-care insurance premiums up to a dollar limit** (depending on age).

●**"Long-term-care services"**—up to any amount—provided to a person who is chronically ill. The meaning of "long-term-care services" is liberally interpreted to include rehabilitative services and personal care services. This is so even though personal care service probably would not qualify as a deductible medical expense were it not a *long-term-care* service.

Taxes: Some part of the benefits provided under a long-term-care policy may be taxable.

How to Get the Care You Want When You're Too Sick to Ask for It

Susan H. Evans, PhD, research scientist, Institute for Health Promotion and Disease Prevention, University of Southern California School of Medicine, Los Angeles. She is coauthor of *Surviving Modern Medicine: How to Get the Best from Doctors, Families & Friends.* Rutgers University Press.

If you're like most Americans, you've failed to sign an *advance medical directive*—a living will and/or a medical power of attorney.

A *living will* is used to spell out in detail what sort of health care you wish to receive should you become incapacitated—unable to communicate in *any* way—and doctors judge that you are near death.

A *medical power of attorney* is used to appoint a health-care agent. That's a person who makes medical decisions on your behalf if you are incapacitated—whether you are near death or not.

Having an advance medical directive brings peace of mind for you and your loved ones. It frees them from the burden of having to make tough medical decisions at a time of great upheaval and psychological distress.

Having a directive can also help avoid the family conflict—and protracted legal battles—that often arise when there is disagreement about what sort of treatment you should get.

No one knows when an illness or accident may strike, so every person age 18 or older should complete an advance medical directive—either a living will or a medical power of attorney.

LIVING WILL

A living will specifies your wishes regarding health care at the end of life. It takes effect only if you are terminally ill or permanently unconscious.

If you recover, of course, you're free to make your own decisions. You may also revoke a living will at any time as long as you are able to communicate your wishes.

The living will covers decisions about the use of feeding tubes, respirators and antibiotics. Pain medications would still be administered, even if your living will called for life support to be withdrawn in case of terminal illness.

MEDICAL POWER OF ATTORNEY

A medical power of attorney for health care—also known as a durable power of attorney for health care or a health-care proxy—is broader and more flexible than a living will. It lets you designate as your agent someone close to you—a friend, relative, member of the clergy, etc.

This person legally makes medical decisions for you if you become incapacitated.

Unlike a living will, a medical power of attorney applies to survivable illnesses, such as a stroke, as well as to terminal ones.

Also unlike a living will, a medical power of attorney does not generally state such specifics as whether doctors should attempt to prolong your life by administering cardiopulmonary resuscitation (CPR), placing you on a respirator, etc.

Instead, your health-care agent will express your wishes.

MEDICAL DIRECTIVE

Statutes governing advance directives vary from state to state. A few states recognize only a single basic form known as a medical directive. In this document, you can explain what you want in terms of life support...and appoint a spokesperson. It takes effect only in cases where a living will would apply.

To obtain copies of the appropriate documents for your state, contact Partnership for Caring, 1620 Eye St. NW, Suite 202, Washington, DC 20006 (800-989-9455/*www.partnershipfor caring.org*). None of the medical directives requires a lawyer's help.

PICKING A HEALTH-CARE AGENT

Your health-care agent must be at least 18 years of age. To prevent conflicts of interest, avoid picking your primary-care physician or any other health-care professional involved in your care. Many states prohibit you from doing this—unless the practitioner is related to you by blood, marriage or adoption.

Discuss your wishes with your health-care agent before you execute the medical directive. Be sure the person you select is psychologically resilient enough to make critical decisions under stressful circumstances.

Good idea: Designate an alternate health-care agent, just in case your first choice is unable to fulfill the role.

As you consider potential agents, ask yourself...

●**Is this person comfortable talking about death?**

●**Is he/she assertive enough to see to it that I get the care I want** even in the face of opposition from my doctors or members of my family?

●**Does he understand and respect my values?**

●**Is he capable of exercising good judgment** in case an unforeseen situation arises?

Once you decide whom you'd like to be your agent, spend some time rehearsing how you'll broach the subject. Many people find it best to begin the discussion when the whole family is present.

Whatever you say, make sure to explain things in detail. Many people complete advance directives too hastily, without considering all their options and without describing fully their wishes for end-of-life care. Don't try to cram everything into a single discussion. Several may be necessary.

During these conversations, tell your agent just what you think about "extreme measures" doctors might use to prolong your life. Do you want every treatment available, no matter how limited the benefit might be? Or would you rather forgo treatment once it becomes clear that death is inevitable?

After considering these questions, you may find that there is no one you trust sufficiently to become your health-care agent. If so, it's probably best to stick with a living will—which does not require you to appoint an agent.

WHERE TO KEEP THE DOCUMENT

Whichever advance medical directive you choose, be sure that key family members and/or friends have a copy.

Your loved ones should be able to press photocopies of the document into the hands of your doctors and nurses.

Your physicians and your HMO should also have a copy—just in case. Many hospitals and nursing homes also request copies upon admission.

If you have multiple residences: Prepare an advance medical directive for each location.

If you spend half the year in one state and half in another, have forms filed with your doctors in both states. Make sure each document conforms to the requirements of that state.

Medical Directives: The Legal View

An adult has the right to decide on the type of medical treatment to receive—or not receive. Advance "medical directives," such as living wills and health care proxies, ensure that your wishes are followed if you can't speak for yourself.

• Is refusing medical treatment the same as suicide?

No. From a legal view, the refusal of medical treatment, which in turn results in your death, is not considered by law to be suicide.

When treatment is refused, the US Supreme Court has held that the cause of death is the underlying medical problem, not the refusal.

• Does one need a living will to enforce the right to die?

No. As long as you can speak or express your wishes regarding medical treatment, your doctors must follow them. But having a living will or other advance medical directive will protect your wishes when you can no longer communicate them.

Peter J. Strauss, Esq., a partner in the law firm Epstein Becker & Green, PC, 250 Park Ave., New York 10177. He is a fellow of the National Academy of Elder Law Attorneys and coauthor of The Elder Law Handbook—A Legal and Financial Survival Guide for Caregivers and Seniors. *Facts on File.*

Secrets of Happier Recuperation

Regina Sara Ryan, a Prescott, Arizona, wellness consultant. She is author of After Surgery, Illness or Trauma: 10 Practical Steps to Renewed Energy and Health. *Hohm Press.*

Convalescing after illness, surgery or injury can be frustrating and tedious—or productive and life-affirming. Much depends on how you spend your time during your period of forced confinement.

Here's how to flourish while you're recovering...

FACING YOUR EMOTIONS

Illness or injury can spark strong emotions like anxiety, anger and grief. Painful though they may be, these emotions are normal and healthy responses to what you've been through. *To express them...*

• **Keep a personal healing journal.** Record your feelings, sketch, write poetry, compose letters you'll never send. Don't edit yourself. Accept the full range of your emotions.

• **Let go by yelling.** Scream into a pillow. Or practice "silent screaming": Open your mouth... let out your breath...contort your face...and gesture as if you were shouting at the top of your lungs.

• **Enlist a sounding board.** Choose one or two people who agree to let you vent—uninterrupted—without advising, reassuring or judging you.

STRESS REDUCTION

Breathing and relaxation techniques reduce stress, aiding your body's efforts to heal. *Useful exercise...*

Focus your gaze on something you find soothing, like a painting or a vase of flowers. Silently count "one thousand," "two thousand," "three thousand," "four thousand" as you inhale through your nose. Then exhale through your mouth, repeating the same slow count. Keep breathing this way for three minutes.

Next, tense every muscle in your body—jaw, fists, abdomen, calves—whatever your condition allows. Hold for a count of 10, then slowly release the tension. Breathe deeply again.

Finally, make a loud noise such as "bah" or "dah" over and over until you start to relax. Stop and repeat to yourself, "I am here, I'm alive, I can cope, I survive."

EXERCISING THE BODY

It's important to keep moving to improve muscle tone, blood flow, digestion and sleep. Do what you can. Wriggle and stretch your fingers and toes. *Or, if your doctor permits, try these in-bed exercises...*

• **Inner leg isometrics.** Lie flat on your back, knees bent, feet a few inches apart. Put a pillow between your thighs. Inhale, then squeeze the pillow with your legs, holding for a count of five. Exhale and release. Repeat five times.

●**Glute sets.** From the same starting position (but without the pillow), inhale, squeeze your gluteal (buttocks) muscles and hold for a count of five. Exhale and release. Repeat five times.

●**Head and neck.** Imagine that you have a pencil protruding from your chin. Inhale, turn your head left and begin to draw the biggest circle you can. At the halfway point, exhale slowly but continue to draw.

Make three circles to the left, rest, then turn to the right and make three circles.

●**Total body stretch.** Lying on your back, raise your arms above your head. Extend your feet and hands in opposite directions as if you were being stretched. Hold this position for 10 seconds, being sure to breathe normally. Repeat three times.

EXERCISING THE MIND

Nothing is more frustrating than feeling as if you're wasting time. *But time recuperating can be time well spent...*

●**Read about countries you'd like to visit or heroes who inspire you.**

●**Delve deeply into a subject that's always fascinated you**—art, astronomy, politics, economics, etc.

●**Use audiotapes to practice a foreign language.**

●**Master chess, backgammon or bridge.**

●**Draw or paint.** If you don't want to draw freehand, use a coloring book. Terrific ones made for adults are available at book and art supply stores.

●**Listen to music.** Now is the time to enjoy entire symphonies, operas or albums.

Trap: Television can be a harmless escape... or an energy-depleting crutch. Before tuning in, ask yourself, "Does TV make me laugh more? Does it leave me feeling better about myself and my life? Does it distract me from my pain or problems?" Should you answer "no" to any of these questions, explore other, more energizing pastimes.

A HEALTHFUL ENVIRONMENT

Where you heal affects how you heal. Your immediate environment should make you feel calm and uplifted—not agitated or depressed.

●**Declutter your room.** Clear off surfaces ...ask a friend to remove excess furniture... and toss old magazines and newspapers.

●**Use incandescent lights, not fluorescent ones.** Experiment with rosy lightbulbs that cast a soothing glow.

●**Give yourself new vistas.** Have new paintings or posters hung or old ones rearranged.

●**Surround yourself with mood-enhancing color.** Drape beautiful fabric over an old table or nightstand. Festoon windows with bright curtains.

●**Add fragrance to the room with incense or fresh flowers.**

●**Fill your room with plants** or grow an herb garden in an ice-cube tray on a window ledge.

WELCOMING VISITORS

Illness and injury can make visitors uncomfortable. Family and friends may be unsure of what to say or do. Put your guests at ease by voicing your wants and needs. *Be very specific...*

●**If talk is tiring, ask your visitor to hold your hand** and pray, meditate or do a breathing exercise with you.

●**Suggest a game of cards** or ask your guest to read to you.

●**Request a back or foot massage** from a close relative or friend.

●**Ask to have groceries picked up or library books returned.** Most loved ones appreciate having concrete ways to help you.

If you're too tired for visitors or need to cut a visit short, say so. Be gracious but firm. Your guests will understand.

Secrets of Better Living With a Terminal Illness

Ed Madden, a columnist for the *Dorchester Reporter*, a weekly newspaper in Dorchester, MA, and author of *Carpe Diem: Enjoying Every Day with a Terminal Illness*. Jones and Bartlett Publishers.

Several years ago, my doctor told me that the excruciating back pain that had plagued me for six months was caused by *multiple myeloma,* a rare bone marrow cancer that was attacking my spine and ribs.

Multiple myeloma accounts for only 1% of all cancers—and it's incurable. I was 53 years old, and I knew it was unlikely that I would survive more than a few years.

I hate the cancer, and there have been times that I railed against it. But I decided early on to try to put my disease in its place and go about my business.

Today is the only day I have. I'm going to enjoy it. This philosophy can benefit not only people with terminal or chronic illness, but also those who are healthy. *Here are some of the other lessons I've learned...*

●**View terminal illness as the key that opens the vault to unknown treasures.** Since I got sick, I've experienced more love, concern, compassion and care on a single day than I used to experience in an entire year.

Even though I know my days are numbered, I really enjoy life. I have a good time with my family and friends. I realize that I am one of the richest people in the world.

●**Accept help.** My close friends and relatives all felt powerless when I told them I had cancer. They wanted to help, but there wasn't much they could do. So they did what they could. Some came and did yard work for me. My brother-in-law put up a banister. A friend dropped by once a week to have dinner with me.

They couldn't cure my cancer or take away my pain, but they could help in other ways. And their help has helped me not only in practical terms, but also emotionally.

My friends all say, "You'll beat this." Of course, I won't. They're in denial, but I don't let that bother me. It's their way of coping. It's also their way of trying to be kind to me.

●**Don't worry about the things you can no longer do.** Instead, try to focus on what you still can do.

My cancer has caused my bones to deteriorate. As a result, I now have severe osteoporosis. If I attempt heavy physical labor or try to lift more than 20 pounds, I risk a fracture.

It would be easy to feel sorry for myself. But I'm not in pain, and I've been able to resume gardening and biking—two pleasures I'd thought were history—so I'm content. Sure, it would be safer to avoid these activities, too, but I refuse to wrap myself in a protective sheath.

●**Don't view yourself as a patient.** When you do, you see yourself sick, lying in a hospital bed with tubes sticking out of your body. That's not a pleasant concept, and it's certainly not one you have to dwell on.

Although I might be a bit more physically flawed now than I used to be, I'm really not too different from you or anyone else. We're all flawed. It's the daily struggle to better ourselves physically, spiritually, intellectually and emotionally that makes life interesting and challenging. Illness is just another imperfection that we can strive to overcome.

●**Take charge of your health care.** If you're used to being "in control" of your life, suddenly being diagnosed with an uncontrollable illness can be overwhelming.

I've always been a take-charge person. While I can't control the course of my illness, I refuse to give up power over the one thing that I do have control of—my treatment.

I've become a partner in my health care. My doctor and I decide on all treatments together. I stay on top of the latest medical advances. I read medical journals and I discuss the things I read about with my doctor.

If you or a close friend or family member has a serious illness, you should do the same. Hospital libraries are an excellent place to start your search for helpful information.

●**Decide what you want in a hospital.** Many of us have a choice between teaching hospitals and community hospitals. Teaching hospitals tend to offer the most up-to-date care, *but they have certain drawbacks…*

- **You'll often be seen by a medical resident instead of your regular doctor.**
- **You may have to wait a long time before you're seen.**
- **You may have to commute to get to the hospital.**

I decided to go to a local four-doctor practice because I wanted to get individualized care. Each of these doctors knows who I am and what my condition is. I don't have to reeducate them each time I come in for a checkup.

- **Practice positive thinking.** The latest research shows that the mind has at least some control over the body. And how you feel can control the mind. To keep myself optimistic, I focus on all the great things in my life—especially my family and close friends.

When my cancer was diagnosed, one of my greatest disappointments was that I wouldn't live to see my 25th wedding anniversary. But I did! Joy is great medicine.

- **Decide whether the side effects of treatment are worth its benefits.** For cancer that's curable, you go ahead with chemotherapy or radiation regardless of the side effects. But some people with incurable cancer decide against chemo and radiation because they don't want to suffer the nausea, fatigue and other side effects that often accompany these treatments.

I take chemotherapy treatments that don't abuse my body terribly but suppress the cancer sufficiently to give me some more and better days.

I know that eventually my cancer may destroy my kidneys. But I've decided not to go on dialysis. Getting hooked up to a machine three times a week and knowing I'll never quite feel well again is not the sort of life I can bear to live. If you want to maintain your quality of life, you must know when to say no to treatment.

- **Root your hope in reality.** People living with terminal illness need hope, but a hope that denies reality is a false one. It makes you prey to charlatans who seek to profit off your suffering.

I know that I'm going to die in a few years. I can't keep thinking that maybe there's some-thing out there to cure me. If my bones start breaking, if I get pneumonia and my kidneys are going…then it's time to say good-bye.

- **Join a support group.** I've always hated meetings. And I never thought I needed any psychological counseling. But support groups are different. They let you share your concerns and feelings with others who are just like you.

Midway through the first meeting of my support group, I realized something very powerful—that I was able to help everyone in the room—and that everyone was helping me. Some people say they don't feel comfortable opening up. If you're one of them, realize that in a support group, nobody forces you to talk.

If you'd like information on cancer support groups in your area, contact a hospital social worker or the American Cancer Society at 800-227-2345.

- **Plan for your future.** Tending to the business of dying is not easy. But it's something that we must do—both for ourselves and for our loved ones. I've made a living will. It says that when I'm near the end and I can no longer express myself, I want to die as quickly as possible.

I also have a durable power of attorney, which gives another person—my wife—the right to carry out my wishes. If you don't get your affairs in order, hospitals and doctors are liable to use mechanical marvels to keep you alive—even if you'd simply prefer to die.

- **Appreciate the spirituality of illness.** A terminal illness forces you to look inward and find what's important in your life. It's comforting to know that if your priorities have been misplaced, you can correct them for whatever days remain.

Those of us who believe in God can make ourselves fit for the journey to come. That might mean squaring ourselves with people with whom we've quarreled in the past.

Those who do not believe in a divinity probably feel even more strongly about leaving behind favorable and healing memories.

- **Seize the day.** My motto is the Latin phrase *carpe diem* (literally "seize the day"). I think of it as "enjoy today." Those of us with terminal illness have had life's brevity impressed upon us.

Yet because our tomorrows are limited, our todays become much more important. In reality, of course, we all have a limited number of days. We should enjoy each one as if it were our last.

My wife and I are very much living in the moment. Recently, after dreaming of seeing Rome for years and years, we finally made the trip. We also visited Nova Scotia, where my maternal grandparents were born.

I'm storing up great memories, not so much for myself but for my wife and daughter. My attitude is, *Let's get on with the good times.* You may not be able to have them later.

Getting the Government Aid You Are Entitled to For Health Care and Medical Bills

Charles B. Inlander, president of the People's Medical Society, a nonprofit consumers' health organization, 462 Walnut St., Allentown, PA 18102. He is coauthor, with Karla Morales, of *Getting the Most for Your Medical Dollar.* Pantheon.

Given the skyrocketing costs of medical care and health insurance, it is particularly important to make sure you receive the benefits you're entitled to…and to minimize the expenses for which you are liable.

The primary federal health-care programs are Medicare…and Medicaid—for the needy.

Other government programs, for which fewer people are eligible, include Veterans Administration (VA) benefits and Supplemental Security Income (SSI).

Medicare and Medicaid aren't charity programs. They are tax-funded insurance programs you have paid premiums for—through Social Security—and that you are entitled to. Most beneficiaries of Medicaid, which now covers half of the US nursing-home population, have paid premiums for most of their working lives.

Even with an employer-provided health insurance plan—and we recommend you keep any plan you have—you should enroll in Medicare Part A (hospital insurance), when you turn 65…and purchase Part B (doctor insurance) within three months of your 65th birthday. Otherwise, you will have to pay an additional 10% premium for every year you wait. Enrolling keeps that cost to your employer down and maximizes the benefits of your existing plan.

Medicare was never intended to cover all of its beneficiaries' health costs. Everyone's share is rising. Today, the elderly spend up to 20% of their income on health care, even with Medicare.

Money-saving solutions: Make sure you have supplemental private insurance ("Medigap" coverage)…and try to keep all medical costs as low as possible.

HOW TO GET THE MOST FROM MEDICARE

Maximize your coverage by tuning into Medicare's best-kept secrets…

●**Doctors' fees are very negotiable.** A doctor who accepts Medicare assignments agrees to accept the fee that it pays for the procedure or treatments provided, and handles the paperwork. You remain responsible for your deductible and 20% co-payment.

Seventy-five percent of physicians and other limited licensed practitioners accept assignments for all of their Medicare patients. Ninety percent of all Medicare-allowed charges are now billed by participating practitioners. This shows how consumers have used their power to persuade providers to accept assignment.

If your physician does not accept assignment, you can try to persuade him. *Helpful approach:* "I believe that Medicare pays a fair rate, and I hope you will respect my request, as I cannot afford more than the 20% co-payment. However, if you do not accept assignments, perhaps you could refer me to another practitioner who does." Most people who take the trouble to negotiate assignments are successful.

●**You never have to pay more than the balance billing limit for any service,** even if your doctor does not take assignments.

Medicare has set a maximum fee of 115% above the Medicare-approved amount for all services that doctors who do not take assignments may charge Medicare patients. (Some states have set lower limits.) To find out a specific balance billing limit, call the Medicare carrier in your area. If your doctor bills you for more than the balance billing limit, neither you nor your insurance company has to pay the difference.

Example: Your doctor charges $3,000 for a procedure. Medicare pays $2,000 for the same procedure, and has set the balance billing limit at $2,300. Medicare will pay 80% of the $2,000 "reasonable cost," or $1,600. If your doctor accepts assignments, you would only have to pay the 20% co-payment, or $400. If the doctor does not take assignments, you must pay the difference between $1,600 and the $2,300 balance billing limit, or $700, and the doctor must absorb the other $700. (The difference between the doctor's charge of $3,000 and the balance billing limit of $2,300.) But if you didn't check the balance billing limit, you may be billed for the full $3,000, less Medicare's $1,600, and unknowingly pay the $1,400 difference.

● **The fact that Medicare refuses payment does not necessarily mean that you must pay.** You are not responsible for any medical bill that you could not reasonably have been expected to know wasn't covered. You must be informed in writing from an official source, such as a Medicare notice or pamphlet, that a service isn't covered. If your doctor tells you something is covered by Medicare and it isn't, then the doctor—neither you nor your insurer—is responsible.

● **You cannot be discharged from the hospital before you are medically able to go.** You cannot be discharged because your Medicare payments or "DRG" (Diagnosis-Related Group system) days have been used up. When you are admitted to the hospital, you will be issued a form outlining your rights as a Medicare patient. If you think you are being discharged too soon, request a review by your state's PRO (Peer Review Organization), a group of doctors who review Medicare cases. The PRO will decide if your Medicare coverage can be extended, based on medical necessity.

SHOPPING FOR "MEDIGAP" INSURANCE

Employer-provided retiree health insurance is usually as good as the available high-option Medigap policies, and often better. But several million Medicare beneficiaries continue to purchase duplicate policies to supplement their Medicare coverage. Changes in the law prohibit an insurance company from *knowingly* selling a second or third Medigap policy to a Medicare beneficiary. *Unfortunately,* these companies are not prohibited from selling *disease-specific* insurance (such as cancer, heart, accident) to Medicare beneficiaries. If you have an employer-sponsored plan you may not need more coverage. If you don't, consider supplemental insurance.

WHAT TO LOOK FOR

The federal government certifies insurance policies as meeting the standards established for Medicare Supplemental Insurance or "Medigap" policies. As a result of reforms in the Medigap insurance market, one basic policy and nine optional plans have been approved for sale. It is illegal for an insurance company to sell you a policy as a Medigap plan if it does not conform to these standards.

Key: Since the coverage offered by each plan is the same regardless of the insurance company selling it, the only difference is the premium. Comparison shop on premium once you have determined which plan best meets your needs. Also, be aware that all 10 policies may not be available in your state. Check with your state insurance department to learn which policies are approved in your state, and which companies are authorized to sell policies.

If you have had a Medigap policy for at least six months and you switch policies, the replacement policy may not impose a waiting period for any pre-existing conditions. *The only exception:* Your new policy offers a benefit that was not in the old policy. However, some states prohibit any exclusions.

Rule of thumb: Don't change an existing policy unless you know that your new policy will cover your existing conditions.

SAVING ON OUT-OF-POCKET EXPENSES

You can minimize your co-payments and keep premiums down by trying to keep your medical expenses as low as possible.

● **Take advantage of low-cost or free health services** offered by counties, organizations, or health fairs.

Examples: Inoculations, screenings.

- **Make sure you are aware of your health plan's limits and exclusions.**

    Example: Number of chiropractic visits.

- **Shop around for prescription prices,** and buy generic drugs when possible.

- **Guard against unnecessary or excessive testing.** Many physicians have adopted new, costly tests while continuing to administer the old ones—often less expensive and just as effective.

- **Avoid hospitalization and surgery unless absolutely necessary.** Avoid for-profit hospitals—they're up to 23% more costly. Avoid weekend admission.

- **Bring your own food, vitamins, and drugs.**

- **Specify in writing that surgery or invasive procedures must be done by the person you are paying,** i.e., your fully-trained physician, not a resident or intern.

- **Keep track of all bills and services** while hospitalized.

Common errors to check for: Additional services not covered by the DRG for your condition, physician visits that actually occurred, as opposed to those routinely billed. Report any irregularities to the Medicare Inspector General at 800-447-8477.

Cold Defense

Avoid colds this winter by being active. A study of middle-aged adults found that those who were most active throughout the day had fewer colds.

Men with the highest levels of physical activity accumulated at work, at home and in regular exercise experienced a 35% reduction in risk of colds compared with less active men. Highly active women experienced a 20% reduction in risk.

Any kind of activity, as long as it was at least moderately intense and performed for two to three hours per day, provided cold-reducing benefits—from structured exercise to gardening and yardwork to brisk walking.

Chuck Matthews, PhD, research assistant professor, department of epidemiology and biostatistics, University of South Carolina, Columbia.

Weight Control and Aging

Beginning in their mid-30s, most people begin losing one-third to one-half pound of muscle each year.

Muscle burns calories and drives metabolism. As you lose muscle, you'll begin to accumulate fat even if your diet is unchanged.

This sequence affects both men and women —but after age 35, women tend to lose twice as much muscle, and accumulate twice as much fat, as men.

Result: Effective weight control requires exercise as much as diet—to combat age-related muscle loss. By maintaining muscle mass or restoring lost muscle, one can maintain a desired weight—or get back to it—without "deprivation" dieting…and be stronger and healthier overall as well.

Good news: It's possible to restore lost muscle with moderate exercise. Studies show that even women in their 70s can restore their muscles to what they were when 40 years younger, with only two exercise sessions per week.

Required: Building muscle mass requires resistance training—lifting weights or working on an exercise machine—in addition to aerobic exercise such as walking or jogging. Get inexpensive advice on strength training at your local YMCA or seniors center.

Miriam Nelson, PhD, director, Center for Physical Fitness, Tufts University, Boston, www.strongwomen.com, and coauthor of Strong Women, Strong Bones. Putnam.

15

Medical Problems And Solutions

Lifesaving Breakthroughs In Asthma Care

Asthma is a growing problem in the US. Today, more than 15 million Americans suffer from the disease, and 5,000 die of it each year. That's more than twice as many as died from asthma 20 years ago.

Here's what asthma sufferers should be doing to gain control of the disease…

•**Control allergies.** More than half of all cases of asthma are associated with allergies to food or environmental factors, such as pollen, mold, pet dander and microscopic dust mites.

A doctor can perform a "prick" test—dotting the skin with small amounts of suspected allergens—to show which substances cause trouble for you.

Armed with this knowledge, you can avoid environmental allergens…and avoid foods that might cause an attack.

Minimizing the allergens in your home is critical to asthma control. If you have an allergy to pet dander, for instance, it's best to find a new home for any dog or cat you might have. If that's impossible, keep the animal out of your bedroom and off upholstered furniture. Bathe your pet weekly to reduce dander.

To control your exposure to dust mites and their feces—the leading culprit in allergies—encase your mattress and pillows in zippered, airtight covers.

Covers range in price from $2 to $80. Two reputable mail-order sources of the covers are National Allergy Supply (800-522-1448)…and Allergy Asthma Technology Ltd. (800-621-5545)

Leather furniture is unlikely to harbor mites. If your furniture is upholstered in fabric, cover it with a sheet that can be removed and washed every week.

Betty B. Wray, MD, chief of allergy and immunology, and professor of pediatrics and medicine at the Medical College of Georgia in Augusta, and former president of the American College of Allergy, Asthma and Immunology. She is author of *Taking Charge of Asthma: A Lifetime Strategy.* Wiley.

For allergies that interfere with work, school or daily living, allergy desensitization injections may be needed.

The injections contain tiny doses of the substances that cause allergic reactions. Over time, the body adjusts and reacts less strongly.

Initially, shots are given once or twice a week. Once the maintenance dose is reached, shots are given every two to three weeks. Improvement may take six months to be apparent.

●**Make sure heartburn is under control.** Asthma is sometimes caused by spasms of the bronchi, the tubes that connect the lungs to the windpipe.

Bronchospasms are often triggered by gastroesophageal reflux (heartburn), in which stomach acid flows "upstream" from the stomach to the esophagus. Reflux is especially likely to occur when you're lying in bed. To control heartburn, lose weight, eat smaller meals and avoid trigger foods. Common triggers include caffeine, alcohol and fatty or spicy foods.

●**Avoid medications that aggravate asthmatic symptoms.** Twenty percent of asthma sufferers experience an attack after taking aspirin or another nonsteroidal anti-inflammatory drug (NSAID), such as *ibuprofen* (Motrin) or *naproxen* (Aleve). NSAIDs can cause airways to narrow. *Acetaminophen* (Tylenol) does not have this effect. It's often a better choice for people with asthma. Ask your doctor.

Beta-blockers such as *propranolol* (Inderal) —often prescribed for high blood pressure or congestive heart failure—can cause the bronchi to constrict. If your doctor prescribes a beta-blocker, ask if you can take a diuretic, an ACE inhibitor or another alternative instead.

●**Take vitamin C.** Recent studies suggest that vitamin C supplementation boosts lung function in people with asthma. *Usual dosage:* 1,000 mg a day.

●**Do breathing exercises.** Deep breathing exercises, tai chi, qi gong and yoga are all good for breath control—and strengthening the diaphragm. That's the sheet-like muscle between the chest and abdomen that is used to draw air into the lungs.

Breathing exercises are taught by respiratory therapists and speech therapists.

Tai chi, qi gong and yoga are best learned from an instructor. Check with a local hospital, college or health food store for classes in your area.

●**Be careful about taking your asthma medications.** If other methods don't work, medication can help you prevent an attack—or short-circuit an impending one.

Several medications are used, depending on the severity of your asthma…

●Nonsteroidal inhalers, such as *cromolyn* (Intal) and *nedocromil* (Tilade) can help prevent asthma attacks—if used before you exercise or encounter an allergen. Because these prescription drugs have few side effects, they're often the first line of defense.

Caution: Over-the-counter inhalers, such as Primatene Mist, should be used only in a breathing emergency. Most contain epinephrine, a compound that can cause rapid heart rate, increased blood pressure and dizziness.

●Antihistamines control histamines, the body chemicals that are released in an allergic reaction. Histamines can cause bronchospasm.

Mild asthma can often be controlled by using *loratadine* (Claritin), *fexofenadine* (Allegra), *cetirizine* (Zyrtec) or another prescription antihistamine.

●Inhaled beta-agonists, such as *albuterol* (Ventolin) and *terbutaline* (Brethine) can be used to stop an attack that is just beginning…or on a regular basis to prevent attacks.

These prescription drugs work by relaxing bronchial muscles, opening air passages.

●Steroids are the most potent asthma drugs. Inhaled steroids, such as *fluticasone (Flonase)* and *beclomethasone* (Vanceril), are used mainly to prevent attacks.

After a few weeks of regular use, these prescription drugs cause the lungs to become less reactive to allergens.

Oral steroids, such as *prednisone* or *dexamethasone,* are used to treat severe attacks.

Since long-term use of oral steroids can lead to osteoporosis, high blood pressure and heart trouble, these drugs are generally a good idea only if no other medication has worked.

Caution: If you must rely on long-term oral steroids to control your asthma, ask your doctor if you are taking the lowest possible dose.

•Leukotriene modifiers—the newest asthma drugs—prevent asthma attacks by blocking *leukotrienes*. Those are substances released from cells during an asthma attack.

Taken in tablet form, leukotriene modifiers, such as *zafirlukast* (Accolate), *zileuton* (Zyflo) and *montelukast* (Singulair), have few side effects but may interact with other drugs. Rare complications include joint pain or shortness of breath.

•**Use a peak flow meter.** This handheld device is used to measure how forcefully you can exhale. A low reading might suggest that an asthma attack is imminent.

Using a peak flow meter twice a day—when you first wake up and then again at bedtime—will enable you to predict attacks and tailor your medication accordingly.

Look for meters with both high and low ranges. They're sold in drugstores for about $35.

Natural Year-Round Allergy Remedies

Richard Firshein, DO, physician practicing in complementary medicine in New York. He is author of *A Guide to Nutritional Therapies: The Nutraceutical Revolution* (Riverhead) and answers health-related questions at *www.drcity.com*.

More than 20 million Americans suffer from springtime allergies. Over-the-counter and some prescription antihistamines can cause drowsiness. Decongestants can raise blood pressure and steroid nasal sprays may cause nasal bleeding and may have other yet unknown effects.

Here are some natural remedies that can often be used instead of—or in conjunction with—medications. Consult a doctor before trying any of these, especially if you are pregnant, planning surgery or taking other medications.

•**Quercetin.** This supplement is a bioflavonoid—the component in fruits and vegetables that gives them their vibrant color. It has natural antihistamine and anti-inflammatory effects.

Typical dosage: If you have spring allergies, start taking quercetin when spring weather begins, and continue through the end of June. Take 300 mg twice a day for one week. If that doesn't work, increase to 600 mg.

If you also suffer from fall allergies, begin again in mid-August and continue through the first frost. In hot climates, you may need to take quercetin year-round.

•**Stinging nettle.** Like quercetin, this plant extract is an excellent antihistamine and anti-inflammatory. It can be used in conjunction with quercetin or on its own.

Typical dosage: 400 mg twice a day during allergy seasons.

On-the-spot treatment: If you find yourself in the throes of an allergy attack despite taking quercetin and/or stinging nettle regularly, take an extra dose. I tell my patients to reach for these remedies whenever they would take an antihistamine.

Most allergy sufferers find quercetin and/or stinging nettle highly effective. But if they don't work for you, one of the following natural antihistamines and anti-inflammatories may help—either in conjunction with each other or alone. Try them in this order—but, of course, talk with your doctor first.

•**Vitamin C.** Take 1,000 mg once or twice a day during allergy season. This should be reduced or eliminated during the off-season. Recent studies suggest vitamin C in high doses may cause thickening of arteries and interfere with certain cancer therapy. Caution is advised for patients with these conditions.

•**Pycnogenol.** An antioxidant derived from the bark of pine trees. Take 50 mg twice a day.

•**Ginkgo biloba.** Take 60 mg twice a day. Once symptoms subside, stop taking this herb. Used in excess (more than 200 mg per day), it can cause diarrhea or sleeplessness.

Caution: People using blood thinners should avoid ginkgo biloba.

•**Feverfew.** Buy a product standardized to contain at least 0.7% parthenolide. That is the component of this herb that reduces swelling in the sinuses. Take 500 mg two or three times a day.

MORE ALLERGY DEFENSES

●**Rinse pollen out of your nasal passages before bedtime.** Use a saline nasal spray, or make your own nasal wash by dissolving one-half teaspoon of salt in one-half cup of water. Place a few drops of the solution in your nose with a dropper, then blow your nose.

●**Keep home and car windows closed**—to keep pollen outdoors. Run an air conditioner continuously to filter air and fight allergy-causing molds.

●**Run a HEPA filter all the time during allergy season**—to purify your air of pollen and other allergens. A HEPA vacuum cleaner may also help.

●**Shampoo your hair, eyebrows, eyelashes, mustache and beard** at bedtime and after outdoor activities. Dust mites and other allergens cling to hairs. Change clothes when you come inside.

●**Strengthen your immune system.** Better overall health means reduced allergy symptoms. Take a daily multivitamin/mineral supplement...eat healthfully...get adequate rest... exercise regularly...and don't smoke.

New Weapon for Fighting Sinus Congestion

*S*inupret, a highly effective German herbal remedy, is available in the US under the name Quanterra Sinus Defense. It is a combination of five herbs—gentian root...elder flower...European vervain...primrose flower... and sorrel. *Best for:* Persistent mild-to-moderate sinus congestion brought on by changes in weather. It may be used in place of a decongestant. Consult your doctor before using any herbal treatment.

Andrew L. Rubman, ND, associate professor of clinical medicine at College of Naturopathic Medicine, University of Bridgeport, and director of Southbury Clinic for Traditional Medicines, Southbury, CT.

Stopping a Nose Bleed

*I*f your nose starts bleeding, blow it gently to remove any blood clots...sit upright with your head leaning forward...and pinch both nostrils below the nose bridge for 15 minutes, using your second and third fingers of both hands. *If bleeding doesn't stop:* Go to the hospital emergency room. The ruptured blood vessels may need to be treated by a physician.

Ronald Charles, MD, assistant professor of emergency medicine, University of Texas Southwestern Medical Center, Dallas.

Inhaling Steam Doesn't Help Get Rid of a Cold

*P*revious studies suggested that steam inhalation kills the cold-causing rhinovirus in the respiratory tract. But in a newer study, volunteers who breathed steam long enough to raise the temperature inside their nostrils to 109° Fahrenheit—the minimum needed to inactivate the virus—reported no differences in their symptoms compared with those who simply inhaled warm air.

G.J. Forstall, MD, assistant professor of medicine and staff physician, department of infectious disease, McLaren Regional Medical Center, Flint, MI.

Treating Chronic Coughs

*C*hronic coughs should not be treated with over-the-counter remedies. Most short-term coughs clear up on their own within a week or two. A chronic cough may signal an allergy, asthma or another more serious condition—which should be evaluated by a doctor.

Steven Lamm, MD, clinical assistant professor of medicine, New York University School of Medicine, New York.

Heartburn Help

Two promising treatments for chronic heartburn have been approved by the FDA. Both were successful when tested on approximately 200 patients with moderate chronic heartburn. *How they work:* Each treatment involves passing a tiny device through an endoscope—a tube inserted into the esophagus—to fix the faulty valve that allows acid to escape from the stomach and cause heartburn. The Stretta System emits pulses of radio-frequency radiation to burn spots on the muscle that controls the valve. The endoscopic suturing system tightens the valve with tiny pleats.

James C. Reynolds, MD, chief of gastroenterology at MCP Hahnemann University, Philadelphia.

Beat Heartburn Without Drugs

Avoid foods that can trigger heartburn—alcohol, chocolate, peppermint, spearmint and fat. Avoid caffeine in foods and over-the-counter pain medications. Avoid carbonated drinks. *Also:* If you are overweight, lose weight …if you smoke, quit smoking.

For nighttime heartburn: Raise the head of your bed on four- to six-inch blocks, or use a wedge-shaped support to elevate the upper half of your body. Do not lie down with a full stomach.

Marvin Lipman, MD, chief medical adviser, Consumers Union, writing in *Consumer Reports on Health,* 101 Truman Ave., Yonkers, NY 10703.

How to Beat Dizziness

Brian Blakely, MD, PhD, associate professor of otolaryngology and director of the dizziness clinic at Wayne State University School of Medicine in Detroit. He is coauthor of *Feeling Dizzy: Understanding and Treating Dizziness, Vertigo and Other Balance Disorders.* Macmillan.

In the absence of other symptoms, occasional mild dizziness is nothing to worry about. But see a doctor right away if dizzy spells recur …if they're severe enough to force you to lie down…*or if they're accompanied by…*

- **Double vision.**
- **Incontinence.**
- **Arm and/or leg weakness.**
- **Difficulty with speaking or swallowing.**
- **Severe headache.**

These symptoms are suggestive of stroke, brain tumor, aneurysm or another potentially life-threatening problem.

COMMON TYPES OF DIZZINESS

A mild turning sensation. Caused by almost any systemic ailment, including transient ischemic attacks, multiple sclerosis…even AIDS.

Some women have mild turning during menstruation—or as a side effect of hormone replacement therapy or menopause.

Imbalance. This swaying or wobbling feeling can be caused by flu, infection, arthritis, compression of the spinal cord, diabetes or another metabolic disorder.

Imbalance can also be caused by alcohol abuse, depression or anxiety (rapid breathing reduces the flow of oxygen to the brain)…or by certain medications, including cough medicines and blood pressure drugs.

Vertigo. This sensation of spinning often accompanies migraine headaches and many diseases.

Presyncope (feeling of faintness). This is often a result of *postural hypotension,* the brief period of reduced blood pressure that occurs when someone abruptly stands or sits up.

Several medications can contribute to postural hypotension, including antihypertensives, antihistamines, sedatives and antipsychotics.

EAR AND BRAIN DISORDERS

Persistent dizziness not linked to an underlying illness usually involves brain or inner ear trouble. *Most common forms of inner ear/ brain dizziness…*

Benign paroxysmal positional vertigo (BPPV) occurs when a person moves his head in a certain position—typically when he lies on his back, then rolls quickly to one side.

BPPV itself isn't life-threatening, but it can be deadly if it occurs while driving an automobile or standing up.

211

BPPV in people under 50 is often caused by head trauma. Even a light bump can be enough. In people over 50, BPPV can occur after illness, or be caused by degeneration of the nerves in the middle ear. In some cases, BPPV appears for no apparent reason.

• **Vestibular neuronitis** is sudden vertigo that occurs a few days or weeks after recovery from a viral infection. Often it's accompanied by nausea and/or vomiting. *Likely cause:* Inflammation of the vestibular nerve, which connects the brain and inner ear.

• **Ataxia** is a loss of coordination. It's usually caused by the death of brain cells, although it can also be caused by vitamin deficiencies or heavy drinking. Most common among elderly people, it often comes on gradually, and is generally irreversible.

• **Ménière's disease** is a set of related symptoms, including vertigo attacks...roaring, ringing or hearing loss in one ear...a feeling of fullness in the ear. Most cases are caused by fluid buildup in the inner ear.

Ménière's usually strikes between the ages of 30 and 50. Symptoms tend to recur, lasting an hour or more at a time. They range from mild to debilitating.

• **Ear infection** that causes fluid to accumulate in the middle ear can cause everything from mild imbalance to severe vertigo.

GETTING GOOD TREATMENT

There's no easy way to test the balance mechanisms in the ear and the brain, so your doctor may have trouble pinpointing the cause of your dizziness.

If he/she fails to take a complete medical history...or does not take your dizziness seriously...or has little experience with dizziness, find another doctor.

Best: An otolaryngologist or neurologist working in a dizziness clinic. For the name of an otolaryngologist near you, call the American Academy of Otolaryngology-Head and Neck Surgery, 703-836-4444. For a neurologist, call the American Academy of Neurology, 651-695-1940.

Doctors use several tests to check for inner ear damage. The tests I use most often are the hearing test (audiogram) and two more specialized tests, *electronystagmography* (ENG) and the *rotary chair exam.*

ENG looks at eye movements caused by electrical stimulation of the vestibular system. The rotary chair exam measures eye movements as the patient sits in a computer-controlled rotating chair.

The best antidote for inner ear ailments is time. Inner ear damage usually heals within a few weeks or months. Fluid buildup from ear infection also tends to disappear in a few weeks.

Even persistent nerve damage usually stops causing dizziness after several months. The brain simply learns to re-sort incoming information (much as it adjusts to the rocking of a ship).

Vestibular neuronitis often persists until the underlying inflammation clears up. That can take years—though medicine, bed rest and rehabilitation exercises are helpful.

Dizziness may be permanent in those suffering from ataxia, multiple sclerosis or other central nervous system disorders.

Treatment for Ménière's disease may involve surgery to relieve accumulation of fluid, but diuretics and/or steroids can provide significant relief.

If you do have surgery, make sure the surgeon is board certified in otolaryngology. *To check credentials:* Call the American Board of Medical Specialties, 866-275-2267.

Dizziness usually subsides within eight weeks of surgery. In some cases of dizziness, the mild sedative *meclizine* (Antivert) brings short-term relief. *Scopolamine* is even more effective...but also causes more side effects, including drowsiness and dry mouth. *Caution:* These drugs should be used for no more than a week or two, during severe episodes.

Causes of Trembling Hands

Hand and head tremor are often attributed to Parkinson's disease, the debilitating neurological disorder. But tremor can also be the result of a condition known as essential tremor. *Telling the two apart:* Parkinson's-related tremor is typically seen at rest. Essential tremor is typically seen when the afflicted body part is in use. Alcohol has no effect on Parkinson's, but a drink can reduce the severity of essential tremor for a couple of hours. *Good news:* Most essential tremor sufferers can be helped by the beta-blocker *propranolol* (Inderal) or the anti-seizure drug *primidone* (Mysoline).

William C. Koller, MD, president, International Tremor Foundation, 7046 W. 105 St., Overland Park, KS 66212. *www.essentialtremor.org.*

Shingles Alert

Pain from shingles can be relieved very effectively by the Lidoderm patch. Nerve injury from a shingles outbreak often causes postherpetic neuralgia (PHN), excruciating pain that continues for months or years, particularly in people over age 60. The most effective topical method of easing the pain is the Lidoderm patch, an adhesive patch about 4" by 5.5" that releases the analgesic lidocaine directly onto the affected area. Recently approved by the FDA, the patch relieves PHN pain without causing numbness or any of the side effects caused by other methods of relief. *Caution:* People with a history of drug sensitivity should be cautious in using the patch.

Michael C. Rowbotham, MD, associate professor of neurology and anesthesia at the School of Medicine at the University of California, San Francisco.

Chicken Pox Vaccine May Prevent Shingles In Older People

And—those over age 60 are especially prone to shingles. A study of 200 people aged 55 to 80 who were inoculated with chicken pox vaccine were found four years later to still have their immunity boosted to the virus that causes shingles. A pilot study of the vaccine's effec-

tiveness against shingles is currently being conducted nationwide.

Myron J. Levin, MD, professor of medicine and chief of pediatric infectious diseases, University of Colorado Health Sciences Center in Denver.

Fight Bug Bites ...Naturally

To protect yourself from bug bites, take a multi–B-vitamin complex twice daily. A preliminary study indicates that riboflavin, one of the B vitamins, causes the body to emit an odor that repels mosquitoes, stinging ants, wasps, yellow jackets and bees.

Important: Use one that contains an average of 50 mg of most B vitamins.

Also: Apply a sports rub or an aromatic compound that contains menthol or eucalyptus. These odors temporarily scare off bugs.

Natural remedies: Sprinkle monosodium glutamate (MSG) powder—available in supermarkets and pharmacies—on the bite as often as needed. Or use After Bite, a penlike device that delivers a safe amount of sodium hydroxide (lye). Both penetrate the skin and break down the offending compounds that cause stinging and itching.

Andrew L. Rubman, ND, associate professor of clinical medicine at College of Naturopathic Medicine, University of Bridgeport, and director of Southbury Clinic for Traditional Medicines, Southbury, CT.

About Lyme Disease

Deer ticks usually require 24 hours or more to transmit Lyme disease. If you remove a tick promptly, you shouldn't have a problem. Always check yourself and your children carefully for ticks after leaving a potentially infested area. *Hot spots:* Armpits, groin and hairline.

Ticks that carry Lyme disease are tiny—as small as a poppy seed—so they can easily be missed.

Allen Steere, MD, chief of rheumatology and immunology, New England Medical Center, Boston.

West Nile Virus Update

State and local health departments and the Centers for Disease Control and Prevention are closely monitoring mosquitoes, which carry the virus, and bird populations, which are the first to be afflicted, for early signs of the return of the potentially deadly virus along the eastern seaboard and Gulf Coast. Currently there is no treatment. *Self-defense:* Curb outdoor activities during the early morning and early evening hours, when mosquitoes are most likely to be feeding...wear long-sleeved shirts and long pants when outdoors...use insect repellent that contains DEET...and remove any standing water, such as birdbaths, near your home—it attracts mosquitoes.

Tom Skinner, Centers for Disease Control and Prevention, Atlanta.

Leg Cramp Reliever

Nighttime leg-cramp relief: "Acupinch." *How it works:* With thumb and forefinger, pinch your upper lip—yes, lip—just below the nose for 20 to 30 seconds. This works about 80% of the time.

Donald Cooper, former US Olympic team doctor, quoted in *Minute Health Tips: Medical Advice and Facts at a Glance* by Thomas G. Welch, MD. DCI/Chronimed Publishing.

Foot Pain Relief

To relieve foot pain from high arches, a protruding bone or a nerve or tendon injury, try leaving a space in your shoelaces. Skip the eyelets at the painful point and draw the laces to the next set of eyelets.

Carol Frey, MD, chief, foot and ankle clinic, University of Southern California, Los Angeles.

Knee Pain Relief

Knee pain associated with arthritis can be eased with injections of *hylan GF 20* (Synvisc).

The drug curbs pain by increasing the viscosity of synovial fluid, which cushions the knee joint.

Treatment: Three injections, spaced one week apart.

Knee pain sufferers who got the injections reported less pain while walking. Some needed less pain medication.

Others were able to resume participation in sports that they had abandoned.

Jane Servi, MD, a sports medicine specialist in private practice in Fort Collins, CO. Her study of 43 arthritis sufferers 34 to 94 years of age was presented at a meeting of the American Medical Society for Sports Medicine.

A Sign of Osteoporosis

An unexplained foot fracture may be an early sign of osteoporosis. A bone-density study of 21 men and women who suffered from small fractures of their foot bones found that 19 of them had significant bone loss. Nine of those tested, mostly women in their 50s and 60s, had osteoporosis in their hips and spine. Researchers suggest that people who suffer foot fractures that are not due to accidents or repeated stressful motion should ask their physicians to consider giving them a bone-density test for osteoporosis.

Rodney L. Tomczak, DPM, EdD, assistant professor of orthopedics, Ohio State University, Columbus.

Osteoporosis Warning

Osteoporosis can be a complication of chronic illnesses. That includes chronic obstructive pulmonary disease (COPD) as well as asthma and other chronic diseases treated with steroids. At-risk patients should ask a doctor about bone-density testing and calcium supplements. Men may need to have testosterone levels tested.

Jeffrey Michaelson, MD, senior research fellow, pulmonary and critical care division, Emory University School of Medicine, Atlanta.

New Drug Fights Fractures

Bone-boosting drug makes sense for women who already have osteoporosis as well as for those at risk for the disease. In a new study, the prescription medication *raloxifene* (Evista) cut risk for additional fractures by up to 50% in women who had already sustained one fracture. In previous studies, raloxifene was shown to help prevent breast cancer. The drug may be a good alternative for women at risk for osteoporosis who fear the increased breast cancer risk associated with hormone-replacement therapy (HRT). HRT is often prescribed as a means of preventing osteoporosis.

Bruce Ettinger, MD, senior investigator, division of research, Kaiser Permanente Medical Care Program, Oakland, CA. His three-year study of 7,705 women 31 to 80 years of age was published in *The Journal of the American Medical Association,* 515 N. State St., Chicago 60610.

Tranquilizers and Hip Fractures

Elderly people who take tranquilizers that remain in the body for more than 24 hours are 70% more likely to fracture their hips in falls than those taking tranquilizers that remain in the body for less than 24 hours or those who don't take any at all.

Long-acting: *Diazepam* (Valium), *flurazepam* (Dalmane), *chlordiazepoxide* (Librium).

Short-acting: *Alprazolam* (Xanax), *lorazepam* (Ativan), *oxazepam* (Serax).

T. Franklin Williams, MD, director, National Institute on Aging, Bethesda, MD.

You Can Beat Arthritis

Hani El-Gabalawy, MD, clinical investigator with National Institute of Arthritis and Musculoskeletal and Skin Diseases in Bethesda, MD.

Osteoarthritis (OA)—the most common form of arthritis—affects nearly 21 million Americans.

It primarily strikes the hands...knees... hips...feet...and back. It occurs when cartilage in the joints begins to wear down after injury—usually after age 45.

Here are answers to some frequently asked questions about the best ways to prevent and treat this troubling condition...

How can I prevent osteoarthritis if I have a family history of the disease?

The best way is to maintain an ideal body weight. Excess weight stresses the joints—especially hips and knees.

How can I slow the progression of OA if I already have it?

There are no medications currently available to stop OA, but the over-the-counter supplement glucosamine sulfate may. A recent three-year Belgian study of 202 people with OA of the knee found that taking 1,500 mg of oral glucosamine daily slowed joint deterioration and eased pain and stiffness.

There's also limited evidence that antioxidant vitamins may retard OA. I suggest my patients take the same daily doses recommended for prevention of heart disease—1,000 mg of vitamin C...400 IU of vitamin E...and 15,000 IU of beta-carotene.

What other drugs are available?

Most other OA medications minimize pain. They include *aspirin, acetaminophen* (Tylenol) and non-steroidal anti-inflammatory drugs (NSAIDs)—*ibuprofen* (Advil)...*naproxen* (Aleve, Naprosyn)...*nabumetone* (Relafen)...*piroxicam* (Feldene)...and *etodolac* (Lodine).

The safest drug is acetaminophen. NSAIDs can cause stomach upset, gastrointestinal bleeding and ulcers.

Other agents, including *misoprostol* (Cytotec) and *omeprazole* (Prilosec), can be prescribed along with NSAIDs to protect the stomach from these side effects.

Newest agents: Celecoxib (Celebrex) and *rofecoxib* (Vioxx). Compared with other NSAIDs, these "COX-2 selective inhibitors" are just as effective and seem to have a less harmful impact on the gastrointestinal tract. But not all insurers will pay for them.

Have any alternative therapies proven to be effective?

Besides glucosamine and antioxidants, the alternative remedy for which there is good data is acupuncture. Several trials indicate it alleviates pain that originates from extremities, such as legs or arms. So it's worth a try.

It's possible you could benefit from using magnets or another alternative remedy. Even though there's no proven reason they should work, they may work for you.

If you try an alternative remedy, tell your doctor to make sure it won't interfere with your conventional treatment.

What foods are associated with increased or decreased arthritis problems?

Foods that contain high levels of antioxidants, such as fruits and vegetables, may reduce risk of arthritis. Eat as much of those as you can. There's no scientific evidence to support the common belief that nightshade plants —tomatoes, potatoes, peppers and eggplants —exacerbate arthritis.

I always wake up feeling stiff. What can I do to get my day started faster?

Ask your doctor about taking a long-acting NSAID or Celebrex at night. The drug's effects will carry over into the morning, when you take your next dose.

Performing some stretches and range-of-motion exercises in the morning can also help.

Sleep on a firm mattress and pillow that support your neck and back. Avoid caffeine, nicotine and alcohol, which can prevent you from sleeping well.

What are some particularly useful products for people with arthritis?

The Arthritis Foundation (800-283-7800 ...*www.arthritis.org*) offers a wealth of well-balanced, scientifically validated information and products.

Reliable companies that have useful catalogs...

●**Aids for Arthritis, Inc.,** 800-654-0707.

●**MOMS Home Healthcare,** 800-232-7443.

●**Smith & Nephew, Inc.,** 262-251-7840... *www.rehab.smith-nephew.com.*

●**Center for Assistive Technology and Environmental Access** (404-894-4960... *www.catea.org*), an information clearinghouse for people with disabilities.

When should I consider joint replacement?

Most orthopedic surgeons recommend arthroplasty (joint replacement) only when there is no cartilage left in the hip or knee and you're experiencing pain even when at rest. Some people who have great problems with the pain have it done sooner.

Disadvantage: The prosthesis will loosen in about 10 years and will need to be replaced.

If you have arthroplasty before age 70, ask your surgeon about getting an *uncemented* prosthesis, which is easier to replace than a cemented one.

What about injectable drugs for arthritis? Do they work?

They certainly are worth trying. You're probably referring to *Hyalgan* and *Synvisc*. These products contain hyaluronic acid to lubricate the joint. I've used these devices often, with mixed results.

Cost: $200 to $300 for a full course of treatment—usually three injections given one week apart. Few insurance companies cover it.

Corticosteroid injections are also used. But unlike hyaluronic acid, they are proven to work. Three or four injections per year seem to be safe.

What does the future of arthritis treatment hold?

There's a tremendous amount of research. *Most exciting:* There are specialized stem cells in the body that make all sorts of connective tissue, such as bone, cartilage and tendons. We're hoping to use these cells to replace the damaged cells and "fix" the joint.

How to Overcome Headaches, Arthritis, Backache and Other Common Sources of Chronic Pain

Norman J. Marcus, MD, president, International Foundation for Pain Relief, and medical director of the New York Pain Treatment Program at Lenox Hill Hospital, both in New York City. He is author of *Freedom from Chronic Pain*. Simon & Schuster.

Our brains are programmed to interpret pain as a sign of acute injury. Almost instinctively, we stop what we're doing...we limit our movement...and we get help. When pain is chronic, however, these instincts are counterproductive. Inactivity won't heal a bad back, constant headaches or arthritis—it just creates more problems.

People come to our pain center seeking total relief. But that isn't always possible. What they must really learn is to *manage* their pain, to focus on quality of life. That way, they can learn to live happily, even with pain.

OVERREACTING TO PAIN

One of the first things I ask new patients to do is to describe their pain. More often than not, they describe not the sensation of pain, but what the pain means to them.

Typical responses: "Pain makes my life miserable...pain drives away my friends...it means that something is terribly wrong...it consumes my whole life...it makes me irritable and angry."

Such negative thoughts can be more devastating than the pain itself. This "pain-button thinking" turns every twinge into a catastrophe. Do any of these "catastrophizing" thoughts sound familiar?

- **Things are bad and getting worse.**
- **This pain will destroy me.**
- **My body is falling apart.**
- **Poor me.**

Thinking that severe pain must mean some dreadful disease adds mental anguish to physical discomfort. Many people experience pain as a form of punishment—like being spanked as a child. That only makes it worse.

None of these negative thoughts makes sense. Becoming aware of your pain-button thinking is the first step to getting rid of it.

ENDURING DISCOMFORT

One of the most important strategies for coping with chronic pain is to develop a capacity to endure discomfort.

Modern Americans are so accustomed to comfort and convenience that we expect it. As a result, we're less able to withstand pain than people were a century ago. A minor ache that our ancestors might not have given a second thought to can debilitate us.

To have a full life, you must be willing to tolerate some discomfort.

THE REAL CAUSE OF CHRONIC PAIN

Although few pain sufferers are aware of it, chronic pain usually goes hand in hand with tense, weak muscles.

Example I: Most chronic headaches are the result of muscular tension. You may feel the pain in the front of your head, but it's really coming from tight muscles in your neck and shoulders.

Example II: Pain blamed on osteoarthritis sometimes comes not from the joints themselves but from stiff muscles around the joints. Exercising to strengthen those muscles and make them more limber will diminish your pain—even if your joints remain stiff.

Example III: Weakened or tense muscles are responsible for at least 80% of chronic back pain. Even when a high-tech test like magnetic resonance imaging (MRI) shows evidence of herniated disks, there's no proof that these are causing the pain. In fact, 40% of people who display spinal abnormalities on an MRI (including herniated disks) have no pain.

Perhaps the most effective way to tame chronic pain is to relax, stretch and strengthen your muscles.

PAIN-RELIEF STRATEGIES

•**Breathe from your belly.** Most people move their chests in and out when they breathe. *Problem:* This type of breathing places constant strain on the muscles of your neck and shoulders, exacerbating headaches and back pain.

Better way: Place your hands on your belly or over your head and relax your shoulders. Breathe so that your abdomen goes in and out while your chest remains still. Once you get the hang of it, practice belly breathing without using your hands—and try to breathe that way all the time.

•**Get regular exercise.** If your pain is too severe to permit aerobics classes, jogging or weight-lifting, try walking or swimming. They will increase the flow of blood and oxygen to muscle cells without causing more pain.

Pacing is essential. Plan to finish your walk or swim before you become tired. If necessary, start off by going only a very short distance. Increase the distance gradually. Concentrate on gentle, stress-free motions.

•**Reduce psychological stress.** Stress intensifies pain by restricting blood flow and tightening muscles. And negative feelings speed the transmission of pain impulses from the body to the brain. Pleasant emotions help block the transmission of pain signals.

Learn to recognize the links between tension and pain. Notice the situations that cause back pain or headache to flare up. Consider what role might be played by your thoughts and emotions. Once you've tuned in to the triggers, look for better ways to solve problems and eliminate hassles.

Helpful: Keep a "pain diary" that details what you're doing and thinking when pain strikes.

If you notice that you can sit for 45 minutes before your back starts to hurt, for example, you can then make it a point to get up before that time is up.

Once you break the association between a specific activity and pain, you'll avoid the anticipation that makes pain a self-fulfilling prophecy. This way, you'll gradually increase your endurance.

•**Be more assertive.** If chronic pain limits your energy, you must learn how to set limits —to say "no" in a reasonable way, without anger or guilt.

Also important: Good planning skills. Each morning, make a list of what needs to be done that day. Recognize that focusing wisely on the top 20% of your list will fulfill 80% of your needs. Intelligent management of your time prevents the fall behind/catch-up spiral that exacerbates chronic pain.

•**Get enough sleep.** Go to bed and get up at the same time every day...and avoid caffeine, alcohol, sleeping pills and naps. Use your bed for sleeping and sex only.

If you're not sleepy—or if you wake up in the middle of the night—get out of bed. Read or listen to music until you're drowsy.

Essential: A firm mattress. If your body "gels" into position on a soft mattress, you'll wake up in more pain than if you had moved around throughout the night.

•**Steer clear of painkillers.** While they're helpful for acute pain, long-term use often causes severe side effects. Regular use of painkillers can actually *cause* some forms of chronic pain.

As your ability to tolerate discomfort grows, cut back gradually—under your doctor's supervision, of course.

Migraine Prevention

Magnesium and vitamin B-2 can help prevent recurrent migraines. In separate studies, migraineurs who took 400 mg a day of either supplement reported fewer headaches—

often within a couple of weeks. *Helpful:* An over-the-counter product called *Migra-Lieve.* It contains magnesium, vitamin B-2 and feverfew, an herbal remedy that has also been shown to be effective against migraines.

Alexander Mauskop, MD, director, New York Headache Center, New York.

Hidden Cause of Stomach Problems

Bloating and stomach pain may be caused by *tight pants syndrome.* The "condition" was named by a doctor who treated a male patient who complained of mysterious abdominal pains. After a series of tests proved negative, the doctor discovered that the man's waist size was at least three inches greater than his pants size.

Octavio Bessa, Jr., MD, clinical assistant professor of medicine, New York Medical College, Valhalla, and an internist practicing in Stamford, CT.

An Often Undiagnosed Disease

Celiac disease affects one million Americans—and many have no idea they have it. The disease is caused by an intolerance to gluten—the main protein in wheat, barley, rye and oats. The resulting intestinal inflammation hampers absorption of nutrients and can lead to diarrhea, cramps, anemia, osteoporosis, infertility and seizures. Because many different conditions can cause these same symptoms, the average individual with celiac disease goes 11 years before receiving a diagnosis. *Good news:* Once celiac disease sufferers eliminate bread, pasta, beer and other gluten-containing foods from their diets, most begin improving in as little as one week.

Peter Green, MD, clinical professor of medicine, Columbia University College of Physicians and Surgeons, New York. For more information, contact the Celiac Disease Foundation, 13251 Ventura Blvd., #1, Studio City, CA 91604. 818-990-2354.

Epilepsy and Aging

Epilepsy in elderly people often goes undiagnosed. The condition's incidence rises steeply in people age 60 or older. But the symptoms of the most common seizure type in the elderly—the complex partial seizure—are often blamed on dementia. These include facial movements such as chewing or lip-smacking, memory loss, wandering, intermittent altered mental status and clumsiness. *Self-defense:* Call your doctor at once if you or a loved one experiences an apparent seizure.

A. James Rowan, MD, professor of neurology, Mount Sinai School of Medicine, New York.

It May Not Be Carpal Tunnel Syndrome

A numb wrist does not necessarily mean that you have carpal tunnel syndrome (CTS). A recent study of 2,500 people reporting numbness and tingling in the wrist or hands found that 80% of the cases did not have carpal tunnel syndrome, which comes from compression of the median nerve in the wrist. If your doctor cannot diagnose your problem quickly, ask for a carpal compression test. The doctor presses the median nerve with his thumb. If this does not reproduce tingling in your fingers within 60 seconds, CTS is unlikely to be the cause.

Robert A. Werner, MD, associate professor and chief of physical medicine and rehabilitation at the Ann Arbor VA Medical Center at the University of Michigan.

The Mint/Gallstone Connection

In England, gallstones are often treated with an over-the-counter mint preparation called *Rowachol.* In a recent study, 42% of gallbladder patients who took Rowachol were stone free after four years, compared with 73% of those who took Rowachol plus a stone-dissolving prescription drug, which can cause diarrhea and liver damage. Rowachol is hard to find in the US. *Instead:* Ask your doctor about taking one or two enteric-coated 0.2 ml peppermint oil capsules three times daily, with meals. The capsules are sold in health food stores.

Melvyn R. Werbach, MD, a physician in private practice in Tarzana, CA. He is author of *Nutritional Influences on Illness.* Third Line Press.

Lower Your Risk of Kidney Stones

Kidney stone risk can be lowered by consuming less protein. It has long been known that high protein intake boosts risk for stones. But in one of the first studies of its kind, researchers found that moderate protein reduction lowers levels of urea, calcium, uric acid, phosphate and oxalate in the blood and urine. All of these are considered markers for kidney stone formation. *If you have kidney stones:* Limit your daily intake of protein to 1g per kilogram of body weight daily (with a maximum of 90 g). To calculate your weight in kilograms, divide your weight in pounds by 2.2.

Sandro Giannini, MD, PhD, assistant professor of medical science and surgery, Institute of Internal Medicine, University of Padova, Padova, Italy.

Accident Complications

Car crash survivors can develop post-traumatic stress disorder (PTSD).

Most often associated with combat veterans and victims of natural disasters, PTSD can cause vivid, crippling memories, disabling anxiety, severe anger, depression and guilt.

Helpful: Talk with friends and relatives about the accident...stay active physically and mentally...get back to your daily activities ...consider taking a defensive driving class to bolster your confidence.

If necessary, your doctor should be able to refer you to a psychotherapist and/or prescribe an antidepressant or another helpful medication.

Dennis J. Butler, PhD, director of behavioral science, Medical College of Wisconsin, Milwaukee.

Good News for Those with Macular Degeneration

There is a breakthrough drug treatment for vision loss to slow progress of macular degeneration, the leading cause of blindness in the elderly. The FDA has approved the prescription medicine *Visudyne,* which is injected into the arm and then light-activated, so it should act only in the eye and have limited side effects. Visudyne is for the *wet form* of macular degeneration—not for the more common, but less serious, dry form.

Jennifer I. Lim, PhD, is associate professor of ophthalmology, Keck School of Medicine, University of Southern California, Los Angeles.

For Better Vision

Vision-enhancement "goggles" improve vision dramatically in those with very poor eyesight. The Low Vision Enhancement System (abbreviated LVES and pronounced "Elvis") contains three separate black-and-white video cameras. A control unit worn on the belt allows the user to adjust contrast and magnify images from three to 10 times. The LVES is available to individuals who have experience using low-vision devices. Obtaining the LVES requires a low-vision evaluation and individual training. *Cost:* $4,000–$5,000. *Information:* Call the Lions Vision Center at Johns Hopkins Wilmer Eye Institute, 410-955-0580.

Robert W. Massoff, PhD, professor of ophthalmology, Johns Hopkins Wilmer Eye Institute, Baltimore.

All About Dry Eyes

Dry, red eyes aren't always caused by irritation or lack of sleep. *Another possibility:* Rosacea, a progressive skin disease marked not only by facial redness, but occasionally by burning, stinging or a feeling that there's something in the eye.

Danger: Severe cases of ocular rosacea can cause scarring and even vision loss. Although the condition cannot be cured, it can be managed and controlled with oral antibiotics and possibly corticosteroid eye drops.

See an ophthalmologist about any eye rash associated with redness, burning or itching that lasts for more than a couple of days.

Jerome Z. Litt, MD, assistant clinical professor of dermatology, Case Western Reserve University School of Medicine, Cleveland.

Custom eyeglasses offer relief for severe eye dryness (Sjögren's syndrome). This condition can be very painful, particularly when outdoors. The custom glasses have plastic "moisture chambers" that hug the wearer's face to slow the evaporation of tears from the eye surface. Customizing a pair of eyeglasses takes at least three visits to the optometrist. The work is covered by some insurance plans. For more information on moisture-chamber glasses, write Dr. Dean Hart at 185 Woodbury Rd., Hicksville, NY 11801.

Dean E. Hart, OD, associate research scientist, Harkness Eye Institute, Columbia University, New York. His report on moisture-chamber eyeglasses was published in the *Journal of the American Optometric Association,* 243 N. Lindbergh Blvd., St. Louis 63141.

Glaucoma—Prevention And Treatment

Martha Motuz Leen, MD, assistant professor of ophthalmology, glaucoma specialist, University of Washington, Seattle.

A leading cause of blindness,* glaucoma afflicts approximately two million Americans—half of whom may not even know that they have the disease.

*The other two leading causes of blindness in the US are *age-related macular degeneration* and *diabetic retinopathy.*

Glaucoma occurs when the *optic nerve*—the nerve in the back of the eye that transmits visual information to the brain—is damaged by an abnormal rise in the pressure of the fluid filling the eyeball.

Normally, this fluid—called *aqueous humor*—drains out of the eye as new fluid is produced. In some individuals, however, the drainage system can become blocked.

Result: Increased *intraocular pressure* (pressure inside the eye).

Some people think that abnormal pressure itself constitutes glaucoma. But a patient is usually considered to have the disease only once the optic nerve is damaged.

Some people with high intraocular pressure, as measured by eye exams, have no nerve damage. Other patients with normal pressure readings, but a more vulnerable optic nerve, suffer vision loss.

There are two major types of glaucoma…

• **Closed-angle glaucoma** occurs when drainage becomes blocked. This can happen suddenly or gradually. Sudden (acute) closed-angle glaucoma is usually accompanied by eye pain or redness, seeing colored halos around lights and/or nausea. With this type of glaucoma, permanent vision damage can occur within a few days. See an ophthalmologist immediately if you notice any combination of these symptoms. The disease is usually treated with laser surgery. Gradual (chronic) closed-angle glaucoma is usually asymptomatic.

• **Open-angle glaucoma** is much more common. Unlike the acute closed-angle type, open-angle glaucoma rarely causes symptoms until the disease has caused a significant amount of damage to the optic nerve. Loss of peripheral vision may occur during the early stages of open-angle glaucoma—but so gradually that the person fails to notice it.

RISK FACTORS

People in their 60s are six times more likely to develop glaucoma than those younger than 60. But the elderly aren't the only ones at increased risk for the disease. *Also at risk:*

• **People with a family history of glaucoma.**

• **African-Americans.**

- **People who use steroids in any form** —including drops, creams and inhalers.
- **Nearsighted people.**
- **Those with a past eye injury.**
- **Migraine sufferers.**
- **Diabetics.**

DETECTING GLAUCOMA

By the time glaucoma starts to produce symptoms, it may already be in an advanced stage. For this reason, every adult at increased risk for glaucoma should have annual eye exams.

A thorough glaucoma exam will include…

- **Intraocular pressure measurement.** Some doctors still measure pressure using a device called an air-puff tonometer. More accurate, however, is the *applanation tonometer*. It touches the eye directly, after the eye has been numbed with anesthetic drops.
- **Visual field testing.** This procedure checks for loss of peripheral vision, which is often an early sign of glaucoma. Usually, patients are asked to spot tiny lights as they appear on a screen.
- **Optic disk exam.** The most important part of the three-part exam because it can detect glaucoma in the earliest possible stages. The ophthalmologist uses a special lamp or viewing scope to peer into the back of the eye. The instrument does not actually come in contact with the eye.

TREATMENT

Although glaucoma has no known cure, it can be arrested—usually with drug therapy. *Essential:* Early treatment.

Glaucoma medications—taken in drop form or as pills—are designed either to decrease the rate of aqueous humor production or improve the flow of the fluid out of the eye. A combination of drugs may be needed to achieve the correct fluid balance. In most cases, the medication must be taken indefinitely.

If drug therapy fails, laser surgery may be required to open up the eye's drainage system. A third treatment alternative—incisional surgery—involves creating a completely new drainage system. This system bypasses the eye's own blocked system. This treatment is now quite effective, thanks to medications that prevent scar formation.

You Don't Have to Put Up With Hearing Loss

Donna Wayner, PhD, clinical director of The Hearing Center at Albany Medical Center in Albany, NY, and director of science and education for the Deafness Research Foundation's National Campaign for Hearing Health (www.drf.org). She is author of Hear What You've Been Missing: How to Cope with Hearing Loss. *John Wiley & Sons.*

It's a shame. Despite the availability of highly effective hearing aids, many of the 28 million Americans with hearing loss are failing to get help for their frustrating—and potentially dangerous—condition.

Many hearing loss sufferers aren't even aware that they have a problem. But if you've been having trouble making out what others say—or if you've been told that you speak too loudly or watch TV with the sound turned up too high—stop making excuses. Effective help is available.

What should I do if I suspect that I have hearing loss? Have your doctor check your ears for wax blockages, infection or some other easily treatable problem.

If no such problem is found, consult an audiologist for a comprehensive hearing exam. The exam takes about 45 minutes and costs about $150.

If your doctor is unable to refer you to an audiologist, call the American Academy of Audiology at 800-222-2336 for a referral.

Generally, hearing aids are appropriate if you're having trouble hearing the telephone or a car horn. That can be dangerous. Hearing aids are also a good idea, of course, if you cannot make out speech clearly.

Hearing aids are now sold on a 30-day trial basis, so there's little downside to trying them out.

How effective are hearing aids? The newest "digital" models are custom-programmed to amplify the frequencies that trouble you most. They're much more effective than the standard "linear" models that were popular just five years ago.

Some people think that hearing aids are useless for so-called "nerve deafness." In fact, more than 80% of all hearing aid users have nerve-related hearing loss—and most of them get substantial help.

Which kind of hearing aid is best? Behind-the-ear models are more powerful and more versatile than the inside-the-ear models that have become popular in recent years. They can correct a wider range of hearing loss.

The only drawback to behind-the-ear models, of course, is that they're a bit more conspicuous than inside-the-ear models.

Ask the audiologist which type of hearing aid is most suitable given your problem.

Besides using a hearing aid, what else can I do to hear better? Turn off the TV, radio, etc., if it's not the focus of your attention…and do your best to avoid loud restaurants.

In conversation, try to have your partner's full attention. Watch his/her face carefully.

Doing so not only helps you read his lips but also helps you pick up facial expressions that can clue you in to what's being said. If you find yourself having trouble understanding someone, don't ask him to speak more loudly. Ask him to speak more slowly. That gives your brain more time to interpret the meaning.

If trouble persists, ask the other person to reword what he's saying rather than simply having him repeat himself.

Hearing loss often involves problems with the brain's ability to process spoken language. So if one wording causes trouble, another might be easier for your brain to process.

What about phones that flash and other assistive devices? If your hearing loss is particularly severe, the audiologist can equip you with assistive listening devices and systems —lights that flash when the phone or doorbell rings, vibrating alarm clock, telephone amplifier, etc.

Don't forget to take advantage of the captioning available for many TV programs—and, in some cities, theatrical movies.

To protect yourself against additional hearing loss, avoid exposure to loud sounds.

If you must be in a noisy environment, pick up a pair of $1 sound-dampening earplugs at a drugstore. Better yet, buy a pair of sound-deadening ear muffs. They're better at protecting against hearing loss. They're sold by sporting goods stores and audiologists for $15 to $25.

Free Hearing Test

Free hearing test identifies hearing problems in your own home.

How it works: Call 800-222-3277 from 9 am to 5 pm, EST, Monday through Friday. Request your local Dial-A-Hearing-Screening-Test number. Call that number from a quiet room using a corded telephone (not a cordless or cellular phone). A recording will play four tones for each ear. If you don't hear all eight, see a doctor or audiologist.

Occupational Hearing Services, Box 1880, Media, PA 19063.

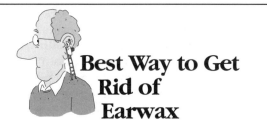

Best Way to Get Rid of Earwax

Most of the time, earwax dries up and falls out on its own. Using a swab to clear out wax can push it against the eardrum. That can interfere with hearing—or damage the eardrum. If earwax does accumulate, use a rubber bulb to flush your ears gently with warm water. If that doesn't work, see a doctor.

M. Lee Williams, MD, associate professor of otolaryngology and head and neck surgery, Johns Hopkins University School of Medicine, Baltimore.

Controlling Tinnitus

Ringing in the ears (tinnitus) can, in many cases, be controlled with the antianxiety drug *alprazolam* (Xanax). After three months on the drug, 75% of tinnitus sufferers reported a lessening of symptoms.

Caution: See a doctor to rule out any underlying problems.

Robert M. Johnson, PhD, professor of otolaryngology, Oregon Health Sciences University, Portland.

Protect Yourself from Gum Disease

Robert J. Genco, DDS, PhD, professor and chair of oral biology and director of the periodontal disease research center at the State University of New York in Buffalo.

Four out of five American adults have some form of periodontal (gum) disease —from swollen gums to bleeding gums to loose teeth.

The damage isn't limited to the mouth. Gum disease contributes to heart disease and can cause trouble for diabetics and pregnant women, recent studies show.

HOW GUM DISEASE DEVELOPS

Gum disease is caused by bacteria that breed in plaque. That's the substance formed by food debris that accumulates around the gum line.

If it's not removed by brushing, plaque eventually turns into tartar *(calculus)*. Tartar roughens tooth surfaces, making plaque adhere even more tightly to teeth.

Toxins produced by the bacteria in plaque inflame gums, making them red, swollen and prone to bleeding. This condition is called *gingivitis*.

Unless inflammation is arrested, gums eventually pull away from teeth. Bacteria then collect in the resulting pockets, further promoting tissue destruction.

Over time, the infection and inflammation destroy bone and tissue. Teeth then loosen and fall out.

Although gum disease usually has obvious symptoms, it can lurk in the mouth even if gums don't bleed. *Among the lesser-known warning signs:* Persistent bad breath...a change in the way teeth fit together when they bite...a change in the fit of partial dentures.

Anyone can develop gum disease. But some factors put people at special risk. These include smoking...diabetes...stress...and low bone density.

THE THREATS TO YOUR HEALTH

Severe gum disease (periodontitis) poses serious health risks...

●**Heart disease.** People with periodontitis have nearly twice the risk for fatal heart attack as do those without the disease.

However, recent studies suggest that the milder form of gum disease—gingivitis—is not associated with heart disease.

How does gum disease harm the heart? The same bacteria that cause gum disease may also raise heart attack risk by provoking a barrage of inflammatory substances that exacerbate coronary artery plaques. They're the sticky deposits that clog blood vessels and lead to heart attack.

●**Diabetes.** Diabetics are more likely to develop gum disease. And, for unknown reasons, diabetics with gum disease have more trouble controlling their blood sugar than do other diabetics. The more severe the gum disease, the worse their blood sugar control.

REVERSING GUM DISEASE

The same oral hygiene regimen that prevents gum disease can reverse it if it's caught early.

●**Brushing.** Twice a day, brush gently for three minutes with a soft-bristled brush. Don't brush side-to-side or in circles. Hold the brush at a 45-degree angle to the gums and sweep from the gum line to the tip of the tooth. Brush the back of each tooth, too.

What about the special grips and bristles common in toothbrushes nowadays? They're frills. Use them if they make brushing more enjoyable. But they're no more effective than straight-handled, straight-bristled versions.

Electric toothbrushes are not necessarily better than manual ones. But they can be useful for people who have difficulty brushing properly because of arthritis or other conditions.

The newest devices—sonic toothbrushes—use sound waves to dislodge plaque and debris. These brushes can help with plaque removal. But good flossers do just as well with old-fashioned manual toothbrushes as with sonic ones.

●**Flossing.** Floss at least once daily. Guide the floss between each set of adjacent teeth in sequence, so you don't miss any. Slide the floss gently down the side of one tooth, then up the side of the other.

Some flosses are waxed or Teflon-coated. Some are flavored. Some are thin filaments. Others are broad ribbons or tapes. None is inherently better than the others. Use the type you prefer.

To make sure you remove all plaque and debris between teeth, add at least one of these strategies to your flossing routine…

●**Use a rubber-tipped stimulator or an interproximal brush**—a tiny flexible brush perched atop a metal wand. The brush is useful for people with spaces between their teeth. Insert the brush or stimulator between teeth at the gum line and move gently back and forth.

●**Try an irrigator such as a Water Pik.** The stream of water dislodges debris caught between teeth.

●**Mouthwash.** Some mouthwashes have been proven to fight gingivitis. Look for the American Dental Association seal of approval.

●**See your dentist.** Even if you're doing everything right, regular dental checkups and professional cleanings are essential. Twice-yearly cleanings suffice for most people. But some need more frequent attention, no matter how scrupulous their home regimen.

Ask your dentist what schedule is right for you. Make sure he/she examines your mouth for signs of bone loss at every visit.

FIGHTING ADVANCED DISEASE

Periodontitis is most often treated with root "scaling" and "planing." Scaling removes plaque and tartar below the gum line at the tooth's root. Planing smooths the root to keep plaque from accumulating along rough surfaces.

In especially severe cases, surgery is needed to cut away detached gum tissue and regenerate bone.

Treatment for periodontitis usually includes antibiotics. New strategies have been developed to deliver antibiotics and germicides directly to gum tissue. These include a gel that hardens in the gum pocket…and a tiny chip that's inserted into the pocket.

Surprising Causes of Dental Problems

●**Cough drops, antacids and chewable vitamin C tablets.** These typically contain lots of cavity-causing sugar.

●**The antiseizure medication *phenytoin* (Dilantin)…**and calcium channel blockers *nifedipine* (Procardia) and *diltiazem* (Cardizem) used to treat blood pressure. They can cause gums to swell, increasing the risk for periodontal disease.

●**Chemotherapy drugs.** These can cause dry mouth, which encourages growth of decay-causing dental plaque.

If you take any of these drugs, be especially careful to practice good oral hygiene.

See a dentist at least three times a year for a cleaning and checkup. Tell him/her if you are taking a drug that can affect teeth and gums.

Alan Winter, DDS, a periodontist in private practice in New York.

Answer for Chronic Pain

Dharma Singh Khalsa, MD, founding director of the Acupuncture Stress Medicine and Chronic Pain Program at the University of Arizona College of Medicine in Tucson. He is president and medical director of the Alzheimer's Prevention Foundation in Tucson, and is author of The Pain Cure. Warner Books.

Twenty-five million Americans are bedeviled by some form of chronic pain—sciatica, migraine, arthritis, muscle pain, etc. There are effective ways to curb chronic pain, but these aren't the ways typically recommended by mainstream physicians.

Here are 10 pain-relieving strategies that really work…

●**Eat more fish and poultry.** Doctors often prescribe *fluoxetine* (Prozac) for chronic pain. This prescription antidepressant helps curb pain by boosting levels of the neurotransmitter *serotonin* in the brain. Serotonin blocks synthesis of *substance P,* one of the main chemical messengers involved in chronic pain.

But many people can keep serotonin levels high simply by eating foods rich in *tryptophan,* an amino acid that the body converts into serotonin.

Two excellent sources of tryptophan are poultry and fish. If you have chronic pain, try eating three ounces of either one five days a week.

In addition to blocking substance P, serotonin helps make people less aware of pain by improving mood and regulating disturbed sleep cycles.

●**Eat a banana every day.** Most chronic pain stems from arthritis, muscle pain or another inflammatory condition, which invariably goes hand in hand with muscle spasms. These spasms contribute to chronic pain.

Eat one banana a day—along with a bit of the lining of the peel that you've scraped off with a spoon. Doing so will supply you with lots of magnesium and potassium. Both minerals help control spasms.

●**Get regular exercise.** Exercise triggers the synthesis of natural painkillers known as *endorphins*.

If you're experiencing severe pain, of course, you probably don't feel like doing vigorous exercise. That's fine. Endorphin synthesis can be triggered by any form of activity that pushes the body a bit harder than it's accustomed to.

If you've been sedentary for a long time, something as simple as rotating your arms for a few seconds can work. So can sitting in a chair and raising your legs a few times.

●**Take steps to control psychological stress.** Stress plays a central role in chronic pain. Meditation and other relaxation techniques reduce muscle spasms, limit the release of pain-causing stress hormones and improve breathing. Each of these helps reduce pain intensity.

One recent study found that pain sufferers who meditated for 10 to 20 minutes a day visited a pain clinic 36% less often than did their nonmeditating peers.

What to do: Carve out at least 15 minutes of quiet time each day. If you aren't comfortable meditating, use the time to pray...visualize a tranquil scene...or sit quietly.

●**Avoid harmful fats.** Red meat and cooking oil stimulate production of *arachidonic acid,* a compound that the body converts into hormone-like substances that trigger inflammation. These substances are known as *prostaglandins.*

Chronic pain sufferers should avoid red meat entirely...and use cooking oil sparingly.

●**Take omega-3 fatty acid supplements.** Taking 1,000 mg to 3,000 mg of fish oil or flaxseed oil each day helps block synthesis of prostaglandins.

In addition to blocking prostaglandin synthesis, a type of omega-3 fatty acid known as *eicosapentaenoic acid* (EPA) improves circulation by making the platelets—cell-like structures that are responsible for blood clotting—less "sticky." This helps keep blood from pooling and causing inflammation and irritation.

Fatty acid supplements are unnecessary for individuals who eat cold-water, dark-flesh fish several times a week. Salmon, tuna, mackerel and sardines all fit the bill.

●**Take a vitamin B complex supplement.** Chronic pain is often accompanied by fatigue. When you feel more energetic, your pain is more manageable.

Ask your doctor about taking a daily supplement that contains at least 50 mg of B complex vitamins.

Vitamin B helps increase energy levels by facilitating the production of ATP, the high-energy compound found in mitochondria, the "power plants" inside cells.

●**Season food with turmeric.** Its primary constituent, *curcumin*, has been shown to be as effective at relieving pain as cortisone or ibuprofen—without any risk for side effects. A pinch or two a day is all you need.

●**Try acupuncture.** There's now solid evidence that acupuncture can be more effective than drug therapy for relieving many types of chronic pain.

Acupuncture that is done by a physician seems to be especially effective. So-called medical acupuncture often involves the application of electrical current to needles inserted into the skin. This variant of traditional acupuncture is called electroacupuncture.

For referral to an acupuncturist in your area, call the American Academy of Medical Acupuncture at 800-521-2262.

●**See a chiropractor or osteopath.** Most physicians rely upon drug therapy and surgery for controlling pain. Chiropractors and osteopaths incorporate physical manipulation into their treatments. For back pain especially, manipulation often works better than drugs or surgery.

16

Surviving Major Medical Threats

All You Need to Know About Alzheimer's and Other Age-Related Dementias

Many people who dread the idea of getting older are especially worried about dementia. For about four million Americans, dementia is not a fear but a reality.

Alzheimer's disease accounts for 60% of all cases of dementia, and at least 30% more are attributable to vascular dementia—the type caused by a major stroke or a series of small "mini-strokes." The remainder of cases are caused by other brain diseases, such as Parkinson's and Huntington's.

●**What's the difference between dementia and normal age-related mental changes?** Some slowdown in the formation of new memories—and some memory loss—is a normal part of aging. By contrast, dementia involves not just forgetfulness but also declines in language, visual and spatial skills…and impaired judgment and problem-solving ability. These grow steadily worse.

Example: A healthy person might forget where he/she left the house keys. But he would solve the problem by calling a neighbor or a locksmith. Someone with dementia would have no idea what to do.

●**Is dementia preventable?** We don't know how to prevent Alzheimer's. All we have are some studies that point to possible Alzheimer's risks and suggest ways to lower them.

On the other hand, strong evidence indicates that vascular dementia *is* preventable.

High blood pressure is the main cause of the strokes that cause this type of dementia. To prevent strokes, get your blood pressure checked

Muriel R. Gillick, MD, associate professor of medicine and director of the geriatrics fellowship program at Harvard Medical School and staff physician at the Hebrew Rehabilitation Center for the Aged, both in Boston. She is author of *Tangled Minds: Understanding Alzheimer's Disease and Other Dementias*. Dutton.

227

regularly. Your systolic pressure (the upper number) should be 160 or less. If it's higher, work with your doctor to lower it through diet, weight loss, exercise and medication.

●**If Alzheimer's can't be prevented, what can be done to minimize the risk?** Inflammation is thought to play a key role in Alzheimer's disease, and a recent study suggests that nonsteroidal anti-inflammatory drugs (NSAIDs) such as *ibuprofen* (Advil) and *naproxen* (Naprosyn) have a small protective effect. The study compared sets of identical twins in which one twin had Alzheimer's and one didn't. It found that the healthy twin was more likely to be taking NSAIDs for another condition—such as arthritis—or to have taken them recently.

I don't think the data are strong enough to recommend that everyone take ibuprofen in the hope of preventing Alzheimer's. NSAIDs can cause side effects ranging from gastrointestinal bleeding to kidney problems. But for people who have recently been diagnosed with Alzheimer's, it might be worth taking 400 mg of ibuprofen three times a day.

●**What about estrogen supplementation and Alzheimer's risk?** Postmenopausal women on estrogen replacement therapy are less likely to have Alzheimer's than women who don't take estrogen.

The problem is that it's hard to separate estrogen's effect from that of other factors. Women who take estrogen tend to be better educated—and for some unknown reason, higher levels of education are associated with lower Alzheimer's risk.

●**Is aluminum exposure a risk factor for Alzheimer's?** Studies in England conducted in the mid-1980s showed higher rates of Alzheimer's in areas with a high concentration of aluminum in drinking water. But the increase was slight. I do *not* make any recommendations based on the studies.

●**What are other risk factors for Alzheimer's?** Serious head injury is one. Several studies have shown that injury resulting in a loss of consciousness is associated with a two-fold increased risk of developing Alzheimer's.

●**How much does family history matter?** Up to 15% of Alzheimer's cases have a clear hereditary basis. Most of these involve a particular version of a gene called *ApoE*. For people with this form of the gene, the lifetime risk of developing Alzheimer's is 29%. For the general population, the risk is 15%.

Having this specific version of the gene does *not* guarantee that you'll get Alzheimer's…and not having it doesn't ensure that you won't get it. That's why I don't recommend genetic testing for Alzheimer's. It won't tell you anything certain and might cause needless anxiety.

Genetic testing *can* be useful to help confirm a diagnosis of Alzheimer's after an individual begins to show symptoms of dementia.

●**How effective are the medications used to treat Alzheimer's?** The FDA has approved *tacrine* (Cognex) and *donepezil* (Aricept). These prescription drugs work by preventing the breakdown of acetylcholine, a neurotransmitter essential for nerve signaling.

Both drugs lead to slight improvement on tests of memory and language in the early stages of Alzheimer's.

Donepezil, the newer of the two drugs, is taken once a day and has few side effects. Tacrine can cause vomiting and liver damage and must be taken three times a day.

●**Do any alternative treatments work against Alzheimer's?** In one recent study, Alzheimer's patients who took high doses of vitamin E or the prescription antioxidant drug *selegiline* (Eldepryl) stayed out of nursing homes longer. This suggests that the antioxidants may have delayed the disease's progression by mopping up cell-damaging "free radicals."

Unfortunately, the study didn't measure the patients' cognitive function, so we don't really know what impact vitamin E had. It may or may not be effective, but at low dosages of 200 to 400 international units (IU) a day, it probably won't hurt.

Some studies also suggest that *ginkgo biloba* boosts memory in patients with Alzheimer's and other forms of dementia. It does not work as well as donepezil or tacrine, but it might be an alternative for people who can't tolerate even donepezil's minimal side effects.

Ginkgo can interact with other medications, so check with a doctor before taking it.

● **What's the outlook for future Alzheimer's treatments?** The most promising research involves *amyloid*. That's the protein that forms abnormal deposits in the brains of Alzheimer's patients. One line of research aims to find medicines that halt production of amyloid. Researchers also hope to create a vaccine that would prevent amyloid deposition. But such a vaccine probably won't be available for at least a decade.

Alzheimer's Care Basics

Establish a daily routine for the person suffering from Alzheimer's...remove items that might encourage the person to wander, such as a coat rack near the door...have the person wear an ID bracelet in case he/she does leave home unattended...plan at least one regular daily outing, such as a walk or trip to the grocery store...reduce clutter so that misplaced items can be more easily found...respond to agitation by distracting and reassuring rather than arguing or correcting the person...make others a part of the regular care routine.

Rebecca Logsdon, PhD, clinical psychologist, University of Washington, Seattle.

 Parkinson's Hope

New Parkinson's drug quells the characteristic tremors and muscle rigidity with few side effects. In a recent study, *ropinirole* (Requip) was just as effective at relieving symptoms as *L-dopa* (Sinemet). That's been the main drug used to treat Parkinson's for more than a decade. Only 20% of the ropinirole group developed sudden, involuntary twisting motions (dyskinesia) compared with 46% of the L-dopa group.

Carl Clarke, MD, associate professor of neurology, University of Birmingham, Birmingham, England. His study of 268 Parkinson's patients was presented at an International Congress on Parkinson's Disease in Vancouver.

Staying Healthy Despite Diabetes

Peter Lodewick, MD, medical director of the Diabetes Care Center in Birmingham, AL. A diabetic himself, Dr. Lodewick is author of *A Diabetic Doctor Looks at Diabetes—His and Yours*. Lowell House.

Have you developed diabetes without realizing it? If so, you've got lots of company. One in three individuals with the more common form of the disease—adult-onset, or type 2 diabetes—has never been diagnosed.*

Even more alarming, more than half of those who have been diagnosed with type 2 diabetes aren't getting adequate treatment. As a result, their blood sugar (glucose) levels remain perilously high. That places them at risk for heart disease, blindness and other complications of diabetes.

There's no excuse for this. As a diabetes specialist—and as a diabetic myself—*I've found that most cases of type 2 diabetes can be controlled if the following key steps are taken...*

● **Be on the lookout for symptoms.** In its early stages, type 2 diabetes causes only subtle symptoms—fatigue...increased thirst and/or hunger...frequent urination...weight loss...blurred or double vision...anxiety...faintness or irritability.

If you suspect you have diabetes, ask your doctor about having a blood glucose test. This in-office test checks your glucose level before and after eating. You probably have diabetes if your fasting blood sugar level exceeds 126...or if your blood sugar level after eating exceeds 200.

IF TESTING REVEALS DIABETES

● **Adopt a low-carbohydrate diet.** Just how far diabetics should cut back on carbohydrates remains a matter of debate among diabetes specialists.

The American Diabetes Association recommends a diet in which 50% to 60% of daily calories come from carbohydrates. But I've found that my diabetic patients fare much better if they limit carbohydrates to 30% of their total calories—maybe as little as 30 g a day.

*The other form of diabetes, juvenile or type 1, typically requires a lifetime of insulin injections.

229

This is especially true during the first few days of treatment, when glucose levels are still very high.

To cut back to the 30% level, you must limit your consumption of corn, rice, wheat, barley, potatoes and pasta. Fruits and fruit juices should be avoided completely. So should breads and other baked goods, including bagels, pancakes and waffles...sugary drinks and candy...and milk, yogurt, cottage cheese and dairy substitutes.

You can eat liberal amounts of fowl, fish, meat, cheese, eggs, green vegetables (including broccoli, asparagus, spinach and brussels sprouts), cabbage, avocado, mushrooms, sauerkraut, zucchini, yellow squash, peppers, almonds, walnuts, tea and coffee.

Caution: A very-low-carbohydrate diet should be undertaken only with a doctor's help. The doctor should carefully monitor your cholesterol and triglyceride levels and your kidney function until cholesterol and blood sugar levels are acceptable.

•**Get aerobic exercise every day.** Walking, bicycling, swimming or jogging—or doing some other form of aerobic exercise—for at least 30 minutes a day is even more important for diabetics than for nondiabetics.

A recent study of 70,000 nurses published in *The Journal of the American Medical Association* found that those who exercised aerobically for 30 minutes a day had a 41% reduction in risk for diabetes.

•**Be vigilant about blood sugar testing.** During the initial stages of diabetes treatment—when glucose levels are still fluctuating—I recommend doing a finger-stick blood test just before and two hours after your morning and evening meals. That's a total of four times a day.

Even more frequent testing may be helpful if blood sugar levels are not optimal.

Your blood sugar should fall between 70 and 100 before eating...and below 150 two hours after eating.

Once your blood sugar has stabilized, ask your doctor about cutting back on testing.

•**Get a hemoglobin A-1C test every three months.** This $30 test, performed in your doctor's office, lets you know your average blood sugar over the previous three months. We now know that average glucose levels are much more significant than any single spot reading.

Ideally, hemoglobin A-1C should be 6.2% or lower.

•**Take antioxidant supplements.** Tissues exposed to high glucose levels undergo oxidation, a process in which free radicals are formed. Free radicals can damage cells, nerves and blood vessels.

To minimize oxidation, take a daily multivitamin supplement such as *Alpha Betic* along with five additional supplements...

- •Alpha lipoic acid . . . . . .200 mg divided into two 100-mg doses
- •Chromium . . . . .200 mcg
- •Folic acid . . . . .400 mcg
- •Vitamin C . . . . .500 mg
- •Vitamin E . . . . .400 international units (IU)

•**Take oral diabetes medication if necessary.** Few people with type 2 diabetes need insulin injections, but some do require oral diabetes medication.

If your blood sugar level remains high after several weeks on a low-carbohydrate diet, your doctor should prescribe one or more hypoglycemic agents.

Examples: Glyburide (DiaBeta)...*metformin* (Glucophage)...*pioglitazone* (Actos)...and *repaglinide* (Prandin).

New diabetes medications are being introduced every few months. Discuss with your doctor which medication is right for you.

Drinking and Diabetes

Moderate drinking is beneficial for people with diabetes. Diabetics who routinely had one or more drinks a day had one-fifth the risk of dying from heart disease than that faced by nondrinking diabetics, a study found. *However:* This finding does *not* necessarily mean that all diabetics who don't drink should start. Nor does it mean that those who already drink should drink more. But if you have diabetes, ask your doctor about the potential benefits of moderate drinking.

Ronald Klein, MD, MPH, professor of ophthalmology and visual sciences, University of Wisconsin, Madison, Medical School. His study of 983 diabetics was published in *The Journal of the American Medical Association*, 515 N. State St., Chicago 60610.

If Lyme Disease Just Won't Go Away…There Are Things to Do

Joseph J. Burrascano, Jr., MD, an internist in East Hampton, New York. He has treated Lyme disease patients and conducted research on the illness for more than 15 years.

Lyme disease is the most common tick-borne illness in the US, infecting about two million Americans in the past 20 years.

No one knows the exact number of Lyme cases because the usual blood test used to diagnose it is unreliable.

While most medical authorities question the notion of chronic Lyme disease and its treatment with repeated courses of antibiotics, some doctors do believe it. They believe that up to half of all Lyme patients still have symptoms after they undergo the standard treatment—a one- to two-month course of antibiotics. Of those, 20% are believed to suffer from chronic Lyme disease (post-Lyme syndrome).

One prominent proponent of this theory, Joseph J. Burrascano, Jr., MD, has treated more than 7,000 Lyme patients. *His advice:*

•**See a specialist.** While an internist or family practitioner can treat you, a select group of physicians—primarily in the Northeast, where the disease is prevalent—specializes in Lyme disease care.

To find a specialist, contact the Lyme Disease Foundation referral program (*www.lyme.org* or 800-886-LYME).

Lyme specialists are more likely to know about the latest in treatments, medications and clinical trials.

•**Keep a daily diary of your symptoms and treatment.** This will help your doctor identify the most effective therapies.

Track any pain, confusion or other symptoms. Also note what you were doing when the symptoms occurred.

This helps to rule out other conditions, such as neurological disease, arthritis and depression.

•**Get tested for other tick-borne diseases.** Like Lyme, ehrlichiosis, babesiosis and bartonella cause chills, high fever, headache and fatigue.

When Lyme is combined with another tick-borne illness, symptoms include sudden severe headache…drenching sweats…and high fever (above 101°F).

Of 100 ticks recently collected in Hunterdon County, New Jersey, 43 carried Lyme…17 carried ehrlichiosis…and five carried babesiosis. Ten ticks carried two of the three diseases.

Antibiotics that help relieve Lyme disease symptoms do not fight babesiosis.

•**Ask your doctor about other antibiotics.** There is no universally effective antibiotic for treating Lyme. The choice of drug depends on many factors, such as age…body size…and how long you've had the disease.

•**Have a polymerase chain reaction (PCR) test after each round of antibiotic treatment.** This $100 blood test detects the DNA of the Lyme bacterium.

You may need to repeat the test because the Lyme bacterium, though present in your body, may not appear in each blood sample.

A negative test result doesn't prove that the disease has disappeared. A positive result means that it still exists.

•**Adjust your lifestyle.** Stop smoking… avoid alcohol and caffeine…get enough rest… avoid stress, which weakens immunity.

•**Eat right.** That means low-fat, low-carbohydrate foods.

Each day, eat eight ounces of yogurt containing active cultures. Or take two acidophilus capsules after each meal to control the overgrowth of yeast that antibiotic treatment can cause.

•**Exercise.** If you're sick with Lyme disease, you may be spending too much time in bed. This can leave you stiff and weak.

Work with a professional trainer to develop a program that stretches and tones your muscles.

Avoid aerobic exercise until you have recovered. High-intensity exercise actually weakens immune function. Your doctor can recommend a physical therapist or exercise physiologist.

●**Ask your doctor about helpful herbs and supplements.** In addition to a multivitamin/mineral, consider taking…

● *Cordyceps.* This herb from Tibet has been shown to improve stamina, enhance lung function and reduce fatigue.

● *Essential fatty acids (EFAs).* Derived from plant and fish oils, EFAs curb achiness, depression, fatigue, memory loss and poor concentration.

Take four plant oil capsules (borage oil, evening primrose oil or black currant seed oil) and four fish oil (omega-3) capsules a day.

Caution: See your doctor before taking plant or fish oil if you already take a blood thinner. The combination can cause bleeding.

● *Coenzyme Q10.* Lyme patients may be deficient in this naturally occurring compound (also known as *ubiquinone*). Take 200 mg to 300 mg daily of a standardized brand.

Warning: Do not take coenzyme Q10 if you take *atovaquone* (Mepron). This antibiotic may negate the effect of coenzyme Q10.

● *Vitamin B complex.* Supplemental B vitamins help relieve neuropathy, poor memory and mood disorders. Take one 50-mg B-complex capsule every day.

● *Magnesium.* Lyme patients may be deficient in this mineral, which eases headaches, tremors, twitches, cramps, sore muscles and irregular heartbeat. The best source is magnesium L-lactate dihydrate. Take 168 mg every 12 hours.

●**Treat symptoms even if you can't cure the disease.**

● *Depression.* Nearly 75% of Lyme patients are depressed. Ask your doctor about antidepressants and psychotherapy.

● *Fibromyalgia.* This related disorder causes stiff, sore muscles. Ask your doctor about anti-inflammatories, such as ibuprofen (Motrin), and low-dose tricyclic antidepressants, which restore sleep patterns and relieve muscle pain.

New Treatment for Multiple Sclerosis

Severe attacks of multiple sclerosis (MS) and similar neurological disorders that fail to respond to the usual treatment may be eased by treatment with plasma exchange. In a recent study, half of MS patients who underwent this new therapy regained their ability to move their limbs and speak. During plasma exchange, the fluid portion of blood is replaced with a synthetic substitute. Seven two-hour treatments are given over a two-week period. Plasma exchange is *not* a cure for MS.

Brian G. Weinshenker, MD, consultant, department of neurology, Mayo Clinic, Rochester, MN. His study of 22 MS patients was published in *Annals of Neurology,* 5841 Cedar Lake Rd., Suite 204, Minneapolis 55416.

Up to 70% of Cancers Can Be Avoided

Melanie Polk, MMSc, RD, director of nutrition education, American Institute for Cancer Research, 1759 R St. NW, Washington, DC 20009.

People often assume that cancer is out of their hands because it is "genetic." In fact, lifestyle decisions are much more important in determining who gets cancer—and who doesn't.

Even if your genes place you at risk for cancer, 60% to 70% of all malignancies can be avoided by paying attention to four lifestyle factors—diet, weight control, physical activity and not smoking.

IF YOU MAKE JUST ONE CHANGE

Eating a plant-based diet is the single most important thing you can do to lower your cancer risk.

Foods should be minimally processed and as close to their natural state as possible. Processed foods may have lost some of their nutritional value.

Example: Eat a potato rather than potato chips.

Also limit intake of foods with added sugar, such as soft drinks and sweetened cereals.

If you eat red meat, have no more than three ounces per day.

Eating at least five servings—about one-half cup each—of fruits or vegetables every day can decrease your risk of cancer by 20%.

OTHER IMPORTANT STEPS

• **Maintain a healthful weight, and be physically active.** Try not to gain too much weight after reaching your full height (at about age 18 for women…24 for men).

Start by walking every day—working your way up to a brisk, one-hour walk daily. In addition, work up a sweat by engaging in some form of vigorous physical activity for at least one hour each week.

• **Drink alcohol in moderation—if at all.** There is no evidence that alcohol reduces cancer risk, though some evidence suggests that moderate alcohol consumption helps prevent coronary artery disease in men and possibly women. If you do drink, limit your consumption to one drink a day for women…two drinks a day for men.

Avoid alcohol entirely if you are a woman with an increased risk of breast cancer.

• **Select foods that are low in fat and salt.** Limit your intake of fatty foods. Use a moderate amount of monounsaturated oils, such as olive and canola.

Avoid animal fat and hydrogenated fat, which are commonly found in shortening, margarine and bakery items.

Watch those snack foods, salty condiments and pickles.

• **Prepare and store foods safely.** Keep cold foods cold and hot foods hot.

If you eat meat, avoid charring it. Limit cured or smoked meat. Take precautions when grilling —trim fat from meat, marinate it, microwave it for half the cooking time before grilling.

• **Avoid tobacco in any form.**

CANCER RISK FACTORS

Anticancer precautions are particularly important for individuals at increased risk for cancer.

These risk factors include*…

• **Family history of genetically linked cancers,** such as breast, ovarian and colon cancers.

• **Inflammatory bowel disease.**

• **Human papillomavirus (HPV) infection.**

• **Alcoholism.**

• **Hepatitis B or C virus (HBV/HCV).**

Additional risk factors for women…

• **First menstrual period before the age of 12.**

• **First child born after age 30.**

• **Childless and over age 50.**

• **Postmenopausal and on hormone-replacement therapy.**

*This information is based on a major study by the American Institute for Cancer Research that reviewed more than 4,500 studies to determine the relationships among diet, lifestyle and cancer risk.

Colon Cancer Prevention Secrets

Samuel Meyers, MD, clinical professor of medicine at Mount Sinai School of Medicine in New York. He is coauthor of the medical textbook *Bockus Gastroenterology*. W.B. Saunders.

Colon cancer is diagnosed in 130,000 Americans each year…and 50,000 die of the disease. That makes colon cancer second only to lung cancer as the leading cause of cancer deaths in this country.

These statistics are doubly tragic because colon cancer can almost always be prevented.

Tumors in the colon—and rectum—usually begin as tiny mushroom-shaped growths. Most of these *polyps* are harmless, but a small percentage turn cancerous.

The progression from benign polyp to cancerous tumor takes at least five years. That's ample time for detecting and removing any polyps before they threaten your health.

If cancer cells are detected in the colon, removal of the polyps is curative in 92% of all cases.

Unfortunately, only one in four Americans undergoes the periodic screenings necessary to check the colon for growths.

Not smoking and getting regular aerobic exercise help cut your risk. *Here's what else you can do to prevent colon cancer...*

• **Have periodic colonoscopies.** Colonoscopy is an outpatient procedure in which a long, flexible viewing tube inserted through the rectum is used to examine the entire length of the large intestine. If polyps or tumors are detected, they often can be removed on the spot—the colonoscope doubles as a cutting tool.

People are understandably reluctant to undergo colonoscopy. If you are properly sedated, however, you should not feel any discomfort.

There is a small risk of complications—about one in 1,000. The most common complication is a perforated intestine, which requires immediate surgery.

The test is extremely accurate. When you have periodic colonoscopies, there's no need for sigmoidoscopy, barium enema or any of the other tests often recommended by doctors.

If you're in good health and have no family history of colon cancer, ask your doctor about having a colonoscopy once every 10 years, starting at age 50.

If you have a family history of colon cancer, have your first colonoscopy no later than age 40...and perhaps even earlier.

The starting age—and the frequency of exams—depends on how many of your first-degree relatives had colon cancer...and the age when it was diagnosed. A first-degree relative is a parent, sibling or child. Ask your doctor which schedule is right for you.

An experimental technique called *virtual colonoscopy* uses X rays and computer technology to create a 3-D view of the colon's interior. Less invasive, virtual colonoscopy is a bit like having a computed tomography (CT) scan.

Virtual colonoscopy should be available within the next few years. Whether it will prove as accurate as the real thing remains to be seen.

• **Consume at least 25 g of dietary fiber a day.** Fiber binds to special digestive juices known as *bile acids* in the intestine and carries them out of the body in the stool.

This is critical, because the interaction of bile acids with intestinal bacteria releases carcinogenic by-products.

It's fine to boost your fiber intake with fiber supplements such as Metamucil. But research suggests that it's more effective to have at least five servings a day of fruits, vegetables, beans, peas and whole grains.

Unlike fiber supplements, these food sources of fiber contain vitamins and minerals that reduce your risk for cancer.

Examples: Yellow, orange and dark-green vegetables and fruit are rich in vitamins A and C. Peppers, squash, broccoli and cauliflower are rich in vitamin E, folic acid and selenium.

Colon cancer occurs much less often in parts of the world where people eat lots of plant-based foods. Fiber is found only in plant foods.

• **Eat less fat.** Fiber gets most of the attention, but cutting back on dietary fat may be even more critical for preventing colon cancer. That's because bile acids are produced largely in response to the presence of fat in the small intestine.

Reducing fat consumption to 20% of total calories is ideal. If that level is unrealistic for you, keep your fat intake under 30% of total calories. That means roughly 45 g of fat a day.

Cutting back on or eliminating red meat, butter and snack foods—and switching to non-fat dairy foods—is often enough to lower fat to the right level.

• **Don't eat charred meats.** When animal fat is exposed to barbecuing with charcoal or to a direct flame in the broiler, carcinogens similar to those in tobacco are created.

Self-defense: When broiling or grilling, don't let the flames touch the meat. Avoid grilling with charcoal.

• **Eat fish three times a week.** Fish contains fatty acids that the body uses to reduce the potency of *prostaglandins* and other tumor-promoting chemicals in the body. Salmon and mackerel have the most fatty acids.

People who don't like the taste of fish sometimes take fish oil supplements. There isn't enough research to show they work, however, and they can give perspiration a fishy odor. Eating fish is better.

• **Get 1,000 to 1,500 mg of calcium a day.** Three servings of low-fat milk or other dairy foods supply about 1,000 mg. Calcium fights colon cancer by preventing rapid growth of cells in the colon.

Helpful: Antacids such as Tums contain more than 500 mg of calcium per tablet. They're a less costly source of calcium than calcium supplements. Use the sugar-free kind.

•**Ask your doctor about taking aspirin.** Aspirin, *ibuprofen* (Motrin) and other non-steroidal anti-inflammatory drugs (NSAIDs) seem to help keep polyps from forming by inhibiting prostaglandin production.

These drugs seem to have a cancer-inhibiting effect when taken over the course of many years—even at low dosages.

Caution: Regular use of NSAIDs can cause ulcers and other problems, especially in people with a history of gastrointestinal bleeding and those over age 65. NSAID therapy should be implemented only with your doctor's okay.

Beating Pancreatic Cancer

Ordinarily one of the fastest-growing malignancies, pancreatic cancer can be slowed dramatically. In a pilot study, pancreatic cancer patients lived an average of three times longer than would otherwise have been expected when they ate a vegetarian diet...took vitamin, mineral and pancreatic-enzyme supplements...and had twice-daily coffee enemas, which are thought to clear the body of metabolic wastes. In light of these impressive results, the National Cancer Institute has funded a new, larger trial to study the regimen. *More information:* 800-4-CANCER.

Nicholas J. Gonzalez, MD, an immunologist in private practice in New York. His study of 11 pancreatic cancer patients was published in *Nutrition and Cancer,* 12433 Galesville Dr., Gaithersburg, MD 20878.

Lung Cancer Treatment

Certain lung cancer patients in remission live longer when they receive radiation therapy to the brain. *Background:* Treatment for lung cancer has improved, decreasing the risk for recurrence in the lung. Ironically, this good news means that a spread (metastasis) of lung cancer to the brain has become one of the main types of relapse. In a recent study of 987 patients whose small-cell lung cancer was in remission, "prophylactic cranial irradiation" cut the death rate 16% by reducing the risk that the cancer would later spread to the brain.

Jean-Pierre Pignon, MD, PhD, senior statistician, department of biostatistics and epidemiology, Institut Gustave-Roussy, Villejuif, France. His study was published in *The New England Journal of Medicine,* 10 Shattuck St., Boston 02115.

Drinking More Water Reduces Risk Of Bladder Cancer

A 10-year study of almost 48,000 men found that those who drank six glasses of water a day had only half the chance of developing bladder cancer as those who drank only one glass...and those who drank 10 glasses of fluids (including water) had an even lower risk.

Dominique Michaud, ScD, is a research fellow at the Harvard School of Public Health in Boston.

Better Bladder Cancer Therapy

Conventional surgery for bladder cancer that invades surrounding muscle tissue calls for removing the entire bladder along with the tumor. Without a bladder, patients who undergo this treatment must—for the rest of their lives—use an uncomfortable and inefficient urine-collection bag.

Now: An experimental treatment spares the bladder. The surgeon simply cuts out the tumor using instruments attached to a slender fiber-optic scope that's passed through the urethra. The operation is followed by chemotherapy and radiation.

235

Outlook: Half of patients who underwent this procedure were still alive after four years with no signs of the cancer spreading. That's the same cure rate as obtained via the old method.

Donald S. Kaufman, MD, associate clinical professor of medicine, Harvard University Medical School, and oncologist, Massachusetts General Hospital, Boston. His study of 53 bladder cancer patients was published in *The New England Journal of Medicine*, 10 Shattuck St., Boston 02115.

Cancer Pain Problem

One-fourth of all cancer patients fail to get adequate pain relief.

Reason: They assume that pain is inevitable …they don't complain because they want to be "good" patients…they fear addiction…and they are afraid that pain management will distract the doctor from treating the disease.

Reality: Pain management is an integral part of cancer treatment. Patients should not hesitate to communicate their needs.

Jamie H. Von Roenn, MD, associate professor of medicine, section of medical oncology, Northwestern University Medical School, Chicago. Her survey of 897 cancer doctors was published in *Annals of Internal Medicine*, Independence Mall West, Sixth Street at Race, Philadelphia 19106.

Good News About Irritable Bowel Syndrome

Gerard Guillory, MD, clinical professor of medicine at the University of Colorado Health Sciences Center in Denver and an internist in private practice in Aurora, Colorado. He is author of *IBS: A Doctor's Plan for Chronic Digestive Troubles*. Hartley & Marks. He maintains the Web site *www.ibsinformation.com*.

Thirty million Americans have irritable bowel syndrome (IBS). The condition is characterized by bloating…abdominal pain…urgent need to defecate…mucus in the stool…and episodes of diarrhea or constipation —or alternating bouts of both.

Only a few years ago, IBS sufferers awaiting diagnosis endured months of fear as doctors first ruled out other conditions like cancer and Crohn's disease.

When these patients finally got their diagnosis, all too often doctors told them that the ailment was "all in their head"—due simply to stress or emotional problems.

Today, IBS is usually diagnosed after just one doctor's visit. Patients have more treatment options…and no longer have to endure put-downs from skeptical doctors.

DIAGNOSING IBS

IBS experts now agree on a set of criteria to diagnose the condition without first excluding many other possibilities. *These criteria include…*

●**Presence of abdominal pain** and at least two of the following symptoms for at least 12 weeks in the preceding year…

●Unusually frequent or sporadic defecation during periods of abdominal pain.

●Unusually hard—or soft—stools during periods of abdominal pain.

●Relief of abdominal pain with defecation.

●**Absence of the following: Fever, weight loss, abdominal pain at night, blood in the stool or anemia.** These signs and symptoms are suggestive of another diagnosis, such as colon cancer or Crohn's disease.

WHAT CAUSES IBS?

Recent research shows that certain nerves in the colons of IBS sufferers are overreactive. These are the nerves that control sensation (what is felt in the colon) and motility (how colon muscles move).

Result: Mild stimuli that would not bother most people cause the colon to spasm. These stimuli include the pressure of intestinal gas…colon contractions triggered by eating *(peristalsis)*…and psychological stress.

GETTING RELIEF

Self-help strategies can be remarkably effective in easing IBS symptoms…

●**Prevent excess gas.** People with IBS are intolerant of even normal amounts of intestinal gas. *To minimize it….*

●Avoid gum and candy. They stimulate salivation, which increases the number of swallows.

With each swallow, a little air goes into the intestine.

- Eat slowly. Quick eaters gulp their food... and swallow more air.

- Avoid carbonated drinks.

•Avoid trigger foods. IBS symptoms often occur after consumption of sugary and/or fatty foods. Undigested sugar ferments in the colon, causing more gas. Fat causes the body to release *cholecystokinin,* a hormone that stimulates colon contractions.

Other common food triggers are caffeine, nicotine and alcohol. *Monosodium glutamate* (MSG) and *aspartame* (NutraSweet) can also trigger IBS symptoms.

Sources of MSG include commercially prepared soups, bouillon, low-fat salad dressings and most restaurant foods.

Products that contain aspartame or MSG must say so on the labels.

To identify triggers: Keep a "look-back" diary. After every IBS attack, jot down a list of all the foods you consumed in the previous 12 hours. You should spot patterns that point to foods you should avoid.

•Get more fiber. Fiber helps IBS sufferers who are constipated or whose constipation alternates with diarrhea. It's not helpful for diarrhea-predominant IBS.

Gradually add fiber-rich foods such as fruits, vegetables and whole grains to your diet. Add foods one at a time to make sure they're not trigger foods.

Another option: Use psyllium seed supplements such as Konsyl or synthetic fiber supplements such as FiberCon. Take them at mealtime so they mix with foods. This produces a soft stool that is easy to pass. Avoid supplements that contain sugar or aspartame.

•Reduce stress. Eliminate as many stressors as you can...and increase your use of stress-reduction techniques. Good ones include exercise and yoga.

MEDICATION

If self-help strategies fail to alleviate symptoms, medications may help.

Historically, doctors have treated IBS using muscle relaxants, laxatives, antidiarrhea drugs and antidepressants.

A new generation of drugs block serotonin, a neurotransmitter that stimulates supersensitive nerves in the colon.

Unfortunately, *alosetron* (Lotronex) was recently pulled from the market due to side effects.

Treatment for Ulcerative Colitis

Ulcerative colitis that fails to respond to steroids may respond to cyclosporine, a drug long used to prevent organ rejection.

Study: Nine of 11 patients taking the drug had relief from bloody diarrhea and other symptoms—within a week. The drug was so effective that researchers cut the study short—they felt it would be unethical not to treat those subjects taking placebos.

Payoff: Cyclosporine therapy may eliminate the need for intestinal surgery.

Simon Lichtiger, MD, assistant professor of medicine, Mount Sinai School of Medicine, New York.

What You Should Know About Hepatitis A, B...and C

Suzanne Cotter, MD, epidemiologist in the Hepatitis Branch of Centers for Disease Control and Prevention in Atlanta. For more information on hepatitis, go to *www. cdc.gov/ncidod/diseases/hepatitis.*

Millions of Americans are infected with hepatitis, a highly contagious inflammation of the liver...yet many don't know it.

Symptoms of the three most common forms—A, B and C—are the same. They include vomiting...fever...abdominal pain...lethargy...loss of appetite...yellow eyes and skin...and dark-yellow urine.

However, many people with hepatitis don't experience any symptoms.

A vs. B vs. C

- **Hepatitis A is transmitted primarily by the fecal-oral route** by either person-to-person contact or ingesting contaminated food or water. The only treatment is bed rest and a healthful diet. Symptoms may last up to two months.

- **Hepatitis B is transmitted through blood or body fluids via sexual contact** ...contact with contaminated equipment (such as syringes)...and from mother to child during delivery (perinatal transmission). Symptoms usually last up to two months. Ten percent of infected adults may become virus carriers, meaning they can infect others and can have chronically inflamed livers. There are antiviral drug treatments available (such as *lamivudine*) for chronic carriers.

- **Hepatitis C is transmitted predominantly via blood**—through cuts or needle sticks...via sexual contact...and from perinatal transmission. Combination antiviral drug therapy with interferon and ribavarin is sometimes effective.

Up to 70% of infected people develop chronic hepatitis, making them vulnerable to cirrhosis (scarring of the liver) and liver cancer or liver failure. Then the only cure is a liver transplant.

At greatest risk: People who had blood transfusions before 1992...intravenous drug users (even those who experimented just once)...hemodialysis patients before 1992...organ transplant recipients...infants born to infected mothers.

PREVENTING HEPATITIS

Vaccines are available for hepatitis A and B. Speak with your doctor about whether the vaccine or screening is appropriate for you. There is no vaccine for C. *Other self-defense strategies...*

- **Wash your hands after going to the bathroom and changing diapers.**

- **Follow precautions for safe food preparation.**

- **Bandage cuts and wounds.**

- **Practice safe sex.**

- **Don't share personal-care products,** such as razors, toothbrushes, toothpaste tubes, nail clippers, etc.

Syndrome X—The Little-Known Cause of Many Heart Attacks

Gerald M. Reaven, MD, professor of medicine at Stanford University School of Medicine in Stanford, CA. He is coauthor of *Syndrome X: Overcoming the Silent Killer That Can Give You a Heart Attack.* Simon & Schuster.

It's well known that a high cholesterol level—especially a high level of LDL (bad) cholesterol—is a major risk factor for heart attack. Now, another risk factor is finally getting the attention it deserves as a major contributor to heart disease. That factor is insulin resistance.

Insulin—produced by the pancreas—is the hormone that ushers blood sugar (glucose) into cells. Cells can become resistant to insulin's action. When they do, the pancreas pumps out more insulin in an attempt to "force" sugar into the cells.

Excess insulin directly damages coronary arteries. It also triggers an array of metabolic abnormalities that contribute to the development of artery-clogging fatty plaques and to blood clots.

The constellation of abnormalities, which affects 70 million Americans, is called "syndrome X." *It includes...*

- **Excess fibrinogen,** a substance that promotes blood clots.

- **Excess plasminogen activator inhibitor-1 (PAI-1),** a substance that slows clot breakdown.

- **High levels of triglycerides,** the body's main fat-storage particles.

- **Low levels of HDL (good) cholesterol,** which sweeps fat out of arteries.

Many people with syndrome X also have high blood pressure. And they're likely to have glucose intolerance—a condition characterized by slightly elevated blood sugar levels.

Important: Glucose intolerance is not diabetes. But up to 5% of people with syndrome X go on to develop type-2 diabetes annually. That's the form that occurs later in life among people, typically overweight, who become increasingly insensitive to the effects of insulin.

DIAGNOSING SYNDROME X

The results of five simple tests point to a diagnosis of syndrome X. Risk for heart attack rises with each out-of-bounds test score.

- **Fasting triglyceride level in excess of 200 milligrams per deciliter (mg/dl).**
- **Fasting HDL cholesterol level under 35 mg/dl.**
- **Blood pressure higher than 145/90.**
- **Being overweight by 15 pounds or more.**
- **Fasting blood sugar level higher than 110 mg/dl**…or a level higher than 140 two hours after drinking a glucose solution.

FIGHTING SYNDROME X

- **Eat the right diet.** Americans are besieged by a glut of high-concept diets, all of them purporting to be best for weight loss and health.

The American Heart Association diet counsels cutting down on fat and boosting consumption of carbohydrates. *The Zone* diet advises boosting protein intake and lowering fat.

These diets may work for people who don't have syndrome X. But protein and carbohydrates stimulate insulin production—which is a dangerous outcome for people with the syndrome.

The Atkins diet counsels consumption of low levels of carbohydrates and as much fat as desired. But that diet is too high in artery-clogging saturated fat.

The ideal diet to combat syndrome X supplies 45% of calories from carbohydrates…15% from protein…and 40% from fat.

Key: Emphasize beneficial mono- and polyunsaturated fats. These should supply 30% to 35% of the diet. Only 5% to 10% should come from saturated fats.

Good sources of healthful fats include avocados…fatty fish (such as sea bass, trout, sole and salmon)…natural peanut butter…nuts and seeds…canola, corn, olive, safflower, peanut, soybean, sesame and sunflower oils.

- **Lose weight.** Shedding pounds improves insulin resistance. *Recent study:* Insulin resistance fell an average of 40% in overweight individuals who lost 20 pounds.
- **Exercise.** People who exercise daily use insulin 25% more efficiently than those who do not exercise. Forty-five minutes of aerobic exercise a day is ideal.
- **Stop smoking.** Smoking promotes insulin resistance.

MEDICATION

If lifestyle changes alone don't overcome syndrome X, medication can help…

- **Triglyceride-lowering medication.** Three drugs can lower triglyceride levels. They also lower PAI-1 levels and raise HDL cholesterol.

One of them—nicotinic acid—has the added benefit of lowering LDL cholesterol. A common side effect of nicotinic acid is facial flushing.

Self-defense: To minimize flushing from nicotinic acid, increase the dose gradually.

Two other effective drugs are *gemfibrozil* (Lopid) and *fenofibrate* (Tricor). In rare cases, however, they can cause liver damage.

Self-defense: Talk to your doctor about testing liver function periodically.

- **Blood pressure medication.** Fifty percent of people with high blood pressure have syndrome X. But some blood pressure drugs can worsen the condition.

Talk to your doctor about the potential risks of high-dose diuretics and beta-blockers if you have syndrome X.

Because syndrome X is caused by insulin resistance, it's logical to ask whether *thiazolidinediones*—drugs that increase insulin sensitivity—might be helpful.

Such drugs are currently used to treat type-2 diabetes.

Ongoing research will determine if thiazolidinediones improve syndrome X. Until the studies are completed, these drugs should *not* be used to treat the condition.

About Defibrillators

People with implanted defibrillators are less likely to die suddenly from cardiac arrest than those who rely on anti-arrythmia drugs. In a study of more than 700 cardiac patients with dangerous heart arrythmias, those treated with drugs were four times as likely to die suddenly from cardiac arrest as those with a defibrillator. In fact, drug treatment produced no better results than doing nothing. Researchers suggest that a defibrillator be used for cardiac patients with arrythmias reproducible during electrophysiological testing.

Alfred E. Buxton, MD, professor of medicine, Brown University Medical School, Providence, RI.

New High-Tech Weapons To Help You Win the War On Heart Disease

Gary Francis, MD, director of the coronary intensive care unit at the Cleveland Clinic.

Regular exercise, low-fat eating, not smoking and other "low-tech" approaches remain the cornerstones of heart health. *But recently there have been several exciting "high-tech" advances...*

CHOLESTEROL-LOWERING DRUGS

A class of drugs known as "statins" have become the drugs of choice for people with elevated cholesterol.

These prescription medications can cut cholesterol levels up to 40% in a matter of weeks.

And—new research shows that statins can reduce the risk for heart attack even in individuals with so-called "normal" cholesterol levels.

In light of this new evidence, doctors have begun prescribing statins for most heart attack patients...as well as certain patients at high risk for heart attack. Because these drugs have side effects, be sure to discuss the pros and cons with your doctor.

BYPASS ALTERNATIVE

An experimental technique called *transmyocardial revascularization* (TMR) is a boon for people with severe coronary artery disease, who are unlikely to benefit from angioplasty or bypass surgery. It involves the use of a laser to "punch" a dozen or so small holes in the heart's muscular wall.

Some cardiologists had considered TMR a bogus, pseudoscientific procedure. But now there's compelling evidence that TMR can improve blood flow to the heart, reducing angina pain.

How does TMR work? Most cardiologists now believe that TMR works by promoting the growth of new "micro-blood vessels" in the heart muscle...or by causing death of small sensory nerve endings in the heart.

MEDICATED STENTS

Angioplasty has become one of the most common procedures for reducing the fatty deposits (plaques) that threaten to occlude coronary arteries. In this procedure, a tiny balloon is inflated inside a coronary artery, squashing the plaque deposits against the artery wall and thus opening the artery for resumed blood flow.

The problem with angioplasty is that the cleared artery often clogs up again—sometimes in a matter of months.

To prevent this phenomenon (restenosis), doctors often line the cleared arteries with metallic mesh tubes. Called stents, these tubes act as scaffolding to keep the artery from clogging again.

Unfortunately, there can be regrowth of artery-clogging tissue in the artery even after the stent has been inserted.

Doctors have found that this form of restenosis can be treated via an experimental technique in which a tiny radioactive pellet is inserted into the stent.

HEART FAILURE SURGERY

Congestive heart failure (CHF) occurs when a person's heart becomes enlarged and weak. The condition has long been treated with digitalis, diuretics and other drugs. No surgical fix was available.

In the mid-1980s, a Brazilian surgeon named Randas Batista, MD, surprised cardiologists in the US when he reported having had success treating CHF surgically.

In the Batista procedure, the heart is effectively made smaller by removing a triangular piece of the heart and then sewing the heart back together. The Batista procedure is sometimes effective at controlling breathlessness, fatigue and other symptoms of CHF. But it is now being supplanted by the Dor procedure, which may be more effective. The Dor procedure was developed by Vincent Dor, MD.

The Dor technique gets rid of scar tissue (the aftermath of a heart attack) that underlies many cases of CHF. Once this scar tissue is removed, the heart can pump efficiently again.

HEART PUMP

Another important new development for heart failure patients is left-ventricular assist devices. These fist-sized devices—implanted in the patient's chest or abdomen—take over some of the heart's pumping duties. They're typically used as a "bridge" treatment for people awaiting heart transplantation.

Most Common Times for Heart Attacks to Strike

Most heart attacks occur during the morning or late evening. In a poll of heart attack sufferers, 25% said they were awakened by heart attack symptoms in the early morning. Another 25% said their heart attacks occurred within four hours of waking...and 20% said their attacks came 11 to 12 hours later—often following a heavy supper.

Robert W. Peters, MD, chief of cardiology, Veterans Affairs Medical Center, Baltimore. His study of more than 3,000 heart attack patients was published in the *Journal of the American College of Cardiology*, 9111 Old Georgetown Rd., Bethesda, MD 20814.

Heart attack deaths peak during December and January, when there are 33% more deaths from heart attacks than in summer and early fall. *Possible reasons:* Increased food, alcohol and salt consumption...additional stress...respiratory infections...and reduced hours of daylight.

Robert Kloner, MD, PhD, professor of medicine, University of Southern California, Los Angeles, leader of a study of deaths from heart disease during a 12-year period in Los Angeles, quoted online at *www.medscape.com*.

When Chest Pain Means Heart Attack And When It Doesn't

Chest pain is psychosomatic almost half the time, according to a study.

Key: If the pain is sharp and stabbing, or it's on the left side of the chest, it's likely caused by psychological stress. But a heavy, gripping sensation in the central chest is a typical heart attack symptom, especially if it lasts five or more minutes. Consult your doctor in either case.

Dr. Christopher Bass, King's College Hospital, London.

Heart Attack Symptoms ...Gender Differences

What are considered the classic signs of a heart attack are actually the symptoms experienced by men. Unfortunately, heart attacks in women are often undiagnosed—and untreated—because the signs of heart trouble are different. It is important to know the symptoms for each gender.

FOR WOMEN

- **Chest, stomach or abdominal pain that does not necessarily feel acute or crushing.**
- **Nausea or dizziness.**
- **Shortness of breath.**
- **Heart palpitations.**
- **Fatigue.**
- **General feeling of weakness.**

FOR MEN

- **Uncomfortable pressure,** fullness, squeezing or pain in the center of the chest that lasts more than a few minutes or quickly fades in and out.
- **Pain radiating to shoulders, neck, arms or jaw.**
- **Any of the above symptoms** accompanied by lightheadedness, sweating, nausea or shortness of breath.

Important: Whether man or woman, if you are having any of the above symptoms, immediately chew a full-strength (325 mgs) aspirin and get to the hospital as soon as possible.

Lynn Smaha, MD, PhD, president, American Heart Association, Dallas.

Controlling Blood Pressure Without Medication

Sheldon G. Sheps, MD, emeritus professor of medicine at Mayo Medical School, Clinic and Foundation, Rochester, MN, and chairman of the working group that produced the NHLBI guidelines on managing high blood pressure. He is editor in chief of *Mayo Clinic on High Blood Pressure*. Mayo Foundation.

High blood pressure is a time bomb—but it's one that ticks very quietly. This "silent killer" causes no symptoms, but elevated pressure in the arteries can, over years, cause severe damage to several organs.*

This damage sets the stage for stroke, heart attack, kidney failure...and premature death.

Fifteen million Americans are unaware that they have high blood pressure (hypertension). Of the 35 million who know they have it, only two out of five are getting adequate treatment.

A generation ago, doctors tended to think of blood pressure as being "normal" or "high." Now the National Heart, Lung and Blood Institute (NHLBI) recognizes six levels of blood pressure. *Each succeeding level is associated with a higher degree of risk...*

- **Optimal**...120/80 or below.
- **Normal**...121/81 to 129/84.
- **High-normal**...130/85 to 139/89.
- **Stage 1 hypertension**...140/90 to 159/99.
- **Stage 2 hypertension**...160/100 to 179/109.
- **Stage 3 hypertension**...180/110 or higher.

If you don't know your blood pressure, have a doctor check it. *If your pressure is elevated, here's how to get it down...*

---

*Blood pressure readings are expressed as fractions—130/80, for example. The numerator (top number) represents systolic pressure—that existing in the arteries when the heart's main pumping chamber (left ventricle) contracts. The denominator (bottom number) represents diastolic pressure—that which exists between beats.

- **Follow the DASH diet.** In 1997, the Dietary Approaches to Stop Hypertension (DASH) study concluded that high-normal people and stage 1 hypertensives could achieve significant reductions in blood pressure simply by switching to a diet that stresses fruits, vegetables, grains and dairy products.

On average, study participants who followed the DASH diet lowered their blood pressure by 11 points systolic...and 5.5 points diastolic.

That was virtually the same level of reduction that is typically achieved with pressure-lowering medication—without the side effects associated with medication.

The daily DASH meal plan consists of...

- Seven or eight servings of grains, bread, cereal or pasta—preferably whole-grain varieties.
- Eight to 10 servings of fruits and vegetables.
- Two or three servings of nonfat/low-fat dairy products.
- Two or fewer servings of meat, poultry or fish.

The DASH diet also calls for four or five servings per week of beans, peas, nuts or seeds.

- **Eat less salt.** Only about 40% of people with high blood pressure are salt-sensitive, but it's hard to know who falls into this category. For this reason, everyone should limit sodium intake to 2,500 mg a day...
  - Read food labels and tally the sodium content of all the foods you eat in a typical day.
  - Cut out offending foods—such as fast food, cheese, bacon, pickles—as required.
  - Avoid salt at the dining table...and in food preparation. Flavor foods instead with red pepper, cumin, onion, dill, lemon, etc. It can take up to six weeks for your taste buds to adapt to less salt—so be patient.

- **Cut back on caffeine—and nicotine.** The caffeine in coffee, tea and soft drinks causes blood vessels to narrow for several hours, causing a transient rise in blood pressure. People with hypertension should limit their daily caffeine intake to two cups of coffee, four cups of tea or four cans of caffeinated soda.

Like caffeine, nicotine causes a transient rise in blood pressure. Smoking just two cigarettes boosts systolic *and* diastolic pressure by up to

10 points. This increase persists for up to 90 minutes.

●**Limit your drinking.** Excessive drinking—more than two drinks a day for men or one for women—is clearly a major contributor to hypertension. If your drinking exceeds these levels, cut back. Do so gradually, over a few weeks. Going "cold turkey" can cause a rapid and potentially dangerous rise in blood pressure.

●**Lose weight.** The heavier you are, the larger the network of blood vessels your body must maintain. The larger this network, the more forcefully your heart must pump. This means higher blood pressure. If you're overweight, losing even 10 pounds is often enough to lower your blood pressure one full level on the six-part scale.

●**Alleviate psychological stress.** Stress causes the body to produce hormones that constrict blood vessels, thereby raising your blood pressure. Get organized...make lists of tasks...set priorities...clean out clutter...say "no" to additional responsibilities...delegate work...try meditation and other relaxation techniques.

●**Get more physical activity.** Walking, cycling, running and other forms of aerobic exercise boost your heart's pumping efficiency. The more efficient your heart, the wider the arteries open and the less forcefully the heart must contract.

Bonus: Regular exercise helps alleviate stress and promotes weight loss—thereby augmenting its pressure-lowering effect. Aim for five to seven 30-minute workout sessions weekly.

Silent Stroke Warning Sign

Sudden depression in someone over age 50 may signal a "silent stroke."

These silent strokes occur when small blood vessels in the brain become blocked or rupture, interfering with the brain's ability to produce the mood-regulating chemicals serotonin and norepinephrine.

Silent strokes don't result in classic symptoms (severe headache, dizziness, loss of motor skills), but are often the precursor to full stroke.

Older people who show signs of sudden depression, such as apathy or loss of interest in usual activities, should be closely monitored by their doctors.

David C. Steffens, MD, assistant professor of psychiatry, Duke University Medical Center, Durham, NC.

Seven Out of 10 Stroke Patients Suffer Disability or Death

Thomas G. Brott, MD, professor of neurology at the Mayo Clinic in Jacksonville, Florida. While serving as director of the Stroke Research Center at the University of Cincinnati Medical Center, Dr. Brott helped to develop one of the most successful citywide emergency stroke treatment programs in the US. He is coauthor of a review of stroke treatment published in The New England Journal of Medicine, *10 Shattuck St., Boston 02115.*

Every 53 seconds, an American suffers a stroke. Unfortunately, one in three people does not recognize the symptoms quickly enough to benefit fully from state-of-the-art diagnostic methods and treatments.

If you—or someone you know—suffers a stroke, your response time in seeking medical treatment can mean the difference between full recovery and permanent disability or death.

CAUSES OF STROKE

Think of stroke as a "brain attack." It occurs when the flow of blood—and the oxygen it carries—to the brain is interrupted.

Result: Body functions controlled by oxygen-deprived brain cells may be weakened or lost.

In an *ischemic* stroke, the more common type, a blood clot blocks a blood vessel, usually an artery. It is typically painless but causes weakness, paralysis or loss of sensation on one side of the body...loss of vision in one eye...sudden confusion, trouble speaking or understanding...and/or staggering or inability to walk.

In a *hemorrhagic* stroke, rarer and more dangerous, a blood vessel bursts, leaking blood into the brain or surrounding area. This usually causes a severe headache…difficulty breathing …nausea…and/or vomiting.

Good news: A clot-busting medication known as *tissue plasminogen activator*—or tPA (Activase)—is effective at preventing brain damage—but only in ischemic stroke victims and only if it is administered within three hours of the onset of symptoms.

EVERY MINUTE COUNTS

If you experience or witness even one stroke symptom, call 911 immediately. Stroke victims may be unable to speak to medical personnel, but a family member or friend can help ensure proper care. *Here's how…*

An up-to-date list of all medications the patient takes is crucial for appropriate stroke treatment. Make sure such a list is in his/her wallet and/or posted on the refrigerator. That's where emergency medical technicians (EMTs) routinely look for this information.

Next best: Put the patient's medications in a paper bag and take it to the hospital.

When the ambulance arrives, ask the EMTs to take the patient to the nearest hospital that uses tPA.

Remind the EMTs to alert the hospital's emergency room (ER) that a possible stroke patient is en route. This allows the ER staff to notify the hospital's stroke team or neurologist on duty…and ask the pharmacy to be ready to do immediate (stat) blood tests.

DIAGNOSIS

In the ER, a physician should take the patient's vital signs and request a computed tomography (CT) scan or magnetic resonance imaging (MRI) scan to identify the type of stroke that has occurred, its precise location in the brain and the extent of the damage.

CT scans are routinely used, but MRI scans provide more information. CT scans are preferable if the patient is agitated, however, because MRIs require him to remain still during the procedure.

When tPA is administered intravenously for about one hour or via a catheter directly into the brain, it dissolves 60% to 80% of stroke-related blood clots.

Danger: The drug can cause life-threatening brain hemorrhage if it is used beyond the three-hour cutoff…in patients who have suffered a hemorrhagic stroke…or in people who take the blood thinner warfarin (Coumadin).

In patients who are not candidates for tPA, treatment involves controlling the heart rhythm, stabilizing blood pressure and monitoring brain function.

For all stroke patients, the doctor should also order tests that examine blood flow to the brain to determine the cause of the stroke.

Common causes of stroke: Blockage of the blood vessels in the neck or brain from hardening of the arteries…blood clots in the aorta, the artery that leads to the heart…and blockage of the small blood vessels in the brain, often related to high blood pressure.

HOSPITALIZATION

Stroke patients who have suffered a hemorrhagic stroke…received tPA…or are in serious or unstable condition are typically transferred from the ER to the intensive-care unit (ICU). Other stroke patients are admitted to a general neurological unit. Doctors then watch for medical complications. Because a stroke can affect breathing, movement and swallowing, pneumonia can develop. A blood clot in a leg vein can move to the lungs, causing a life-threatening pulmonary blood clot (embolus).

REHABILITATION

Within two days of the stroke, rehabilitation typically begins in the hospital's rehab unit. Patients work with physical, speech and occupational therapists to relearn basic skills, such as eating, dressing and walking.

Depending on the severity of the stroke, patients continue their rehabilitation at home or at an inpatient rehabilitation facility. Although some patients require long-term care in a skilled nursing facility, up to two-thirds of stroke survivors regain their independence within one year.

Important: Notify a physician if the stroke patient develops a fever of 101°F or higher. This can be a sign of infection or another serious complication.

Up to 30% of stroke patients develop depression. Signs include persistent sadness…and/or changes in sleep habits or appetite. Such patients should consult a psychiatrist or other experienced psychotherapist.

PREVENTION

Of course, the best way to minimize damage from strokes is to prevent them in the first place. *Best:*

- **Eat a diet that is low in fat.**

- **Exercise regularly.**

- **Eliminate risk factors such as being overweight and smoking.**

- **See a doctor on a routine basis for blood-pressure checks.** Seek regular treatment if you have medical risk factors, such as diabetes or heart disease.

- **Don't take oral contraceptives if you smoke.** If you live with a smoker, consult your doctor to determine whether or not contraceptives are safe for you.

- **Avoid over-the-counter diet pills.** Most contain ingredients that increase the risk of stroke.

Finally, people who have aneurysms can elect to have surgical treatment that can prevent stroke.

What happens: Blood flow to the aneurysm is prevented with the placement of a permanent metal clip at the base of the aneurysm that allows blood to flow normally through the rest of the artery.

When Stroke Treatment Is Most Effective

Treatment for stroke is most effective when administered within six hours of the onset of symptoms. Seek help immediately if you experience unexplained weakness on one side of the body…loss of vision or double vision…difficulty speaking…numbness on either side of the body…severe dizziness or loss of balance.

David Sherman, MD, professor and chief, department of medicine/neurology, University of Texas Health Science Center, San Antonio.

Dangerous New Infectious Diseases

Mohammad N. Akhter, MD, MPH, executive director of the American Public Health Association and clinical professor of family and community medicine at Georgetown University Medical School, both in Washington, DC.

Nowadays, it's very easy for people to travel to and from places that used to be too remote to visit. When people travel, infectious diseases travel with them.

From West Nile virus and Ebola virus to Marburg virus and hantavirus infection, new diseases can crop up anytime, anywhere.

We're also threatened by Lyme disease and variants of "old" diseases, such as tuberculosis. Even influenza remains a major threat. Each flu epidemic kills 20,000 to 40,000 people in the US.

HANTAVIRUS INFECTION

This potentially lethal virus is contracted through contact with feces of infected rodents. It first appeared in the southwest US in 1993 and has shown up in a dozen states since.

The people most likely to contract hantavirus include workers who enter the crawl spaces under houses…and anyone who spends time in places where they could touch or inhale rodent droppings.

Many victims say they didn't even *see* rodents or droppings.

Symptoms: Fatigue, fever and muscle aches in the beginning. Later on, coughing and shortness of breath.

Treatment: None for the hantavirus itself. But people who seek emergency care have a better chance of surviving respiratory distress—the deadliest problem associated with this infection.

Prevention: Protect yourself against rodents. Keep your kitchen clean. Whenever possible, stay out of barns and sheds. Clear away brush that could provide nesting places. If rodents are a problem in your neighborhood, alert your local public health department at once.

INFLUENZA

New flu strains emerge every year. A flu shot provides some protection—but it's not foolproof.

Symptoms: Headache, runny nose, sore throat, fever and fatigue. Serious complications, such as pneumonia, can be fatal.

Treatment: Liquids, good nutrition, bed rest and aspirin help control symptoms. Ask your doctor about the antiviral drugs that are now available for influenza—*amantadine* (Symmetrel), *rimantadine* (Flumadine), *oseltamavir* (Tamiflu) and *zanamivir* (Relenza).

Prevention: Get an annual flu shot as soon as it becomes available (typically in October).

Especially if the vaccine is in short supply—wash your hands frequently…stay in good physical shape…get adequate sleep…and eat healthfully to support your immune system.

LYME DISEASE

This tick-borne viral illness is a growing problem in the Northeast, mid-Atlantic and upper Midwest.

Symptoms: A rash that resembles a bull's-eye and swollen lymph glands near the bite. As the illness progresses, joint pain, facial palsy and fever. In the worst cases, arthritis, personality changes and memory loss may also occur.

Treatment: Oral antibiotics can usually cure Lyme disease if it has been caught early. Once the infection has progressed, intravenous antibiotics are used—but may not always be effective.

Prevention: Before going into wooded areas, use insect repellent containing DEET. Wear closed-toe shoes, a long-sleeved shirt and long pants. Choose light-colored clothing, which makes it easier to spot ticks.

Walk in the center of trails to avoid brushing against vegetation that might harbor ticks. Avoid sitting on the ground. Once a day, do a full-body "tick check."

You might also consider getting the Lyme vaccine. Lymerix appears to prevent the illness, but there have been reports of severe reactions, including arthritis.

WEST NILE VIRUS

Over the past few years, this mosquito-borne illness has caused a potentially deadly brain inflammation known as West Nile encephalitis.

Symptoms: Flu-like illness, headache, rash, neck stiffness, muscle weakness, incoherence and paralysis.

Treatment: None for the illness itself. Anyone who exhibits suspicious symptoms should seek immediate medical help.

Prevention: During warm weather, protect yourself against mosquitoes when outdoors. Apply insect repellent containing DEET. Wear long pants and a long-sleeved shirt.

Remove any standing water, where mosquitoes like to breed. Stay inside at dawn and dusk, when mosquito populations are at their highest.

17

All About Hospitals, Surgery, Medical Procedures and Tests

How to Prepare for Common Diagnostic Tests And Surgical Procedures

Each day, millions of Americans endure difficult medical procedures. From colonoscopy to biopsy to bypass surgery, these diagnostic tests and surgical procedures affect us psychologically as well as physically.

Will the procedure hurt? Are there risks? Will it put me in an embarrassing position? Even worse, we fear the outcome. Do I have cancer? Will I need surgery? Will the treatment work? Could I die?

At the crux of these anxieties lies the fear of losing control. *Here's how to regain that sense of control...*

●**Make sure you know *why* you need the test or procedure.** People who lack a clear understanding of why they need a particular procedure require more pain medication and recover more slowly than do people who undergo the procedure with all their questions answered. *Ask the doctor...*

●Why do I need this test or treatment?

●What will happen if I don't have it? If it's a diagnostic test, how will the results affect my treatment?

●What risks and side effects are associated with this procedure? How common are they?

●Are alternative procedures less invasive and/or less costly?

●How likely is a successful outcome?

Do not shy away from asking any question that occurs to you. Worried that you'll be left with an unsightly scar? That your sex life will be affected? Discuss your concerns with the doctor.

●**Find out exactly what to expect.** Videotapes that detail what you'll experience may be available through your doctor's office, hospital or diagnostic treatment center.

Bernie Siegel, MD, author of several books, including *Love, Medicine & Miracles* (HarperPerennial), and creator of *Getting Ready* (Hay House), an audiocassette that helps patients prepare for medical tests and procedures.

247

If not, contact the practitioner slated to administer the test or procedure to ask if you can stop by for a quick preview of the equipment that will be used.

This can be especially helpful if you're unusually apprehensive about the procedure.

Example: If you are afraid that a magnetic resonance imaging (MRI) scan will make you feel claustrophobic, you may be relieved to discover that newer MRI scanners are "open"—that is, during the procedure you won't have to lie in a narrow tube.

Once you've gotten all the information you need to make the decision about whether to undergo the procedure, it's *your* decision to make. After all, you are in charge of your own life.

•**Mentally rehearse the experience.** I recommend *guided imagery,* a visualization technique often used by athletes.

What to do: Sit in a comfortable chair, close your eyes and breathe deeply for a minute or so. Picture yourself undergoing the procedure one step at a time. See yourself walking into the exam room…chatting calmly with the nurse…positioning yourself. Notice that you feel relaxed, pain free and "in control."

As you see yourself completing the procedure, imagine yourself feeling energized and happy that you took the steps necessary to get your health back on track.

Use this technique four times a day for the week leading up to the procedure, and you'll have "completed" 28 successful procedures before the actual event.

In addition to giving you more confidence, this "programs" your body to experience less pain and fewer side effects.

•**Seek help from family and friends …and from other patients who have "been there, done that."** Share your concerns with those closest to you. If you'd like someone to accompany you on the day of the procedure, ask. Be sure to make it easy for the person to say "no" if he/she doesn't feel up to the task.

Many hospitals conduct support group and group therapy sessions for breast cancer patients, heart patients, etc. But if you just want to chat with someone who has had, say, a liver biopsy or thallium stress test, ask your doctor if he can put you in touch with someone.

Most people are happy to share their experiences.

•**During the test or procedure, "go" someplace else you'd rather be.** Close your eyes, breathe deeply and visualize yourself in an environment where you feel safe and relaxed.

Maybe it's lying on a beach, listening to the surf…hiking in a forest…or just sitting at home in your favorite easy chair.

Focus on *every* detail of the setting, including sights, sounds and odors. If you lose track of time, you'll forget about your fear—and may not even feel any pain.

If you have trouble being visual, consult a hypnotherapist. Ask him to help you prepare a visualization audiotape that you can listen to during the procedure.

To find a hypnotherapist in your area, contact the American Society of Clinical Hypnosis, 33 W. Grand Ave., Suite 402, Chicago 60610. 630-980-4740.

Another option: Many people find slow baroque music, such as Pachelbel's *Canon,* especially tranquilizing during a procedure. But any music you enjoy and associate with positive feelings can be beneficial.

Ask your surgeon or anesthesiologist if you may bring along your own tape player or CD player and headphones.

You might even ask about aromatherapy. Doctors at Memorial Sloan-Kettering Cancer Center in New York City reported recently that the percentage of patients who panicked during MRIs dropped dramatically once the exam room was scented with vanilla and music was played.

•**Keep smiling.** Rent a humorous videotape or buy a book of jokes to keep your spirits high in the days before and after the procedure. Laughter is a terrific antidote to tension. What's more, studies show that it alters brain chemistry, producing more of the body's natural painkillers.

How to Get VIP Treatment In a Hospital

The first thing an admitting clerk does when you're brought into a hospital is slip a plastic tag with an identity number onto your wrist. From that point on, like it or not, you are a number to most of the hospital staff.

Being a number instead of a name can be an awful shock. It means that you may be treated as if you have no identity—except for your symptoms, vital signs and medical treatment.

Fortunately, there are steps you can take to improve that treatment. And those steps, if successful, not only will make you feel more comfortable and human during your hospital visit, they could dramatically affect your state of health by the time you're ready to be discharged. In fact, it may be the issue that determines whether you leave alive or dead.

So how do you get the hospital to treat you like a person instead of a number?

In general, you've got to use the same techniques you use in other aspects of your personal and business life. The key word is assertiveness.

FINDING THE RIGHT DOCTOR

The first step in getting VIP treatment in a hospital should be taken long before you're admitted—and that's finding a doctor who can provide the leverage you'll need. You want someone with more than an MD after his name.

Every community has a clique of doctors who have "political" clout. Usually, these are physicians who serve on the local hospital's board of directors. Be aware, however, that a doctor with clout doesn't necessarily have the skills or any other attributes that make a physician a superior healer. Do you want such a person as your personal physician? Generally speaking, the answer is no, but there are exceptions. If you're satisfied that such a doctor can serve double-duty, so to speak, then you need go no further.

The drawbacks: Aside from the possibility that such a doctor may be more expert in a boardroom than an operating room, there are other potential problems.

The most serious: He may be more interested in keeping his professional calendar and the institution's beds filled than in your welfare.

If he wants to admit you to the hospital for treatment and there is any doubt in your mind about this decision, ask for a consultation with another doctor.

We've heard of many instances where doctors are annoyed when a patient wants a second opinion. If you ever face a less-than-cooperative response to such a request, seek out another doctor immediately. It's well within your rights to consult with as many physicians as you wish.

THE PERSONAL TOUCH

To guarantee better attention once you know that you're going to spend time in the hospital, make a date with the hospital administrator. Introduce yourself. Tell him that you're a little concerned about your hospital stay and that you'd appreciate it if he'd take a personal interest in your case.

He'll get the message, and in all likelihood, he'll make sure that you're well cared for. Now that you've made your presence known, he will probably, out of courtesy, call the head of nursing and the admitting office and tell them you're coming to the hospital and that they should be expecting you. It's just such words, without pressure, that may make all the difference in the way you're subsequently treated.

ONCE YOU'RE IN THE HOSPITAL

There are still things you can do to ensure good treatment, if not VIP treatment.

●**During the admission procedure, ask what rooms are available.** You may prefer a private room, or for the sake of company, you may want to share a room with someone else. If you do want to share, ask about your potential partner's medical status to be sure that you can deal with his illness.

●**After settling into your room, ask to see the dietitian.** Explain that you understand that the hospital is not a hotel, but within reasonable bounds, and limited by doctor's orders, there are foods that you do and do not like. Itemize them. If you present your request with tact, the dietitian will probably try to meet your reasonable requests.

●**Go out of your way to be polite to the nursing staff.** They are your lifeline—literally. If the nurses take a dislike to you, the recuperation period will not be smooth.

●**It's not tacky to provide small favors,** such as a box of candy, and even flowers, on each of the three nursing shifts: the 8 am to 4 pm, the 4 pm to midnight and midnight to 8 am. Don't offer a gratuity until you're ready to be discharged. Nurses are professionals, and most would resent the offer. But if you received extra special care from a nurse during your stay, a tasteful gift isn't inappropriate.

●**Make it clear that you'd like to know what medication or treatment is being given to you beforehand.** That will require a discussion with your doctor. Most doctors work on the premise that patients don't want to know too much, and so only provide information as it's necessary or if the patient specifically requests it.

Why you should want this information: Unfortunately, mistakes are made now and then, but if you ask the nurse, "What are these pills?" or, "What exactly will you be doing to me?", and she has orders from your doctor to provide that information on request, then it gives the staff the opportunity to double-check what they are doing and it gives you a chance to say, "Wait a minute!" if an obvious error is being committed.

How to complain: If you're not happy with your care, explain your complaint firmly and politely to the nurse. If that gets you no place, ask to speak to the head nurse. And if that fails, you may have to speak to either your doctor or the hospital administrator. Usually, when you reach that level, and you're not being unreasonable, steps will be taken to satisfy your complaint and resolve your problem.

Planning Pays: How to Get the Best Care in a Medical Emergency

Peter Canning, EMT-P (emergency medical technician-paramedic) in Hartford, Connecticut. He is author of *Paramedic: On the Front Lines of Medicine*. Fawcett Columbine.

If you or a loved one ever requires emergency care, here's how to get the fastest, most effective help possible…

●**Make sure your home is easy to spot.** Emergency Medical Service (EMS) personnel often waste precious time trying to locate the victim's home—especially at night, when house numbers are hard to identify.

Mark your house with large, reflective numbers and/or paint your house number on the curb with fluorescent paint. Trim any foliage that might obscure your address.

If an emergency occurs, turn on all the lights—including your porch light. If possible, ask someone to stand out front to wave down the ambulance.

●**Post your medical information in a prominent place.** EMS workers also waste time searching patients' homes for medicine bottles and other clues about their health status.

To save time: Write a brief medical history of yourself (and anyone else living in the house) on an index card. Tape the card to your refrigerator door. Be sure to include…

●Your doctor's name and telephone number.
●Medical conditions you have.
●Allergies you have.
●Names and dosages of all drugs you take.
●Name of your insurance carrier, plus your group and personal identification numbers.

●**Prepare your phones for emergency use.** If you have a chronic ailment, install a phone in every room of your house.

If your community lacks 911 service, program the phones with the local emergency number (typically the police or fire department).

●**When phoning for help,** be sure to give the right information. Be as specific as possible.

Sample script: "My husband is having chest pains and severe dizziness. He has a history of heart disease."

●**Don't delay calling for help.** People experiencing persistent chest pain or pressure sometimes tell themselves, "It's probably just indigestion. I'll wait to see if it goes away." Some wait so long that doctors cannot save them.

Especially if you're having a heart attack or stroke, the sooner you get medical attention, the better. Emergency personnel can administer lifesaving drugs before you get to the hospital…and alert the emergency room staff so that they can prepare to care for you without delay.

Reused Medical Device Warning

Single-use medical devices—such as syringes, cardiac catheters, obstetrical forceps, laser tips and intubation tubes—are increasingly being cleaned, sterilized and reused by doctors and hospital workers to cut costs, putting patients at greater risk for infection. *Self-defense:* At the time a procedure is to be performed, tell the doctor or nurse that you do not want a resterilized single-use product. Request that only new devices be used for your care.

Charles Inlander, president, People's Medical Society, 462 Walnut St., Allentown, PA 18102.

Tape Trap

Hospital tape—often used to secure intravenous lines to the body—is sterile when it comes out of the box. But in a recent study, 74% of opened rolls were found to harbor bacteria. And 92% of tape samples removed from patients were contaminated. This finding may help explain why one in 20 patients develops an infection while hospitalized. *Self-defense:* Ask hospital workers to use a new roll of tape—or to unravel it at least one full turn—before using it on you.

Don Redelmeier, MD, associate professor of medicine, University of Toronto Faculty of Medicine. His study of bacterial growth on hospital tape was published in the *Journal of General Internal Medicine,* University and Woodland Aves., Philadelphia 19104.

Medication Alert

Medication errors at hospitals would be cut in half if all hospitals used computerized drug-dispensing systems. *Reasons:* These systems eliminate handwriting problems...labels are scanned at the patient's bedside to confirm that the correct drugs have been dispensed. *Problem:* Currently, few US hospitals have these systems.

Charles Inlander, president, People's Medical Society, 462 Walnut St., Allentown, PA 18102.

Intravenous Fluid Danger

Emergency intravenous fluids may do more harm than good when given to patients with severe bleeding. For decades, bleeding has been treated with an intravenous solution of saline or Ringer's lactate—given immediately, in an attempt to elevate the patient's blood pressure and to prevent organ damage and shock.

Finding: Among patients given intravenous fluids immediately, 62% survived. The survival rate among patients given intravenous fluids after the bleeding had stopped was 70%. *Also:* Patients given fluids after the stoppage of bleeding left the hospital sooner and had fewer complications.

Theory: Fluids encourage bleeding both by keeping blood pressure high and by diluting coagulants in the blood.

William H. Bickell, MD, director of research, St. Francis Hospital, Tulsa. His 37-month study of 289 trauma patients treated at Houston's Ben Taub General Hospital was published in *The New England Journal of Medicine,* 10 Shattuck St., Boston 02115.

Better Hospital Recuperation

Patients whose rooms contained water-dominated nature photographs reported substantially less postoperative anxiety than those whose rooms contained photos of trees, abstract paintings...or a blank wall. Those exposed to the water photo also needed the least-strong pain medications.

Self-defense: Bring your own pictures for the hospital wall—ones that you like and find relaxing to look at.

Study of 160 Swedish cardiac patients, led by Roger Ulrich, PhD, professor, College of Architecture, Texas A&M University, College Station.

When You Need More Time In the Hospital

Timothy McCall, MD, an internist based in Boston, and author of *Examining Your Doctor: A Patient's Guide to Avoiding Harmful Medical Care.* Citadel Press.

In an effort to boost their bottom lines, HMOs and other managed-care plans have dramatically reduced the lengths of their patients' hospital stays. To remain competitive, many traditional insurers are adopting similar tactics.

For bypass surgery, stays of two weeks were common just a few years ago. Now it's down to four days. Women having hysterectomies sometimes get as few as two days in the hospital.

This isn't all bad. There's good scientific evidence that hospital stays were too long in the past. Under the old system, doctors and hospitals had a financial incentive to keep patients hospitalized as long as possible. Under managed care, doctors can be penalized—or even fired—if their patients stay longer than the HMO deems necessary.

Unfortunately, the logic used by HMOs seems to be, "If cutting a little was good, then cutting more is better."

Example: Childbirth is the leading cause of hospitalization. In 1970, women having normal deliveries stayed an average of four days. By 1992, it was two days. A few years later, however, some California plans were hustling mothers out of the hospital after only eight hours.

In response, laws were passed mandating that insurers pay for two-day stays for normal deliveries and four days for C-sections. Unfortunately, these laws don't help people who are hospitalized for other reasons.

PROTECT YOURSELF

How can you prevent your loved ones or yourself from being thrown out of the hospital too early? *Be assertive.* Keep in mind that in calculating when to send you home, managed-care plans rely on best-case scenarios. Be prepared to explain why your case may not fit that definition.

If your specified number of days is up but you don't feel well enough to go home, tell your doctor (or have a family member do so for you). Though they don't always tell their patients, doctors have the ability to challenge the discharge decisions of insurance companies and hospital "utilization reviewers." If necessary, make your case to the hospital ombudsman.

The major determinant of whether it's okay to go home early is your medical condition. Any fever should be resolved. You should be able to take food by mouth. You shouldn't be so confused or lightheaded that you risk falling when you walk to the bathroom. If you've had surgery, you should be able to urinate on your own, and your pain must be controllable with oral medications.

The other important determinant is the situation at home. Is the environment conducive to healing? Will someone be there to take care of you? Will your insurer arrange for visiting nurses or other home care? Is there adequate backup if a problem arises? If these conditions aren't met, alert your doctor and your insurance company.

Many people prefer to recover at home—if it's feasible. The surroundings are familiar, and there's more privacy. And given the risk of catching infections or developing other complications in the hospital, it makes sense to be discharged as soon as you can.

But the decision should be based on what makes sense medically—not on the HMO's bottom line.

Most Frequent Hospital Bill Mistake

Ninety-seven percent of hospital bills are wrong, and less than 2% of those errors are in the patient's favor. *Average error:* $1,400.

Frequent mistake: Billing for items or services never delivered (lab work, medication, thermometers, wheelchairs, etc.).

Self-defense: Insist on completely itemized bills...and review them carefully.

Harvey Rosenfield, head of the watchdog group Bills Project.

Secrets of Successful Anesthesia for Very Successful Surgery

Jeanette Liska, PhD, founder of Awareness with Anesthesia Research Education (AWARE), 1563 Summit Ave., Cardiff by the Sea, CA 92007.

In the 28 million surgical procedures performed each year, about 250,000 patients report being painfully and traumatically aware during the operation. Here's what to do to reduce the odds of that happening to you.

Questions to ask your anesthesiologist or nurse anesthetist—prior to your surgery…

● **Will I need a muscle relaxant?** Anesthesia is usually a combination of drugs. This mix typically includes a drug to knock you out…a hypnotic drug to help hinder memories…and a muscle relaxant to prevent movement during surgery. But if a muscle relaxant is used, it might be impossible for you to signal anyone if the anesthesia isn't working properly.

● For surgery under 30 minutes, a muscle relaxant might not be necessary. If a muscle relaxant isn't necessary, ask that it not be used. Without it, signaling the surgeon will be easy.

● For longer procedures—such as heart, spine or brain surgery—a muscle relaxant is a must.

● **What hypnotic drug will I be given?** Based on my study of 11,000 patients, the drug *Versed* led to the fewest awareness episodes, however, it appears to last for less time than *Propofol,* the common alternative.

Request a monitor that measures consciousness. These monitors have sensors that are attached to your head to track brain-wave activity.

Example: Aspect Medical (Natick, Massachusetts) makes a monitor now used in more than 175 hospitals nationwide.

If an awareness monitor is not available at the hospital your surgeon chooses for a procedure, consider asking to use a hospital that has one.

Blood Transfusion Self-Defense

James P. AuBuchon, MD, professor of pathology and medicine at Dartmouth–Hitchcock Medical Center in Lebanon, NH. He is coauthor of an article on transfusion medicine that appeared recently in *The New England Journal of Medicine,* 10 Shattuck St., Boston 02115.

Just when Americans were feeling reassured about the safety of the nation's blood supply, a new scare has emerged concerning mad-cow disease (bovine spongiform encephalopathy, or BSE). That's the deadly neurological disease that swept through cattle herds in England a few years ago.

James P. AuBuchon, MD, a distinguished specialist in transfusion medicine, answers some important questions.

● **Is it possible to get mad-cow disease from a blood transfusion?** In 1999, US blood banks began turning away potential donors who had spent more than six months in the United Kingdom between 1980 and 1996. The move was prompted by the fear that people who had eaten beef from cattle with BSE might themselves become infected…and pass on infectious blood.

There's *no* evidence that the disease can be transmitted through blood. We know that a related human disease—Creutzfeldt-Jakob disease—is not transmissible via blood.

● **How about getting AIDS from a transfusion?** The risk of contracting AIDS from donated blood plummeted in the 1980s. That's when blood banks started using screening tests that detected antibodies to the AIDS virus—a sure sign that the virus was present.

But some risk remained, because of the two-week "window" between the time of infection and the time that antibodies appear in the blood.

By 1995, when additional tests were added, the risk that a particular unit of blood was infected with the AIDS virus was one in 676,000. That's a very tiny number, but still worrisome.

Today, the risk of getting AIDS-infected blood from a transfusion is about one in a million. That's because blood banks have added *nucleic-acid testing* (NAT), in which the AIDS virus itself—and not antibodies to it—is detected.

●**How about other viral infections?** Several other viruses can be spread via transfusion. The most serious is hepatitis C, which can lead to cirrhosis and possibly liver failure or liver cancer.

The good news is that NAT ferrets out the hepatitis C virus as well as the AIDS virus, so the risk that a unit of blood contains hepatitis C is now one in 500,000.

NAT does not detect the hepatitis B virus, which typically causes muscle aches, fever and fatigue but which can also destroy the liver. Fortunately, other tests do detect it. The risk of getting a unit of blood that contains the hepatitis B virus is one in 63,000.

●**I've seen ads for "premium" blood that's guaranteed to be safe. Is that a good idea?** The ads, which have been appearing in newspapers, are for a product called *Plas+SD*.

Actually, this isn't "whole" blood. It's blood *plasma* that's been chemically treated to destroy the viruses that cause AIDS and hepatitis B and C.*

A one-pint unit of Plas+SD costs about $85, as compared with $45 or so for a unit of untreated plasma.

Since NAT effectively screens out AIDS and hepatitis C, the only meaningful advantage of Plas+SD is a reduced risk for hepatitis B.

In any case, most transfusions involve red cells—not plasma.

●**What about donating blood for myself?** You can set aside a pint or more of your own blood before surgery. Called *autologous donation,* this technique became popular when the AIDS virus threatened the nation's blood supply.

Now that blood is carefully screened, however, there's less advantage in going this route. Your blood is only a tiny bit safer than a stranger's blood. And, of course, autologous donation does nothing to prevent the possibility that a mix-up in the blood bank could cause you to receive the wrong—incompatible—blood.

Receiving incompatible blood kills two dozen Americans a year—and there's really nothing patients can do to eliminate this small risk.

*Plasma is a straw-colored liquid that's left over when blood has been stripped of its oxygen-carrying red cells. It's typically given in cases of massive blood loss.

Autologous donation should be considered only if you're facing orthopedic surgery or some other operation that's likely to cause significant blood loss.

Make the donation well in advance of the surgery to give your red cell count time to recover. Red cells can be stored for about six weeks.

●**What can I do to reduce the need for transfusion?** If you're anemic and/or facing major surgery, ask your doctor about taking the hormone *erythropoietin*. Administered a few weeks before surgery, it can crank up production of red cells.

During certain operations, special cell-washing devices can be used to collect and reinfuse red cells that come out of your body.

Some surgeons have begun doing so-called "bloodless" surgery, in which various techniques are used to minimize blood loss. These include reducing blood pressure, administering certain drugs and careful cutting and suturing.

These blood-saving techniques may be appropriate if you are undergoing surgery in which there is potential to lose a lot of blood, such as cardiovascular or orthopedic surgery. Discuss the matter with your doctor.

Good News for Hemorrhoid Sufferers

Painful hemorrhoid surgery may soon be a thing of the past. Patients who underwent *neodymium:YAG* laser surgery reported 65% less pain than did those who had traditional scalpel surgery. *More:* The laser surgery group experienced fewer complications…and returned to work faster.

Khalique Zahir, MD, plastic surgery fellow, Vanderbilt University School of Medicine, Nashville, TN. His study of 50 hemorrhoid sufferers was presented at a recent meeting of the American Society for Laser Medicine and Surgery.

Safer Gallstone Surgery

The *laparoscopic* technique reduces the likelihood of death by 80%, compared with the traditional "open" surgical technique. In laparoscopic surgery, stones are removed via a narrow "telescope" inserted through four small incisions in the abdomen. Conventional "open" gallbladder surgery necessitates a much larger incision.

Claudia A. Steiner, MD, MPH, senior fellow, Johns Hopkins University, Baltimore. Her review of discharge records at 54 Maryland hospitals was published in *The New England Journal of Medicine,* 10 Shattuck St., Boston 02115.

New Hernia Operation

The "plug-and-patch" method is cheaper, safer and faster-healing than the standard surgical techniques. The plug, shaped like a badminton birdie, fills the hernia defect. A mesh patch covers the repair site. Plug-and-patch is done with local rather than general anesthesia. Patients can resume normal activity in three days, as opposed to weeks or months with standard techniques. The recurrence rate with plug-and-patch is virtually zero, in contrast to 10% to 15% for other methods. The technique is now widely available.

Keith W. Millikan, MD, associate professor of surgery, Rush–Presbyterian-St. Luke's Medical Center, Chicago.

No More Stitches

The surgical zipper is often a good alternative to sutures and staples as a means of closing incisions. The device consists of a polyester patch with a polyethylene zipper running lengthwise down the middle. An adhesive backing secures the patch to the skin. To close an incision, the surgeon places one edge of the zipper on each side, then pulls the zipper's tab to bring skin edges together. The zipper is quicker to apply than sutures and staples,

leaves a smaller scar and can be peeled off in the shower after about 10 days.

Mitchell Roslin, MD, director of bariatric surgery, Maimonides Medical Center, Brooklyn, NY.

Eight Questions That Could Save Your Life

Ervin Moss, MD, executive medical director of the New Jersey State Society of Anesthesiologists in Princeton Junction and clinical professor of anesthesiology at Robert Wood Johnson Medical Center in New Brunswick, NJ.

Surgery has moved outside the hospital surgical suite. Thirteen percent of all surgical procedures are now done in doctors' private offices. By 2005 that figure is expected to rise to 20%. That's almost 10 million operations a year. These include cataract surgery...biopsies...ear tube insertions...cosmetic and plastic surgery...and hernia repairs.

Office surgery costs less than similar procedures done in hospitals or outpatient surgical facilities. It can be more convenient and "patient friendly," too. But office surgery also poses potential risks.

Even the best-equipped doctor's office lacks the state-of-the-art surgical suites and extensive support staffs found in hospitals. Some in-office surgeons lack the training required of their hospital counterparts. And office surgery generally isn't regulated by state or national agencies.

That's not to say that surgical procedures can't be done safely in doctors' offices. But before bypassing the hospital, patients should ask the surgeon...

●**Do you have hospital privileges to perform this procedure?** Surgeons earn hospital privileges—the right to operate in the hospital—by undergoing intensive scrutiny. Only surgeons who provide exemplary care get the privileges.

Surgeons who work in office settings may not have those privileges. And if they have a high rate of poor outcomes, they normally aren't required to report it.

Also important: Ask your doctor if he/she is board-certified for the type of surgery to be done. Certification means that the surgeon has completed an accredited residency program and has passed a rigorous certification exam.

●**How many similar procedures have you performed?** Surgeons get better with practice. A surgeon who has done only a few dozen procedures is still learning. Patients should choose surgeons who have performed many operations similar to the one they will undergo.

●**Who will administer the anesthetic?** The person administering the anesthetic should be a board-certified anesthesiologist or a certified nurse-practitioner-anesthetist. That's a registered nurse (RN) who has had two years of specialized training in anesthesiology.

States have standards regarding the types of anesthetic that nurse-anesthetists can administer in the hospital and the circumstances under which they can do so. These standards vary among states. Ask your doctor which standards his hospital follows. His in-office surgical practice should follow the same standards.

●**Is your office prepared for emergencies?** Are resuscitation and life-support equipment and medicine on hand in case things go wrong during surgery?

At a minimum, this equipment should include a "crash cart" with a defibrillator and airway resuscitation equipment.

●**Do you have an ongoing relationship with an ambulance company?** The drivers should know exactly where the office is...the best routes to get there and from there to the hospital...and which entries and exits are large enough to accommodate a stretcher.

●**Who staffs your office?** The doctor's office should employ at least one RN who, like the surgeon and anesthesiologist, has training in advanced cardiac life support.

All nurses assisting during surgery should be RNs specializing in operating room procedures. And—all RNs caring for patients after surgery should be specialists in post-anesthesia recovery.

●**Has your facility been accredited?** Several agencies inspect physicians' offices, protocols and procedures to certify that they meet standards for quality in-office surgery.

The most demanding agency is the Joint Commission on Accreditation of Healthcare Organizations (JCAHO).

Facilities offering in-office surgery aren't required to be JCAHO-accredited, but some go through the procedure voluntarily. Ask to see the accreditation certificate. It assures you that the facility is well-run and up-to-date.

●**How long will my procedure take?** In-office surgery is safest when it does not exceed four hours. Any operation lasting longer should be done in a hospital.

Bypass Surgery: Who Really Needs It?

Thomas B. Graboys, MD, associate professor of medicine at Harvard Medical School and director of the Lown Cardiovascular Center at Brigham and Women's Hospital, both in Boston.

The number of heart bypass operations performed in the US is soaring. For individuals whose heart vessels are so blocked that they feel chest pain (angina) even while resting, bypass surgery can be a lifesaver. But estimates are that up to half of bypass operations may be unnecessary—exposing patients to needless expense and risk of death.

Self-defense: If a doctor recommends bypass surgery for you, *be sure to get a second opinion if...*

●**You feel no chest pain while resting.**

●**You feel slight chest pain *only* when you exert yourself**—when running to catch a bus or taking a hike up a hill, for instance.

In these instances, medications and lifestyle changes—quitting smoking, exercising more and eating less fat—are better.

Why? Because although generally safe, bypass surgery is not without risk. Two percent of patients younger than 70 who undergo bypass die from the surgery, and 3% to 4% of people older than 70 die.

And bypass surgery is only a quick fix. Heart vessels can clog up again—especially if lifestyle changes aren't made.

Don't get a second opinion from another doctor in your own doctor's practice or HMO. *Better:* A doctor who practices at a local hospital—especially one that's affiliated with the cardiology department of a university.

If bypass surgery is necessary, shop around. Surgeons and hospitals that do the most bypass surgery procedures have the best survival rates.

Helpful: *US News & World Report's* annual guide to the best hospitals in America, published in the magazine each July. Articles and rankings, segmented by specialty and region, are available at its Web site, *www.usnews.com.*

Death-from-Heart-Disease Predictor

The *ankle/arm blood pressure index (AAI)* is a fast, noninvasive test that compares blood pressure in the upper and lower extremities. A reading of 0.9 or lower suggests an increased risk of death—even in persons who seem healthy.

Finding: Women 65 and older with low AAI values were five times more likely to die of heart disease than women of the same age with higher values. A separate study yielded similar results for men.

Self-defense: Periodic measurement of AAI in a physician's office or screening center may be appropriate to identify older men and women at high risk of premature death.

Molly T. Vogt, PhD, assistant professor of epidemiology, Graduate School of Public Health, University of Pittsburgh. Her four-year study of almost 1,500 women was published in the *Journal of the American Medical Association,* 515 N. State St., Chicago 60610.

A Test That's a Must If You're Over 60

Have your protein status checked at your next physical exam if you are in your 60s or older or have surgery scheduled. A simple blood test for *albumin* can indicate whether your body has enough stored protein. Adequate protein is important for fighting off postsurgical complications—particularly infection. *Cost:* Generally less than $10.

Bruce Yaffe, MD, gastroenterologist and internist in private practice, New York.

To Detect Heart Disease

Experimental diagnostic test detects heart disease faster, more safely and at lower cost than X-ray angiography. *Three-dimensional coronary magnetic resonance angiography* (MRA) pinpoints the location of blocked coronary arteries using powerful magnets. MRA takes just 30 minutes, unlike traditional X-ray angiography, which can take up to six hours. It is noninvasive and involves no injected dye and no radiation exposure to the patient. *Bonus:* MRA costs only 30% as much as X-ray angiography.

René M. Botnar, PhD, clinical scientist, Cardiac MR Center, Beth Israel Deaconess Medical Center, Boston.

A Test That Predicts a Second Heart Attack

Blood flow imaging predicts second heart attacks better than an exercise stress test. A study found that when blood flow imaging (called myocardial perfusion imaging) was performed after giving patients a drug to increase blood flow to the heart, it could be given three to five days sooner after a heart attack—and was better at predicting repeat cardiac attacks—than the traditional exercise stress test. Blood flow imaging gives physicians an opportunity to act more quickly to prevent repeat heart attacks.

Kenneth A. Brown, MD, professor of medicine, University of Vermont, Burlington.

Unnecessary Chest X Rays

Half of all chest X rays performed prior to surgery are unnecessary. Doctors often order them anyway out of habit or because they fear being sued for failing to diagnose a problem that an X ray might have revealed.

Perry G. Pernicano, MD, assistant chief, radiology service, Veterans Affairs Medical Center, Ann Arbor, MI. His study of 108 pre-op chest X rays was presented at a meeting of the Radiological Society of North America, 2021 Spring Rd., Oak Brook, IL 60521.

Unnecessary Tests for Migraine Sufferers

Migraine sufferers do not benefit from routine MRIs and CAT scans—although many physicians continue to order these costly and potentially frightening tests for their migraine patients.

Exceptions: To rule out brain tumors, these scans may be appropriate for individuals whose headache patterns change…who have a history of seizures…or who are experiencing numbness, weakness, changes in vision, difficulty maintaining balance or other neurological problems.

B.M. Frishberg, MD, clinical assistant professor of neurology, Georgetown University School of Medicine, Washington, DC, and a neurologist in private practice in Bethesda, MD. His review of 17 studies involving 2,722 headache sufferers was published in the *American College of Physicians Journal Club,* Independence Mall West, Sixth Street at Race, Philadelphia 19106.

18

Medications and Vaccines

Wise Ways to Buy Prescription Drugs Online

Many people like the idea of purchasing drugs from online pharmacies. Some find it more convenient than standing in line at the local drugstore. Others hope to save money. Still others are too embarrassed to ask their doctors to prescribe drugs like the baldness remedy *finasteride* (Propecia) or the impotence drug *sildenafil* (Viagra).

I think online pharmacies are going to play an increasingly big role in coming years. They offer many advantages—especially to older people, individuals with disabilities and people living in remote areas. But many kinks in the system haven't been worked out yet. Before you buy drugs online, here's my advice.

• **Stick with reputable sites.** Look for sites certified by the National Association of Boards of Pharmacy (NABP). Its Verified Internet Pharmacy Practice Sites (VIPPS) program ensures that an online pharmacy complies with the licensing requirements of each state in which it sells drugs. Certification also ensures that the pharmacy protects patient privacy, verifies prescriptions and gives meaningful consultation to patients.

A seal on the online pharmacy's site identifies it as VIPPS-approved. Two popular online pharmacies, *www.planetrx.com* and *www. yourpharmacy.com*, display the seal. So does *www.cvs.com,* the online site of CVS drugstores. Approval is pending for several other sites. If you don't see the seal on the site, you can check to see if it's certified by going to the NABP Web site: *www.nabp.net*.

• **Don't assume that the Internet is always cheaper.** Thanks to increasing competition, significant discounts are often available online. Some chains price drugs on their Internet sites lower than in their own stores.

But watch out. A recent study in the *Annals of Internal Medicine* found that sildenafil and

---

Timothy McCall, MD, a Boston internist and author of *Examining Your Doctor: A Patient's Guide to Avoiding Harmful Medical Care.* Citadel Press.

finasteride cost more online than at Philadelphia pharmacies. To be sure of a bargain, compare prices at several Internet vendors with those at the drugstore or mail-order outfit you normally use.

●**Don't use Internet pharmacies for urgent prescriptions.** You could easily wait several days for drugs to arrive from an online vendor. That's fine for blood pressure medication if you've got enough to last awhile. It's not okay if the prescription is for an antibiotic to treat a sinus infection.

●**Think about confidentiality.** Reputable online pharmacies have safeguards in place to protect confidentiality, but even then there is no guarantee of complete privacy. If confidential medical information is intercepted—such as data about cancer or AIDS treatments —you could wind up harming your chances of getting insurance or a job in the future.

●**Steer clear of online prescribing.** Some sites employ doctors who dispense prescriptions online. As tempting as it may be to use this service to obtain, say, Viagra, I don't recommend it. You usually know nothing about the qualifications of an online doctor. Worse, he or she knows almost nothing about you. It's only by actually talking with and examining a patient that a doctor can determine if a drug is appropriate.

That brings up a final point. If you do get a prescription from an online physician, overcome your embarrassment and tell your regular doctor. He or she might otherwise fail to recognize side effects or prescribe another drug that causes dangerous interactions.

There's no room for fear or shame in doctor–patient communication. If you find it hard to be honest with your doctor, work together to pinpoint and correct difficulties in your relationship. If they seem insoluble, switch to a doctor with whom you feel more comfortable.

Reduce Medication Mix-Ups

Ask your doctor to spell aloud the name of any drug he/she prescribes for you. Ask

what the drug is for and what the pills look like. Jot this information down, and use it to double-check that the pharmacist has given you the right drug. *Also helpful:* A pill reference book, such as *Complete Drug Reference* (Consumer Reports Books). *Trap:* An estimated 1,100 pairs of drugs have similar brand names or generic names. Fosamax *(alendronate)* treats osteoporosis, while Flomax *(tamsulosin)* is for prostate enlargement. Nicoderm *(nicotine)* helps smokers quit, while Nitro-Derm *(nitroglycerin)* treats angina.

Bruce L. Lambert, PhD, associate professor of pharmacy administration, University of Illinois, Chicago.

Customized Medications

Medications can be customized with doctor's approval to meet patients' needs. *Example:* If you cannot tolerate an oral medication, such as ibuprofen, a compounding pharmacist sometimes can prepare suppositories or transdermal (skin) gels. *When compounding may help:* For a dosage that is not commercially available…more natural formulation, such as for hormone-replacement therapy…better-tasting version…one that has no dye, lactose, preservative, etc. *Drawback:* Few health insurers cover compounded medications. *To find a compounding pharmacist:* Ask your doctor…or contact International Academy of Compounding Pharmacists, 800-927-4227, or Professional Compounding Centers of America, 800-331-2498.

Robert GiaQuinto, RPh, pharmacist/owner, Rye Beach Pharmacy, Rye, NY.

Medication Wallet Card

A medication wallet card lists all the prescription and over-the-counter medications you take…drug allergies…emergency telephone numbers.

National Council on Patient Information and Education, 4915 St. Elmo Ave., Suite 505, Bethesda, MD 20814.

Best Times to Take Medicines

Time medicines for the most benefit. *Examples:* Many asthma attacks occur between 2 am and 4 am—so medication taken in late afternoon works better at preventing attacks than medication taken at other times of the day. Hay fever often flares overnight as the body's cortisol and adrenaline levels drop—so taking an antihistamine right before bedtime may help. *Caution:* Check with your doctor before changing any medication schedule.

Monica Kraft, MD, assistant professor of medicine, University of Colorado Health Sciences Center, Denver.

Painkiller Danger

Taken in high doses and for long periods of time, Advil, Nuprin, Motrin, Aleve, Naprosyn, Indocin and other nonsteroidal anti-inflammatory drugs (NSAIDs) may cause elevated blood pressure. Often used to treat arthritis, gout and other painful conditions, NSAIDs have long been known to cause small increases in blood pressure.

Now: A study has linked these drugs to an increased need for antihypertensive therapy, particularly among the elderly. Although the link was found with prescription NSAIDs, users of over-the-counter versions of these drugs often take more—sometimes much more—than the label recommends.

Self-defense: Take only as much of any NSAID as is prescribed or indicated on the label, or switch to Tylenol or another pain reliever containing acetaminophen. Aspirin in low doses has not been linked to increases in blood pressure.

Jerry H. Gurwitz, MD, assistant professor of medicine, Harvard Medical School, Boston. His study of NSAID use among 9,411 Medicaid patients was published in the *Journal of the American Medical Association,* 515 N. State St., Chicago 60610.

Dangerous Drug Mix

Anticoagulants such as *warfarin* (Coumadin), taken in combination with aspirin, ibuprofen or another nonsteroidal anti-inflammatory drug (NSAID) could cause problems. Those who combine both drugs have a 13-fold risk of developing a bleeding peptic ulcer, compared with those who use neither drug. Patients taking anticoagulants should ask their doctors about substituting a NSAID alternative, such as acetaminophen.

Ronald I. Shorr, MD, assistant professor of pharmacoepidemiology, Vanderbilt University School of Medicine, Nashville. His study of anticoagulant use was published in *Archives of Internal Medicine,* 515 N. State St., Chicago 60610.

Herb Alert

Drug–herb interactions can complicate surgery. Herbs such as St. John's wort can make narcotics and anesthetics last longer. Many herbs can interfere with blood clotting, causing potentially dangerous bleeding during surgery. Some herbs can cause rapid heartbeat or high blood pressure. *Self-defense:* Avoid all nonprescription natural medicines for two weeks before surgery…or consult an herbalist, licensed naturopathic physician or knowledgeable medical doctor.

Andrew L. Rubman, ND, associate professor of clinical medicine at College of Naturopathic Medicine, University of Bridgeport, and director of Southbury Clinic for Traditional Medicines, Southbury, CT.

Sexual Side Effects of Commonly Prescribed Drugs

M. Laurence Lieberman, a pharmacist in New York and author of *The Sexual Pharmacy.* New American Library. His book lists 226 drugs that are known to influence sexual performance or enjoyment.

In the past, doctors attributed most sexual disorders to psychological causes. But there is a growing awareness—fueled by a growing number of studies—that more than half these conditions are triggered by physical ailments or, more surprisingly, the drugs used to treat these ailments.

Many commonly prescribed drugs produce sexual side effects that most patients—no matter how frightened or delighted they are by the effects—are too embarrassed to discuss with their doctors. Knowing about these drugs ahead of time can help to alleviate the problems.

DRUGS THAT ENHANCE SEXUAL PERFORMANCE AND ENJOYMENT

We've all heard about Viagra (sildenafil) but many other drugs can enhance sexual performance and enjoyment.

• **Labetalol** is an antihypertensive drug. But unlike most drugs of its kind, which are notorious for causing impotence, this one may actually delay loss of erection after intercourse.

• **Levodopa,** used to treat patients with Parkinson's disease, increases the body's level of dopamine (a natural sexual stimulant) and causes patients to feel sexually aroused. As a result, the drug has been used to treat impotence in otherwise healthy subjects. *Success rate in one study:* 70%.

• **Nitroglycerin** is a vasodilator used to treat patients with angina. It may also increase blood flow to the genitals, thereby facilitating erections in men who have trouble achieving them.

• **Oral contraceptives** can work both positively and negatively. Many women experience a decreased sexual drive when taking the Pill, while others report an increased sex drive. Researchers are still unclear as to why these contradictory effects occur.

• **Papaverine** is another vasodilator which increases the flow of blood to the genitals and is often prescribed to treat impotence. The patient simply injects the drug at the base of his penis immediately prior to intercourse. An erection is almost instantaneous.

Caution: If an erection lasts more than four hours or becomes painful, contact your doctor immediately.

• **Phenoxybenzamine** and **phentolamine** are alpha-blockers that are most commonly used to lower blood pressure. But since they prevent the constriction of blood vessels, they are also being used to treat impotence.

• **Valium** and valium-like drugs inhibit sexual performance when taken in high doses. But when given in very low doses to patients with psychologically caused sexual problems, they enable these patients to relax and become sexually aroused. These drugs can also delay ejaculation and orgasm.

• **Yohimbine** is designed specifically to enhance sexual performance and enjoyment. As a result, it has been touted as the ultimate aphrodisiac. While that overstates the drug's effectiveness, it does help some impotence sufferers.

DRUGS THAT INHIBIT SEXUAL PERFORMANCE AND ENJOYMENT

• **Alcohol,** ingested alone or in liquid medications (cough medicine, etc.), can cause inhibited erection, decreased sexual desire, delayed ejaculation, male infertility and gynecomastia (painful breast growth in men).

• **Anabolic steroids** are analogs of testosterone that are prescribed to build muscle tissue in malnourished patients. While they are not widely prescribed, they are widely abused by athletes, especially bodybuilders. In males these drugs can cause reduced sex drive, impotence, decreased testicle size and sperm production, gynecomastia and priapism (prolonged, painful erections). In females, they can cause male-type hair growth and balding, deepening of the voice, reduction in breast size, clitoral enlargement, decreased uterine size, irregular menstruation and cessation of ovulation.

• **Digoxin** is prescribed to regulate heart beat. It very closely resembles the female hormone estrogen, and can cause decreased sex drive, impotence and gynecomastia.

• **Isotretinoin** (Accutane) is an extremely effective drug for severe cases of acne. It has received a lot of attention, however, because of the risk of birth defects in the children of women taking it. It can also cause impotence, decreased sex drive, menstrual irregularities, galactorrhea (discharge from the female breasts) and vaginal dryness.

• **Lithium,** prescribed for the treatment of manic depressive disorder, can cause decreased sex drive, inhibited erection, male infertility and the discharge of milk from female breasts.

• **Nicotine** is a vasoconstrictor that often blocks blood flow to the genitals. As a result, it can cause impotence, vaginal dryness and even early menopause.

• **Penicillin** and related antibiotics can accumulate in the semen, triggering allergic reactions in susceptible partners.

• **Thiazide diuretics,** which account for about 90% of diuretics, cause a loss of zinc through the urine. Since zinc is vital to male potency, men using this drug often become impotent.

• **Timolol,** a beta-blocker, is the only eyedrop that has been associated with impotence and decreased sex drive.

nausea or stomach upset results, discuss it with your physician or pharmacist. *Common drugs that fall into this category include:*

• **Acetaminophen*** (Tylenol, etc.)
• **Enteric-coated aspirin**
• **Ampicillin**
• **Erythromycin**
• **Epsom salts**
• **Levodopa**
• **Mineral oil**
• **Magnesium hydroxide** (milk of magnesia)
• **Penicillin G and V**
• **Tetracycline**
• **Procainamide**

50+: The Graedon's People's Pharmacy for Older Adults by Joe and Teresa Graedon. Bantam Books.

*Generic names are given.

Anticoagulant Danger

Anticoagulants taken to reduce risk of cardiovascular disease can lead to severe internal bleeding—if doses are too high.

Self-defense: If you're on anticoagulants, ask your doctor about prescribing the lowest effective dose. Have periodic blood tests to check your anticoagulant levels. Avoid aspirin. Alert your doctor if there are any changes in your diet or use of alcohol.

C. Seth Landefeld, MD, senior research associate, department of medicine, Cleveland Veterans Affairs Medical Center, and associate professor of medicine, Case Western Reserve University, Cleveland. His review of risks from anti-coagulant-related bleeding was published in the *American Journal of Medicine,* Box 7722, Riverton, NJ 08077.

New "Last Chance" Antibiotic

Many bacteria have become resistant to some or even all antibiotics. The trend is especially pronounced in hospitals. Without effective antibiotics, patients die of once-curable infections. *Now available:* A combination of *quinupristin* and *dalfopristin* called Synercid. This intravenous drug works against most resistant strains of *Enterococcus faecium,* a common hospital-acquired pathogen.

Alexander Rakowsky, MD, team leader, medical review team, anti-infective division, Center for Drug Evaluation and Research, Food and Drug Administration, Rockville, MD.

Drugs That Work Best When Taken on an Empty Stomach

Food slows the absorption of certain drugs, so they are best taken without food. If

Dangerous Over-the-Foreign-Counter Drugs

Many drugs available by prescription in the US are sold over the counter in other countries. Don't buy them online or while traveling.

Reasons: They may be poorly regulated and it can be hard to verify if a drug is legitimate or dosage is correct.

Charles Inlander, president of People's Medical Society, America's largest nonprofit consumer health advocacy organization, 462 Walnut St., Allentown, PA 18102.

When You Need a Tetanus Shot

Get a tetanus shot at least once every decade. If you sustain a serious puncture wound five or more years after your last shot, ask your doctor about getting another booster.

Also: Be sure to thoroughly wash any cut, abrasion or puncture wound—no matter how minor—with soap and water. You may wish to apply an over-the-counter antibiotic ointment …and keep the wound clean and dry with a bandage. If redness surrounding the wound extends more than one-quarter inch, see a doctor right away. It may be infected.

James Brand, MD, assistant professor of medicine, University of Oklahoma Health Sciences Center, Oklahoma City.

19

Very, Very Personal

Jump-Start Your Sex Life...Naturally

Well before *sildenafil* (Viagra), people relied on aphrodisiacs to increase sexual desire...boost stamina...improve performance...and increase pleasure.

Many of these compounds owe their reputation to folklore, but several herbs and dietary supplements have proven sex-enhancing effects.

Good news: Products that improve sex naturally may be less likely to cause serious side effects than prescription drugs. Many strengthen the cardiovascular system and help regulate hormone production. That's as important for good sex as having an erection or being sufficiently lubricated.

Unlike sildenafil, sex-enhancing herbs and supplements aren't taken just an hour or so before sex. They're taken daily until there's a noticeable improvement in sexual performance.

At that point, some people take a pause to see if the herbs and supplements are no longer necessary. Others continue taking the preparations indefinitely.

Important: Use herbs and supplements only under medical supervision. That way you'll be sure to get the product and dosage that's right for you.

Caution: Fresh or dried herbs differ greatly in potency from batch to batch. Use capsules or tinctures, ideally ones that have been standardized to contain the proper amounts of active ingredients.

For better sex, try one of the following natural enhancers. Select the one that best suits your needs. Give each preparation a few months to work. If you see no effect, try another.

GINKGO BILOBA

Ginkgo contains a variety of compounds that relax blood vessels and increase circulation to the brain and pelvic area.

For women, increased blood flow improves vaginal lubrication and sexual responsiveness.

Chris D. Meletis, ND, dean of clinical affairs and chief medical officer of the National College of Naturopathic Medicine in Portland, OR. He is author of *Better Sex Naturally*. HarperResource.

For men, adequate blood flow is essential to achieve and sustain erections.

Typical dosage: *Capsules:* 40 mg to 60 mg of 24% standardized powdered extract three to four times daily. *Tincture:* 30 drops three to four times daily.

Side effects: Ginkgo may cause dizziness, headache or heart palpitations.

Caution: Ginkgo is a blood thinner and can increase the blood-thinning effects of aspirin and *warfarin* (Coumadin). Check with your physician before using ginkgo if you're taking either medication.

MUIRA PUAMA

Also known as "potency wood," this herb contains sterols and other compounds that boost levels of testosterone, a hormone that plays a critical role in sexual desire in women as well as men.

Muira puama also contains volatile oils that are thought to restore sex drive by stimulating the brain's pleasure center.

Typical dosage: 250 mg three times daily in capsule form.

Side effect: Muira puama may lower blood pressure by as much as 10%. Check with your doctor before using this herb if you have low blood pressure (hypotension).

GINSENG

This herb is an "adaptogen," meaning it helps the body compensate for extended periods of stress. Stress can cause sexual desire and performance to plummet.

Compounds in ginseng root lower levels of adrenaline and other stress hormones.

These compounds also improve blood flow to the penis, help tissues use oxygen more efficiently and boost production of testosterone in men and progesterone in women.

Typical dosage: *Capsules:* 10 mg to 50 mg one to three times daily. *Tincture:* 30 to 60 drops daily.

Side effect: Ginseng may cause diarrhea… high blood pressure…sleeplessness.

ASHWAGANDA

A member of the pepper family, this herb contains *withanolides,* substances that increase the activity of testosterone and progesterone.

Ashwaganda also relieves stress and anxiety.

Typical dosage: *Capsules:* 1,000 mg once or twice daily. *Tincture:* 60 to 90 drops two or three times daily.

Side effects: Because ashwaganda has anti-anxiety properties, it should not be used by anyone taking medications to treat anxiety and/or depression. The herb could intensify the drugs' actions as well as their side effects. Ashwaganda may also trigger miscarriages.

ARGININE

Taken in supplement form, this amino acid has been shown to relax smooth muscle contractions. This boosts arterial dilation, bringing more blood to the pelvic area.

The body uses arginine to produce nitric oxide, a chemical needed to achieve erections. (Sildenafil works in part by making nitric oxide more readily available in the body.)

Typical dosage: 1,000 mg to 2,000 mg twice daily in capsule form. Take capsules between meals, since many foods contain lysine, an amino acid that counteracts arginine's effects.

Side effect: Don't take this herb if you get cold sores caused by the herpes simplex virus. Arginine stimulates viral replication.

FOR MEN ONLY

The herb *yohimbe* is approved by the FDA for treating impotence and low sex drive.

Yohimbe contains a compound called yohimbine, which helps dilate blood vessels in the penis. Most men who take yohimbe experience an increase in sexual desire within an hour.

Typical dosage: 15 mg to 25 mg daily in capsule form. Divide into several doses throughout the day to minimize side effects. Take smaller amounts at first—for example, 5 mg or 10 mg a day—then gradually increase the amount over several weeks.

Side effects: Elevated blood pressure, nausea, racing heart and anxiety. Use yohimbe only under medical supervision.

FOR WOMEN ONLY

The herb *dong quai* contains plant sterols that help correct estrogen deficiencies.

Studies suggest that dong quai can increase sexual desire as well as the intensity of orgasms.

Typical dosage: *Capsules:* 1,000 mg three to four times daily. *Tincture:* 45 to 60 drops two or three times daily.

Caution: Pregnant and lactating women should not use dong quai. The herb also increases sensitivity to sunlight.

Viagra Warning

Heart patients bothered by impotence should undergo a treadmill stress test before starting to take the impotence drug Viagra *(sildenafil)*. A man who is capable of exercising up to at least five METs (metabolic equivalents of oxygen consumption) without chest pain, abnormal heartbeats or other problems is unlikely to suffer a heart attack during sexual intercourse. It's safe for him to use Viagra. Viagra should be off-limits to men who cannot exercise at this level without problems. They're at risk for a sex-triggered heart attack.

Sanjay Kaul, MD, assistant professor of medicine, University of California, Los Angeles, School of Medicine, and associate director of the coronary care unit, Cedars-Sinai Medical Center, Los Angeles.

Don't Take Viagra Before Surgery

Viagra dilates blood vessels so blood flows easily to the penis. But dilation affects the rest of the body, too—lowering blood pressure. This can be dangerous during surgery because some anesthetics have the same effect on blood pressure. Do not use Viagra within 24 hours of surgery—and tell your doctor and anesthesiologist when you last took it.

Patrick C. Walsh, MD, urologist-in-chief, Johns Hopkins Medical Institutions, Baltimore.

Sex Is Good for Your Health

Sex boosts the immune system—and can help prevent colds and headaches. People who averaged one to two sexual encounters per week had higher levels of *immunoglobulin A*—which protects against disease. And people who had sex two or three times a week reported fewer migraine headaches—because sex releases hormones that prevent migraines.

Alexander Mauskop, MD, director, New York Headache Center, New York.

For Women Only

Women's sexual desire may grow stronger following hysterectomy—that was the surprising conclusion of a study of 1,000 women by the University of Maryland School of Medicine. Researchers discovered that after surgery, 15% more of the women desired sex at least once a week, 12% more made love at least five times a month and 9% more experienced orgasms. Only 5% felt the quality of their sex life had deteriorated.

Kristen H. Kjerulff, PhD, associate professor of epidemiology, University of Maryland School of Medicine, Baltimore.

Older Men and Sex

It is a myth that older men are dissatisfied with the quality of their sex lives, according to the largest research study on impotence since the famous Kinsey report.

It is true that more than half of men between 40 and 70 experience some difficulty in obtaining and maintaining erections. But they expect a decline in performance to occur as they age, so their level of satisfaction with sex remains the same as when they were younger.

John McKinlay, PhD, an epidemiologist with the New England Research Institute, Nine Galen St., Watertown, MA 02472.

Older men who have trouble attaining erections at night can do better with morning sex. Testosterone levels are higher earlier in the day.

Medical Aspects of Human Sexuality.

Sex for Seniors

To improve your sex life as you grow older—*take your time.* Stick to easy positions, and try alternating occasions—each of you is touched one day and does the touching the next. *For men only:* Thinking about sex or looking at sexy pictures may no longer be enough to arouse you. But touching yourself—or having your partner touch you—usually works.

Ruth Westheimer, PhD, authority on human sexuality and intimacy, writing in *Are You Old Enough to Read This Book? Reflections on Midlife* (Reader's Digest Association), a collection of writings from prominent individuals over age 50.

Treatment for Penis Curvature

Severe penis curvature *(Peyronie's disease)* can be minimized via injections of *verapamil,* a calcium channel blocker. Peyronie's is caused by scar tissue resulting from injury to the erectile bodies, the two long chambers within the penis that fill with blood to form an erection. If severe enough, this curvature can make intercourse impossible.

Now: Regular injections of verapamil into the scar resulted in better erectile function in 80% of the men who received treatment. Seventy percent of the men noted a reduction in the curvature. All the men reported a significant decrease in the narrowing of the penis, another common result of Peyronie's. If you have a curved penis, ask a urologist about verapamil.

Laurence Levine, MD, director of the male sexual function and fertility program, Rush-Presbyterian/St. Luke's Medical Center, Chicago. His study of 14 men with Peyronie's disease was published in the *Journal of Urology,* 1120 N. Charles St., Baltimore 21201.

Overcoming Premature Ejaculation

Premature ejaculation can be overcome with *clomipramine* (Anafranil)—a drug long used to treat depression and obsessive-compulsive disorder. A dose of 50 milligrams (mg) increased time before ejaculation from an average of 81 to 409 seconds. At 25 mg, ejaculation was delayed to an average of 202 seconds. *Side effects:* Dry mouth and constipation.

Stanley Althof, PhD, psychologist in sexual disorders, Case Western Reserve University, Cleveland. His study of 15 monogamous couples 21 to 65 years of age was presented at a meeting of the American Urological Association, 1120 N. Charles St., Baltimore 21201.

Love Handles—Impotence Connection

Love handles often go hand in hand with impotence. *Recent finding:* Men with a 42-inch waist were twice as likely to be impotent as were men with a 31-inch waist. *Theory:* In overweight men, inability to achieve or maintain erection is an early sign of heart disease—which is often associated with impotence. *Best advice:* Shape up. Inactive men are 40% more likely to experience impotence than those who exercise.

Eric Rimm, ScD, assistant professor of epidemiology and nutrition, Harvard School of Public Health, Boston. His survey of 1,981 men was presented at a meeting of the American Urological Association.

Impotence Predicts Heart Disease

Twenty-five percent of men who see doctors for impotence caused by vascular problems have a heart attack or stroke within five years of the start of impotence. *Reason:* Sexual impotence is often caused by the same problems that cause heart trouble, including diabetes, smoking, high blood pressure and high cholesterol levels.

Kenneth Goldberg, MD, director, Male Health Center, Lewisville, TX.

Genital Bites

Treatment of genital bites is often delayed because victims are embarrassed. Men bitten by dogs typically go to an emergency room within an hour. But men whose penises are bitten or scraped during oral sex often ignore the injury even after infection sets in—and may not seek help for 24 hours to six weeks.

Danger: Infected human bites can be more serious than dog bites. Bitten men need to be treated for infection and tested for sexually transmitted diseases.

J. Stuart Wolf, Jr., MD, associate professor of urology, University of Michigan Medical Center, Ann Arbor.

Prostate Cancer— How to Outsmart the #2 Cancer Killer of Men

Gerald W. Chodak, MD, professor of surgery at the University of Chicago Hospitals, and director of the prostate and urology center at the Louis A. Weiss Memorial Hospital in Chicago.

Prostate cancer is the second-leading cause of cancer death in men (after lung cancer). It kills an estimated 38,000 men a year.

Experts disagree on how to fight the disease. Should men take the blood test to detect prostate cancer? And how should they treat the cancer if it's detected? *We asked Gerald Chodak, MD, to clear up the confusion…*

Dr. Chodak, what causes prostate cancer?

We don't yet know the precise causes, but we have identified several factors that put men at increased risk…

• **Being African-American.**

• **Having a father, grandfather or uncle who had the disease.**

• **Eating a diet high in fat, especially animal fat.**

• **Possibly infrequent sexual activity.**

Exposure to sunlight seems to help prevent prostate cancer, although the reason for this protective effect is unknown. But it's possible to get prostate cancer even in the absence of these risk factors. Any man can get prostate cancer.

What's the best way to detect prostate cancer?

In the past few years, doctors have begun to rely on the prostate-specific antigen (PSA) test. This test measures the blood level of PSA, a protein released in microscopic amounts by the prostate gland. The digital rectal exam is also an important diagnostic tool.

But I've heard that the PSA test isn't always accurate.

That's true. A high PSA reading may be a sign of cancer. But high readings sometimes occur in men who are cancer-free—causing needless alarm and the expense of additional tests.

Even if prostate cancer is accurately detected, it may grow so slowly that the man dies of an unrelated ailment long before the cancer has a chance to harm him.

Prostate cancer experts still don't know whether aggressive treatment of these slow-growing tumors is beneficial—especially since surgery and radiation have severe side effects, including incontinence and impotence. Some doctors think it's better to do nothing—to try "watchful waiting" instead.

Even if surgery or radiation is performed, there's no guarantee that the cancer won't spread to other areas of the body. Men who take the PSA test might be setting themselves up for needless expense, worry and treatment-related complications, without gaining any survival benefit.

What's your view of the PSA test?

I tell my patients that if their desire to minimize their risk of prostate cancer outweighs their concern about being subjected to possibly unnecessary, possibly harmful medical care, then they should get tested. You can discuss the matter with your own doctor, but ultimately it's your decision.

269

What role does a man's age play in determining whether he should be tested?

For men younger than 50, there's not much to be gained by getting tested. *Reason:* Prostate cancer is very rare in men that young. If you have a family history of the disease or if you're African-American, however, you might benefit from getting the test before age 50. That's something to discuss with your doctor.

If you are older than 70, or if other ailments have cut your life expectancy to 10 years or less, odds are you won't benefit much from the test, either. Even if you did have prostate cancer, you'd probably die of another cause. There would be no reason to treat the cancer.

Men between the ages of 50 and 70 are most likely to benefit from PSA testing. Men at the lower end of that age range are especially likely to benefit.

Have you had a PSA test?

I probably will get tested when I'm 50. I'd like to reach 80. I'd prefer to reach 90, and I don't want prostate cancer to get in the way.

How often should men get tested?

Men who are especially concerned about prostate cancer can get a PSA test once a year. Even once every six months is not too often. That way you'll know what's normal for you—and be able to see if the numbers shoot up, signaling cancer growth.

What do the test results mean?

The traditional view has been that any PSA level over 4.0 suggests trouble. But evidence suggests that numbers well below 4.0 might be risky for younger men...while higher numbers might be normal in elderly men.

For a 40-year-old man, a PSA above 2.5 is now considered abnormal. But among 60-year-olds, a reading as high as 6.5 might be normal.

What if my PSA reading is suspiciously high?

Your doctor should refer you to a urologist, who will perform an ultrasound exam to try to locate a tumor site. If a tumor is found, you'll have a biopsy to determine whether it is malignant. Don't worry—a biopsy does not spread the cancer.

What if cancer is found?

The decision about treatment is about trade-offs. The older the patient and the shorter his life expectancy, the smaller a chance of benefiting from aggressive treatment. But at any age, some of the treated men will probably benefit. The question is whether the benefit is worth the risk.

For younger men who are otherwise healthy, the benefits of treatment outweigh the risks. If the cancer were to remain untreated, your risk of dying of prostate cancer in the next 20 years would be about 60%.

What's the best treatment for prostate cancer?

Complete surgical removal of the prostate (a procedure called radical prostatectomy) offers the best chance for a cure. But surgery has drawbacks. Studies of Medicare patients have shown that up to 70% of men experience impotence following surgery. Of course, many older men are already impotent due to other diseases.

Good news: It's often possible to remove the prostate without injuring the nerves to the penis. Ask your surgeon if you're a candidate for nerve-sparing surgery.

About 18% of men will experience at least minor incontinence after surgery. But only 2% to 4% say that postsurgical incontinence is a serious problem.

What about radiation therapy?

Radiation is roughly comparable to surgery in terms of its ability to prolong life. And radiation controls the cancer while avoiding some of the complications of surgery.

Problem: For at least two years following the treatment, it's hard to tell whether radiation therapy has worked. In cases where radiation therapy does not work, it becomes very difficult to find a cure. And when incontinence and impotence occur following radiation, they're often harder to treat than the same problems caused by surgery.

Bottom line: Either surgery or radiation is a reasonable alternative, depending on your own preferences.

I read that it's possible to treat prostate cancer with radioactive "seeds." Is that effective?

While definitive evidence is not in, some experts believe that radioactive seed implants may be a viable alternative to radical prostate surgery and radiation therapy in the treatment of localized prostate cancer. Studies in coming years should help sort out the treatment options.

Prostate Cancer Trap

Prostate cancer is misdiagnosed more often than many men realize.

Most malignancies, including breast cancer and lung cancer, produce solid grape-like tumors. But prostate tumors are often diffuse, spreading finger-like throughout the gland. That makes them easy to be overlooked.

Self-defense: Get a second opinion for any prostate biopsy.

Jonathan I. Epstein, MD, professor of pathology, urology and oncology, Johns Hopkins University School of Medicine, Baltimore.

Seed Therapy Safety

Radiation used for prostate cancer poses no danger to a patient's family members. The dosage in the tiny radioactive seeds is too low to affect others.

Jeff Michalski, MD, radiation oncologist, Washington University School of Medicine, St. Louis.

Testicular Cancer Self-Defense

Self-exams for testicular cancer should be performed monthly. After a bath or shower, when the skin of the scrotum is relaxed, look for any swelling on the skin. Examine each testicle separately by rolling it between the index and middle fingers. Look and feel for any hard lumps or a change in the size or shape of testicles. It is normal for one to be slightly larger than the other. If you notice any changes from the previous month, see your doctor. This is especially important for men ages 20 to 40, who are at the highest risk.

Patrick C. Walsh, MD, urologist-in-chief, Johns Hopkins Medical Institutions, Baltimore.

Baldness/ Heart Trouble Link

Men who are losing the hair on the crowns of their heads have a 36% greater risk of heart problems than men who are not going bald…or who have mildly receding hairlines. Going bald at the crown is an inherited characteristic that may be linked to elevated male hormone levels. Anyone going bald in this way should carefully watch his blood pressure and cholesterol levels, and be especially careful to exercise regularly, not smoke and eat a heart-healthy diet.

JoAnn Manson, MD, DrPH, chief of preventive medicine, Brigham & Women's Hospital, Boston, and coauthor of a study of 22,000 male doctors, ages 40 to 84, reported in *Archives of Internal Medicine.*

Women Continue to Get Shockingly Substandard Medical Care

Leslie Laurence, coauthor of *Outrageous Practices: The Alarming Truth About How Medicine Mistreats Women.* Fawcett Columbine.

For the past several decades, American women have been systematically excluded from most research on new drugs, medical treatments and surgical techniques. As a result of this neglect, women are often denied the life-saving and life-extending treatments routinely offered to men.

Example I: Women are less likely than men to be referred for angioplasty, a surgical technique proven to clear blocked coronary arteries.

Example II: Among sufferers of kidney failure, women are 30% less likely than men to receive kidney transplants.

This sex bias pervades medicine, directly undermining the treatment women receive in clinics, hospitals and doctors' offices across the country.

271

Common problems women face when seeking medical care...

•Having your symptoms dismissed as being "all in your head." Medical mythology has it that women are "complainers" whose symptoms often stem from emotional stress. This insidious attitude among doctors keeps women from getting the diagnostic tests they need.

In one study, only 4% of women with abnormal stress tests received follow-up tests necessary for pinpointing arterial blockages. But these important tests were ordered for 40% of men with abnormal stress tests.

Similarly, because women's physical complaints are often viewed as evidence of psychological problems, women are more likely than men to receive prescriptions for psychiatric drugs.

Women make up 66% of those diagnosed with depression, yet they receive 73% of prescriptions for psychiatric medication—and 90% when the prescribing doctor is not a psychiatrist.

Self-defense: Communicate your problem to your doctor as clearly and concisely as possible.

Before your office visit, make a list of the questions you want to ask—in order of importance. If you get interrupted before you're through, at least you'll have covered the most crucial information.

If you feel your doctor is being dismissive, say so. If he/she still refuses to take your problem seriously, find another doctor.

•Having your symptoms of heart disease go unrecognized. Unlike men, women experiencing a heart attack often do not experience the classic symptoms—pain radiating down the arm or the elephant-sitting-on-your-chest type of pain.

Self-defense: Women should realize that vague abdominal discomfort, nausea, vomiting and shortness of breath can all be signs of heart attack. Take these symptoms very seriously. Make sure your doctor does, too.

•Not being told to have routine mammograms and Pap smears. Women over 65 account for almost half of the deaths from cervical cancer and are at greater risk of breast cancer than women of other age groups. But these older women are less likely than younger women to get the appropriate screening tests, often because their doctors fail to refer them for testing.

Self-defense: Annual mammograms, clinical breast exams and pelvic exams are recommended for all women 50 to 64 years of age.

The National Cancer Society recommends mammograms every one to two years for women 40 to 49 years of age.

A panel convened by the National Cancer Institute and the National Institute on Aging urges women 65 to 74 to have a clinical breast exam annually and a mammogram every two years, and women 75 and older to have both tests every two years. After three consecutive Pap smears with normal results, older women should have a Pap at least every three years. Younger women also need routine Pap smears.

•Not being told that lumpectomy is a safe alternative to mastectomy. Ninety percent of women with breast cancer are eligible for lumpectomy (removal of the tumor and a small margin of tissue), yet many undergo mastectomy (removal of the entire breast). The type of surgery a woman receives depends on such nonmedical factors as where she lives, her age, income and race.

Most likely to have a mastectomy: Black women, Medicare recipients, older women and women who live in the Midwest or South.

Self-defense: If your doctor says you need a mastectomy, get a second opinion—from a surgeon unaffiliated with your doctor's institution. Ask your doctor if he/she is aware of studies showing that lumpectomy followed by radiation is just as effective as mastectomy in treating early-stage breast tumors.

For more information on lumpectomy, call the National Cancer Institute at 800-4-CANCER.

•Not having your early warning signs of AIDS recognized in time for effective treatment. AIDS is now the fifth-leading killer of reproductive-age women. Not all doctors recognize female-specific symptoms of AIDS.

Self-defense: If you're involved in a new sexual relationship or if you're in a relationship with a man who may be unfaithful, insist that he wear a condom.

If you have recurrent vaginal yeast infections, genital herpes or cervical dysplasia, get tested for the AIDS virus. These conditions may be an early sign of infection.

•Being subjected to a needless hysterectomy. Many of the hysterectomies performed annually in the US are medically unjustified.

Self-defense: Women should know about the proven alternatives to hysterectomy. *Example:* Uterine fibroid tumors, which are usually benign, can often be shrunk with medication, then removed in a comparatively minor surgical procedure called myomectomy.

Women should also ask about subtotal hysterectomy—a procedure in which only the top of the uterus is removed and the cervix is left intact. This method, which is common in Europe, helps women maintain sexual responsiveness.

•Being prescribed drugs that were never properly tested in women. Women may suffer more or different side effects than men who take the same medication. *Example:* Doctors are often unaware that some drugs cause adverse reactions when combined with estrogen-replacement therapy or oral contraceptives.

Self-defense: If you're experiencing troublesome side effects, ask your doctor if you can switch to another medication. Realize that anti-anxiety drugs and postmenopausal estrogen taken together increase the risk of seizures and reduce the effectiveness of estrogen in treating hot flashes and other symptoms of menopause.

Hormone-replacement therapy (HRT) and oral contraceptives decrease the liver's metabolism of tricyclic antidepressants, leading to a greater risk of toxicity in women. For some women, doses of antidepressants may also need to be increased premenstrually.

•Being urged to go on hormone-replacement therapy despite the continuing debate over its long-term safety. Estrogen must be used continuously to maintain its benefit on bones. But most women—fearful of the link between estrogen and breast cancer—take HRT for a few years to relieve hot flashes and other menopausal symptoms and then stop.

Self-defense: Women may get almost as much protection if they take HRT to relieve short-term symptoms, discontinue it and start up again in their 70s. It's something to discuss with your doctor.

•Being overmedicated. Many common medical complaints of older women—including confusion and incontinence—may be caused by overmedication. Older women take drugs at twice the rate of older men, and are more apt to take multiple medications, increasing their risk of toxic side effects.

Self-defense: Older women should be aware that they metabolize many drugs differently than men. In women older than 65, for example, psychotropic drugs have a longer half-life, meaning that they remain in the body longer. To reduce the risk of side effects, physicians may need to reduce the doses of these drugs by one-third.

Elderly women also need to know that high doses of antipsychotic medication may increase their risk for chronic side effects such as tardive dyskinesia, a neurological disorder that results in abnormal movement of the mouth and tongue.

•Receiving medical care that is haphazard or fragmented. While men may see one doctor for all their health-care needs, women may see a gynecologist for a Pap smear and pelvic exam, an internist for a general physical exam and a radiologist for a mammogram.

Typically, one doctor doesn't know what the other is doing. Services often overlap, wasting time and money—and leading to inadequate care.

Self-defense: Find an internist with training in gynecology, qualifying him/her to perform pelvic exams and Pap smears. Find out whether there's a comprehensive women's health center in your community. These centers, generally affiliated with a major teaching hospital, offer one-stop medical care. Practitioners with training in gynecology, general medicine, cardiology, menopause care, oncology, infectious diseases, endocrinology and bone metabolism make themselves available to you during a single appointment.

With this trend toward women-centered care, women may finally be seen by the medical establishment not as a collection of reproductive organs but as human beings with hearts and lungs and colons and kidneys—just like men.

Mammography Report

Doctors should tell their patients of abnormal results, but they don't always do so.

Good news: The FDA now requires mammography testing facilities to send results directly to women within 30 days. Women who fail to get a report should call the testing facility.

Sharon Snider, press officer, Food and Drug Administration, Rockville, MD.

Mammogram Advice

Annual mammograms are a good idea for all women 40 or older. Annual screening permits detection of tumors at the earliest possible time. Early detection means better chances for survival, more treatment options and less disruption of daily life.

Christine E. Williamson, MD, director of breast imaging, Providence Medical Center, Seattle, and a member of the American Cancer Society's breast cancer task force.

HRT & Mammograms

Hormone replacement therapy (HRT) can raise the risk for falsely negative mammogram readings.

Recent finding: Mammograms detected only 64% of breast cancers in women 50 to 69 years of age who were on HRT. The test detected 80% of cancers in women of that age who were not on HRT.

Theory: HRT increases the density of breast tissue, making it more difficult to detect signs of cancer.

Important: Despite these findings, mammograms remain the most effective way to screen for breast cancer.

Anne M. Kavanagh, PhD, senior research fellow, Australian Research Centre for Sex, Health and Society, La Trobe University, Melbourne. Her two-year study of 103,770 women was published in *The Lancet,* 84 Theobald's Rd., London WC1X 8RR.

Benign Breast Lumps

Benign breast lumps occur in more than half of all women at some point in their lives. For 97% of these women, such lumps represent no significant increase in their risk of developing breast cancer. But any woman who notices a lump, particularly one that doesn't come and go with her menstrual cycle, should see her doctor right away.

James R. Dolan, MD, assistant professor of obstetrics, gynecology and gynecologic oncology, and codirector of the Breast Care Center, Loyola University Medical Center, Maywood, IL.

Breast Cancer Scandal

Women who've had a lumpectomy (removal of the breast tumor alone) should not be alarmed by reports of falsified data in breast cancer studies. Thousands of breast cancer patients opted for lumpectomy after several studies concluded that this procedure was just as safe and effective as mastectomy (removal of the entire breast). The fact that one of these studies has been questioned does not affect the validity of the others. Lumpectomy is still a valid option.

Harmon Eyre, MD, chief medical officer, American Cancer Society, 1599 Clifton Rd. NE, Atlanta 30329.

Lumpectomy Myth

Lumpectomies alone do *not* cure breast cancer. Standard treatment guidelines call for radiation and lymph node biopsies. *Troubling:* One-third of American women who had breast-conserving operations from 1990 to 1995 did not receive other needed treatment. *Self-defense:* Get second opinions…be treated by a team that includes surgeons, chemotherapists and radiation specialists.

Ann Butler Nattinger, MD, MPH, professor of medicine, Medical College of Wisconsin, Milwaukee, and leader of a study of nearly 145,000 women treated from 1983 to 1995, reported in *The Lancet,* 84 Theobald's Rd., London WC1X 8RR.

Pelvic Exams and Aging

Continue periodic pelvic exams even after menopause. Some cancers are more common in older women, including cancers of the vulva, vagina, cervix, uterus and ovaries. These cancers may have no obvious symptoms—but could be discovered by a doctor during a pelvic exam. This regular appointment also allows for discussion of health issues, sexuality and screening and prevention of major diseases that affect women as they age. *But:* After three consecutive normal tests, a postmenopausal woman at low risk for cancer may not need Pap tests every year. Ask your doctor.

Vicki Mendiratta, MD, clinical physician, obstetrics and gynecology, University of Washington Medical Center, Seattle.

Frequently Misdiagnosed: Vaginal Infections

Most women being treated for chronic yeast infections—either by their internists or by themselves with over-the-counter preparations —actually have a different condition.

Other causes of symptoms: Bacterial vaginosis or herpes infections, which require different treatments than that for yeast infections.

Caution: Never diagnose yourself. Over-the-counter treatments could make your symptoms worse. If you think you have a vaginal infection, ask your doctor to perform a complete physical examination and comprehensive medical history.

Karen Carroll, MD, departments of pathology and infectious diseases, and Paul Summers, MD, department of obstetrics and gynecology, both at the University of Utah Medical Center in Salt Lake City.

Cancer Warning

Vaginal bleeding or "spotting" following menopause can signal cancer of the cervix,

uterus or vulva. Postmenopausal women too often disregard such bleeding, but a doctor's exam is important to rule out these serious ailments. Cervical, uterine and vulvar cancer kill nearly 12,000 American women a year.

Katherine O'Hanlan, MD, associate director of the gynecologic cancer service, Stanford University Medical Center, Palo Alto, CA.

Surgery Preventive For Women

Precancerous lesions of the cervix may not always require treatment with surgery or lasers. Repeated topical application of the acne drug *retinoic acid* (Retin-A) reversed early (stage 2) lesions. However, retinoic acid was ineffective against stage 3 lesions. *Side effect:* Mild vaginal inflammation.

Frank L. Meyskens, Jr., MD, director, Clinical Cancer Center, University of California, Irvine. His five-year study of more than 300 women with cervical lesions was reported in *The Medical Post*, 777 Bay St., Toronto, Ontario, M5W 1A7, Canada.

Pelvic Pain Trap

Pain caused by varicose veins around the ovaries and uterus often goes undiagnosed. *Reason:* Few doctors are familiar with the condition, known as *pelvic congestion syndrome*. When doctors do diagnose the ailment, they often recommend hysterectomy. That rarely solves the problem. *Better:* A new nonsurgical procedure that uses a catheter to plug the varicose veins with either coiled springs or a liquid agent that causes the veins to clot. These plugs prevent the pooling of blood that causes the pain.

Anthony C. Venbrux, MD, director, interventional radiology, Johns Hopkins Hospital, Baltimore.

Estrogen Trap

Estrogen replacement therapy (ERT) may contribute to asthma. *Recent finding:* Menopausal women on ERT have an 80% higher risk of developing asthma than women not taking hormones. *Theory:* Estrogen affects cells involved in the body's allergic or inflammatory response. *Important:* Women considering estrogen therapy should discuss these findings with their physicians. Asthma risk must be weighed against the potential benefits of ERT.

Graham Barr, MD, fellow, Channing Laboratory, Brigham and Women's Hospital, Boston.

Treatment for Hot Flashes

It's no surprise that many postmenopausal women experience hot flashes. But hot flashes also afflict some men being treated for prostate cancer. In a study, the drug *megestrol acetate* (Megace) cut symptoms by 80%. Some women experienced menstrual bleeding one to three weeks after the medication had been discontinued...but that was the only side effect.

Charles L. Loprinzi, MD, associate professor of medical oncology, Mayo Clinic, Rochester, MN.

A Safer, Gentler Estrogen

Most women are familiar with estrogen replacement therapy (ERT), which is used to prevent menopause-related problems—hot flashes, vaginal dryness and osteoporosis. However, not all women are aware that there are two kinds of estrogen. Most doctors prescribe *estradiol* even though some studies have linked this form of estrogen to breast cancer. Another, less frequently prescribed form—called *estriol*—fights symptoms of menopause without promoting breast cancer.

Most women on ERT also take a synthetic hormone called *medroxyprogesterone* to offset some of the increased risk caused by estrogen. But the natural form of this drug—*progesterone*—not only reduces these risks but also stimulates bone growth, helping prevent and treat osteoporosis.

In my practice, I use estriol and progesterone exclusively. Although they cost a bit more, they cause fewer side effects, including bloating, irritability and breast tenderness. Both substances are available by prescription at compounding pharmacists. These "old-fashioned" practitioners can mix and encapsulate the hormones and other medications not widely marketed.

Robban Sica-Cohen, MD, director of the Center for the Healing Arts, Orange, CT. She specializes in environmental and nutritional medicine.

Estrogen Update

Women who take estrogen after menopause tend to do better on memory tests than those who do not take the hormone. Estrogen may even reduce the risk of Alzheimer's disease. But hormone-replacement therapy can have side effects of its own—be sure to discuss it in detail with your doctor.

Sanjay Asthana, MD, Puget Sound Health Care System, American Lake Division, Tacoma, WA.

Pacemaker Surgery For Women

One type of pacemaker surgery for women allows the device to be implanted beneath the breast tissue. The technique leaves only small scars near the shoulder and under the breast, hidden from view.

Result: Patients can wear low-cut dresses or bikinis without the stigma of having a long scar along the neckline. Surgery takes about two hours and is performed under local anesthesia. Recovery takes less than a week.

Marc Roelke, MD, attending physician in cardiac pacing and electrophysiology, Beth Israel Hospital, Newark, NJ.

Conquering Incontinence

Mary Dierich, RN, a nurse-practitioner at the Center for Bladder and Pelvic Dysfunction at the University of Minnesota in Minneapolis. She is coauthor of *Overcoming Incontinence: A Straightforward Guide to Your Options.* John Wiley & Sons.

Urinary incontinence—leakage of urine—is a mainstay of TV and magazine ads. But the condition is rarely discussed where it ought to be—in doctors' offices.

At least 30% of the estimated 17 million Americans who have incontinence—two-thirds of whom are women—fail to bring it up with their physicians.

Many are silent because they believe incontinence is an inevitable part of aging...and that it's incurable.

They're wrong on both counts.

Incontinence has many causes besides aging. These include vaginal and urinary tract infections...constipation...medication side effects...childbirth...prostate disease...and neurological conditions.

Good news: Regardless of the cause, incontinence can usually be ameliorated.

TYPES OF INCONTINENCE

There are three different types of urinary incontinence...

• **Stress incontinence**—leakage that occurs with activity.

This is most commonly caused by weakness of the pelvic floor muscles that support the bladder and control the urinary sphincter. That's the muscle at the base of the bladder that controls urine flow.

• **Urge incontinence**—a sudden and uncontrollable need to urinate. Common causes of urge incontinence include bladder infection, medication and neurological disease.

• **Overflow incontinence**—leakage from an overly full bladder. It is common in men with enlarged prostates.

Other causes include blockage of the urethra or inability of the bladder to contract efficiently.

HELPFUL MEDICATIONS

Many incontinence medications are now available. *These include medications that...*

• **Reduce bladder contraction.**

• **Increase muscle tone of the urinary sphincter.**

• **Alleviate blockage of the urethra.**

Medications are often recommended as the first line of defense against incontinence. Drug therapy can be effective for the condition and is relatively inexpensive.

Trap: The medications can cause side effects, including heart palpitations, high blood pressure, dizziness, dry mouth and constipation. And using medications doesn't usually correct the *cause* of the problem—such as pelvic floor muscle weakness.

By contrast, individuals who are willing to go a nonmedical route can usually correct the problem's cause, not merely treat its symptoms.

SELF-HELP STRATEGIES

Nonmedical approaches do require commitment and follow-through—sometimes for a lifetime. *Eight self-help strategies can be remarkably effective...*

• **Avoid irritants that trigger bladder contraction.** These include caffeine, aspartame (NutraSweet) and alcohol.

• **Drink plenty of water.** Consume at least six eight-ounce glasses daily. This dilutes urine so it won't irritate the bladder.

• **Boost consumption of fruits and vegetables.** Five servings daily help prevent constipation, a potential trigger of stress and urge incontinence.

• **Avoid sleep medications.** Even over-the-counter sleeping aids induce sleep so deep that the signal to get up and urinate can be missed.

• **Do Kegel exercises.** These exercises work for stress and urge incontinence. Effective for men and women, they strengthen the pelvic floor muscles.

What to do: Two to three times daily, contract the muscles used to hold back intestinal gas and urine flow. To begin, do five contractions at a time while lying down. Hold each contraction for five seconds. Relax for 20 seconds after each contraction. Gradually work up to a total of 40 contractions daily, holding each for 10 seconds.

Once perfected, Kegels can be performed standing or sitting.

Some people have trouble doing Kegels. *If you do, ask your doctor about trying...*

•*Biofeedback.* A sensor placed in the vagina or rectum monitors pelvic floor muscle contractions. A computer analyzes the contractions and points out problems. Biofeedback typically requires about five sessions—at home or at an incontinence specialist's office—to learn how to correct the errors and do Kegels reliably.

•*Pelvic muscle stimulation.* Pelvic muscles are stimulated by a device briefly inserted into the vagina or rectum. Equipment is used in medical offices or at home. Treatment typically takes at least three months. After it's completed, the muscles are strong enough to do Kegels effectively.

•*Pulsed magnetic therapy.* In this newest method, a mild magnetic current flows through the seat of a special chair called the "NeoControl" chair. The current stimulates contraction of pelvic floor muscles. No device is inserted into the body. Individuals remain clothed during treatment.

Therapy usually involves two 20-minute sessions each week for eight weeks. After treatment, muscles are strengthened and Kegels are done more effectively. The chairs are not yet widely available. To locate a practice that uses the NeoControl chair in your area, call the manufacturer at 877-636-2668.

•**Try bladder retraining.** People who get the hang of Kegels can use them to "retrain" their bladders to empty less frequently. This approach—which helps with urge incontinence—trains people not to respond to every signal the bladder sends.

Begin by permitting yourself to respond to the signal to urinate only every 90 to 120 minutes. Increase the time between voiding by 15 minutes each week for six weeks. Use Kegels to prevent urination outside these times.

AND FOR WOMEN ONLY

•**Use a vaginal cone.** This tampon-like weight—available by prescription—takes advantage of Kegel contractions to strengthen pelvic floor muscles.

As the device works its way down the vagina, the muscles automatically contract.

•**Try pessaries, continence rings and bladder prostheses.** Inserted into the vagina, these devices support a fallen bladder (pessary)... press the bladder neck closed (ring)...or lift the urethra to position it correctly (prosthesis). They need not be removed before urination.

GETTING COVERAGE

Some health insurers cover biofeedback, pelvic muscle stimulation and the NeoControl chair. *If yours doesn't...*

•**Contact your insurer's customer service department.** Most companies will provide coverage if you can show that self-help methods are more economical than other approaches, such as surgery.

•**Get permission to try self-help strategies for two months.** At that point, your health-care provider must send a letter documenting your progress.

•**Choose an incontinence specialist experienced in working with insurers.**[*]

WHEN SURGERY IS NECESSARY

Surgery is an option if self-help strategies and drug therapy fail. Surgical procedures include adding bulk to the urethra to increase its resistance to urine flow...repositioning the base of the bladder and the urethra...and inserting a "cuff" around the urethra to keep it closed until urination is desired.

[*]To find a qualified incontinence specialist, contact the National Association for Continence (800-252-3337).

Incontinence Update

The incontinence drug *tolterodine* (Detrol) works just as well as older drugs—and is less likely to cause dry mouth and other troublesome side effects. The first new drug for overactive bladder in 20 years, Detrol may be effective in curbing symptoms of urinary frequency and urgency.

Harold P. Drutz, MD, professor and head of urogynecology, University of Toronto Faculty of Medicine.

Natural Relief

To relieve constipation, mix one-half cup of unprocessed bran, one-half cup of applesauce and one-third cup of prune juice. Refrigerate the mixture. Take two tablespoons after dinner, followed by a glass of water. If this does not relieve constipation, increase the dose to three or four tablespoons. *Diet hints:* Eat plenty of fresh fruit, vegetables and fiber. If the extra fiber causes excess gas, try the herbal remedy *epazote. Note:* For people with restricted mobility, more fiber can aggravate constipation.

Craig Rubin, MD, professor of internal medicine and chief of geriatrics, University of Texas southwestern Medical Center, Dallas.

Easy Steps to Avoid Irregularity and Constipation

St. Luke's Episcopal Hospital, Houston, TX, a member of the Texas Medical Center.

Irregularity and constipation are common in children and in older adults and, although there may be many causes, including diet, stress and even medications, there are some easy ways to deal with these problems.

What they are: The experts at St Luke's Episcopal Hospital, Houston, Texas, explain that irregularity means bowel movements that do not occur regularly, while constipation means infrequent or difficult bowel movements, or hard, dry stools. Because there is no normal pattern for bowel movements, and frequency ranges from as many as three a day to as few as three or four a week, frequency alone is not necessarily an indicator of irregularity and constipation. But a change in normal pattern and difficult bowel movements may suggest that they are present.

Whatever the diagnosis, the common symptoms of irregularity and constipation include a bloated, full feeling, sluggishness, headache, loss of appetite, straining to move the bowels, a general sense of feeling out of sorts and occasionally nausea.

How to avoid problems: Six simple changes in your habits can go a long way to freeing you of suffering from these maladies:

● **Set aside a time for regular bowel movements,** and do not delay when you feel the urge to have a bowel movement.

● **Avoid straining when going to the bathroom.**

● **Drink lots of liquids**—six to eight 8-ounce glasses a day—unless otherwise instructed by your doctor.

● **Increase the soluble fiber in your diet gradually** by eating more cereals, breads and whole grains (such as bran, whole wheat, oatmeal and brown rice), and fresh fruits and vegetables (such as celery, beans, prunes and leafy vegetables). Your physician may recommend soluble fiber supplements.

● **Eat regular meals,** and chew food thoroughly and slowly.

● **Exercise daily.**

Men and Menopause

Barbara Sherwin, PhD, co-director of the McGill University Menopause Clinic in Montreal and associate professor of psychology and obstetrics and gynecology at McGill University.

Not enough men understand what menopause is. As a result, even the most sympathetic man may be thrown completely off balance when the woman in his life begins to exhibit the physiological and emotional symptoms of menopause. Sadly, his ignorance will prevent him from helping the woman he loves …and may even cause him to inadvertently do and say things that make matters worse.

Thanks to books like Gail Sheehy's *The Silent Passage* and Germaine Greer's *The Change,* magazine articles and TV talk shows, the whole subject of menopause has come out of the closet. But plenty of myths and misconceptions remain…and they often lead to problems between men—who see in menopause their own mortality—and their menopausal wives. *Answers to basic questions:*

What is menopause? Menopause occurs when the ovaries stop producing the female hormone estrogen and menstruation ceases.

When does menopause typically occur? Menopause is actually a prolonged series of events that occur over years. On average, it starts at around age 51, but the symptoms are the most intense during perimenopause—about two years before and two years after.

What's causing my wife's physical and emotional changes? The hot flashes, the thinning of the vaginal tissues, the decreased vaginal lubrication, the mood swings are all the result of the ovaries producing little or no estrogen now. Any or all of these changes are perfectly normal and to be expected.

Why is my wife less interested in sex now? *A couple of reasons:* The changes in the reproductive tract may make intercourse painful. And hormonal changes may cause a decrease in her sexual desire.

Is there any good news? Definitely! Most of the worst symptoms of menopause can be alleviated with hormone-replacement therapy. Even if she doesn't take hormones, some of the troublesome symptoms may naturally wane in time. She should discuss her course of action with her gynecologist. *Advantages of hormone therapy:* Control of hot flashes…restoration of integrity of genital tissues…women generally feel better. *Long-term bonus:* Hormonal therapy helps protect against osteoporosis and possibly Alzheimer's disease. *Disadvantages:* Women with an intact uterus also receive progestin to prevent endometrial cancer, and this can cause resumption of menstruation. *Long-term risk:* Estrogen therapy for more than 15 years can cause a slightly increased risk of breast cancer.

How can I be more supportive of my wife now? Visit the gynecologist with her, so that you can show your support and get your own questions about menopause answered—just as more and more husbands are going to prenatal classes to learn about pregnancy and labor and to be there for their wives.

Give your wife a break. If she's more tired than usual these days, tell her you won't mind if she isn't up to attending the theater or going out after work. *Better:* Make dinner for the two of you, order in…or take her out to eat more often. Don't gripe when she wants to fling open the windows in mid-December—just get yourself another blanket. Offer to rub her feet or bring her a cup of tea. You get the idea.

Anything else? Avoid such inflammatory comments as:

"It's all in your mind!"…"There's nothing wrong with you!"

We have to be careful not to make menopause sound like an illness. Without the fear of pregnancy now…with the children perhaps grown and out of the house…with greater time for recreation and for each other, many couples report that this is the happiest time in their life…and that sex is better than ever. Menopause can actually be the start of a wonderful new phase for you both.

Tips for Denture Wearers

Removing dentures at night can lead to aching jaws, headaches and insomnia.

Reason: Jaws adapt to closing over teeth. If you sleep without your dentures, you may "over-close"—which strains the jaw joint and muscles.

Recommended: If you have morning-after pain, try leaving dentures in at night (but remove them for four hours during the day).

An Army study of 200 denture wearers, cited in *American Health*, 28 W. 23 St., New York 10010.

Music vs. Rectal Exam Pain

Colorectal cancer is the second-leading cause of death by cancer in the US, but many patients are reluctant to undergo a sigmoidoscopy because the exam can be embarrassing and uncomfortable.

Good news: 88% of patients who listened to music during a sigmoidoscopy reported reduced levels of anxiety and pain. Their blood pressure and heart rates were also lower than those of people who didn't listen to music.

Brian Sweeney, MD, assistant professor of surgery, University of Massachusetts Medical Center, Worcester. His study of 50 men and women 20 to 76 years of age was presented at a meeting of the American Society of Colon and Rectal Surgeons, 85 W. Algonquin Rd., Arlington Heights, IL 60005.

Try Plato, Not Prozac!

Lou Marinoff, PhD, associate professor of philosophy at City College of New York, New York. He is founding president of the American Philosophical Practitioners Association and author of *Plato, Not Prozac! Applying Eternal Wisdom to Everyday Problems.* HarperCollins.

L ife isn't always to our liking. Marriages can be filled with strife. We fall ill. We lose those we love. We retire…and find leisure empty.

Faced with problems, worry and confusion, more and more people today seek help by talking through their painful emotions with a psychotherapist, or taking potent medications. Sometimes, these are absolutely necessary. But in many cases, they're not.

Often, suffering isn't a matter of emotional maladjustment or brain chemistry, but understanding. What we need to examine are our lives and our beliefs…what we need to change is how we see things. What we need isn't therapy, but philosophy.

WHY PHILOSOPHY?

What are you? On the one hand, you're a biological creation—flesh, blood and chemical reactions. Something goes awry in your metabolism, and you get diabetes. Or a disorder in brain cells with which you think and feel can cause misery or anxiety and require medication.

On the other hand, you're a psychological creature, shaped by decades of experience. If you were abused as a child or grew up in a family where anger must be buried at all costs, you may have emotional difficulties that require the help of a psychotherapist.

But human beings are also thinking beings governed by beliefs, not biology or emotion. How you explain the world to yourself, what you see as truly important, why you're here and where you're going…these can create and dispel turmoil. That's where philosophy comes in.

Philosophy has much to offer. All you need is a willingness to lead an examined life, to take a step back, look inside the things that bother you, consider what you truly believe and explore what you can do about it.

LOOKING AT LIFE PHILOSOPHICALLY

A "philosophy of life" may sound like something for gurus, but actually everyone has one—although most of us don't put it into words.

Everyone, that is, has beliefs about how the world works, what counts and what doesn't, what's right and what's wrong.

An important step in resolving problems is becoming aware of what you already believe: To look at what's troubling you in an analytical way…to see—and understand—what turns a "situation" into a "problem." And to understand how your philosophy of life can help you make the most of it.

Many people have found help in this process from a new breed of counselors, "philosophical practitioners" who have studied philosophy intensively and are experienced in applying ideas to life problems. But you may be able to do it on your own. *Here's how…*

"PEACE" IS THE WAY

It's best to work systematically using the "PEACE" process…

- **Identify the *problem.***
- **Take stock of the *emotions* that it evokes.**
- ***Analyze* your options.**
- ***Contemplate* the entire situation.**
- **Reach an *equilibrium* through understanding and effective action.**

Although we usually think we know what's bothering us, sometimes introspection takes us deeper. What seems like just bad luck or ill treatment may turn out, on closer inspection, to be more complex.

Example: The company where you've worked for 30 years has downsized, forcing you to retire sooner than you wanted. The "problem" seems obvious—you've lost your job and suddenly have less money than you're used to. But closer thought makes you recognize that you can get by quite easily. Then why do you feel so anxious and unhappy? Your *reaction* is the real problem.

Looking analytically at your emotions, you see that underneath the dismay and worry lies anger…you feel you've been treated unfairly by those you gave much of your life to. You're also feeling insecure and disoriented by the sudden change in circumstances.

What are your options? Your job is gone. You can nurse a grudge or spend hours fuming and fantasizing revenge. Or, you can put it behind you and seek other employment. Or make a virtue of necessity, planning how to make your retirement full and rewarding.

Contemplating the situation means thoughtfully pondering these alternatives, weighing their consequences and trying to develop the philosophical outlook that works best for you. The first two options, you realize quickly, are unlikely to bring you happiness or lasting pleasure.

You know it would be best to go beyond the setback and enjoy the rest of your life, but you hurt!

Making peace with the situation takes time… it may take weeks, even months, of thoughtful contemplation to put the problem in perspective. You may need to ponder just why you're angry—perhaps at the "unfairness" of it all—and resolve this with the realization that the cost-cutting move wasn't directed at you personally. You're upset by the change, but come to the recognition that change is simply an inexorable fact of life.

Contemplation may involve searching exploration of yourself—who are you? What's most important to you? Which of your feelings come from deep inside you…and which did you simply learn from others? If being independent emerges as a powerful value, then you can see this situation as an opportunity to develop that trait.

Finally, you put the fruits of your contemplation into action. The "problem" is no longer a problem, but a fact of life, and the understanding you've attained tells you where to go from there. You've achieved a new equilibrium that allows you to go on with your life.

20

Self-Defense

The Ultimate Guide to Avoiding Violent Crime

The first rule of avoiding violent crime on the street or in the home is to understand this—*it can happen to you.* No neighborhood is immune.

You can improve your odds that the bad guy won't pick you. How? Make yourself a tough target.

Just as the lion chooses the weakest antelope to pick off from the pack, the bad guy chooses the easiest victim—the weak one, the one who isn't paying attention, the one least likely to resist.

But there's a trick to this game. It's not how tough you really are—it's how tough you *look.*

Psychologists use the term, "displaying the weapons of aggression." Dogs bare their teeth, cats show their claws and you should show the bad guys you have something to fight back with, too.

Example: A woman who jogs with a dog might be no tougher than one without a dog, but she looks tougher. The dog is an unknown quantity to any would-be muggers—and muggers don't like to take unnecessary chances.

PEPPER SPRAYS AND PERSONAL ALARMS

Another weapon of aggression you should consider is pepper spray. It's easy to use. Pressing the button sprays a stream of oleoresin capsicum more than 1,000 times more powerful than Tabasco sauce. Unlike tear gas, pepper spray deters even crazed drug users and vicious animals. That's why mail carriers use it.

If you're afraid you wouldn't be able to use pepper spray on someone, consider a personal alarm. Pull out the pin, and it emits a piercing alarm until you reinsert the pin. They're better than whistles, because whistles stop making noise the moment you stop blowing.

Important: To scare off potential attackers, keep the spray in your hand, ready for fire. Keep

J.J. Bittenbinder, a retired detective with the Chicago Police and a frequent lecturer on personal safety.

283

the alarm attached to your waistband or in a jacket pocket.

Personal alarms and pepper sprays are available in hardware stores and gun shops. If you have trouble finding them, call your local police department and ask where they get theirs.

People often ask me whether it's a good idea to own a gun. It's always a personal choice, but I don't recommend it. A gun in the home is far more likely to be fired by accident, during a domestic dispute or in a suicide, than used to protect the family from an intruder. Any situation that reaches the point where you need to use a gun has already gone too far. Prevention is much better.

AVOIDING SEXUAL ASSAULT

To keep a date from turning into date rape, a woman should resist unwanted sexual advances strongly and clearly, or she runs the risk of being misunderstood.

If a man kisses you against your will, bite down on his lower lip...or grab his scrotum and wring it like a towel.

Teach your children that it's okay to say no to adults—especially in the area of forced affection. Never insist that a child allow Grandpa to kiss her—give her the choice. Otherwise, you'll be giving her the message that it's okay for adults to force themselves on her.

When kids go somewhere together, remind them never to leave one another behind. If they have to run, the faster one should always wait for the slower one.

BANK MACHINE SELF-DEFENSE

Automatic teller machines (ATMs) are certainly convenient, but they can leave you exposed to muggers.

To minimize risk: Use a drive-through ATM whenever possible. If anyone approaches, drive away. Failing that, stick to an ATM in an enclosed kiosk—one that requires a magnetic card for entry and which is equipped with a security camera. ATM kiosks inside a building or store are safer than stand-alone kiosks.

Avoid ATMs located directly on the street—especially if it's a deserted street at night. If the ATM is next to an alley, where someone can pop out with no warning, that's even worse.

If you must use a street ATM, do so during the day or with a friend—in an area with people around.

Special problem: ATMs with vertical keypads. They allow a robber to watch as you punch in your personal identification number—increasing the odds that he'll try to steal your card. Try to use an ATM with a horizontal keypad—one that's parallel with the ground.

ON THE STREET

Don't make things easy on muggers by wearing headphones and listening to loud music. Headphones prevent you from hearing someone coming up behind you—making you an easy target.

Don't flash jewelry on the street, subway or bus either—even if it's fake.

Women: Carry your purse in front of you, not bouncing on your hip.

Men: Keep your wallet in your front pants pocket or in the vest pocket inside your coat. Using the back pants pocket only invites pickpockets.

If you're approached by a suspicious-looking character, cross the street or walk in the middle of the street to maintain your distance. Don't worry about appearing overly cautious.

Helpful: Wrap two $1 bills inside a $5 bill and put them in a money clip. If a robber demands your money, toss the clip in one direction, say, "That's all I've got," and run as fast as you can in the other direction.

IN YOUR HOME

There's no doubt about it—good locks and bright lighting are your best bet against a break-in. Keep shrubs pruned so that they don't hide your windows from neighbors' view.

The best alarm systems are those monitored by the company that sells them. Typically, these alarm systems call the police or fire department when a signal goes off.

You're provided with code numbers to use in case you set it off accidentally...and a "hostage code" to secretly alert police that you're being held.

At the first sound of an intruder, dial 911. If you own a cellular phone, keep the recharger near your bed. That way, if an intruder cuts your phone lines, you can still call 911.

THWARTING CARJACKERS

A car phone is a great investment in safety. You can use it to dial 911 in any emergency. And just the sight of it is often enough to deter would-be attackers.

Some motorists are now equipping their cars with electronic homing devices that automatically alert the police if their car is stolen—and lead them to it. These devices are effective—but expensive for many people.

Every car is already equipped with the best possible anti-carjacking device—the door locks. Use them even when you're inside the car. It's hard for a carjacker to be successful if he cannot get inside your car.

If someone does get in—get out. No car is worth dying for.

If someone orders you into a car—his or yours—don't do it. Odds are you'll never come back. *Instead:* Run for it. Statistics show that 95% of people who run from an armed kidnapper survive. Most kidnappers won't shoot. The few who do usually miss.

Protecting Yourself Against Muggers

Ken Glickman, coordinator of Educational Services, Greenwich Institute for American Education, Greenwich, CT 06830.

The best defense against becoming a crime victim is to avoid a setup. Muggers, like most people, don't take more risks or work harder than they have to. *Point:* They choose victims who seem easy to handle. And they create situations that make the attack simpler.

Chief defense: Don't allow yourself to be distracted, isolated or simply stopped on the street by a stranger. Muggers prefer victims who have stopped moving. They use every technique to accomplish that—asking for directions, a match or a handout.

First and most important rule: When spoken to by a suspicious stranger, don't stop. Move away quickly. Don't slow down to watch an argument or any other commotion on the street. Fake street fights are a favorite way to set up a robbery.

DEFENSIVE TACTICS

Walk down the middle of the sidewalk near the street. Be wary of corners and doorways. Reduce the possibility of being grabbed from the shadows. Hugging the curb permits you to see around the corner while at a distance. Be alert to someone hiding between or behind parked cars.

Walk a couple of extra blocks to take a safe route, especially late at night. Keep to known neighborhoods. Identify in advance where the places of refuge are, in the event of trouble.

Look ahead, up the street (not down) to see what's happening. Be alert, especially to people loitering or moving suspiciously. *Example:* Two men up ahead who suddenly separate and begin walking apart. They could be preparing to set you up.

However foolish or rude it may seem, don't get on any self-service elevator if there's somebody at all suspicious on it. Never let an elevator you are on go to the basement. *How to avoid it:* When entering an open elevator, keep a foot in the door while pressing the floor number. Keep your eyes on the elevator indicator. If the arrow is pointing down, don't get in.

Don't get into a self-service elevator late at night without making sure nobody is waiting on an upper floor to intercept you. *How to do it:* Push the top floor elevator button, but don't get in. If the elevator does not stop on any floor on the way up or down, it's safe.

Avoid places where gangs of juveniles congregate. They can be more dangerous than professional muggers because they will often hurt a victim rather than take the money and run.

Get into the habit of automatically saying *excuse me* when you bump into someone on the street. Say it no matter whose fault it is.

Never show money in public, whether at a newsstand, market, bank or getting out of a cab. Muggers are watching.

If you are mugged: Cooperate. Above all, communicate the willingness to cooperate. Keep calm. It can help relax the mugger, too, which is crucial. *Reason:* If a mugger is pointing a cocked revolver, nervousness on his part could be fatal to you. *Ways to calm the situation:* Say something reassuring, or ask a distracting question that establishes the mugging as a businesslike transaction. *Example:* "You can have anything you want. Do you mind if I just keep my driver's license?"

Never move suddenly. *Tell the mugger where your wallet is and ask:* "Do you want me to get it or do you want to get it?"

A woman mugger with a knife or gun can kill just as easily as a man. Letting macho feelings interfere with cooperating is suicidal.

Don't show the slightest condescension or hostility. Be careful of your tone of voice. Cooperating with disdain can set off violence. *Best attitude to project:* You've got to earn a living, too. *Or:* I don't hold this against you at all; times are tough.

Don't make jokes. They are too risky, and the chance for misinterpretation is too great.

Avoid direct or steady eye contact.

If a mugger is particularly hostile, be supercooperative. Offer money or possessions he has overlooked.

Bottom line: Always carry mugger money. Keep $25 to $100 in your pocket as insurance. A happy mugger is much less likely to do harm than one who comes away empty-handed.

What You Can Do To Avoid Terrorism

Susan Blum, former editor, *Bottom Line/Health,* 281 Tresser Blvd., Stamford, CT 06901.

The enormity of recent terrorist attacks have made us all vigilant. But what specific steps are necessary to avoid being hurt in the midst of an attack?

We spoke with Michael Zanker, MD, assistant professor of clinical emergency medicine at the University of Connecticut in Hartford and a well-known expert on terrorism. He offered several pointers on how to avoid being hurt in a terrorist attack…

●**If you see several people vomiting or having seizures,** do not rush over to help. These symptoms can be caused by chemical agents such as the nerve gas released in the Tokyo subway in 1995. Good Samaritans who offer assistance could wind up being exposed to the same agent.

It's probably okay to give aid if only one person is ill. But stay away and alert the authorities if two or more people exhibit the same odd symptoms.

●**In case of a bomb blast while you're indoors,** crouch under a heavy desk or table or a door frame. If outside, run for it. Do not stick around. Terrorists often set a second bomb to go off minutes after a first.

●**And…if you see an unattended suitcase or parcel in a public place**—airport, train station, etc.—alert the authorities at once. It could harbor a bomb or a biological or chemical weapon.

If you're headed overseas, you can get details on recent terrorist activity at your destination from the US State Department. Go to *www.state.gov,* and click on "travel."

Police-Impersonator Self-Defense

The color of the flashing lights atop police cars are not standardized across the United States. While red flashers are common, many police forces use combinations on their vehicles, such as blue-and-red and blue-and-white. Other police forces use just blue lights.

Self-defense: To protect yourself from criminals impersonating highway police—without violating the law—turn on emergency flashers when an unmarked vehicle signals you from behind …stay on the road…slow down…then stop at the first well-lighted, populated area, such as a gas station.

Phil Lynn, manager, National Law Enforcement Policy Center, International Association of Chiefs of Police, Alexandria, VA.

How Not to Be Swindled

J.L. Simmons, PhD, author of *67 Ways to Protect Seniors From Crime*. Henry Holt and Co. Inc.

Here's some very good advice to help you steer clear of swindlers and avoid being an easy mark…

●**If any offer sounds too good to be true,** you can be virtually certain that it is.

●**Never rush or impulse buy.** Swindlers don't want to give you any time to think the deal over because your common sense might prevail.

●**Responses to help separate the good guys from the bad guys:** "Well, let me talk this over with my attorney."…"I'll check this out with the Better Business Bureau and get back to you."

●**If an offer is in person or by phone,** insist on getting details in writing before making a decision.

●**Check out any offer or recommendation thoroughly.** Call your local Area Agency on Aging or Better Business Bureau.

●**Investigate and comparison shop as you would with any major purchase.** Check it out with knowledgeable people.

●**Don't sign anything until you've done your investigation.**

●**Use credit cards, or at least checks—** never cash. With credit cards and checks there is a legal record of your payment.

●**Never give out your credit card,** Medicare, Social Security, telephone calling card or bank account numbers to solicitors.

●**The fact that an offer appears on network TV** or in a respected magazine or major newspaper means nothing. Acceptance

standards for ads are notoriously lax and virtually anyone can buy advertising.

●**Beware of anyone touting "little or no risk."**

●**If you get taken, don't be too embarrassed to report it to the police,** your local attorney general, the Better Business Bureau and any relevant professional association. You might help save others from being hurt.

Before You Give To Charity…

Check on how a charity spends its money before you donate. Send the name of the charity and a self-addressed, stamped envelope to the National Charities Information Bureau (NCIB), 19 Union Square W., Sixth Floor, New York 10003. You can also request a free copy of the NCIB's *Wise Giving Guide,* which evaluates 300 charitable organizations.

Also: You can request free information on up to three charities by sending a letter accompanied by a self-addressed, stamped envelope to the Philanthropic Advisory Service of the Council of Better Business Bureaus, 4200 Wilson Blvd., Arlington, VA 22203.

Nancy Dunnan, financial columnist, writing in *Your Money,* 5705 N. Lincoln Ave., Chicago 60659.

High-Tech Scams

Beware: Criminals are using new technology to perpetuate old scams. *Examples:* Work-at-home schemes still promise untold riches—but solicitations now arrive by e-mail and tout medical-billing software instead of envelope-stuffing kits…official-looking notices of travel "bargains" are faxed to companies to trick employees into booking scam vacations with their credit cards. *Increasingly important:* Check out a company by calling your local Better Business Bureau or visiting *www.bbb.org. Caution:* Burgeoning area

287

codes make it hard to tell whether a phone number is domestic or international. *To identify unfamiliar area codes: www.555-1212.com.* If your money leaves the country, it is nearly impossible to get it back.

Holly Cherico, vice president of communications, Council of Better Business Bureaus, Inc., Arlington, VA.

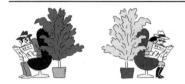

How to Keep *Them* From Knowing Too Much About *You*

Robert Ellis Smith, publisher of *Privacy Journal*, Box 28577, Providence, RI 02908. He is author of *Ben Franklin's Web Site: Privacy and Curiosity from Plymouth Rock to the Internet.* Privacy Journal.

New technology allows more scrutiny than ever of your public and private actions—your data are available to everyone from con artists and telemarketers to your bank, employer, insurance companies and more.

You can't prevent disclosure of *some* of your private information. But you can do a personal risk assessment. Often, a small amount of caution can neutralize large risks to your privacy.

ONLINE ACTIVITY

Every Web site you visit collects information about your surfing habits.

Result: Your e-mailbox is flooded with unwanted solicitations.

With just your e-mail address, anyone can find out your spouse's name, where you live, how much you paid for your house, etc. *Self-defense...*

●**Use a special e-mail address for surfing the Internet**—especially if you visit chat rooms, newsgroups or register on Web sites. That's where junk mailers harvest information. This way, you can more easily sift through undesirable e-mail.

If you want to use your regular e-mail address in newsgroups, insert "no-spam-"* when you are asked to give your e-mail address.

*Spam is unsolicited e-mail.

Example: *no-spam-john-doe@isp.com.* If junk mailers try to reach you at this e-mail address, their mail will be returned.

Individuals who really want to reach you can simply strip off the "no-spam" portion of the address when they reply.

●**Don't reply to spam or junk e-mail,** even if it's to ask the sender to remove you from its list.

Reason: Responding confirms your e-mail address and invites more spam.

Better: Send a complaint e-mail to your Internet Service Provider (ISP). It should contact the spammer's ISP.

You can also use antispam software. It works in conjunction with your e-mail software to filter out junk e-mail.

Popular: SpamScan97 *(www.webster-image.com/SpamScan97)*...and Spam Buster *(www.contactplus.com).*

●**Alter your browser to reveal less information about you** when you download files from Web sites. If you use Netscape, choose Communicator from the system menu and select *Messenger.*

●Under *Edit* menu, select *Preferences.*

●Scroll down and click *Advanced.*

●Remove the checkmark in the *Send e-mail as anonymous FTP password* box.

●Click on *OK.*

If you use Microsoft Internet Explorer 5, go to Tools–Internet Options.

●Click the *Security tab.* Highlight the *Internet* icon.

●Click the *Custom Level* tab.

●Scroll down to *User Authentications/ Logon.*

●Click *Anonymous Logon.*

Warning: Don't disable your cookies. Cookies are data strings in your Internet browser that identify you when you visit a Web page. If you turn off this function to remain invisible, most sites will not allow you to enter.

●**Examine the "privacy policy"** before you use a Web site regularly. Some sites enable you to check an "opt-out" box if you don't want to receive e-mail from marketers.

●**Investigate yourself online**—to see how much about you is available to the public. Type your name into search engines, such as *www.lycos.com* and *www.excite.com*. To check your postings in Internet newsgroups, search *www.dejanews.com*. Ask directories that list e-mail addresses, home addresses, phone numbers, etc. to remove yours. *Big ones include…*

- *www.anywho.com*
- *www.bigfoot.com*
- *www.people.yahoo.com*
- *www.infospace.com*
- *www.switchboard.com*
- *www.whowhere.lycos.com*

Use a specific credit card only for online purchases. That way you can conveniently cancel the card if it is stolen or misused.

Warning: Purchases made through conventional retail stores may also be monitored if you pay by credit card or check—or if you are a member of the store's "customer club." To keep your purchases anonymous, pay by cash and don't give any personal data—not even a phone number.

YOUR MEDICAL RECORDS

More and more nonmedical employees in the health industry have access to your confidential information. *Self-defense…*

Check your medical records the same way you would your credit reports. Look over HMO, Medicare and Medicaid files twice a year. Check for incorrect, embarrassing or outdated entries.

Example: If you haven't had high blood pressure for five years, ask your health-care provider to remove—or at least segregate—the item.

Helpful resource: The Medical Information Bureau (MIB), a central database of personal medical information on millions of Americans. It is used by many insurance companies.

Get a copy of your file by writing to: MIB, Box 105, Essex Station, Boston 02112…or call 617-426-3660. *Cost:* $8.50, or free if you receive a letter from an insurance company stating that it used MIB information to make a decision about you.

●**Talk with your physician and his/her staff.** Request in writing that the office physician give out the minimum amount of medical information from your file that is required. Many doctors hand over a patient's entire file without thinking about the potential consequences.

Example: If you have an auto accident, the insurance company should get the information that it needs to settle the claim. But it doesn't need to know that you once took antidepressants or that you are diabetic.

In court: If your medical records are ever subpoenaed, they become public record. Ask the court to allow only the relevant portions of your medical record as evidence. A judge will decide what parts should be kept private. After the case is over, ask the judge to "seal" the court records containing your medical information.

●**Never sign a standard "blanket waiver."** It authorizes the release of all information regarding your medical history, symptoms, treatment, exam results or diagnosis.

Better: Edit the waiver. Write in your own specific terms to limit what's released…

I authorize information from my records to be released from hospital X as relates to my condition Y.

Be sure to add an expiration date to the release.

FINANCIAL INFORMATION

Large banks and credit card companies routinely sell your financial data—from account balances to payment histories—to marketers. This leads to a deluge of promotional mail and phone calls. *Self-defense…*

Find out about the "opt-out" provisions before you use a financial service.

Example: American Express never gives detailed account information to outside merchants. It also sends customers a notice asking if they want to receive product offers from American Express or other marketers.

●**Diminish mail and dinner-time phone calls from direct marketers.**

●Add your name to the "Telephone Preference Service" and "Mail Preference Service" lists maintained by the Direct Marketing Association, Box 9008, Farmingdale, NY 11735.

•List your telephone number but not your street address in the telephone book. This will foil compilers of many marketing lists.

•Ask each of the four major credit bureaus not to disclose your credit information to marketers. Call 888-5OPTOUT—this number reaches the four credit bureaus.

Send a check to yourself if you do electronic banking. This is an excellent way to test your bank's privacy loopholes. See if the bank sends you as the payee any unnecessary data.

SOCIAL SECURITY NUMBER

Social Security Numbers (SSNs) are commonly used in computer recordkeeping.

Your SSN gives a thief access to your entire identity—and all information that is associated with it financially. *Self-defense...*

•**Only disclose your Social Security Number to private companies** when there are tax consequences, such as opening an interest-bearing account at a bank. Most insurance companies and some credit card companies will back off if you refuse to give your SSN. As a fallback position, offer to provide the last four digits.

•**Review your Social Security statement,** which the government now automatically mails annually to every worker over age 25 (about three months before his/her birthday). *If needed sooner: www.ssa.gov.*

•**Never put your Social Security Number on your checks** or any identifying information.

If your state's Department of Motor Vehicles uses the SSN as the driver's license number, ask for an alternative number. Most states will grant one.

If a private business requests your SSN on an application, simply leave the space blank or write "refused." Most companies will not question this—or will back off when you ask to see a written policy requiring your SSN.

Web Site Trap

Medical Web sites do not protect visitors' privacy—even if they claim they do. Georgetown University's recent study found that most leading health sites share the information they collect with other companies—from health-care providers and direct marketers to manufacturers of drugs or health-care products. The study also found that visitors to health Web sites are not anonymous, even if they think they are. *Trap:* Many medical organizations require online registration to access their Web sites. *Self-defense:* Give as little personal information as possible ...do not complete surveys.

John Featherman, president, featherman.com, consumer privacy consultants, Philadelphia.

Choose Your Passwords Carefully

A recent security test at Stanford University found that a simple password-cracking program could deduce one-fifth of all university account passwords. *Helpful:* Choose longer passwords...mix letters, numbers and special characters...use different passwords for different applications...change passwords at least every six months. *Avoid:* Your name...mother's maiden name...birthday...Social Security number. *Critical:* If you suspect someone is trying to determine your password, report it to relevant authorities.

John Featherman, president, featherman.com, consumer privacy consultants, Philadelphia.

New Privacy Danger

A federal court decision allows phone companies to sell data about customers to third parties—without customers' permission. Phone companies successfully argued their right of free commercial speech lets them use data they collect any way they wish. *Troubling trend:* Many Web sites collect browsing preferences...banks sell account information...and even medical files are not fully protected. The court decision on phone data is being appealed. If it stands, contact your local and long-distance companies and opt out of all data-transfer arrangements.

John Featherman, president, featherman.com, consumer privacy consultants, Philadelphia.

Phone Bill Alert

Check your long-distance phone plan quarterly to find out if it is still best for you. Rates and calling plans change continuously. If your monthly long-distance bills exceed $50, inquire *monthly*. Ask your carrier to check your calls to see if it has a cheaper plan. To check among many carriers, visit *www.trac.org*, and use the free *Web pricer*. You enter your calls from a recent bill, and the pricer compares costs among six top companies and picks the best carrier for your calling pattern.

Samuel Simon, founder of TRAC—Telecommunications Research & Action Center, Box 27279, Washington, DC 20005.

Slamming Self-Defense

Slamming—the unauthorized switching of long-distance telephone service—is still common. *Helpful:* Call your local phone company, and ask for a Primary Interexchange Carrier (PIC) freeze. This locks you into your current long-distance carrier so your service cannot be switched unless you call the local phone company.

Holly Anderson, director of communications, National Consumers League, 1701 K St. NW, Suite 1200, Washington, DC 20006.

Dangers Where You Least Expect Them

Melinda Muse, a health journalist and author of *I'm Afraid, You're Afraid: 448 Things to Fear and Why.* Hyperion.

As a health journalist, I read and write a lot about medical advances. One big lesson I've learned is that life today is no longer survival of the fittest—but of the wariest.

Here are some surprisingly dangerous places, things and situations…

●**Personal computers and the Internet.** The Web is a virtual downer. People who spend even just a few hours a week online are more depressed and feel more isolated than those who log on less frequently.

Hunching over your computer for hours isn't good for your physical health, either. After observing elementary school students slumped at computer workstations, Cornell University researchers concluded that at least 40% were at risk for serious repetitive stress injuries.

●**Frequent flying.** Hazards of flying include luggage carts, which have those elastic tethers with metal hooks on each end. They have snapped back into eyes, causing dislocated lenses, internal bleeding, retinal detachment and temporary loss of sight.

Think twice before grabbing that aisle seat. Every year, some 4,500 passengers are hit by items falling from overstuffed luggage bins. Briefcases are the most common missiles in the carry-on arsenal, but it also includes laptops, golf clubs and heavy backpacks.

●**Long flights.** An estimated 350 passengers die in-flight in the US every year, with heart attacks the leading cause. Sitting for four hours or more in arid cabins risks dehydration and reduces circulation in the legs by half, which could cause blood clots. If a piece of the clot breaks off and makes its way to the lungs, it can be deadly.

What to do: During long flights, walk the aisles often…and drink plenty of bottled water (unbottled airline water can carry additional health risks).

●**Hotel rooms.** Check out your room before you check in. Blood, semen and other bodily fluids have been found on purportedly "clean" sheets, blankets and bedspreads.

According to Johns Hopkins School of Public Health, it is possible to contract hepatitis from soiled bed linens, as well as to pick up body lice, which burrow in mattresses and covers.

What to do: Never lie on a hotel bedspread —strip it off. Check sheets for freshness. And don't pad around barefoot, since bathroom floors may host athlete's foot fungi.

●**Yard work.** Need good reasons not to spend hours grooming your lawn?

Americans scatter 70 million pounds of pesticides on their yards every year. Your hands are most likely to be exposed, but your forehead, abdomen and crotch absorb pesticides faster than other body parts.

Research at Memorial Sloan-Kettering Cancer Center in New York suggests that sunscreen, while preventing sunburn, gives people a false sense of security, making them feel they can indulge in more sun time. One million Americans are diagnosed with skin cancer every year. Protect yourself by covering up.

●**Garage sales.** These hagglers' havens are notorious for unloading unsafe products, including bunk beds that can strangle…cribs that can suffocate…dangerous baby carriages …collapsing playpens…beanbag chairs stuffed with foam pellets that have choked children.

●**Money.** Coins and greenbacks are cruddy with germ colonies, including fecal bacteria… Staphylococcus, which causes food poisoning …and acne-causing Propionibacterium. It seems the smaller the denomination, the more dangerous.

A test of $20 bills uncovered money's other dirty secret—cash is contaminated by cocaine. The *Journal of Forensic Sciences* says, "…most Americans handle small amounts of cocaine every day…on dollar bills." Follow Mom's advice about keeping your hands out of your mouth.

●**Gemstones.** Radiation is sometimes used to deepen the color of gemstones, which greatly enhances their value. Although "nuked" gems should be kept in lead casings for several years while their radiation levels taper off, unscrupulous traders have released to the market "hot" cat's-eye gemstones, some registering 51 times the US radiation limits. Experts estimate that thousands of radioactive stones are in circulation in the US, Europe and Asia.

●**Mondays…Fridays…and Saturdays.**

●Mondays produce more suicides than any other day, says the American Association of Suicidology. It is also the day when the most heart attacks occur.

●Fridays produce more car accidents than any other day of the week.

●Saturdays produce the greatest number of fatal motor vehicle crashes. Most occur between 4 pm and 4 am.

●**Casinos.** The odds are lousy. Only 150 of 736 high rollers who suffered a heart attack in Las Vegas casinos lived to place another wager, according to a recent study. Paramedics must maneuver through throngs in the mammoth gaming halls, wasting valuable life-saving time. Hedging their bets, many casinos have installed defibrillators.

●**Kissing your dog.** Each year, more than one million Americans get parasites, such as roundworms, hookworms and pinworms, from kissing their canine pals. Since parasitic infections are difficult to diagnose in humans, people often never discover the causes of their headaches, liver ailments or sinus infections. Teach Rover to shake.

Although in my book I chronicled 448 things to fear, I urge people to not let their fears overwhelm them. After all, optimism is a tonic for a longer, healthier and—dare we hope—safer life.

Health Scams

Stephen Barrett, MD, a retired psychiatrist, consumer advocate and board member of the National Council Against Health Fraud, Box 1276, Loma Linda, CA 92354. He is coauthor of *The Health Robbers: A Close Look at Quackery in America.* Prometheus Books.

If you think quacks are sleazy-looking characters whom you can spot a mile away— think again.

Many of today's medical hucksters have so much medical knowledge and are so familiar with medical jargon that they're capable of fooling doctors. In fact, some quacks are themselves doctors who believe in the ill-conceived treatments they offer. *The trendiest and most dangerous health scams now...*

•**False memory syndrome (FMS).** The darling topic of afternoon talk shows, FMS involves adults undergoing psychotherapy who suddenly recall long-repressed cases of physical and/or emotional abuse. As a result, many FMS "victims" falsely accuse, disown or sue once-loved relatives.

Recovered memories may be legitimate in rare cases. But I'm convinced that many of these people—with the help of misguided or incompetent psychotherapists—are "recalling" past events that never occurred.

These therapists—some of whom call themselves "traumatists"—often misuse hypnosis, meditation or guided imagery to help patients regress to their childhood or even to "past lives." Or the patient may be inspired by FMS books or talk show guests, and the therapist fails to help the patient distinguish fact from fantasy.

As someone who practiced psychiatry for more than 35 years, I find it very hard to believe that a person could forget such abuse. Indeed, it's much more common for victims of abuse to have trouble putting memories of abuse out of their minds.

•**Diet hocus-pocus.** Beware of any weight-loss product or program that purports to melt off pounds by suppressing appetite through hormonal manipulation or by blocking the absorption of fats, carbohydrates, sugar or calories. Such products are always phony.

And while very-low-calorie diets can help obese people under medical supervision, do-it-yourself starvation plans are dangerous. They force the body to burn lean body mass for fuel. These plans can also cause anemia, liver damage, kidney stones and mineral imbalances. In some cases they are fatal.

Some diets—including many of those spelled out in popular diet books—are pure nonsense. Authors of these hugely profitable books, who often have no training in nutrition, claim they've discovered weight-control secrets.

For example, one popular book says that when certain foods are combined in the body, they rot, poison the system and make a person fat. To avoid this, dieters are urged to eat fats, carbohydrates and protein at separate meals, concentrating on fruits in the morning and vegetables in the afternoon. The premise is utter nonsense.

Commercial weight-loss programs and diets are very popular. While these programs may help people lose weight, they don't teach dieters how to maintain their weight loss with proper eating and exercise. *Result:* The weight comes right back on.

The only sensible way to lose weight is to exercise more and eat less. Bringing about these changes may require help from a registered dietitian or another professional.

•**Chelation therapy.** This treatment involves intravenous injections of EDTA, a synthetic amino acid.

While chelation therapy is a legitimate treatment for lead poisoning, some advocates maintain that it can prevent or even reverse the accumulation of fatty deposits along artery walls (a process known as atherosclerosis).

Duped by this claim, some patients with badly blocked coronary arteries are forgoing the bypass surgery that they so desperately need, opting instead for worthless chelation injections. At least one person suffered a heart attack while on chelation therapy. Others undergoing the treatments have died of kidney failure (EDTA can be very toxic to kidneys if not properly administered).

Some proponents of chelation therapy also claim that it is effective against arthritis, Parkinson's disease, emphysema, multiple sclerosis, gangrene and psoriasis. But there's absolutely no scientific evidence to back up these contentions.

•**"Environmental illness."** Certain practitioners called clinical ecologists say the immune system can become overloaded by constant exposure to toxins in the environment.

As a result of being exposed to these toxins, these practitioners claim, certain people develop a host of ailments ranging from depression, irritability, inability to concentrate and poor memory to fatigue, respiratory problems, rashes, headache and muscle and joint pain.

Clinical ecologists "diagnose" their patients by injecting them with suspected chemical culprits and then observing their reactions—even though careful research has invalidated this provocation and neutralization test. And scientific panels have deemed the entire field of clinical ecology speculative and unproven.

Still, desperate patients agree to treatment. Some go so far as to move to the desert or rip apart their houses to get rid of synthetic chemicals...or even avoid contact with certain people suspected of giving off irritating odors.

Some patients ultimately become hermits in their own homes—afraid to venture out into a toxin-tainted world.

In fact, the symptoms these people suffer are real. But the origin of these symptoms is usually psychological, not chemical. Once patients understand this, psychotherapy may help them.

SPOTTING A QUACK

While it's essential to maintain a healthy level of skepticism when discussing medical treatments, skepticism alone is not enough to protect yourself against quacks. *I also recommend avoiding any doctor who...*

• **Claims that everyone needs to take vitamin supplements.** There's simply no evidence for this.

• **Recommends vitamins for a large number of ailments.** In fact, vitamin supplements are useful only against a very limited number of conditions.

• **Uses anecdotes and testimonials to support his/her claims.** Look instead for carefully controlled clinical studies.

• **Says that most diseases are caused by hidden allergies.** This is untrue.

• **Claims that large numbers of Americans suffer from low blood sugar** (hypoglycemia) or hidden yeast infections. Again, not true.

Beware of Nutritionists Who Advertise

Fewer than half of the so-called professionals listed in the *Yellow Pages* in 32 states were reliable sources of sound, scientifically based nutrition information. Seventy percent of those who claimed to be PhDs had phony degrees or delivered fraudulent information. Others boasted nonexistent degrees—certified nutritionist (CN), doctor of nutrimedicine (NMD) and nutrition counselor (NC). Still others had "degrees" from nonaccredited schools.

Bottom line: Don't trust nutritionists who cannot show their credentials from an accredited college or university. For a directory of accredited schools, see the *Accredited Institutions of Postsecondary Education* in your local library.

Survey by the National Council Against Health Fraud, reported in *Tufts University Diet & Nutrition Letter,* 10 High Street, Suite 706, Boston 02110.

Pacemakers and Store Security Scanners

In-store security scanners pose little threat to people with an implanted cardiac defibrillator (ICD) or pacemaker. Cases have been reported in which ICDs or pacemakers went off inappropriately when exposed to the electromagnetic beams used by the scanners, which are positioned at store exits. But in each case, the individual with the ICD lingered near the machines instead of passing through quickly. *Also:* ICD and pacemaker patients should ask airport security agents to pass security wands over the devices quickly.

Douglas P. Zipes, MD, distinguished professor of medicine and pharmacology, Indiana University School of Medicine, Indianapolis.

Self-Defense for Older Drivers

Older drivers need to take precautions to compensate for the physical and perceptual changes associated with aging.

Self-defense: Plan your trips—and drive your plan. Knowing your route lets you concentrate on driving, not navigating...choose less demanding routes, such as intersections with safer left-turn arrows...drive with a large "anticipation zone," giving yourself room to react.

For a copy of the American Association of Retired Persons' handbook, *Older Driver Public Policy Institute Fact Sheet* (Item #AC 1613) contact AARP at 800-424-3410.

How to Drive Safely Through Bad Winter Weather

Dave Phillips, tactical driving instructor at International Training Inc., the country's leading defensive driving school for businessmen, bodyguards and chauffeurs, Box 709, West Point, VA 23181. He is an ex-police chief and former special agent for the Office of Special Investigations in the US Air Force.

Winter rain, snow and ice can cause even good drivers to make dumb mistakes. Even the most cautious drivers panic when their vehicles slide out of control.

I've taught hundreds of good drivers how to be great drivers in the worst road and weather conditions. *Best self-defense techniques...*

BETTER BRAKING

●**Use heel-to-toe pivot.** This is the most efficient way to move your foot between the brake and gas.

How it works: Keep your right heel on the floor...swivel it as you switch the top half of your foot between pedals. You can move your foot twice as fast this way as you can by lifting your leg and foot each time you change pedals.

If you wear boots while driving in the winter, be sure the heel is no higher than on regular

shoes. Or remove boots in the car, and slip on flat shoes or sneakers.

●**Learn your car's brake threshold.** This is the point at which you can apply brakes hardest before they lock up. When brakes lock up, wheels lose traction and the car skids.

If you don't have antilock brakes: Drive to an empty parking lot. Accelerate to 40 miles per hour. Engage the brakes with varying pressure to see how well you can control the car. Repeat at different speeds and on different surfaces.

Avoid jamming down the brake and releasing it completely when you feel the wheels lock up—commonly known as *pump braking*. You'll only be using half of your car's braking potential. Pump braking pulls the car's weight away from front tires—causing loss of traction for steering.

Better: Apply more constant pressure to the brakes. Press the brakes until the car starts to skid. Then ease up slightly. This will keep the front tires in contact with the road.

If you have antilock brakes: Push the pedal down firmly with your foot until it stops, and hold it there. The antilock mechanism applies constant pressure-and-release automatically and in a fast, efficient way.

Antilock brakes need a longer braking distance to stop. They are designed to keep the front wheels rolling so that you can continue to steer.

CAREFUL CORNERING

●**Decelerate and brake before a turn.** Braking hard while your wheels are on a curve greatly increases your chance of a spinout. Let the momentum of the car carry you through the turn. Lightly squeeze the brake pedal. Take the widest possible turn in the road if there aren't any other cars next to you.

Example: On a bend that hooks to the right, enter the turn on the far left of your lane. Then move across the middle to the far right of your lane as the curve straightens out. This angle will reduce the weight shift of the vehicle.

Don't accelerate until the car's front tires are pointed straight again in the direction you want to go.

●**"Shuffle" your hands along the steering wheel as you turn**—rather than using the hand-over-hand method. Taking your hands off the wheel crosses up your arms and makes it easier to lose your grip. Shuffle steering is performed with both hands on the wheel. Your physical size will determine your hand placement at positions of 10:00 and 2:00...9:00 and 3:00...or 6:00 and 4:00.

These hand positions on the wheel also are safer should your airbag go off. Your hands are less likely to be thrown directly into your face.

• **Inflate tires four pounds above your carmaker's recommended level.** Your car manufacturer's recommended tire pressure will give you a smooth, comfortable ride—but slightly overinflated tires in winter will stiffen up the sidewalls, maximizing the amount of tread on the road and providing much better control in turns.

Your vehicle's tire pressure information is in your owner's manual...on the sticker inside the glove-compartment door...or on the portion of the chassis that holds the driver's side door.

• **Look beyond the car in front of you.** When driving, it's natural to focus on the rear bumper of the car ahead of you. But if there's a problem on the road ahead of that driver, you won't react until the driver in front of you does.

By training yourself to constantly scan as far ahead as possible, you can anticipate obstacles and other drivers' reactions.

USING YOUR EYES

• **Position the rearview mirror so it reflects the entire rear window.** Now turn your head and look at the left sideview mirror. Maneuver it until you can no longer see the side of your car. Repeat for the right sideview mirror.

This shrinks the blind spot so you should only have to turn your head as far as your shoulders to see a car passing on either side.

• **Swing your gaze left and right to find safer options** if you are skidding toward an object. Many people get into accidents because their natural reaction is to look at the object they are about to hit.

To avoid or get out of a skid: Lift off the brake slightly to allow the front wheels to roll, which will enable you to steer the vehicle where you are looking.

BAD-WEATHER MOVES

• **If you hit an area of the road that has collected water and ice** and you feel your car's wheels losing contact with the road, remove your foot from the gas to slow down the car. Keep the wheels pointed straight, and resist the urge to brake hard. If you turn your wheels, you risk losing even more traction.

• **At lights, stop while you can still see the rear tire of the car in front of you.** Most people stop when the car's bumper in front of them disappears from view. But if you're hit from behind on a wet or icy surface, you could hit the car in front of you.

Air Bag Warning

Measure precisely how far you sit from your car's air bag. Check the distance between the center of your chest and the hub of the steering wheel. Anything less than 10 inches may subject you to serious injury if the bag inflates.

Maria Segui-Gomez, MD, ScD, assistant professor of health policy and management, Johns Hopkins University School of Public Health, Baltimore.

Lemon Law vs. Manufacturer's Responsibility

If your new car is a lemon, first give the dealer a chance to fix it and keep copies of all the repair orders. After the second unsuccessful repair attempt—or after the car has been out of service for 15 days—contact the manufacturer's regional office and ask for assistance in getting the car repaired. After three repair attempts—or after the car has been out of service for 20 days—write to the manufacturer's headquarters and explain that you will invoke your lemon law right to a refund or replacement unless repairs are successful. After four repair attempts or 30 days out of service, demand a refund or replacement. If the manufacturer refuses, go to court or arbitration—attorney fees can be redeemed under federal or state lemon laws.

Clarence Ditlow, executive director of the Center for Auto Safety. For a lemon-lawyer referral, write to Center for Auto Safety, 2001 S St. NW, Washington, DC 20009. Include a self-addressed, stamped, business-sized envelope.

Snow-Shoveling Self-Defense

Do not hold your breath and strain when lifting a shovelful—this slows blood flow to the heart. When breath is released, blood pressure suddenly rebounds and becomes significantly elevated—which can create a dangerous heart overload.

Correct way to shovel: Breathe out as you lift the shovel and toss the snow off to the side.

Cardiac Alert, 7811 Montrose Rd., Potomac, MD 20854.

New Drinking Water Threat: Cryptosporidium

The threat posed by this microbe is smaller than media reports suggested. There's no need to boil tap water or drink bottled water unless your water utility issues an alert. Utilities are usually extremely vigilant. If there is an alert, boil *all* the water you ingest—that used for brushing your teeth, washing produce, etc., as well as for drinking. If you were to ingest crypto, you'd experience diarrhea and nausea lasting one to two weeks.

Exception: Crypto may be fatal to AIDS patients and others with weakened immune systems. Several experts now urge these individuals to boil their water even in the absence of a crypto alert, although there's really not enough evidence to say that this precaution is necessary.

Rosemary Soave, MD, associate professor of medicine and public health, New York Hospital-Cornell Medical Center, New York.

The Importance of Washing Your Hands

Inadequate hand-washing is responsible for most cases of diarrhea and vomiting.

Self-defense: Always wash your hands before eating or handling food. Always wash after handling uncooked food—especially meat…after handling money or garbage…after using a bathroom or changing a diaper…after blowing your nose, sneezing or coughing into your hand…after playing with a pet.

Most effective: Apply soap to hands, rub vigorously for at least 10 seconds in warm water, then rinse thoroughly. Be sure not to miss your cuticles and underneath your fingernails.

Mayo Clinic Health Letter, Mayo Foundation for Medical Education and Research, 200 First St. SW, Rochester, MN 55905.

Lighting and Your Health

An 85-year-old needs more light than a 15-year-old to see the same thing. Make sure lights are bright wherever possible. *Also:* Use contrasting colors. It is easier for older people to see furniture, toilet seats and counters if they are a different color from the floor.

Maria Meyer, cofounder of CareTrust, Inc., a firm that helps develop affordable housing and assisted living for the elderly, Portland, OR, and coauthor of *The Comfort of Home: An Illustrated Step-by-Step Guide for Caregivers.* CareTrust Publications.

Skin cancer risk is boosted by exposure to fluorescent lighting—but only slightly. Eight hours under an unshielded fluorescent light is equal to 1.2 minutes of July sunlight in Washington, DC. To eliminate this slight risk, cover lights with *acrylic transmission diffusers*—plastic covers.

W. Howard Cyr, PhD, senior biophysicist, office of science and technology, Center for Devices and Radiological Health, Food and Drug Administration, Rockville, MD.

Diagnosing Difficulty

Hypothyroidism, or an underactive thyroid, is often underdiagnosed because symptoms are subtle. See your doctor if you have two or more of the following symptoms for two weeks or more: Fatigue...sluggish thinking...dry skin...and cold sensitivity. Anemia and high total cholesterol (above 220) are also warnings.

Paul W. Ladenson, MD, director, division of endocrinology and metabolism, John Hopkins University Medical School, Baltimore.

Thyroid Treatment Trap

Treatment for thyroid cancer and hyperthyroidism may involve swallowing a solution containing radioactive iodine. But an individual treated this way emits radiation for up to one week afterward. This can pose a threat to those who spend a lot of time in close proximity. *Helpful:* For at least one week following treatment, patients should sleep at least 18 inches from their partners and stay away from children younger than one year old. Talk to your doctor about other precautions that may be necessary.

Kichiro Koshida, PhD, associate professor of health sciences, Kanazawa University, Kanazawa, Japan. His study was published in *Radiation Protection Dosimetry,* Box 7, Ashford, Kent TN23 1YW, England.

21

Keeping Up in a High-Tech World

New Technologies to Improve Your Life

There is a lot of speculation about how cutting-edge technologies will change the planet. To find out what is theory—and hype—and what is possible, we spoke to noted futurist Arnold Brown.

WITHIN TWO YEARS

Smart cars: The transformation of the car into a global communications center. Drivers will interact with a voice-activated computer that is continuously linked to the Internet. *Benefits…*

•**Instantaneous suggestions for local restaurants.**

•**Gas price comparisons in the area.**

•**Centralized monitoring of driving performance by automakers**—as well as engine maintenance and upgrades.

Available: General Motors' OnStar Virtual Advisor gives drivers voice access to Web-based information.

Biometrics: Applications for biological data, such as using scans of body parts (eyes, fingerprints) for identification.

•**As more personal information about you goes online,** the need for foolproof security will become vital.

•**Today's technology enables anyone to intercept private information**—medical information…credit card and Social Security numbers…etc.

•**Biometrics will be more convenient than plastic cards,** metal keys and personal identity numbers.

Example: Veincheck, now being tested, scans the vein patterns on the backs of hands to allow students entry into dormitories.

Interactive entertainment: The convergence of television, radio, computers and the Web into a single appliance. Expect to see it soon now

Arnold Brown, chairman of Weiner, Edrich, Brown, Inc., consultants in strategic planning and management of change for businesses and nonprofit organizations, 200 E. 33 St., Suite 91, New York 10016. He is coauthor of *Office Biology*. MasterMedia.

that most of the US cable infrastructure can receive digital and video data. *Benefits...*

• **Free digitized books and music will be disseminated easily.**

• **Authors will make money by adding value to their products,** such as lecturing, rather than just from book sales.

• **"T-commerce" ("T" for television)**—the integration of entertainment and consumerism —will become hot.

    Examples: While watching your favorite sitcom, you might see a chest of drawers you like. A click on your remote control takes you to a shopping channel that gives information on the make, model, price and where you can buy it.

• **Your TV set will alert you to upcoming films or sports shows you may like based on your past viewing patterns.**

• **Your stock portfolio will scroll across the bottom of the screen while you watch the evening news.**

• **An interactive Judge Judy will let you select particular cases to watch.**

WITHIN FIVE YEARS

Wearable computers: Built into clothing, these will enable fabrics to receive and transmit data. *Examples...*

• **Apparel with global positioning technology will allow you to track kids at all times.**

• **Clothing will adjust to temperature** —if it is cold, the insulation will warm you...if it is hot, the weave will loosen to cool you.

Virtual spaces: Advanced video-communications to alter the environments in which we live, work and learn. *Examples...*

• **Virtual reality guru Jaron Lanier is heading an effort to create electronically linked work spaces.** Instead of walls, you'll have screens that let you see and interact with distant colleagues.

• **Distance learning in schools will solve educational problems,** such as the lack of good teachers and funding. The lectures by the best instructors will be broadcast to thousands of schools. On-site teachers will function more like teaching assistants.

Sense augmentation: Medical devices—implants, surgical tools and diagnostic machines—that make up for physical shortcomings. *Examples...*

• **Battery-powered exoskeletal muscle suits will give you more "lift power"** and help avoid hernias and lower-back problems.

• **Eyeglasses will self-adjust to fit almost any prescription**—the fluid-filled lenses will be altered with a small pump.

• **For the more seriously visually impaired,** Johns Hopkins University researchers are creating a retinal implant. It restores partial vision by sending wireless images from a camera in a prosthetic eye to electrodes implanted in the retina.

Smart appliances: Semiconductor chips imbedded in even the most common household tools. *Examples...*

• **You'll be able to use your voice mail to control your appliances.**

• **Dial up your kitchen on the way home from work,** and tell your stove to heat up a casserole.

• **Ask your VCR to record a favorite television show.**

• **Your refrigerator will have a flat-panel computer screen** connected to a bar-code scanner to order groceries from the Web when you run low.

• **A Web-enabled dishwasher will transmit diagnostic problems directly to the manufacturer.**

    Special example: Japanese electronics giant Matsushita has developed a toilet with sensors that monitor body fluids for irregularities. For instance, it checks levels of sugar and protein in urine of diabetes patients and sends the data to their doctors. This product is now available in Japan.

IN 10 YEARS OR MORE

Brain chips: Small computer chips embedded in the brain. *Benefits...*

• **You'll trigger electronic devices by looking at them or just thinking about them.**

• **Advanced contact lenses will project images,** allowing you to read e-mail and scan documents sent wirelessly from a computer.

• **Your brain will be able to scan databases** all over the world for information.

Potential problem: The two-way nature of such communication. If your thoughts can influence a computer, will commands from that computer be able to influence your thoughts?

Nanotechnology: Robots too small for the eye to see. *Benefits...*

• **So-called "nanobots" will move through your bloodstream,** delivering accurate drug doses to select tissue or killing diseased or dangerous cells.

• **Nanobots will also revolutionize preventive medicine.** They'll be programmed to live inside your body as early warning sensors providing, for example, your doctor with X rays to detect diseases like lung cancer.

The Brave New World of Genius Computers

Raymond Kurzweil, PhD, founder and chairman of Kurzweil Technologies Inc., pioneer in the application of artificial intelligence, 15 Walnut St., Wellesley Hills, MA 02481. He is author of three books, including *The Age of Spiritual Machines.* Viking. He was named Inventor of the Year by Massachusetts Institute of Technology.

Advances in computing speed and capacity won't merely continue at today's pace into the next century. They will accelerate as technology moves beyond today's two-dimensional silicon microchips to three-dimensional circuits created from microscopic particles.

In fact, there will be incredible technological change in the next 20 years...

• **By the year 2004,** cell phones will have enough computing power to automatically translate your words into the language of the person to whom you are speaking.

• **By 2009,** a $1,000 personal computer will operate 1,000 times faster than current models.

• **By 2019,** a $1,000 personal computer will match the computational ability of the human brain—20 million billion calculations per second.

Instead of being housed in large plastic boxes, tiny but enormously powerful computers will be embedded everywhere—in walls, furniture, jewelry, even human bodies.

Far from being something to fear, this age of genius machines will bring advances to human life that were never before possible. You will lead a more prosperous life—in better health, with more career choices and personal challenges open to you.

Here's how to make the most of the opportunities this age of genius machines will provide...

• **Prepare for unparalleled prosperity.** Innovation creates new wealth, which is why the economy grew much faster in the 1990s than economists of the 1980s thought possible. Silicon Valley alone has created $1 trillion in new stock market capitalization over the past 10 years. The creation of wealth through innovation will only accelerate in the next century.

Advances in technology will change the economic landscape beyond recognition. Everyone must learn to be entrepreneurial in the coming age of genius machines.

The barriers to launching a new business will become lower than ever. All that will be needed to achieve great economic success in the next century will be a $1,000 computer and the idea for a more intelligent product.

Genius machines hold out the promise of new enterprises involving very small groups of people creating substantial wealth.

• **Expect to succeed even if you don't have technological skills.** Those with engineering skills will build tomorrow's genius computers. But those with the ability to create knowledge of any kind will be the ones who are best able to extract great value from them.

The way to create value in the age of genius machines will be to compile and disseminate knowledge that other people will find useful—from medicine to golf to Florentine painting.

The more specialized the knowledge on a Web site, the greater its value to users.

Find your passion, and then find a way to express that passion online. In tomorrow's world of machine intelligence, interactive computers and virtual reality, you can make that passion come alive in ways that will captivate your audience.

• **Become a lifelong student.** Learn everything you can about as much as you can.

You must keep up with the advances in technology because each one will create more opportunities for your success.

But you must expand your studies far beyond technology. It is impossible to know today all the skills that might make you successful in the age of genius machines.

When you discover your passion, pursue it because that is where you can make your real contribution in the age of genius machines.

Learning must last your whole life. Even now, the model in which you had a specific skill that would carry you for a whole career is dying.

You will not have to attend school in order to gain these new skills. Instead, genius machines will deliver the interactive learning courseware to you, wherever and whenever you want it. All you must have is the desire to keep learning.

•**Assume that no ailment or handicap will limit you.** The age of genius machines will remove all physical and mental limitations from what humans can accomplish.

Examples: Soon bioengineering treatments for cancer and heart disease will greatly reduce the mortality from these diseases. Such technological answers to medical problems will become commonplace as computers become vastly more powerful and far smaller.

In less than 20 years, blind people will use "seeing" machines to explore and understand their visual environment.

The deaf will "hear" what other people are saying through computers mounted in eyeglasses. A combination of computer-controlled nerve stimulation and robotic devices will help quadriplegics walk and climb stairs.

Potential medical problems will be diagnosed by doctors using telemedicine—and resolved before they become limitations on your life.

Your brain: Within 30 years, implants of microcomputing devices directly into the brain will enhance human intelligence and learning. People will be able to acquire and transfer knowledge as never before.

Prevent Computer Screen Eyestrain

Adjusting room lighting conditions can help prevent the eyestrain problems often caused by spending hours staring at a computer screen. *Some suggestions...*

•**Adjust window coverings to reduce reflection of sunlight by the screen.**

•**Set up the computer screen to show black letters on a white background and adjust the brightness so the screen,** the room lighting, the keyboard and any reading matter you are using all appear equally bright.

•**Wear dark clothes to minimize reflections in the screen.**

•**Adjust sitting position so your eyes are equidistant from the screen,** keyboard and anything else you are reading as you work.

Sylvan R. Shemitz, FIES, CEO of Sylvan R. Shemitz Associates, lighting consultants in West Haven, CT.

Computer Virus Rx

If you think your computer has a virus, stop using the computer immediately. Quit all programs, and run a virus-checking program. *Better:* Run two separate ones, since different programs may identify different viruses. Do not use any floppy disks—they may be infected or may pick up a virus and spread it. Use the antivirus software to scan all floppies—before you work from them—and destroy any viruses found on them.

John Edwards, high-tech consultant and writer, Gilbert, AZ.

How to Get Started On the Internet

John R. Levine, coauthor of *The Internet for Dummies,* Sixth Edition (IDG Books WorldWide), and an Internet Web host, consultant and lecturer.

Ten years ago, few people had even heard of the Internet. Today, it is an integral part of the lives of millions, young and old, at home and at work.

Recent estimates put the number of Internet users worldwide at more than 200 million, and project nearly half a billion will be online within five years.

If you're not already among them, you're missing one of the most significant communications revolutions ever to shake the planet.

The Internet literally places all the information resources of the *world* at your fingertips. *Bonus:* You can use the Internet to find and communicate with people who share your interests.

Until you explore the Internet, you can't begin to comprehend the breadth or depth of all it offers. There's really not much required. All you need is a system, a connection…and curiosity.

THE BASICS

For most users, the *system* is synonymous with *computer.* Any new computer you buy today is Internet-ready. *Included in the computer package are…*

- **Internet browser**—such as *Netscape Navigator* or *Microsoft Internet Explorer.*
- **Modem for connecting to the Internet over a phone line.**
- **E-mail program.**

Expect to pay around $1,000 for a new Internet-ready computer.

Minimum requirements in a Microsoft Windows system…

- **Pentium II processor.**
- **32MB RAM.**
- **CD-ROM drive.**
- **56K modem.**

All of Apple's iMac models are Internet-ready.

Alternative: If you have no real need for a computer but still want access to the Internet, look into MSN® TV. *Cost:* Around $100 to $350.

The system/service includes a box you connect to your TV, a remote and optional keyboard. It empowers your TV to bring the World Wide Web to your living room.

NO-RISK INTRODUCTION

Most public, college and university libraries have one or more computers connected to the Internet. You can use these to sample how the Internet might benefit you before making any investment.

Before any system can connect with the Internet, it must first connect with a server, which is owned and maintained by an Internet provider.

YOUR CONNECTION

Servers are your gateway to the Internet, and charge a monthly fee for the privilege. You have a couple of choices, but the basic package you get from any Internet service provider (ISP) is about the same. *You get…*

- **User name and password.**
- **CD-ROM loaded with the required software tools for getting you on the Internet.**
- **E-mail account.**
- **Access to the Internet.**

Most providers offer unlimited access, but some impose a surcharge after you've exceeded a set number of hours.

Average cost: Around $20 a month (depending on provider and services).

America Online (AOL) is the best known of the commercial online services. Others include CompuServe and the Microsoft Network.

Well organized, they offer subscribers the company's unique content, events and services along with the Internet connection.

INTERNET SERVICE PROVIDERS

If all you want is access to the Internet and none of the many other options that services such as AOL provide, an Internet service provider may be a better bet than a commercial online server. As the name implies, its only service is connecting you with the Internet and providing technical help over the telephone when you have problems.

You're probably best served by a local ISP familiar with the local operating environment. Check the *Yellow Pages* under *Internet service providers.*

Other choices: MSN® TV (mentioned earlier) or your local cable company, which may now be an Internet provider.

The cable modem access ISPs provide is considerably faster than basic telephone connections, but costs about twice as much.

The quality of service from ISPs can vary greatly, so carefully consider these points for comparison…

- **Make sure you can connect by a local call.**
- **Find out how many hours of Internet access the monthly fees allow you.**

•**Ask if there are surcharges in addition to the monthly fee.**

•**Ask about the speed and types of connections the provider's system supports.**

•**Find out the number of users the ISP can handle at any given time.**

Put these questions to the Internet service provider's customer/tech support line. Polite, informative answers are a good sign.

Caution: Be wary of any ISP whose tech support line is always busy or doesn't answer calls.

Get recommendations: Your best insight into the provider will come from other users. Ask around and find out how satisfied they are with the service, and what, if any, problems they may have had.

JOINING THE REVOLUTION

Before you can connect to the Internet, you must create an account. The software supplied by your ISP reduces account creation to simply filling in the blanks with basic information about you and your system configuration.

You'll need to give a "user name," a password of your choice, the name and possibly a number address of your Internet provider and the addresses of its e-mail and news servers.

This takes only a couple of minutes to complete. If you have any trouble, the provider's tech support will guide you through the process.

Once your account is established, making the connection to the Internet is as simple as launching your Internet browser or e-mail program—just click on the provider's icon.

Once the Internet connection is established, your browser fills the screen with a "home page." You can change it later, but first time out it's usually the home page of your ISP or the supplier of your computer or browser.

Helpful: Every location, or site, you'll find on the World Wide Web has a name: *www.what youwant.com*. If you know a Web site address you want to visit, just type it on the address bar of your browser and hit "enter" on your keyboard.

The best way to understand the way the Web works is simple—just start exploring.

Learn to use search engines. They can locate whatever you want online. (Try *www.yahoo.*

com or, better still, *www.google.com* or *www. excite.com*.)

Experiment with a few research projects. Track down information on a medical condition a relative is concerned about or a recipe that you have always wanted to try.

Best Ways to Use the Web For Better Health

Tom Ferguson, MD, adjunct associate professor of health informatics at the University of Texas Health Science Center in Houston and editor of *The Ferguson Report* (*www.fergusonreport.com*), a free online newsletter covering the online health industry. He is author of *Health Online: How to Find Health Information, Support Groups, and Self-Help Communities in Cyberspace*. Addison-Wesley.

It's no secret that the Internet is a terrific source of medical news and information. But getting the latest on specific diseases and treatments is just the most obvious of what health-minded people can do online.

Here are six other ways to use the Internet for better health—with a choice of the best sites…

CONSULT A PHYSICIAN

There's no substitute for a face-to-face meeting with a doctor. But you can get basic medical questions answered via online medical consultation services. *How it works:* A doctor answers queries that you type in while logged on.

•**AmericasDoctor.com (*www.americas doctor.com*)** offers free, real-time consultations with board-certified or board-eligible physicians 24 hours a day. All communications are private and one on one.

The physicians answer your questions and suggest reliable sources of information. They do not diagnose any condition or recommend treatment.

FIND A DOCTOR

Selecting a family doctor or specialist can be difficult. Online referrals are a useful adjunct to referrals from family members, friends and other physicians.

•**Physician Select (*www.ama-assn.org*)**, operated by the American Medical Association

(AMA), provides detailed information about virtually every physician licensed to practice in the US.

Listings include the physician's medical school and year of graduation, residency training and primary practice specialty. You can search by name, location, specialty, etc. To get to Physician Select, click on "Doctor Finder" on the AMA home page.

GET SUPPORT

Nowadays there's an online support group for virtually every ailment. These can be of great help to patients and their families alike.

●**Self-Help Sourcebook Online** *(www. mentalhelp.net/selfhelp)* offers links to more than 800 national and international self-help support groups. You can search by ailment or by keyword—cancer, depression, heart disease, etc. There's also guidance on starting your own group or linking up with a traditional off-line support group in your area.

MAINTAIN MEDICAL RECORDS

Having all your medical records in one place isn't just convenient. In an emergency, it can be a lifesaver. Some sites require you to do the work yourself. Others work with your doctor to keep records up to date.

●**PersonalMD.com** *(www.personalmd. com)* is a free service that acts as an electronic repository of your medical records, including details about your blood type, allergies, etc. These records can quickly be accessed from anywhere in the world via the Internet or fax. You are responsible for entering and maintaining data and can decide who gets access (through the appropriate password and personal identification number).

Electrocardiograms and other graphical documents can be faxed to the service to be scanned into your personal records.

FIND A CLINICAL TRIAL

Patients who have exhausted all standard treatment options or are interested in being on medicine's cutting edge may be able to enroll in clinical trials—studies of promising experimental treatments. Online services help steer patients to these studies.

●**Drug Study Central** *(www.drugstudy central.com)* lets you search for trials by dis-

ease name, medical condition or geographic location. The site provides details of each study and sends e-mail alerts about new ones.

BUY HEALTH INSURANCE

Online health insurance is no cheaper than health insurance obtained through traditional channels. But it's easier to compare policies online—and you don't have to deal with high-pressure salespeople.

●**Healthaxis.com** *(www.healthaxis.com)* sells health and prescription medicine coverage. It also provides instant quotes and insurance-buying advice.

Important: Not all policies are available in all states.

E-Mail Your Doctor

Use e-mail for simple queries if your doctor or pharmacist is equipped for it. A two-minute e-mail exchange may eliminate the need for a time-consuming office visit. Managed-care doctors who are paid a set amount per patient are especially likely to use e-mail. Doctors who are reimbursed based on office visits may discourage it.

Consensus of doctors—some who use e-mail and some who do not—reported in *The Wall Street Journal.*

Better Online Bill Paying

Use an Internet-based bill-payment service, not a bank. Internet services make a contractual commitment to protect users' privacy. Not all banks do this—most banks want to cross-market products or sell customers' names. *Also:* Internet-based services are usually more comprehensive. *Example:* They let you arrange to have all your bills sent to them...then notify you by e-mail when bills arrive. Check offers at

www.paymybills.com...www.paytrust.com...
and *www.statusfactory.com.*

Susan Wyland, managing editor, *Real Simple,* Time-Life Building, Rockefeller Center, New York 10020.

How to Use the Internet To Cut Your Taxes

James Glass, Esq., a New York–based tax attorney.

Now you can obtain free tax information that formerly you could get only by paying a tax professional—if you could get it at all.

FREE FROM THE GOVERNMENT

●**IRS Web site, *www.irs.gov,*** is the most important tax Web site of all. *It offers a huge array of resources...*

●Forms and publications. No more trips to the IRS office or waiting for tax forms to arrive by mail.

●Local resources. Get help from your local IRS office that you may not know is available.

Examples: Free tax counseling for seniors ...schedules of problem-solving days...small-business workshops...citizen advocacy groups...and much more.

●Latest news. The IRS's e-mail letter provides national tax news and news of your local IRS district.

●Tax research. Official IRS regulations, rulings, procedures and announcements, along with the IRS manual and many other official documents.

●Questions answered. Submit questions to the IRS through its Web site. Receive responses via e-mail.

This is just a sampling. The IRS site is well worth examining in detail.

●**US Tax Court, *www.ustaxcourt.gov.*** Learn how to use the Court's "small case division" to contest a tax bill involving up to $50,000 (excluding penalties and interest) per year—without a lawyer...and under simplified rules. This site also lists all Tax Court decisions issued since the beginning of 1999.

●**State and local tax agencies.** A great many of these agencies are now on the Internet. You can find a comprehensive listing at *www.tax sites.com/state.html.* This site, maintained by Professor Dennis Schmidt, PhD, CPA, of the University of Northern Iowa, Cedar Falls, also lists many local taxpayer advocacy groups, which can assist individuals and local businesses.

ANSWERS FROM PROFESSIONALS

One of the best features about the Internet is that you can use it to get your questions answered by tax professionals—*for free.* These groups are a great starting point for tax research, but you should still contact a tax professional.

●**Tax newsgroups.** These are open, ongoing discussion groups that anyone can join. *The two major newsgroups for US taxes are...*

●*misc.taxes.moderated.* This has a number of tax professionals as "regulars" who answer questions from anyone. A tax professor moderates the group, screening questions so discussion is polite and focused on practical tax issues.

●*misc.taxes.* This group is not moderated, so "anything goes."

Newsgroups are *not* part of the World Wide Web. To reach them, use your Web browser's "News and Message" function—Internet Explorer's *Outlook Express* or Netscape Communicator's *Collabra* message center.

A complete, searchable archive of all the messages that have appeared in these groups is also available on the Web at DejaNews, *www.deja.com.* And—visit the Usenet Info Center Launch Pad, *http://metalab.unc.edu/usenet-i/home.html.*

●**E-mail discussion groups.** If you want to focus on a specific tax issue, you can join one of many specialized Internet discussion groups that are hosted by professional groups and universities. Questions and comments are submitted via e-mail to a moderator, who compiles them in a document that is e-mailed to all group members.

To find a discussion group on a particular topic: Use the University of Chicago's Law Lists search engine, *www.lib.uchicago.edu/cgi-bin/law-lists.* Type in "tax" for a list of tax groups.

TAX-FILING HELP

You don't have to buy software every year to prepare your tax return and keep records. Some Web sites do it for you. *The best...*

- **TurboTax for the Web,** *www.turbotax. com,* is the online version of the popular Turbo Tax return-preparation software. *Cost:* $29.95-$39.95 per federal and $12.95 per state return.

- **H&R Block TaxCut OnLine,** *www.tax cut.com,* offers free services to help you prepare and file your federal and state tax forms electronically. Ideal for students and those with simple tax returns.

MORE RESOURCES

Still more useful sources of free tax information on the Web...

- **Nolo Legal Encyclopedia,** *www.nolo. com/encyclopedia/.*

- **Fairmark Press Tax Guide for Investors,** *www.fairmark.com.* Includes one of the most extensive explanations of Roth IRAs, as well as tax news and discussion boards on investment tax subjects.

- **TaxWeb,** *www.taxweb.com.* Includes lists of frequently asked questions as well as perhaps the broadest collection of links to tax discussion groups, taxpayer organizations and other tax resources.

Cyber-Directories Save Time—Big Time

Business directories available online can quickly locate firms and their phone numbers for free. *Useful...*

- **Anywho,** *www.anywho.com,* provides the AT&T directory of business and personal phone numbers.

- **Bigfoot,** *www.bigfoot.com,* is a leading directory of phone numbers and e-mail addresses for individuals.

- **Global Yellow Pages,** *www.globalyp. com,* gives links to the *Yellow Pages* for more than 40 countries.

- **Verizon Super Pages,** *www.superpages. com,* provides more than 16 million business listings in the US and links to the Web pages of many.

Nancy Tanker, managing editor, Specialty Retail Report, *293 Washington St., Norwell, MA 02061.*

Thinking About a New Cell Phone?

Here is what to do if you're in the market for a cell phone or service provider...

- **Pick a service plan before you pick a phone.** New cell phone designs are so seductive that many people sign up with providers only if they carry the phones they want. That can leave you with excessive calling charges.

Consider before signing up...

- The number of minutes you'll likely be on the phone each billing cycle.

- How often you'll use your phone outside your local region. Long-distance "roaming" charges are expensive.

- Phone size and options you prefer.

Also, most people are unaware that if they decide to switch service providers, they will have to buy new phones.

Reason: While service providers sell identical-looking phones built by the same manufacturers, each phone is designed to access the network of one carrier—and one carrier only.

- **Don't sign a service contract that lasts longer than one year.** Some firms offer two- and three-year deals with what appear to be attractive rates. But considering how far prices have fallen and how much cell phone technology has improved in the past three years, any contract today will be a terrible deal three years from now. Also, any phone will be obsolete in three years.

Mike Feazel, managing editor, Communications Daily, *a magazine for the telecommunications industry.*

Guarding Against Potential Cell Phone Dangers

Timothy McCall, MD, a Boston internist and author of *Examining Your Doctor: A Patient's Guide to Avoiding Harmful Medical Care.* Citadel Press.

Recently, I became one of the 100 million Americans who carry a cell phone. I had resisted for a long time—primarily because I don't like to be accessible at all times. But I finally gave in.

Like many of you, I've been following the ongoing debate about cell phone safety. Some scientists argue that the phones can cause everything from memory problems to brain cancer—and some preliminary findings do seem to support this view. Other scientists say there is no danger.

The central issue is whether microwave radiation given off by the phones affects the brain. Studies involving rats suggest that long-term memory can be affected by cell phone use. And a new study from Sweden found that—among brain tumor patients who used a cell phone—tumors tended to develop near where the cell phone was habitually held.

Since cell phones have only recently come into widespread use—and since cancer can take decades to turn up—it will be years till we can sort out this controversy. In the meantime, here's what I suggest to stay on the safe side:

● **Use cell phones sparingly.** Cell phones can be lifesavers in an emergency, and they're a great convenience when no conventional telephone is handy. It's prudent to use a land line whenever possible—especially for conversations that last more than a few minutes. Of course, conventional phones usually cost less to use and offer better sound quality.

● **Choose the model carefully.** Studies suggest that digital phones give off less radiation than do older analog models.

Another important feature to look for is a built-in speakerphone. That lets you put more distance between your head and the cell phone antenna—the source of the radiation. The greater this distance, the lower the potential risk.

I often switch my cell phone to the speakerphone and put it on the desk in front of me—especially when the other person is doing most of the talking.

● **Forget about "radiation blockers."** Several devices now on the market are said to reduce radiation from cell phones. But recent tests cast doubt on their effectiveness. Some recent research suggests that headsets—sometimes touted as a way to reduce radiation exposure—can act as antennas, actually increasing the dose to your brain. But other studies have found they could decrease the radiation.

● **If you have a pacemaker, watch out.** Cell phone radiation can interfere with pacemaker signals, so it's best to keep the cell phone as far as possible from the pacemaker. Use the phone on the opposite side of the body from the pacemaker, and don't keep the phone in a breast pocket.

● **Take extra care with children.** If cell phones do turn out to affect brain tissue, kids could pay the highest price. Their skulls are thinner, their neurological systems are still developing and they are more sensitive to the effects of radiation. I believe it's prudent to limit kids' use to emergency situations.

● **Limit cell phone use in cars.** Unless the phone is connected to a roof-mounted antenna, using a cell phone inside a car exposes your brain to more radiation.

But the biggest risk faced by motorists who use cell phones is distraction. Talking on a phone while driving is just as dangerous as driving drunk, according to a *New England Journal of Medicine* study. If you must use your phone while driving, dial only when you're stopped—or have a passenger dial for you.

The New World of Digital Imaging

Bill Schiffner, editor in chief of the imaging industry publication *Photographic Processing* and a contributor to *Digital Photographer* magazine and *JetPrintPhoto.com*. Mr. Schiffner has been covering the photo industry for more than 15 years.

Digital imaging now offers a practical, affordable complement to film photography.

With a digital camera you can take a picture, view it immediately, share it on the Web—or make a print. A scanner lets you convert favorite photos into image files that you can retouch and restore on your computer and distribute online…or as prints.

Most photo centers can now upload pictures captured on film to the Internet, as well.

While film still offers the most economical solution for quality prints, digital imaging's advantage and appeal is as an extension of your computer system for visual communications.

HOW IT WORKS

A digital image begins as a file of information. That file is the digital equivalent of a negative, but you can work with it in ways never practical with film: Revise it, enhance it, archive it to disk or transmit it over the Internet. *Some basics…*

● **Resolution.** The quality of a digital image is defined by its *resolution,* expressed in pixels—the more pixels the better.

Most digital cameras offer several resolution modes, from standard to super fine. Typically, the higher the resolution, the higher the quality of the image. Resolution determines the size of the image file.

● **Image capture.** This is accomplished with a CCD (Charged Coupled Device) or CMOS (Complementary Metal Oxide Semiconductor) image chip. CMOS is better for dim lighting situations, but CCD is said to deliver cleaner images generally.

Pictures are stored in microchips or PC cards as a kind of "digital film." These are removable memory cards, such as CompactFlash, Miniature Card or SmartMedia. With removable storage cards you can take unlimited pictures by just replacing the storage cards.

● **Printing.** Producing a quality print from a digital image at home requires buying inks and paper. Even then, the results may not be what you'd expect from film. However, you can also have them printed at a photo lab, as well as share them online.

WHAT YOU'LL NEED

● **Imaging system.** The computer is the core of any digital-imaging system. Know your system specs when you shop for a camera. Suppliers publish the minimum requirements in computer RAM, processor speed and hard drive needed to support their cameras or scanners.

● **Cameras.** Digital cameras start in the $200 range and climb to more than $1,000. Available from traditional suppliers of photographic, computer and electronics equipment, they are best purchased in stores specializing in these products where experts are available to advise you.

If you merely want to share photos online, an entry-level camera will prove adequate. These are the digital equivalent of a point-and-shoot 35mm camera and offer basic features.

● **Scanners.** A scanner offers a less-expensive entry into digital imaging. Basic flatbed scanners, adequate for home users, sell for $100 or less. These "read" your photos, reflective art or text documents and convert them into a digital file within seconds.

Many people find the scanner the ideal way to copy treasured family photos, preserve them on disk and share them with family and friends. With the right paper, some photo realistic printers can give the images from your digital camera or your scanner the look and feel of prints from regular 35mm film.

● **Digital services.** Want to experiment with digital imaging without buying new equipment? Inquire at local photofinishing centers about what digital services they offer. Most now "digitize" film as part of basic services.

Along with prints, you can copy photos to CD-ROM or upload to the Internet to a photo-sharing site such as *www.ofoto.com*—where they can be shared by family and friends.

You'll also find more of these centers equipped with digital minilabs and self-serve kiosks. These minilabs combine traditional print and digital services, regardless of what camera you use. With the kiosks, you step up, insert your digital "film," place your order and it's ready in minutes.

TAKING IMAGES ONLINE

There are two ways to share images online…

•**E-mail.** Compose a message, attach an image file and send. All the recipient needs to do is click on the message and view the image. Or, you can upload images to your Web page or a commercial Internet site for viewing.

•**Upload to the Internet.** You can also have your photofinisher digitize and upload your pictures to the Internet. Once there, the images are assigned a URL, which you and others can use to view the pictures.

Buying a DVD Player

If you've been waiting to buy a DVD player, now is the time. A wide range of movies is available on digital videodiscs—for $15 to $30

each…renting costs the same as renting videocassette tapes. You can buy a low-end player for as little as $169. Brand names—Panasonic, Sony or Toshiba—start at $249. If you own a Dolby Digital audio/video (A/V) receiver, hooking it up to a DVD player will give you top-quality digital sound suitable for a home theater. *Cost:* $250 and up. If your audio requirements are less ambitious, don't spend more for a DVD player with a built-in Dolby digital receiver. *Better:* A DVD/CD changer that handles five discs—$350 to $450.

David Elrich, an independent reviewer of electronic devices and a freelance writer for a number of consumer and trade publications.

Global Positioning On Your Wrist

Casio's *GPS Satellite NAVI* pinpoints your location anywhere, using the global satellite system. Latitude and longitude coordinates help you plot your location on a map. Good for hikers, bikers, boaters, balloonists, drivers or anyone traveling in unfamiliar territory. Strap-on unit, about the size of a wristwatch. Also tells time. *Cost:* $500. *More information:* 800-962-2746…*www.casio.com.*

22

Travel Tips and Traps

Handling Money When You Travel

Before you leave on a trip, accommodations must be made to cover financial matters while you're away from home, especially if you plan to be gone for an extended period of time. *Here are a few areas to consider…*

●**Consolidate and simplify.** Arrange to have as few bills coming in as possible while you're away. *Helpful:* Limit the number of credit cards you carry.

  Example: Instead of carrying five gasoline credit cards in your wallet, pay for fuel using a single Visa or MasterCard.

Contact creditors about setting up automatic payment plans to pay regular monthly bills directly from your checking account. *Including:* Mortgage payments…utility bills…insurance premiums. Arrange for direct deposit of regularly arriving checks. *Including:* Social Security…dividends…pension payments.

●**Have a trusted friend or family member pick up your mail.** Leave a supply of presigned checks so they can pay any unexpected bills that arrive. *Also:* Have them review your mail to make sure nothing important—such as a notice from the IRS—goes unanswered.

  Alternative: If you're going to be traveling on a schedule or will be in only one location, have your mail forwarded directly to you.

  How: If you will be in only one location, have your local post office forward your mail. If you'll be moving around, contact a mail forwarding service—listed in the *Yellow Pages* (look under "Mail Receiving Services"). These services will receive your mail from the post office, bundle it up and forward it to you anywhere in the world. *Including:* To a private mailing address …a hotel…RV campsite office…post office general delivery.

●**Get an Automated Teller Machine (ATM) directory.** Contact your bank or ATM card network for a directory of locations. In the US,

---

Bob Howells, correspondent for *Outside Magazine* and writer for *National Geographic Adventure*. He is author of *The RVer's Money Book.* Trailer Life Books.

machines are easy to find, but in some countries, machines are tied into only one network.

ON THE ROAD

Gaining access to your money when you're on the road can be a problem. *There are several useful options...*

● **Traveler's checks.** The old standby for travelers, traveler's checks are readily negotiable in an emergency—or when you are temporarily unable to find an ATM for some reason.

Carry—at most—only several hundred dollars in traveler's checks. *Reason:* You usually have to pay a 1% service charge, plus you'll tie up money that could otherwise be earning interest.

● **ATMs.** ATMs give you instant access to your money, and with so many available in the US and Canada, one is always nearby. Plus, more and more businesses are accepting ATM cards for purchases.

Strategy: Keep most of your funds in an interest-bearing checking or savings account linked to your ATM card so you'll continue to earn interest on your money until the day you withdraw it.

Important: ATMs often charge transaction fees of $1 to $2 for network withdrawals, so compare charges when selecting a bank.

● **Credit cards.** A great convenience for travelers, credit cards eliminate the need to carry a lot of cash and allow you to "float" your money for as long as 60 days—the time from when you make a purchase to when you have to pay for it.

You may need to carry two credit cards. One for making purchases and the second for checking into hotels or renting cars.

Background: When a hotel or car rental company makes an imprint of your card, a portion of your credit line is tied up as a security measure to cover damage to the room or car. It may be two to three weeks before that amount is released—usually only when payment is received from the card company.

Problem: If you rent a few cars or stay in several hotel rooms, your credit limit can easily be exhausted, making the credit card worthless.

Self-defense: Carry another emergency card or a charge card—such as American Express or Diner's Club—which has no credit limit. In an emergency, most credit cards can be used to withdraw cash from ATMs.

Note: These withdrawals—via credit card—are considered cash advances and begin accruing interest from the moment the money is withdrawn.

Cash-advance fees: Most cards charge cash-advance withdrawal fees of up to 3% of the total amount withdrawn, not to exceed a maximum of $10 to $25.

● **Carry a telephone calling card.** Available from AT&T, MCI, Sprint and other long-distance providers, they let you bill telephone calls to a personal account, use the provider of your choice and avoid the exorbitant rates charged by no-name long-distance companies.

Precaution Before a Trip

Before taking a trip, put valuables that you usually keep at home in a safe-deposit box or leave them with a friend or relative. Pay bills before you leave so they are not overdue when you return. Have your burglar and fire alarms checked to be sure they are working properly. Leave an itinerary with a friend, neighbor or relative so you can be reached in case of emergency.

Ira Lipman, president, Guardsmark, Inc., one of the world's largest security services companies, Memphis.

How to Save Big Money And Prevent Big Travel Hassles

Deborah Burns, acquisitions editor with Storey Books, Williamstown, MA, and author of *Tips for the Savvy Traveler*. Storey Books. She has visited 42 countries—traveled from Hong Kong to Cochabamba, Bolivia, trekked in the Himalayas, ridden cargo boats down the Amazon, cruised through the Caribbean—and has visited every state in the US.

Travel provides an education—about yourself and about the places and people you encounter. But there are some things travelers really don't want to learn.

I learned the hard way that not every doctor in the world speaks English. I also learned that after a long airplane flight, it is dangerous to drive a car in a country where they drive on the left.

MONEY LESSONS

•**Plan for the worst.** Currency rates can change suddenly, sometimes just before or even during a foreign trip. That can turn a budget holiday into an unexpectedly expensive splurge.

Always budget for 20% more than current prices. If exchange rates change in your favor, you'll have an extra cushion.

•**Choose your indulgences in advance.** On some trips, I make eating well a priority—and skimp on hotel rooms. Of course, in developing countries, paying more for food is not an extravagance—but a necessity.

If you're going to a beach resort, lodging near the surf might be the place to spend money. In cultural capitals, such as London or New York, the theater might be your priority.

•**Learn the local currency.** Knowing the value of foreign coins and bills will facilitate quick conversions.

Helpful: Know the dollar value of 10 units of foreign currency. *Example:* 10 UK pounds is worth about $16.

A currency converter is helpful, but most savvy travelers prefer doing quick, rough calculations so they don't feel so obviously foreign—and at a bargaining disadvantage.

•**Monitor your spending.** Keep track of the traveler's check serial numbers—in case any checks are lost or stolen.

Keep an eye on how much credit you're charging...and the fact that ATMs are giving you local currency.

Best exchange rates: Banks, ATMs, American Express or Thomas Cook offices. Many hotels and shops tack on stiff surcharges.

Reminder: Convert $100 before departing on your trip. Keep $100 in US dollars for your return home...and for emergencies.

HEALTH LESSONS

•**Know your prescriptions.** Have your physician write out the chemical name for any prescription you might need refilled while traveling. Foreign pharmacists can be confused by US brand names.

•**Keep all essential drugs with you.** Do not pack them in your checked luggage. Older travelers should bring along a medical history that lists blood type and other important health information.

•**Plan for medical emergencies.** Join the International Association for Medical Assistance to Travelers. Subscribe to this free service and you'll get a list of English-speaking doctors around the world. *Information:* 519-836-0102.

Another group worth knowing about is HouseCallsUSA. This service will send a doctor to a hotel room within 40 minutes of a call. *Cost:* $150 for doctor's visit, plus medications. *Information:* 800-468-3537...or *www.hotel docs.com.*

PACKING LESSONS

•**Take half the clothes you planned to pack.** "Just in case" items probably will never leave the suitcase—but you'll feel them every time you pick it up.

If you need something once you reach your destination, buy it there. You'll have a better feel for the weather and local style. You might also find regional bargains—silk in Asia, woolens in Europe—that become treasured souvenirs as well.

Exception: Business travelers should always pack an extra outfit—in case other business clothes become soiled or are lost.

•**Bring an inexpensive camera.** Taking pictures will be more enjoyable if you're not worried that your expensive camera might be stolen. And pack extra film and camera batteries, which may cost much more abroad.

TRANSPORTATION LESSONS

•**The Internet has made a huge difference in airfares,** and I don't mean just the auctions and lowest-fare searches. The Internet has empowered travelers.

Often the local travel agent will quote a price that is twice the fare available online—and if you tell the agent of the lower price you found, he/she will often match or beat the lower fare. Always do fare searches both through the Internet and with a travel agent.

•**Bring your own snacks when flying.** Surrounding passengers will look enviously at you munching on fresh apples, crackers and Brie while they nibble on airline peanuts.

•**Rent a bicycle.** Bicycling is often the best way to see the land. If you want to bring your own, most airlines accept bikes as luggage. Get a shipping box from a local bike shop.

FOOD LESSONS

•**Read up on the cuisine before departing.** Travelers in France, for example, should learn the words for different animal body parts—unless you don't mind ordering feet, blood sausage, brains or other organs that are considered delicacies in that country.

•**Photocopy the food section in your favorite guidebook**—so you have a reference to pull out at the table.

SHOPPING SMARTS

•**Never buy anything on your first day in a new city.** You'll usually find something cheaper...or something you like better.

Best times to bargain: Early morning and late afternoon. Early in the morning, vendors are eager to start selling. Late in the day, they are more anxious.

Caution: Duty-free doesn't necessarily mean cheaper. Know the approximate prices of liquor and other goods you might be tempted to buy in a duty-free store. Make sure they are a better deal than what you can get at home.

Health Tips

Prevent traveler's stomach trouble by taking an acidophilus supplement. Start a few days before your trip, and continue following the package instructions until you return home. Acidophilus, which is a healthful bacteria, helps maintain your intestinal environment—making you less susceptible to traveler's diarrhea and similar problems.

Allison Clough, MD, MPH, Travel and Geographic Medicine Clinic, Tucson, AZ.

Antibiotics can be taken to prevent traveler's diarrhea. But the best approach in many cases is to take chewable bismuth tablets. Bismuth is the active ingredient in over-the-counter remedies such as Pepto-Bismol. Chewing two tablets four times daily throughout the trip should keep traveler's diarrhea at bay. *Still important:* When traveling in developing countries, don't drink tap water...avoid salads...and eat only well-cooked foods served hot.

Bruce Yaffe, MD, a gastroenterologist and internist in private practice in New York City.

You Don't Have to Travel Alone

Travel-companion matching helps single people find travel companions. Most clients are over age 45. More than 70% either request a companion of the opposite sex or are willing to accept one. Profiles of all members are required, and clients are urged to meet and spend time together before any trip. *More information:* Travel Companion Exchange, 800-392-1256 or *www.whytravelalone.com.*

Smarter Trip Planning

Save big on airfares by studying a map before you purchase tickets. Make a list of cities within driving distance of your destination and ask about the fares to those cities.

Example: A round-trip fare from Chicago to Cincinnati for a family of four was $1,028. By flying to Louisville, a route with a "friends fly free" program to a city that is one hour's drive from Cincinnati, the round-trip fare was $196.

Tom Parsons, editor of *Bestfares.com.*

Airline-Ticket Buying Savvy

When ordering airline tickets, pay for them with credit cards. People who pay cash are in danger of losing their money if a carrier goes under or there are any other unforeseen circumstances. Credit card customers usually can get a refund.

New Choices for the Best Years, 28 W. 23 St., New York 10010.

How to Fly Free

Linda Bowman, author of *Freebies (and More) for Folks Over 50.* COM-OP Publishing.

Big bargains on air travel are available and are easy to get. The hard part is getting someone to tell you what these deals are and how you can take advantage of them. *Examples...*

●**If you fly to a nearby "secondary" airport,** you may be able to save 10% to 34% on your ticket, and avoid many of the hassles associated with overcrowded primary airports.

●**If you fly on Thanksgiving, Christmas or New Year's day,** you can save up to 70% on your ticket—and still arrive in plenty of time for dinner.

●**If you fly as a senior citizen,** you can save 10% to 100% on your ticket. The older you get, the more you save. At 99 you can get 99% off your ticket on some airlines. When you reach 100, you'll be eligible for a 100% discount.

RESEARCH PAYS

If you take the time to do the research and analyze your options, you will be able to take advantage of special fares and money-saving situations. Examples...

●**Hidden city flights.** The trick here is to get off or on in the connecting city, rather than take the plane to its final destination.

Example: A one-way fare for the nonstop, direct flight from Dallas/Ft. Worth to Phoenix might cost $393, but if you booked a nondirect flight from Houston to Phoenix where you changed planes in Ft. Worth, you might pay as little as $207 and beat the higher fare. You would get on the plane in Ft. Worth and only use that part of your ticket.

●**Split ticketing.** Beat the mandatory Saturday night stay on excursion fares to cities you'll visit more than once by buying two round-trip discount tickets.

Here's how to do it...

●Ticket A from your home town to your destination and back again.

●Ticket B from your destination to your home, and back to your destination.

You use the outbound part of your ticket A to get you to your destination, but use the outbound ticket from ticket B to get home. The airline will not realize that you didn't stay over on a Saturday. Use the remaining portions of your two round-trip tickets for your next trip.

●**Special member discounts.** Members of the clergy, Red Cross workers, military personnel, medical students, children, job corps trainees and seamen all can qualify for as much as a 50% discount on air travel.

●**Consolidator fares.** Independent discount travel brokers buy blocks of surplus seats on international flights and sell these seats at fares far less than those a retail travel agent or the airline can offer you directly.

Check the travel sections of major metropolitan newspapers or ask your travel agent if he/she uses consolidators or wholesalers.

●**Bumping from an overbooked flight.** Some people hope to be bumped from flights so that they can receive a free flight voucher as compensation. To help make this happen, book your flight during a time when there is a great likelihood that there will be bumping. Take only carry-on luggage. Seat yourself very near the check-in clerk so that you can be the first to volunteer when volunteers are called for.

You'll have lost a few hours in travel time, but gained a free ticket for your next adventure.

THE FLEXIBLE TRAVELER

If you've always got your bags packed, and you are ready to go, but are interested in the best deals to the best places, subscribe to *Best Fares* (800-635-3033), *Travel Smart* (800-FARE-OFF) or *Consumer Reports Travel Letter* (800-234-1970).

These are very thorough monthly publications specializing in the latest information about travel promotions and discounts being offered by cruise lines, airlines, hotel chains, car rental agencies and frequent flyer programs.

TRAVELING ABSOLUTELY FREE

● **Group leader.** Organize your entire extended family for a trip, or get together a group of friends with similar interests.

If you can put together a big enough tour group—sometimes six is big enough—you can go free.

If you can recruit 12 fellow travelers, you may be able to bring a friend free, too.

Work with your travel agent or directly with an airline group travel representative to set it up.

● **Tour escort.** If you are fluent in a foreign language, you can become a tour escort. Check with large travel agencies or tour operators.

● **Courier.** Volunteer your services as an air courier and escort freight (usually documents) to a distant client. Air couriers fly free to exotic spots all over the world. Check the *Yellow Pages* or metropolitan papers for advertisements.

KNOW IT ALL

The key to traveling inexpensively is to do the research yourself by creating a file of cheap flight advertisements, subscribing to travel publications, scouring the travel sections of the Sunday newspapers and comparing all your options before you pick up the phone to book your trip.

Bottom line: Always use a charge card to pay for your trip so you'll have some recourse if your trip doesn't go as planned.

And if you're hoping to sleep en route, bring along a U-shaped, blow-up pillow—they're great.

Information Source

Weather conditions and airport delay information for the 40 busiest US airports always are available free on the Web site of the Weather Channel, *www.weather.com.* The site also provides driving conditions around the country, a database of hotels and restaurants and other resources for business travelers.

Airport Scams Are Multiplying...Self-Defense Made Simple

Alvy Dodson, director of public safety at Dallas–Fort Worth Airport, where he oversees more than 300 officers who patrol an area the size of Manhattan. He has been with DFW Airport for 22 years.

Airport thieves have devised very clever schemes to separate you from your valuables...

Scam: **Stealing your luggage left with strangers.** It is not a good idea to entrust your property to strangers...*ever.*

Scam: **Stealing luggage in men's rooms.** A popular area for theft in airports is at the small, crowded entrance to the urinal area. Thieves wait for travelers to pile up their bags and turn their backs for a moment.

Also popular—the shelf above sinks, where travelers place rings, watches or cell phones while washing their hands.

Self-defense: If possible, wait until an end urinal or stall is available, so luggage can be placed against the wall. At the sink, place valuables in your front pockets while you wash. Put your luggage on the floor between your feet.

Scam: **Looting your luggage cart at the airport.** Thieves look for a cart loaded with bags and follow it until you stop to hail a cab or buy a magazine. Then one or two of them create a diversion while a third slips one of your bags out from the bottom.

Self-defense: Always push luggage carts —never pull them behind you.

Also, run twine through the handles of your luggage, especially smaller ones. That way a thief trying to grab a bag will make a commotion as he/she pulls the others along with it. If you must stop with your cart, do so in an area away from the flow of the crowd or against a wall where no one can get behind you.

***Scam:* Cutting your fanny pack.** These are the wraparound pouches people wear on their waists.

Thieves follow you up an escalator. One gets on in front of you...the other behind you. The lead person stumbles as he gets off the escalator, causing you to nearly fall over him. The second person sandwiches you and uses a knife or razor to slice the pack's waistband.

Self-defense: If you wear a fanny pack, wear it with the pouch in front and keep it under a jacket or sweater.

***Scam:* Stealing luggage off the carousel.** Thieves take the black, pull-along suitcases that are so common now. If challenged after they grab yours, they claim it was an honest mistake.

Self-defense: If you must use a black pull-along, make it distinctive. Put your initials in reflective tape on the side. Arrive at the baggage claim area as quickly as possible so you can retrieve your luggage as soon as it is delivered.

***Scam:* The baggage-handler rip-off.** Some dishonest airport employees who load and unload bags from planes run their hands through bags looking for valuables. This is hard to prevent—even if you use small locks on your bags. Small locks are easily broken...although they are better than nothing.

Self-defense: If you must carry valuables, keep them in your carry-on bag. If you must pack them, roll valuables in your clothing and place those garments in the middle of the bag. Thieves will open a zippered compartment or rummage through the top of the contents of your luggage.

Also, make your bags "tamper-obvious." Thieves avoid luggage that will show obvious signs of pilfering.

Helpful: Many airports have kiosks that will wrap checked luggage in a thick layer of transparent plastic. *Cost:* About $6/bag.

***Scam:* Picking the pockets of victims at food kiosks.** Thieves move in close to see in which trouser pocket or zippered luggage compartment you keep your wallet. They also want to see your money and credit cards.

Self-defense: Remove the money and credit cards you need *before* entering the airport terminal. Keep them in a clip in your front pocket. Women should avoid carrying their wallets in their purses. Instead, conceal them in a coat or sweater pocket where they do not show.

***Scam:* Stealing at checkpoints.** A favorite place for distraction is screening checkpoints. When you are presenting your carry-on articles for X-ray inspection, be ready to proceed *immediately* through the magnetometer. This can be accomplished by removing all metal objects—coins, jewelry, keys, etc.—*before* you approach the checkpoint.

The Best Airline Seating

To get the best airline seating, make a reservation as early as possible—and ask immediately about seat assignment. If your travel agent or airline says that seat assignments open at a later date, mark your calendar and call then—or make sure the travel agent does. If boarding passes become available at still another time before the flight, be sure to call again for them.

Bottom line: Seat-assignment policies vary by airline. Most reserve some of the best seats for their most-frequent travelers and people paying the full fare. This leaves fewer good seats available for others.

Consensus of airline officials reported in *The New York Times.*

317

Visit National Parks Off-Season

Jim Yenckel, former chief travel writer for *The Washington Post* and a freelance travel writer based in Washington, DC.

Hate camping but want to see beautiful parks? Here are affordable places to stay at five of our national treasures. These sites are breathtaking year-round—but contact the lodge to find out when peak season is so you can avoid the rush.

DEATH VALLEY (CALIFORNIA)

•**Stovepipe Wells Village.** In the summer, this is one of the hottest places on earth. But in winter, it's a perfect spot for hiking, biking and four-wheel driving. Stay in the heart of the park, near breathtaking Mosaic Canyon, the Sand Dunes and an abandoned mining town, among other unique attractions. The village has 83 rooms, starting at $70 a night.

760-786-2387...*www.stovepipewells.com.*

YOSEMITE (CALIFORNIA)

•**Curry Village** is a small city of tent cabins. The spartan accommodations—a bed... canvas "walls"...and shared bathrooms—start at only $54 per night. The setting, however, is spectacular—woods and boulders near the famous Half Dome. In summer, there's a pool. In winter, an outdoor ice-skating rink. There are also more expensive wooden cabins ($92 per night).

Even in the summer, you can sometimes find a vacancy without a reservation. Bring a flashlight to find your way around at night.

559-252-4848...*www.yosemitepark.com.*

GRAND CANYON (ARIZONA)

•**Maswik Lodge** is about one mile from the canyon's South Rim in a spectacular pine forest. It is a quiet place, located away from the crowds. Cabins with bath and TV cost $64 a night in the summer. Motel-style rooms start at $76.

Reservations are necessary during the summer peak, but rates are cheaper and crowds sparse during the winter, when the weather may still be lovely.

Just a few feet from the rim, the **Bright Angel Lodge and Cabins** has rooms that start at $48 for a shared bath and no TV. The lodge is located in the historic section of Grand Canyon Village.

303-297-2757...*www.grandcanyonlodges.com.*

YELLOWSTONE (WYOMING)

This vast park has nine separate lodges. Most have budget cabins that start around $42 per night with shared bath. Booking early is essential.

Alternative: Stay in West Yellowstone, just outside the park entrance in Montana. The town is packed with motels. It's a beautiful, 30-mile drive to Old Faithful, and you can plan different loop drives through Yellowstone for different days. If you need a reservation quickly, this is the place.

Yellowstone Park: 307-344-7311...*www.travel yellowstone.com.* **West Yellowstone Chamber of Commerce:** 406-646-7701...*www.westyellowstonechamber. com.*

MAMMOTH CAVE (KENTUCKY)

•**The Mammoth Cave Hotel,** located near the entrance to the caves—the world's biggest cave system—offers cottages from spring through fall. They start at $36 a night for a single. Rooms in the hotel and lodge cost more but are available year-round.

If descending hundreds of feet into the earth doesn't thrill you, the park is loaded with aboveground activities, such as hiking, fishing and boating.

270-758-2225...*www.mammothcavehotel.com.*

How to Stay Healthy While Traveling By Air

Thomas N. Bettes, MD, MPH, southwest area medical director for American Airlines in Fort Worth, TX. He wrote about medical advice for commercial air travelers in a recent issue of *American Family Physician*, 11400 Tomahawk Creek Pkwy., Leawood, KS 66211.

The time you spend on airplanes can leave you tired, stiff and dehydrated... and, if you have a chronic health condition, raise your risk of serious complications.

Here are the leading threats to airline passengers' health—and how to counter each…

●**Dehydration.** During flight, cold, dry air inside the cabin can dry the skin, throat, eyes and nostrils.

To protect yourself, drink noncaffeinated beverages—six to eight ounces per hour while aloft. Pass up caffeine and alcohol. They're diuretics. Use moisturizer to keep your skin from drying out. Over-the-counter saline eye drops can help prevent dry eyes.

If you're flying overseas: Ask to be booked on a nonsmoking flight. If no such flights are available, ask to be seated well away from the smoking section.

All domestic airlines are now smoke-free.

●**Altitude sickness.** Airliner cabins are typically kept at a pressure equivalent to that found at 8,000 feet above sea level. This reduced pressure can cause mild *altitude sickness*— headache, fatigue and trouble concentrating.

There's no way to prevent altitude sickness, but being aware of it can ease any anxiety you might feel as a result of the symptoms.

If altitude sickness doesn't cause you to have headaches, engine noise might.

Self-defense: Ask for a seat far away from the engines. Bring along earplugs and *acetaminophen* (Tylenol) or another nonprescription pain medication.

●**Blood clots.** Stiffness isn't the only problem that can result from spending long hours in a cramped airplane seat. If blood pools in the legs, dangerous blood clots can form.

If your flight is longer than three hours, try to get up once an hour to stretch and walk around. While seated, periodically extend and flex your feet.

Caution: If you're already at risk for blood clots—because of smoking, obesity, oral contraceptive use or a history of deep venous thrombosis—ask your doctor about taking aspirin and wearing support stockings during the flight.

If possible, get a bulkhead seat. It will provide more legroom.

Prolonged sitting can also cause swelling of the feet and ankles, especially in pregnant women and people with kidney trouble or heart failure.

To minimize swelling: Elevate your legs …walk around the cabin…and avoid nuts, pretzels and other salty foods.

AVOIDING COMPLICATIONS

If you've had recent surgery or have a chronic health problem, ask your doctor if you're stable enough to fly…

●**Recent surgery.** Postpone flying at least one week after major surgery—two weeks after coronary bypass surgery.

The danger is that air that might have been trapped inside the body during surgery could expand under reduced air pressure. This could cause torn sutures and other problems.

●**Special oxygen needs.** If your doctor recommends that you have supplemental oxygen during the flight, you'll need to call the airline to order it at least 48 hours in advance.

You'll also need to provide the airline with a medical certificate that spells out the proper flow rate and other important points.

●**Heart disease.** Anyone who has had a heart attack should wait at least two weeks before flying. Wait at least six weeks if there were complicating factors, such as arrhythmia or left ventricle dysfunction.

If there's any doubt as to your ability to fly safely following a heart attack, your doctor should give you a treadmill stress test.

If you take an antihypertensive drug or another heart medication, be sure to bring enough to last the entire trip. Keep it in your carry-on luggage.

It's also a good idea to bring along a copy of your most recent electrocardiogram.

Caution: Flying is off limits to individuals with unstable angina, severe heart failure, uncontrolled hypertension and certain heart arrhythmias.

●**Diabetes.** Be vigilant about monitoring your blood glucose levels while flying…and about scheduling meals and medication dosing—especially if you'll be traveling across time zones.

Pack *twice* as much medication and supplies as you think you'll need. Bring half the supply on board with you in your carry-on luggage. Bring *all* of your insulin on board with you to avoid exposure to freezing temperatures in the cargo hold.

Important: Bring a "diabetes alert card" and a doctor's note specifying your dosages and explaining why you're carrying syringes. To obtain a free card, contact the American Diabetes Association at 800-342-2383.

IN-FLIGHT EMERGENCIES

Domestic airlines are required to carry basic medical equipment, and crew members are trained in basic first aid.

Unfortunately, the first-aid kit can be used only by a physician or another trained medical professional, such as a nurse or paramedic. Whether there'll be one on your flight is a matter of luck.

Good news: Many airlines recently upgraded their medical kits. A wider range of medical problems can now be treated on board, including heart attacks, asthma attacks and seizures.

These days some airliners are equipped with automatic defibrillators, which can shock an erratically beating heart back into a normal rhythm. These devices can be operated by flight attendants.

AVOIDING JET LAG

Many travelers rely on over-the-counter supplements, such as melatonin. But recent studies have had conflicting results. And since melatonin is not regulated by the FDA, its purity and long-term safety are uncertain.

To minimize fatigue and disorientation after your arrival, remain active during daylight hours...adopt local mealtimes and bedtimes... eat small, well-balanced meals...avoid alcohol...and get moderate exercise.

Second Passports: The State Department's Best-Kept Secret

Information from our insiders at the US State Department.

Some countries won't permit entry to travelers whose passports show that they've previously visited certain other countries. Most Arab countries, for example, won't allow entry to people whose passports have a stamp showing that they've visited Israel. A similar situation confronts people traveling among some African countries. Traveling freely among these countries is a matter of carrying two passports and knowing when to use them.

You can get a second passport that looks just like a regular US passport and is only valid for a limited period of time, usually two years.

Apply for one at your regional passport office, but be prepared to document your legitimate need...itinerary, assignment from your employer specifying that you need to do business in a particular country, etc. Take two passport-sized photos.

To find out if you'll need a second passport, check the "Visa Information Sheet" available from any passport office. That document will help you to determine if there are visa or passport conflicts among the countries on your itinerary. *Extra protection:* Check with the consulate or embassy of each country you plan to visit.

Reason: Customs regulations of foreign governments change so quickly that even the State Department is unable to keep its information on these regulations absolutely up-to-date.

Avoid relying on information from travel agencies. They use the Travel Information Manual put out by an airline organization. Because the compiling, distribution, etc., can take a long time, the manual can be out-of-date as soon as it's issued.

While traveling, be sure to stay on top of possible entry-rule changes at borders you plan to cross. If entrance to a country depends on the second passport, show only that document. Put away your regular passport. Using two passports is officially frowned upon by most governments, so there could be repercussions.

If you use the wrong passport on arrival, you'll probably be refused entry. If you're caught with the wrong document when leaving, on the other hand, chances are the border guards will let you depart.

Combating Air-Travel Fatigue

Warren Levin, MD, and Howard Bezow, MD, World Health Group, New York.

Before takeoff: Eat and drink lightly for 24 hours before a flight. *Recommended:* Salads, fish, chicken, wine. *Avoid:* Liquor, bon voyage parties.

Forty-eight hours before departure: Ask the airline for a special severe hypoglycemia (low blood sugar) in-flight meal. You will probably get a nice seafood salad from the first-class galley, even if you have an economy ticket. On boarding, remind the chief flight attendant about the special meal you ordered.

Clothes: Wear loose-fitting clothing. Bring slip-on shoes. *Reason:* Long hours of sitting can cause swelling of the legs and, especially, of the feet.

Women: If possible, plan to fly within seven to 10 days after the onset of the menstrual cycle.

Medication: Take an adequate supply and a copy of your prescriptions. A note from your doctor can often avoid hassles with overzealous customs officials.

●**In the air.** Avoid consuming all the food and drink offered. Alcohol, soft drinks and other foods that have empty calories can cause a swing from high to low blood sugar.

You go from feeling great to feeling tired, cramped and headachy.

Don't do important business work while flying. *Reason:* Decision-making and complicated paperwork add to an already increased stress level. *Better:* Accomplish as much as you can before departure. *Aboard:* Read nondemanding work-related material. *Preferred:* Relax by reading an absorbing book.

●**At your destination.** Changes of time, space and place can cause a feeling of dislocation. Continue following the airborne guidelines of moderation suggested. Realize that your tolerance level for everything from decision-making to dining are below average while on a short trip abroad.

Foreign Airport Danger

Airport thieves target tourists *traveling* to their destinations, not returning from them. That's because tourists carry more money early in a trip.

This means that if you travel abroad, you will be more at risk when you arrive in a foreign airport than later when you depart from it.

Also, when you first arrive in a foreign land, you are least familiar with your surroundings—which increases your vulnerability to thieves.

More risk: Travelers are at special risk after changing money at an airport bank or ATM. Thieves watch these areas to see how much money travelers are carrying and where they are keeping it.

Jens Jurgen, president of Travel Companion Exchange and editor of *Travel Companions,* Box 833, Amityville, NY 11701.

Better Car-Rental Rates

Quote the advertised discount directly from the company's ad when calling the reservation number. *Problem:* Reservation agents often will not volunteer the best available price up front.

Helpful: Mention the promotion's discount code, usually listed in small print beneath the boldly displayed rate, or in the description of the terms and conditions of the rental.

Ed Perkins, editor, *Consumer Reports Travel Letter,* 101 Truman Ave., Yonkers, NY 10703.

Money Savers

Don't prepay for gasoline when you rent a car at an airport. Rental-car employees often urge travelers to prepay for a tank of gas when renting a car.

Reality: Most off-airport gas stations charge less than rental car firms do. And people who prepay get no refund for gas left in the cars when they return them.

Better: Fill up the gas tank on your own before returning the car.

Survey of 58 rental car employees at 12 airports, reported in *USA Today,* 1000 Wilson Blvd., Arlington, VA 22229.

Renting a car in Europe costs much more if you want an automatic transmission. Most Europeans drive stick shifts, and European car rental companies have a difficult time selling cars with automatic transmissions, so they get their profits by charging more for renting them.

Result: You may save a lot by renting a car with a manual transmission in Europe.

Brent Rolfe, vice president of operations, Auto Europe, quoted in *Travel Holiday,* 1633 Broadway, New York 10019.

Great Ways to Cut Hotel Costs

Christopher J. McGinnis, director of Travel Skills Group, a communications and consulting firm specializing in the business travel industry, Box 52927, Atlanta 30355. He is author of *The Unofficial Businesss Travelers Pocket Guide.* McGraw-Hill.

Why not get a great hotel room for the same money, or less, than you'd pay for a standard room? *Try these strategies I recommend to my business-traveler clients...*

•**Consolidators.** National consolidators provide deep discounts. Try Quikbook (800-789-9887 or *www.quikbook.com*)...Hotel Reservations Network (800-964-6835)...or Priceline *(www.priceline.com).*

Example: The Beverly Plaza in Los Angeles charges $179 to $228 for a room...Quikbook's rate is $125.

Downside: Some consolidators require advance payment.

Beware: Hotels that are "frayed around the edges" often unload rooms with consolidators. But some desirable properties—such as Chicago's Drake and Palmer House hotels—do work with consolidators. Know your hotels before you book.

•**Travel consortia.** Many travel agencies belong to networks that can provide discounts and upgrades. Leaders include Hickory Travel Systems (800-448-0349).

•**Be specific when you book a room.**

Example: Nonsmoking, lake view, between floors three and 10, away from the pool, etc. This way, if the hotel can't meet your specifications, it might give you an upgrade.

•**Get out of the mainstream.** Check out lesser-known boutique hotels, such as those of...

•The Kimpton Hotel Group (no 800 number...call hotels individually, listed at *www.kimptongroup.com*) on the West Coast.

•Manhattan East Suite Hotels (800-637-8483 or *www.mesuite.com*).

•Boutique Hotels (877-847-4444…call hotels individually, listed at *www.boutiquebg. com*) in New York.

Example: Boutique's five Manhattan properties are known for their stylish period designs and architectural integrity. They offer breakfast…dessert buffets…VCRs and CD players… libraries of videos and CDs—all free. *Cost:* $265 to $355 per night at the deluxe Shoreham, compared with $415 to $615 at the superdeluxe Carlyle.

•**Use clout on the right people.** A couple of weeks before you leave, send a note to the manager of guest relations or the front-desk manager. Introduce yourself…suggest that you might be staying often…and that you might refer business.

When you get to the hotel, say hello to these people. You may get a better room or free breakfast. If you do, write a thank-you note.

•**Work the wiggle room.** Rates are not set in stone. Smoke out the lowest price in town, and ask the manager you've met to match it. Also, ask for the corporate rate of the company that you are visiting. Often the hotel has a local rate that only in-house reservationists are aware of. If you can't get a break on the room, ask for free upgrades—breakfast, valet services, transportation.

•**Call right after 6 pm.** This is when hotels wipe out all reservations unsecured by a credit card…and may offer rooms at a bargain rate. In high-occupancy cities—New York or San Francisco—many hotels have a 4 pm deadline.

•**Join the club**…a frequent-guest program will get you a few extras—and it costs nothing to join.

Example: Starwood Preferred Guest Program offers Gold Preferred Guest Benefits…10 stays within one year, upgrade, late checkout and three star points per dollar spent toward a free night. For more information, call 888-625-4988.

Credit Card Calling

When you have more than one phone call to make from a hotel or pay phone, don't hang up after each call. Push the # button between calls. This will allow you to stay connected with your chosen long-distance carrier.

Added benefit: Most hotel computers will register several calls made this way as a single local call, saving you surcharges.

Travel and Leisure, 1120 Avenue of the Americas, New York 10036.

Best Places to Eat

To save money while traveling abroad, don't eat in a hotel unless breakfast is included in your room rate. Look for tasty ethnic restaurants—they're real bargains in cities such as London, where traditional fare can be very expensive. Plan to eat only two big meals a day and snack the rest of the time. You can almost always buy fresh fruit or wrapped sandwiches at take-out groceries.

Family money-saver: Ask at museums and historic spots for a family pass. They are often available—and provide significant savings over the price of individual admissions.

Alex Kennedy, editor, *Family Fun,* 114 Fifth Ave., New York 10011.

Bed & Breakfast Club For Seniors

Bed & breakfast club for persons 50-plus has hosts in more than 1,500 cities in North America. You may stay in a private home, condo or farm for $15/day for two, breakfast included. To be a member, you must be willing to be a host. There are more than 4,000 members and growing. Contact the Evergreen Bed & Breakfast Club, *www.evergreenclub.com* or

800-962-2392. *Dues:* $75/year for two people, $60 for a single membership.

Herbert J. Teison, editor, *Travel Smart,* 40 Beechdale Rd., Dobbs Ferry, NY 10522.

Grandchild Trap

Travel with grandchildren may require special documentation. Many countries require specific forms for minors traveling alone, with only one parent or with an adult who is not a parent. Check the rules before you go.

Christopher Lamora, press officer, Bureau of Consular Affairs, US Department of State, Washington, DC.

How to Get Paid To Take a Vacation

Cruise lines hire many retirees, semiretirees and students to work on their luxury cruise ships. And with many new ships entering service, hiring is increasing.

Trade-off: Cruise ship employees receive spartan accommodations compared with those provided to passengers, and are required to work to high standards. But they are paid for traveling the high seas and great rivers and lakes of the world, and for visiting exotic ports of call.

Jobs of all kinds are available on ships that often now resemble floating cities.

Examples: Purser, photographer, beautician, casino staff, counselor, host, clerk, doctor, nurse, youth counselor, sports trainer and many more. Persons with special skills may be hired as lecturers on subjects such as investing and the arts.

Pay range: From $1,700/month (bartender) to as much as $7,500/month (cruise director).

For more information...

•*How to Get a Job with a Cruise Line,* by Mary Miller (Ticket to Adventure Press), 800-929-7447.

•**New World Cruise Ship Employment Agency.** Read the "Frequently Asked Questions" list at *www.cruiseshipjob.com.*

•**Cruise Lines Employment Guide 2001,** *www.cruiselinejob.com.* Provides job descriptions, profiles cruise lines and offers a CD-ROM of contact numbers, employment contracts and other information for different cruise lines.

•**Small Ship Cruises,** *www.smallshipcruises. com,* provides a directory of small ships, windjammers and river barges that visit ports of call ocean liners never reach—for persons seeking special ventures.

When you find a cruise line that visits ports attractive to you, contact it directly or visit its Web site—many now post job openings online.

Herbert J. Teison, editor, *Travel Smart,* 40 Beechdale Rd., Dobbs Ferry, NY 10522.

23

Doing Your Own Thing

High-Quality, Affordable, Educational Adventures For Anyone Over 55

Go behind the scenes at an archeological dig. Take part in reef research in Hawaii. Study American Indian, Scottish, Irish or Afro-American culture at historic sites. Take field trips to rarely visited birding sites with an expert ornithologist. Learn the art of woodcarving. Attend a guided tour of American music from the colonial times to the end of the 20th Century. Explore Canada by train, guided by historians and naturalists.

All this and much more is available through the Elderhostel program, founded in 1975 as a not-for-profit organization. They offer stimulating adventures in lifelong learning across the 50 US states, Canadian provinces and territories and in 85 countries. Elderhostel also sponsors exciting educational programs that explore the world from the unique vantage point of a floating classroom.

In addition to travel-based education/adventure programs you can take part in community-based educational opportunities or volunteer as an aid in doing meaningful research.

What does an Elderhostel program cost and what's included? Participants are responsible for getting themselves to and from the program, but once you start, the cost of registration, accommodations, all of your meals, classes and field trips noted in the program description are covered. All Elderhostel program costs also include limited accident insurance. The cost of a six-night program in the US averages $450, while for a five-night program it is $430, with programs in Hawaii and Alaska slightly more.

What's the catch? There really is no catch. Elderhostel is committed to providing high-quality, educational opportunities to older adults at very affordable prices. The many colleges, museums, national parks and learning

Elderhostel, Inc., 75 Federal St., Boston 02110.

institutions that make up their 'campus' share this commitment.

Who's eligible? Anyone 55 or over. (Younger adults are welcome if accompanying a senior.) Singles are welcome. On a typical Elderhostel program, there is always a mix of couples and singles and the atmosphere is very friendly and social. Accommodations can be made for special diets and disabilities.

Do you have to participate in every activity? The sponsors believe that a complete Elderhostel experience means full attendance in every aspect of the program! If you feel, however, that a particular excursion or field trip may be too strenuous for you, or you would like to take the afternoon to explore on your own, you may forgo a lecture or activity.

To learn more: Call toll-free at 1-877-426-8056, Monday through Friday, 9 am–9 pm (Eastern Time). *TTY line:* (toll-free) 1-877-426-2167. *Callers outside the U.S. and Canada dial:* 1-978-323-4141. Elderhostel's online catalog is a fast way to quickly search out a program by season, subject and location. You can also check program availability and even register online at *www.elderhostel.org.*

Golf Smarts

To improve your golf game: While waiting your turn at the tee, take some practice swings from the opposite side—if you are right-handed, take swings left-handed. Start slowly, and do not go more than 70% of your normal swing speed. Do the swings a few times on the first three or four holes of every round. Also do a few opposite-side swings at the driving range. They will help strengthen and balance your muscles, making it easier to hit longer drives.

Gregory Florez, golf trainer, Salt Lake City, quoted in *Men's Health*, 33 E. Minor St., Emmaus, PA 18098.

Book golf tee times over the Internet. The new Golfextras.com Web site lets you book tee times up to 120 days in advance at more than 300 golf courses nationwide. The service is free, and convenient if you want to book a round of golf at a location you plan to visit during a vacation trip. The site also offers an extensive selection of golf accessories and instructional items. *www.golfextras.com.*

Improved Backswings For Older Golfers

Backswings get shorter as golfers get older. When the swing gets too short, you'll lose distance, accuracy and consistency.

Remedies: Hold the club lightly. *Reason:* Too tight a grip tenses the arm and shoulder muscles and restricts the backswing.

Put more weight on your right foot, especially on full swings with woods and longer irons. *Result:* A head start on your swing and less weight to shift.

Turn your chin to the right (or to the left, if you're a southpaw) as you start your backswing. If it throws your timing off, cock your chin in the direction of the backswing before you swing.

Appropriate Tips for Helpful People

●**Golf caddie.** If you are a guest at an upscale course, offer to pay the customary $25/bag club fee for the caddie. If your host declines the offer, discreetly give the caddie a tip of $5 (stingy) to $15 (generous).

●**Tennis pro.** $5 to $10, unless you are at a private club, where no tipping is required.

●**Crew members on a yacht or a power-boat.** For first-class service, tip the captain $50 and crew members $25 each. If they were surly and unhelpful—not too likely, of course—reduce these amounts to $10 and $5.

●**Captain or mâitre d' at a club.** In addition to the club's service fee and the annual collection for a holiday gift...if you give a party at the club, tip between $15 and $50 (no one should see you do it).

Letitia Baldrige, leading authority on practical etiquette and author of *In the Kennedy Style*. Doubleday.

Fishing a New Lake

If you know where to start looking, you can fish any lake successfully.

WHERE BASS CONGREGATE

●**Near trees that have recently fallen into the water.**

●**In hot weather.** Under lily pads, especially in the only shallow spots around.

●**In consistently mild weather.** In backwater ponds and coves off the main lake. *Best:* Good weed or brush cover, with a creek running in.

●**Any time at all.** In sunken moss beds near the shore.

Outdoor Life, Two Park Ave., New York 10016.

Surf Casting—a Different Kind of Fishing

For more than just a day at the beach, try surf fishing. It is easy to learn, and basic gear is inexpensive—rod-and-reel combinations can cost $50 or less. Talk to tackle-shop personnel about fishing. Ask which bait to buy and how to thread it onto the hooks. Find out if casting lessons are available. If you decide to buy a rod and reel, the lessons may come free.

T. Edward Nickens, freelance writer, *Cooking Light,* Box 1748, Birmingham, AL 35201.

Best Guides for Bird-Watchers

Sheila Buff, author of many books about birding and the outdoors, including *The Complete Idiot's Guide to Bird Watching*. Macmillan.

Birders now have a number of excellent guides from which to choose. *Following is a short list to get you started...*

●***The Sibley Guide to Birds,*** written and illustrated by David Sibley (Knopf).

This comprehensive new book is on bestseller lists across the country for good reason. Its 6,600 detailed illustrations show the birds in realistic positions and include field identification marks, how the birds look in flight and more.

The book also contains detailed identification tips and up-to-date range maps.

Every birder needs this book. *One drawback:* At 544 pages, 6" x 9" and about 2.5 pounds, it's too large and heavy to use easily in the field.

●***Birds of North America,*** by Kenn Kaufman (Houghton Mifflin).

This new field guide by a legendary birder uses more than 2,000 digitally enhanced photographs to illustrate the birds and emphasize their field marks. The organization by related bird families is especially helpful for beginning birders.

●***Peterson Field Guides: Eastern Birds/Western Birds,*** by Roger Tory Peterson (Houghton Mifflin).

The classic and in some ways still the best, particularly for new birders. Peterson's lifelike illustrations feature arrows indicating important field identification marks. The crisp text describes birds and their songs in terms so memorable that many experienced birders can quote the descriptions by heart.

The dividing line for the Eastern edition and the Western edition is the 100th meridian, or roughly the Rocky Mountains.

●***National Geographic Field Guide to the Birds of North America,*** by Jon L. Dunn (National Geographic Society).

This volume—a favorite among experienced birders—features excellent illustrations, range maps and good text. The pages are larger than the pages of most field guides. They have some white space, which is handy for making notes.

●*Birds of North America: A Guide to Field Identification (Golden Field Guide),* by Bertel Bruun, Chandler S. Robbins and Herbert S. Zim (St. Martin's).

More than eight million copies have been sold. Outstanding illustrations, informative text, range maps and sonograms (visual depictions of bird songs).

●**The Birder's Handbook,** by Paul R. Ehrlich, David S. Dobkin and Darryl Wheye (Simon & Schuster).

This book takes up where field guides leave off. It provides detailed, condensed information (but no pictures) about each species, along with highly readable and informative essays about birds and bird ecology, behavior and evolution.

How to Turn Your Yard Into a Haven for Wildlife

Sheila Buff, author of many books about birding and the outdoors, including *The Complete Idiot's Guide to Bird Watching.* Macmillan.

Gardens designed to attract birds and other wildlife are both beautiful and good to the earth. And as a bonus, they're easier to plant and maintain than conventional ornamental gardens.

TO ATTRACT MORE WILDLIFE, YOU NEED...

●**Plants that provide food.** Any plant that produces nectar-filled flowers, seeds, berries or nuts will attract butterflies, birds and small animals. The more variety, the better.

●**Plants that provide shelter.** Just as important to wildlife as the right food is the right kind of shelter. Birds need places to perch safely and to build their nests. Other wildlife such as squirrels, chipmunks and rabbits need shelter to rest safely from predators and raise their families.

●**Watering holes.** Especially in developed urban areas, fresh water for wildlife can be scarce. In addition to attracting wildlife, a bit of fresh water adds interest and beauty to any garden. You'll find that a birdbath, a fountain or a small pond (artificial or natural) will attract animals and birds you've never seen in your garden.

GETTING STARTED

1. *Use only organic methods.* Commercial pesticides, fungicides, fertilizers and other yard chemicals harm the very insects, birds and animals you're trying to attract. *Key organic gardening methods...*

●Use compost instead of chemical fertilizer.

●Use insecticidal soap rather than commercial pesticides.

●Mulch heavily instead of using chemical sprays to cut down on weeds and fungus infections.

●Let nature control the insect population. Some easily attracted animals can noticeably reduce the number of annoying insects in your garden.

Examples: A single tree swallow will eat hundreds of mosquitoes in a day. A bat can do the same in a single night.

2. *Look for good garden areas* that could be made more attractive to wildlife. *Possibilities...*

●A corner of the yard you don't use much. Turn it into an easy-to-care-for mini-meadow of wildflowers and grasses, or plant some food shrubs such as cotoneaster or serviceberry there.

●A fence around the yard. Make it more attractive to wildlife by planting climbing vines—such as trumpet vine, Virginia creeper or euonymus (wintercreeper)—to run along it. The fruits and flowers of these vines will attract birds. The foliage provides shelter.

Even better: Replace the fence with a hedge of boxwood or American holly.

●An open area near shrubbery. That's a good spot for a birdbath, garden fountain or small pond.

●Against the foundation of your house. For attractive covering, consider planting barberry and pyracantha (firethorn) for food and ornamental evergreens, such as creeping juniper, for shelter.

3. *Add a variety of levels to your garden.* A greater range of levels will increase the amount of bird and animal life in your garden. *To add levels…*

●Plant vines that climb up walls, tree trunks and fences.

●Build stone walls, rock gardens and raised beds.

●Plant shrubs and small trees.

CHOOSING THE RIGHT PLANTS

Many ornamental plants—azaleas, for instance —are very attractive to human eyes, but they don't do much for butterflies, birds and other animals.

Your goal: Add plants that are attractive to both you and wildlife. And if the plants are easy to care for, so much the better.

●**Plants that attract butterflies.** Any flowering perennial or annual with flat-topped, sweetly scented blossoms will do the trick.

Good perennial choices are aster, butterfly bush, coreopsis, hollyhock, lilac, Shasta daisy and wallflower.

Good butterfly-friendly annuals include ageratum, cosmos, heliotrope, Johnny-jump-up (viola), marigold, Mexican sunflower, sweet alyssum, sweet william, verbena and zinnia. Herbs such as thyme and basil, if left to flower, are also good choices.

●**Shrubs that attract birds.** Shrubs provide both food and shelter. *Best:* Shrubs that produce berries and/or bushy foliage.

Good choices include arrowwood (viburnum), bayberry, blackberry, cotoneaster, dogwood, elderberry, juniper, holly, Oregon grape, serviceberry and sumac.

●**Plants that attract birds.** The seeds of flowering plants—perennials and/or annuals —attract birds.

Sunflowers, for example, work magic on wildlife. And because they're very easy to grow, they're a great way to introduce kids to gardening.

Other useful easy-to-grow annuals and perennials include ageratum, blazing star, candytuft, cornflower, cosmos, Indian paintbrush, phlox, purple coneflower, sage, sweet rocket, valerian and zinnia.

Caution: Don't "deadhead" these flowers— that is, remove the seed heads after the blossoms fade. Deadheading will get you more flowers, but few seeds.

●**To attract hummingbirds.** Any flowering plant or shrub with red or orange tubular blossoms will attract hummingbirds. Bee balm (monarda) is highly attractive and very easy to grow. Other good choices include columbine, fire pink, flowering tobacco, honeysuckle, jewelweed (wild impatiens), penstemon, phlox and trumpet vine.

●**Trees for birds and small animals.** Smaller fruit-bearing trees will attract both birds and small animals such as chipmunks, squirrels and rabbits. Autumn olive, cherry, crabapple and mulberry are all good choices for backyards.

Bigger trees: Bats roost in the natural cavities found in larger trees. Other small animals— such as foxes, raccoons and squirrels—use tree cavities or dig dens under the roots of large trees for sleeping areas and to raise their young.

Don't cut down dead trees: Dead trees are just as useful as live trees for attracting wildlife. Woodpeckers and other birds—such as chickadees and nuthatches—dig nesting holes in the soft wood, for example, and bats roost in hollow trees.

Unless a dead tree is truly unsightly or threatens to fall over, consider leaving it in place and letting it be gradually covered by food-bearing vines such as wild grape and Virginia creeper.

Senior Softball World Series

For people over 50, series includes teams for age groups up to 80-plus. Women and men play on separate teams. Last year's playoffs involved 139 teams from 40 states.

More information: National Association of Senior Citizens Softball (NASCS), 810-792-2110.

Ken Maas, president and founder, NASCS, Box 1085, Mt. Clemens, MI 48046.

Small Towns with Great Antiques

Glendale, Arizona, 30 minutes northwest of Phoenix, has more than 45 antique shops downtown. 877-800-2601.

•**Essex,** Massachusetts, 30 miles north of Boston, has more than 35 shops. 978-283-1601.

•**Abingdon,** Virginia, 135 miles southwest of Roanoke, near the Tennessee border, has a 20-block historic district with a dozen antique shops. 800-435-3440.

•**Waynesville,** Ohio, 40 miles northeast of Cincinnati, has more than 30 antique shops. 513-897-8855.

Malcolm Katt, an antiques dealer and owner of Millwood Gallery, which specializes in Nippon and Pickard porcelain, Box 552, Millwood, NY 10546.

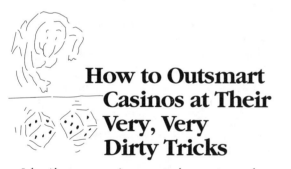

How to Outsmart Casinos at Their Very, Very Dirty Tricks

John Alcamo, a gaming expert who spent several years interviewing Atlantic City card counters. He is author of *Casino Gambling Behind the Tables.* Gollehon Books.

No matter how much we hope for big wins, casino odds are stacked against gamblers.

You can still have fun gambling—and dramatically improve your odds and limit your losses—*by knowing the strategies that casinos use to get gamblers to lose...and lose...*

•**Casinos want you to forget you're gambling.** The carefree, party atmosphere in a casino helps soften the blow when a player loses. The last thing a casino wants a player to do is dwell on how much he/she has lost.

•**Greed is good—for the casino.** It's hard for gamblers to stop while they're winning. That's why casinos have pictures of big winners displayed when you enter. They want you to think, "Hey, I could win a pile, too." That way, if you win a few hundred dollars—even $1,000—you'll feel unsatisfied and try to parlay it into a huge win.

•**Casinos hate players with a plan.** A casino's nightmare is a bettor who refuses to lose more than a certain amount, no matter what. Luckily for the casino, few players have such discipline. The majority of players violate the mental limits they set. After losing the allotted bundle, a player thinks he can break even by risking just a little more. So the losses add up. The more the player loses, the more desperate—and foolish—his bets become.

•**Cashing out is purposely difficult.** By design, gamblers who want to cash out have to get past a gauntlet of table games and slot machines before they get to the cashier's window. *Don't be tempted to bet more.*

You'll also often find a line of customers at the cashing-out windows. The casino wants you to become impatient and resume play. Don't give in.

•**Every comp is strategic.** Casinos give out complimentary tickets—freebies—to customers because they want them to keep playing and eventually visit again.

Casinos roll out the red carpet for big winners because they don't want them to leave. The longer a player stays in a casino, the more likely he is to lose money.

Strategy: Accept comps...but don't be swayed by them.

GAME TRICKS

•**Blackjack.** Card counting doesn't work. Skilled counters can *theoretically* get a mathematical edge in blackjack. But casino employees are adept at spotting card counters. When they do, the pit boss can order the cards to be shuffled, negating the counter's hard work.

•**Keno.** Worse than a lottery—because there is no guaranteed winner.

•**Roulette.** Tracking numbers is a sucker's game. It gives you no mathematical edge. But casinos will gladly give you a scorecard because they know that people who keep "score" play longer—and lose more money.

•**Slot machines.** Credits are diabolical. Years ago, slot machines dispensed actual coins if you won. Today's slot machines register "credits." Casinos changed their methods because gamblers are more likely to fritter away credits since "they're not real money."

Remember: Credits are real money—with or without a dollar sign.

•**Video poker.** Can be misleading. If you're playing Jacks-or-Better and you end up with a pair of jacks, the machine will tell you that you won. If you bet five coins, five coins will be returned to you.

But you didn't win. You tied and got back only what you wagered. In blackjack, this would be called by its right name—a *push*. Video poker machines call it a win so you'll feel better and keep playing...and lose more money.

The Best Slot Machines

Las Vegas rules are most chaotic for slot machines. In Atlantic City, all machines must return at least 83% of the amount wagered...and a few return even more than 83%. But in Nevada, one machine might pay back 99%, while the one right next to it pays back only 60%. The bettor's problem is that it's impossible to identify the hot machines. Their placement is the casino's closely guarded secret.

The best-paying machines are usually found third or fourth from the end of a busy aisle, where the most people will see and hear the payoffs.

Worst payoffs: Any machine near the door of a casino showroom.

Among Atlantic City's casinos, the variations are narrower than in Vegas, but they can still be worked for or against you.

Lee Pantano, Box 47, Atlantic Highlands, NJ 07716.

Vacation Traps...and Wonderful Alternatives

It's a shame to waste money on a vacation that fails to meet your expectations. *Overrated destinations...*

Trap: **Hawaiian "fantasy" resorts.** In both architecture and amenities, these multimillion dollar resorts completely lack any feel for the culture of Hawaii. Guest activities include Clydesdale horse riding and gondola sailing on man-made lakes. If fantasy is what you're looking for, go to Disney World instead.

Better: The island of Lanai, once home to pineapple plantations. Though the island has seen the opening of several major resorts, it still retains the atmosphere of early Hawaii.

Trap: **Bermuda in winter.** Many vacationers don't realize that this island is located in the Atlantic Ocean, not the Caribbean—at about the same latitude as North Carolina. Winter weather is often rainy and chilly.

Better: Cancun or Cozumel on the Mexican Caribbean. Both offer good winter rates.

Trap: **Venice in the summer.** Poor sanitation, hordes of tourists, and heat and humidity combine to make Venice smelly and unpleasant in the summer. Visit at another time of year.

Better: If you want both art and canals, try Amsterdam.

Trap: **Miami Beach.** The city lost its luster long ago. Hotel Row has become crowded and expensive.

Better: Fort Morgan Island on the Alabama Gulf Coast. This 25-mile breaker island is quiet and offers a pleasing southern atmosphere. *Drawback:* Winter weather isn't as mild as in South Florida.

Trap: **The overbuilt Caribbean islands.** These include Nassau/Paradise Islands in the Bahamas, the Montego Bay area in Jamaica and the Dutch side of St. Maarten.

331

Better: The quieter Bahamian islands of Eleuthera and Exuma. If you want quiet and excitement, Anguilla is only a 20-minute ferry ride from the shopping and casinos of St. Maarten.

Summer Camps For Adults

These summer camps offer grown-up versions of the fun kids have at camp, *plus a chance to follow specific interests...*

•**The Clearing in Ellison Bay,** Wisconsin, 877-854-3225—one-day to week-long classes in such fields as music, painting, photography, writing and bird identification.

•**Camp Mom in southern California,** 760-806-4582, is for women—mothers or not —interested in traditional camp activities plus manicures, facials, massages and line dancing.

•**Camp Cheerio in Roaring Gap,** North Carolina, 800-226-7496, is for people over age 50. Swimming, tennis, arts and crafts, guided walks, bingo and beautiful mountain scenery.

Alycia Borer, travel writer, quoted in *Good Housekeeping*, 959 Eighth Ave., New York 10019.

Bike Tours for People Over Age 50

Cycle along flat or gently rolling terrain. Tours usually start with easy mileage—defined as 15 to 50 miles per day.

•**Canadian Trails Adventure Tours,** 800-668-2453 or *www.canadiantrails.com,* run three to eight days—prices start around $600.

•**Cape Cod Bicycle Adventures,** 888-644-4566 or *www.capecodbybike.com,* offers six-day tours for $1,895.

•**Elderhostel,** 877-426-8056 or *www.elder hostel.org,* has 14-day European bike tours starting around $2,400—including airfare. It also has five- to nine-night North American tours—prices start at about $500.

Herb Teison, editor, *Travel Smart,* 40 Beechdale Rd., Dobbs Ferry, NY 10522.

America's Very Special And Very Different Little Museums

Lynne Arany and Archie Hobson, coauthors of *Little Museums: Over 1,000 Small and Not-So-Small American Showplaces.* Henry Holt.

CALIFORNIA

•**Musee Mécanique** (San Francisco). Arcade games ranging from Victorian-era carnival fortune-tellers to computer games are all playable. *Admission:* Free.

1090 Point Lobos Ave., 415-386-1170.

DELAWARE

•**Treasures of the Sea** (Georgetown). Gold bars, silver jewelry and treasures from a royal Spanish vessel that sank off Florida's coast 300 years ago. *Admission:* $2 for adults ...$1 for children and seniors.

Delaware Technical and Community College, Rte. 18, 302-856-5700.

ILLINOIS

•**The Cookie Jar Museum** (Lemont). A half-hour south of Chicago, this museum displays 2,000 rare cookie jars. *Admission:* $2 for adults...$0.50 for children.

111 Stephen St., 630-257-5012.

MICHIGAN

● **American Museum of Magic** (Marshall). Magicians' secrets of the past 200 years, including many of Houdini's props. *Admission:* $4 for adults...$2 for children.

107 E. Michigan Ave., 616-781-7666.

VIRGINIA

● **Money Museum** (Richmond). Located in a Federal Reserve Bank, exhibit shows the history of money over the past 3,000 years. *Must see:* Uncut sheets of $100,000 gold certificates. *Admission:* Free.

701 E. Byrd St., 804-697-8108.

WASHINGTON

● **World Kite Museum** (Long Beach). Hundreds of exotic kites. *Activities:* 28 miles of open beaches and brisk winds provide the best kite-flying conditions in the country. *Admission:* $1.50 for adults...$1 for children and seniors.

112 3rd St. NW, 360-642-4020.

Search for Volunteer Opportunities Online

Visit the Web sites of well-known organizations that depend on volunteer help.

Examples: Peace Corps, *www.peacecorps. gov*...Red Cross, *www.redcross.org*...Volunteers of America, *www.voa.org.* Or look for positions near your home by checking the databases at Impact Online, *www.impactonline.org*...SERVEnet, *www. servenet.org.*

Carey Millsap-Spears, writer, *Consumers Digest,* 8001 N. Lincoln Ave., Skokie, IL 60077.

Volunteer Vacations

Mix work and pleasure—and maybe get a tax deduction. In *Hawaii,* 10-day Sierra Club trips monitor humpback whales. $1,395 plus airfare. 415-977-5522 or *www.sierraclub. org/outings.* In *Georgia,* the Caretta Research Project helps protect endangered loggerhead turtles. $550/week. 912-447-8655 or *http:// members.aol.com/wassawcrp.* Cross-Cultural Solutions in *India* uses volunteers for teaching and community-planning in New Delhi. $1,950 for three weeks, plus airfare. 800-380-4777 or *www.crossculturalsolutions.org.*

Travel Holiday, 1633 Broadway, New York 10019.

Millennium Trails develops new cycling and hiking trails and restores historic routes. *www. millenniumtrails.org* or 877-645-8757. Millennium Service Project works with local people on community projects—and needs volunteers who can contribute at least a week of their time. There is a tax-deductible service project fee of $450. *www.globalvolunteers.org* or 800-487-1074. Earth Day Network goes beyond the official April 22 Earth Day to plan year-round activities about health, wildlife, land use and more. *www.earthday.net* or 206-876-2000.

Cooking Light, Box 1748, Birmingham, AL 35201.

Here's How to Make Working at Home Work For You!

Barbara Weltman, an attorney practicing in Millwood, NY, *www.bwideas.com.* She is author of *The Complete Idiot's Guide to Making Money After You Retire.* Alpha Books.

More than 43 million Americans now work from home either full-time or part-time. Many millions more are expected to join these ranks as our economy changes.

HOW TO MAKE THIS WORKING ARRANGEMENT SUCCESSFUL

Problem: Separating business from personal time and space. Many people work from home because they want to balance work with family obligations—caring for a child, grandchild or parent. Or they want the time to do other things—exercise, volunteer, write or simply kick back and relax. They expect that an at-home work arrangement will afford them the flexibility to plan out their day so they can do it all.

Reality: People who work from home usually work longer hours than they did in an office. This can make it harder to balance business and personal concerns.

If they're starting a business from home, then general start-up issues—organizing the business, making connections, getting the ball rolling—eat up time. And whether they're running their own business or telecommuting, the plain fact is that the business is always there.

Discipline: To maintain the balance you want to achieve, you need to use discipline. *Set boundaries for both space and time...*

●**Fix your business hours.** While you may not always stick to your schedule, at least you'll have a guideline for your time.

●**Separate your business from your personal life**—use separate phone lines for each.

Bonus: You'll earn a tax deduction. The first line to a home is not deductible even if used for business...the second line is.

●**Answer your business phone only during business hours.**

●**Advise clients and customers of your business hours.** Tell them you don't work weekends or after a certain hour during the week.

SETTING UP YOUR WORK SPACE

You're going to be spending considerable time in your home office, so set it up right. *Two things to make your home office function properly...*

●**Sufficient space.** You need to find room for the office furniture and equipment you'll use in your business. List the equipment you'll need to fit into your office space—a computer, an easel or anything else required for you to function properly. Then map out where everything will go. You may also need space for samples or inventory.

●**Separate space.** You need office space apart from your personal living space. It's difficult to make a kitchen table function as an office if you also use it for family meals.

Note: Setting up separate space for a home office is necessary if you want to claim a home-office deduction.

The tax law requires that your space be used regularly and exclusively for business. This means you can't use your den as an office by day and a family room by night. You don't necessarily need an entire room for business or even a partitioned space within a room. All you need is a clearly defined area devoted solely to business.

MAINTAINING A PROFESSIONAL IMAGE

Working from home may allow you to go to the office in a robe and slippers. But you need to present a professional image to the outside world. *This means infusing quality into everything you do...*

●**Consistently use your business identity.** Answer the phone with the name of your business.

●**Be prompt in returning calls and correspondence**—snail mail or e-mail.

●**Keep your office space neat**...and free from personal effects. This is especially important if clients or customers come to call.

Office address? It may be helpful to use a post office box—or other box number—as your official mailing address. Doing this will maintain your privacy. (Customers and other business associates won't know your home address.)

A mailbox can also afford you a prestigious address if you think it will help your business image.

Example: You live down a dirt road outside a small town that nobody knows. Consider renting a commercial box from a service, such as Mail Boxes, Etc. This will give you a known address, probably one on the main street of your home town. *Other benefits of a box...*

•Deliveries can be made to the box, even if you're away from home.

•Neighbors won't know about your business.

MORE ABOUT HANDLING PERSONAL ISSUES

Working from home presents a range of issues you won't have at a downtown office. *List the issues that trouble you and devise ways to minimize or avoid problems...*

•**Distractions.** Working at home means that the demands of running a home are always at hand. Laundry, cleaning and home repairs are never out of sight.

Solution: Set business hours and stick to them. Do household chores only after business hours.

For some, a big distraction in working at home is the refrigerator. While about half of those who start working from home don't have any weight change, about one-third do gain weight. To maintain your weight, stay away from the refrigerator during business hours.

•**Interruptions.** An at-home spouse...a needy neighbor...calls from friends.

These and other interruptions eat into your concentration and detract from your business performance.

Solutions: Set limits. Put a "do not disturb" sign on the door. Give strict instructions that you don't want to be interrupted during business hours.

•**Isolation.** Working at home means no more juicy conversations at the office water-cooler. While some people thrive on being alone during work hours and are more productive because of it, others suffer from feelings of isolation.

Solutions: Working from home doesn't mean you're locked in. Just the opposite. It means you're free. *You can...*

•Schedule outside appointments. Instead of having clients or customers come to you, visit them at their place of business.

•Join business and professional groups. This will give you the opportunity to network and make important business connections. It will also give you an incentive to get out of the house.

•Make breakfast and lunch dates. Meet friends or business associates for a meal, at least once a week.

Earn Money in Your Free Time The Way You Want

The new Freetimejobs.com service matches people looking for freelance work of all kinds with those looking to hire them, nationwide. Jobs range from high-tech to basic.

Examples: Jobs recently were posted for computer network specialists, baby-sitters, financial consultants, translators, advertising copywriters, bartenders, bookkeepers and persons willing to make wake-up calls. Categories of jobs include law, sales, marketing, education, household, writing and many others. The service is free to those looking for jobs. Those looking to hire someone can post one job at a time free, or an unlimited number for $50 per month. On the Web at *www.freejob.com.*

Cristina Gair, writer, *Home Office Computing,* 156 W. 56 St., New York 10019.

How to Make Money As a Consultant

Charles Moldenhauer, VP, Lefkowith, Inc., marketing and corporate communications consultants, New York.

At one time or another, most executives consider selling their expertise on their own, as consultants. The majority are at least moderately successful, but many fail. Most commonly, they overestimate the salability of their services and underestimate the effort needed to sell them.

PITFALLS FOR NEW CONSULTANTS

•**Not realizing that consultants,** especially new ones, spend more time selling their services than performing them.

• **Wasting time on unproductive prospects.**

• **Choosing too broad a field in which to consult.**

• **Not learning to talk the client's language.** This is essential because many consultants sell a highly specialized service with its own vocabulary to an equally specialized customer who uses a completely different language. *Example:* A computer expert who is hired to automate market research for a diaper manufacturer.

To sell their services, successful consultants…

• **Maintain pressure by keeping in touch with clients and prospects.**

• **Master sales and marketing tools,** such as writing effective letters, making convincing phone calls and developing presentations.

• **Start at the top,** contacting the chief executives of the Fortune 1,000 companies.

How to Put Together an Inspiring Reading Group

David Laskin, author of numerous books, including, with Holly Hughes, *The Reading Group Book: The Complete Guide to Starting and Sustaining a Reading Group, with Annotated Lists of 250 Titles for Provocative Discussion.* Plume.

Reading groups are blooming and booming across the country. These groups provide intellectual stimulation and are a great way to socialize with friends and make new ones.

CHOOSING MEMBERS

Reading groups typically start with a small cluster of friends who decide to get together. Find, create or expand yours by word of mouth, notices posted on bulletin boards at the library, "Y" or bookstore, ads in a college magazine or the newsletter of a local chapter of a national organization such as the American Association of University Women.

Hook up with fellow book lovers when a novelist or poet comes to town for a book signing.

Mixed-gender groups tend to be livelier and more challenging than single-sex groups. For me, the most rewarding combination is 10 to 12 men and women of assorted backgrounds and ages who are able to discuss books passionately.

Not everyone must be a lifelong bookworm. People grow with the group. One member of my former book group in Seattle had read mostly detective fiction, but was eager to widen his literary horizons.

WHERE TO MEET, WHAT TO EAT

Rotating among members' homes is the most common method. Other groups meet at libraries, alumni clubs, bookstores, schools and restaurants.

Meals run the gamut from brown-bag lunches to elaborate dinners designed around the book's theme or setting. See what your group wants and try it. Many groups find that limiting food to snacks or dessert helps focus conversation on the book.

WHO LEADS?

Start the meeting with a presentation by a pre-arranged leader other than the busy host. A member with special knowledge or experience in the topic at hand may wish to lead that session.

Hiring a professional book group leader can solve common problems, such as not knowing how to get started…falling into the "I loved it"/ "I hated it" trap…getting bogged down by the repeated recitation of personal anecdotes or agendas.

SETTING GROUND RULES

• **Socialize selectively.** As members become friends, they'll want to discuss matters besides books. Set aside a time at the beginning or end of the meeting for this.

• **Finish reading every book.** Insist that all members read to the end. If not, they should attend anyway, but meetings will not be disrupted by plot summaries, nor will the ending be kept secret.

• **Limit the length of meetings.** Participants should go home refreshed, not exhausted. Three hours is a good maximum.

• **Ban filibusters.** Limit the amount of time an individual can talk before someone else has a say. Ten minutes is plenty.

•**Participate.** Everybody must say something or at least ask a searching question at every meeting. Prolonged silence from one corner creates a black hole that sucks energy from the group.

•**Welcome guests.** Inviting new faces can refresh the group.

•**Communicate.** Agree to air problems as they arise.

•**Have fun.**

KINDS OF BOOKS TO READ

While your group can focus on a single genre, period or author, limitations lead to boredom. Discussions soon feel like classes, not open-ended and freewheeling.

Variety is the spice of book groups. The best ones allow themselves the freedom to choose different things and surprise themselves. One of the greatest joys of reading groups is discovering a wonderful book or author. Delve beyond novels into short stories, nature essays, poetry, biographies, travel writing and plays.

SELECTING BOOKS TO READ

Choosing books is one of a group's most intensive experiences. Some groups use the last 15 minutes of each meeting to select the book for the next meeting.

Disadvantages: This method steals time from the discussion and invariably involves someone saying, "You decide. Gotta go."

Try setting aside one meeting per year to determine the entire next year's schedule. All participants must come prepared to suggest (and fight for) books they have read.

Your picks shouldn't merely have pleased or inspired you. They should be controversial, packed with discussable issues and likely to elicit strong opinions.

SOURCES OF BOOK IDEAS

Some independent bookstores maintain shelves of books that have worked well for book groups. A knowledgeable staff member might agree to give your group a presentation. *Other sources of good ideas…*

•**Subscribe to *The New York Review of Books* or *The New York Times Book Review*** (you can get it without the rest of the paper).

•**Read the book sections** of the *Los Angeles Times, Chicago Tribune* or *The Washington Post.*

•**At your library, look for the March 15 issue of the ALA** (American Library Association) magazine *Booklist,* which summarizes the previous year's best books. Also check out *Publishers Weekly* and *Kirkus Reviews.*

•**Scan lists of winners of The Pulitzer Prize,** National Book Award, PEN/Faulkner Fiction Prize, Booker Prize and Whitbread Book Awards (both in England), Goncourt Prize (France) and Nobel Prize in Literature, awarded for the complete work of a writer of international stature.

In our New York group, we set aside 15 minutes at our "anniversary" meeting each year to discuss what we read the previous year. This sparks new ideas and reminds us of a favorite author to try again.

•**Troll the Internet.** Many publishers post reading group suggestions and guides or offer free pamphlets listing topics for discussion about specific books.

My book with Holly Hughes, *The Reading Group Book,* includes more than 60 pages of annotated group-friendly book lists in dozens of categories.

"DOING" THE BOOK

Discussion topics that cover the book thoroughly…

•**Context and background.**

•**Meaning of the text.**

•**Content.**

•**Technique.**

•**Appreciation.**

Write Your Lifestory

Denis Ledoux, director, Soleil Life-story Network of Lifewriting Seminar Leaders. He is author of several books, including *Turning Memories into Memoirs: A Handbook for Writing Lifestories.* Soleil Press.

There are good reasons why you should go to the trouble of writing your lifestory and all the family stories you can remember…

•**Preserve the past.**

●**Through your stories, show children, grandchildren and future generations** how the family was shaped and how they all fit in.

●**Record and celebrate personal as well as professional accomplishments.**

Key to lifewriting: Simply getting started. Don't waste time thinking about it, talking about it or wishing you could do it. Sit down right now and get started. *Helpful...*

●**Make a lifelist of the relationships and experiences** that have formed you and determined your path in life.

Your lifelist is likely to be long and may take several weeks—or months—to create. Add to it freely as significant people or events occur to you. *Examples...*

●Incidents of serious illness, death and divorce in the family.

●Facts about the ethnic or religious group you grew up in.

●Key events and relationships.

●A decision to go to college or not, marry or not, have children or not, etc.

●Falling in love.

●Natural disasters.

●**Create a core lifelist.** From your lifelist, choose the 10 most crucial events or relationships—those which, had they not happened, would have made you become a different person.

On a separate sheet of paper, briefly describe the 10 events or relationships and explain how each influenced you. *Examples...*

●My parents' divorce in 1940 surprised me and made me feel uncertain of the world and my place in it.

●The flood that destroyed my father's print shop in 1950 forced me to reconsider plans for college and my career as a doctor.

●Deciding not to marry Larry Smith because of his drinking led to my renting an apartment and learning to be self-sufficient.

●**Pick a memory—write a story.** Select one item from your core lifelist and write three to five pages about it. Repeat this process until you've tackled all 10. *Helpful...*

●Write vignettes, scenes or dialogues without worrying about chronology or how they'll fit together.

●Concentrate on writing many short stories instead of one long one.

●*Use an active voice, writing from your own point of view:* "I remember Grandpa wheeling himself over to the oak cabinet, looking around to make sure Grandma wasn't in sight, and sneaking a piece of chocolate from the hidden panel."

●Writing down your stories will prime the pump of your memory. If it doesn't, try jogging your memory with photographs, conversations with family members, old journals, yearbooks, period-specific songs or newspaper clippings.

●If you have trouble getting started, write down a well-loved family story. It will help get your story-telling juices flowing.

●Don't worry about spelling, grammar, sentence structure, etc. You'll take care of all that in the editing process. It's best to use a computer or typewriter. Double-space. Type only 6" to 6½" wide.

●**Write down all the facts.** Precise dates and descriptions are helpful for preserving your family's history. To make your writing as factual as possible, check dates and details with others who've shared your experiences, or spend time in the library researching a particular time period.

EDIT YOUR WORK

After you've finished a story, put it away and don't look at it for two to four weeks. Time will give you the emotional distance you need to look at the story with a fresh eye and consider how you might improve it. *Other editing ideas...*

●**Give the story to a friend or family member who can read it objectively.** It helps to send written questions along with the story. Ask the reader if the story is easy to understand, what he/she liked about it, what he didn't like about it, what he would change about it, etc.

●**Read the story aloud to yourself.** Hearing the story read aloud will alert you to awkward sentences, false-sounding dialogue and more.

●**Turn your lifestory into a real book.** When you've finished your lifestory, add photographs, poems, old family letters and other items that illustrate your stories. Then, have 10 or fewer copies of your book bound by a local copy shop at a cost of around $8 to $15 per book.

Inscribe them. Donate a copy to your local public library or historical society. Your lifestory will be a gift your children and grandchildren and your community will treasure forever.

Index